MW01627600

Teaching Music through Performance in Choir Volume 3

Also available from GIA Publications

Teaching Music through Performance in Band
Volume 1, second edition • G-4484
Grades 2–3 Resource Recording • CD-418
Grade 4 Resource Recording • CD-490
Grade 5 Resource Recording • CD-817

Volume 2 • G-4889
Grades 2–3 Resource Recording • CD-446
Grade 4 Resource Recording • CD-551
includes selections from Grade 5

Volume 3 • G-5333
Grades 2–3 Resource Recording • CD-473
Grade 4 Resource Recording • CD-510

Volume 4 • G-6022
Grades 2–3 Resource Recording • CD-552
Grade 4 Resource Recording • CD-603

Volume 5 • G-6573
Grades 2–3 Resource Recording • CD-623
Grade 4 Resource Recording • CD-638

Volume 6 • G-7027
Grades 2–3 Resource Recording • CD-683
Grade 4 Resource Recording • CD-684

Volume 7 • G-7436
Grades 2–3 Resource Recording • CD-780

Volume 8 • G-7926
Grades 2–3 Resource Recording • CD-849

Teaching Music through Performance in Jazz • G-7268
Resource Recording • CD-772

Teaching Music through Performance in Beginning Band
Volume 1 • G-5337
Grade 1 Resource Recording • CD-485

Volume 2 • G-7264
Resource Recording • CD-750

Teaching Music through Performing Marches
• G-5684
Resource Recording • CD-563

Teaching Music through Performance in Orchestra
Volume 1 • G-5565
Grades 1–3 Resource Recording • CD-536

Volume 2 • G-6091
Grades 1–3 Resource Recording • CD-615

Volume 3 • G-7191
Grades 1–4 Resource Recording • CD-751
for String Orchestra

Teaching Music through Performance in Choir
Volume 1 • G-6534
Levels 1–4 Resource Recording • CD-650

Volume 2 • G-7100
Levels 1–5 Resource Recording • CD-719

G-7522

Teaching Music through Performance in Choir

Volume 3

Frank S. Albinder
Philip Brunelle
Bruce Chamberlain
Rodney Eichenberger
Sandra Snow

Compiled and Edited by Heather J. Buchanan and
Matthew W. Mehaffey

GIA Publications, Inc.
Chicago

For a complete, searchable index of works covered in the Teaching Music Series, as well as audio clips of more than 900 pieces, visit the website TeachingMusic.org.

Teaching Music through Performance in Choir, Volume 3
Frank S. Albinder, Philip Brunelle, Bruce Chamberlain, Rodney Eichenberger, and Sandra Snow
Compiled and edited by Heather J. Buchanan and Matthew W. Mehaffey
www.teachingmusic.org

layout: Martha Chlipala

GIA Publications, Inc.
7404 S. Mason Ave.
Chicago IL, 60638
www.giamusic.com

G-7522
ISBN: 978-1-57999-753-3

Table of Contents

Acknowledgments xi

Introduction by Heather J. Buchanan xvii

Part I: The Teaching of Music

CHAPTER 1 MALE CHOIRS AND MALE SINGERS
by Frank S. Albinder

History 3
Working with Male Voices 5
Recruitment and Retention Strategies 7
- Get Them Out There Performing 7
- Organize a Small Ensemble 8
- Use Your Members to Recruit 8
- Organize a Festival 8
- Bring in a Guest Chorus 8
- Invite a Guest Clinician 8
- Participate in Local Competitions 9

Repertoire and Resources 9
- The Barbershop Quartet 10
- A Cappella Singing 10
- Intercollegiate Men's Choruses, Inc. 11
- The American Choral Directors Association 11
- GALA Choruses 11
- Associated Male Choruses of America 11
- Publishers 12
- Online Libraries 12
- Extended Works 13

CHAPTER 2 THE JOY OF COMMISSIONING 15
by Philip Brunelle

Communicate with Composers 16
Commissioning by Collaboration 20
Co-commissioning 22
Hold a Contest 22
Finding a Composer 24
Share Strengths and Weaknesses 25

CHAPTER 3 ARTICULATION: ENABLING THE MEANING IN MUSIC TO BE UNDERSTOOD 27
by Bruce Chamberlain
Introduction—Setting the Scene 27
What Is Style? 28
Applying the Appropriate Articulation. 30
Rehearsal Implications. 35
Putting Pedagogy into Practice 37
Settle the Articulation 37
Balance the Texture 38
Elucidate the Subtler Meanings
and Relationships in the Score 38
Concluding Observations 38

CHAPTER 4 WHEN WORDS FAIL 41
by Rodney Eichenberger
The Power of Gesture 42
Using Gesture to Solve Pitch Problems 43
The Character of Music 43
The Four Functions of Rhythm 44
Down 44
Away 44
Off 44
Into 44
Using Gesture to Enliven Singing 45
Creating Entrances with Forward Motion. 45
Phrasal Direction 45
Tuning a Downward Scale. 45
Well-supported Dynamics 46
Fortissimo 46
Piano. 46

Chapter 5 BRAINSTORMING FOR IMPROVISATION: DEVELOPING IMAGINATIVE TEACHING STRATEGIES IN THE CHORAL REHEARSAL 49
by Sandra Snow
The Conductor-Teacher 50
Listens-in-Sound 50
Analyses Scores 50
Contextualizes 50
Adapts 50
Reflects 51
Improvises 51
Facilitates 51
Listening Deeply 51
Exercise 1: Hearing Individual Vocal Parts 53
Exercise 2: Working from Recordings 53
Exercise 3: Increasing Keyboard Facility 54
The Rehearsal Plan 55
The Rehearsal Plan Is the In-Action Implementation of Conductor/Teacher Philosophy 55
The Rehearsal Process Is Adaptive and Flexible, Encouraging Experimentation and Learning by Ensemble Members Towarda Collective Interpretation of the Music Under Study 55
Unlocking Imagination in Teaching 56
Brainstorming out of Real-Time 57
Visual Mind Mapping/Webbing 57
The First Dimension: Musical Interpretation 57
From Imagination to Inspiration: The Productive Rehearsal . . .63
Making Choices about Teaching Moves: Developmentally Appropriate Strategies 64
Active and Passive Strategies: Thinking in Music Versus Thinking in Language 64
Learning-Based Stratification: Visual, Aural, Kinesthetic 64
Applications for Teacher Training 64
Improvising from the Podium 65
expertise with a Little "e": The Path to an Engaged Choral Classroom 66

Rehearsal Is a Parallel Highway 67
Assessing-in-action Is a Constant .67
Gesture Is Our Most Powerful Teaching Tool 67

PART II: The Choral Conductor as Music Teacher

Teacher Resource Guides

Introduction to the Teacher Resource Guides
by Matthew Mehaffey. 71

LEVEL ONE

Mixed voices:

God Is Our Refuge	Mozart, W. A. 77
Sing We and Chant It	Morley, Thomas 81
Sorida	arr. Powell, Rosephanye . . . 87
The May Night (Die Mainacht)	Brahms, Johannes/ arr. Frackenpohl, Arthur. . . 93

Treble voices:

Nine Hundred Miles	Silvey, Philip 99

Men's voices:

Fillimiooriay	arr. Beery, Lon. 105
Medieval Gloria	Singh, Vijay. 111
Viva Tutti	anonymous 18th century . 115

LEVEL TWO

Mixed voices:

City Called Heaven	Poelinitz, Josephine. 121
Ahrirang	arr. De Cormier, Robert . . 127
Bile Them Cabbage Down	arr. Wilberg, Mack 131
Domaredansen	arr. Collins, Drew 137
Ev'ry Time I Feel the Spirit	arr. Dawson, William 145
God Is Seen	arr. Parker, Alice. 151
Ipharadisi	arr. Ulrich, Jerry 155
It Takes a Village	Szymko, Joan. 159
O Occhi, manza mia	de Lassus, Orlande. 163
Old Time Religion	arr. Hogan, Moses 167

Requiem Gilkyson, Eliza/ arr. Craig Hella Johnson . . 173
"The Pasture" from *Where the Earth Meets the Sky* Stroope, Z. Randall 179
Wantimg Memories Barnwell, Ysaye M. 185
Where the Music Comes From Hoiby, Lee 191

Treble voices:
Dance on My Heart Koepke, Alan 195
Gate, Gate arr. Tate, Brian 199
Japanese Garden Culloton, Matthew 205
Jordan's Angels Dilworth, Rollo 209
Measure Me Sky Mulholland, James 215
Scarborough Fair Goetze, Mary 221
The Birds Britten, Benjamin 225
Weep No More Childs, David 229
Yo Le Canto Todo El Dia Brunner, David 235

Men's voices:
Back to Ethiopia arr. Rardin, Paul 241
Byker Hill arr. Sandler, Mitchell 247
Flanders Fields Emerson, Roger 253
How Can I Keep from Singing arr. Ellingboe, Bradley 257
Streets of Laredo Takach, Timothy 261

Level Three
Mixed voices:
Ave Maria Dett, Nathaniel 267
Hodie Whitbourn, James 271
In Remembrance Ames, Jeffery 275
"In Splendoribus Sanctorum" from *The Strathclyde Motets* MacMillan, James 281
Jesu dulcis memoria Victoria, Tomás Luis de. . . 285
Lebenslust Schubert, Franz 291
Magnificent Horses arr. Ling-Tam, Jing 297
O vos Omnes Casals, Pablo 301

Oremus Sisask, Urmas 305
Pater Noster Stravinsky, Igor 309
Prayer Before Sleep Robinovitch, Sid........ 315
Psalm 100 (Jauchzet dem Herrn) Mendelssohn, Felix...... 321
Revoici venir du Printemps Le Jeune, Claude........ 327
Sir Christèmas Mathias, William 333
The Water Is Wide Paulus, Steven.......... 339
This We Know Jeffers, Ron 345
To the Mothers of Brazil: Salve Regina arr. Eriksson, Gunnar 349
We Shall Walk through the Valley Moore, Undine Smith ... 355

Treble voices:

Magnificat in A minor Porpora, Nicola......... 361
Vus vet zayn Hatfield, Stephen 371

Men's voices:

Greater Love Chatman, Stephen 375

Level Four

Mixed voices:

A Boy and a Girl Whitacre, Eric.......... 381
Also hat Gott die Welt geliebt Schütz, Heinrich........ 385
Balulalow Custer, Gerald.......... 393
Best of Rooms, The Thompson, Randall ..... 399.
Calme des Nuits Saint-Saëns, Camille .... 403.
Chindia Pascanu, Alexandru 409
El Hambo Mäntyjärvi, Jaakko 413
In Paradisum Fissinger, Edwin......... 419
Lay a Garland Pearsall, Robert......... 423
Lo, How a Rose E'er Blooming Sandström, Jan 429
My Flight for Heaven Henson, Blake.......... 433
Stars I Shall Find Dickau, David 439
Sure on This Shining Night Lauridsen, Morten....... 443
Valiant for Truth Vaughan Williams, Ralph. 449

Treble voices:

Ain't No Grave Can Hold My Body Down arr. Caldwell, Paul/Ivory, Sean 55

Hotari Koi arr. Ogura, Roh 463

I Thank You God Walker, Gwyneth 469

LAWA Sadler, Katheryn 477

Les étoiles Sirett, Mark. 483

O bone jesu Brahms, Johannes 489

Psalm 121 Raminsh, Imant 493

There Is Sweet Music Here Gawthrop, Daniel 499

Men's voices:

Come Sing to Me of Heaven arr. McDermid, J. Aaron. . 503

Credo Martini, Giovanni Battista 507

Crucifixus Lotti, Antonio/ arr. Davison, Archibald. . . 515

Four Cummings Choruses, Opus 98 Persichetti, Vincent 519

Love Never Ending Zinter, Aaron 527

Ramkali arr. Sperry, Ethan 533

Rustics and Fishermen Britten, Benjamin 539

LEVEL FIVE

Mixed voices:

Come to Me My Love Dello Joio, Norman. 545

I Find My Feet Have Further Goals Larsen, Libby. 551

The Hour Has Come Glick, Srul Irving 555

Treble voices:

Jerusalem Luminosa Betinis, Abbie 561

MASTERWORK: Gloria, RV 589 by Antonio Vivaldi
Analysis and commentary by Bruce Chamberlain
Biographical Sketch and Brief History by Emilie Amrein 567

Index by Title for Teaching Music through Performance in Choir: Volumes 1–3. 593

Index by Publisher for Teaching Music through Performance in Choir: Volumes 1–3. 602

Index by Composer and Arranger for Teaching Music through Performance in Choir:
Volume 3 611
Index by Title for Teaching Music through Performance in Choir:
Volume 3 614
About the Editors 617

Acknowledgments

The following research associates are gratefully acknowledged for their scholarly contributions to the Teacher Resource Guides:

Jeffrey Ames
Director of Choral Activities
Belmont University • Tennessee

Emilie Amrein
Director of Choral Activities
Lake Forest College • Illinois

Christopher L. Bartley
Instructor of Music
University of Pittsburgh at Greensburg

Lon Beery
Chorus Director
Spry Middle School • New York

Abbie Betinis
Composer

Geoffrey Boers
Director of Choirs
University of Washington

James Bowyer
Lecturer in Music
University of Wyoming

Gregory Brown
Lecturer in Music
Smith College • Massachusetts

David L. Brunner
Director of Choral Activities
University of Central Florida

David Childs
Associate Professor of Choral Studies
Vanderbilt University • Tennessee

Drew Collins
Assistant Professor of Music
Wright State University • Ohio

Andrew Crow
Assistant Professor of Music
Ball State University • Indiana

Matthew Culloton
Artistic Director
The Singers, Minnesota Choral Artists • Minnesota

Gerald Custer
Composer

David Dickau
Director of Choral Activities
Minnesota State University

Rollo Dilworth
Associate Professor of Choral Music Education
Temple University • Pennsylvania

Jeffrey Douma
Associate Professor of Music
Yale University

Bradley Ellingboe
Director of Choral Activities
University of New Mexico

Dan Gawthrop
Composer

W. Bryce Hayes
DMA candidate
University of Minnesota

Michele Holt
Director of the Concert Choir
University of Connecticut

Richard Hutton
MM candidate
Westminster Choir College of Rider University • New Jersey

Joni Jensen
Coordinator of Choral Activities
Texas Women's University

Brandon Johnson
Director of Choral Activities
Houghton College • New York

Karen Kennedy
Director of Choirs
Towson University • Maryland

K. Steve Kim
MM candidate
Westminster Choir College of Rider University • New Jersey

Anthony Maglione
Director of Choral Studies
William Jewell College • Missouri

Bradley Miller
DMA candidate
University of Arizona

Joseph Ohrt
Director of Choral Activities
Central Buck High School West • Pennsylvania

Christopher Owen
DMA candidate
University of Minnesota

Mary-Jane Pagenstecher
Director of Fine and Performing Arts
Holton Arms School • Maryland

Amelia Nagoski Peterson
DMA candidate
University of Connecticut

Paul Rardin
Director of Choral Activities
Temple University • Pennsylvania

David Scholz
Director of Choral Activities
California State University-Chico

Philip Silvey
Associate Professor of Music Education
Eastman School of Music • New York

Ethan Sperry
Director of Choral Activities
Portland State University • Oregon

Timothy Takach
Composer

John Trotter
Assistant Conductor
Vancouver Chamber Choir • Canada

Jerry A. Ulrich
Director of Choral Activities
Georgia Tech University

Giselle Wyers
Assistant Professor of Choral Studies
University of Washington

Introduction

Heather J. Buchanan

The response to the *Teaching Music through Performance in Choir* series has been tremendous, and we continue to receive positive feedback from many people in the choral profession who are effectively utilizing both the books and companions CDs for Volumes 1 and 2. In addition to the high school choral directors for whom that volume was specifically targeted, college and university directors, students studying choral methods, and community choir directors have found the series a valuable resource.

As with Volumes 1 and 2, Volume 3 has been written primarily with the needs of high school choral directors in mind. The repertoire selection and rating system specifically reflects that. This book is a practical, multi-faceted companion for your artistic journey and is intended to be used often. It can be used as a reference or a guide for the selection and teaching of repertoire. It can also be used to investigate topics of interest and in doing so confirm or challenge your choices—either way, there is information that will support and facilitate the continuing education and development of choral directors worldwide. We also know that this book will be of great interest to conductors in other forums and sincerely hope it will continue to be used for the teaching of choral methods in colleges and universities.

The content of this volume is divided into two parts. Part I features five chapters written by leaders in the choral field: Frank Albinder, Philip Brunelle, Bruce Chamberlain, Rodney Eichenberger, and Sandra Snow. Part II comprises the Teacher Resource Guides, which includes historical, biographical, and analytical information about choral octavos for mixed voice, women's, and male-voice ensembles. My co-editor and compiler, Matthew Mehaffey, gives a comprehensive explanation of the Teacher Resource Guide in his introduction to Part II. Volume 3 also contains analysis of Vivaldi's *Gloria*, prepared by Bruce Chamberlain and Emilie Amrein.

Chapter 1, "Male Choirs and Male Singers," was written by Frank Albinder who is nationally recognized as an authority on male voices and ensembles. His chapter presents a comprehensive perspective on the many facets associated with male-voice pedagogy, repertoire, and performance opportunities. Philip Brunelle's chapter, "The Joy of Commissioning," describes the process of choral commissioning and highlights key elements that contribute to a successful and satisfying experience for all concerned. As one of America's foremost proponents of new music, Philip's experience with commissioning is extremely valuable and relevant for choral directors at all levels. Chapter 3, "Articulation: Enabling the Meaning in Music to be Understood," emphasizes the importance of articulation in relation to musical style. Bruce Chamberlain systematically explains how to achieve clarity and accuracy in the choral ensemble, and the direct relationship between diction and stylistic finesse.

Rodney Eichenberger's contribution to Volume 3 is "Starting Out." His choice of topic is directed at the newest conductors in our profession and is written after reflecting on his many years on the podium. That chapter addresses a range of topics designed as "lifelines" for immediate success and draws heavily on connections between the physical gesture and desired musical result. Chapter 5, "Brainstorming for Improvisation: Developing Imaginative Teaching Strategies in the Choral Rehearsal," presents Sandra Snow's innovative approach to choral pedagogy through the paradigm of improvisation. Her extensive chapter guides the reader through a range of concepts, exercises, and repertoire references with the ultimate goal of stimulating the imaginations of both conductors and their singers. The end result is dynamic and engaged music making. This chapter is a must-read for all choral music educators!

We wish to express our heartfelt gratitude to each of the authors and researchers who worked with us to complete Volume 3. We also sincerely appreciate the ongoing commitment to the series from the team at GIA Publications, in particular GIA President, Alec Harris. James Jordan and Jerry McCoy's recordings in the companion CDs also provide excellent role models of the repertoire we present, and we thank them and their choirs for their dedication to the music.

As the *Teaching Music through Performance in Choir* series continues to evolve, we look forward to your feedback as we develop subsequent volumes. We will continue to present chapters from choral leaders because we believe that providing access to the richness of the collective experience of our colleagues is essential. We encourage choral pedagogues at all stages of their journey to remain open to embracing new ideas while upholding the wisdom acquired from their own experiences. We sincerely trust that Volume 3 will find a worthy place in your library as a resource that supports the artistic and educational needs of you and your choirs.

PART 1

THE TEACHING OF MUSIC

CHAPTER 1

Male Choirs and Male Singers

Frank S. Albinder

History

The male voice choir is the oldest type of organized singing ensemble in the Western (and some Eastern) musical tradition. The origins of the men's chorus date back centuries, to the performances of Christian and Jewish chant as part of worship services in which women were not allowed to participate. These early "men's choruses" evolved over time. In some countries, women joined their male singing colleagues and the mixed choir was born. In other countries, the adult male vocal range was expanded upon by adding boys to tenor-bass ensembles, thus keeping them all male but affording them a larger vocal compass.

It wasn't until the eighteenth and nineteenth centuries that men's choruses took on the form familiar to us today. In Great Britain, Glee, Catch and Part-song Societies became an important part of the cultural fabric of everyday life. These choruses performed both sacred and secular repertoire as a form of recreation, occasionally giving public concerts but also serving as social clubs for both the upper and the developing middle class. These societies held competitions and commissioned new music, but they also served as business and political roundtables, providing a variety of valuable social functions to society at large. Among the hundreds of composers writing repertoire for these choruses one can find the names of some of the greatest musicians of the nineteenth and twentieth centuries: Edward Elgar, Gustav Holst, Charles Villiers Stanford, and Ralph Vaughan Williams are but a few.

An offshoot of the English male chorus tradition can be found in Wales, where organized groups of male singers grew out of the coal and steel industries that once flourished there. These choruses found a home in the country's Eisteddfodau, large festivals of music and literature that date back to the twelfth century. The National Eisteddfod of Wales is the largest of these festivals, which are held all over the world. During this annual eight-day event, thousands of singers and poets compete and perform, almost exclusively in Welsh. The Eisteddfodau are credited with keeping Welsh language and culture alive.

As the English singing societies blossomed, so did the *Männerchor* in the German-speaking parts of Europe. Similar in many respects to their English brethren, these German men's choruses also commissioned works, held concerts and contests, and served as social gathering places in cities large and small. Among composers who wrote for *Männerchor* one finds these musical luminaries: Johannes Brahms, Anton Bruckner, Franz Liszt, Felix Mendelssohn, Josef Rheinberger, Franz Schubert, and Robert Schumann.

The German *Männerchor* tradition had a strong influence on the development of men's choirs in the Nordic countries, with three of the finest groups in the world coming from that region: The Estonian National Male Choir (Tallinn, Estonia, since 1944), Orphei Drängar (also known as OD, in Stockholm, Sweden, since 1853) and Ylioppilaskunnan laulajat (also known as YL, from Helsinki, Finland, since 1883). These choruses, some with roots in the nineteenth century, have commissioned great quantities of music from their native composers that have become part of the standard repertoire, including important works by Arvo Pärt, Einojuhani Rautavaara, and Veljo Tormis.

Another important branch of the men's choral world can be found in Russia, where all-male ensembles have been singing both sacred and secular music for centuries. Perhaps the most famous of the Russian men's choruses was the Don Cossacks, a group consisting of former officers of the Russian Imperial Army that gave its first formal concert in 1923. The group toured the United States (and much of the world) extensively in the mid-twentieth century, bringing Russian sacred music, folk songs, and military music to thousands of new listeners. Many of the greatest Russian composers wrote music for men's chorus, including Dmitry Bortniansky, Pavel Chesnokov, Sergei Rachmaninoff, Nikolai Rimsky-Korsakov, and Pyotr Tchaikovsky.

Male chorus singing in the United States evolved from all of these traditions and culminated in the formation of numerous community and collegiate men's choruses during the nineteenth century. The oldest community group in the United States, the Liederkrantz of New York, was founded in 1847; the oldest continuously-performing group is the Mendelssohn Glee Club of New York, founded in 1866. The oldest collegiate men's chorus is the Harvard Glee Club, founded in 1858. Other schools with men's choruses over one hundred years old include the University of Michigan (1859), the University of Virginia (1871), The Ohio State University (1874), and The Pennsylvania State University (1888). With the advent of the federal equality laws known as Title IX in 1972, many all-male colleges and universities became coeducational, as did some of their men's choruses. Among these groups are the Glee Clubs from Yale University (1861) and Princeton University (1874), which are now mixed ensembles.

Working with Male Voices

Traditional voicing for a men's chorus, like a mixed chorus, is for four parts: first tenors, second tenors, baritones, and basses; this voicing is abbreviated as TTBB. Because of the relative proximity of the ranges of these four vocal parts, the tessitura for first tenors in a men's chorus is a bit higher than for tenors in a mixed chorus. The second tenor part is more like a high baritone part, and the tessitura of the bass part may be somewhat lower than in standard mixed chorus repertoire. First tenors usually have the main melodic material, though in some repertoire, especially barbershop quartets, second tenors sing the melody.

One need treat the voices in a male chorus no differently than those in a mixed chorus. However, there are some obvious, fundamental differences between male and female singers that come into clearer focus when dealing with a single-gender choir. One should also note that men behave differently in a male chorus setting than they do when women are present. When singing in a male chorus, men are generally more willing to take risks and do exercises they might find somewhat embarrassing to perform in front of the opposite sex.

While women regularly sing in both upper and lower registers, most of their speaking occurs in the lower register while much of their singing is in the upper register. Men normally sing and speak in the same (lower) register. While this makes some aspects of vocal production easier for men, one must take care to exercise the upper register in both tenors and basses.

While there are many schools of thought on the best ways to teach solid vocal technique, most pedagogues agree that vocalizing men in both upper (head or falsetto) and lower (chest) registers will increase a singer's range and improve overall vocalism. One might remind choristers that singing is both "enhanced speaking" and "toned-down yelling." A good sense of how breathing works is key to good singing, so working regularly on making singers better aware of their breath and its effect on their singing is key to good vocal production.

Simple breathing exercises (panting like a dog is excellent) help a singer to activate the muscles used to control the breath. Exercises involving slow inhalation through the nose (it filters and warms the air) are good for increasing capacity. Ask singers to imagine the air filling the stomach or reaching all the way down to the feet to help avoid the pitfalls of shallow, clavicular breathing (raising the collarbone and shoulders while pulling in the abdomen), which is antithetical to good singing. In addition to expansion in the front of the torso, ask singers to be aware of expansion on the sides and even the back (where most of the lungs are located). Placing one hand on the abdomen and another in the small of the back during breathing exercises will help singers to become more aware of the physical aspects of breathing.

After a deep inhalation is achieved, ask singers to hiss on exhalation. This will allow them to gauge their progress and learn to control the breath exclusive of vocalization. One can also ask singers to exhale and hiss in rhythmic patterns indicated by the conductor. If the starting and stopping of the hiss is properly controlled by the breathing muscles and not the tongue, it can strengthen these muscles and make singers more aware of their function and their ability to control them.

Two of the most common buzzwords encountered in discussions of breathing technique are "diaphragm" and "support," as in, "Breathe from the diaphragm!" or "Support the sound!" The diaphragm (more properly, the thoracic diaphragm) is a thin sheet of muscle that extends across the bottom of the ribcage. During inhalation, the diaphragm contracts, increasing the space in the thoracic cavity and creating a vacuum that draws air into the lungs. The diaphragm is an involuntary muscle that must move in order for one to breathe. Therefore, encouraging singers to breathe from the diaphragm is a useless and misleading instruction. When the diaphragm is contracted, the intercostal rib muscles are activated; these are the muscles over which a singer has some control. So the idea of breathing into the stomach, while not anatomically accurate, creates a more realistic image of the actual movement of the diaphragm and external intercostal muscles. Singers might imagine trying to hold up a large inner tube (without using their hands!) while inhaling and expanding to full capacity.

The idea of breath support, while not unhelpful in the abstract, tends to be vague and ill-defined for most singers, even those with extensive vocal training. When one admonishes a choir to "Support the sound," the results often include tightening of muscles that impede rather than enhance and control the flow of the breath. One could define good breath support as the dynamic tension that exists with the skilled control of the breath for the most efficient vocalization. This might be a complicated concept for most choral singers to grasp, so many conductors simply abbreviate the concept by using the word "support" regularly, as both admonition and exhortation. Teaching singers the fundamental aspects of breathing will go much farther toward helping them create a healthy vocal sound and a well-grounded vocal production.

For the next step in coordinating the breath with the voice, try using a controlled shout or yell. Start by asking singers to take a deep breath and then slide up and down at their own pace on a neutral (schwa) vowel. After they have a sense of how these spoken glissandos feel, ask them to take a deep breath and shout in unison, in the manner of a sports team breaking a huddle or a group of soldiers shouting a group response. Care must be taken to keep an open throat during the accented shout, most especially at the end. This exercise, like the hissing exercises mentioned above, help singers strengthen the muscles involved in the process of breathing.

There are an infinite number of pitched vocalizations one can use to warm up a choir and strengthen vocal production. One common practice is to isolate specific passages from the repertoire a choir is singing and design vocalizes around that music. Don't hesitate to vocalize men well into their upper registers, using nonpitched exercises like the so-called "yawn-sigh," and pitched exercises using simple three- or five-note patterns. A simple vocalize allows singers to concentrate on breathing and vocal production without thinking too hard about what pitches they might have to remember in a more complicated exercise.

Recruitment and Retention Strategies

Recruitment and retention of male singers, whether for a mixed or men's chorus, is one of the principal challenges facing conductors. In some parts of the country it's not unusual to find a ratio of ten women to one man signed up for a choral audition. Yet there are successful programs throughout the United States that have ample supplies of men for both mixed and male choirs.

How do they do it? When starting from scratch, it takes a lot of work on the part of the conductor and singers already in the chorus. Though the recruitment of male singers might seem a daunting task, evidence suggests that creating a strategy for each individual situation from the many successful techniques used by others can yield positive results. Once you've started increasing the ranks of men in your chorus, more singers will follow and the program will become more self-sustaining.

While there's no single "silver bullet" to guarantee tenors and basses will flock to your chorus, there are a number of ideas that have worked well for others.

Get Them Out There Performing

At the top of any list should be the determination to make your men better known to the students and faculty at your own school. Whether you have a men's chorus, an a cappella group, or barbershop quartet from your mixed choir, get them out there performing. They could sing the national anthem before a school assembly or serenade passing students during lunchtime or between classes. If you have a collegiate men's chorus, consider doing a dorm sing. Or "round up" your newest members by having your current singers appear at their dorm room to sing the alma mater and present them with their letter of acceptance. Others will hear your group and want to know more about it. While one can't accept every opportunity to provide singers for events at school, don't cloister your groups, saving them exclusively for your own concerts. The more students see them, the more they'll want to learn more about them, and then become a part of the group.

Organize a Small Ensemble

If you can't always bring your whole chorus to a performance, find some men in one of your existing groups who want to do more singing and organize them into a small ensemble. A cappella groups and barbershop quartets can be great calling cards for your choral program. Information and resources on how to start a small group are below.

Use Your Members to Recruit

Use the members of your choir to recruit new ones. This seems like an obvious strategy, but it's surprising how many conductors fail to exploit this easy way to bring more singers to your ensembles. The conductor can also do some of this recruiting. Find a popular sports figure on campus (this works best in high schools) and see if he's interested in singing. He might enjoy performing in an extracurricular a cappella group, and his presence will create new audiences for all your groups. Ask the women in your mixed choir to each bring a male friend to audition. You'd be amazed at how effective this can be.

Organize a Festival

If you have several small groups at your school, organize your own a cappella festival. These events, when well-publicized, can bring out far more students than a standard choral concert. Make sure you feature your small ensembles on regular concert programs as well.

Bring in a Guest Chorus

Bring in a guest group to perform for your students (or a school-wide assembly). If you teach in a high school, perhaps a nearby university has a men's chorus, or even an a cappella group that would be willing to come and perform. Contact the local chapter of the Barbershop Harmony Society to find a quartet to perform at your school.

Invite a Guest Clinician

Invite a guest clinician to come and work with your choir. If you're a female conductor working with a men's chorus, then bring in a male clinician for contrast. If you're a tenor, bring in a bass, and vice versa. It always wakes up students a bit to have something different from what they experience every day. It will provide a boost for your singers and give you a chance to take a step back and see your choir from a different perspective.

Participate in Local Competitions

If you have a small group, seek out a local festival or competition in which they can participate. This will help build their confidence and allow them to hear other similar groups. If you have a men's chorus, take them to a festival or other outside event. Many colleges and universities sponsor men's choral festivals. If there's nothing in your area, consider starting something. It could be as simple as a Sunday afternoon in your auditorium, with your chorus and two or three other groups singing for each other. If the idea takes hold, consider bringing in a guest clinician to work with the singers and conduct a combined number. Some colleges and universities sponsor high school men's singing festivals with their own chorus as the featured ensemble, a guest clinician to work with all the students, and an opportunity for the visiting groups to perform for each other.

One doesn't have to have a men's chorus to participate in these types of events. Some school districts sponsor a day of men's singing, when students from all the local schools can come and sing together with a guest conductor. Remember, you don't have to have a men's chorus to send students to these events, or to participate in an honor choir! Send some men from your mixed chorus. They might get so inspired at an outside festival or concert that they'll want to start a small group on their own. Mission accomplished!

Whatever strategies you use, remember that starting out might not be easy. Stick with it, try a variety of events, enlist students to aid in the effort, and chances are you'll be able to build up your program enough to keep the men auditioning and singing for years to come.

Repertoire and Resources

In addition to the large quantities of sacred music engendered by the many branches of the male chorus tree, secular music is a mainstay of the modern men's choir. There are hundreds of arrangements of folk songs, Broadway musical numbers, popular songs, and other unique secular forms, including the barbershop quartet. Secular men's choral music tends to fall into broad thematic groupings: love, war, drinking, hunting, patriotism, and nature are all popular themes found in a great deal of this repertoire.

Voicing in the male chorus repertoire ranges from the serene beauty of unison plainchant all the way up to complex works in more than a dozen parts or for multiple choirs. For younger singers, there are many two- and three-part works with limited ranges that can serve as fine introductions to this vast repertoire.

Part II of this volume, as well as those in *Teaching Music through Performance in Choir, Volumes 1 and 2*, contains an extensive list of varied repertoire appropriate for choruses of different age levels and abilities. There are a number of additional resources that can be enormously helpful when looking for music for whatever men's ensemble you might conduct. And remember, just because you don't have a formal men's chorus doesn't mean you can't have the men in your mixed chorus sing a number or two in a concert, or create a small group and have them sing a contemporary a cappella piece or a barbershop quartet. These are certain crowd-pleasers that might also help bring more men to your choral program.

The Barbershop Quartet

The barbershop quartet is a uniquely American musical genre, with roots in the African-American musical traditions of the turn of the twentieth century. We imagine that the specific musical language we associate with the barbershop quartet sprang from the imaginations of men in actual barbershops, creating their own harmonies to the popular tunes of the day. This image is driven home by Norman Rockwell's iconic illustration of four gents in a barbershop, engaged in song. However, the original barbershop quartets appeared on the vaudeville stage and in minstrel shows, and the musical language has roots in the call-and-response style of singing found in spirituals and gospel music.

As the music grew more popular, a support organization was born in Oklahoma in the 1930s, the Society for the Preservation and Encouragement of Barbershop Quartet Singing in America, often known simply as SPEBSQSA. Now known as the Barbershop Harmony Society, the organization boasts hundreds of chapters and thousands of singers throughout North America. The organization publishes music and recordings, and has a great deal of useful information available at its website (www.barbershop.org). To encourage your men to embrace this uniquely American art form, contact a local chapter of the Society and ask a quartet to some sing for your choir. They'll also be happy to help with repertoire suggestions and other information about the genre.

A Cappella Singing

Another prominent genre for male singers revolves around the world of a cappella singing. We're not talking about the standard definition of a cappella; this genre is all about student-run ensembles performing everything from Renaissance madrigals and Gregorian chants up to the latest rock-and-roll hits. Though the emphasis of most a cappella groups is on pop music, there are a cappella groups that sing virtually every type of choral literature.

The a cappella movement is alive and well on most college campuses in the United States, with some schools boasting more than a dozen single-sex or mixed a cappella groups. Because most of these groups are student-run, the quality can be highly variable. Nevertheless, these groups attract large audiences and can draw men into a more traditional choral program.

The Contemporary A Cappella Society of America (CASA) has created a web-based clearinghouse for all things a cappella (found at www.casa.org). They publish a cappella news, concert and job listings, repertoire lists, and even collections of arrangements useful in starting such a group with your male singers. Many a cappella groups learn their music by copying recordings, an illegal practice that CASA helps combat by providing clear and helpful guidance on all aspects of performing this repertoire.

Intercollegiate Men's Choruses, Inc.

There are other service organizations that can provide useful information about men's choruses. Intercollegiate Men's Choruses, Inc., was founded in 1914 as an offshoot of the University Glee Club in New York City. IMC sponsored festivals and competitions throughout most of the twentieth century. Today the organization is open to choruses and conductors of all levels, though most members are collegiate groups in the Glee Club tradition.

IMC holds a National Seminar every two years, featuring concerts, interest sessions, and reading sessions relating specifically to the male chorus. The organization also publishes a newsletter and maintains a library of unpublished works for male chorus (available at www.imci.us).

The American Choral Directors Association

The American Choral Directors Association (ACDA) counts Male Choirs as one of the fourteen official categories of Repertoire and Standards within the organization. ACDA has Male Choir chairs at the national, division, and state levels who are available to assist conductors, and the ACDA website (www.acdaonline.org) has a section specifically for male choirs.

GALA Choruses

GALA Choruses, the Gay and Lesbian Association of Choruses (www.galachoruses.org), provides links to gay men's choruses around the world as well as concert listings and articles about composers and repertoire.

Associated Male Choruses of America

This organization sponsors "big sings" in the United States and Canada as well as other activities. See www.amcofa.net for more information.

Publishers

Though nearly all music publishers have some repertoire for men's choruses, some are especially noteworthy for their broader focus on such works. The E. C. Schirmer Music Company (www.ecspublishing.com) has a vast archive of compositions and arrangements for men's chorus written by some of the early luminaries in the field. They also publish new works for men's chorus, providing a broad overview of the genre through most of its history in the United States. Their music never goes out of print, so if you're looking for historic arrangements by A. T. Davison or Marshall Bartholomew written for the Glee Clubs of Harvard or Yale, this is your destination.

There are a number of sources for Russian repertoire, but one publisher stands above the rest: Musica Russica (www.musicarussica.com). Their music is published in clean, clear editions with a sensible system of transliteration. They also feature recordings and make available pronunciation discs for those who need help with the language.

Yelton Rhodes Music (www.yrmusic.com) publishes a great deal of music for men's chorus, including many engaging and inventive arrangements of contemporary and traditional songs for most choral occasions.

Online Libraries

There are a number of library resources on the Internet, including Subito, the library of Orphei Drängar (www.od.se). OD's web site boasts that "Subito is the world's largest catalogue of music for male-voice choirs."

Ylioppilaskunnan Laulajat (YL) has a number of publications and recordings available through their web site (www.yl.fi) as well.

The Washington Men's Camerata in Washington, DC maintains the National Library of Men's Choral Music known as The Demetrius Project (www.camerata.com) that serves as a storehouse for music from colleges and universities that no longer have men's choruses.

In addition to the Camerata's substantial library, there are collections from Colgate, Davidson, Georgetown, Princeton, Temple, Yale, and other college and community groups. All of the collections contain some out-of-print and manuscript editions, which can be very valuable to the inquisitive conductor. The library's searchable database can be accessed on the Camerata's web site (given above).

You can also search Musica's Virtual Choral Library (www.musicanet.org). The goal of Musica's library project is to list every choral work ever published, so you might find many things of interest there!

Extended Works

Though much of the programming for men's choruses focuses on shorter works, there are a number of extended works of varying lengths for male chorus, either a cappella or accompanied by orchestra, band, chamber ensemble, or keyboard. Though no extended work for men's chorus rises to level of popularity attained by large-scale works for mixed chorus, there are a number of works worth investigating should the opportunity arise to perform such a piece.

There are a number of pieces in the ten- to fifteen-minute range with various accompaniments that could fit nicely into a program if accompanying forces are available. Perhaps the most frequently-performed shorter work for men's chorus and orchestra is the *Alto Rhapsody* by Johannes Brahms. Other pieces that fall into this category include Daniel Pinkham's familiar *Christmas Cantata* in a version for brass, organ, and men's chorus, published by Robert King.

Kurt Weill's *Berlin Requiem* for male chorus and stage band is a fascinating setting of Bertolt Brecht texts and is published by Universal Edition. Randall Thompson's grand setting of the words of Thomas Jefferson, *The Testament of Freedom*, is for male chorus and either piano, jazz band, or orchestra. Arnold Schoenberg's *A Survivor from Warsaw* is another fascinating shorter work for narrator, male chorus, and orchestra.

There are a number of Romantic-period mass settings, including two by Josef Rheinberger for male chorus and organ or wind ensemble. Franz Liszt wrote two quite different masses: the *Requiem* for male chorus and organ with optional brass instruments and the *Szekszárd Mass* for male chorus and organ. Maurice Duruflé's *Messe cum jubilo* for men's chorus and organ is an excellent example of twentieth-century French composition, along with the *Messe Solennelle* by Jean Langlais, for men's chorus, brass, and two organs.

For a large-scale Russian work, look for Pavel Chesnokov's *Panikhida*, a concert-length a cappella memorial service. There are also many Renaissance mass settings that work for men's chorus, though the style and length of these works might be challenging for the average singer.

With the constant growth of internet resources, it's easier than ever to obtain information on men's chorus repertoire, recruitment, recordings, festivals, and anything else you might want to know about the genre. By singing in a men's chorus, your students will gain an invaluable experience that can affect them throughout their lives.

In 2003, Chorus America (www.chorusamerica.org) sponsored a study entitled "America's Performing Art: A Study of Choruses, Choral Singers, and Their Impact." Among the study's many interesting findings was the fact that more people participate in choral singing than in any other performing art. There are more than 250,000 choruses nationwide, with more than twenty-eight million choral singers. These singers tend to be better informed and more politically aware than the average citizen. They are major culture consumers and frequent volunteers in community-building endeavors. Choral singers also donate more to charity and help to bridge social gaps in their communities.[1] So singing in a chorus, while also recreational, is important in creating better, well-rounded citizens through music.

While many singers who begin their choral training in school continue to sing avocationally as adults, some go on to careers in professional ensembles in the United States and abroad. Although these opportunities are limited, the work of professional men's ensembles can also help to inspire students, build membership, and increase audiences.

The most prominent professional men's groups in the United States are Chanticleer (www.chanticleer.org), Cantus (www.cantusonline.org), and the U. S. Army Chorus (www.usarmyband.com), though there are plenty of other part-time ensembles that sing at a professional level and have done many things to expand the repertoire and bring greater awareness of the male choral art to the public. Though there might be fewer men singing in organized male choirs than there were one hundred years ago, the long and proud tradition of these choruses still inspires singers and audiences through the beauty and power of the unique sound of male voices raised together in song.

CHAPTER 2

The Joy of Commissioning

Philip Brunelle

VocalEssence celebrated its fortieth season in 2008–2009 with its mission unchanged: "to explore the interaction of voices and instruments through innovative programming of music, past and present." This mission has given us the exciting prospect of working with many living composers (over 120 so far), premiering their music in concert as world or United States premieres.

There are many benefits from such collaborations:

1. The thrill of being involved in the creative process. We all have performed music where we wondered how the composer would want his or her music to sound. Working directly with the composer allows us to have questions answered by the source and also solve matters involving a specific choir's sound, the style the composer wishes, and the tempo desired (which may not end up being what is marked).
2. The second thrill is for the choir—the opportunity of creating a new work with the composer's assistance. It is a marvelous experience for both composer and choir to share in this creativity, and definitely a real learning experience for the choir. And for the composer, it offers the opportunity to be more precise based on the questions offered by members of the choir as to the result in performance.
3. The third thrill is for the audience—giving them the opportunity of being present for a first performance, a debut which no one has heard before. It is a very special feeling to be present when history is made, and I can assure you that the audience loves it!

It is not necessary for the composer to be present when premiering a work by a living composer (or presenting a subsequent performance), but it is an added bonus for everyone if this can happen. If it cannot happen, one still has the opportunity of being in contact with the composer to ask questions, and composers are delighted to be consulted and to know that their music is being performed.

Communicate with Composers

Whether or not a composer is present, one thing I strongly urge is sending the composer a copy of the concert program or bulletin. When a piece of music (such as an orchestral work or an opera) is performed, the composer is likely to hear about it because of the rental agreement with a publisher. In the case of a choral work (an anthem, motet, or longer work from your library or purchased from a music store), the composer has no idea of the possibility of performance and is *delighted* to know of your presentation.

I began doing this when I founded VocalEssence and concurrently began my music directorship at Plymouth Congregational Church in Minneapolis. If I didn't have a composer's address, I simply sent the program in care of the publisher with a short note of thanks. The responses received over these forty years have been heartwarming and exciting, resulting in many warm friendships and discovering more music of many composers.

When the Plymouth Choir first performed an anthem by the English composer, Ian Kellam (*A Hymn to Jesus*), I sent a bulletin with a note to the publisher, not knowing Kellam's whereabouts. I didn't expect a reply, but was delighted some six months later to receive a note from him *and* a new anthem he had composed especially for me (see figure 1)! Now this is an unusual situation, but what a wonderful one it was, for it has resulted in a friendship spanning decades and the subsequent performance of many other Kellam anthems and hymns—to the delight of the Plymouth Choir and congregation.

FIGURE 1. Anthem written for the author

For Philip Brunelle
and the choir of Plymouth Congregational Church, Minneapolis

NOW WELL MAY WE MIRTHËS MAKE

For SATB Chorus & Organ

Medieval Carol

Music by
Ian Kellam

5

Soprano *f*
Now well may we mir - thës make. Al - le - lu - ia,

Alto *f*
Now well may we mir - thës make. Al - le - lu - ia,

Tenor *f*
Now well may we mir - thës make. Al - le - lu - ia,

Bass *f*
Now well may we mir - thës make. Al - le - lu - ia,

How did this idea of communicating with composers first occur to me? It was actually due to my wife, Carolyn (then my fiancée), who was very moved by an early performance of Benjamin Britten's *War Requiem* and wanted to send Britten a note of thanks. I knew he lived in the small town of Aldeburgh, England, and figured that the post office would find him if the address was only the town and country.

Imagine her surprise when some months later she received a handwritten note from Benjamin Britten personally thanking her for taking the time to write to him! This became our first framed note from a composer, which have been followed by a number of others. And this convinced me to start communicating with composers whenever I perform their music.

Working with a composer can take many forms, depending on the piece of music at hand and the questions you may have. Sometimes a piece is very straightforward with clear instructions from the composer, whereas at other times notes may be unclear or questionable; you may wonder about specific places for breathing or have questions about dynamics or tempos. A composer may respond in a general way to your concerns, or at other times will be very precise about the desired effect. In any case, it is wonderful to have the composer's insights...sometimes leaving the interpretation totally in your hands!

For the inaugural season of VocalEssence (then named the Plymouth Music Series), I knew I should start with a "bang" and placed a phone call to Aaron Copland, inviting him to come to Minneapolis to conduct his choral music. I knew this was a long shot, but figured I wouldn't know if I didn't try. His response "Young man, I have never been asked to conduct my choral music, just my orchestral music. Tell me the date you have in mind—I'll cancel whatever I have and be there!" So, you never know.

What I especially remember from his first visit besides his very natural way of making music was his comment about interpreting his music: He strongly urged me to use my own musical sense. "It is impossible for a composer to write down every little rubato and intention . . . that's what we composers are counting on you conductors for! Trust your instincts and I'm sure my music will come out just fine!"

* * *

Commissioning a composer is an exciting opportunity and one I hope you will consider doing so again and again. It will give you a special relationship with a composer which will delight you and your singers. It may be that you will have a composer in mind or a text that you want to have set to music.

Before contacting a composer, try to decide on the basics involved:

- The composer
- The text (if you have one, or you wish to explore that with the composer)
- The length of the piece
- The performing forces (a cappella or with piano or other instruments)
- SATB or divisi, and any soloist(s) featured
- The date of performance (if a specific one is needed.)
- Dedication (if desired)
- Fee

Of course, you can begin by contacting the composer of your choice and work out all the details together, but the more specifics you provide, the more responsive the composer will be. It is important to plan ahead, giving the composer adequate time to write the piece and sufficient time for you to rehearse it.

My first commission was to Dominick Argento, Regents Professor of Music at the University of Minnesota and a beloved teacher and friend of mine. At the time I commissioned him, VocalEssence was in its earliest years and I had only rudimentary ideas of how the commissioning process worked. I knew I wanted Dr. Argento to compose a thirty-minute work for my chorus of fifty singers accompanied by a small instrumental ensemble to celebrate our fifth anniversary.

I contacted Dominick and the idea of writing a work pleased him. As I didn't have a text in mind, he agreed to give it some thought and get back to me. After discussing several possibilities we settled on a medieval setting of "Jonah and the Whale," a work of thirty minutes duration for chorus, three soloists, and nine instrumentalists. A fee was set as well as a date to receive the music and a dedication. All of this was drawn up in a contract prepared by the composer's publisher.

When the music arrived I discovered that it was forty-five minutes in length and I wondered how I would find the funds to pay for the extra fifteen minutes of music. Dominick informed me that he had gotten carried away by the text and that the fee we had agreed on would be the same, no matter the length.

The work was a resounding success, a wonderful piece—not easy, but worth the effort—and one that has received additional performances and has appeared on several recordings. Subsequent commissions have not always been on that scale, but it started me on a path that has provided me and my singers with many pleasurable occasions.

FIGURE 2. Descriptive label

Moderato mosso (♩= 69 ca.)

S. Pa - tience is a prince-ly thing,

A. Pa - tience is a prince-ly thing,

T. Pa - tience is a prince-ly thing,

B. Pa - tience is a prince-ly thing,

Moderato mosso (♩= 69 ca.)

(ORG.) *mp* *poco* *mp*

Commissioning by Collaboration

Another way of thinking about commissioning is by collaboration. I have been involved in three unique ways:

In 1980, the American Guild of Organists' national convention was held in Minneapolis-St. Paul. Because of the (then) new and vibrant Minnesota Composers Forum created by Libby Larsen and Stephen Paulus (now the American Composers Forum), I contacted Libby to see if we might celebrate and call attention to the burgeoning number of outstanding composers in the community. My idea was to line up as many churches as possible and have each one commission a local composer; each church would receive an anthem and it would be performed on the opening Sunday of the convention.

Most of the churches contacted had never commissioned an anthem but were eager to be involved. A total of twenty-nine Twin Cities churches commissioned twenty-nine Minnesota composers for that June 1980 Sunday morning! Each church paid a similar commissioning fee, with the monies being raised in all manner of ways, from bake sales and memorial gifts to special offerings and endowed funds. In return, each church received a bound copy of all twenty-nine anthems in camera-ready manuscript for each choir member. Libby and I sat down together and paired the composers with the churches, and it was a great celebration!

FIGURE 3. Descriptive label

One of the special benefits was, of course, the ability to consider some of the other twenty-eight anthems in a service and many choirs opted to do so. It definitely made an impact on the convention attendees, helping them understand the depth of composer talent in the Twin Cities area.

Co-commissioning

A second way of collaborating which VocalEssence has pursued has been to co-commission with another organization, resulting in performances in multiple locales. We have collaborated with such diverse organizations as the BBC Singers, Three Choirs Festival in England, Opera Theatre of St. Louis, The Library of Congress, and King's College Choir, Cambridge. Each collaboration was unique and required special negotiation's to satisfy each of the commissioning partners, but the end results have been wonderful, providing additional opportunities for composers' music to be heard and a wider network of friends for VocalEssence.

Hold a Contest

A third unique collaboration has continued for twelve years now with the American Composers Forum (ACF): the commissioning of two new carols every Christmas. My concern has been with the renewal of the carol form, helping listeners and performers to understand that carols can be as alive today as they were hundreds of years ago when "The First Nowell," "Deck the Halls," and hundreds more were first created.

Each year my artistic associate, Sigrid Johnson, and I decide on an accompaniment for the new carols, and with the support of the ACF, the call for scores goes out to its 1700 members and beyond. The rules are simple:

World premiere	No prior performance of submitted work
Eligibility	Composers of all ages whose permanent residence is North America
Form	Carol (defined as a strophic song, which may or may not have refrains, that is associated with Christmas)
Voicing	SATB with an instrument
Duration	Maximum of 3 minutes
Text	Sacred or secular, medieval to present, appropriate for concert setting; Christmas or seasonal winter themes accepted; proof of public domain or author's written permission for use of text is required

The hope is to find two outstanding carols to premiere every December at our five *Welcome Christmas!* concerts which are broadcast on National Public Radio. The result has been marvelous, with wonderful new carols being submitted (over 100 entries every year) and a very enthusiastic response from our audiences. Many of them are now published and a number of them are included on the VocalEssence CD, *Beloved This Heavenly Night*, (Gothic Records). including many of the carols in the future.

FIGURE 4. Descriptive label

UN NACIMIENTO
(A Nativity Scene)

Music and Lyrics
by Diegc Luzuriaga

(Duration: 3 minutes)

Soprano — solo: Es-
tre-lli-ta, es-tre-lla fu-gaz, que vas del mar a la sie rra, de - cí, de-cí en dón-de_es-ta-rá

Alto: que vas a la sie rra

Tenor: sie rra

Bass

Guitar

One of the outcomes of such a contest is coming in contact with new composers. The carol submitted by Ecuadorian composer, Diego Luzuriaga, a 2006 Carol winner, led to our commissioning Diego to write an extended Christmas piece, *The Child of the Andes* for choir, soloists, and an instrumental ensemble of Ecuadorian instruments: quena, quenilla, quenacho, zampoña, charango, and tiple. It was a marvelous premiere!

As you can see, working with composers is exciting and rewarding. Often, the results are artistically unexpected: In the mid-1980s I spoke with Libby Larsen, suggesting that she consider composing a more extended work. She told me that she had this very thought after composing a number of shorter works. We decided to think about a poet for a forty-five-minute work. I had heard about the interest of Jehan Sadat, Egypt's First Lady, speaking and writing about peace and wondered if a meeting with her would be of interest to Libby. Of course it was!

Several months later the two of us flew to Cairo, Egypt and presented the idea of a work on peace for chorus, soloists, and orchestra to Mrs. Sadat. She was surprised, as she had never been involved in such a project, but she was interested and a subsequent meeting laid out plans for a four-movement choral symphony. Mrs. Sadat did not feel competent to write the text herself, but together with Libby, they discovered texts from many faiths and countries that brought this theme together.

As the work progressed, Libby realized that the piece needed a narrator and we persuaded Jehan Sadat to travel from Egypt to Minnesota to narrate the work. It was, as you can imagine, a very moving occasion to hear this eloquent woman speak—this woman whose husband had been assassinated and who was speaking about peace, and on the very evening that President Reagan ordered U. S. planes to bomb Libya. An extraordinary event.

FIGURE 5. Descriptive label

Finding a Composer

Finding a composer can happen in many ways:

1. It might be a composer whose music you have performed and admired. If you don't have an address, begin by contacting the publisher...or researching the composer's online!

2. Search your community to see if there is a composer of interest—perhaps someone whose music fascinates you but whom you have not performed.
3. Consider investing in a young composer who is studying composition at a local college or university. Consult the composition teacher to see if there is someone of merit for whom the encouragement of a commission might be *the* moment the composer has been waiting for. Of course, it will be important for you to meet the composer and work to make the relationship positive.
4. Consult with a choir director whom you admire and seek a suggestion.

Share Strengths and Weaknesses

No matter which route you take, it is important that you and the composer understand the choir's skill level so that the composer can write to the choir's strengths. The best thing is to have the composer hear the choir before beginning the composition. If the composer lives far away send a recording from a concert, worship service, or rehearsal—something that gives a healthy representation of what the choir can do. If one section of the choir is weaker than the others, let the composer know this. Likewise, if there are range concerns, address them. Anything that can help the composer approach the writing with positive energy will be to your advantage.

* * *

The important thing is to take the leap and commission a composer! You will be so pleased that you did and wonder why you didn't do it before. For all of the reasons that I stated earlier you will find that commissioning will help your choir grow in many ways: musically, intellectually, emotionally, and positively. Wonderful as it is to perform the beautiful music of the past, it is equally important to encourage the composers of today, and this is a responsibility that each of us in the choral profession must share: ours is a profession of music that lives!

CHAPTER 3

Articulation: Enabling the Meaning in Music to be Understood

Bruce Chamberlain

Introduction—Setting the Scene

Having been a director of choral activities in higher education for thirty-one years, I have had plenty of time to consider and prioritize the things that are important to impart to choirs and aspiring young choral conductors. Various aspects and components of this pedagogic curriculum have changed over the years and received varying levels of attention from time to time, depending mostly upon the needs of students and the mission of the institution. However, the one component that has remained a constant for me is that the primary role of the conductor is to function as the composer's advocate. If the literally millions of decisions that a conductor makes every day are predicated upon what is in the best interests of the composer's creation, then the art form that we all know and love will continue to thrive, flourish, and nurture the souls of humankind for years to come.

Many would argue that this advocacy for the primacy of the score must of course be predicated upon the experience level and maturity of the ensemble. No conductor can really expect an elementary school choir to represent the desires and concepts of a beautifully composed phrase as can an auditioned choir of highly trained college students. The obvious response here is "Bunk!" Everyone of us have marveled at the glorious, stunningly beautiful and profoundly moving experience of hearing the voices of children who fully understand and represent the intent of the composer's language. There is no magic here; it rests upon the conductor's ability to impart, elicit, inspire, cajole, and ultimately understand the language and style of the music.

I have used the terms *language* and *style* in the sentence above very purposefully, for all music is language, with syntactical principles and communicative capabilities. It was after reading John Ciardi's fascinating book, *How Does a Poem Mean?*, that I began to make the connection between meaning in language and meaning in music. The common denominator here, the conduit through which meaning is enabled to flow from poetic/musical language to the reader/listener, is style. When the style of the music is matched, enhanced, and enabled by the style of the performance, meaning and understanding become possible. Thus an understanding of musical styles is critical for the conductor at every level of performance.

Central to the educational process for choirs and conductors is an understanding of salient style features, characteristics, if you will, to enable the meaning of the music to be expressed, communicated, and understood. We conductors, for example, must be able to recognize Brahms' musical language when we see it on the page and hear it performed, and most importantly, "speak in Brahms" when we stand on the podium to rehearse and conduct our ensembles.

The inherent style features of music, when addressed from the first rehearsal, have at least a two-fold positive impact upon the rehearsal process and allow for the composer's intentions to be more readily understood. First, rehearsal time is saved and reduced since there will not be any need for unlearning or relearning. Rehearsals work best when the music is digested in a natural, sequential way, maximizing the learning curve of the choir. If these layered rehearsal sequences are always tempered and formulated with the salient style features in mind, the layering process becomes most efficient.

Secondly, by fostering style awareness from the outset, the music making can rise to a higher plane of understanding, ensuring that performances are not about "getting the notes and rhythms," but rather speaking the meaning of the music. It is paramount that we conductors do not devolve into "keepers of the time" but evolve into "makers of the music."

What Is Style?

We conductors often discuss style and stylistic characteristics of performances, but what are these style features? We all recognize the differences between the style of an oratorio chorus by Handel and a movement from Brahms' *Ein deutsches Requiem*, but what are those differences and how do we impart those to our choristers? Here then, is a preliminary list of eight basic style features:

Melody	conjunct or disjunct
Harmony	diatonic, chromatic or non-tonal
Texture	homophonic, polyphonic or contrapuntal
Rhythm	reflects a single meter or is multi-metric
Phrase shape and length	symmetrical or asymmetrical, long or short
Form	standardized formal principle or through-composed

Timbre	bright or dark, etc.
Articulation	legato, non-legato or staccato

Of these basic style features that help delineate meaning in music, it seems that articulation is the least understood and consequently the most ignored by conductors. During the last decade or so, I have participated in hundreds of clinics, festivals, adjudications, and guest conducting events with choirs from all over the country and in varying parts of the world. Invariably I discover that aspects of the approach to articulation are undefined or mismatched, causing a confusion or barrier to fully understanding the musical meaning these choirs are trying to convey. When I pause the process to inquire about which articulation they are using and why, the response usually ranges from inquisitive silence to that pained look that signifies "What are talking about?" This leads to a second question: "What is articulation; what does articulation mean?" The response now yields a laundry list of symptoms:

1. How to pronounce the words
2. Accent
3. Cutoffs
4. Diction
5. Good rhythm

All of these are good observations that can affect and certainly are affected by articulation. However, given this muddled reaction to the simple request for a definition of an English word that is central to creating meaning in music, there is no wonder that so much of choral music performance fails to reach its potential for meaning and understanding.

The dictionary definition of *articulation*, according to the *Webster's New World Dictionary*, states:

1. a joining or being joined
2. the way in which parts are joined together

Thus, by definition, articulation is the relationship between things or events and how they are or may not be connected. In musical terms, articulation is the relationship of one sound event to the next. It really is that simple, but also that profound. It is this inner connectedness with its varying degrees, that really delivers the meaning of musical statements and allows our musical language to be understood.

Distilled down to its basic elements, there are only three basic articulations. When musical events are performed as long and connected as possible with absolutely no release of intensity between them, we call that articulation *legato*.

When the events are foreshortened and separated by intervals of silence, the articulation is called *staccato*. The varying degrees of shades of intensity release between sound events that ranges from the extreme of *legato* to the extreme of *staccato* can be lumped together into one large generic grouping called *non-legato*. Thus the very essence of syntactical musical meaning can be governed by these three basic means of articulation: *legato*, *non-legato*, *and staccato*.

We all have experienced live presentations of glorious music expression to be frustrated by the fact that the orchestra was too loud or too present and the choir seemed muffled or in the background. The solution to this problem is not to have the orchestra play artificially softer, putting the players "on eggshells," so to speak, which only engenders a tentative performance riddled with instances where players are unable to make their instrument speak for fear of being too loud. Conversely, the choir may not, cannot, and perhaps should not simply phonate louder to rectify balance issues. The solution lies in articulation. When the choir is articulate, rhythmically "supercharged," and pristinely together, almost all balance issues with the instrumental complement will be corrected.

Notice that I have chosen the term "instrumental complement," not accompaniment. I firmly believe that the instruments which complete a choral score, whether piano, chamber ensemble, or full orchestra, are just as important to the understanding of the music as the choir. It is when the totality of the score complement articulates together, is a matched and calculated syntactical unison, that the profundity of the music expression can be understood.

Applying the Appropriate Articulation

The artistry of musical performance and our responsibility as conductors is knowing when and how to employ each articulation to enable the meaning of the music to be understood. The decision-making process or processes to determine which articulation to use can be varied and multifaceted. In addition to matching, then changing articulation by subtle degrees within various style periods and single compositions, the conductor needs to be sensitive to the articulation requirements even within single phrases. The single most significant guiding principle here is to allow the music to be understood. Conductors must constantly monitor and ask themselves: Can everything in the texture be heard? Is the music conveying the meaning the composer intended?

As daunting as the task of determining which articulation to choose may seem, there are some overriding principles or axioms that can assist and inform the process. Here are three initial points of departure for choosing a basic articulation:

1. Music written prior to 1600 is basically text driven and should use text stress and diction principles to determine articulation. A really good rule of thumb for pre-1600 music (compositions which are essentially guided rhythmically by tactus and not beat) is for non-stressed syllables to intensify (move forward/crescendo) to the stressed syllable and the stressed syllable should relax (diminuendo) to the unstressed syllable. This process allows the polyphonic conversation between voices to be heard and understood while eliminating the dreaded tyranny of barline stress on downbeats. Figure 1 shows an example of text-stress articulation in the first few vocal entries of Palestrina's famous motet

2. The second guiding principle involves music written between 1600–1800. Music from this period should be performed basically *non-legato* unless indicated as *legato* by the composer. The implications in this statement are truly illuminating. It means that essentially all Baroque and early Classic music should have a certain kind of articulation "bounce" unless the composer has indicated slurs or *legato*. This means that the basic relationship of one pitch to another has a degree of decay or waning of intensity.

The term and image I have found that works best for choristers to understand and replicate this process is *handbell articulation*. Everyone is familiar with the attack and decay sound that a handbell makes automatically. When applied to singing highly melismatic Baroque choral music, this articulation allows texture to become transparent and understandable. This putting small spaces of less intensity between pitches allows the ear to "hear into the texture" and follow each individual line, much like an intricately woven sweater has spaces between the strands of wool and allows the eye to "see into the textile." Notice that texture and textile, both products of weaving strands of material (whether music or wool), come from the same root word. Figure 2 shows an example of *non-legato* or handbell articulation applied to the opening motive in "For Unto Us" from Handel's *Messiah.*

FIGURE 2. Mm. 7–9, "For Unto Us" from *Messiah*, Handel

The indications on the score excerpt in figure 2 necessitate some degree of interpretation. The list below endeavors to clarify the articulation axioms:

a. One flip of the "r" in the word "For" on pitch
b. Begin the words "unto" and "us" with a light glottal stroke
c. The sibilant sound of "s" in "us" articulates the beginning of the word "a" to become "sa"
d. The four repeated notes on "us a child is" should all bounce lightly, using a handbell articulation
e. The two-note figure on "born" must *diminuendo* from C to B using an umlaut "o" vowel (ö), thus eliminating the possibility of treating the "r" as a vowel sound

3. Finally, music written between 1800–1900 should be performed *legato* unless the composer indicates otherwise. As music became "democratized" in the nineteenth century and moved from the salons and chambers of the falling aristocracy into larger performance venues for a greater mass-market audience, the need for instruments to be able to fill these larger spaces was created. Combined with the technical advances in instrument construction that were a collateral result of the industrial revolution, the mechanism of musical instruments became heavier and allowed for greater range on the *forte* end of the dynamic spectrum and a much greater resonant tone color. This contributed to the shift in articulation foundation from the basic separated articulation and light tone color of the eighteenth century to the basic legato articulation and darker tone color of the nineteenth century. One need only to compare the opening of the seventh movement of Brahms' *Ein deutsches Requiem* (see figure 3) with the Handel excerpt in figure 2 to see and hear the dramatic shift in articulation that is needed to impart the full understanding and meaning of the music.

FIGURE 3. Mm. 1–7, movement 7, *Ein deutsches Requiem*, Brahms

7. Selig sind die Toten

Blessed are the dead

Feierlich [Solemnly]

2 Flöten

2 Oboen

2 Klarinetten in B

2 Fagotte

Kontrafagott (ad lib.)

2 Hörner in F

2 Hörner in E

3 Posaunen

Harfe

Sopran

Alt

Tenor

Baß

1. Violine

2. Violine

Bratsche

Violoncell

Kontrabaß

Orgel (ad lib.)

Se - - - - - - lig— sind die To - ten, die in dem Her-ren ster - -

a 2

div.

Ped.

Feierlich

Composers of the twentieth and twenty-first centuries have become much more careful and exacting with regard to indicating the articulation and tone color necessities for their music. For example, one need only to examine *The Last Words of David* by Randall Thompson to see and hear how much information and instruction he provides for the conductor and performers. Thus the guiding principle for articulation for music from 1900 to the present is simply to follow carefully the composer's indications.

Obviously the dates given in the above discussion are only landmarks and not to be interpreted strictly and precisely, as though on January 1, 1800 concepts of articulation changed for all music. Think rather of an evolutionary process that happened over a period of time as socio-political climates changed and helped change artistic taste, and vice versa.

Rehearsal Implications

Once some parameters for stylistic articulation have been set and are in place, the imperative for implementation during the earliest stages of the rehearsal process is obvious. Warm-ups fashioned to elucidate and facilitate the complexities of articulation will prove most helpful. Rehearsing the entire choir together on one motive employing the articulation axioms enable the conductor to place more responsibility upon the choristers for monitoring the implementation of the axiomatic principles as they present themselves throughout the work at hand. This ability for "transfer of learning," recognizing the axiom implementation in one section and applying it likewise at a similar section later in the work, is a real sign that true understanding is taking place within the ensemble. This rehearsal approach is very effective for encouraging independence and personal responsibility in each choir member.

For orchestral rehearsals, carefully marked parts and an immediate and consistent insistence upon matters of articulation yields the best results. When the conductor has a clear understanding of the style and articulation of the music, is able to show it in the delivery system of the conducting technique, and aurally demonstrate on occasion, the orchestra is enabled to produce the desired results. These suggestions, designed to make each rehearsal much more efficient, become paramount as performance schedules increase and rehearsal periods decrease.

Finally, it is important to mention the articulation approach during contrapuntal works in which more than one text phrase and associated musical motive are pitted against one another. In situations like this it works best to give each line of text/musical motive its own articulation and shape, reflective of the text meaning, resulting at times in opposing, not matching, articulations sounding at once. A very clear and instructive example of this occurs in the eighth movement of the "Symbolum Nicenum" of Bach's *B Minor Mass*.

In this movement, the text phrase "Confiteor…" and "in remissionem…" are given very distinctive and exclusive musical material as seen in figure 4.

FIGURE 4. Ms. 31-37, Confiteor from *B Minor Mass*, Bach

The "Confiteor" motive with its longer note values works best when given a lighter, more delicate *non-legato* articulation while supporting the melodic shape with a corresponding dynamic shape. The more active "in remissionem" motive benefits from a more heavily bounced handbell articulation that allows it to remain separate and distinct but in coordination with its textural/motivic partner. This concept of opposing articulations for textual and musical material allows the ear to follow each line clearly and distinctly even through quite complicated contrapuntal texture. It is amazing how the ear can understand this multi-layering of text and music. When each line has its own integral articulation, it renders a powerful theological statement that is enhanced by the musical association.

On the contrary, when actors in a play step on each others' lines and two lines of dialogue sound at once, the result is almost chaotic. The audience is left confused and frustrated by not being able to fully comprehend what has been said. Music's ability to provide meaning, understanding, and clarity when several ideas are expressed simultaneously is one its endearing and exciting characteristics. One need only to think of the famous Mozart "Finale to Act II" of *Le nozze di Figaro* to witness the genius of composer, librettist, and art form. In this dramatic scene, duet becomes trio, trio becomes quartet, quartet becomes quintet, quintet becomes sextet, and sextet becomes septet, with many competing plot lines and dramatic issues happening at once, and all are perfectly comprehendible by the audience when text and music are carefully sculpted and articulated.

Putting Pedagogy into Practice

In my present position as Director of Choral Activities at The University of Arizona I have the distinct honor and privilege to teach exclusively at the graduate level, working with many gifted aspiring choral conductors seeking instruction and guidance to begin or continue established careers in choral music. When these students are confronted with the complexities of the choral/orchestral score they very often seem overwhelmed by the amount of information that is coming at them, and they begin to "fix" things or prioritize issues with which they feel the most comfortable, namely minute details in the choir. Since for any given project most choral conductors get at best only two or three rehearsals with the orchestra (but have usually had significantly more rehearsal time with the choir), my advice and pedagogical instruction is to focus initially upon the orchestra.

Settle the Articulation

I go even further to advocate a three-part priority system to enable the music to get a thorough and artistic rehearsal. First, as you might expect, get the articulation settled, uniform, and in service to the style of the music. It is imperative that the ensemble plays and sings together, matching the lengths of notes and beginning and ending each sound event together, "together" being the operative word here. The generic name of our choirs and orchestra is "ensemble," which literally means "together." If the music is not together, there is no possible way that the composer's intentions can be met and the audience perceive the intended meaning.

Balance the Texture

Secondly, and closely related, get the texture balanced. Be sure that what is most important in the texture can be heard and what is supportive is only that: supportive. Balance issues between choir and orchestra can be a little tricky at times. However, many balance issues will be solved automatically if the groups are absolutely together and articulating appropriately. Once everyone is able to hear clearly the priorities of the texture, balance issues begin to go away. Many inexperienced choral directors begin to fix balance problems by asking the orchestra to play softer. This can often result in players trying to accommodate the request to the point that their instrument will not speak reliably, thereby leaving silences or holes in the texture. A better approach is to ask the choir to articulate more and then listen for the balance to change. I don't know why, but when the choir stops singing absolutely together, in essence "primitizes" articulation and creates pristine ensemble, it becomes louder!

Elucidate the Subtler Meanings and Relationships in the Score

Finally, after everyone is together and the texture is balanced, then it is appropriate to elucidate that "gem of an idea" about what motive X might mean or the existential relationship between text, music, and form. Save these observations for exactly the right moment when the ensemble can make sense of the information and use it to enhance the understanding of the meaning of the music. How often have ensembles been asked to "think about idea X" while rehearsing a particular section when in reality it is still struggling for correct articulation, ensemble, balance, and intonation! Provide for the singers and players what they need at the moment in order that they may give you what you want the audience to hear and experience.

Concluding Observations

The choral art is truly amazing. Having things to say to the world through music is unbelievably rewarding and yet so incredibly humbling. It is quite difficult to have a life in music, but once music has chosen you, you have an obligation to your musicians and audience to communicate fully the meaning and understanding inherent in the art form itself. It is my hope that these observations and ideas will enable conductors to find their voice and communicate more fully through their chosen art.

CHAPTER 4

When Words Fail

Rodney Eichenberger

The choir one dreams of conducting is not always the one that shows up for rehearsal. I well remember the first high school choir rehearsal I held as I began my teaching career. I had graduated from St. Olaf College, and as a member of the choir had sung in some of the most important concert halls in the country at that time: Carnegie Hall in New York, Boston's Symphony Hall, Orchestra Hall in Chicago, the Los Angeles Shrine Auditorium, and the San Francisco Opera House. When I began my choral conducting career, those sounds rang in my ears, and for some inexplicable reason, those were the sounds I dreamed I would hear on that morning in early September in the Wapato, Washington High School Choral Room.

What a shock! The singers who finally meandered into the seats in front of me not only seemed to fail to understand that I was "in charge," but appeared to be in the room for a reason far removed from the one I assumed they would have. They wandered about, laughing and chatting, clearly ready to challenge my leadership. I took the bull by the horns. I pounded both fists on the top of a six-foot grand piano and screamed, "Quiet!" thinking this would clearly demonstrate who was in charge! They were stunned into silence. They listened with jaws agape as I yelled at them to either change their registration or be prepared to spend each hour working with me to make beautiful music.

While I have since learned that screaming is not the best class management approach, I was sure I had won, so I began to lead a vocalise. The second shock of the day occurred at that moment: in no way did the sound that filled the room match any of the sounds in my ear. To my dismay, there were actually a couple of students in the rehearsal room who were singing about a fourth below the first pitch I had sounded.

To make things even more difficult, there were some unusually talented musicians with excellent voices in all sections. I'm certain everyone in the room was aware of those singing the wrong note and that the most talented were waiting to see if I could or would do anything about it. I can't remember exactly what I action I took but, it would have been to everyone's advantage had I known something about the power of gesture before I stepped on the podium for the first time.

The Power of Gesture

I wish I had been aware of fact that all choir members have in common some kinetic experiences that can easily be attached to the most sensitive music making. We all use our hands and arms to perform daily tasks. Whether we eat with our hands, forks and spoons, or chopsticks, we all lift food from the plate to our mouth. This lifting gesture is an integral part of every human's experience well beyond feeding oneself. The lifting and laying down of objects is such a integral part of our daily lives that it is easy to fail to observe the affect of these moves on seemingly non-related tasks such as singing.

We also use gestures to clarify points when speaking. Interestingly, many *words* are pitch related. There is some evidence that pitch differences in words are related to the gestures that always accompany them. In testing dozens of languages, I've discovered that the word for "up" is always at a higher pitch than the word for "down."

When gesture accompanies these words, the difference is more pronounced, so that if one points to the ceiling and says "up," the gesture invariably encourages the pitch to be a bit higher and louder. When one points to the floor and says the word "down," the dynamic is louder but the pitch is slightly lower. If, however, one points to the ceiling when saying the word "down," the pitch will likely more closely match the pitch for "up."

Some words have both pitch and projection qualities. The word pairs "here/there" and "near/far" are normally spoken with different pitches and projection. The word "there," if accompanied by a pointing gesture with the arm raised slightly invariably has a higher pitch and a more projected quality than does the word "here" if one points to oneself. The further the distance implied by the word "there" the higher one tends to raise the arm, resulting in a higher pitch and stronger projection.

We have long known that gesture and paralanguage (the inflection that accompanies words) is upwards of ninety percent more believable than words themselves, and that anytime gesture and word inflection is in opposition to normal pitch and gesture relationship we choose to believe the gesture and inflection, thus assigning the word a meaning opposite to its definition. If gesture is so powerful in normal communication, then could it be a valuable tool when attached to singing? If I had known about the power of gestures demonstrating "up" and "there," the frustration of the young men in my first choir who had not yet found their voices could have been quickly alleviated.

Using Gesture to Solve Pitch Problems

Since the room was large enough, I could have had the tenors and basses form a circle in the front of the room. To assure that they added some vitality to their bodies, I could have asked them to turn and start walking in a circle, singing the appropriate note over and over, separated by rests, on a syllable such as "No" or "Do" (see the example in figure 1).

FIGURE 1.

If the vast majority of singers were able to sing the correct pitch it would dominate the sound in the room. It is amazing how quickly this simple exercise helps inexperienced singers begin singing the correct note.

To help a singer having trouble finding the right note, the instructor can walk in the middle of the circle beside the singer, saying such things as "Lift those feet higher" and "Point further away," and by encouraging them to sing a bit louder. This will often get every singer on pitch in less than a minute.

From my point of view, this is step one with the kind of group described above. The inexperienced singer achieves some success, and the talented singers realize that the conductor can solve a problem. Will the singers be able to immediately find the right note next time? If not, repeat the exercise even if singers remain in place on risers.

The Character of Music

There are a number of in common gestural experiences which can easily be used to add subtlety and character to a choir's performance beyond helping inexperienced singers find the correct pitch.

Great music making has imagination, direction, rhythmic viability, accurate intonation, and dynamic variation. The character one prescribes to a work is determined in a large part by the treatment of phrase and rhythmic function of notes in a melodic pattern.

The Four Functions of Rhythm

Each note in a phrase can have a "Down," an "Away," an "Off," or an "Into" function. In order to help singers understand these four possible functions of rhythm it is helpful to let them hear the quality before naming it.

Down

To experience the Down function, place one hand, palm up, directly in front of you and clap down with the other hand.

Away

The Away function can be shown by putting one hand in a forward "there" position and using a forward clapping movement with the other hand.

Off

To experience the Off function, start by clapping Down (as above). Now bring the clapping hand up to the shoulder and hit it with the other hand.

Into

Put one hand in front of the naval. Move that hand slightly forward. Clap it Down and forward with the other hand.

Note that only the Away function suggests no existing or ensuing Down function. If one claps Down while moving the lower hand up and out, the Away function is imposed on Down. This closely resembles the quality we normally seek for the first note of a phrase. It is the Away function that gives life to the phrase.

Many choirs sing the first beat of a measure with a Down quality. It seems that if we changed the terminology from *down*beat to *first* beat, then the first beat in a measure would automatically have more life.

Say "down" and then say "first." Note that there is a difference in the weight of the two words. If one sings the first note in a bar with the word "down" in mind, the pitch and direction of the note is different than if "first" is the focus.

We all know the results of continually singing Down followed by Off beat functions, or the sing-songy effect of singing downbeats on the first beat of every measure. This often occurs when singing one beat to the measure. It is amazing how a dull phrase comes to life by simply using forward movement starting close to the body and slowly moving up and out.

Using Gesture to Enliven Singing

Creating Entrances with Forward Motion

Reaching out a few inches from the naval and picking up the first note of a phrase can bring life and forward motion to an otherwise dull entrance. It adds an Away rhythmic function to a note that can easily be sung as a Down. A conductor can use this same gesture to bring in the choir. The kinesthetic accompaniment to this exercise strengthens the understanding of the quality of the entrance. We can say "Lift the tone," but these words have added meaning if choir members actually use their hands to pick it up.

If the first note of a phrase still has no forward motion, asking the singers to take a step forward when they sing the note will invariably achieve the desired result. Then the conductor need only ask singers to remember that sensation. When they forget, a step forward by the conductor should serve the same purpose; if not, a repetition of the move with the choir will do it.

Phrasal Direction

An entire phrase will automatically gain direction if the choir walks the phrase, taking a step on every note, especially if they do so without making any noise with their feet. Try this exercise:

1. Slowly lift the arm, beginning with the hand beside the knee in the normal relaxed position, palm toward the leg.
2. Slowly turning and lifting the hand to about the level of the sternum to avoid tension in the vocal mechanism will encourage a nice forward-moving phrase and a spontaneous crescendo.
3. The slower the move, the more effective the phrase and the less obvious the crescendo.
4. If singers reach the sternum prior to the climax of the phrase, returning the hand to the beginning position at an appropriate time will still achieve the sense of phrase motion that great performances always enjoy.

Tuning a Downward Scale

There are several things we can do to assure accurate intonation if a downward scale falls out of tune rather than the "You're flat" admonition that often follows this phenomenon.

1. Ask the choir to sing the highest pitch by itself accompanied by a tossing gesture across the room to give more height and direction to the first note.

2. Sing the top note of the phrase, then a note above it to get the top note in tune.
3. If the following downward note is a half step, sing the top note then cut it off with a swinging upward motion of the hand. This produces a pitch-raising release.
4. Since most downward scale pitch problems are caused by anticipating the next lower step while still singing the note above, helping singers think up at the end of each note prior to the downward step is most helpful.
5. Placing rests after each note helps singers hear this upward release, encouraging better intonation when followed by the half or whole step below.

Well-supported Dynamics

Fortissimo

There are a number of bodily activities in our daily lives that can make a huge difference in how we sing if simply transferred into pictorial gestures. Asking a choir to sing *fortissimo* sometimes produces a forced sound. Instead, ask singers to simply reach down with both hands and pick up a large, imaginary object as they sing. This results in a wonderfully well supported and unforced *fortissimo*. If hands are down close to the body when singers prepare to pick up the object, their hands and arms will go out, encouraging a low, full breath. As they pick up the object, the tone will be well supported and full.

Piano

Try this exercise to get a truly beautiful and well-supported *piano*.

1. Circle the right hand clockwise (or the left hand counterclockwise) so that the upward movement is in front of the body, just above the naval. This results in a supported and attractive *piano* sound.
2. Should the choir have some trouble supporting the tone, ask singers to first make big circles in front of their bodies while singing *forte*.
3. Slowly decrease the size of the circle to help achieve a gradual move to a *piano* or *pianissimo* dynamic.

Fortunately, these common gestural experiences can easily be utilized to add subtlety and character in all aspects of a choir's performance.

I have been asking choirs to experiment with the use of gestures that give subtle meaning to words and phrases in normal speech for years now, and have found this to be one of my most useful tools in keeping singers on task, connecting with their artistic side, and keeping a rehearsal positive.

My early years of conducting would have been easier on both my singers and myself had I known how effective singer gesture can be. I also wish I had understood a few conductor habits that interfere with pitch and tone. Inviting the choir in with a nod of the head or upper body bending invariably affects pitch and the clarity of an entrance. Bobbing knees and floppy wrists confuse rhythm and affect pitch, as well. Long ago, I began asking myself "Are you causing the problem?" When I discovered that I often did, I began a very satisfying study into the affect that conductor and singer gesturing had on the elements of sensitive music making. I urge the readers to join me in my search for an ever more effective use of the non-verbal in the rehearsal.

CHAPTER 5

Brainstorming for Improvisation: Developing Imaginative Teaching Strategies in the Choral Rehearsal

Sandra Snow

Improvisation. The word has special and particularized meaning for conductor-teachers. Improvisation is a useful construct for describing what it is that conductor-teachers do in the rehearsal process. As improvisers, we call on knowledge in a variety of ways. Musical knowledge, knowledge of teaching and learning, understanding vocalism, sensitivity to context, and the ability to monitor one's actions in real-time all inform the process of improvisation in the choral setting.

Improvisation is a reflection of open ears, listening deeply, and juggling a musical interpretation against the real-time sounding by the choir. To be effective, an improviser remains open to new possibility while retaining past knowledge and experience. The conductor-teacher is able to draw on a deep well of knowledge about effective rehearsing while living fully in the present with the singers at hand. The toggling between musical interpretation, the immediate sounding by the singers, and the relationship-making between conductor and ensemble require complex acts of assessment and judgment as the conductor-teacher shapes the experience for all.

Brainstorming. Brainstorming is an activation of the imagination, possibility, and action. It is a feature of the creative act and is perhaps a necessary condition for the process of improvisation. Brainstorming is characterized by musing, pondering, reflecting, making connections, firing neurons, and an orientation of openness and expectation. One can brainstorm in the moment, often described as thinking on one's feet, or out of time in free-floating thinking apart from intentional action. It is this free-floating thinking, away from real-time, that can inform improvisation in teaching.

This chapter[1] explores what it means to maximize one's teaching practice in the choral setting. We examine the role of teaching philosophy and its impact on the experience of singers. A system for developing the ability to improvise from the podium is introduced as well as a means for rehearsal planning that supports this process. We emphasize conducting/teaching as a form of improvisation, the skills for which can be deliberately exercised and developed to improve teaching practice and the quality of music-making and learning in the choral classroom.

It is beyond the scope of this chapter to discuss all pre-conditions necessary to engage in rehearsal planning and teaching from the podium, so it is essential that conductor-teachers have a system of score analysis already in place and that is consistently applied.[2]

An ancillary goal of this chapter is to show conductor-teachers how to encourage singers to become fully engaged participants in the learning process, converting passive behavior into active, critical thinking. When singers think "inside the music" and are given the opportunity to meaningfully interact with the repertoire and each other, the choral classroom functions as a learning community working at the highest level.

The term *conductor-teacher* conveys an emphasis on pedagogy while upholding the expectations for artistry embedded in the word *conductor*.

The Conductor-Teacher

Listens-in-Sound

Hears more, imposes less. Listening-in-sound is both a skill set and a philosophical choice. It is difficult to listen when one is not open to receiving sound. Novices are often unable to move past the "noise" of the complex set of tasks to be implemented. Other teachers may miss out on listening by excessive talking or by an inflexible approach to pedagogy.

Analyses Scores

Employs a consistent and meaningful system of score analysis as the basis of planning and conducting effective rehearsals.

Contextualizes

Uses fluid pedagogy to meet the challenges of each particular situation. This includes the skills and experience levels of singers, social factors, and learning styles.

Adapts

Willing to abandon teaching strategies that are not working; to re-direct, re-deploy, extend, refine or change the basic approach to rehearsal. These decisions are based on in-the-moment, ongoing assessments of what students are actually doing.

Reflects

Brainstorms, out of real-time, by reflecting on previous rehearsals. Reflection may include consideration of future action in direct relationship to past experience. This analysis coupled with activation of the imagination for future experiences requires complex acts of discernment, judgment, and prescription.

Improvises

Brainstorms, in real-time, multiple teaching strategies designed to increase ensemble member understanding. Based on rich knowledge of teaching and learning, improvisation at the upper edge of a teacher's abilities encourages continual growth.

Facilitates

Is an agent of change on the podium with a specific emphasis on the development of musical thinking. Includes selecting from a vast array of tools, as well as verbal and nonverbal strategies designed to stimulate critical thinking in the choral classroom.

Listening Deeply

Here we introduce conductor-teacher preparation in two areas: listening in the sound and formulating a musical interpretation of the music under study. There are many valid systems for approaching these ideas. The system presented here is intended to be conductor-friendly. It deals directly with the skills needed to decode the musical score and to open the ear. It encourages an organic approach to musical understanding that can result in a clear musical picture of the repertoire to be taught.

Conductor-teachers must listen-in-sound. Frequently, teachers are proficient at hearing their own voice part but less able to hear surrounding parts. This may be compounded by the following practices:

1. singing along with ensemble members, further reducing the ability to hear
2. unnecessary mouthing of text which diminishes listening ability
3. playing loudly from behind the keyboard

The following exercises are designed to deepen the ability to listen perceptively within the choral sound. Novice teachers will have more success working with two- or three-part textures before tackling four parts. The excerpt in figure 1 is a four-part Bach chorale, "Wachet Auf," from cantata 140.

Figure 1. "Wachet auf," Chorale from Cantata 140

Wachet auf, ruft uns die Stimme
(nach BWV 140, 7, original in Es-Dur)

J. S. Bach

1. Wa - chet auf, ruft uns die Stim - me der Wäch - ter sehr hoch
Mit - ter - nacht heißt die - se Stun - de; sie ru - fen uns mit
3. Glo - ri - a sei dir ge - sun - gen mit Men - schen- und eng -
Von zwölf Per - len sind die Pfor - ten an dei - ner Stadt; wir

auf der Zin - - ne: wach' auf, du Stadt Je - ru - sa - lem!
hel - lem Mun - - de: wo seid ihr klu - gen Jung - - frau - en?
li - schen Zun - - gen, mit Har - fen und mit Cym - - beln schon.
sind Kon - sor - - ten der En - gel hoch um dei - - nen Thron.

Wohl - auf! der Bräut' - gam kömmt, steht auf! die Lam - pen nehmt.
Kein Aug' hat je ge - spürt, kein Ohr hat je ge - hört

Al - le - lu - ja! Macht euch be - reit zu
sol - che Freu - de. Dess' sind wir froh, i - -

der Hoch - zeit, ihr müs - set ihm ent - ge - gen gehn.
o, i - o! e - wig in dul - ci ju - bi - lo.

2. Zion hört die Wächter singen, das Herz tut ihr vor Freuden springen, sie wachet und steht eilend auf.
Ihr Freund kommt vom Himmel prächtig, von Gnaden stark, von Wahrheit mächtig, ihr Licht wird hell, ihr Stern geht auf.

Exercise 1: Hearing Individual Vocal Parts

The conductor-teacher should:

1. Sing the chorale melody while playing the bass part at the piano, ideally on solfege.
2. Choose a different voice part and sing.
3. Play the familiar bass part against the vocal line.
4. Retain the vocal line but change the part played on the keyboard.
5. The final step is to challenge yourself to audiate (sing silently) each vocal part. At the end of each phrase you may check yourself by playing the part.

Exercise 1 also works well to increase facility at the keyboard. Simply substitute playing for singing.

Exercise 2: Working from Recordings

Choose a representative recording of a piece under study.

1. Hearing individual voice parts
   a. Follow a vocal line other than the melody from beginning to end.
      i. Were you able to trace the vocalism throughout?
      ii. Did you identify a tricky section or measure?
      iii. Why might it be challenging?
   b. Follow two outside vocal lines (soprano and bass).
      i. Was the bass or soprano more prominent in your hearing?
      ii. Sing along with the vocal line that was harder to hear.
   c. Follow two inside vocal lines (alto and tenor).
      i. Was one easier to hear than the other?
      ii. Go back and focus your mind's eye on the part that was harder to hear.
   iii. Audiate that part while replaying.
   d. Sing along with the recording. Beginning with the soprano line, pivot downward to the next vocal part at regular intervals.
2. Vocal color and hearing
   a. Isolate a musical excerpt from the piece and play the recording. Describe the vocal color of the excerpt using as many adjectives as possible. Examples:

Rich	Bright	Unified
Warm	Vibrato/non-vibrato	Colorless
Silky	Brassy	Colorful

   b. Listen through soprano, alto, tenor, bass sections.
      i. Do these adjectives apply equally to each section?
      ii. Did you hear differences in color from section to section?
   c. Identify a second recording of the previous piece.
      i. Play the second recording.
      ii. How is vocal color different?
      iii. Imagine the decisions the conductor of each recording made in order to affect the sound.

There are those who would argue listening to a recording precludes the ability of a conductor-teacher to develop an independent interpretation. For those learning the craft of conducting/teaching, this argument seems unrealistic. Sound recordings give us a complete aural context and provide fertile ground for teaching the ears to open. Furthermore, listening to a variety of interpretations stimulates the imagination.

Exercise 3: Increasing Keyboard Facility

Piano skills are essential for the effective conductor-teacher. Invariably, students who enter teacher training programs with weak piano skills work the hardest to learn to hear in the sound, not to mention work from the keyboard in a rehearsal setting. The following principles help guide increasing facility from the keyboard while studying and preparing music:

1. Choose a tempo, usually quite conservative, that allows you to play without stopping. Force yourself to play even if it is inaccurate.
2. Use a metronome and force yourself to play something on each tactus or pulse.
   a. Reduce parts if necessary.
   b. If only a single line can be played, play the bass part.
   c. Disregard changes in tempo and work for a consistent tempo.

3. Learn to read harmonically.
   a. Try blocking chords rather than playing everything on the page.
   b. In the beginning of this practice, block the downbeat of each bar.
   c. If in 4/4, block the downbeat and beat three.
   d. Add more beats per bar as proficiency increases.
4. Learn to read ahead.
   a. Using a metronome, practice jumping eyes two beats ahead at all times.
   b. It is helpful to have another person point two beats ahead until the eye is used to the practice.

5. When accompanying your ensemble, preserve the bass line at all times.

These exercises can be useful to everyone interested in improving their keyboard skills.

The Rehearsal Plan

The Rehearsal Plan Is the In-Action Implementation of Conductor/Teacher Philosophy

Making an explicit focus on the conductor-teacher as a facilitator of student learning, conductor-teachers shift responsibility to the ensemble member for understanding of the score.

Shifting the role of the conductor-teacher to that of active facilitator does not imply that singers are fully responsible for decisions regarding music. After all, the conductor-teacher is the one with the background and experience, and who has studied the music closely. Neither does facilitating mean reorienting the experience to the verbal domain; that is, to talk about the music incessantly rather than experience it directly.

Facilitating instead involves an ongoing commitment to guiding singers to musical understanding by stimulating musical thinking, reflecting actively on musical actions, and providing meaningful ways for singers to experience musical ideas.

The Rehearsal Process Is Adaptive and Flexible, Encouraging Experimentation and Learning by Ensemble Members Toward a Collective Interpretation of the Music Under Study

A pitfall for conductor-teachers both novice and experienced is the undisciplined act of *micro-rehearsing*. Micro-rehearsing is the practice of stopping to fix every mistake as heard, not allowing the choir to sing through entire ideas, and results in a top-down approach that emphasizes perfection through "drill and kill" of each phrase. It may seem efficient in the short-term but does not encourage independence of musical thinking in the long-term. There are important philosophical issues embedded in micro-rehearsing. In this approach, the conductor is the Expert, the singers are passive receivers of information. Technical perfection often trumps the experience of the singers—indeed, such experience may be immaterial in the quest for perfection.

Besides issues of hierarchy, micro-rehearsing is fraught with problems. Singers learn to wait for instructions, and as such, are trained not to think. This is highly inefficient, as the ability to transfer what is learned to new repertoire or situations is undeveloped. Micro-rehearsing disrupts music-making for talking about the music, shifting the periods of singing to talking—a frustrating experience for all.

Micro-rehearsing allows the choir to dictate the pace of rehearsal. When a conductor stops every time a mistake is made, the choir is in charge of the rehearsal experience. The conductor is trapped by the need to fix pitches and rhythms and may neglect the essence of the music at hand. In this way choirs may perform music with no understanding, perhaps executing a technically flawless performance that somehow seems disconnected and unemotional. Further, micro-rehearsing reduces the experience to a process of error detection that risks missing the reason for singing together in the first place.

Rehearsals reflecting a more organic approach are rich with action-guided rehearsal strategies such as:

1. singing
2. chanting
3. solfeging
4. count-singing
5. shaping
6. conducting
7. drawing
8. moving,
9. etc.

Each of these actions require musical thinking and decision-making on the part of each ensemble member. One feature of a more organic rehearsal is the rehearsing of large, global sections or ideas first, details later.

The next section links interpretation to the rehearsal process. Converting interpretation into an active rehearsal involves consideration of the many ways ensemble members can experience the music. It is the responsibility of the conductor-teacher to develop an understanding of the music while inviting choral singers to share in these ideas as they move toward the goal of making the music their own. Linking musical knowledge to teacher knowledge is a central goal for the conductor-teacher.

Unlocking Imagination in Teaching

At its core, artistry in any form can be described as rich imagination. A profound sculpture begins as a solid mass of marble. Unlocking the secrets of the human genome was first in the mind's eye of a scientist—creating order, purpose, and beauty where there was none. The riveting performance is full of imaginative choices, setting it apart by vivid insight.

A key characteristic of the active imagination is the capacity to work on the outer edge of one's competence: to push oneself...probe...problem-solve...adapt and reflect. Working on the outer edge requires an openness of orientation to consider the new, radical, and surprising...*this* is the hallmark of both great teaching and great learning. In this way teaching is the practice of ongoing learning.[3]

How then can we effectively stimulate the imagination to convert our musical images of a piece into a solid rehearsal that cultivates musicianship and active participation by ensemble members?

Brainstorming is a means of engaging the mind in free-form thinking or musing. Next we explore a visual system of brainstorming that encourages the conductor-teacher to marry musical interpretation to a series of teaching moves. The brainstorming process becomes a way of exercising improvisation on the podium by unlocking the imagination toward any number of potential teaching strategies. These strategies are not prescriptive, but are instead available to the conductor-teacher as a possible pathway in rehearsal.

Brainstorming out of Real-Time

It is possible to isolate the process of improvisation in real-time with an ensemble by stimulating the imagination in advance of the choral rehearsal. Brainstorming for teaching is a central means of increasing fluency in teaching. When one brainstorms, thinking opens to make critical connections with knowledge. Connectivity is achieved by activating the imagination to link knowledge to the new, the untested, the daring.

Brainstorming creates a state of receptivity to the unknown.

Visual Mind Mapping/Webbing

Visual mind mapping (or webbing) is a two-dimensional picture of thinking. New teachers will find value in the visual mapping system presented here. Experienced teachers may not need to map every piece for each rehearsal, but they certainly want to exercise the mental habit of openness, imagination, and improvisation that marks an effective conductor-teacher.

The First Dimension: Musical Interpretation

The first dimension represented on the map is a series of teacher decisions about how the music will sound and what aspects of a teacher's musical interpretation will be shared with ensemble members. It is quite literally a picture of your musical interpretation (see figure 2).

Figure 2. Mind map dimension 1

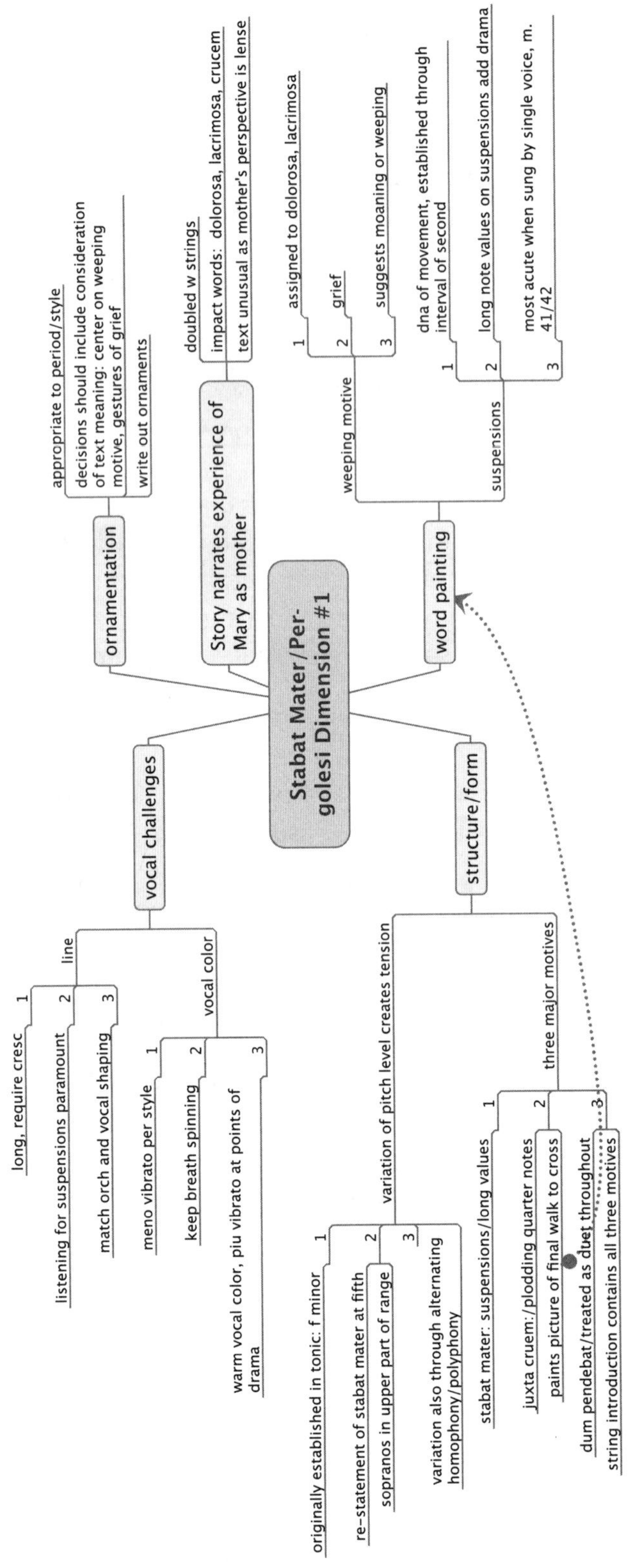

Stabat Mater/Pergolesi Dimension #1

- ornamentation
  - appropriate to period/style
  - decisions should include consideration of text meaning: center on weeping motive, gestures of grief
  - write out ornaments
- Story narrates experience of Mary as mother
  - doubled w strings
  - impact words: dolorosa, lacrimosa, crucem
  - text unusual as mother's perspective is lense
- word painting
  - weeping motive
    - 1 assigned to dolorosa, lacrimosa
    - 2 grief
    - 3 suggests moaning or weeping
  - suspensions
    - 1 dna of movement, established through interval of second
    - 2 long note values on suspensions add drama
    - 3 most acute when sung by single voice, m. 41/42
- vocal challenges
  - line
    - 1 long, require cresc
    - 2 listening for suspensions paramount
    - 3 match orch and vocal shaping
  - vocal color
    - 1 meno vibrato per style
    - 2 keep breath spinning
    - 3 warm vocal color, piu vibrato at points of drama
- structure/form
  - variation of pitch level creates tension
    - 1 originally established in tonic: f minor
    - 2 re-statement of stabat mater at fifth
      - sopranos in upper part of range
    - 3 variation also through alternating homophony/polyphony
  - three major motives
    - 1 stabat mater: suspensions/long values
    - 2 juxta cruem:/plodding quarter notes
      - paints picture of final walk to cross
    - 3 dum pendebat/treated as duet throughout
      - string introduction contains all three motives

Represented in figure 2 are the decisions made by a conductor-teacher as to which features or musical gestures will be highlighted in the rehearsal process. Those trained to write objectives-based lesson plans from the general music education domain will immediately recognize many of these first-level strands as musical elements. In this example, elements include dynamics, harmony, and rhythm. A distinctive difference in this approach is that these elements are derived directly from the music itself. In other words, there is not a preconceived set of musical elements to teach, but rather a close examination of the particular music under study. This approach is inside-out and from the voice of the composer. The music does not serve teaching for musical concepts, but reorients the learning experience to the repertoire. The teacher takes each identified element and richly describes how the music will sound.

The second dimension of the visual mind map is the one most critical for new teachers. The conductor-teacher is required to generate possible teaching strategies in direct relationship to the musical decisions represented in the first dimension. When working with new teachers, one might require them to generate three to five teaching moves for each strand in the first dimension. A benefit of this approach is that one can further coach young teachers in the kinds of strategies chosen. For example, one might require that no more than a single strategy per strand generated is verbal in nature. This reorients the new teacher's imagination toward more meaningful nonverbal experiences for ensemble members.

FIGURE 3. Mind map dimension 2

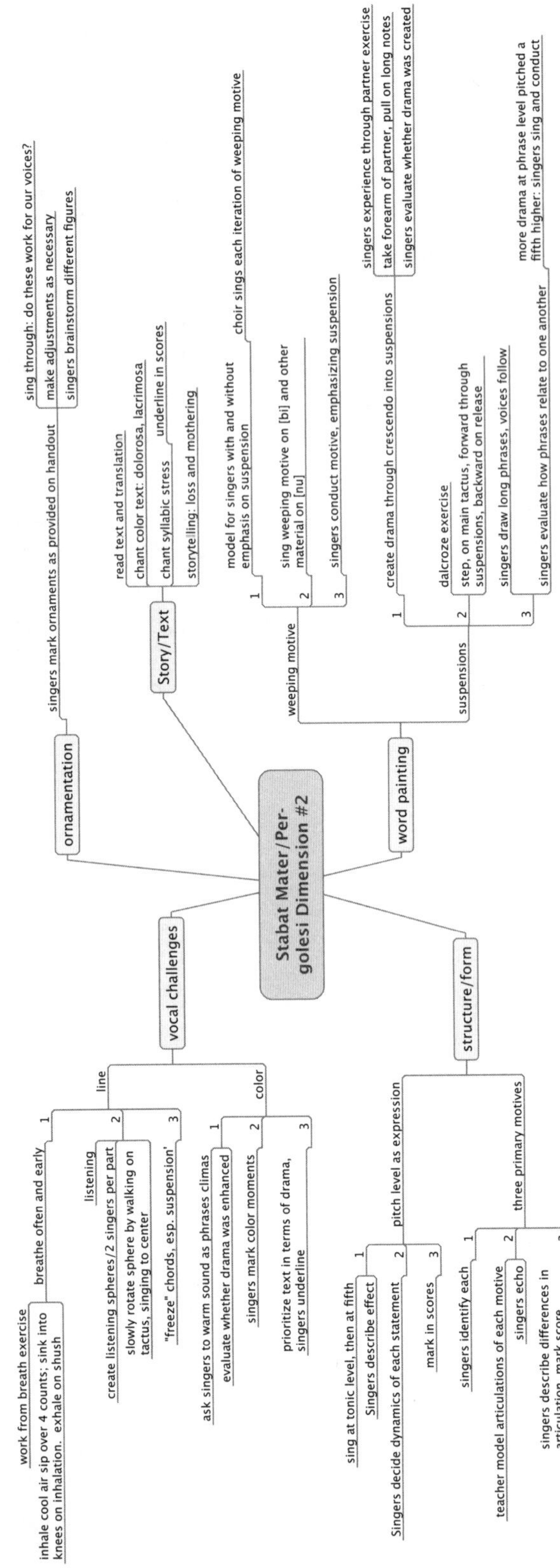

- **Stabat Mater/Pergolesi Dimension #2**
  - ornamentation
    - singers mark ornaments as provided on handout
      - sing through: do these work for our voices?
      - make adjustments as necessary
      - singers brainstorm different figures
  - Story/Text
    - read text and translation
    - chant color text: dolorosa, lacrimosa
    - chant syllabic stress
      - underline in scores
    - storytelling: loss and mothering
  - word painting
    - weeping motive
      1. model for singers with and without emphasis on suspension
         - choir sings each iteration of weeping motive
      2. sing weeping motive on [bi] and other material on [nu]
      3. singers conduct motive, emphasizing suspension
    - suspensions
      1. create drama through crescendo into suspensions
         - singers experience through partner exercise
         - take forearm of partner, pull on long notes
         - singers evaluate whether drama was created
      2. dalcroze exercise
         - step, on main tactus, forward through suspensions, backward on release
      3. singers draw long phrases, voices follow
         - singers evaluate how phrases relate to one another
           - more drama at phrase level pitched a fifth higher: singers sing and conduct
  - vocal challenges
    - line
      1. breathe often and early
         - work from breath exercise
         - inhale cool air sip over 4 counts; sink into knees on inhalation. exhale on shush
      2. listening
         - create listening spheres/2 singers per part
         - slowly rotate sphere by walking on tactus, singing to center
      3. "freeze" chords, esp. suspension'
    - color
      1. ask singers to warm sound as phrases climas
         - evaluate whether drama was enhanced
      2. singers mark color moments
      3. prioritize text in terms of drama, singers underline
  - structure/form
    - pitch level as expression
      1. sing at tonic level, then at fifth
         - Singers describe effect
      2. Singers decide dynamics of each statement
      3. mark in scores
    - three primary motives
      1. singers identify each
      2. teacher model articulations of each motive
         - singers echo
      3. singers describe differences in articulation, mark score

The teacher has now generated any number of teaching strategies to carry out the musical ideas. As a teacher-trainer this is useful in assessing how novice conductors are thinking for instruction. One can specifically coach novices in numbers of strategies devised, signaling growing fluency. One might suggest students reorient strategies away from telling toward a better percentage of nonverbal and verbal tasks. The teacher here is clearly considering the growing knowledge of the ensemble as singers are required to work out musical challenges for themselves. The knowledge represented by the ability to keep an open orientation for the new and unexpected is critical for teachers of all levels of experience. While experienced teaches may not need to mind map or web as they plan, they do need to develop the *habit of mind* to be flexible in the rehearsal process. Figure 4 represents the theoretical starting place for the brainstorming process.

FIGURE 4. Mind map prototype

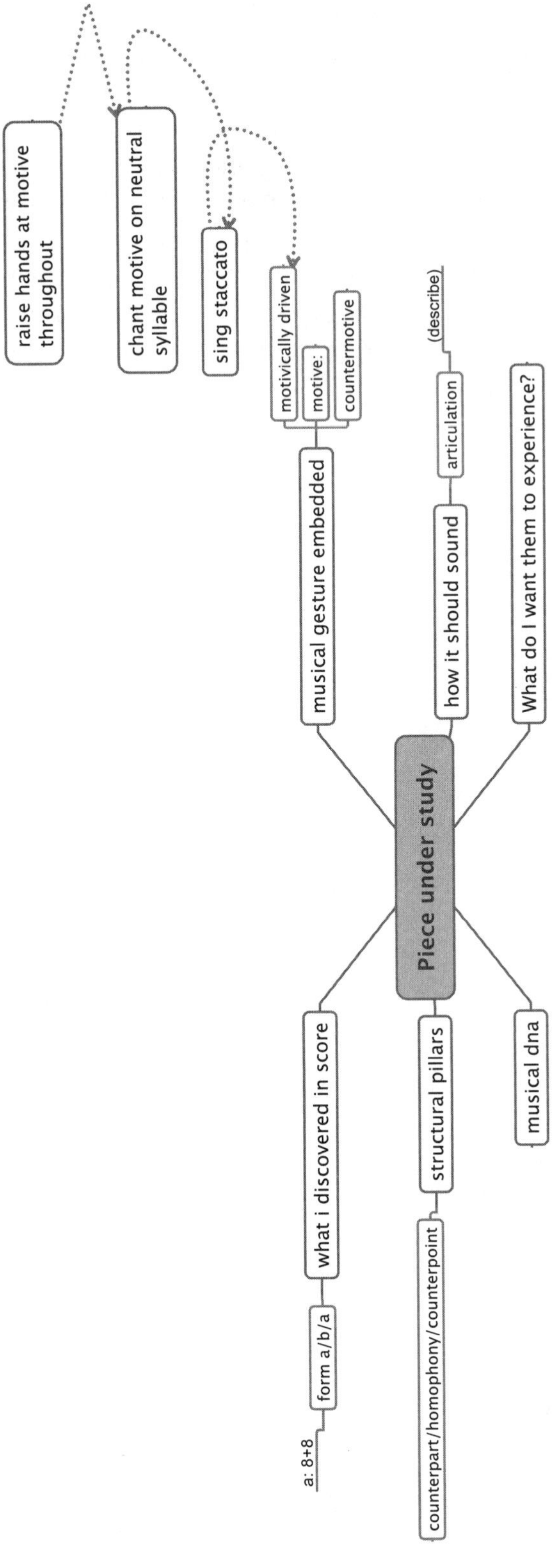

- Piece under study
  - musical gesture embedded
    - motivically driven
    - motive:
    - countermotive
  - how it should sound
    - articulation
      - (describe)
  - What do I want them to experience?
  - what i discovered in score
    - form a/b/a
      - a: 8+8
  - structural pillars
    - counterpart/homophony/counterpoint
  - musical dna
- sing staccato
- chant motive on neutral syllable
- raise hands at motive throughout

A natural critique of this process might be that while many teaching moves are imagined and generated, there is little order or sequence to help conductor-teachers organize rehearsal time. This is absolutely true! It is at this stage that the conductor-teacher is ready to write a rehearsal plan. The visual mind map will yield obvious clues about how and what might be rehearsed in early rehearsals. This preparatory mapping system is an invaluable tool in setting up the pre-conditions necessary to learn to rehearse in a productive manner.

From Imagination to Inspiration: The Productive Rehearsal

Inspiration. What does it take to inspire? to motivate? When students talk about influential teachers, they rarely mention teaching skill or knowledge of content area. For most learners, this is a given. Inspiring teachers are motivating forces in the lives of their students, passionate about their subject and their students, exhibit leadership, and are empathetic and caring. The late great Howard Swan used tell his university students "Teachers should be masters at the art of living."[4] We are, by necessity, powerful models for our students.

Our profession's ongoing rehearsal paradigm makes it hard to be inspirational, as we often rehearse from the outside-in: First, notes and rhythms, then expressive elements; add the facial expression, all in service of a public performance.

How do we, as teachers, continually shape rehearsals that inspire and motivate? Part of the answer comes from a deep understanding of the needs of the ensemble at hand, what we can refer to as knowing one's "context." Some guiding principles, then, in shaping choral rehearsals that acknowledge context include using your visual map or web as a guide to determine what specific strands represent the essence of the musical gestures embedded in the composition.

In other words, what makes the piece under study special? What about it rises to the top as important? What special gestures or "DNA" does the composer use to put the piece together? It is these special characteristics that will grab the interest and imagination of the learner. If you as a teacher are excited by the music you have chosen, your students will likely have a deep interest as well.

One might shape a rehearsal, then, based on these special characteristics rather than the rote teaching of notes and rhythms from the beginning to the end of a piece.

Making Choices about Teaching Moves: Developmentally Appropriate Strategies

Acknowledging context means deciding on teaching moves that match the skill level and developmental needs of the ensemble.

For example, one conductor-teacher had all students in an advanced chamber choir analyze a poem to exercise the concept of text. If the ensemble were less skilled, the teacher might adapt the strategy of having students sing the opening statement in unison before introducing harmony parts. Working right from the music, students might be asked which word or words seemed most important. The reading of the poem might come several rehearsals in, after students have sorted through basic issues of pitch and rhythm.

The significant point here is that the learning of notes and rhythms can coincide meaningfully with larger musical goals in the rehearsal process. In each case ensemble members experience something essential and meaningful about the piece, but in a way each can understand.

Active and Passive Strategies: Thinking in Music Versus Thinking in Language

Inspirational rehearsals occur in environments where learners feel challenged, electric, and alive. Avoiding passive teaching strategies go a long way in shoring up pacing in the classroom. Passive strategies often are verbal in nature, often delivered from the conductor-teacher to the student. Finding means to have ensemble members experience the music without mediating the experience through language is a powerful tool in the conductor-teacher's teaching practice.

Learning-based Stratification: Visual, Aural, Kinesthetic

Shake it up. If a first teaching move is to use the chant voice to practice appropriate syllabic stress, the next move might be kinesthetic in nature. If students listen to a vocal model for style, they might write adjectives describing style on the board the next time around. This variety keeps singers engaged and thinking inside the composition.

Applications for Teacher Training

Here we address thinking on your feet in the choral classroom and provide a series of exercises designed for implementation in choral methods/pedagogy courses or advanced conducting courses. It assumes undergraduate conductor-teachers have learned to analyze scores, develop ideas about how the music should sound, and are fluent in their ability to construct multiple teaching strategies in the form of a visual map or web.

One link remains, however, and that is exercising improvisation in real-time. These exercises are designed to increase the ability to think on one's feet on the podium.

Improvising from the Podium

Exercise 1. Talk-aloud

1. Two class members act as note-takers.
2. Each is instructed to document each teaching move observed by the peer conductor-teacher.
3. The conductor-teacher is asked to construct a mini-rehearsal no more than five minutes in duration.
4. Following the rehearsal the note-takers talk through their observations and reflections.
5. The conductor-teacher may not interrupt or explain choices.
6. Instead, the conductor-teacher listens to two different descriptions of what happened in the words of other peers.
7. At the end of the exercise the conductor-teacher is required to generate one further teaching strategy for a next rehearsal.
8. This exercise sensitizes conductor-teachers to the reactions and perceptions of ensemble members and requires them to think forward to the next rehearsal.

Exercise 2. No-talking rehearsal

1. The challenge here is to reduce the percentage of time spent talking and explaining and maximize the time thinking in music.
2. It is most interesting for teachers to examine *why* they spend so much time talking.
3. Here are the most common reasons I have observed for talking:
   a. *Lack of confidence* in the ability to generate a variety of teaching strategies.
   b. *Nervousness*, especially in new or unfamiliar settings.
   c. *Control*. Teachers want to make the rehearsal successful and talk through each rehearsal strategy at length with the ensemble prior to the actual exercising of the task at hand.

   d. *Edification*. Teachers have a need to explain their thinking to the ensemble members in a near re-creation of their thought process in the planning stage.
   e. *Lack of preparation*. The teacher may not know the material well and talks around this fact.
4. The no-talking rehearsal has the obvious benefit of reorienting rehearsals away from talking. Often there are moments of *great* self discovery for the conductor-teacher.

EXERCISE 3. Tag-team brainstorming

1. The conductor-teacher must react in real-time to the sounding from the ensemble and is required at the same time to generate a teaching strategy that flows in a logical way from a previous action.
2. Teachers are grouped in threes.
3. They are asked to prepare the same section of a musical work.
4. Without prior notice, select a student to begin the rehearsal.
5. The student is allowed three teaching moves lasting no more than three minutes. 6. At the conclusion of the third move, student two takes over, teaching based on what just happened.
7. Student three has the most difficult task, but must also logically extend the rehearsal by finding new ways of presenting the section or assessing whether the choir has accomplished the goals of the section and needs to move on to different material.
8. This process does not substitute for a carefully conceived rehearsal plan, for we are not hoping to create a chaotic, unfocused, or unorganized rehearsal.
9. Instead, it is the consistent habit of mind that prepares the conductor-teacher to make a prescribed rehearsal plan with goals and skills as a focus.

These exercises are all useful procedures. When implemented at regular intervals, they contribute to the teacher-conductor's ongoing growth and development.

expertise with a Little "e": The Path to an Engaged Choral Classroom

In the course of this chapter, we have looked at learning in the choral classroom through the eyes of the conductor-teacher. By first examining the philosophy embedded in our practice then the skills and habits of mind needed to create a rich learning environment we understand the powerful role of the teacher in the choral classroom to stimulate creative thinking among ensemble members.

The critical relationship between an engaged ensemble and an inspiring conductor-teacher is fueled by the choice of great music with which to interact, a caring and open approach, and expecting high levels of accomplishment by ensemble members.

In sum:

Rehearsal Is a Parallel Highway

The conductor-teacher is continually comparing real-time sounding with a mental image of the music. The conductor-teacher provides means for ensemble members to share in the interpretation and relationship-making that occurs among them as a result.

Assessing-in-action Is a Constant

Assessment is something conductor-teachers do at all times. One gauges whether the challenge presented has been met. One knows when to find another path to success, when to move on, and how to motivate singers to do their best.

Gesture Is Our Most Powerful Teaching Tool

Conducting ideas and communicating these through gesture remove the need for excessive talking and is the primary way a conductor-teacher paints interpretative decisions. Meaningful gesture is the most potent means of relaying musical ideas and shaping sound.

Though we all aspire to be master teachers, what is most important is that we work consistently in a way that challenges our own thinking and spurs our own growth as both musician and teacher. This ongoing process can be thought of as expert-like in nature. When we view expertise with a little "e" we see that challenging ourselves and our students to think critically is the central means of improving teaching practice. Such practice improves over time, judgments are more accurate, pacing more natural, and rehearsal strategies more potent.

A little "e" expert, then, has no pressure to be a master teacher overnight. The growing expert, instead, is patient with the present and recognizes that the engaged classroom is a community of learners whose growth is a process, not a product.

Endnotes

1. The content of this chapter is a fuller discussion of the material on the DVD Conducting/Teaching: Real World Strategies for Success (Chicago: GIA Publications, Inc, 2009).
2. Several resources exist to guide development of skills associated with score analysis. The following resource is especially useful for score marking. Jordan, James, *Music for Conducting Study: A Companion to Evoking Sound: Fundamentals of Choral Conducting* (Chicago GIA Publications, Inc., 2008).
3. 3. Yinger, R. J. "The conversation of practice," in Clift, R. T., W. R. Houston, and M. C. Pugach, eds., *Encouraging reflective practice in education: An analysis of issues and programs* (New York: Teacher's College Press, 1990), 73–94) Yinger describes at length the idea of brainstorming *for* teaching.
4. Swan, Howard. *Conscience of a Profession*. (Chapel Hill, NC: Hinshaw Music, 1987). A series of lectures on the humanity of music making and the conductor's responsibility to honor both music and those singing.

PART II

THE CHORAL CONDUCTOR AS MUSIC TEACHER

Teacher Resource Guides

LEVEL ONE. 75

LEVEL TWO 119

LEVEL THREE 265

LEVEL FOUR 379

LEVEL FIVE. 543

Introduction to the Teacher Resource Guides

Matthew Mehaffey

Working on the third volume of *Teaching Music Through Performance in Choir* has truly been a labor of love. Arriving at a list of music that will thrill all readers is no easy task. For this reason, we polled dozens of music educators from across the globe for their insights into repertoire suitable for the high school chorus. Through endless revisions and consultations across the profession, we arrived at the list presented to you in this book. This volume does not include a piece by every great composer who has ever lived; however, you will find that this list includes both familiar titles and new titles, sacred titles and secular titles, *a cappella* and accompanied titles, ancient music and modern music, English language selections and foreign language selections. There is something in this list for everyone, and we are confident it is all of the highest musical quality. When you combine this volume with the first two in the series, you have the beginnings of a very comprehensive list of choral repertoire appropriate for the high school-aged singer. While every piece in this volume may not be immediately appropriate for the choir you conduct, we hope this list will broaden your repertoire knowledge and inspire you to lead your choir to the next level of repertoire.

In each **Teacher Resource Guide**, we have provided you with historical, biographical, and analytical information that is helpful in score preparation and useful fodder for teaching. These resource guides are not meant to be complete studies of each piece but offer a place to begin your musical journey. To complete these resource guides, we enlisted the help of professors, teachers, and graduate students from across the country. These authors have graduated from institutions with some of the richest choral traditions in our country. Because of the great richness of background among our contributors, they were encouraged to write each resource guide from their own perspective instead of sticking to a prefabricated style or form. We hope that as you read each resource guide you will discover rehearsal techniques that you can apply across your teaching and in other repertoire.

It was very exciting to work closely with so many composers and arrangers on this volume. This volume features sixteen teacher resource guides submitted by the composer/arranger. Hopefully their insight will increase your depth of understanding about their works. We are pleased to include the Vivaldi

Gloria as a major work section. Wonderful information is offered on this oft-performed work by Bruce Chamberlain and Emilie Sweet Amrein.

In this volume, we have continued using the new choral rating system we developed for Volumes 1 and 2. We have received many positive comments about the accuracy of this rating system; it is proving to be very helpful when deciding whether a piece is appropriate for one's choir. The rating system employs a five-point scale, with Level Five being the most difficult. Each piece has been assigned an **Overall** difficulty rating, which gives the conductor a quick reference point. In an effort to give teachers and conductors more information, we provide two additional ratings: **Vocal** and **Tonal/Rhythm**. The vocal rating assesses the vocal difficulty of each piece by considering the range, tessitura, dynamics, and diction issues: the higher the number, the more advanced the required technique. Pieces with a higher number will be more likely to contain passages with extreme ranges, long vocal lines, extended vocal techniques, challenging diction, and stylistic issues. The tonal rating assesses how difficult this piece will be to teach/learn from an aural perspective: the higher the number, the more complex the composer's harmonic, melodic, and rhythmic language. Pieces with a higher tonal rating will be more likely to have chromatic and/or modal passages that are outside of the major/minor tonalities, instances of mixed meter, and difficult rhythms. The **Overall** rating is essentially an average of the **Vocal and Tonal/Rhythm** ratings; therefore, to have a complete understanding of the difficulty, consult the additional ratings when choosing repertoire. (N.B. The number of vocal parts, divisi, length of composition, and intangible "musical" elements were taken into consideration but were not weighted as heavily as the aforementioned criteria.) We have calibrated our ratings to the ability of the average high school choir; the average high school choir should be able to perform, without great difficulty, anything with a rating of three or lower.

The chart on the next page summarizes possible characteristics of the music in each level. However, because the repertoire in this volume is very diverse, not all pieces in each level will contain all of the qualities/criteria listed in the chart, and it should be noted that this list is not exhaustive. Each higher level assumes all the criteria of the previous levels.

Level	Vocal	Tonal/Rhythm
1	• Short, simple vocal lines with limited ranges • Conjunct vocal lines prevail • Comfortable vocal range • Manageable tessitura	• Major or minor tonality with little to no chromaticism • No modulations to other keys or tonalities • Straightforward rhythms within simple or compound meter
2	• Phrases of moderately challenging length • Slightly disjunct vocal lines • Brief, yet negotiable forays into extreme ranges • Basic dynamic range • Basic diction challenges in languages commonly encountered in choral music (e.g., English, Latin, German)	• Major or minor tonality with brief, obvious chromaticism • Brief modulations are obvious and move to closely related tonalities • Modal passages • Dissonances are approached and resolved by step • Short passages of challenging rhythm within simple or compound metric structure
3	• Short passages requiring advanced vocal technique • Short passages of challenging tessitura • Long phrases requiring good breath control • Vocal melismas of moderate length requiring martellato technique • Wide dynamic range • Extended *crescendos* and *decrescendos* • Wide range of languages encountered	• Major/minor/modal tonality • Concrete or implied modulations to different tonalities or modalities • Dissonance approached by leap • Added-note harmonies • Imitative and nonimitative counterpoint • Difficult rhythms may occur, but are usually repetitive • Simply constructed mixed meter
4	• Long phrases requiring excellent breath control • Extreme ranges • Vocal lines requiring subtlety of shape, dynamics, and expressivity • Long vocal melismas • Alternative vocal techniques (i.e., non-Western techniques) • Refined diction required as stylistic vehicle	• Extended modal passages • Passages in non-diatonic harmony • Frequent chromaticism • Challenging rhythmic passages may be extended and non-repetitive • Full compositions in mixed meter

Level	Vocal	Tonal/Rhythm
5	• Vocal maturity required • Extreme ranges and tessituras • Repertoire at this level will provide numerous challenges for the experienced choral ensemble	• Atonal passages or passages of extreme dissonance • Unprepared/unresolved dissonant harmonies • Very complex rhythmic/metric structure • Repertoire at this level will provide numerous challenges for the experienced choral ensemble

We encourage you to read this book in many different ways: to learn more about old repertoire, to learn about new repertoire, and to refresh your perspective when you feel rehearsals have become stale. We hope you find these resource guides to be helpful in all levels of your music making and inspire you to venture into choral repertoire with renewed dedication to the choral art.

Level 1

Mixed voices:

God Is Our Refuge Mozart, W. A.. . . .77
Sing We and Chant It Morley, Thomas. . . .81
Sorida Powell, Rosephanye. . . .87
The May Night (Die Mainacht) Brahms, Johannes/arr. Frackenpohl, Arthur. . . .93

Treble voices:

Nine Hundred Miles arr. Silvey, Philip. . . .99

Men's voices:

Fillimiooriay arr. Beery, Lon. . .105
Medieval Gloria Singh, Vijay. . .111
Viva Tutti anonymous 18th century. . .115

Teacher Resource Guide

God Is Our Refuge

W. A. Mozart

(1756–1791)

SATB
National: NMCH168
Overall: 1
Vocal: 1
Tonal/Rhythm: 1

Composer

Leopold Mozart, himself a respected composer, author, violin teacher, and conductor in the service of the Prince-Archbishop of Salzburg, Austria, saw prodigious musical talent in his young son, Wolfgang (b. 1756, Salzburg), and daughter, Maria Anna ("Nannerl"). At age three, Wolfgang demonstrated great affinity for the keyboard, and by age six he was performing on harpsichord and violin with his older sister (herself an exceptional pianist) in courts across Europe. Leopold, as primary teacher and manager of the young children, secured performances first for the Bavarian elector in Munich and then for the Empress Maria Theresa in Vienna. Legend has it that after the Viennese concert, the six-year-old Wolfgang, while playing with the Empress's children, slipped and was caught by the Empress's daughter, Marie Antoinette (who was a year older). He is reputed to have looked into her eyes and said, "I'll marry you someday." (Marie Antoinette declined, and at the age of fourteen married the future King Louis XVI of France instead.)

At age eight, Mozart wrote his first symphony; at eleven, the oratorio *The Obligation of the First and Foremost Commandment*; at thirteen, the opera *The Pretended Simpleton*. Mozart's musical gift was clearly unparalleled. In 1770, at the age of fourteen, Mozart heard a performance on Wednesday of Holy Week of Allegri's *Miserere* in Rome's Sistine Chapel. That evening he transcribed the nine-part polyphonic piece from memory and returned on Good Friday (with the manuscript rolled under his hat) to make minor corrections.

From 1773 to 1777 Mozart was employed as a court musician for the Prince-Archbishop in Salzburg. This period saw Mozart's interest in the piano concerto and violin concerto, but he became increasingly restless with Salzburg's few operatic venues. In an effort to settle into a city with a larger operatic presence, Mozart relocated first to Paris, France, and then to Mannheim, Germany, where he found success with the opera *Idomeneo*. By 1782 Mozart had finally been granted permission to leave his duties to the court, and established himself as a freelance musician in Vienna, where he married Constanze Weber. Vienna welcomed Mozart's operatic genius, and *Abduction from the Seraglio* was a commercial and critical success. Mozart's final years in Vienna, until his death there in 1791, were particularly prolific and included some of his most admired works: *Cosi Fan Tutte*, *The Magic Flute*, and the Clarinet Concerto, among others. On his deathbed Mozart is reputed—although there is little evidence to support this assertion—to have dictated passages of his unfinished *Requiem* to his student Süssmayr. (Süssmayr did, in fact, finish the work following Mozart's demise.) According to official record, Mozart died of "severe military illness," but rheumatic fever, influenza, or mercury poisoning have been postulated as actual causes of death.

In his short life, the composer would compose more than six hundred works in all major genres of the Classical Period, including symphonies, sonatas, string quartets, operas, oratorios, and works for various chamber ensembles. His legacy is, perhaps, that he was able to compose equally well in all genres of the period, making him the most versatile and talented musical mind in history.

Composition, Genre, and Historical Perspective

In 1764, following a highly successful tour of continental Europe, the nine-year-old Mozart, along with sister Nannerl and father Leopold, settled in London, England. At the time, London was a city that offered very lucrative recital venues and gave Mozart the opportunity to study voice with the castrato Giovanni Manzuoli. Mozart's performances for the royal family were tremendously successful. During one of his two concerts for King George III, he was given the task of playing at sight anything that the king set before him and of accompanying the queen in a song. Toward the end of his stay in London, Mozart visited the British Museum in 1765. He presented to the museum several autographed works and an original manuscript titled *God Is Our Refuge* (K20). This work, a short, polyphonic anthem for four voices, is Mozart's earliest surviving vocal work and is his only setting of a text in English.

Musical Elements and Technical Considerations

Conductors will find *God Is Our Refuge* to be quite accessible and a good introduction to the minor mode, imitative polyphony, and tuning chromatic passages. Prepare the chorus to sight-read the piece by first scanning for all necessary solfège syllables. (It is strongly suggested that *la*-based minor be used for reading and teaching this piece. The pure, Latin vowels as used in solfège will model an in-tune, unified melodic line from the outset. In addition, *la*-based minor will tune more successfully than *do*-based minor.) The soprano part is in natural minor, so no chromatic syllables will be required. The alto part, in harmonic minor, will require the addition of *si* to the scale. The tenor part, in melodic minor, will require the addition of *fi* and *si* to the scale. The bass part—the most challenging—will require *ri*, *fi*, and *si*. Invite the choir to sing the natural minor scale *(la* to *la')* ascending and descending using Curwen hand signs. Add in one chromatic syllable at a time until the students are comfortable with the entire scale using the chromatic pitches *ri*, *fi*, and *si*. Next, locate the solfège pitches on the staff and invite the students to silently "sing through" (audiate) their individual parts.

Set the metronome (a bit slower than the ultimate performance tempo) so that the eighth note is pulsating. Sight-sing through the piece on solfège *with the metronome*. Expect the choir, from the very first note, to sing each solfège syllable accurately and in tune within each section. Demand rhythmic precision at all times, as this will alleviate many intonation problems. Finally, even during sight-reading, expect the singers to perform musically.

After the choir is completely fluent on the solfège and is able to perform the piece absolutely in tune with the metronome, move to a neutral vowel. A bright vowel, such as /di/ ("dee"), will pull the sound forward but may encourage "spreading" or an overly bright tone. Be sure with the /i/ vowel to keep the lip position rounded. A darker vowel, such as /du/ ("doo"), produces a warmer, richer sound, but runs the risk of putting the choral tone too far back. Use your discretion, but in any case, choose a neutral vowel that will model the type of tone that you will require when the text is finally added.

After the choir is able to sing the entire piece on a neutral vowel, add the text. If at any time the choir loses its sense of the underlying pulse, add back the metronome. If at any time the choir sings incorrect pitches, return to solfège. If the choir drops pitch or is unable to sing "on the breath," add in lip trills or other vocal exercises to evoke a healthy, vibrant tone.

To this point the choir has used the five Latin vowels with the solfège and then mastered unifying a single vowel with the neutral syllable. Both the solfège and the neutral syllable are devoid of diphthongs, so these will be a focal point in your instruction. Choose British English, since Mozart composed this piece while in England. This means that the "r" is going to be flipped. The text is quite short, so the chorus will unify its diction quite quickly.

Stylistic Considerations

The conductor would do well to approach teaching this piece in the same manner as a Renaissance motet by Byrd, for instance. As with any imitative polyphonic piece, invite chorus members to sing on one line (in their own registers). Follow this process for each of the main entrances to ensure that, as sections enter, they are truly "imitative" in style and color.

A secondary consideration is in the use of the *messa di voce*. The *messa di voce* is the quintessentially Renaissance device that involves a gradual crescendo and diminuendo on a single pitch. The *messa di voce* will be used on any note that is longer than the beat, *except* the last note of the phrase. Take care not to overly inflate the *messa di voce*, such that the musical line is distorted.

A third consideration is the treatment of individual lines. In imitative polyphony, each voice part is of equal importance. Make certain that significant phrase entrances are transparent and that other voice parts listen for these entrances.

A fourth consideration is the choice of tonality for this piece. Originally in G minor, *God Is Our Refuge* might be more ably performed a whole-step lower. The tessitura in the tenor part is high and very "exposed."

Form and Structure

God Is Our Refuge is a very short (23 bars) anthem that, while through composed, is constructed in an imitative, polyphonic fashion that seems to be inspired by the Renaissance motet.

Text and Translation

The biblical text comes from the King James Version and is a setting of Psalm 46:1.

God is our refuge and strength.
A very help in trouble.

Additional References and Resources

Abert, Hermann, et. al. *W. A. Mozart*. New Haven: Yale University Press, 2007.
Deutsch, Otto. *Mozart*. Stanford: Stanford University Press, 1966.
Eisen, Cliff, et al. "Mozart." *Grove Music Online. Oxford Music Online*, 2009.
Keefe, Simon B. *The Cambridge Companion to Mozart*. Cambridge: Cambridge University Press, 2003.
Küster, Konrad et al. *Mozart*. Oxford: Clarendon Press, 1996.
Solomon, Maynard. *Mozart: A Life*. New York: Perennial, 1996.

Contributed by:

James Bowyer

Teacher Resource Guide

Sing We and Chant It

Thomas Morley

(1557/58–1602)

SSATB
G. Schirmer: 50310800
Overall: 1
Vocal: 1
Tonal/Rhythm: 2

Composer

Thomas "Thoroughly Modern" Morley is an example of the modernity that was born in the Renaissance. Morley's perspective on the business aspects of musicmaking, the procedures of composition, and even the content of his music, all resemble twenty-first century concerns of professional musicians.

Born in 1557 or 1558, Thomas Morley, like many composers of the Renaissance, was probably a chorister in a church in his childhood, where he later became choirmaster and organist. Also, like most Renaissance composers, Morley's "day job" made him responsible for teaching music and singing to others, mostly children. He seemed to be interested in doing it well, as inferred from the title of his instructional book, *A Plaine and Easie Introduction to Practicall Musicke*, published in 1597.

This happened to be the year following the end of the monopoly on printing music granted by Queen Elizabeth I to a group of composers including William Byrd, one of Morley's early teachers, to whom the book is dedicated. In 1598, Morley was granted the monopoly, and—centuries before online file sharing—was even involved in lawsuits against others who published works to which he owned the rights. Interestingly, Morley's work is now public domain, but most recordings are protected by copyright. Four hundred years after Morley was concerned about profiting from his intellectual property, scores (of widely varying quality—what would Morley have thought of that?) can be found for free online and can be legally photocopied at will; however, professional recordings of his music are protected by law.

Morley's own study of music earned him a degree from Oxford University in 1588; then he worked for Queen Elizabeth I. He composed for all the existing genres, but is best known for his madrigals.As described in the article about him in the Grove Dictionary of Music and Musicians, Morley was the "guiding force of the whole English madrigal development." Morley focused on the simple style, but within that light form created florid, complex, exciting textures and harmonies that are now the archetype of English madrigals. Many of his songs, including "Sing We and Chant It," are based on Italian *canzonetti*, with small improvements that accommodate language differences and create an English grace.

After long declining health, Morley died around 1602, barely more than fifty years old.

Composition, Genre, and Historical Perspective

"Sing We and Chant It" is representative of a very important genre of music. It's easy for students to be intimidated—or worse, bored—by the song's age and historical significance. But this song can be a tool to teach about the larger connection between Morley's time and ours.

The word *madrigal* has a complicated history, but for the purposes of your students' understanding and application of historical information to their performance, the most important element is its descent from Italian light song forms like *canzonetti* and *balleti*. The word *madrigal* originally described a poetic form and was only applied to music when composers began setting those poems. How all of this vocabulary developed—the poetic forms, the specific musical distinctions among these similar genres, and so on—while fascinating to those of us who love the musicological nitty gritty, won't be memorable or useful for most high school students. The major benefit of this information helps dispel the burden of the word *madrigal* and its historical stodginess.

- *Canzonetta* is the Italian diminutive of *song*, translatable as "little song"—but just as literally and perhaps more evocatively "songling," "songlet," or "song-i-poo"—the point being that it is intended to be light and fun. It's easy to take this great music very seriously, but its successful performance depends on delicacy and grace. If your singers get bogged down with the historical responsibility of performing a "Madrigal" with "Polyphony," remind them that it is just a little song-i-poo.

- *Balletto* is related to the word *ballet*, which might seem stuffy and dull, but it *is* dance. If they can make "Sing We and Chant It" dance, it won't be stuffy or dull! It's also an excellent reason for you to make them use movement—to internalize the beat in their bodies and wholly engage themselves in the music making.

The *balletto* is also where the "fa-la-la" tradition comes from. It was originally an instrumental form with the same sequence of short, repeated sections. Usually, they alternate between homophonic and polyphonic sections, and usually the polyphonic section has nonsense syllables, like scatting. "Nonny nonny" is a more English version seen in other light English songs, and heard in songs Shakespeare included in his plays.

Another significant point that denies the potential for stodginess is the fact that madrigals were pop music. They weren't sung in church for the glory of God, they were sung for celebrations and for fun. "Sing We and Chant It" is representative of the common practice of English composers taking Italian canzonets, making a few changes, and giving them English texts. This same practice exists in pop music today, but we call the result a re-mix.

Musical Elements and Technical Considerations

The song is in five parts, and the middle would fit nicely on a staff with a C clef—it goes as far below middle C as it does above. It's low for altos and high for tenors. On the other hand, the tenor part is not all that high, with just a few Ds and an E above middle C. It might take some imaginative finagling to make this work with a modern choir.

- All of this is assuming your edition has one sharp in the key signature. You might find one in another key or just transpose it to fit.
    - Singing it in A would make life easier for the altos and would be fine for the tenors, but you must also take the soprano tessitura into consideration.
    - Singing it in F would put the middle voice more comfortably in tenor range if you've got enough men to divide three ways and still balance with women, only divide into two parts.
    - Any key will present awkwardness and compromise.
- Have a conversation about the difference between a voice classification and a voice part. Adolescents enjoy having labels to define themselves, and it's convenient to let them consider themselves "altos" and "sopranos" long before their voice classification can truly be identified. The historical origins help us here:

  - The voice "parts" are not SSATB, but "cantus, quintus, altus, tenor, bassus."
  - Any alto in your choir should be able to sing the quintus part perfectly comfortably, as long as they aren't worried about singing "soprano II."
  - The word "tenor" is not there in reference to male singers with high voices, but because the function of that voice has descended from slow-moving *cantus firmus* line, and most of your baritones should be able to sing this one as long as they aren't worried about singing "tenor."
- Once they understand that they aren't violating their section-hood, redistribute singers:
  - Try putting any unchanged or recently changed boys on the middle part ("altus") along with the highest tenors and lowest altos.
  - Divide the remaining girls equally, or with slightly more on the quintus and fewer on the cantus (top part).
  - Add a few of your higher baritones to the tenor section.

The only surprising or challenging pitch concern is the transition between the A section and the B section, where Fs become natural. Isolate this transition and let the singers' ears learn to predict the change, or even solfège the A section with G as *do* and the first phrase of the B section with C as *do*.

The polyphony is not very difficult or very prolonged, but it does require the singers to listen and count. Of particular concern are the rests, when singers tend to stop counting while they stop singing. Count-singing will help singers keep their own parts in line with the rest, hearing the other parts counting while they wait for their next entrance.

The song is repetitive—that's part of what defines an English madrigal. There is temptation from editors to use all manner of dynamic contrast. If you decide to do it differently on the repeat, have a musical reason or have the singers come up with the reason ("it says so on the page" is not a musical reason). Allow them to develop a story that the song tells: Beyond the words, what story is the *music* telling? When they come up with it on their own, they are more likely to internalize the expressive purpose.

If you decide not to follow whatever editorial dynamic markings you may have, you would certainly be free to sing with whatever expressive energy comes naturally without violating any authenticity.

Stylistic Considerations

The important thing is to make connections between this sixteenth-century song and twenty-first century life so that the performance is alive, fresh, and spontaneous.

As described above, the historical roots of the song provide lots of evidence in support of the necessary delicacy and grace in the performance of this song.

Ironically, all of the historical facts also support the fact that the song should be sung from a modern point of view. Of course, that's the point of performing great songs from older historical eras: we can see that the same themes and ideas were important to people in 1585 as today. In this case they are fun, love, money, and pleasure. The students shouldn't be singing as though they were pretending they were Renaissance Faire anachronistic wenches and knights, but rather with the same easy freedom and enthusiasm they use when they sing show tunes on the bus.

The repetitiveness and the intimidating historical significance make it easy for a performance to be boring, but it has to be fun and lively. It has to dance. It cannot be sung on "automatic pilot," where the singers just reproduce the pitches on the page with blank accuracy. They will forget as the song goes on; their minds will wander. Possibly the most difficult thing they will have to practice in "Sing We and Chant It" is staying *in* the song from the first note to the last.

As with teaching any song, encourage students to keep their bodies engaged as they sing. Ask them to use a gesture with their hands or arms, like flicking or brushing motions that look and feel like the articulation and line of the music, as they sing. Have them shift weight with each measure, which could lead to walking in place, or even actually walking, as long as it stays as light and lilting as the music.

Certainly, excellent tone and otherwise healthy singing are required, but precision should not come at the expense of joy. Quality of technique should not exclude excitement. It won't take much detailed explanation about how to create this—the lines are so well written that anyone who likes choral singing will inevitably sense the lilt—but you will have to insist on and model for them staying engaged in the music all the way through, telling the story from beginning to end.

Form and Structure

Measure numbers will vary depending on your edition and whether the verses are written out under the same music, or if they are on separate pages.

Section	Event and Scoring
Verse 1	A (+ repeat)
B (+ repeat)	
Verse 2	A (+ repeat)
	B (+ repeat)

Text and Translation

The text is an easy vehicle for making connections between your diverse population of modern kids and a long dead, white, middle-aged, male composer. Like a stereotypical R&B song, it's about partying and having a great time while you're young. The phrase "care, be packing," is sort of funny: we would use the word *stress* instead of *care*, and tell it to "get packing," but the idea is clear. And the final sentiment of "spare no treasure to live in pleasure" is also a very modern one, and common in a lot of pop music: if you've got it, spend it to have a good time. Songs on the radio get specific about clothing designers and brand names of cars, and son; but again, the idea is clear.

There are also plenty of examples in modern pop music of nonsense syllables in the refrain. The ones your choir members are familiar with will likely change every year, but they will surely make the connections (and play them for you from their phones!) once you point it out.

I do recommend a broad, open "ah" for "chant" and "grant." It sets a nice precedent for vertical space in the rest of the song, and avoids the flat American pronunciation's susceptibility to ugliness. "Lasteth" and "hasteth" constitute a visual rhyme only, so use "ah" for "lasteth," but not for "hasteth."

> Sing we and chant it, While love doth grant it; Fa la la... (repeat)
>
> Not long youth lasteth, And old age hasteth;
> Now is best leisure To take our pleasure; Fa la la... (repeat)
>
> All things invite us Now to delight us; Fa la la... (repeat)
>
> Hence, care, be packing, No mirth be lacking;
> Let spare no treasure, To live in pleasure; Fa la la... (repeat)

Contributed by:

Amelia Nagoski Peterson

Teacher Resource Guide

Sorida

arr. Rosephanye Powell

SATB/a cappella
Hal Leonard: 8703350
Overall: 1
Vocal: 1
Tonal/Rhythm: 1

Composer

Dr. Rosephanye Powell is an internationally recognized composer and arranger of choral music and is currently published by Gentry Publications/Fred Bock Music, the Hal Leonard Corporation, Alliance Music Publications, and Oxford University Press (London, England). During her career, Powell has distinguished herself as a researcher, interpreter, and performer of solo vocal works by William Grant Still and the African-American spiritual. Her doctoral treatise, *The Art Songs of William Grant Still*, is considered an authoritative work on the subject. She has presented numerous recitals and lecture-recitals at churches, concert halls, universities, and professional meetings around the United States.

When asked about her major influences, Powell names her husband, Dr. William C. Powell as her major influence. By requesting compositions for his Gospel Choir at Florida State University (FSU) in the early years, Dr. William C. Powell encouraged his wife to sharpen her skills as a composer. The first such piece was "I Want to Be Ready," which was written for the FSU Gospel Choir. Rodney Eichenberger, then choral director at FSU, was excited about the piece and encouraged Powell to submit it for publication. "I Want to Be Ready" was the first of her pieces to be accepted for publication. Later, when

Powell submitted her motet "The Word Was God" to eight publishers, she received eight positive responses. When this piece was performed by Albert McNeil and the Jubilee Singers, publishers requested more works from Powell.

Powell attempts to express the strong feelings for her heritage through her original melodies. She grew up singing and listening to jazz, R&B, gospel, spirituals, and soul. Powell says that each of these styles has influenced her compositional style. Experiences with the African Ensemble at Florida State University helped to connect her to her African roots in drumming, singing, and dance.

While Powell points out that the lyricism and drama so apparent in her music are highly influenced by Bach, Mozart, Handel, and Verdi, she cites William Grant Still as the most important influence on her compositional style, especially in terms of harmonic colors in piano accompaniments, rhythmic energy, beautiful melodies, and the use of music to bring out the true meaning of the text.

Presently, Powell composes, for the most part, commissions by request. The categories of her music can be loosely organized as:

1. Arrangements of spirituals and folksongs.
2. Ethnic and multicultural songs (*Sorida*).
3. Message songs.
4. Motets, anthems, and psalms.
5. Gospel, worship, and praise songs.
6. Poetry settings.

Composition, Genre, and Historical Perspective

Sorida is an original work, not an arrangement. While serving at Philander Smith College in Little Rock, Arkansas, Dr. William C. Powell (the composer's husband), Director of the PSC Collegiate Choir was looking for an African song to include on the choir's recording project. Rosephanye Powell decided to research the possibility of arranging an African folk song for the project. While researching African folk songs, she came upon the word "sorida," which is an African greeting of brotherhood and unity. Powell also found an African children's song that played on the syllables of the word "sorida." She developed the song using the syllables as a foundation (so-ri-da, ri-da, ri-da). Powell composed her own lyrics, melody, and harmonies to represent the meaning and far-reaching scope of "sorida." After the PSC choir used the song for its title track, there were no plans to have the song published until the conductor, Dr. Andre Thomas (Florida State University), heard the song through a mutual friend and called to say that he would like to have it published so he could use it immediately. Powell was excited at the opportunity to have Dr. Thomas perform her work and *Sorida* was immediately published by Hal Leonard (2002).

Musical Elements and Technical Considerations

Sorida is written for SATB *a cappella* and features percussion, layered vocal patterns, and a call-type solo with optional duet and/or trio that includes both secular and sacred texts. Beginning with bass voices, the word *Sorida* is sung in a two-note ostinato pattern that continues throughout the entire piece as other voices are layered in, from baritones to divided tenors, and eventually adding in alto and divided soprano voices. *Sorida's* simplicity contributes to its charm. The entire piece is composed on a sometimes ornamented A-flat major chord until the very final chord, where the A-flat chord is ornamented with the 6th and 9th, giving the listener an edgy finish. The performance time is approximately four and a half minutes, but *Sorida* can easily be lengthened or shortened due to all the repeated phrase possibilities.

The simplistic ostinato sung in the men's voices for more than half the piece is probably the trickiest part of performing it in that it becomes difficult at times to keep men focused and in tune while elongating the downbeat of every bar. The stress of the downbeat on the syllable "So-" in the first measure of the ostinato and "da" of the second measure of the ostinato is extremely important for the entire choir, not only the men's voices, as this stress point encourages a dipping body movement that should be realized by the entire choir, and which also helps the choir when used as a processional. I think a bit of stylizing is acceptable for the women's voices as they sing all the melodies. I usually encourage my choir not to sing this melody completely as written but to slide into notes a bit.

Although the duets and trios are optional and can be sung quite well with one soloist, I find that the additive effect of bringing more soloists to the front as the piece goes along is very inviting to the audience. I would encourage directors to allow the soloists freedom in terms of vocal style and gesture to make this piece more personal.

Stylistic Considerations

The repeated choral ostinato that is carried by the men's voices throughout features a strong, pressed downbeat in each bar, which almost invites the singers to move. Included with the octavo are suggested African percussion instruments with ostinato patterns. Allowing the percussionists to begin their ostinatos a few bars before the choir begins works very well in setting up the rhythmic mood of the piece. Whether the piece is used as a processional or not, the composer suggests that the singers as well as the percussionists be encouraged to move or sway and engage their whole bodies. Because of its heavy rhythmic feel, *Sorida* works extremely well as a concert processional or call to worship.

Form and Structure

Sorida's characteristic ostinato and repetition make it a wonderful composition to use as a processional. It features a slow harmonic rhythm (one chord) with two simple phrases repeated over an ostinato passage that continues throughout the piece. The overall form is:

A A[1] A[2] Mini Coda (3 bars)
a b a b a b

Measure	Event and Scoring
mm. 1–6 (12 bars with repeats)	Layering of a two-bar ostinato which is repeated each time a new voice enters (bass, then baritone, then tenor 1 and finally tenor 2).
mm. 7–18	4+4+4+4 (with repeats) Women's voices layer in with the melody (alto, soprano 1 and then soprano 2).
mm. 19–30	4+4+4 Female voices sing a secondary melody using a triplet figure over the continuous male ostinato.
mm. 31–38	4+4 Solo (optional duet) features call & response with choir.
mm. 39–46	Same as mm. 7–18 but with solo layered on top.
mm. 47–58	Same as mm. 19–30 with solo layered on top.
mm. 59–66	Same as mm. 31–38 (solo becomes optional trio).
mm. 67–74	Same as mm. 39–46 with optional trio in call and response style.
mm. 75–86	Same as mm. 47–58 with optional trio in call and response style.
mm. 88–90	Mini Coda or "tag." Choir sings "sorida" in block chordal style.

Text and Translation

Sorida is a term of greeting in the Shona language of Zimbabwe, Africa, similar to *shalom* in Hebrew or *jambo* in Swahili.

Sorida

Sorida,
Sorida,
Sorida,
Sorida.

Sorida-rida-rida,
Sorida-rida-rida,
Sorida-rida-rida.

Greetings my brothers,
Greetings my sisters.
Greet everybody,
Love one another.

[Optional sacred verse]
Greetings my brothers,
Greetings my sisters.
O magnify Jehovah,
Let's worship him together.

Sorida,
Sorida,
Sorida,
Sorida.

Sorida-rida-rida,
Sorida-rida-rida,
Sorida-rida-rida.

Wave to your brothers,
Wave to your sisters.
Greet everybody,
Love one another.

[Optional sacred verse]
Sing praise unto the Lord God,
Let's magnify Jehovah.
Greet everybody,
Love one another.

Sorida,
Sorida,
Sorida,
Sorida.

Sorida-rida-rida,
Sorida-rida-rida,
Sorida-rida-rida.

Sorida,
Sorida!

Additional References and Resources

Powell, Rosephanye. "Frequently Asked Questions." The Official Web site of Rosephanye Powell. http://www.rosephanyepowell.com. Copyright 2007.

Dr. Rosephanye Powell,. Faculty and Staff Directory, Auburn University, Department of Music, http://media.cla.auburn.edu/music/bio/bio_display.cfm?contact_id=13. Copyright 2008.

———. *Compositions of Rosephanye Powell.* Auburn University, Department of Music. http://media.cla.auburn.edu/music/bio/r_powell_compositions.cfm. Copyright 2008

Recorded interviews with Rosephanye Powell available on MP3 from the composer at dunnprt@auburn.edu.

Contributed by:

Michele Holt

Teacher Resource Guide

The May Night (Die Mainacht)

Johannes Brahms

(1833–1897)

arr. Arthur Frackenpohl

(b. 1958)

SATB
Hal Leonard: 7777
Overall: 1
Vocal: 1
Tonal/Rhythm: 1

Composer

Johannes Brahms (1833–1897) was born in Hamburg, Germany. Early in his life, he had the benefit of extensive music training in piano, composition, and theory, and began performing as a pianist at age 14. In 1853 he toured Germany, where he had the opportunity to meet Robert and Clara Schumann. Robert heralded Brahms as the composer to carry the symphonic legacy of Beethoven, a challenge that perhaps weighed on Brahms for much of his compositional career. When Robert suffered a mental breakdown, Brahms briefly moved in with Clara, and remained close with her for the remainder of his life.

Having studied with Joseph Joachim in Germany, Brahms composed mostly chamber music from 1856 to 1868; at that time he also served as conductor for various ensembles, including the Weiner Singakademie. From 1868 to 1890, Brahms focused on larger symphonic and choral and orchestral works, beginning with *Ein Deutsches Requiem*, and later followed by his four symphonies. Toward the end of his life, he returned to smaller chamber works, highlighted by the *Vier Ernste Gesänge* (Four Serious Songs), a deep contemplation about death as a response to Clara's stroke in 1896. Brahms himself died of liver cancer the next year.

Arthur Frackenpohl has been an active composer, arranger, and music educator. Born in 1923 in Irvington New Jersey, he earned a master's in music from Eastman, and a DMA at McGill University in Montreal in 1957. He also studied composition with Darius Milhaud and Nadia Boulanger. Frackenpohl taught at the Crane School of Music at SUNY Potsdam from 1948 until retirement in 1985. He wrote the popular textbook *Harmonization at the Piano*, and he composed for band, orchestra, brass and wind chamber ensembles, and solo voice with piano.

Composition, Genre, and Historical Perspective

An example of German Lied, Brahms's setting of "Die Mainacht" (Op. 43, no. 2) is part of the collection *Vier Gesänge* (Four Songs) of 1866. He set the text of 18th-century poet Ludwig Hölty, leader of a poetry movement called the Göttinger Dicthterbund. The version Brahms found, however, was in an 1804 collection edited by Johann Heinrich Voss. Shortly after composing this set of songs, Brahms began to focus on larger choral-orchestral works like *Ein Deutsches Requiem* and *Alto Rhapsody*. Frackenpohl arranged Brahms's work for SATB chorus in 1962, while still teaching at the Crane School.

Musical Elements and Technical Considerations

This arrangement maintains the melody, the piano accompaniment, and the overall form of Brahms's setting. The original melody resides almost entirely in the soprano voice, the only exception being measures 3 through 8, where the tenors and basses introduce the melody in unison. In addition, other voices at times join the sopranos: all voices at measures 33 through 38 and 44, and the tenors often double for a couple of measures at a time. Conductors can easily teach their choirs how this piece sounds as a solo lied by having the sopranos sing their part with piano (tenors and basses singing mm. 3 through 8).

Attending to the sound of music as a solo piece can pay dividends in teaching the choral harmonization. Frakenpohl's arrangement largely draws the new choral parts from the piano accompaniment, and singers should be sensitive to how the piano supports them. For example, much of the bass part comes almost directly from the accompaniment, both in pitch and in rhythm (mm. 9 to 13, mm. 23 to 31, mm. 39–48). Altos and tenors also can hear their parts within the piano harmonies, though this support more often comes in terms of pitch and harmony, and less as rhythm (mm. 9 to 19). At times, the choral arrangement of the tenor and alto parts *anticipates* harmonic change in the piano (mm. 24 alto C-flat on beat 1 before piano at beat 2; mm. 29 tenor D-flat on beat 3 before piano at beat 4). When learning these sections, practice not with the piano part as written, but just with the implied chords. For example, mm. 29 is C9 moving to E-flat7. As written, this can be tricky for tenors, given that they must sing D-flat in the E-flat7 chord, when they have heard D-natural in soprano 2 and the accompaniment. Play the implied chords on beats 1 and 3, and the tenors can better learn where their part fits.

One of the challenges of the piece is the harmonic change of E-flat major to B major from section A to B. The music begins in E-flat, with the first two measures interpreted as V/E-flat. The first phrase (mm. 3 to 8) moves from E-flat to B-flat. At measure 9, the introduction of the pitch C-flat in the melody and the accompaniment along with A-flat in the bass allows the quick chord progression of A-flat minor–D-flat7–G-flat. An immediate move by third relation from G-flat to E-flat minor makes possible the cadencing of section A not in the original E-flat major (E-flat G B-flat), but in E-flat minor (Eb **Gb** Bb); the accompaniment affirms E-flat minor with three measures of i and V chords (E-flat minor–B-flat, mm. 12 to 14).

The G-flat and E-flat, then, are the pivotal pitches, reinterpreted as F-sharp and D-sharp in B major. The altos provide the greatest continuity, enharmonically remaining on the same E-flat/D-sharp pitch. The tenors sing G-flat at measure 13, and it is prominent in the accompaniment in the next two measures. Sopranos then re-enter at measure 15 on F-sharp. To emphasize these pitches as the connectors from section A to B, practice this without the basses and without playing the piano part of measures 13 and 14. This allows singers to hear the continuity between where they finish and where they begin again, without yet the interference of B-flat (in E-flat minor) and B-natural (in B major). Once solid, add back the missing parts to complete this transition.

Stylistic Considerations

This piece highlights Brahms's signature 3-against-2 rhythms. Triplets abound in the piano, and the singers have rhythms with eighth notes above (m. 22, and mm. 33 to the end). The tendency of many singers will be to shorten their eighth notes to match the length of the final triplet eighth. Warmups should include rhythmic practice, whereby half of the singers clap or sing triplets, while the others do straight eighths (then reverse).

This edition keeps the multitude of dynamic markings from Brahms's work that ensure that virtually every phrase crescendos or decrescendos. This enhances the beauty of moments like suspensions (mm. 29 and 30, mm. 41 and 42) and cadences (mm. 9 and 10). No phrase should be dynamically static: longer notes must also move even when not marked as such (ex: m4 half note must crescendo to connect to the rest of the phrase; m5 half note must decrescendo to finish the phrase).

Form and Structure

Form: ABA', where the final A is a combination of elements from sections A and B. The form is identical to the original Brahms.

SECTION	MEASURE	EVENT AND SCORING
mm. 1–2	Introduction	1 phrase (2)
mm. 3–14	A: Verse 1	2 phrases (6+6)
mm. 15–32	B: Verse 2	3 phrases (6+6+6)
mm. 33–51	A': Verse 3	3 phrases (6+9+4). The first 6-bar phrase is the melody from measures 3 to 8. The next 9-bar phrase mimics and then extends the melody of measures 27 to 32, and uses a different choral arrangement. The final 4 bars are piano alone.

Text and Translation

Frackenphol's arrangement includes only English text. Included below is the German poem on which Brahms based his original setting. Neither Brahms nor Frackenpohl used the second verse of the Hölty poem.

Original Text by Ludwig Hölty
English Text by Richard Griffith

1.
Wann der silberne Mond durch
die Gesträuche blinkt,
Und sein schlummerndes Licht
über den Rasen streut,
Und die Nachtigall flötet,
Wandl' ich traurig von Busch zu
Busch.

3.
Überhüllet von Laub girret ein
Taubenpaar
Sein Entzücken mir vor; aber ich
wende mich,
Suche dunklere Schatten,
Und die einsame Träne rinnt.

4.
Wann, o lächelndes Bild, welches
wie Morgenrot
Durch die Seele mir strahlt, find
ich auf Erden dich?
Und die einsame Träne

1.
When the silvery moon shines
thro' the leaves,
When her pale, drowsy light over
the fields she throws,
And the nightingale warbles,
I go sadly o'er hill and vale.

3.
Somewhere, hid in the leaves,
two softly cooing doves
Fill my heart with delight,
Yet do I turn away, Turn to
shadows that are darker,
In my eye is but one tear.

4.
Where, O vision whose smile
streams like the rosy dawn
Through the depths of my soul,
where on this earth are you?
In my eye is but one tear.
It burns me, burns upon my

Contributed by:

Christopher Bartley

Teacher Resource Guide

Nine Hundred Miles

Philip Silvey

(1952–1961)

SATB
Santa Barbara Music: SBMP 438
Overall: 1
Vocal: 1
Tonal/Rhythm: 1

Arranger

Growing up in the rural mountains of central Pennsylvania, Philip Silvey studied piano from an early age and actively participated in school music. He studied composition formally with William T. Allen at Houghton College, and with Burt Fenner and Bruce Trinkley, both at the Pennsylvania State University. He began his career as a school vocal music teacher in 1992 where he had the opportunity to prepare arrangements and original compositions for the choirs he taught in Allegan, Michigan. After seven years of teaching, he returned to graduate school and studied at the University of Illinois in Urbana–Champaign, earning a doctorate in music education. For four years he directed the Women's Chorus at the University of Maryland where he also taught courses in music education and conducted the Maryland Boy Choir for two years. At present, he conducts the Women's Choir and teaches undergraduate courses in music education at the Baldwin-Wallace Conservatory in Berea, Ohio.

Composition, Genre, and Historical Perspective

A folk song belongs to the people who create it and pass it along, usually in rural settings, sung from person to person. The text often depicts a moment, a mood, or a way of life. Essentially a folk song sketches a portrait of people and their lives, often carrying universal themes that relate to people from all walks of life.

The railroad as a theme appears in the texts of numerous American folk songs; it links them in time to an early part of the twentieth century when laborers built the transcontinental railways that transformed the lives of Americans. The railroad was symbolic of the wandering, restless spirit of many young men at this time. American folk singer Cisco Houston called the railroad one of the "last romances of labor," a symbol of both adventure and distant loneliness.

At this time in history, folk music also played a greater role in American life and culture than it does today. "Nine Hundred Miles," like many other songs learned and passed along through oral traditions, has no clear authorship, although it probably originated between the years of 1870 and 1940. As a genre, folk songs defy definition because by nature they are freely recalled, sung, and altered by the many singers and arrangers who come to learn them, often by ear.

My first encounter with this song came when I observed a fifth grade creative arts class singing a simplified version of the tune (without the final two lines of text as the appear in this arrangement), accompanying their singing on mallet instruments by playing a simple, open-fifth ostinato of steady half notes. Between rounds of singing, the teacher invited individuals to read aloud the contents of the letter mentioned in the third line of the lyrics, as imagined by the improvising students pretending to read. While I listened to the class sing, I began to hear alternate harmonies for the melody. I developed these initial ideas, consulting recordings and other sources (where I learned about the additional lines of melody and text), until I felt able to capture the spirit of the song while enhancing it with my own additions and interpretations. This version is set in D minor and the open fifth between the root and the dominant (inspired by the ostinato pattern played by the class I observed) can be found throughout the arrangement in various forms. It first appears in the introduction and then throughout the accompaniment in a more concealed manner (see left hand of piano in m. 13 or vocal parts beginning at m. 38).

Musical Elements and Technical Considerations

I developed this arrangement with young treble singers in mind. I also wanted to use figures from the vocal inflections I heard the singer Cisco Houston perform on the folkways recording I consulted (see references). In this arrangement, the choir sings the entire first verse and refrain in unison. At measure 18, an ostinato figure is introduced that requires singers to repeat the word "miles" numerous times. Most singers need to be reminded to elongate the "ah" vowel while minimizing the last half of the diphthong (the "ee" sound) in this word. I employed a small degree of divisi, purposefully making it accessible for developing choirs. In measure 25, a subgroup of sopranos can easily pivot to the sustained half notes on the word "blow," foreshadowing the eventual stacked minor seventh chord that imitates the sound of a train whistle.

In measures 32 and 33 (and repeated in mm. 34 and 35), two parts fan out into four when each voice part divides into two groups, each moving either up or down one scale degree, doubled at the interval of a fifth. In *la*-based minor, half of the sopranos ascend from *la* to *ti*, while the others descend from *la* to *sol*. Shortly thereafter, half of the altos ascend from *mi* to *fa* and the rest descend from *mi* to *re*. This exercise can easily be introduced out of context during a series of vocal warmups. Using solfège (or a comparable system) in conjunction with a visual chart that reflects half- and whole-step intervals will allow singers to recognize that in both parts, voices that move upward move by half step, while those that move downward move by whole step. Even choirs with a smaller number of singers can achieve this, and the resultant minor seventh chord can be a rewarding sound for both singers and audience.

At measure 38, a variation of the "miles and miles" ostinato requires singers to leap a perfect fifth, with altos echoing this from a minor third below the sopranos in measure 40. For the altos, finding this pitch (hidden inside the fifth outlined by the sopranos) can be challenging, but the left hand of the piano accompaniment asserts the D minor tonality on the downbeat, and this can serve to anchor the alto entrance on beat 3 of that measure. It is important that all singers sustain a pure and rounded "o" vowel on the word "home" for the last note of measures 43 and 44. The last word in this section for all singers becomes "home" rather than "miles." The lower two parts must make this change since they have been singing "miles and miles" in an ostinato pattern for 4 or more measures. This climactic moment in the piece results in a first inversion F chord with a D in the bass of the accompaniment. It will tune well if all singers are producing a pure and rounded "o" vowel.

Stylistic Considerations

Traditionally, singers perform folk music as soloists, often accompanying themselves on traditional folk instruments such as guitar or banjo. When the short refrain first occurs (beginning in m. 13 and again in m. 46), the piano figure imitates the sound of a guitar plucked gently in broken chord patterns of eighth notes. The recorded version I consulted for this arrangement includes Cisco Houston playing an actively picked guitar accompaniment that alternates between the root and dominant in the implied bass line. This accompaniment seemed to simulate the churning action of the wheels on a train. For this arrangement, I used ostinato patterns (where singers sing "miles and miles" numerous times to suggest the vast distance referenced in the title) to generate a similar effect. I also used stark, open fifths in the accompaniment to elicit the hollow, lonely feeling implied in the text. As Charles Edward Smith suggests in his liner notes for the Folkways recording of this folk song: "There is probably no sound in America so universally nostalgic as that of a train whistle at night. It is a siren song for the distant places and a sickness for home, an ache in the stomach and an ache in the heart." With this mood in mind, I attempted to evoke the essence of train whistles in the accompaniment (mm. 17 and 50) and in the voices (mm. 25 and 26, 33, 35, and 44). Some of the embellishment figures in the melody (most readily seen on the word "read" in m. 7) are reminiscent of the yodeling quality heard on the vocals of the recorded version of this song. The original version seemed almost unmetered, but since young singers would have had difficulty trying to follow a similar setting, I chose to establish a metered feel.

Directors should keep in mind the spirit of folk music and how it sounds in authentic renderings. An overly refined choral sound could compromise the "feel" and intent of the source material. Therefore allow singers to use a more relaxed approach to text pronunciation. The apostrophes used in words like "try'n'" and "whistlin'" are clear examples of the relaxed or slang treatment indicative of folk song texts such as this. Also, the natural spoken stress of the words should be clearly followed to achieve a somewhat spoken quality. For example, the first syllable of the word "walkin'" in measure 5 should receive a slight accent and the second syllable should be significantly minimized. This results in a more natural, folk-like character from the onset of the piece. Keep this sensibility in mind throughout.

Form and Structure

This arrangement amplifies the usual folk song structure of verse and, in this case, a short two-line refrain. Introductory material, ostinato patterns, and piano interludes supplement the original material in order to reflect the emotional undertones of the text.

The piece begins and ends with a framing 4-bar piano figure. Within this external frame, the work gradually develops toward two high points that serve to set up the primary trajectory of the piece, which ultimately ends in a stark, wistful manner. The first peak occurs in measure 36 where the voices crescendo to a point that propels the piano to launch into a thick, soloistic treatment of the "miles and miles" ostinato, an inevitable outgrowth of the growing train whistle chords produced by the singers. The music here reflects the intensity and range of feelings experienced by the speaker of the text. The second climax, and perhaps the more poignant one, occurs in measure 45 after a section where the texture builds and accelerates until the voices stop and the accompanist strikes three pairs of notes converging inward in slow succession. In my mind, this signifies a moment of truth, when the train comes to a stop and the next chapter of the unfinished story is about to take place. To maximize this effect, allow for enough time for a molto ritardando in the accompaniment and a sufficient grand pause before the accompaniment commences in measure 46. This can be the dramatic high point of the work if done with artistic and interpretive sensitivity. The overall structure can be outlined as follows:

Section	Measure	Event and Scoring
Introduction	mm. 1–4	2 phrases (2+2)
Verse 1	mm. 5–12	4 phrases (2+2+2+2)
Refrain	mm. 13–17	2 phrases (3+2)
Transition	mm. 28–33	ostinato 1, 2 phrases (2+3)
Verse 2	mm. 23–30	with ostinato 1, 4 phrases (2+2+2+2)
Transition	mm. 32–35	whistle figure, 2 phrases (2+2)
Interlude	mm. 36–37	piano (ostinato 1)
Transition	mm. 38–45	ostinato 2, 3 phrases (2+2+3+1)
Refrain	mm. 46–50	2 phrases (3+2)
Introduction (reprise)	mm. 51–54	2 phrases (2+2)

Text and Translation

The text for this folk song implies a story. The narrator tells the listener what is happening at the moment the song begins ("I am walkin' on this track") and suggests an emotional state ("I've got tears in my eyes"), but the details of what led to this moment are undisclosed. The singer must imagine what might have dislocated the speaker to a place "nine hundred miles" from home. The singer could be some kind of "hobo," a term that derives from the telling designation "homeward bound."

In an article that appears in a songbook with a transcription of this folk song, Cisco Houston writes:

> A folk song is a way of singing out the news—news of a wedding, a murder—good times or bad times—good people and bad people. It's one way of making a record of memorable things that happened. In the days before newspapers, and among people who couldn't have read them even if they existed, the folk song was a kind of chronicle and running commentary on the times. Many of them have lived for years, while nothing is more dead than yesterday's newspapers. The folk songs and story ballads were not the most accurate kind of history of course, because once the event, whatever it was, had been recorded, generations of singers went on elaborating and changing the

> song—smoothing it out, or shaping it up to suit their own ideas of how the event might have happened. Often, the event which started the song was blurred or lost as time went on. The song then took on its own independent life. Aristotle said in his poetics, that art is truer than history because it shows what should have happened rather than simply what did happen.

Although the text, melody, and harmony of a folk song all reflect the flavor of a time and place, Houston suggests a universal quality to this music that invites the singers to make it their own.

> I am walkin' down this track,
> I've got tears in my eyes,
> I'm tryin' to read a letter from my home.
> And if that train runs me right,
> I'll be home Saturday night,
> 'Cause I'm nine hundred miles from my home.
>   And I hate to hear that lonesome whistle blow,
>   that long lonesome train whistlin' down.
> Well this train I ride on
> Is a hundred coaches long
> You can hear her whistle blow a million miles.
> And if that train runs me right,
> I'll be home Saturday night,
> 'Cause I'm nine hundred miles from my home.
>   And I hate to hear that lonesome whistle blow,
>   that long lonesome train whistlin' down.

Additional References and Resources

Asch, Moses and Irwin Silber, eds. *900 Miles: The Ballads, Blues, and Folksongs of Cisco Houston*. New York, Oak Publications, 1965.

"900 Miles" on *900 Miles and other R.R. Songs*, Folkway Records No. FA 02013.

Contributed by:

Philip Silvey

Teacher Resource Guide

Fillimiooriay

arr. Lon Beery (b. 1958)

SATB
Alfred: 24012
Overall: 1
Vocal: 1
Tonal/Rhythm: 2

Arranger

Lon Beery was born on May 11, 1958 in El Paso, Texas. He attended high school in Findlay, Ohio, and graduated from Heidelberg College in Tiffin, Ohio in 1980 with a degree in music composition. He returned to Heidelberg College a year later to pursue Ohio teaching certification. Beery taught middle school and high school vocal music in London, Ohio for several years while he pursued a masters degree in music education at The Ohio State University in Columbus. After completing his masters in 1990, he was offered a teaching assistantship at Ohio State while he pursued a PhD program in music education. He received a PhD in music education in 1994.

Beery accepted a position as an assistant professor at Syracuse University where he taught from 1993–1999. At Syracuse, he directed the Men's Glee Club and served as Chair of the Music Education Department. In 1999, he decided to return to public school teaching. Currently, he teaches vocal music at Spry Middle School in Webster, New York where he directs the 7th and 8th grade choruses and "Spry Select," a select mixed chorus. Dr. Beery has also taught Choral Arranging at the Eastman School of Music in Rochester, NY. He is a frequent guest choral conductor, working especially with adolescent choruses. He has directed middle school honors choirs in Connecticut, Florida, New York, Pennsylvania, and Texas.

Beery has composed or arranged over seventy published choral pieces, which appear in the catalogues of Hal Leonard, Alfred, Alliance, BriLee, and others. His TTBB composition, "I Believe," was performed by the U.S. Army Chorus at President Ronald Reagan's interment service in California. For his compositions, he has received several ASCAP Standard Awards. He has also written several articles that have appeared in the *Choral Journal* and the *Music Educators Journal*, and he has presented sessions at state, regional, and national conferences of ACDA and MENC. Beery currently serves as chair of the Eastern Division ACDA Junior High and Middle School Repertoire and Standards.

Composition, Genre, and Historical Perspective

"Fillimiooriay" is an Irish-American folk song from the middle of the nineteenth century. The title is spelled in a number of ways, including "Filimeooriay," "Fillymeooriay," "Filameeoryay," "Filimeooreay," "Filameomeray," and others. It is perhaps more widely known by the title "Paddy Works on the Railway," or by other alternative titles that include "Poor Paddy Works on the Railway," "Paddy Works on the Erie," "Paddy on the Railway," "Poor Paddy on the Railway," "Paddy and the Railway," among others. It should be noted that the name "Paddy," was a slang term for someone Irish, often used pejoratively. It was taken from the name Patrick or Padraic.

Daniel Cassidy, in his book "How the Irish Invented Slang," notes that Carl Sandburg claimed he discovered this song as a piece of sheet music published in 1850. However, no copy of that edition has been found. The earliest printed version of the "Fillimiooriay," according to Cassidy, is dated 1864.

The song seems to refer back to the experience of Irish immigrants during the decade of the 1840s when over a million Irish people died of starvation and another million were scattered throughout the United States. This song probably originated with Irish laborers in the United States in the mid-19th Century, specifically those who worked to build the First Transcontinental Railroad from the east coast toward the west. It is not known whether this was a completely new folk song coming out of the Irish-American labor experience, or whether it was an adaptation of an earlier Irish folk song.

Although the word "fillimiooriay" has often been considered to be merely nonsense syllables, Cassidy suggests that it is actually an English phonetic spelling of "fillfidh mé uair éirithe," pronounced *fill'ih may oo-er í-ríheh*, which means, "I'll go back, time to get up."

Musical Elements and Technical Considerations

I arranged "Fillimiooriay" to meet very specific range criteria. It was written for, and dedicated to, the Webster Men's Glee Club in Webster, New York, which I directed for several years. This was a unique male chorus that included boys in grades six through twelve. With these grade levels in mind, I was determined to arrange this in a way that met the vocal needs of all the men in this chorus:

1. We had a number of unchanged male voices, especially in the boys in grades six and seven. A number of these were moving into the first stages of voice change, sometimes called cambiata, alto-tenor, or mid-voice. These boys were most comfortable in the octave between the A below middle C and the A above. The purely unchanged voices could obviously sing higher, but by keeping these boys in the same section, there was more security and success. The high school men who generally sing first tenor also found this range accessible. This tessitura became the range used for the tenor 1 part.
2. We had a number of changing voices that were most comfortable in the area of the F below middle C to the D above as their tessitura. There were many of these boys, especially among the seventh through ninth graders. I arranged the tenor 2 part specifically for them. Many of the high school tenors also found this range to be comfortable.
3. We also had a number of guys who were true baritones, especially among the boys from the high school. A number of the middle school boys were also young baritones, but they often lacked the depth and flexibility of their high school counterparts. The high school baritones certainly added vocal support to the middle school guys. The range was also kept rather modest to reflect the ranges of the young baritones in the upper middle school grades.

The range of the melody in both the verse and the chorus spans only a seventh. This made arranging this for middle school and high school men very approachable. By setting the first verse in the key of A minor, I was able to give the melody completely to the second tenors. Since this is the most prominent section in the upper middle school grades, this made sense. At the chorus from measure 17 to 24, the tenor 1 part sings a descant above the melody in the tenor 2 part. By modulating up a fourth to D minor beginning with the third verse at measure 33, I was able to give the same melody now to the first tenors. As an arranger, I have found that modulating up a fourth or a fifth often works extremely well when writing for young male choruses.

With these specific range considerations, this piece works equally well with high school men's choruses as with middle school male ensembles. It is an ideal piece for groups that combine boys of all ages, especially for recruitment purposes.

Form and Structure

Section	Measure	Event and Scoring
Introduction	mm. 1–8	piano (a minor)
Verse 1	mm. 9–16	unison melody, tenor 2 (or solo)
Chorus	mm. 17–24	TTB with melody in tenor 2, tenor 1 descant
Verse 2	mm. 1–24	(repeat)
Interlude	mm. 25–32	piano
Verse 3	mm. 33–40	tenor 1 unison melody (or solo) (d minor)
Chorus	mm. 41–48	TTB with melody in tenor 1
Interlude	mm. 49–50	(in slower tempo)
Verse 4	mm. 51–58	TTB with melody in tenor 1 (in slower tempo)
Chorus	mm. 59–72	TTB with melody in tenor 1

Text and Translation

In eighteen hundred and forty one,
I put me corduroy breeches on.
I put me corduroy breeches on
to work upon the railway.

(chorus)
Fillimiooriooriay, Fillimiooriooriay,
Fillimiooriooriay, to work upon the railway.

In eighteen hundred and forty two,
I left the old world for the new.
'Twas sorry luck that brought me through
to work upon the railway.

(chorus)

In eighteen hundred and forty-three,
'twas then I met sweet Biddy McGee.
An elegant wife she's been to me,
while working on the railway.

(chorus)

In eighteen hundred and forty-sev'n,
sweet Biddy McGee she went to heav'n.
If she left one child, she left eleven,
to work upon the railway.

(chorus)

Additional References and Resources

Cassidy, Daniel, *How the Irish Invented Slang*. CounterPunch/AK Press, 2007.

Contributed by:

Lon Beery

Medieval Gloria

Vijay Singh

SATB
Alfred: Oct-14
Overall: 1
Vocal: 1
Tonal/Rhythm: 1

Composer

Vijay Singh directs the choral and jazz program at Central Washington University in Ellensburg, Washington. He received a master's degree in choral conducting and vocal performance from Portland State University. He has performed regularly as baritone soloist for a variety of groups, including the Oregon Symphony, the Robert Shaw Chorale, and the Disciples of Groove. Having taught in many educational settings, Singh writes music for groups of many different ages and skill levels, and for both classical choral ensembles and jazz groups. ASCAP has honored him eight times with their prestigious Composer's Award.

Composition, Genre, and Historical Perspective

This piece is a two-voice partial mass movement appropriate for young singers, particularly middle school and freshman choirs. Published in 1996, Singh dedicated this piece to the honor choir of the Spokane Public Schools Festival of the Arts, 1995.

Musical Elements and Technical Considerations

This piece has arrangements available for both SA and TB ensembles. It is a relatively easy piece, with frequent step-wise motion, and melodic range not greater than an octave in each voice. In performance, it can serve as an invigorating processional, but its greatest benefit is as an educational piece for young singers.

Mode

Reminiscent of the modal sound of chant, this piece uses the dorian mode for the vocal parts. For singers who have learned the sounds of major and minor scales, the important difference in comparing dorian mode to natural minor is that the sixth scale degree is raised the by a half step. Singh sets this music in E-flat, rather than the more common D of the dorian mode, and thus it is the C pitch (instead of C-flat) that helps to produce the signature dorian sound. The singers will have a tendency of to try to lower the C to C-flat and sing natural minor, particularly when a melody strongly suggests E-flat minor (mm. 9 and 10, followed by the C pitch of m. 11).

It is possible to hear the dorian mode as two sets of 4 pitches, each with the same sequence of intervals. In E-flat, for example, the first four are E-flat, F, G-flat, A-flat—whole step, half step, whole step. The second four are B-flat, C, D-flat, E-flat—also whole step, half step, whole step. Design warm-up exercises that use a range of four pitches, using a simple vocable *la-la-la* singing up and down with this same interval sequence. Move up by step and repeat (E-flat–F–G-flat–A-flat; F–G–A-flat–B-flat; etc.) and then back down to original tonic. Then ask singers to do two in a row, a fifth apart: E-flat–F–G-flat–A-flat; then B-flat–C–D-flat–E-flat. This should help your singers recognize the basic melodic building blocks of the melody of "Medieval Gloria," and permit them to learn it faster and more accurately.

Alternatively, for choirs that have learned some solfège for sight reading, these vocal lines represent good opportunities to show how effective it can be. Have singers treat their melodies as though rooted in B-flat minor/D-flat major (as the key signature would normally suggest). This enables singers to apply their solfège skills to quickly read their parts amid more familiar-sounding modes. For example, all singers can learn the main melody (mm. 1 through 4) by beginning on *la*. Then the first C pitch of measure 2 comes in the context of singing *la–ti–do* (B-flat–C–D); the C pitch of measure 11, which can feel out of place after the E-flat minor mode of measures 9 and 10, is now easy to find in *re–do–ti–la* (E-flat–D-C–B-flat). This approach shows singers how useful and flexible their sight-reading techniques can be.

TEXTURE

This piece teaches singers to sing monophonically, homophonically, and polyphonically. It begins with all singers on the main melody (mm. 1 through 4). The basses/altos then add a second vocal line in the same rhythm as the main melody (mm. 5 through 8). The two vocal parts then separate, with the lower voice singing for two measures, then holding a B-flat while the upper voice enters (mm. 9 through 12). Finally, the voices begin together but sing in different but complementary rhythms (mm. 13 through 16). In other words, built into the structure of the piece are the steps that allow singers to learn independence of vocal line within multi-voice textures.

LANGUAGE

The Gloria from the Ordinary of the Mass is one of the most commonly set choral texts. This piece helps singers new to singing in Latin become comfortable singing in the language. Singers will undoubtedly encounter this text again, and here they gain experience with it. At the same time, one of its advantages is that it uses only about seven lines of the Gloria, rather than the much lengthier full text. From this shorter text, singers can practice all of Latin's pure vowels, and also learn some of its rules for consonants: the silent "h" of Hominibus, the single nasal sound of "gn" in Magnam, the "ch" sound of Benedicimus, and so on.

INSTRUMENTATION

Accompanying the voices is a part for optional hand drum. This part uses a single repeating rhythm: quarter note followed by two eighths. It gives the music greater rhythmic vitality, particularly useful when using it as a processional. Moreover, it provides an opportunity to teach young singers about creative contribution to ensemble performance, and about a sense of personal ownership of music they learn. Encourage choir members to choose any nonpitched instrument, or even percussion instruments they make, and play this part.

Stylistic Considerations

In some senses, this piece is antithetical to its source material inspiration. While the music owes its debt to medieval chant due to its modal scale, it is percussive and highly rhythmic—not like the ethereal quality of relatively freer chants. Performance of this piece should recognize the percussion's emphasis of beats one and three. The vocal lines also stress these beats, though not each and every beat one and three. Identify in the text where these stresses are, such as in the main melody:

Beat	1	2	3	4	1	2	3	4
	GLO	ri-a	GLO	ri-a	in	ex-cel-sis	DE-	o

Most of the piece stresses two beats in each measure; consequently, the final four measures feel faster, as the effect of the polyphonic texture (with the lower voice entering one beat after the upper) is now to emphasize all four beats of each measure, rather than only beats one and three.

Form and Structure

SECTION	MEASURE	EVENT AND SCORING
Introduction	mm. 1–4	2 phrases (2+2), repeated (cantor, all). Monophonic
Refrain	mm. 5–8	2 phrases (2+2). 2-part choir. Homophonic
Stanza	mm. 9–16	2 phrases (4+4). 2-part choir. Polyphonic
Refrain	mm. 17–20	2 phrases (2+2), as before
Stanza	mm. 21–24	1 phrase, same music as first phrase of previous stanza
Refrain	mm. 25–28	2 phrases, as before
Refrain	mm. 29–32	Polyphonic setting

Text and Translation

Ordinary of the Mass—The Latin text uses part but not all of the *Gloria*.

Gloria in excelsis Deo.	Glory be to God on high,
Et in terra pax hominibus bonae voluntatis.	and on earth peace, good will towards men.
Laudamus te. Benedicimus te.	We praise thee, we bless thee,
Adoramus te. Glorificamus te.	We worship thee, we glorify thee,
Gratias agimus tibi	We give thanks to thee
Propter magnam gloriam tuam.	For thy great glory.
Domine Deus!	O Lord God!

Contributed by:

Christopher Bartley

Teacher Resource Guide

Viva Tutti

Anonymous 18th Century

TTB a cappella
Lawson-Gould: LG00778
Overall: 1
Vocal: 1
Tonal/Rhythm: 1

Composition, Genre, and Historical Perspective

The term "glee" comes from the Old English *gleo*, which means "mirth" or "entertainment." Mainly inspired by the English madrigal of 1590–1630, the glee flourished in England from the mid-eighteenth century until the early twentieth century. Most glees were written for male voices in either three or four parts. An interest in the genre was set in motion after a rediscovery of the English madrigal in the early eighteenth century. The glee inherited a number characteristics from the madrigal, including those present in *Viva Tutti*: (1) text divided into sections; (2) short homophonic sections where one or more voices temporarily drop out to give a semi-chorus affect; and (3) close canon. Some contemporary characteristics of the glee include detailed dynamic and articulation markings.

Musical and Technical Considerations

Viva Tutti is a fantastic piece for men's choruses of all ability levels. I have used this piece with a small ninth-grade men's chorus and a collegiate men's chorus. It works especially well as concert opener, closer, or encore.

Although highly accessible, the piece does present a number of challenges for singers; the first is tessitura. Depending on the age and vocal ability of the choir, particularly the tenors, it might be wise to transpose the piece. I found the best key for my ninth-grade tenors to be F-sharp major; it allows both students with changed and unchanged voices to sing comfortably. On the other hand, my collegiate ensemble sang more comfortably in the printed key of A major. I advise experimenting with the key and making a choice that allows the singers to sing with healthy and efficient production.

The Italian language is often challenging for young singers. While teaching the diction, giving the singers a few axioms might help them find success more quickly. For example, the following three concepts should be introduced immediately: (1) no "American" Rs—all Rs should be flipped or rolled; (2) all Ts should be dental, not aspirated; and (3) no diphthongs. The singers must learn the diction correctly the first time because it becomes more difficult to change their habits once they are part of their muscle memory. When working with novice singers, modeling the diction typically produces the most successful results. Remember to be systematic; too much information too fast will confuse them. Speak one word of text at a time and have them repeat it back to you. Repeat this process as necessary. When the singers are successful, go on to the next word. Then work with groups of words, beginning with just a few and gradually adding more text until the singers are proficient with the diction.

The opening section should come together rather quickly with the simple canonic entrances in both tenor parts and the bass entrance on the tonic. Be aware of the voice crossing in measures 9 and 11 in the tenor parts (this figure appears each time this section repeats). At measure 12, the start of the B section, the tenors have the challenge of sustaining an inverted dominant pedal for four measures. Encourage healthy production and a sense of direction and spin as they sustain. Below the pedal, the second tenors and basses sing a repeated pattern in parallel thirds. For young singers, it is often difficult to hear this third relationship. The conductor should also be aware of the contrasting rhythm in the bass part in measure 17 and the first-inversion A-major chord on beat one of measure 19; young basses will be inclined to sing the root. The return of the A section at measure 23 might be difficult for the second tenors, again because they must find the third of the A-major triad.

As one might expect, singers will have a tendency to rush. Throughout the learning of this piece, conductors might find it helpful to use various rhythm and tempo exercises to help their singers internalize the pulse. For example, have the singers tap the pulse quietly on their bodies. When they have mastered this, have them tap the pulse on the shoulder of the person next to them.

Adhere to the barring in the score when conducting this piece. One might be inclined to begin with a downbeat, rather than the anacrusis written in the score; however, the pickup is absolutely critical, as it allows the accented syllables to fall on the strong beats throughout.

Stylistic Considerations

It is imperative that this piece be driven by the text. Phrases should be thought of primarily in groups of four measures; this will allow the rhyme scheme to be heard clearly. As is typical in this genre, Hunter's edition is highly marked with dynamics and articulations. The overarching articulation should be non-legato as per his indication. Be certain to observe the *subito piano* in the final A section (m. 42) to add excitement. Hunter also indicates that the final measures be sung without ritardando and that the final note be cut off on beat two without fermata.

Form and Structure

Viva Tutti is constructed in ABA´BA´ form. The A section differs from A´ in that it has four measures of introductory material where the two tenor parts enter in canon.

Section	Measure	Event and Scoring
A	mm. 1–4	canonic introductory material in tenor parts
	mm. 5–12	homophonic
B	mm. 13–18	tenor inverted pedal; lower two parts move in parallel thirds
	mm. 19–23	alternation between upper voices and bass
A´	mm. 24–31	homophonic
B	mm. 32–37	tenor inverted pedal; lower two parts move in parallel thirds
	mm. 38–42	alternation between upper voices and bass
A´	mm. 43–49	homophonic

Text

Viva Tutti levezzose, *Donne a'mabiliamorose,* *Che non anno crudeltà!*	Long live all the pretty women, The women so pleasant, like roses, Who have no cruelty.
Viva sempre, *Delle donne sol de riva,* *Labramata sedelta.*	Hail always, Those women yearning by the shore. They who have no cruelty.

Contributed by:

Bradley Miller

Level 2

Mixed voices:
City Called Heaven arr. Poelintz, Josephine. . .121
Ahrirang arr. De Cormier, Robert. . .127
Bile Them Cabbage Down Wilberg, Mack. . .131
Domaredansen Collins, Drew. . .137
Ev'ry Time I Feel the Spirit Dawson, William Levi. . .145
God Is Seen arr. Parker, Alice. . .151
Ipharadisi Ulrich, Jerry. . .155
It Takes a Village Szymko, Joan. . .159
O Occhi, manza mia de Lassus, Orlande. . .163
Old Time Religion arr. Hogan, Moses/ad. Harlan, Benjamin. . .167
Requiem Gilkyson, Eliza. . .173
The Pasture" from Where the Earth Meets the Sky Stroope, Z. Randall. . .179
Wantimg Memories Barnwell, Ysaye M.. . .185
Where the Music Comes From Hoiby, Lee. . .191

Treble voices:
Dance on My Heart Koepke, Allen. . .195
Gate, Gate Tate, Brian. . .199
Japanese Garden Culloton, Matthew. . .205
Jordan's Angels Dilworth, Rollo A.. . .209
Measure Me Sky Mulholland, James. . .215
Scarborough Fair arr. Goetze, Mary. . .221
The Birds Britten, Benjamin. . .225
Weep No More Childs, David. . .229
Yo Le Canto Todo El Dia Brunner, David. . .235

Men's voices:
Back to Ethiopia arr. Rardin, Paul. . .241
Byker Hill arr. Sandler, Mitchell. . .247
In Flanders Fields arr. Emerson, Roger. . .253
How Can I Keep from Singing Ellingboe, Bradley. . .257
Streets of Laredo arr. Takach, Timothy C.. . .261

Teacher Resource Guide

City Called Heaven

Josephine Poelinitz
(b. 1944)

SATB/piano
Colla Voce: 21-20105
Overall: 2
Vocal: 2
Tonal/Rhythm: 2

Arranger

Josephine Poelinitz (b. 1944) served for fifteen years as a vocal music teacher in the Chicago Public Schools, working with pre-school and elementary students. For the next seventeen years she served as the Vocal Music Resource Specialist and as one of the coordinators of the Citywide Music Contest for the Chicago Public Elementary and High Schools. In the community, Ms. Poelinitz has served as Minister of Music, clinician, and adjudicator.

In 1982, Poelinitz founded the award-winning All-City Elementary Youth Chorus of the Chicago Public Schools, serving as conductor until 2006. The group has given special performances at Carnegie Hall in New York, the Capitol building in Washington D.C., and Orchestra Hall in Chicago. In 1990, the group made a special appearance at the International Advent Sing in Vienna, Austria where Poelinitz was the guest conductor. The group has also performed under Poelinitz's direction at regional and national conventions of the American Choral Directors Association.

Poelinitz is herself an alumna of the Chicago Public Schools She earned a bachelor's degree in music education at DePaul and her master's degree in education at National Louis University. She now lives in Indianapolis where she fills requests as an adjudicator and elementary/middle school music consultant. In addition to her musical activities, she facilitates meditations in the Quan Yin method (www.godsdirectcontact.org).

Composition, Genre, and Historical Perspective

This arrangement of "City Called Heaven" came about when Poelinitz was teaching elementary students. She was charged with, among other things, teaching them music in the African-American tradition. She created this arrangement originally for SAT voicing so that it would work with young singers, especially those with changing voices. However, she always taught it from memory and by rote. Henry Leck came upon a performance of it, and pleaded with Poelinitz to give him a score so that he could publish it in his choral series. But the arrangement existed only in her head, so no written score was available. Leck dogged her relentlessly for two years until she felt compelled to commit the music to paper. She solicited the help of Dr. Keith Hampton to transcribe the arrangement, giving him recordings of both the accompaniment and the vocal parts (which she played at the piano). Hampton played a later role as well, pressing Poelinitz to add a part for bass so that he could perform it with his own choirs.

This tune was originally a spiritual, but Poelinitz's piano part—originally conceived to support young singers not yet ready to sing unaccompanied—gives it a quasi-gospel feel. These two genres have close ties but there are important distinctions.

The African-American spiritual originated during this country's slavery years. Since slaves were generally not allowed to own instruments, spirituals were originally unaccompanied. (This held over when the so-called "concert spiritual"—harmonizations and arrangements of spiritual melodies with the intention of performance—came into practice.) The gospel genre, though technically originating at the end of the nineteenth century, is essentially a twentieth-century phenomenon that draws on several instrumental genres, most notably blues, ragtime, and jazz. Therefore, gospel music is typically accompanied. Another important distinction is that much of the gospel repertoire is composed (notables include Thomas A. Dorsey, Charles Tindley, Clara Ward, James Cleveland, and other greats), whereas the spiritual is a folk genre, without composer attribution.

So Josephine Poelinitz's arrangement of "City Called Heaven" is best thought of and described as a "spiritual arranged with a gospel feel," and is most accurately attributed in printed concert programs exactly as it appears in the octavo: "Spiritual, arr. Josephine Poelinitz." Poelinitz is careful to note: "It is in a gospel *feel*, not necessarily a gospel *style*." Remember that her intention was to make spirituals accessible to young singers, not to "gospel-ize" a spiritual.

There are several types of spiritual, and "City Called Heaven" belongs to the sub-genre "sorrow song." Poelinitz says: "This is a sorrow song...but a sorrow with hope." Spirituals often have codes and double meanings hidden in the lyrics. In this case, the city called "heaven" may refer to a city north of the Mason-Dixon line. Therefore, freedom was an important part of a slave's concept of "heaven."

In the seventeenth and eighteenth centuries, some colonials and immigrants set out on their own. Many found their way to the Central Appalachian Mountains, which created natural insulation for the stories and songs each culture brought with them. Inevitably, the various cultures combined and influenced one another, which is how we have come to have, for example, bluegrass renditions of spirituals. Be cautious about any online recordings or YouTube videos you find of "City Called Heaven," as such examples will likely be inaccurate sources on which to draw expressive devices and improvisational style when interpreting the Poelinitz arrangement, which is solely in the African-American tradition.

The original melody goes by several titles, including "A City Called Heaven," "Pilgrim of Sorrow," "I Am a Poor Pilgrim of Sorrow," and perhaps others. It has appeared in several hymnals over the years; if you look it up, you may have to check for it under several titles in order to find it. Also note that lyrics vary from rendition to rendition.

Musical Elements and Technical Considerations

- The pitches and rhythms of the piece are easy. Junior high choirs, church choirs short on rehearsal time, and even choirs of first-time singers can get this piece up on two legs with very little rehearsing. However, getting the spirit of this piece can be difficult for singers and conductors who did not grow up in a gospel tradition. Depending on your background and that of your singers, this actually might be where the majority of your rehearsal time with the choir will be spent. Listen to gospel choirs and soloists to get your ear used to the expressive devices specific to that genre (appropriate use of scooping, grace notes, glissando, pronunciation, vocal tone, and so on).
- Spending time outside of rehearsal coaching the soloist(s) and pianist on proper style will be time well spent.
- Poelinitz reports that in mixed choir situations, tenors sometimes sing the melody by accident.
- The SATB octavo can be easily adapted for use by SSA, or SAT (i.e., 3-part Mixed). For SSA, have Soprano 1 sing the soprano part as written, have Soprano 2 sing the alto part as written, and have Altos sing the tenor part in the written octave (the range is appropriate and it won't take them long to adapt to singing in bass clef); the arranger

prefers this approach for treble choirs rather than using the SSA publication. For SAT or 3-part Mixed, simply sing all parts as written, except leave the bass part out.

- This flexible scoring makes this an ideal piece for combined choir situations.
- The solo may be performed by either a male of female singer. In fact, the arranger prefers that it be divided between a male and a female. However you choose to divide the solo, no more than one soloist should sing at any one time.

Stylistic Considerations

- The conductor needs to decide houw the choir will pronounce "pilgrim" and "heaven." Pil-GRIM or Pil-GRUM and Hea-VIN, hea-VEN, hea-VON or hea-VUN. The arranger prefers pil-GRUM and hea-VEN. Poelinitz cautions: "The hea-VON pronunciation is often sung by singers/choirs who have not been corrected by their instructors or choir directors. Never allow hea-VON in singing spiritual or gospel music even if it is pronounced that way by a 'top artist.'"
- In measures 12 and 22, first time *forte*, second time *mezzo forte*.
- It is acceptable to deviate from the score in measures 13 to 14 and 14 to, and have the choir connect "no" and "hope" instead of observing the rests. This is at the conductor's discretion.
- It is stylistically acceptable to repeat the refrain (the B section) extra times as desired. Take care, however, as repeating it too many times may bore singers and audience.
- On the final repeat of the refrain (B section), it can be effective for the choir to put fermatas on "-times" (m. 22), "and" (m. 23), and "-en" (m. 24), holding each while the soloist and or pianist improvises.
- On the final repeat of the refrain (B section), consider isolating and repeating measures 34 and 35 ("Tryin' to make it") 1 or 2 times more for added emphasis and to build anticipation and tension before the final cadence. If this is done, the soloist can "let loose" improvisationally during those added repeats.
- A slow, mournful glissando between measures 12 and 13 can be effective. If the conductor opts for this, no breath should be taken between "alone!" and "Ain't."
- Soloists should feel free to improvise. The given solo works quite well and is a good starting point, but the soloist should listen to gospel and spiritual soloists to get used to those styles and what devices are used for expression. Soloists who do improvise often mistakenly use pop or even jazz stylings on this arrangement instead of taking the time to learn the gospel approach.

- Poelinitz prefers that choirs not clap during performances of this arrangement. In addition, "Snapping in gospels and spirituals is traditionally avoided, though it is coming into vogue with some gospel singers and choirs of today."
- Adding drums and/or electric bass guitar would be appropriate, but is not necessary.
- The text certainly has meaning associated with its spiritual roots. But one of the reasons Poelinitz's arrangement has endured over the years is that the text also has meaning for each of us. Making it personal will help the whole piece come alive. Challenge your singers to think about their own lives: when they have felt alone, forgotten, or in need of outside support. This could happen in a classroom discussion, in silent meditation, or individually outside of class time.
- Finally, it is important to remember that spirituals were originally sung by those doing intense manual labor, who saw as their source of hope a long journey by foot to a land of promise. This context has two ramifications that will directly affect your performance. First, the conductor would be well advised to select a tempo that reflects a sort of weary walk after a hard day's work in the hot southern sun. Taking too fast a tempo can sound oddly cheery. Yes, there should be a feeling of hope, but it should be reflected in the occasional loud dynamics that burst forth, not in the tempo. Second, this sorrowful walk can also be reflected in the singers' bodies. A sway on the downbeat of each bar (left-2-3, right-2-3) either in rehearsal or performance will help achieve a more body-aware and engaged performance. The arranger prefers a metronome range of dotted-quarter note = 48–54.

Form and Structure

Section	Measure	Event and Scoring
Introduction	mm. 1–4	Piano.
A (Verse)	mm. 5–21	First time: Choir with accompaniment pattern. Second time: Soloist sings verse over choir's accompaniment pattern.
B (Refrain)	mm. 22–39	First time: Choir with soloist. Second time: Choir with soloist.

Text

Verse 1:
I am a poor pilgrim of sorrow,
I'm left in this old wide world alone!
I ain't got no hope for tomorrow.
Tryin' to make it, make Heaven my home.

Refrain:
Sometimes I'm tossed and I'm driven, Lord.
Sometimes I just don't know which way to turn.
I heard of a city called Heaven.
I'm tryin' to make it, make Heaven my home.

Verse 2:
Note: An additional verse appears in the Songs of Zion hymnal. Poelinitz has expressed that it would be acceptable to sing the verse again (mm. 4–20) with these words, if desired.

My mother has reached that pure glory,
My father's still walking in sin,
My brothers and sisters won't own me.
Because I'm tryin' to make it in.

Additional References and Resources

Suggested Reading

Armstrong, Anton. "Practical Performance Practice in the African American Slave Song." In *Teaching Music through Performance in Choir*, Volume I, ed. Heather J. Buchanan and Matthew W. Mehaffey. Chicago: GIA Publications, 2005.

Cleveland, J. J., and V. Nix. *Songs of Zion* (Nashville, TN, 1981).

Curtis, Marvin V. "African-American Spirituals and the gospel Music: Historical Similarities and Differences." Choral Journal 41 (March 2001), 9-21.

Johnson, James Weldon, and J. Rosamund Johnson. *The Books of American Negro Spirituals*. New York: Da Capo Press, Inc., 1969.

Southern, Eileen. *The Music of Black Americans*. 2nd ed. New York: W.W. Norton & Co., 1983.

Thomas, André. *Way Over In Beulah Lan': Understanding and Performing the Negro Spiritual*. Dayton: Heritage Music Press, 2007.

Suggested Listening

"City Called Heaven" on *Advance Australia Fair*, St. Olaf Choir, Anton Armstrong, St. Olaf Records, 1997.

N.B. Although the arranger has conducted the piece several times in workshops and in live performance, no recording exists with her conducting this piece. She recommends the St. Olaf Choir recording listed above.

Contributed by:

Drew Collins and Josephine Poelinitz

Teacher Resource Guide

Ahrirang

arr. Robert De Cormier

SATB
Hal Leonard: LG1540
Overall: 2
Vocal: 2
Tonal/Rhythm: 2

Arranger

Prolific composer Robert De Cormier, known for his contribution to a variety of musical genres, has heard his work performed throughout the United States and abroad. His ballet score, *Rainbow 'Round My Shoulder*, remains a staple of the Alvin Ailey Ballet repertoire. His choral works *Legacy*, *Four Sonnets to Orpheus*, *Shout for Joy*, and *Under the Greenwood Tree* all premiered at Carnegie Hall, and his cantata, *The Jolly Beggars*, received critical acclaim in its New York premier. In addition to live performances, his works are featured in over a hundred recordings on various labels.

As a conductor, De Cormier is currently the director of the Vermont Symphony Orchestra Chorus as well as the director of Counterpoint, a Vermont-based professional choral ensemble. He served for 17 years as the music director of the New York Choral Society, and as a music director and arranger for popular singer Harry Belafonte and for folk trio Peter, Paul and Mary.

Composition, Genre, Historical perspective

The melody of the folk song "Ahrirang" is known not only to the people of Korea, but is also recognized by foreign populations around the globe. Although there are many variations of the verses of text, the title celebrates a hill named "Ahrirang Pass." There are many hills throughout the Korean countryside named Ahrirang, but one in particular, in Seoul, was immortalized in the 1926 film of the same name. The film *Ahrirang*, which chronicles the Korean uprising during the time spent under Japanese colonial rule (1910–1945), created a swell of nationalist pride among the Korean viewers, and became one of the first icons in a series of anti-occupation cinema, music, and art. While the most popular incarnation of the poetry associated with "Ahrirang" is a mournful text depicting the parting of lovers, there are also texts reflecting the turmoil of war, the despair of death and destruction, and many more themes too numerous to list. An intensely personal piece, it has become the ersatz national anthem of Korea, and the most recognized folk song associated with the country.

Musical Elements

The pentatonic melody of "Ahrirang" is preserved wonderfully in the opening four measures of this arrangement. Eventually, it will be passed around all the voice parts and the piano accompaniment, but here it is played unadorned in the upper register of the piano. A bridge in measures 4 through 8 grounds the melody in a major key and prepares for the entrance of the accompanied voices in measure 9.

The overall impact of the piece comes from the layering of the voices and acompaniment during the progression of the work. The opening keyboard solo gives way to an opening vocal solo, which then progresses into a canon between the treble and bass voices beginning in measure 41. At measure 65, all four voices are finally together, creating the thickest texture in the piece.

The only dynamic marking given by the arranger is *piano (p)* in measures 1, 9, 41, and 45. Due to the reflective nature of the melody and the text, this is entirely appropriate as a guide to the overall sentiment expressed in the piece. When the voices come together in measure 65, the thickness of the texure may allow for an elevated dynamic, which reaches its apex in measure 73, after which the denoument will allow a diminuendo through the closing measures.

Stylistic considerations

Because of the folk nature of the piece, the vocal production should be kept simple, avoiding extremes of heavy vibrato or of an unnaturally straight tone. A warm, free, relaxed choral tone is very appropriate, the beauty coming from ease of production. There are no extremes in the ranges of the voice parts, most of the pitches lying within a normal speaking range.

The title word is the only Korean language word in the text, and is uncomplicated in its pronunciation. The Romanized "r" in the title word is meant to reflect the Hangul symbol ㄹ, which represents a sound halfway between the English "R" and "L." Also known as an alveolar tap, this consonant may be produced by approximating the tongue on the aveolar ridge while rolling from an R to an L sound in rapid succession. The IPA for the word Ahrirang is below:

[a' ɾi ɾaŋ]

Form and Structure

In keeping with the traditional performance of "Ahrirang," the refrain and the verse are of equal length (eight measures each), with the refrain preceding the verse. De Cormier does, however, add an extra refrain after the end of each verse/refrain combination. Even though he uses only one verse of text throughout, he adds interest by using choral texture to differentiate between occurrences.

Section	Measure	Event and Scoring
Introduction	mm. 1–8	piano only
Refrain-verse-refrain	mm. 9–32	soprano solo or section solo
Interlude	mm. 33–40	piano only
Refrain-verse-refrain	mm. 41–64	soprano and alto unison, in canon with unison tenor and bass
Refrain-verse-refrain	mm. 65–80	four-part chorus, SATB
Refrain	mm. 81–88	four part chorus, SATB
Coda	mm. 88–end	piano only

Text and Translation

As mentioned above, the text makes use of a refrain, followed by a single verse that recurs throughout:

Refrain:
Ahrirang, Ahrirang, Ahrirang-o.
Climbing the mountains of Ahrirang-o.

Verse:
Walk beside me, we'll sing as we go
Over all the little hills of Ahrirang-o.

This verse, adapted to English by Lousie Dobbs, is remniscent of the most popular version of "Ahrirang," focused on ascending Ahrirang Hill in Seoul, Korea. Other versions of the song have an indicator word that precedes the title, such as "Eongseon Arirang," which originated in Jeongseon County in Gangwon Province; "Jindo Arirang," which originated in Jindo County in South Jeolla Province; and "Miryang Arirang," from Miryang in South Gyeongsang Province. Although the versions of the text may differ considerably, the tune remains the bond between and within all provinces of the country.

Contributed by:

Karen Kennedy

Teacher Resource Guide

Bile Them Cabbage Down

arr. Mack Wilberg

SATB to SSAATTBB/miscellaneous instruments
Hinshaw Music: HMC1392
Overall: 2
Vocal: 2
Tonal/Rhythm: 2

Composer

Born and raised in Utah, Mack Wilberg has been associated with the Mormon Tabernacle Choir for much of his career. His bachelor's degree is from Brigham Young University, where he returned to teach after receiving his master's and doctoral degrees from the University of Southern California.

Wilberg has composed and arranged choral music in proliferation, much of it for the groups he has directed. Many works call for instrumental forces and many are elaborate settings of well-known folk songs and hymns.

Composition, Genre, and Historical Perspective

"Bile Them Cabbage Down" is a folk song from the American South. There are recordings and transcriptions from different geographic origins, with variations in the tune and the text. Recordings range from fiddlers showing off to a performance on the Andy Griffith Show.

This arrangement is rather more polished, and comes from Wilber's oeuvre of elaborate folk-song settings.

Musical Elements and Technical Considerations

The only musical challenge is the repeated modulations up by half step. If you regularly do warmups that ascend by half step, as many of us do, you'll find that the singers are perfectly accustomed to making the transitions in their ears.

The sparse accompaniment of the first verses requires that the singers stay mostly in tune during phrases in between instrumental chords. If they drift, they need to recognize it by listening and then re-set. As long as they have a strong foundation of musical skills, it will present no problem at all. When incorporating the piece into your warmups, try having the choir sing a particular warmup without accompaniment except the chord that leads into the next key. If the singers have problems, it would be perfectly appropriate to have the piano or another instrument play with them in performance, or just have a bass play tonic and dominant under them as a pedal.

To deal with the clapping, singers will need to sing from memory, use stands, or share folders so that some will clap and others will hold music. Of these options, singing from memory will be the most fun! Memorization won't be overly difficult because of the high degree of repetition. Remembering which verse is which, when to sing harmony and when to sing melody, and when the modulations happen will be the trickiest parts, but making the singers aware of the structure so that they can count verses and repetitions of the refrain and be aware of the increasing frequency of the modulations will make that easier.

If you don't have strong enough numbers to divide the men into four parts, eliminate the first tenor part. It doubles the first soprano part, which is not likely to need reinforcement, and it is the part Wilberg himself eliminates when he only has one tenor on the part. In the rare moments of bass divisi, choose to keep second bass over first. Again, the first basses double the first alto, and the second bass line follows more roots of chords, making it more useful for hearing and tuning the harmonic progression.

Stylistic Considerations

This song is a big showstopper that is carefully designed to get people worked up and excited. The more you can add to it, the better. Think of the roots of the song: if you were sitting on your front porch of an evening and decided to play some tunes for fun, everyone would reach for whatever instrument was handy. In that spirit, use what resources are available to you.

As the editorial notes in this edition suggest, "a performance of 'Bile Them Cabbage Down' is greatly enhanced with the addition of fiddle(s), guitars, woodblock, tambourine, and string bass." The guitar part isn't easy because of the constant modulating up by half step, leading to some chords that aren't in a lot of high school guitarists' frequent usage, but you've probably got kids in the music theory, history, technology, or appreciation class that take guitar lessons or play in a band who would be willing to give it a try. Many schools won't have a string bass player, but almost every school will have a couple of kids who play electric bass.

There is clapping called for in the choral parts. Toss some hand percussion instruments to the kids who clap reliably to add some extra noise.

As for the singing, technical quality and producing healthy tone are always important, particularly for the extended passages of high notes in the soprano line. But that is certainly not the primary factor in a great performance of "Bile Them Cabbage." Feel free to let the singers off the leash, so to speak, to sing with an easy, natural, youthful shape to the tone even if you would ordinarily insist on absolute vowel purity.

The overarching style is that of a cartoon. It's a highly elaborate setting for quite a silly little tune, and the words are so absurd that it is reminiscent of a Bugs Bunny or Road Runner cartoon: lots of crazy hoopla going on without much story because the entertainment value is in the hoopla. If the singers buy into the fun and the goofiness, the audience will be bowled over.

Form and Structure

The piece grows: it modulates up by half step with increasing frequency and continually divides into more and more parts. The verses alternate between male and female voices in the style of "Anything You Can Do, I Can Do Better." The result is the impression that the sections of the choir are trying to out-do each other.

Section	Measure	Event and Scoring
Introduction	mm. 1–20	instrumental; in G major
Verse 1	mm. 21–36	tenor solo, joined by all tenors with sparse accompaniment
Refrain	mm. 37–44	tenors and basses in unison
Refrain	mm. 45–52	SATB
Verse 2	mm. 53–68	sopranos, joined by altos in unison, then divide into harmony with sparse accompaniment
Refrain	mm. 69–76	SATB
Refrain	mm. 77–84	SSATB
Verse 3	mm. 85–100	suddenly in A-flat major, tenor solo joined by all tenors with sparse accompaniment

SECTION	MEASURE	EVENT AND SCORING
Refrain	mm. 101–108	suddenly in A major, tenors and basses in harmony
Refrain	mm. 109–116	SATB
Verse 4	mm. 117–124	suddenly in B-flat major, SATB
Verse 4, cont.	mm. 125–132	suddenly in B major, SAATB
Refrain	mm. 133–140	suddenly in C major, SSATTBB
Refrain/Coda	mm. 141–168	SSAATTBB

Text and Translation

Because it's a folk song, there are many varying versions of the text. The one Mack Wilberg chose is:

Verse 1:
Went up to the mountain just to give my horn a blow,
Thought I heard my true love say, "Yonder comes my beau."
Took my dog to the blacksmith shop to have his mouth made small,
He turned 'round a time of two and swallowed shop and all.

Refrain:
Bile them cabbage down, down,
Turn them hoe cakes 'round.
The only song that I could sing
Was bile them cabbage down.

Verse 2:
Possum in the 'simmon tree, Raccoon on the ground,
Raccoon says, "Get out of here and shake some 'simmons down."
Someone stole my old black dog, wish they'd bring him back,
Chased the big hogs through the fence, the small ones through the crack.

(Refrain)

Verse 3:
Met a possum in the road, blind as he could be,
Jumped the fence and whipped my dog and bristled up at me.
Then that possum stood right up, he went right and left,
Looked my hound dog in the face and went to take a rest.

(Refrain)

Verse 4:
Once I had an old gray mule, name was Simon Slick,
Rolled his eyes and back his ears and how that mule would kick.
How that mule would kick! Kicked with his dying breath,
Shoved his hind feet down his throat and kicked himself to death.

(Refrain)

Some of the language is confusing, and bright students wonder about some of the words:

- "Bile" is "boil" pronounced with a cartoonish Appalachian accent.
- Hoe cakes are like pancakes, possibly made with corn meal or wheat flour, originally cooked by field hands over a fire using their hoe (a gardening tool like a flat-bladed shovel or spade) as a griddle.
- "'Simmons" are "persimmons."
- "Whipped my dog" means the possum beat the dog in a fight.

Like many folk songs, the text doesn't mean much on the surface. The verses chosen for this arrangement focus on wacky encounters with animals and could, like Bugs Bunny and Road Runner cartoons, seem more disturbing than funny if you think about them too hard. But the content of the text isn't the purpose: the one-upman-ship of story telling is the point; sing the words like it's the tallest tale you can think of.

Web site:

http://www.mormontabernaclechoir.org/

Contributed by:

Amelia Nagoski Peterson

Teacher Resource Guide

Domaredansen

arr. Drew Collins

(b. 1975)

SATB
Earthsongs: S-198
Overall: 2
Vocal: 2
Tonal/Rhythm: 2

Composer

Drew Collins (b. 1975) is Associate Director of Choral Studies and Music Education at Wright State University in Dayton, Ohio and Artistic Director of the Festival Choir of Madison in Madison, Wisconsin.

Collins studied with René Clausen at Concordia College, Moorhead, Minnesota, where he earned the Bachelor of Music degree in Music Education. He completed the Master of Music degree in choral conducting at Boston University, studying with Ann Howard Jones, Daniel Moe, Lukas Foss, and Craig Smith. He is completing doctoral studies in choral conducting and composition at Cincinnati College-Conservatory of Music.

Collins began his career teaching music in the public schools (grades 6–12), and now teaches choral music, conducting, and music education courses at the collegiate level. He has conducted festival choirs in several states, most recently the Kentucky Junior High All-State Mixed Choir and the Maryland All-State Mixed Choir. All told, he has conducted early music, community, school, changing voice, treble, male, church, collegiate, jazz, chamber, worship, festival, symphonic, and professional choral ensembles. He has penned articles and interviews for Choral Director Magazine, which also prints his repertoire forum in each issue.

Collins's professional conducting work includes serving as Artistic Director for Tempus (Boston, MA), Choir of the Lakes (Minneapolis, MN), Trinity Concert Singers (Boston, MA), and Festival Choir of Madison (Madison, WI). He has guest conducted at the AMC Mountains & Music Weekend, and was a resident conductor for the prestigious MusicX new music festival where he worked with Michael Torke.

In addition to his busy conducting schedule, Collins is an active composer, arranger, and editor of choral music. He is frequently asked or commissioned to write choral works. His music is found in the catalogs of Curtis, Earthsongs, E. C. Schirmer, Hal Leonard, Kjos, Mark Foster, Odhecaton, Roger Dean, and Walton Music Company.

Collins has also served as Senior Choral Editor and Senior Choral Consultant for the Neil A. Kjos Music Company and The Drew Collins Choral Collection is published by Curtis Music Press.

Composition, Genre, and Historical Perspective

"Domaredansen" (the "Judge's Dance") is a folk song from Sweden. It is a *ringdans* (ring dance) and game for all ages. The most common Swedish folk dance is the *long dance* in which participants form a long chain, holding hands. Depending on the circumstances, the chain might turn into a ring, with dancers circling a maypole or Christmas tree.

There are many versions of the game with which this song is associated. The gist of it is that there is one person in the middle of the ring holding a candle (called the "judge"). As the others sing, the person holding the candle approaches a member of the opposite sex, illumines his/her face with candlelight, and tries to get him/her to smile or laugh. If successful, the two exchange places, the candle changes hands, and the playing begins again.

The age of this tune is not known. The melody with the current text first appeared in print in the anthology *Traditioner af folk-dansar* (Afzelius/Åhlström, 1814). The text has undergone several changes since the resurgence of folk music in Sweden in the 1800s.

This arrangement came about in 2002 while on faculty at Augustana College in Rock Island, Illinois, a college with Swedish roots. One of my ensembles was Collegiate Chorale. Comprised mostly of singers not yet ready for the upper-level ensembles, the group was at a moderate skill level. Two of my singers, who were Swedish majors, requested that the choir sing some Swedish music. I began searching for such a piece that would be appropriate to the group's abilities. I found two published arrangements of this melody; one was for male chorus, and the other was set in a sort of boogie-woogie fantasia style in English. Thinking this the perfect melody for the ensemble but not satisfied with either of the available publications, I set about creating my own arrangement.

"Domaredansen" was one of my first two publications, and was my first published folk-song arrangement.

Musical Elements and Technical Considerations

I took on the challenge to make this arrangement as "elegant" as possible, both in terms of the constructive elements used, and by limiting the voicing to SATB without divisi. This has the added benefit of lowering the difficulty level, as well as allowing for performances by choirs of almost any size.

There are certain challenges in the piece that seem to crop up no matter who is performing it:

- The words in the "käresta i natt skall" bars seem to be the hardest to get out. This is due both to the fast rhythm and the unexpected pronunciation of "kä-." I suggest isolating and looping measure 15, starting slowly and gradually building in speed. Then, once skill and confidence are built, put it into context by looping measures 14 through 16.
- In measure 34, basses often stay on "le" too long (to match the SAT rhythm).
- In measure 34, basses often want to sing an E instead of the D notated.
- In measure 35, the sopranos often want to delay their entrance instead of coming in as scored, immediately after the altos. I suggest, for rehearsal purposes, isolating the first two syllables of each entrance, so that the result sounds like "Nu vil- Nu vil-."
- In measures 36 through 42, the tenors sing a tonal answer to the SA canon. Since it is a tonal answer and not a real answer, some intervals are different from the original melody. Tenors often have difficulty with the downward leap between their 4th and 5th pitches ("vi be-") and other similar spots. Running this passage slowly and having the singers stop on the trouble note will help resolve this issue.
- In measures 43 through 45, the basses and sopranos often have trouble finding their pitches. It can be helpful to first have SAB sing *mi–fa–sol* together in unison (in C major), next sing only their entrance pitches in tempo, and then sing the passage as written.
- In measure 46, tenors often have difficulty finding their starting pitch. Have the sopranos and tenors sing their parts together as written, pointing out that the sopranos start on G, which is also the tenors' starting note.
- In measures 50 through 51, there is tonal ambiguity since the basses are ending the theme in the previous key while the tenors simultaneously

begin the next statement of the theme in the tonic key. The biggest pitch issue is the B-flat in measure 51, which the basses mistakenly want to sing as either an A or as a B-natural.

- Finally, the singers need to understand that this is a fun, youthful song. It is a dance and a game! The spirit of the piece comes through an understanding of the drama. (See Stylistic Considerations). Any discussions, activities, or performance ideas that make the singers body-aware will likely result in a more engaged, spirited performance.

Stylistic Considerations

As an arranger, I often approach folk songs from a dramatic perspective. *What story does the text tell? Is anything implied by certain word choices, but not said outright? How might indigenous people have sung this melody and text? During what kind of activity would the song have been sung?* In approaching *this* tune, I first did some research in the library, talked with colleagues in the Swedish department, and contacted a Swedish heritage society to learn about the game, dance, time of year, instruments, and other traditions associated with it.

This led to the next question. *What compositional devices can bring this drama to the fore?* While arranging, I created a mini-drama in my head and tried to illustrate the plot using established compositional devises. Granted, it may not necessarily be very accurate of Swedish indigenous life, nonetheless, here is the plot I had in mind while writing:

- Statement 1—The girls of the village walk together down the main street, attempting to lure the men with this familiar melody, enticing them away from the village to do the Judge's Dance. Their ploy works, and the men end up following the women, joining in the singing.
- Statement 2—Anticipating the game and dance, everyone is very aware of the distinction between genders. A quasi-ostinato accompaniment pattern for TBs while SAs are flitting about in thirds, highlights the distinction between male and female.
- Statement 3—They arrive at the location of the game and excitement and confusion ensues as decisions are made about who will be next to whom, how big the ring needs to be, and who is going to start off as "judge." This flurry of activity and discussion is illustrated by use of stretto, the rapid entrances and overlapping texts giving an effect of many conversations happening at once.
- Statement 4—Finally, the game begins. The judge looks for a young lady who he thinks he can get to smile (mm. 46 to 53). He chooses one, and the girls near her giggle (m. 53 to 58) while the boys look carefully to see if their friend is succeeding (mm. 58 and 59). Failing at first (mm. 60 to 62), he tries a different, sweeter tactic (mm. 63 to 66), but is ultimately unsuccessful and forced to move on to another girl (mm. 66 to 68).

- Coda—The game and song continue long beyond the end of the arrangement.

Instruments that commonly accompany Swedish dance include flute, fiddle, accordian/concertina, cowherd's horn, and ancient trumpet. At the conductor's discretion, any of these instruments (or reasonable substitutes) may be used to double vocal lines, or to improvise a part. An optional piano part is included and may also be used.

If sung unaccompanied, the conductor might experiment with singing the piece a semi-tone higher or lower if this helps the choir stay in tune.

I suggest that "Domaredansen" be conducted in 2, and that the tempo chosen not feel rushed or frenetic.

"Domaredansen" can be sung any time of year, including spring and yuletide.

Errata

In some first printings, the tempo marking reads "[quarter note] = 84–92." It should have been "[half note] = 84–92." This was corrected in some later reprints, but older scores may have a different marking.

Form and Structure

"Domaredansen" is in Theme & Variations form. Each of the four statements of the theme has the same words.

Section	Measure	Event and Scoring
Statement 1 (mm. 1–17)	mm. 1–17	Choral unison starting with S, with other parts added every 4 or 2 bars
Statement 2 (mm. 1–17)	mm. 17–34	Theme in S, harmonized by A; TB have accompaniment pattern
	m. 34	B leads to dominant key
Statement 3 (mm. 34–50)	mm. 34–42	Stretto: SA in canon at the unison, T has tonal answer at the P5
	mm. 43–47	A has melody, B in canon at the m2
	mm. 47–50	A has melody, B in canon at the unison
Statement 4 (mm. 50–68)	mm. 50–53	T has melody in original key; Tonal ambiguity, due to B overlapping the end of statement 3 with the beginning of statement 4.
	mm. 53–58	SA have early, syncopated entrance for rhythmic interest.
	mm. 58–59	T has melody, B harmonizes
	mm. 60–62	S has melody, A harmonizes; cadence on the dominant
	mm. 63–66	Snippet in augmentation
Coda	mm. 69–end	Coda

Text and Translation

Translated by Lars Jenner, Professor of Scandinavian Studies (ret.), Augustana College, Rock Island, Illinois.

Nu vilja vi begynna en domaredans, *Medan domaren själv är hemma.* *Alla de som i domardansen gå,* *deras hjärtan de skola brinna.*	Now we want to begin a judge's dance, while the judge is home. All those who join in the judge's dance, their hearts will burn [with love].
Alla säga de hå, hå, hå! *Alla saga de nå, nå, nå!* *Har du drömt om din käresta i natt,* *Skall du mot ljuset le.*	They all say, "hå, hå, hå!" They all say, "nå, nå, nå!" If you have dreamt of your sweetheart tonight, you will smile toward the [candle]light.

A pronunciation guide is available from the publisher.

Additional References and Resources

Web site: www.DrewCollins.com.

Contributed by:

Drew Collins

Teacher Resource Guide

Ev'ry Time I Feel the Spirit

arr. William Dawson
(1899–1990)

SATB
Neil A. Kjos: T117
Overall: 2
Vocal: 2
Tonal/Rhythm: 2

Composer

Born in 1899 in Anniston, Alabama, William Levi Dawson ventured from his home as a teenager to attend the Tuskegee Institute. There he worked to support himself, joined the band and orchestra, and finished his education in 1921. Over the next six years, he studied with numerous composers including Henry V. Stearns, Sir Carl Busch, Adolph Weidig, and Thorvald Otterstrom. He earned a Bachelor of Music Degree in theory at the Horner Institute of Fine Arts in Kansas City, Missouri and a Master of Music Degree in composition from the American Conservatory of Music in Chicago. Dawson played first trombone in the Chicago Civic Orchestra for the next four years and in 1930 won the Wanamaker Contest prizes for song and orchestral compositions.

In 1931, Dawson was appointed to the faculty of the Tuskegee Institute to establish and oversee the School of Music and conduct the one-hundred voice Tuskegee choir, a position he held until 1955. Under his leadership, the choir gained international notoriety as they appeared in prestigious concert halls around the United States, including a performance at the opening of Radio City Music Hall in New York City in 1933, which led to performances before presidents and television audiences. His post as music director of Ebenezer

Baptist Church stirred his interest in black American folksong. This facilitated his work in preparing and publishing arrangements of spirituals. At this time he established his own publishing company and recorded performances of his settings of numerous spirituals. After leaving the Tuskegee Institute, Dawson appeared as guest conductor and speaker throughout the world, including important engagements in West Africa, Spain, and the Virgin Islands.

In addition to his imaginative settings of spirituals (fifteen appear on the recordings he made), Dawson's compositional output includes the *Negro Folk Symphony* and other instrumental and choral works. Dawson received a number of honorary doctorates and was honored by the American Choral Directors Association in 1975 for his inspiration, leadership, and service to the choral art. He died in 1990. Dawson can be counted as one of a small number of significant black American composers of the first half of the 20th century. Although black American folksong constituted a primary influence, he also drew from jazz and contemporary concert music idioms. His arrangements of spirituals maintain a consistent presence as staples in the canon of choral repertoire.

Composition, Genre, and Historical Perspective

The origins of African American spirituals, or "religious folk-songs," as Dawson himself described them, can be traced to West Africa. In his essay "Practical Performance Practice in the African American Slave Song," Anton Armstrong recounted: "This song form originated in the southern region of the United States during the nineteenth century and developed from the music of West Africa, where many of the slaves who were eventually brought to the New World originated." In the late 1800s and early part of the twentieth century, composers began setting these melodies for solo singers in a newly composed manner; shortly thereafter, spirituals became the source material for choral settings such as those crafted by Dawson. Despite the tragic and unjust circumstances surrounding its origins, the spiritual represented an important contribution to the musical heritage of the United States of America. Concert arrangements of these songs sought to achieve a balance that respected the emotional and spiritual intensity of such works without losing an awareness of the events that initially gave rise to the words and music. Indeed, the profound nature of both melody and text has made them emotionally stirring to all peoples.

Most spirituals fall under the category of folksong and therefore leave little or no evidence of authorship. They are expressions of a group of people. As Dawson writes in his 1955 essay:

> Negro religious folk-songs contain the experiences and feelings of a people who suffered much. The gamut of emotions contained in them

> is extremely wide. We must therefore first seek, by sincere study and insight, the real message of the music itself before we can pass it on to the listener.

According to Dawson, the singers are interpreters of these songs and should reflect upon the circumstances that led to their creation. In other words, the key to approaching a lively spiritual such as "Ev'ry Time I Feel the Spirit" is to understand the dire circumstances of the originators, which makes the text not only a declaration of faith, but even more poignant as it was declared by a people facing horrific circumstances. In essence, it is the persistent expression of hope in the midst of trouble.

In his essay "A History of the Spiritual," Dominique-René de Lerma outlines Dawson's skillful treatment of these spirituals in his *a cappella* settings, which show "remarkable insight into vocal potentials." He specifically acknowledges Dawson's noteworthy sensitivity to the additive rhythms (3+2+3) in his 1946 setting of "Ev'ry Time I Feel the Spirit," which de Lerma calls "a heritage from the patterns of West African languages." Dawson arranged spirituals between the early 1930s and late 1960s, near the midpoint of this compositional period of his life.

Musical Elements and Technical Considerations

This arrangement presents few major challenges to singers, making it accessible to many choirs. The work is set in common time and in almost every measure of the refrain (including the first entrance) the singers are required to accent the second half of beat three. This syncopated gesture permeates the refrain and must be felt collectively. Choirs often have a tendency to anticipate such a syncopated pattern, causing the tempo to gradually increase. Singers should intentionally place these accented offbeats in a manner that might feel delayed or late. This approach will allow the choir to internalize the correct "feel" of this motive. The director must show beat three with utmost clarity and in a manner that prompts the singers to place the appropriate accent on the second half of the third beat.

Additional challenges lie in the treatment of the four refrains, each slightly more developed than the previous. In the opening refrain, the sopranos sing the melody (created from a pentatonic scale) as the other parts provide a homophonic harmonization beneath. When the refrain returns at the end of measure 16, the sopranos repeat the melody with only a small alteration. In this second refrain, the other three voice parts all have subtle changes throughout, with some added chromaticism in the alto and bass parts. Urge singers to compare the two refrains early in the learning process to distinguish both the similarities and contrasts. It may be worthwhile to have students use spatial gestures to show their understanding of repeated notes and step-wise movement in each setting. For example, the altos repeat their first note three times in the second refrain, whereas in the first version they move down stepwise on the third note, on the word "time." The third and fourth appearances of the refrain occur in succession. In the fourth, sopranos are tacit as tenors and baritones combine to perform the melody in their octave. The second bass part (the bass line is now divided) imitates a "walking bass" as the altos harmonize with them at the interval of a tenth above. Initially, these even quarter and half note rhythms provide a contrast and reference point for the syncopations of the melody. In measure 38, the altos introduce additional syncopated material and more developed counterpoint. The sopranos enter again and double the melody an octave above the tenors for the final refrain. The basses (now consolidated again) increase their counterpoint to eight-note scalar patterns as the altos continue on with a developed countermelody of their own before carrying the melody for one phrase in measures 44 and 45. The melody must not be obscured when it changes hands. Dawson creates a full-blown homophonic harmonization for the final phrase.

There are some discrepancies between printed editions of this work. In some editions, the first two notes have fermatas notated over them. Dawson's recorded performance does not observe these and thus it seems advisable to not follow them. Also, in the penultimate measure of some editions, the basses are asked to sing the word "I" on beat three with the other voices entering on the second half of that beat. Dawson's recording has all singers entering on the upbeat of three, so that also seems preferable. The verses can be sung by an able bass or baritone (or divided among more than one), but Dawson has a group of basses sing the verses in unison. The rest of the choir provides a hummed accompaniment, which allows a soloist to be easily heard. Sing the accompanying hum with a forward and resonant tone, energizing the syncopated entrances through an active abdominal breath pulse.

Stylistic Considerations

Dawson's recording offers an aural guide for conductors who seek to properly approach the style of this work. In other settings of spirituals, Dawson spells words in the text to reflect the original dialect (notably seen in "soon ah will be done a-wid de troubles ob de worl'"). Although Dawson does not spell the word "I" as "ah" in this instance, singers should use that approach to the pronunciation of this word in "Ev'ry Time I Feel the Spirit." The final "t" of the word "spirit" should be minimized, not sharply articulated. Acceptable practice shows that a relaxed approach to final consonants is appropriate for a folk-song setting such as this.

Dawson makes liberal use of accent markings throughout this arrangement. His own recording suggests that he preferred a moderate interpretation of these markings. However, the observance of these accent markings can make a performance of this work more dynamic. The accents must be created through a breath pulse and not by way of forced tone production, or a tightened larynx. In addition to being vocally unhealthy, the latter creates intonation problems and could disrupt a grounded sense of meter across the group. Singers can practice producing accents effectively by hissing the rhythms, feeling the abdominal engagement, and recreating this when singing. To further help singers highlight accents, ask them to de-emphasize the unaccented notes by softening (or as an exaggerated rehearsal technique, silencing) those notes

Form and Structure

The straightforward form of the work can be outlined in a simple manner. The refrain alternates with two verses, and another repetition of the refrain is added at the end. Each new time the refrain occurs, the composer treats it in a more developed way. Thus the form almost functions as a kind of theme and variations. The verses are identical except for the text.

Section	Measure	Event and Scoring
Refrain	mm. 1–8	2 phrases (4+4)
Verse 1	mm. 9–16	2 phrases (4+4)
Refrain	mm. 17–24	2 phrases (4+4)
Verse 2	mm. 25–32	2 phrases (4+4)
Refrain	mm. 33–40	2 phrases (4+4)
Refrain	mm. 41–48	2 phrases (4+4)

Text and Translation

The text of this spiritual is brief and repetitive. The verses use biblical imagery alluding to figures such as Moses or Abraham who encountered God at the summit of a mountain. The Jordan river serves to symbolize the boundary between heaven and earth. This suggests that although death is foreboding, the soul persists eternally. The reference to a train, along with the aforementioned metaphors, can all also be suggestive of an escape to freedom sought by those held captive.

Ev'ry time I feel the spirit,
Moving in my heart, I will pray;
Yes, Ev'ry time I feel the spirit,
Moving in my heart, I will pray.

Upon the mountain my Lord spoke,
Out of His mouth came fire and smoke;
Looked all around me, It looked so fine,
Till I asked my Lord if all was mine.

Jordan river is chilly an' cold,
It chills the body, but not the soul;
There ain't but one train upon this track,
It runs to heaven—an' right back.

Additional References and Resources

Armstrong, Anton E. "Practical Performance Practice in the African American Slave Song" in Buchanan, Heather, and Matthew W. Mehaffey, eds. *Teaching Music through Performance in Choir, Volume 1*. Chicago: GIA Publications, 2005.

Dawson, William L. "Interpretation of the Religious Folk-Songs of the American Negro." *Etude Magazine*. Theodore Presser Music Company. 1955.

Thomas, André J. *Way Over in Beulah Lan': Understanding and Performing the Negro Spiritual*. Dayton, OH. Heritage Music Press. 2007.

Suggested Listening

The Spirituals of William L. Dawson. The St. Olaf Choir. Anton Armstrong, conductor. (St. Olaf Records E-2159) [The essay "A History of the Spiritual" by Dominique-René de Lerma appears in the liner notes.]

Spirituals. Tuskegee Institute Choir. William L. Dawson, director. (MCA Records MSD-35340)

Websites

http://www.tuskegee.edu/
http://marbl.library.emory.edu/dawson/web/main/papers

Contributed by:

Philip Silvey

Teacher Resource Guide

God Is Seen

arr. Alice Parker

SATB/a cappella
Hal Leonard: LG1333
Overall: 2
Vocal: 2
Tonal/Rhythm: 2

Composer

Alice Parker, renowned American composer, conductor, and teacher, was born in Boston, Massachusetts, in 1925 and began composing at a very young age, completing her first orchestral score while still a teenager. Following her graduation from Smith College, she spent the summer in Tanglewood at the Birkshire Music Center, where she first met Robert Shaw. This meeting would lead her to the Juilliard School and a lifelong friendship and partnership with the famed conductor. Their joint arrangements of folksongs, hymns, and spirituals have become educationally sound standards in the canon of popular choral repertoire. Still an active composer, one can experience her work in many forms, from her composition of instrumental and vocal works to her many North American conducting and teaching engagements. Parker, founder of Melodious Accord and board member of Chorus America, has published numerous books and videos, and received many awards including four honorary doctorates and the Smith College Medal.

Composition, Genre, and Historical Perspective

"God Is Seen" can be found in William Walker's 1834 publication *The Southern Harmony, and Musical Companion*, a compilation of shape-note hymns, tunes, psalms, and songs. This tune appeared in early American shape-note sources and can be traced back to ballads relating to the story of Captain William Kidd (1645–1701). Kidd, an English sailor commissioned to hunt pirates, supposedly turned pirate himself and murdered one of his crew, an action for which he was hanged in 1701. This story became the source of numerous ballads for which the tunes are still in existence. The "Captain Kidd' type of tune has, for several centuries, been the impetus for many beautiful songs, including "The Wars of Germany," "Johnny, I Hardly Knew Ye," "Sam Hall and Sugar Babe," and "Wondrous Love."

Musical Elements and Technical Considerations

When preparing any *a cappella* work, a conductor faces a myriad of challenges. Intonation is the first and most obvious of these issues and can be addressed several different ways. Immediately upon opening the score one sees the basses and tenors "Hum"-ing on a unison "A." Having a single note held for as many as ten measures can be an intonation challenge for even the best singers. Therefore, this issue should be addressed from the very first rehearsal. There are several exercises that may prove helpful not only for the men's sustained notes, but for the whole choir's intonation throughout the work. Here are some rehearsal suggestions:

- Lip trills – proper breath support always helps intonation
- Solfege – especially for leading tones!
- Count-singing – maintaining a clear sense of the inner pulse is key

This work also contains some divisi in the tenor and bass lines (mm. 29–40 and 57–62). However, there are never more than three parts. That makes the conductor's job a little easier, as a simple three-part division will suffice. It may require some baritones and second tenors to switch staves at times, but with a little rehearsal, they'll make the switch just fine. The only other major issue this work might present is on its final note. The last chord is voiced with the tenors holding the highest sounding pitch. The tenors should sing lightly to achieve the desired effect.

Stylistic Considerations

The score is marked "Lightly; non-legato" and should be performed as such. It will be easy to fall into the legato trap that will burden the ensemble singing intonation (and the hearts and minds of your audience!). This is a folk tune and should be performed with the appropriate levity and a strong sense of the inner pulse to allow the music to move easily.

Form and Structure

God Is Seen is an arrangement of a strophic folk tune turned hymn tune. Therefore, each verse is the same length with the exception of a short tag on the end of the final verse. The text will determine the minor changes where breaths appear or may be taken. Also, while acquainting yourself with the form presented here, take into consideration the pick-up, which occurs over the second half of the measure prior to each indicated measure in the analysis.

Verse 1 (S/A have melody)

mm. 1–8	2 phrases (4+4)
mm. 9–20	3 phrases (4+4+3)

Verse 2 (S/A then continues with TB div.)

mm. 21–28	2 phrases (4+4)
mm. 29–40	3 phrases (4+4+3)

Verse 3 (SATB some div.)

mm. 41–48	2 phrases (4+4)
mm. 49–60	3 phrases (4+4+3)
mm. 61–62	2-measure tag

Text and Translation

1. Through all the world below,
   God is seen all around;
   Search hills and valleys through,
   There he's found.
   The growing of the corn,
   The lily and the thorn,
   The pleasant and forlorn,
   All declare God is there,
   In the meadows drest in green,
   God is seen.

2. See springs of water rise,
   Fountains flow, rivers run;
   The mist that veils the skies
   Hides the sun;

Then down the rain doth pour
The ocean it doth roar,
And beat upon the shore,
And all praise, in their ways,
That God that ne'er declines
His designs.

3. The sun with all his rays
Speaks of God as he flies:
The comet in her blaze
'God' she cries;
The shining of the stars
The moon as it appears,
His awful name declares;
See them fly through the sky,
And join the solemn sound,
All around.

Bibliography and Suggested Resources

Bonner, Williard Hallam. "The Ballad of Captain Kidd." *American Literature* 15, no. 4 (1944): 362–380.

Bronson, Bertrand H. "Samuel Hall's Family Tree." *California Folklore Quarterly* 1, no. 1 (1942): 47–64.

Gurney, Robert. "Music of Thanksgiving and Harvest." *San Francisco Lyric Choruss*. 2006. <http://www.sflc.org/concerts/programs/harvestprogram.pdf> (August 20, 2008)

Parker, Alice. "Biography." *Alice Parker: Composing, Conducting, Lecturing.* <http://aliceparker.com/html/apbio.html> (August 20, 2008)

Contributed by:

Anthony Maglione

Teacher Resource Guide

Ipharadisi

arr. Jerry Ulrich

SATB divisi
Neil A. Kjos: 8990
Overall: 2
Vocal: 2
Tonal/Rhythm: 2

Composer

ASCAP award-winning arranger-composer Jerry Ulrich is originally from Illinois, where he received his early training in music and developed an interest in and passion for songwriting. His numerous compositions and arrangements are in the catalogs of six publishers in the United States and abroad. His music has been performed at Carnegie Hall, Lincoln Center, throughout New York City, and on national radio and television, as well as throughout Europe, Asia, and Australia.

Ulrich has composed commissioned works for professional choirs and orchestras, including the Grammy-award winning Orchestra of St. Luke's. He has also written music for colleges and universities throughout the United States, including the University of Minnesota, University of Washington, George Washington University, as well as honors choirs in California, Alaska, Montana, Tennessee, Ohio, New York, Texas, North and South Carolina, Virginia, and Hawaii. His composition *Harpenden Psalms* was commissioned by the English organist and recording artist Robert Crowley and was premiered in St. Giles Cathedral, Edinburgh.

Dr. Ulrich is currently Associate Professor of Music and Director of Choral Activities at the Georgia Institute of Technology, where he directs two mixed choirs and the all-male Georgia Tech Glee Club. Ulrich came to Atlanta from the Fiorello H. LaGuardia High School of Music & Art and Performing Arts (the *Fame* school) in New York City, where his choirs had been featured in all major NYC concert venues and on national and international television and radio.

Dr. Ulrich's prior teaching experience includes university positions in New York and Ohio. During 1990–1991 he was Visiting Fulbright Professor of Music at the Royal Scottish Academy of Music and Drama in Glasgow, Scotland. His early training included four years singing with legendary conductor Robert Shaw in the Atlanta Symphony Chorus and Chamber Chorus. Additional academic study included a Master of Music degree from Southern Methodist University, where he was a student of Lloyd Pfautsch, and the Doctor of Musical Arts degree in choral conducting from the University of Cincinnati College-Conservatory of Music.

Over the years, his choirs have shared the stage with Paul Simon, Judy Collins, Hugh Masekela, Kenny Chesney, Joe Walsh, and Stephen Schwartz, as well as the Atlanta Symphony Orchestra and the Orchestra of St. Luke's. In the past ten years, five different choral ensembles under his direction have appeared over a dozen times at New York City's Carnegie Hall.

Ulrich's commitment to music education and familiarity with the choral instrument is evident in the accessibility of his choral writing. Yet his music also includes harmonic and rhythmic interest in a fresh, original style.

Composition, Genre, and Historical Perspective:

Ipharadisi is one of the historic freedom songs from South Africa. Apartheid (meaning *separateness* in Afrikaans, cognate to English, to *apart* and -hood) was a system of legal racial segregation enforced by the National Party government of South Africa between 1948 and 1990. Apartheid had its roots in the history of colonialism and settlement of southern Africa, with the development of practices and policies of separation along racial lines and domination by European settlers and their descendents. Following the general election of 1948, the National Party set in place its program of Apartheid, with the establishment and expansion of existing policies and practices into a system of institutionalized racism and white domination. Apartheid was dismantled in a series of negotiations from 1990 to 1993, culminating in the elections of 1994, the first in South Africa with universal suffrage. The vestiges of apartheid still shape South African politics and society.

Probably nowhere in the world has music so powerfully shaped the political climate as it did from 1960–1990 in South Africa. Similarly, while vestiges of racism continue to pervade the country and culture, it is a testament to the power of music that Nelson Mandela moved from 27 years of imprisonment to become the first elected person of color in the history of the country.

Musical Elements

Ipharadisi uses stylistic features indigenous to the vocal music of the South African culture. The bass and tenor use an upward slide/scoop with neutral phonemes that imitate vocal percussion. It is important to emphasize that this ostinato must never become complacent or "boring," but must undergird the entire performance. Also, with each statement of the pattern, the dynamics should increase ever so slightly.

Unison women introduce the opening line of the melody. After learning the entire piece, younger choirs may have a tendency to forget that this opening section is *not* the same as the introduction of the complete melody in measures 17 to 25.

The first complete statement of the melody is presented in measure 17 with soprano and alto a'2. In the next phrase, the altos begin a contrasting rhythm that uses quarter-note triplets and a bright, nasal tone. Simultaneously, the sopranos divide, with the S2 part taking the original alto line.

In the third complete statement of the melody, the S2 voice assumes the role of melody and the S1 moves to upper harmony. During the final statement (mm. 53 to 62), the basses divide, with the baritone imitating the original tenor part. The tenor assumes the alto rhythmic part, and the soprano line is divisi a'3.

The introduction of body percussion is an interesting and captivating addition to the performance of this work. However, it can be surprisingly difficult for many young singers (and even mature musicians) to sing and execute percussion simultaneously. It is important to introduce this element early on in the learning process.

The body percussion is intended to be an outgrowth of the vocal performance. In order to make it seem natural and not pedantic, the choir will need adequate time to integrate it into their performance.

A very gradual increase in dynamics throughout the piece is most effective. In my experience, achieving a very soft dynamic in the opening 24 bars is the most challenging aspect of creating a powerful *forte* on the last few pages.

Finally, choral tone for South African music is slightly more forward, or nasal than the Western Bel Canto style of singing. This is most evident in the alto rhythmic pattern that begins in measure 26.

It is essential to perform this piece from memory, particularly as the hands and fingers of the singers will be engaged in the percussion and unable to hold the music. Additionally, South African music is an oral/aural tradition, and this printed music is simply a guideline for the overall effect of the composition.

Stylistic Considerations

Again, South African music is an aural and oral tradition. The printed music for *Ipharadisi* is but a guide for both music and text. While the notation should be a starting point, the students must ultimately ingest the music and text into their bodies and express it intuitively. The work is also a cumulative piece; meaning that with each successive statement of the melody or introduction of a new idea, the volume and intensity increase. This is reinforced through the addition of more complex body percussion as the piece develops. Creative directors and students may also introduce whole-body movement to supplement the performance.

Form and Structure

Measure	Event and Scoring
mm. 1–4	Introduction of bass ostinato
mm. 5–8	Addition of tenor ostinato at the interval of a fifth
mm. 9–12	Initial statement of the opening motive by the women
mm. 13–16	Return to the original ostinato motive
mm. 17–24	Chorus 1: a'2 women, Sop melody, Alto harmony
mm. 26–28	Addition of the alto ostinato pattern
mm. 29–36	Chorus 2: a'2 women Soprano (divisi) S1 melody, S2 harmony
mm. 37–40	Introduction of women percussion
mm. 41–48	Chorus 3: a'2 women with S2 melody, S2 upper harmony
mm. 49–52	Tenors take alto rhythm, addition of a'2 women percussion
mm. 53–58	Chorus 3: a'3 women
mm. 59–62	Extension of final melodic phrase
mm. 63–66	Tenor/Bass ostinato conclusion

Text and Translation

Ipharadisi, ikhaya labafile	*Ipharadisi where all the dead are living*
Kulapho sophumla khona	*May we one day join them all there*

Contributed by:

Jerry Ulrich

Teacher Resource Guide

It Takes a Village

Joan Szymko

(b. 1957)

SATB/percussion
Santa Barbara Music: SEMP 328
Overall: 2
Vocal: 2
Tonal/Rhythm: 2

Composer

Joan Szymko is a choral conductor, composer, teacher, and performer in the Pacific Northwest. She has been conductor of the Seattle Women's Chorus, the Aurora Chorus, and founding conductor of Viriditas, a select women's chamber ensemble. Szymko has been resident composer with Do Jump! Movement Theatre in Portland, Oregon since 1995, and has toured and performed with the company on Broadway in New York, at the John F. Kennedy Center for the Performing Arts in Washington, DC, and at the Los Angeles Geffen Playhouse. She was recipient of the prestigious 2010 Raymond W. Brock Memorial Commission from the American Choral Directors Association.

Szymko has written a significant amount of music for women's choirs but has several works for mixed and men's choirs as well. She also composes chamber music, art songs, and music for the stage, including musicals, modern dance collaborations, and other theater music.

Composition, Genre, and Historical Perspective

"It Takes a Village" is an engaging work that has a very simple tonal structure (the whole work centers on B-flat) but generates excitement with repetition and layering of contrasting rhythmic patterns. The effect of juxtaposing divergent ideas connecting and melding into a whole is riveting. It is imperative that the performers feel the pulse and understand their relationship to both it and the ensemble at all times. Joan Szymko says: "The four vocal rhythms in the main portion of the work, each with its own character and function, are essential to creating the unique energy and movement of 'Village.' Only when they are sung together does a truly joyful spirit arise."

The addition of body percussion (open palm on chest), shekere (West African beaded gourd), and medium and low congas help to establish the West African feeling of the work. A strong soloist is needed to sing the opening statement of the main theme and then again when the theme returns at the end of the work, where the soloist must prevail over the entire ensemble.

This work has a strong world music feeling and uses a universal text (adapted from a West African proverb) with which everyone can connect. Our world has continually become smaller through technology and still we sometimes fail to see our interconnectedness and recognize our relationship and responsibilities to each other. This song can inspire thought, build bridges, and help to create community for those who perform or hear it.

Musical Elements and Technical Considerations

"It Takes a Village" begins with the choir hitting open palms on their chests to a simple rhythm that sounds and feels much like a heartbeat. The choir must be able to keep this pounding powerful and in consistent tempo. They can practice by stepping, clapping, or moving on the silent beats. The singers may also say "two, three" on the rests so that the beat structure is maintained. Conductors who have studied Dalcroze Eurhythmics can make effective reference to time, space, and energy here.

A strong soloist is needed to present the initial statement of the main theme. The soloist should maintain a free improvisatory feeling at the same time she or he is grounded in the pulse. It is possible to do a little free improvisation over the B Section or at the return of the A Section. When the main theme recurs at the end of the work, one might consider using a group of soloists so that the theme will more audible over the four rhythmic patterns underlaying it.

The four vocal rhythms mentioned above require independence in each voice part. The patterns that are established repeat over and over with slight variations (except in the soprano part, which remains constant), creating an aurally exciting whole. The ranges are moderate throughout but take care that the intonation does not suffer with so much repetition. Choirs tend to stray from the pitch, usually flatting on repeated notes or patterns. The singers should be encouraged to think slightly higher with each repetition and to continue to breathe and support the sound. In the B Section, tenors have an E-flat4 for seventeen measures. This is an example of a simply written part that could become problematic due to range and repetition.

Competent percussionists are required for maintaining a firm foundation throughout the piece. The notated part in the score for percussion is simple. Undoubtedly, use of improvisation can be employed as long as the pulse and, of primary importance, the downbeat of every measure maintains weight and clarity.

The use of body percussion and the style of the music suggest that the work is best performed from memory. With this in mind, singers will need to clearly understand the structure of the work and how the repetitions and variations in their parts fit into that structure. This is paramount not only so the singers maintain a sense of direction but so that everyone comes together at the end (return of the A Section) for the restatement of the main theme.

Stylistic Considerations

This work has an English text and music written by an American composer but the feeling is very West African in nature. The work projects the idea of calling people to come together as a group or "village." One can picture the soloist summoning other members of the society to come forward and to contribute their part (four different sections/vocal rhythms). This idea necessitates that the choir sing in a full, robust way with a great deal of freedom in the tone. Sliding to and bending of pitches should be incorporated to give the work a more earthy and organic feeling. It is possible to add improvisatory solos over various sections of the work.

Form and Structure

The overall form of the work is ABA.

Section	Measure	Event and Scoring
A	mm. 1–4	body percussion
	mm. 5–21	solo of main theme, full statement of text
	mm. 21–24	percussion
	mm. 25–42	establishment of the main theme by the choir (m. 25 sopranos and tenors, m. 29 altos, m. 37 basses)
	mm. 41–45	percussion

Section	Measure	Event and Scoring
B	mm. 45–84	middle section with four independent vocal rhythms adding one part at a time in a layering process (m. 45 soprano on the syllable "hé," m. 49 tenors on "mm ah," m. 53 alto on "we all," m. 55 basses on "ev'ry one")
	m. 77	soloist reintroduces the main theme over the rhythmic layers
A	mm. 85–104	reestablishment of main theme by the choir (m. 85 sopranos and altos, m. 89 tenors, m. 97 basses)
	mm. 103–104,	percussion ending

Text and Translation

Joan Szymko adapted the text from the traditional West African saying: "It takes a village to raise a child." The composer says: "I've sought to embody the cultural concept behind this proverb—that it is truly ALL the individual parts linked and working together that create and support the whole."

It takes a whole village to raise our children
It takes a whole village to raise one child
We all every one must share the burden
We all every one will share the joy.

Additional References and Resources

Octavo notes:
Szymko, Joan. *It Takes a Village*. Santa Barbara: Santa Barbara Music Publishing, Inc., 2000. (SBMP 331).

Website:

www.joanszymko.com

Contributed by:

Joseph Ohrt, DMA

Teacher Resource Guide

O Occhi, manza mia

Orlande de Lassus

(1532–1594)

SATB
G. Schirmer: 50321340
Overall: 2
Vocal: 2
Tonal/Rhythm: 2

Composer

Orlande de Lassus [Orlandus Lassus, Orlando di Lasso, Roland de Lassus, Roland Delattre] was likely born in 1532 at Mons in Hainaut, a Franco-Flemish territory that now lies in Belgium. It is said that as a young man he was kidnapped no less than three times because of the beauty of his singing voice, although this has never been substantiated. At the age of twelve, Lassus entered the service of Ferrante Gonzaga and traveled with him through Paris, Mantua, and Sicily, eventually spending several years in Milan. In 1548–1549, Lassus went to Naples where he entered the service of Gonzaga's brother-in-law, Giovan Battista d'Azzia, marchese della Terza. It was there in Naples that he likely began to compose the music that was later published in Antwerp—including the *villanesca*, "O Occhi, manza mia." Following his time in Naples, in 1551 Lassus went to Rome, where he later became *maestro di cappella* at San Giovanni in Laterno. He left this position after only one year in order to travel to his sick parents; sadly, though, they died before he arrived. His youthful wanderings then continued, with possible journeys to England and France. He settled in Antwerp in 1554 or 1555, where a collection of his "*madrigali, vilanesche, canzone francesi, e motetti*"—his so-called "Opus 1"—was published by Tielman Sasuto in 1555. This volume helped to launch his young career onto the international stage.

In 1556, Lassus entered the court of Duke Albrecht V of Bavaria in Munich as a tenor in the chapel. He remained in Munich, taking over the leadership of the chapel from 1563 until his death, thirty years later. During his years in Munich he became known, along with Palestrina, as one of the main exponents of mature Renaissance polyphony. His impressive compositional output includes both sacred and secular music with over 2,000 known pieces. His works display an unusual versatility and span a wide variety of genres, though intriguingly, there are no known instrumental works. By the time of his death, Lassus was among the best known musicians and composers in Europe.

Composition, Genre, and Historical Perspective

The *canzona villanesca alla napolitana*, or simply, *villanesca,* was a secular genre that adopted the rustic stylings of Neapolitan street songs. The texts often included thinly veiled ribaldry, word play, and double entendre. They were most often scored for three voices with the melody in the top voice. The harmonic language and voice leading were purposefully unlearned and parallel fifths were sometimes included as a way of imitating the improvisations of untrained musicians. The word *villanesca,* along with the nearly synonymous *villanella* and *villota,* all derive from the Latin *villanus* (peasant), from which we also get the modern English word "villain."

The original "O Occhi, manza mia" was an anonymous three-voice *villanesca* that Lassus probably learned as a young man in Naples. The practice of arranging *villanesche* had been established by Adriano Willaert in his 1544 compilation of both literal and free arrangements. Lassus's arrangement follows Willaert's literal arrangement style, in which the melody is moved from the top voice to the tenor line to allow for a more balanced harmonization, along with some additional minor changes and interpolations that somewhat gentrify the more rustic original.

Musical Elements and Technical Considerations

The fact that the melody is in the tenor requires some thought in terms of balance. The first step is to draw the choir's attention to this fact and to teach the tenor line to all the singers in the choir in their own octave so that they know what to listen for. In addition, you might also add a handful of altos to the tenor line for measures 1 through 21, and a couple of baritones to the tenor line for measures 22 through 39.

In measure 5, the word "mia" is set to one dotted-half note. I would suggest performing the "mi-" on a half note and gently finishing off the "-a" on a quarter note followed with a slight lift at the comma.

Villanesche have their roots in common speech and rely on local sayings and dialectal variations for both humor (parody) and authenticity. These variations may not be familiar even to native speakers of Italian. For instance, *tienemi mente* is Neapolitan for *ricordare* (remember me), and the word *manza* literally means "heifer"—a pun on *amanza* (beloved). (A southern Italian accent omits the initial "a" of *amanza*.)

The sequential passage in measures 22 through 24 (repeated in mm. 31 through 33) may present problems in terms of tuning. The harmonies are unexpected, especially in the context of the harmonies that have come before them. Rehearse the passage slowly out of tempo using the syllable [di] instead of the text. Take time to point out the parts that share unison octaves in each chord and ensure that those octaves are in tune before shifting focus to the fifths and finally to the thirds.

Be wary of over accenting the downbeat of measure 20, as it does not line up with the textual accent. All vocal parts should accent "lu-," "stra-," and "-cen-" in measures 19 through 21 when they appear in their own part. When done properly this will result in rhythmic interplay between the soprano and the other three voices.

Stylistic Considerations

In contrast to the serious love poems of the time, which focused on idealized courtly romance, *villanesche* tended to be lighthearted adventures into feminine deceit, masculine frustration, and other matters of love on a more human scale. They poke fun at human foibles and are meant to be fun to perform and fun to listen to. Expressive singing, perhaps overdone at times for humorous purposes, is invited, and it is essential that the audience knows and understands the text.

Though technically not a madrigal, the *villanesca* was one of its precursors and, as one might find in a madrigal, there are instances of word painting. In "O occhi, manza mia," the most clear instance is found in measures 25 to 27 (and repeated at mm. 34 to 36). The last two words of the phrase "Guardam'un poc'a me" are pulled out and repeated antiphonally as a sort of onomatopoetic pleading to the object of the narrator's desire. These two note figures—"a me"—should be performed with a lighter tone and a noticeable *decrescendo* on "me" to bring out the sighing qualities of the text and the music.

Form and Structure

"O occhi, manza mia" follows the usual *villanesca* format: the text consists of a couplet with a refrain, and the music is in AABCC form.

Section	Measure	Event and Scoring
A	mm. 1–7	2 phrases (3+4)
A	mm. 8–14	2 phrases (3+4) (repetition of mm. 1–7)
B	mm. 15–21	2 phrases (3+4)
C	mm. 22–30	2 phrases (4+5)
C	mm. 31–39	2 phrases (4+5) (repetition of mm. 22–30)

Text and Translation

It should be noted that Lassus used only the first verse of four from the original.

O *occhi, manza mia, cigli dorati,*	O my beloved's eyes, set in gilded lashes,
O *faccia d'una luna stralucenti.*	O face luminous as the moon.
Tienemi mente,	Remember me,
Gioia mia bella,	My lovely treasure,
Guardam'un poc'a me, fami contiento.	Look after me a while, satisfy me.

(Translation from RRMR, p. lv, see below for citation.)

Additional References and Resources

Orlando di Lasso et al. *Recent Researches in the Music of the Renaissance.* Edited by James Haar. Vols. 82–83, *Canzoni Villanesche and Villanelle,* edited by Donna G. Cardamone. Madison, WI: A-R Editions, 1991. (This volume includes an excellent preface and modern editions of both the original three-voice *vallanesca* and Lassus's arrangement.)

Contributed by:

Gregory Brown

Teacher Resource Guide

Old Time Religion
Traditional

arr. Moses Hogan
(1957–2003)
adapted by Benjamin Harlan

SATB
Hal Leonard: 8740181
Overall: 2
Vocal: 3
Tonal/Rhythm: 2

Arranger

Moses George Hogan (1957–2003) was a pianist, conductor, and arranger. He received his training at the New Orleans Center for Creative Arts and the Oberlin Conservatory of Music, and completed additional studies at the Julliard School of Music and Louisiana State University. Though he has received critical acclaim as a concert pianist, he is best known as an arranger/ composer of spirituals. Hogan founded the Moses Hogan Singers and was the editor of the Oxford Book of Spirituals.

Dr. Benjamin Harlan holds BM and MM degrees from Baylor University and a DMA from Southwestern Baptist Theological Seminary in Ft. Worth, Texas. He is currently Professor of Church Music at the New Orleans Baptist Theological Seminary and remains an active composer and arranger of Resources for Congregational Singing.

Composition, Genre, and Historical Perspective

Moses Hogan's arrangement of "Old Time Religion" has its roots in the oral tradition of slave music. Because slaves were kept from gaining an education in order to keep them subservient, they did not have the ability to write songs down, so they passed songs from person to person through singing and listening.

"Old Time Religion" moved from the oral to the written tradition at the hand of Rev. Charles D. Tillman (1861–1943) in Lexington, South Carolina. He was, like his father before him, a Methodist Evangelist Reverend. A large tent would be set up on the edge of town, and church goers and sinners alike would come to participate in singing and listening to the preaching of Reverend Tillman and his Father during their revival services. On Sunday afternoons the Tillmans would turn the tent over to African American worshippers and Reverend Tillman would stay close by to listen in to the music. He heard the group singing "Old Time Religion" and later he met with an African American blacksmith named Rawlings. The blacksmith did not know the origins of the tune since it was passed down from generation to generation but he helped Reverend Tillman write it down.

The written form eventually made its way into the songbook of the Fisk Jubilee Singers. Fisk University was founded in Nashville, Tennessee in 1866 for the purpose of educating freed slaves. The University faced a dire financial crisis and sent their small choir on tour to the northern states to raise money to fund construction of additional buildings on campus. The choir faced racism in its travels but also gained acceptance for the first black performances outside of minstrelsy. The Jubilee Singers were instrumental in introducing the genre of spirituals to the north and to Europe.

Technical Considerations and Musical Elements

"Old Time Religion" is an excellent way to begin singing Spirituals, in that it is mostly a homorhythmic, textured choral accompaniment to an alto or baritone soloist with an optional obligato. The solos and obligato give the conductor an excellent opportunity to highlight some exceptional individual singers while teaching the choir how to listen for the most communicative balance.

The choir can determine which part needs to be heard over the others. I like using the question: "What do you want the audience member to be whistling on their way out of the auditorium?" Have individual sections sing excerpts to highlight their part; there will soon be an ensemble consensus that the melody is indeed the most important and interesting. It would be much easier for the conductor to simply say that the melody needs to be loudest. However, the key to this strategy is to allow the singers to listen to all of the sections to develop their listening skills. Once they know what they are listening for they will be set for greater listening success when singing tutti. The next step is to rehearse altogether to check for the ensemble members' listening skills, which will be evidenced through proper balance. If the melody is becoming muddled the conductor could whistle along with a small segment of the melody to see if that redirects the singers to listen for balance.

However, the choir might need a more formal question in order to reflect on the objective: "Based on our performance, what would you have whistled?"

The chorus sings the vowel [oo] in a mostly stepwise ascending pattern frequently supporting the soloist; one such example is located in measures 18 through 21. Each of the choral accompaniment chords is labeled tenuto and the choir is directed to crescendo from piano to forte over the 14 beats. The choir's tendency will be to sing the tenuto as an overly percussive accent and to ignore the inner music line on the subdivisions of the held notes. One possible approach to this section is through scaffolding the elements to train the physiology and kinesthetic memory of the singers. Begin by counting the excerpt aloud on numbers with subdivisions [One and two and ti and four and].[1] The choir can now progress to the Shaw count-singing method of singing the pitches on the numbers and subdivisions. After the notes and rhythms are accurate, replace the numbers and eighth-note subdivisions with the neutral syllable [du] to allow the choir to focus on creating a 14-beat crescendo, with each successive [du] syllable getting louder. To incorporate the tenuto, have the choir sing [tu] on each note marked tenuto and [du] for the following subdivisons of that note. The [t] will require more air than the softer [d] and will effectively train the diaphragm to pulse with greater energy on the tenuto as well as continue the support through the held notes. The last step is to transfer the elements of musicality while singing the excerpt with the [oo] vowel.

The arrangement moves away from the hymn-style homorhythmic accompaniment and becomes much more syncopated at measure 49. All choral parts will need to enter on a syncopated beat; the basses have the first syncopated entrance off of beat one in measure 49. To practice the skill, stomp on each beat and clap the eighth-note subdivision. Once success is reached, continue to stomp only on beat one of each measure but continue the clapping the subdivisions to reinforce the syncopation. When this becomes part of the singers' rhythmic lexicon, you can superimpose the text while stomping and clapping until the section is fully learned and understood. This technique can be applied to the syncopated entrances of the soprano, alto, and tenor in the sections from measure 50 to the end. The conductor and singer alike must be aware of which notes are accented and which are non-accented in the syncopated section of measures 50 and 51, and all 2-measure phrases like it. The dynamic marking of *piano*, low tessituras, and accents on the first note of each cluster suggest a swinging feel for this repetitive phrase.

The optional obligato at measure 73 is fantastically high and the conductor should consider adding it if there is a singer capable of singing in that register. The obligato is very effective in extending the range of this piece and adds to the layering effect of the texture throughout the work. Unless you have an extraordinarily large choir, one or two sopranos on this part will add color to

1 I use [ti] rather than [three] as the [t] allows for a greater definition of rhythm than the [th].

the overall piece while still allowing the soloist to be heard from within the texture of the piece. If balance is an issue, consider adding more voices to the solo from measure 73 to the end to make the solo melody line more formidable against the accompaniment.

Stylistic Considerations

There is much debate over what type of tone should be used in spiritual singing. When listening to the Moses Hogan Singers perform this song, there is a rich, dark, and open tone being employed. Adolescent singers could strain their vocal mechanism if they are forcing to replicate this sound. An alternative would be to allow these singers to produce sound effectively and freely according to their vocal maturity; present them with the sensibilities of the text and have them decide how their understanding of the emotive qualities can inform their tone.

"Old Time Religion" is sometimes seen as "Old Time 'ligion" and may be sung in dialect. An excellent resource is "A Note on Dialect" by James Weldon Johnson, which is contained in the preface of the *Oxford Book of Spirituals*, edited by Moses Hogan.

Form and Structure

Section	Measure	Event and Scoring
Refrain	mm. 1–9	(4+4) soloist or all women
Refrain	mm. 10–17	(4+4) soloist, homorhythmic choral accompaniment
Verse 1	mm. 18–25	(4+4) soloist, antecedent phrase, choral "ooh," consequent phrase, homorhythmic choral accompaniment
Verse 2	mm. 26–33	(4+4) soloist, antecedent phrase, choral "ooh," consequent phrase, homorhythmic choral text accompaniment
Verse 3	mm. 34–41	(4+4) soloist, antecedent phrase, choral "ooh," consequent phrase, homorhythmic choral text accompaniment
Refrain	mm. 42–49	(4+4) soloist, homorhythmic choral accompaniment
Refrain	mm. 49–56	(4+4) syncopated choral variation
Refrain	mm. 57–64	(4+4) soloist, syncopated choral variation
Refrain	mm. 65–72	(4+4) soloist, syncopated chorus, bass variation
Refrain	mm. 73–80	(4+4) obligato, soloist, syncopated chorus, bass variation
Refrain	mm. 81–89	(4+4+1) obligato, soloist, syncopated chorus, bass variation

Text

Refrain
Give me that old time religion, give me that old time religion.
Give me that old time 'ligion, it's good enough for me.

It was good for the Hebrew children, it was good for the Hebrew children.
It was good for the Hebrew children, it's good enough for me.

It was good for Paul and Silas, it was good for Paul and Silas.
It was good for Paul and Silas, it's good enough for me.

It was good for my grandmother, it was good for my grandmother.
It was good for my grandmother, it's good enough for me.

Additional References and Resources

Benziger, Barbara, and Eleanor Dickinson. *That Old-Time Religion: 100 Hymns, Songs, and Stories*. New York: Harper and Row, 1975.

Emurian, Ernest. *Forty True Stories of Famous Gospel Songs*. Natick, MA: W.A. Wilde, 1959.

Hogan, Moses, ed. *The Oxford Book of Spirituals*. New York: Oxford University Press, 2002.

Johnson, James Weldon, and J. Rosamond Johnson. *The Books of American Negro Spirituals*. New York: Da Capo Press, 1969. Reprint, New York: The Viking Press, 1989.

Pike, G. D. *The Jubilee Singers, and their Campaign for Twenty Thousand Dollars*. New York: Lee, Shepard and Dillingham, 1873. Reprint, New York: AMS Press, 1974.

Websites

Friends of Moses Hogan Society: www.moseshogan.com (accessed June 20, 2008)

New Orleans Baptist Theological Seminary: www.nobts.edu/Faculty/AtoH/HarlanB (accessed August 28, 2008)

Suggested Listening

Moses Hogan, *Spirituals*, Volume 2, 2005 Barbara Hendricks and the Moses Hogan Singers, EMI Records Ltd.

Contributed by:

Christopher S. Owen

Teacher Resource Guide

Requiem

Eliza Gilkyson

arr. Craig Hella Johnson

SATB choir/piano
G. Schirmer: 50486569
Overall: 2
Vocal: 2
Tonal/Rhythm: 1

Composer

Eliza Gilkyson is an American folk musician from Hollywood, who is now based in Austin, Texas. She has composed and recorded prolifically since 1999. Recordings of note include *Times in Babylon* (2000), which focuses on reflections of her own life, including the death of her songwriter father Terry Gilkyson, and her Grammy-nominated *The Land of Milk and Honey* (2004), which highlights her political activism, including critique of United States presence in Iraq. Prior to her recent successes, in the late 1960s she performed and recorded in New Mexico, releasing her first solo album *Eliza* in 1969, and later *Love from the Heart* in 1979. She lived and worked in places like Austin and Los Angeles in the early 1980s before spending several years in Europe, promoted as a new-age artist. She returned to Austin in the mid-1990s, where she created her own record label (*Realiza*) to record and distribute her own new folk songs. Red House records signed her in 2000, helping her gain a greater national presence in folk music.

Arranger

Craig Hella Johnson is Founder and Artistic Director of the professional choral ensemble Conspirare, based in Austin, Texas. Johnson and the ensemble have received international acclaim for their award-winning recordings and provocative "collage" programs in performance. Johnson is also conductor of the annual Victoria Bach Festival. From 1990 to 2001, he was Director of Choral Activities at the University of Texas at Austin, additionally serving as Artistic Director of Chanticleer from 1998 to 1999. He has appeared as guest conductor with several U.S. symphonies. He composes and arranges frequently for G. Schirmer, through which this setting of "Requiem" is available.

Composition, Genre, and Historical Perspective

Gilkyson originally wrote "Requiem" as a response to the 2004 tsunami in southeast Asia that claimed at least 225,000 lives, destroyed homes, and prevented access to water and food for 5 million more. She composed it as a duet for her and her daughter, and released it on her 2005 album *Paradise Hotel*. Johnson found the music moving: "I 'heard' the invitation for it to be sung communally." In 2008 he arranged it for SATB choir and piano and dedicated it to the victims of natural disaster. In 2009, the American Choral Directors Association held its annual conference in Oklahoma City; "Requiem" was the musical centerpiece of a ceremony honoring those who died in the Oklahoma City bombing.

Musical Elements and Technical Considerations

The signature element of this music is the recurring phrase of the A section, first heard in the piano at measure 7, and then with text in the choir at measure 11. Its rhythm is a series of quarter notes and its texture homophonic. Set in B-flat major, it employs the basic harmonic progression I–V–ii–iv–V. What stands out is the way the progression arrives at the second V chord becasue the harmonization often leaves the B–flat pitch of the preceding iv chord suspended in the choral texture (mm. 13, 22, 34, 49, 60, 85). In these places, while the piano does resolve the suspensions in the next measure, the effect of the prolonged suspension in the voices is at times penitent, fearful, prayerful, and eternal. Be mindful, however, of how the same phrase at other moments will resolve the suspension immediately (mm. 17, 26, 53) or does not use it at all (mm. 19, 28, 55). The challenge for the singers is precision needed for ensuring that each cadential structure stands apart from the others. The onus of making these differences clear is on the altos, who always have the B-flat and A pitches of the suspension. Rehearse the main phrase of the

A section *without* altos so that the rest of the choir can practice arriving on the tonic and fifth of the V chord (F and C). Add the altos, using measures 18 and 19 as the sample segment; this will attune your singers to the sound of the phrase without suspension. Back up to measures 15 through 17 and sing again (first without altos and then with), as this now adds the 4-3 suspension with immediate resolution. Back up again to measures 11 through 13, and sing this phrase (without and then with altos). Your singers will become sensitive to the fine differences in each cadence, and the altos can feel and learn their responsibility in making the cadences effective.

The B section is essentially a soprano and alto duet, with tenors and basses supporting on "ooh." The women's parts expand the ranges of the voices, as their music in the A section is set relatively low. The men's parts frequently move in parallel fifths. They will benefit from rehearsing this *a cappella* without the women's parts so that they can be sensitive to the intonation challenge this setting can create. A warm-up exercise for all parts prior to rehearsing the piece will also help:

- With basses and altos on *do* and tenors and sopranos on *sol*, sing "mi me ma mo mu" together, then stop.
- Without playing a new chord, ask your singers to raise their pitches by a whole step (or half step) and sing again. Singers can repeat this with additional steps up or down, practicing their intonation as they move in perfect fifths.

This arrangement uses a piano accompaniment, adapted from Gilkyson's scoring for guitar, cello, and piano. It provides early support to the choir, playing the choir parts when the voices first have the main phrase of the A section (mm. 11 through 19). For the rest of the work, the arrangement provides welcome textural and rhythmic contrasts, such as lightening the piano texture at the first introduction of the B music (mm. 24 through 34) or employing short, arpeggiated eighth-note figures reminiscent of the original guitar part (e.g., mm. 30, 36, 47).

Stylistic Considerations

Because so much of the music moves homophonically in quarter notes, paying attention to the shape and direction of each phrase is paramount, to prevent the repetition of the recurring phrases from plodding along. Every new line of text has choice of emphasis. For example, in measures 20 through 22:

- "mother mary CALM our fears, (have mercy)"
- "mother mary calm our fears, Have MER-cy"

One of Gilkyson's strengths is the poetry of her texts; let your interpretation of each verse and phrase be thoughtful, and even evolve from the beginning to the end of the piece.

It is also possible to remove the piano part entirely and perform the work *a cappella*. In this case, the music can begin at measure 5 with a single or a small number of female voices (Gilkyson's original version does not have the 4-bar introduction that Johnson's does); the choir then hums the piano chords in measures 7 to 10. Conductors can be flexible with the time between choral phrases (e.g., shortening the silence by 4 beats in mm. 28 and 29). Not only does an *a cappella* performance highlight the charm of melodies, but it enhances the effects of the suspensions; without the piano, many remain beautifully and magically unresolved.

Form and Structure

Form: ABA'B'

Section	Measure	Event and Scoring
Introduction	Mm. 1–10	2 phrases (4+6). First phrase foreshadows B music, second phrase is music of A section.
A	Mm. 11–29	4 phrases (4+5+4+6)
B	Mm. 30–46	3 phrases (6+4+7)
A'	Mm. 47–55	2 phrases (4+5). Like the first two phrases of A section.
B'	Mm. 56–82	5 phrases (6+4+7+4+6). 4th phrase based on 2nd phrase; 5th phrase is mostly *a cappella* version of 3rd phrase.
Coda	Mm. 83–86	1 phrase. Derived from A music.

Text

mother mary, full of grace, awaken
all our homes are gone, our loved ones taken
taken by the sea
mother mary, calm our fears, have mercy
drowning in a sea of tears, have mercy
    hear our mournful plea

our world has been shaken, we wander our homelands forsaken
in the dark night of the soul bring some comfort to us all,
o mother mary come and carry us in your embrace,
    that our sorrows may be faced

mary, fill the glass to overflowing
illuminate the path where we are going
    have mercy on us all

in fun'ral fires burning each flame to your mist'ry returning
in the dark night of the soul your shattered dreamers, make them whole
o mother mary find us where we've fallen out of grace,
    lead us to a higher place
in the dark night of the soul our broken hearts you can make whole,
o mother mary come and carry us in your embrace,
    let us see your gentle face, mary

Contributed by:

Christopher Bartley

Teacher Resource Guide

The Pasture

from *Where the Earth Meets the Sky*

Z. Randall Stroope

(b. 1953)

SATB piano
Colla Voce Music: 45-21102
Overall: 2
Vocal: 2
Tonal/Rhythm: 2

Composer

Z. Randall Stroope was born in Albuquerque, New Mexico in 1953. He holds a master's degree in vocal performance from the University of Colorado and a doctorate in choral conducting from Arizona State University. Stroope is currently the Director of Choral and Vocal Studies at Oklahoma State University where he conducts the Concert Chorale and Chamber Choir and coordinates the conducting program. Previously, he was Director of Choral Studies at Rowan University in Glassboro, New Jersey. Stroope is the Artistic Director of summer international choral festivals in Somerset, England and Rome, Italy. In 2004 he was the recipient of the prestigious Raymond W. Brock Memorial Commission from the American Choral Directors Association. He has published ninety-five musical works with Alliance Music Publishers, Colla Voce Music, Heritage Music Press, MorningStar, and Walton Music.

Stroope's compositional output includes works for all choral voicings. The compositions are *a cappella*, or with various accompaniments including: piano, organ, brass, band, and orchestra. He has written songs for solo voice and instrumental ensembles. His larger works include *An American Te Deum*, *Cantus Natalis*, *American Rhapsody/American Christmas*, and *Hodie*. These are all choral works ranging in length from eleven and a half to nineteen minutes with various accompaniments.

Composition, Genre, and Historical Perspective

"The Pasture," with text by Robert Frost, for SATB choir with piano accompaniment, is the second of three movements in a choral cycle entitled *Where the Earth Meets the Sky*.

The set takes its title from the translation of the Mohawk word *karoniakatie* and the three songs are set to texts of poets who represent the diverse cultural heritage of America. This set is tied together by the composer in a way that illuminates different cultures coming together as one and the poet's thoughts about the resources and gifts of the earth. The first movement, "In Time of Silver Rain," is based on a text of African-American poet Langston Hughes and is for SATB choir accompanied by piano four hands. The third movement, "Song of the Earth," is composed using a traditional Mohawk text and is set for SATB choir, piano accompaniment, and flute solo.

"The Pasture" was published in 2000 by Colla Voce Music, Inc. It is one of many exceptional pieces of choral music written by Stroope over many years. The chosen text, especially in context of the set of three pieces, is relevant to current world concerns about bringing people together as well as the growing concern over caring for our earth. This composition can be programmed independently from the set of three.

Musical Elements and Technical Considerations

"The Pasture" is lyrical, beautiful, and accessible. A middle school choir could potentially perform the work but the deep musicality, deftly crafted phrases, and exceptional text make it a very satisfying work for high school and older choirs as well. There is nothing immature about it.

There is a significant amount of unison and two-part homophonic singing in this piece. The first stanza of poetry is sung by only the women and the second stanza by the men. The coda section that closes the work is the only time the men and women join together. The vocal exposure, due to minimal part singing, in this composition magnifies the importance of the choir singing with pure vowel sounds (vowel unification) in order to create a homogenous and beautiful tone. Extreme care must be taken by the conductor to teach the choir how to pronounce and enunciate all words in identical fashion.

The phrases are very lyrical but the notes are frequently disjunct. The choir will need to be able to sing the pitches as though they are all on the same plane, without shifting the vocal mechanism. The lines need to be legato and sung on a steady stream of breath so that none of the pitches or word syllables unintentionally sounds louder in the phrase.

Frequently, the larger musical idea or phrase is made up of several microphrases. The ensemble will need to understand the grand phrase structure to perform the work musically. The phrases don't necessarily end when rests occur. For example, measures 5 through 8 constitute a 4-measure phrase built on two smaller phrases: measures 5 and 6 plus measures 7 and 8. Similarly measures 21 through 26 make a 6-measure phrase that breaks into three 2-measure smaller phrases, with rests between them. In performing the work, stopping the phrase momentum when rests occur and not carrying over through the larger idea would produce a very unsatisfying musical experience.

The challenges in this seemingly simple piece are actually quite plentiful. "The Pasture" can really engage and help singers in any level ensemble to learn or reinforce many aspects of good vocal technique and musicianship.

The piano accompaniment has an integral relationship with the voices in this composition. The pianist needs to play expressively, frequently bringing out the melody in the right hand as it grows out of and enhances the vocal lines. The accompaniment often takes over a melodic passage as the singers sustain the final notes of a phrase.

Stylistic Considerations

The beauty of this work lies in the simplicity of the text setting. Z. Randall Stroope follows in the tradition of composers who giftedly set and skillfully craft music around exquisite poetry. The work brings to mind previous American masters like Samuel Barber, Howard Hanson, and Randall Thompson. Robert Frost's pastoral poetry influences the style and sound of the music. The music is fully marked with dynamics, tempo alterations, and many other expressive elements. The work is meaningfully and sensitively crafted, and it is clear that the composer's intensions are for a communicative and expressive performance. Singers must be engaged with the text and its delivery, as well as deeply committed to the musical expressiveness, as is always very important in the best music of the current era.

Form and Structure

The overall form of the work is very simple and straightforward, there are two verses and a coda. After a brief piano introduction of four measures the women of the choir sing the first stanza of poetry. A piano interlude leads to the second stanza with the men. The men and women do not sing together in this work until the very end. A brief repeat of the last line of text, "you come too" brings the work to a close.

Section	Measure	Event and Scoring
Introduction	mm. 1–4	piano
Verse 1	mm. 5–12	women in unison
	mm. 13–18	women in two parts
Interlude	mm. 18–20	piano (begins under last note of women in m. 18)
	mm. 21–26	final phrase(s) of women
Interlude	mm. 26-34	piano (begins under last note of women in m. 26)
Verse 2	mm. 35–38	men in unison
	mm 39–46	men in two parts (this differs from the women's verse)
Interlude	mm. 46–48	piano (begins under last note of men in m. 46)
	mm. 49–54	final phrase(s) of men
Coda	mm. 54–64	men and women sing for the first time together here (begins with women's entrance on the last note of the men in m. 54)

Text and Translation

Robert Lee Frost (1874–1963) was one of America's greatest twentieth-century poets. He was a four-time winner of the Pulitzer Prize. Frost's poems often reflected on pastoral themes and rural life in New England.

Excerpt:
I'm going out to clean the pasture spring:
I sha'n't be long. [inserted here by composer]
I'll only stop to rake the leaves away:
I sha'n't be long. [inserted here by composer]
And watch the water clear I may: [altered by composer from "and wait to watch"]
I sha'n't be gone long.
You come too.

This beautiful setting of poetry includes text painting on words such as "long," which is given a note of greater duration than those around it. The phrase "I may" is repeated several times as if to make us think about the possibility. The phrase "I sha'n't be gone long" is also continually repeated, evoking a feeling of longing.

Additional References and Resources

Wine, Tom, ed. *Composers on Composers for Chorus*. Chicago: GIA Publications, Inc. 2007.

Suggested Recording

Passages Volume I: The Choral Music of Z. Randall Stroope. Multiple Choirs. Z. Randall Stroope, conducting. (available at www.zrstroope.com)

Website

www.zrstroope.com

Contributed by:

Joseph Ohrt, DMA

Teacher Resource Guide

Wanting Memories

Ysaye M. Barnwell

SSATB
Musical Source: YMB 103
Overall: 2
Vocal: 2
Tonal/Rhythm: 3

Composer

Dr. Ysaye M. Barnwell is best known as a member of Sweet Honey in the Rock, an African-American women's *a cappella* group. A founding member of the group saw Barnwell sing and interpret sign language and then asked her to join the ensemble in 1979. Barnwell is also a speech pathologist with the Bachelor's, Master's (SUNY–Geneseo, 1963–1968), and PhD (University of Pittsburgh, 1975) degrees and was a professor in the College of Dentistry for over a decade. In 1981 she completed post-doctoral work and earned the Master of Science in Public Health.

Barnwell has worked as a commissioned composer on numerous and varied projects including Sesame Street, Dance Alloy of Pittsburgh, David Rousseve's Reality Dance Company, Liz Lerman Dance Exchange, Women's Philharmonic of San Francisco, Redwood Cultural Work, The New Spirituals Project, The Steel Festival of Bethlehem, Pennsylvania, The Plymouth Music Series, and numerous choirs—all outgrowths of her understanding of creative arts inextricably bound to society. Dr. Barnwell was named after the Belgian violinist, Eugéne Ysaÿe.

Composition, Genre, and Historical Perspective

"Wanting Memories" is a work that sings like a folk song even though it is an original composition. Like many of Barnwell's compositions, the poem comes from her own hand. It is a poignant text, reflecting on the love of a parent: "You used to rock me in the cradle of your arms, you said you'd hold me till the pains of life were gone. You said you'd comfort me in times like these and now I need you, and you are gone."

I asked Dr. Barnwell to comment on this work and its context, and she offered the following thoughts:

> "Wanting Memories" was one section of a suite of songs for a dance theater work called CROSSINGS. In the dance choreographed by David Rousseve, a Black child is called a nigger by a class mate or play mate and when the Nana (grandmother) finds out what happens she tells the child that the comment was more a reflection of the teller than the child, and says if you want to know who you are, "look into my eyes." This is what precedes "No Mirrors in My Nana's House." When the child has grown into a woman and the Nana has died, the woman reflects on what she learned from the Nana in "Wanting Memories."
>
> "No Mirrors in My Nana's House" is based on the true story told to me by a friend about her growing up. "Wanting Memories" has in it all the values taught to me by my own parents. I am an only child and what I did not know when I wrote the song (prior to my parents' death) was that they had saved thousands of family photos, over 300 hand written letters, family documents and many other items which I found after their death and which are the memories I had unconsciously wished for and written about. Many of these items can be found on my website http://www.barnwellarchives.com.

Musical Elements and Technical Considerations

"Wanting Memories" is not musically complex, and singers will enjoy the experience of learning and performing this moving work. The women present the poignant text in three-part diatonic harmony. Conductors should equally balance the three female voice parts, and consider swapping the top voices to the middle line (which sits higher than the top line).

Below the three-part women's writing, the work contains an ostinato bass pattern that is repeated identically in each of the 90 measures. This poses one of the only difficult rehearsal issues—keeping the basses engaged while the others learn their lines. The tenors join on each refrain, imitating a gentle percussion shaker. You might consider allowing the tenor section to lightly double the bass ostinato when they do not have a printed part of their own.

One other suggestion to consider involves the key of the score (C major). The altos spend a lot of time below the staff, and directors of high school singers might find this a difficult register to encourage healthy production for the work's nearly four minutes. With my adult chorus, I have performed the work up a half step in C-sharp major, and I know that some choruses have performed the work up a minor third to E-flat major. This brings the octave leap of the ostinato above the *passagio* for the basses and allows a lighter production from that section.

Stylistic Considerations

To get a true idea of Dr. Barnwell's intention, consider listening to a recording sung by Sweet Honey in the Rock (recorded on the 1993 album *Still on the Journey*); there is a sound clip at their Web site. Allow for slight vocal scoops and avoid a purely classical approach to the vocal production. Dr. Barnwell does not indicate dynamics in the score, so teach the singers to phrase according to the text and the natural contours of the score.

The score is written with many syncopated rhythms, but at no point should these feel jagged or accented. Try to encourage a gentle, storytelling approach to the performance of this piece. I suggest allowing the choir to move expressively during the rehearsal and performance of the work. Movements should allow the natural speech patterns to emerge, but they should not reinforce the syncopated rhythms.

Form and Structure

Measure	Section
mm. 1–12:	Introduction and Refrain
mm. 13–22:	Verse 1
mm. 23–30	Refrain
mm. 31–40	Verse 2
mm. 41–48	Refrain
mm. 49–58	Verse 3
mm. 59–66	Refrain (new text)
mm. 67–76	Verse 4
mm. 77–90	Refrain and conclusion

Text

I am sitting here wanting memories to teach me
to see the beauty in the world through my own eyes.
I am sitting here wanting memories to teach me
To see the beauty in the world through my own eyes.
You said you'd rock me in the cradle of your arms.

You said you'd hold me 'til the storms of life were gone.
You said you'd comfort me in times like these and now I need you.
Now I need you...
And you are—
gone.
So, I am sitting here wanting memories to teach me
to see the beauty in the world through my own eyes.
Since you've gone and left me, there's been so little beauty,
but I know I saw it clearly through your eyes.
Now the world outside is such a cold and bitter place.
Here inside I have few things that will console.
And when I try to hear your voice above the storms of life,
then I remember all the things that I was told.
Well, I am sitting here wanting memories to teach me
to see the beauty in the world through my own eyes.
Yes, I am sitting here wanting memories to teach me
To see the beauty in the world through my own eyes.
I think on the things that made me feel so wonderful when I was young.
I think on the things that made me laugh, made me dance, made me sing.
I think on the things that made me grow into a being full of pride.
I think on these things, for they are true.
I am sitting here wanting memories to teach me
to see the beauty in the world through my own eyes.
I thought that you were gone, but now I know you're with me.
You are the voice that whispers all I need to hear.
I know a "Please", a "Thank you", and a smile will take me far.
I know that I am you and you are me, and we are one.
I know that who I am is numbered in each grain of sand.
I know that I am blessed,
again, and again, and again, and again,
and, again.
I am sitting here wanting memories to teach me
to see the beauty in the world through my own eyes.
I am sitting here wanting memories to teach me
To see the beauty in the world through my own eyes.

Additional References and Suggested Resources

E-mail correspondence with Dr. Barnwell.
http://www.barnwellarchives.com
http://www.sweethoney.com/
http://www.ymbarnwell.com/

Contributed by:

Matthew Culloton

Teacher Resource Guide

Where the Music Comes From

Lee Hoiby
(b. 1926)

SATB/piano
G. Schirmer: 50-488947
Overall: 2
Vocal: 2
Tonal/Rhythm: 2

Composer

Lee Hoiby, born in Wisconsin in 1926, is a major voice in American music. He studied piano with Gunnar Johansen and Egon Petri but gave up his intentions to be a concert pianist when he received an invitation to study composition with Gian Carlo Menotti at the Curtis Institute in Philadelphia. Unable to refuse, Hoiby made the move to Philadelphia and there begins his compositional career. He has since composed a wide array of works from opera to solo piano. Perhaps Hoiby's most important contribution is to American song repertoire: his beautiful, elegant settings of texts have great literary and civic value.

Composition, Genre, and Historical Perspective

Hoiby is in no way a stranger to choral composition. In fact, some of his more substantial work is for choir, including the Christmas cantata *A Hymn of the Nativity* and his oratorio *Galileo Galilei*. "Where the Music Comes From" was composed for The Pathwork, a consciousness-raising group, of which he was a member in the 1970s, and whose goals were to learn how to grow, feel, and love. Once Hoiby put it in a collection of his songs, the work began receiving great success and even wound up on recital programs of Leontyne Price. Now this arrangement for SATB choir combines his sophisticated and elegant setting for solo voice, his innate understanding of the piano, and his extensive experience with choral composition.

Musical Elements and Technical Considerations

Unison voicing

This work begins with tenor and bass voices in unison, and contains several unison SATB points thereafter. Unison passages in a score might seem easy to prepare. However, many choirs do not perform unison singing well at all! A unison passage is the perfect time to make sure that each and every singer is performing with the same shape, style, articulation, and vowel formation. After all, there is no harmony or polyphony to mask any errors. One might try a series of exercises like this:

Pitch

1. Rehearse on solfège (for pitch accuracy);
2. Count-sing (for rhythmic accuracy);
3. Rehearse on a neutral syllable (for nuances);
4. Try combinations of the above (to further solidify previous concepts);

Rhythm

5. Practice text speaking (for consistency of vowel formation);
6. Practice text in rhythm;
7. Practice text on a single pitch (carefully watching vowel consistency);

Combine Pitch and rhythm

8. Combine text and pitches in rhythm.

Obviously this series can be applied to every passage regardless of voicing and, if step 8 is reached and there are still inconsistencies, simply move up the list and start again. Also, asking singers to audiate the pitch ahead of time can ensure thinking! Inconsistencies of ensemble will clear up if given the proper time and attention.

Tessitura

The tessitura might be a bit low for some young tenors. However, singing lightly with great diction in their lower registers will help to circumvent that issue. Also there are some passages that contain notes that are fairly low for altos as well. Of course the same solution can help the altos, but at instances like measure 33 (where altos have the G below middle C and the tenors have the D below that) it might be best, should you have the numbers, to split the bass section up to the low tenor line and add some higher tenors to the alto line. This will provide a more consistent sonority as the lines dip down.

Accidentals and Modulations

There are a few accidentals in each verse that should be approached with caution, and the singers should find the top side of the pitch to avoid pulling the melodic line down. Also, each new verse modulates. If there are any issues finding the new tonic, one might try:

1. Isolate the approaching measure and work to land solidly in the new key;
2. Have your singers audiate while the piano accompaniment approaches the modulation, and have them sing just the downbeat in the new key.

Most importantly, be creative and try to break down concepts into their simplest forms. This will allow for maximum retention and ease of learning.

Stylistic Considerations

Text setting and rubato

As with any art song, the text setting of the work offers room for interpretation. A slight ebb and flow to the verses would be completely appropriate and perhaps the ending of each verse could slow slightly. For example, a *poco ritardando* at measures 20 and 21 and measures 41 and 42 would help to ready the audience for the *ritard* to *largamente* at measure 62. However, the text should always be the first and foremost factor when determining where and when to take time, speed up, or breathe.

Dynamics, phrasing, and articulation

Hoiby is extremely straightforward in how he notates his music. Dynamics and crescendi/diminuendi should be followed closely as they are notated clearly and effectively to bring out the dramatic shape of the text.

Form and Structure

This strophic setting is composed simply and provides interest through both the modulations and the changes of voicing for each verse. Also, while acquainting yourself with the form presented here, please take into consideration the pickup, which occurs over the second half of the measure prior to each indicated measure in the analysis.

SECTION	MEASURE	EVENT AND SCORING
Verse 1	mm. 1–7	piano introduction and pickup to first verse (A major)
	mm. 8–15	2 phrases (4+4) tenor and bass
	mm. 16–25	1 long phrase (10)
Verse 2	mm. 26–28	piano modulation to B-flat major and pickup to verse 2
	mm. 29–32	1 phrase (4) soprano and alto
	mm. 33–36	1 phrase (4) SATB
	mm. 37–46	1 long phrases (10)
Verse 3	mm. 47–49	piano modulation to C major and pickup to verse 3
	mm. 50–57	2 phases (4+4) SATB
	mm. 58–69	extended long phrase (12)
	mm. 70–72	piano

Text

I want to be where the music comes from,
Where the clock stops,
Where it's now.
I want to be with friends around me,
Who have found me,
Who show me how…

Additional References and Resources

Lee Hoiby Web site: "Biography." http://www.leehoiby.com/biography.php (August 20, 2008)

Contributed by:

Anthony Maglione

Teacher Resource Guide

Dance on My Heart

Alan Koepke

(b. 1939)

SSA/piano
Santa Barbara Music: SBMP–34
Overall: 2
Vocal: 2
Tonal/Rhythm: 2

Composer

Born in Chicago in 1939, Allen Koepke has been a choral director and music educator at elementary, junior and senior high schools, and collegiate levels throughout Iowa since 1960. He currently serves as director of choirs at St. Mark's Lutheran Church in Cedar Rapids, Iowa. While teaching at Kirkwood Community College in Cedar Rapids, Iowa, he was named "1996 Iowa Professor of the Year" by the Carnegie Institute, and in 1997 he was awarded the Robert M. McCowen Memorial Award "for outstanding contribution to choral music in Iowa" by the Iowa Choral Directors Association. In addition to leading award-winning choirs throughout his career, he is also a frequently commissioned composer, and has published over 60 works with numerous publishers. Many of his compositions have been performed on state, regional, and national choral conventions, as well as in Europe, Asia, and Canada. Well known for his choral writing, his output also includes instrumental works, and for two years he served as Composer-in-Residence for the Cedar Rapids Symphony. Mr. Koepke holds degrees from Luther College and from the University of Northern Iowa.

Composition and Historical Perspective

"Dance on My Heart" is a light-hearted madrigal set for 3-part treble choir with piano accompaniment, and was the winning composition of the 1991 Iowa Choral Directors' Association competition. The text was written by Koepke and tells the story of a young woman being wooed by three different men, each asking what he must do to "win her kind affection." The first man tells her he is strong, brave, and "adoringly sweet"; the second offers her "diamonds and pearls" and "power and riches." She declines the offers of both these men, telling them that her "heart is not pounding" and therefore she cannot marry either of them. The third man tells her that he "can only promise to love you, be at your side through all of my life," and it is to this third man that she exclaims "you dance on my heart, and you sing to my soul... Yes, kind sir, I will marry you!"

Technical Considerations and Musical Elements

The melodic and tonal aspects of "Dance on My Heart" are easily taught. A change of key from F to D at measure 21 (where the young woman responds to her suitors) comes naturally to the ear, as does the transition back to F major at measure 33. The melody, found in the top soprano line, is quite delightful, and the melodic lines of the soprano II and alto parts are easily taught as well. Momentary passages in individual lines, such as brief chromatic motion in the soprano II and alto lines (e.g., soprano II m. 5), and a somewhat unexpected resolution to an E-flat in the alto line (m. 17), should be taught slowly and independently of the other vocal parts to ensure clarity of the line. The range of each vocal line is certainly not extreme (the soprano I line has only a single high E in the coda), but the alto line does require the singing of low A numerous times and there are several instances of a low G.

Although the piece contains both 4/4 and 7/8 time signatures, rhythmic issues are not problematic, as the piece is entirely homophonic. In addition, Koepke has done an exceptional job of bringing out the rhythm in the inflection of the words and textual phrases—even the measures in 7/8 feel entirely natural. Therefore, the director might be wise to begin teaching the work by having the group speak the rhythm of the text in unison before adding the melodic aspects.

By far the most difficult aspect of the piece is in negotiating the score itself. There are numerous repeats and a *DS al Coda* that almost invariably require the singers (and accompanist and director) to flip pages back or forward. Additionally, the repeats are not meant to be observed for all the various verses and do not necessarily return the singers to the same point in the music every time. Koepke has provided detailed instructions in the printed score, but this piece will come off with more ease and effectiveness in performance if both the choir and conductor memorize it. (A page turner for the accompanist would be most helpful as well).

Stylistic Considerations

This is a wonderfully playful piece that is sure to be a favorite of not only the singers but the audience as well. Encourage singers to use light, crisp diction in order to effectively transmit the story to the audience, and above all, maintain the rhythmic vitality of the piece, especially in consideration of the "sprightly" tempo marking of quarter note = 126. Although a fairly short articulation should be used for the majority of the piece, certain words and phrases can be sung with a more legato feel to bring out the meaning of the text (e.g., the triplets on the word "adoringly" at m. 18). Nonetheless, you may suggest to the singers that they experiment with various articulations throughout. The director should take careful consideration of the dynamic markings indicated in the score, as well as the slight tempo change at the pickup to measure 29 ("a bit slower") and the *a tempo* at measure 33. Although nothing is indicated in the score, the conductor might wish to suddenly broaden the tempo at in measures 42 and 43, which will make the *tenutos* over the last two chords in measure 43 seem less abrupt.

Form and Structure

Measure	Event and Scoring
1–2	piano introduction
3–19	verse 1 (repeat to m. 11, v. 2)
11–19	verse 2 (go on to m. 20)
20–36	transition to D major (piano) and verse 3 (repeat to m. 3, v. 4)
3–19	verse 4 (go on to m. 20)
20–27	transition to D major and verse 5 (go to coda, m. 37)
37–47	coda (completion of verse 5)

Contributed by:

David Scholz

Teacher Resource Guide

Gate, Gate

arr. Brian Tate

SSA/piano
Earthsongs: W-050
Overall: 2
Vocal: 2
Tonal/Rhythm: 3

Composer

Brian Tate's eclectic career as a composer, conductor, and vocal performer has taken him from his home in Vancouver to venues throughout the world. After receiving a Bachelor of Music degree from the University of British Columbia, he continued his music studies in London and Toronto. A two-time recipient of Vancouver's Jessie Richardson award for original theatre music, Mr. Tate enjoys the diversity of his output, which includes choral and orchestral conducting, West African drumming, jazz vocals, and composing music for film, television, stage, and concert hall.

Tate currently serves on the faculty of Langara College, as well as at the Banff Centre for Leadership Development. He was the director of Vancouver's Universal Gospel Choir for eight seasons, and continues to give choir workshops throughout North America. Tate also performs regularly as a vocal soloist, and has created a solo performance incorporating live digital looping and visual arts.

In addition to his extensive music career, Tate is a sought-after public speaker and facilitator. His workshops focus on teambuilding, innovation, and leadership through the use of musical improvisation. His goal is to help participants grow not only in their chosen careers but also in all areas of their lives.

Composition, Genre, and Historical Perspective

Gate Gate, composed in 1992, takes its name from the final lines of the *Prajñ p ramit H daya S tra*, commonly known as the "Heart Sutra," thought to be a central tennet of the Buddhist teachings. Scholars date the origin of the text to circa 100 BCE. There has been some debate as to whether the original text was originally written in a Chinese or Indic language, and then later translated into Sanskrit, the language Tate used in this work. Composed by a Buddhist monk, the "Heart Sutra" belongs to a larger group of texts known as the "Wisdom Sutras," that encompass over 8,000 lines of text.

George Boeree, a psychology professor at Shippensburg University who specializes in Buddist philosophical psychology, offers the following translation of the Heart Sutra, the text to *Gate Gate* found in the closing lines—

Avalokiteshvara, the Bodhisattva of Compassion, meditating deeply on Perfection of Wisdom, saw clearly that the five aspects of human existence are empty*, and so released himself from suffering. Answering the monk Sariputra, he said this:

Body is nothing more than emptiness,
emptiness is nothing more than body.
The body is exactly empty,
and emptiness is exactly body.
The other four aspects of human existence—
feeling, thought, will, and consciousness—
are likewise nothing more than emptiness,
and emptiness nothing more than they.

All things are empty:
Nothing is born, nothing dies,
nothing is pure, nothing is stained,
nothing increases and nothing decreases.

So, in emptiness, there is no body,
no feeling, no thought,
no will, no consciousness.
There are no eyes, no ears,
no nose, no tongue,
no body, no mind.
There is no seeing, no hearing,

no smelling, no tasting,
no touching, no imagining.
There is nothing seen, nor heard,
nor smelled, nor tasted,
nor touched, nor imagined.

There is no ignorance,
and no end to ignorance.
There is no old age and death,
and no end to old age and death.
There is no suffering, no cause of suffering,
no end to suffering, no path to follow.
There is no attainment of wisdom,
and no wisdom to attain.

The Bodhisattvas rely on the Perfection of Wisdom,
and so with no delusions,
they feel no fear,
and have Nirvana here and now.

All the Buddhas,
past, present, and future,
rely on the Perfection of Wisdom,
and live in full enlightenment.

The Perfection of Wisdom is the greatest mantra.
It is the clearest mantra,
the highest mantra,
the mantra that removes all suffering.

This is truth that cannot be doubted.
Say it so:

Gaté,
gaté,
paragaté,
parasamgaté.
Bodhi!
Svaha!

Musical Elements and Technical Considerations

Conducting challenges abound in *Gate, Gate*, which employs styles from flowing chant to angular, accented, mixed meter passages. Easing transitions between sections with gesture is essential to helping singers move through the piece with confidence.

Opening chant, measures 1 through 10

The first measure is clearly to be sung in imitation of chant, with emphasis on the strong syllables of text and retreat on the weak, making for a very speech-like production of the text. The key to this section is to empower independence in the chorus so that the conductor is cueing perhaps only every word change, allowing the speech pattern to dictate the flow.

Measure 11 and beyond

Here, the tempo indication is 6/8 and 3/4, which allows for a different rhythmic emphasis in each measure while keeping the tactus steady. The composer notes, "the feeling of 6/8 may be alternated with 3/4, at the conductor's discretion." Many conductors opt to use a "2" pattern for the 6/8 measures, followed by a "3" pattern for the 3/4 measures. Others choose to conduct in "one" to ease the transition into measure 35, which, because of the speed of the tempo and the sustained pitches in the soprano and alto parts, is more efficiently executed in one. If a conductor chooses to use the 2 + 3 pattern, it is helpful to transition into "one" in measure 34 to set up measure 35.

Whatever the pattern, it is essential to keep in mind that the pulse is grounded in the piano. Singers will naturally join in and "feel" the pattern, allowing the conductor to use a minimal gesture. Though most of the piece has a rhythmic, nonlegato feel, this changes to legato in measures 91 to 106 and 122 to 133.

Stylistic Considerations

The opening chant section, though intoned on a single pitch, should remain as speech-like as possible. The syllabic stress carries the direction and pace of the line, and, as stated above, the chorus should be empowered to chant freely with a minimal amount of conducting, to avoid the chant becoming stilted. At measure 2, when the 3/8 time signature appears, the conductor may choose to use a simple 1 pattern, again allowing the chorus freedom to direct the chant.

The remainder of the piece uses a combination of English and Sanskrit texts. For both languages, Tate has used rhythm in the music to reinforce the natural speech rhythm of the text. Thus, the dance-like rhythms are naturally achieved by observing syllabic stress.

Form and Structure

The primary musical subject is 8-measures long, and is crafted into a refrain of sorts when repeated into a 16-measure period. There is a primary melody (introduced in mm. 19 to 34), and a countermelody (introduced in mm. 52 to 58). The distinct rhythm that defines the original melody unifies each strophe, even when the melody is not present in its original form. The form is basically strophic (melodic motive and rhythmic motive are the unifying factors), with an introduction and small coda, and includes a short bridge between strophes in measures 122 to 133.

Section	Measure	Event and Scoring
Introduction	mm. 1–9	*a cappella* chant, first in unison, then in canon
Introduction	mm. 11–18	piano only, now in 6/8 and ¾ alternating time
Strophe 1	mm. 19–34	melody presented in unison in all voices
Strophe 2	mm. 35–50	melody in soprano 2, outer voices on long notes, as in a drone; accompaniment changes to a legato feel
Strophe 3	mm. 52–58	(repeated) melody in soprano 1 and 2, echo-like countermelody in A, English text
Strophe 4	mm. 59–66	English language melody in soprano and 2, English countermelody in alto
Strophe 5	mm. 67–74	(repeated) rhythmic motive intact, all voice parts *a cappella*
Strophe 6	mm. 75–90	Here, all voice parts join to maintain the rhythmic motive, featuring a melody that is reminiscent of the countermelody usually found in the alto line.
Strophe 7	mm. 91–106	Original melodic motive is now in the alto line, new countermelody in the soprano 1 and 2.
Strophe 8		repeat of Strophe 6
Bridge	mm. 123–133	This section transitions, with the help of the piano, into a new key and a new time signature—7/8.

SECTION	MEASURE	EVENT AND SCORING
Strophe 9	mm. 134–154	This is an extended strophe, which features not only the original melody, but the countermelody (mm. 134–141) and rhythmic motive (as originally demonstrated in mm. 67–74).
Strophe 10	mm. 154–168	repeat of Strophe 6, but now in B-flat major
Coda	mm. 170–end	

Text and Translation

The text pronunciation is written phonetically below, along with the translation provided in the score. Tate uses a combination of the Sanskrit language along with English to project the meaning of the text.

Although the original mantra employs *schwa* sounds, directors may opt to move toward a more open "a" to improve resonance, projection, and overall beauty of tone.

Gate gate	[gə'te gə'te]	Gone, Gone
P ragate	[pɑ'rəgəte]	Everybody Gone
P rasa gate	[pɑ'rəsəm gə'te]	Gone all the way over
Bodhi sv h	[bo'dhɪ svɑ'hɑ]	Awake! Hallelujah!

Contributed by:

Geoffrey Boers

Teacher Resource Guide

Japanese Garden

Matthew Culloton

(b.1976)

SA/piano and clarinet
Neil A. Kjos: C9301
Overall: 2
Vocal: 2
Tonal/Rhythm: 2

Composer

Matthew Culloton is the Founding Artistic Director and Conductor of The Singers—Minnesota Choral Artists. He holds degrees from Concordia College, Moorhead (B.M. in Music Education) and the University of Minnesota (M.M. in Choral Conducting). He is currently completing coursework towards a D.M.A. in Conducting at the University of Minnesota. Matthew has studied conducting with René Clausen, Kathy Romey, Paul Nesheim, Matthew Mehaffey, and Bruce Houglum.

An experienced and celebrated music educator, Culloton began his teaching career in the Long Prairie—Grey Eagle School District. From 2000 to 2006, he was Director of Choral Activities at Hopkins High School, overseeing a choral program of six performing ensembles. His Hopkins Concert Choir performed at the 2002 and 2004 Minnesota ACDA Fall Conventions and the 2005 MMEA Mid-Winter Clinic. In November 2004, Colloton was presented with the Minnesota ACDA Outstanding Young Choral Conductor of the Year Award. In the fall of 2003, he was the recipient of the VocalEssence/ACDA of Minnesota Creative Programming Award for his work at Hopkins High School. From 1999 to 2004, Colloton was a member of the

Dale Warland Singers, having served as music advisor to Dale Warland, as assistant conductor, and as bass section leader.

As a composer, Colloton has received commissions from The Singers—Minnesota Choral Artists, the Dale Warland Singers, Choral Arts Ensemble of Rochester (MN), Ames Chamber Artists, Chanson, the Minnesota MMEA All-State Choir, and numerous high school, collegiate, and church choirs. He is co-editor of the *Matthew and Michael Culloton Choral Series* with Santa Barbara Publishing Company. His music is published by Santa Barbara Music Publishing, Hinshaw Music, Mark Foster Music (Shawnee), Kjos Music, and Graphite Publishing.

Composition, Genre, and Historical Perspective

I composed "Japanese Garden" in 1999 while teaching vocal music in Long Prairie, Minnesota. My colleague in the vocal music program was Marilyn Bengtson, a wonderful educator who connected beautifully with her students. Her husband David Bengtson taught in the English department and is a talented poet whose words have inspired a handful of my compositions as well as those of other composers.

Although this work is an art song for female chorus, the premiere performance was sung by my twin brother Michael and me. David Bengtson had arranged a school residency with renowned poet Lucille Clifton, and we were to premiere a new choral work that I composed on a text by Clifton. Unfortunately, she took ill and had to cancel the residency just days before her scheduled appearance. David had worked so diligently to bring Ms. Clifton to Long Prairie and I felt bad for him, so I wrote this piece on his text so he could have a premiere work of his own to celebrate instead.

In Little Sauk, Minnesota there exists a Japanese garden that a man has cultivated for some time. A local company commissioned David Bengtson to write a poem for a secular winter card to be given to employees; an artist was commissioned to paint the garden for the front of the card. As it turns out, the music for this work is the third artistic tribute to this small gem of a garden in rural Minnesota.

Musical Elements and Technical Considerations

This score is a brief, through-composed work that is fairly modest in its use of vocal register. The foundation of the work is a gentle, pulsing ostinato pattern that occurs in the piano below the smooth vocal lines. Do not let the activity of the piano obstruct the overall legato character of the score. The vocal lines should never feel syncopated when dotted rhythms occur, as in measure 16 (soprano), measure 18 (alto), and measure 24 (both parts).

It is important to balance the vocal parts evenly throughout. Although the score is primarily for two-part treble choir, there are two instances of three-part writing occurs in measures 25 to 27 and for one beat in measure 63. Allow for an equal three-part split to balance those chords as well.

As a composer and arranger, I love writing unison lines for full choirs, and this work includes a fair amount of unison singing. Phrases often begin in unison before splitting into countermelodies. Moving into harmonies was a purposeful handling of the text, most notably on the verb *blossom* in measures 41 to 44 and the *outstretched hands* in measures 58 to 61. In this case, the phrase begins in unison in measure 57, splits into two parts, and closes with a unison ending in measure 61.

Homophonic writing dominates the texture of this work. There is a brief imitative passage in measures 13 to 20 before all parts come together in measure 21. Pay attention to the altos in measure 18, as their intervals are slightly different from those in the soprano statement. Try to bring out the melodic contours in measures 22 to 24 because they depict the *wave* described in the poem.

The altos will likely sing an incorrect note in measure 54 unless this is pointed out early in the rehearsal process. The printed alto E is correct, but it is a dissonance with the F-sharp in the piano's ostinato. Along with the C-sharp in the soprano line, it will be too tempting to sing F-sharp instead of E.

I would like to point out a mistake in the score that can be easily corrected if the conductor so wishes. Bengtson's original poem ends with the line "as petals fall silent as snow." In my earliest manuscript I inadvertently substituted "softly" for "silent," and it simply stayed that way. Being true to the wonderful poem, I invite conductors to sing the word "silent."

Most altos will find that the vocal line sits quite comfortably. The soprano scoring is somewhat lower than is found in a lot of repertoire, the part moves above the passagio only in measures 52 and 53. While singing below the passagio, encourage the sopranos to imagine the lightness of their higher range. The score should not be performed with a "belted" or "chesty" vocal quality in either vocal part. Conductors may try to mix sopranos and altos on both lines to blend the vocal colors present in their choirs.

The instrumental writing for the piano and clarinet is fairly accessible for high-school aged or more experienced players. As mentioned earlier, the piano part is consistently active, with eighth notes gently propelling the music forward. The clarinet part consists of melodic fragments from the vocal lines, as well as counterpoint with the voices. The clarinet should dominate in measures 24 to 34, rising slightly above the dynamic of the singers. In measure 55, the clarinet assumes the opening melody (indicated in the score), and this should also be brought out against the vocal line.

"Japanese Garden" also includes tempo nuance that should be observed closely. The overall tempo should flow nicely, but pay close attention to the indications in measures 46 through 47, 59, 62, 64, and 67.

Two instrumental scores are included, one for clarinet in B-flat and one for instrument in C. An oboe or violin would be preferable to a flute, as I do not recommend its timbre for this score.

Stylistic Considerations

As in any art song, the vocal style can be free and expressive. Sensible singing dictates that vibrato should be unified throughout the sections. This work is not meant to be sung in a straight-tone style. A natural vocal approach will serve the music and the text appropriately. The altos should not feel as though their part accompanies the soprano melody. Instead, the altos should perform their countermelodies with the same vocal care given to a melody line. Expressive and warm singing is to be employed throughout the work.

Form and Structure

Measure	Event
mm. 1–33	(4+8+8+5+7)
mm. 34–49	(12+5)
mm. 50–70	(7+5+2+7)

Text

In this garden one tree is weeping
While another's bent branch waits for God to sit
And the lantern rides a frozen wave.
All winter we waited for these few days
When plum and apple blossom.
Tomorrow we will walk this path again
And stand here with outstretched hands
As petals fall silent as snow.

Bibliography and Suggested Resources

For more information about poet David Bengtson, visit http://web.mac.com/dbengtson1/iWeb/Site/Home.html.

To hear a recording of "Japanese Garden" performed by members of The Singers—Minnesota Choral Artists, visit www.kjos.com.

Contributed by:

Matthew Culloton

Teacher Resource Guide

Jordan's Angels

Rollo A. Dilworth
(b. 1970)

SSA/piano
Hal Leonard: HL 08551668
Overall: 2
Vocal: 2
Tonal/Rhythm: 2

Composer

Rollo Dilworth is Associate Professor of Choral Music Education at Temple University's Esther Boyer College of Music and Dance in Philadelphia, PA. Dr. Dilworth holds degrees from Case Western Reserve University, the University of Missouri-St. Louis, and Northwestern University. From 1996 to 2009 he served on the music faculty of North Park University in Chicago, IL.

Dilworth has composed and/or arranged over 150 published choral works, co-authored two choral textbook series and is the author of *Choir Builders: Fundamental Vocal Techniques for General and Classroom Use*. He is also the co-author of *Choir Builders for Growing Voices*. In addition to composing for developing choirs and guest conducting all-state/festival choirs, his scholarly interests are in the areas of multicultural and urban choral music education.

Composition, Genre, and Historical Perspective

"Jordan's Angels" is a composition that reflects both the African-American spiritual and gospel genres. It depicts the image of a child who receives solace and comfort from a vision of being surrounded by a "band of angels."

When composing this piece, I decided to incorporate the spiritual "All Night, All Day." I learned this particular spiritual as a child and I thought it would be most appropriate to integrate it with the text of "Jordan's Angels." Like many African-American spirituals, this religious folk melody represents themes of freedom, hope, and deliverance.

The African-American gospel tradition began to take shape during the early part of the twentieth century. This religious form, pioneered by musicians such as Thomas A. Dorsey (1899–1993), recognized as the "Father" of gospel music, combines African rhythms and melodic elements, with elements from the spiritual, hymnody, and the blues. Like the spiritual, gospel music (referring to "good news") inspires the singers and listeners alike, communicating a message of deliverance from earthly sorrow and strife. From a stylistic perspective, "Jordan's Angels" typifies the African-American gospel tradition through its use of a lilting 6/8 meter, close vocal harmonies, call-and-response patterns, and idiomatic chord progressions. Typical of many gospel style songs, "Jordan's Angels" includes a layered chorus (mm. 56–63) in which vocal lines enter the texture in a sequential fashion.

Musical Elements and Technical Considerations

Much of the choral music from the early gospel years (1920s–1940s) was written and performed by female ensembles, resulting in an SSA vocal texture. Similar to this early gospel music tradition, this arrangement of "Jordan's Angels" features three-part treble voices with close harmonies in parallel motion. Ensembles performing this piece should strive for a consistently even balance among the three vocal parts.

Maintaining rhythmic vitality and integrity throughout the piece is paramount. This concept is very important when performing most music rooted in the African and African-American traditions. All singers must internalize the rhythmic pulsation of the piece when rehearsing and performing. Even though the piece is written in 6/8 meter (with six eighth notes to the bar), it is probably more important to internalize a dotted eighth note pulse—thereby allowing a compound metric feel to become dominant.

The vocal lines are mainly diatonic. All vocal parts are of medium difficulty. As a means of enhancing musicianship skills, the singers should attempt to sight sing the pitches. By using solfège in the rehearsal, singers will reinforce diatonic singing, and they will also experience the following altered pitches: *te* (lowered 7th degree of the scale); *me* (lowered 3rd); *fi* (raised 4th); and *si* (raised 5th).

Vocal blend in the unison passages (mm. 8–11 and mm. 53–55) will be best achieved using two strategies. First, make sure that all vowels are unified. Second, work to develop a blend of vocal color among voice parts by asking sopranos (who typically sing brighter) to sing with a slightly darker tone and by asking the altos (who typically sing darker and heavier) to sing a bit brighter. Essentially, the soprano and alto voices should work toward a compromise—"meeting in the middle," if you will—so as to obtain a unified vocal color.

Stylistic Considerations

Vocal Tone

In general, you will find that singers in the African-American gospel tradition exhibit an expansive palette of vocal tones—from tones that are colored by pharyngeal resonance (sounding "throaty") to tones that are more forward and focused with nasal resonance ("in the mask"). Some gospel singers use the "chest" voice exclusively, to create a "belting" effect, while others employ a mixture of both "chest" and "head" voice. I often suggest that choirs comprised of younger singers use a singing tone that employs a blend of both "head" and "chest" voice ("voix mixte") so as to avoid potential vocal problems in the future. More experienced singers who are well versed in the African-American gospel tradition may choose a different approach. In my opinion, both approaches are equally valid when performing gospel music.

Tenuto Markings and Syllabic Stress

Tenuto markings serve a special purpose in the performance of gospel music. In addition to holding a note for its fullest value, tenuto markings tell the singer to sing a pitch using a slightly breathy crescendo. This process adds stress to a particular word or syllable that needs to be emphasized for dramatic effect. People have often associated the gospel style tenuto marking with a "scooping" of the pitch. To the contrary, the pitch is not necessarily "scooped." I often instruct my singers to expand or lengthen the vowel as they sing through the pitch, which creates a nuanced attack that is emotive and expressive. This vocal technique is in stark contrast to the Western Classical tradition in which singers are taught to "go straight for the vowel" when attacking a pitch.

Movement

The lilting 6/8 metric scheme of "Jordan's Angels" demands that the piece be sung with rhythmic motion. Since rhythm is the most important element in music of the African and African-American traditions, the vocal lines must have "motion." In my research, I have found that there is really no separation between music and movement when it comes to music of African origin. Beginning at measure 56 (the "special chorus"), it is appropriate for the choir to gently sway from side to side (to the dotted-eighth pulse) while performing. If the singers choose to stay still on eighth-note beats 1 and 4, optional handclaps may be added on beats 2, 3, 5, and 6.

Dialect

All of the action verbs in this piece ("comin'," "playin'," and "watchin'") are spelled without the final "g." In an effort to remain stylistically authentic and historically consistent with African-American dialect, singers should make certain that they do not pronounce the final "g."

Swinging of the Sixteenth Notes

With specific reference to this piece, people have often asked me if the sixteenth notes should be performed with a "swing." Historically, much of gospel music that is rooted in the African-American blues tradition can be performed with a buoyant swing style. Personally, I prefer that the 16th notes remain "straight." However, there is certainly latitude for interpreting the 16th notes with a modest swing.

Call and Response

Several episodes of call and response occur throughout the piece. Specifically, there are call-and-response vocals in which the respondents repeat portions of the text that have been delivered by the caller. During these instances (mm. 24–31, for example), the singers should be aware that this type of call-and-response repetition requires the responding voices to convey the text in a manner that is confirming and reassuring.

Accompaniment

The pianist should play all eighth notes with a slightly separated articulation, allowing the music to have a percussive and "soulful" groove. If the accompanist is comfortable, he or she is encouraged to improvise.

Form and Structure

This choral work, written in an ABA'C form, can be divided as follows:

Section	Measure	Event
Instrumental (piano) Introduction	m. 1	
Choral Introduction	mm. 2–7	3 phrases (2+2+2)
A section (2+2+2+2+2+2+4)	mm. 8–23	7 phrases
B section (2+2+1+1+2+2+2+4)	mm. 24–39	8 phrases
A' section (2+2+4+2+2+4)	mm. 40–55	6 phrases
C section (special chorus)	mm. 56–63	2 phrases (4+4)
Codetta	mm. 64–67	2 phrases (2+2) (using similar material from the choral introduction)

Text and Translation

Loookin' out over Jordan, all I could see:
A band of angels comin' after me.
Gabriel was playin' the trumpet,
David was playin' the harp.
Someday my soul shall be free, I shall be free.

All night, all day, the angels keep a-watchin' over me, my Lord.
All night, all day, angels watchin' over me. I shall be free.

Similar to the water images found in other spirituals ("Deep River," "I Stood on the Ribber of Jordan," "Roll Jordan, Roll," and "Wade in the Water," for example), the Jordan River symbolically represents safety, peace, and freedom. It is believed that slaves often made references to water while they sang if a planned escape was to involve crossing a creek or river as a means of covering up a trail. Although the slaves would often acknowledge the hardships and struggles in the spirituals they composed, they relied upon their faith in God and His celestial angels to guide, protect, and sustain them. As the slaves sang in the hope of one day being free, they were usually referring to both an *earthly* freedom from bondage as well as an anticipated *heavenly* freedom in the afterlife.

Additional References and Resources

Agordoh, Alexander A. *Studies in African Music*. Accra, Ghana (West Africa): Printhony Press, 1994.

Barnwell, Ysaye. *Singing in the African American Tradition*. Woodstock, NY: Homespun Tapes, Ltd, 1989.

Boyer, Horace Clarence. *The Golden Age of Gospel*. Urbana and Chicago, IL: University of Illinois Press, 1995.

Caldwell, Hansonia. *African American Music: Spirituals*. Culver City, CA: Ikro Publications, 2004.

Curtis, Marvin V. "African-American Spirituals and Gospel Music: Historical Similarities and Differences." *Choral Journal* 41, March 2001: 9–21.

Heilbut, Anthony. *The Gospel Sound: Good News and Bad Times*. New York, NY: Limelight Editions, 1997.

Newman, Richard. *Go Down Moses: Celebrating the African-American Spiritual*. New York, NY: Clarkson N. Potter, Inc., 1998.

Reagon, Bernice Johnson, ed. *We'll Understand It Better By and By: Pioneering African American Gospel Composers*. Washington, DC: Smithsonian Institution, 1992.

Smitherman, Geneva. *Talkin' and Testifyin': The Language of Black America.* Detroit, MI: Wayne State University Press, 1977.

Thomas, André J. *Way Over in Beulah Lan': Understanding and Performing the Negro Spiritual.* Dayton, OH: Heritage Music Press, 2007.

Walker, Wyatt T. *Somebody's Calling My Name: Black Sacred Music and Social Change.* Valley Forge, PA: Judson Press, 1979.

Warren, Gwendolyn Sims. *Ev'ry Time I Feel the Spirit: 101 Best-Loved Psalms, Gospel Hymns, and Spiritual Songs of the African-American Church.* New York, NY: Henry Holt and Company, 1997.

Contributed by:

Rollo A. Dilworth

Teacher Resource Guide

Measure Me Sky

James Mulholland

(b. 1935)

SSA/piano
Colla Voce: HL–202
Overall: 2
Vocal: 2
Tonal/Rhythm: 2

Composer

James Mulholland was born March 7, 1935 in Laurel, Mississippi to parents of Irish descent. Mulholland showed signs of intellectual curiosity and musical ability from a very young age, due in part to his father's love for reciting poetry and his mother's background as an amateur musician. His parents' nurturing influence may be part of what allowed Mulholland to skip both the first and third grades, and enabled him to receive music lessons during high school from five different teachers in organ, voice, piano, and composition.

At the young age of fifteen, Mulholland was hired to direct an eighty-voice church choir at the First Baptist Church in his hometown. This was the first chorus for which he composed choral music. Mulholland earned BM and MM degrees at Louisiana State University, where he studied voice, composition, and choral conducting, and he composed music for the LSU A *Cappella* Choir. Mulholland came close to receiving a doctorate at Indiana University, achieving ABD status in the area of Performance and Literature. Surprisingly, his primary studies while at Indiana were not in composition but in opera, where he performed many major roles as a baritone.

After a brief stint as Director of Choral Activities at Southwest Missouri University, Mulholland assumed his present post at Butler University, where he has taught since 1964. He served his first seventeen years at Butler as Director of Choral Activities and professor of voice, followed by a shift toward teaching composition, arranging, and music history.

Mulholland is an outspoken advocate for arts education and considers teaching to be a primary aspect of his life. He has said: "My intellectual juices are revitalized by academia. I have to teach. I have to talk about music. My reflection away from the creative process is students. I have to teach as much as I have to compose." ACDA now offers a special scholarship in Mulholland's name, intended for doctoral students pursuing degrees in choral music.

Mulholland's primary composition teacher was Samuel B. Wilson, but he also mentions Britten, Vaughan Williams, Finzi, Warlock, Ireland, and Holst as defining influences on his musical style. Mulholland is one of the most widely commissioned and performed composers living in America, with over 200 choral pieces in print. Over forty all-state choruses have programmed his music, and his compositions have been featured at ten national ACDA conventions. A full CD of his choral music performed by the Kansas City Chorale is now available entitled *Words & Music: The Music of James Mulholland.*

Composition, Genre, and Historical Perspective

"Measure Me Sky" is a modern part song composed in 1993, which rounds out a three-movement set entitled *Songs of Naiveté*, with the following order of movements:

"Reeds of Innocence"
"There Was An Old Farmer"
"Measure Me Sky"

"Measure Me Sky" had its treble choir version premiered by the Indianapolis Children's Choir and the New World Chamber Orchestra in 1992. It is also available in an SATB version as well as a fully orchestrated version.

Musical Elements and Technical Considerations

Below is a list of musical and technical issues that arise in this piece, and suggestions for how to address them.

Large melodic skips

The most memorable motive in "Measure Me Sky" occurs in the opening bars, where Mulholland displays remarkable text painting with a melodic skip of a ninth on the word "sky." Encourage your singers to keep the entire melody in their head voice, lightly dipping into a head-chest mix on the B below middle C. Another skip occurs in measures 10 and 11, up to the word "stars," and here singers will benefit from preparing the phrase as if they are starting on the highest note (E). Learn the main melodies on a neutral vowel to allow vocal freedom, as if one is singing a vocalise.

In the B section, Mulholland's opening melody on the words, "Horizon, reach out, catch at my hands, stretch me taut," spans the range of an octave and a half within three bars (mm. 37–39). This is a stunning example of text painting. When singers are invited to "stretch themselves taut," with a sense of opening their hearts and bodies upwards to the sky, this challenging melody will feel easier to sing. Mulholland's background as singer has helped him to compose melodies that are innately singable and in keys designed to minimize register transition problems.

Very few rests in the A section

The lack of rests in the A section is a powerful method of building intensity, but can pose a challenge to singers. Each new phrase needs to sound as well prepared as the first. Coach your singers to take their new breaths immediately off of the releases, in a continuous cycle of inhale–exhale. Use "relay" or "stagger" breathing for longer phrases, such as in measures 24 to 29, which Mulholland has requested be sung without communal breaths. Most of the words begin with consonants; to preserve legato, use the consonants as "pilots" into the resonance of the vowel.

Challenging piano accompaniment

Mulholland takes pride in writing challenging piano parts that are akin to orchestrations, with frequent shifts of color and intensity. The lush fullness of the piano line could lead confident pianists to overbalance the singers. Pianists should be asked to bring out important motives and to "swell" into the texture in interludes, but in the middle of sung phrases, they must listen to the chorus and be aware of the potential for balance problems. Peter Durow's dissertation about Mulholland tells of how a publisher once thought "Measure Me Sky" shouldn't be published because the piano part "could not be played." This is not the case. However, pianists need to be advised about places, such as in bars 40 through 43, where they must play the lowest octave notes first, right before the downbeat, and then use both hands to play the rest of the pitches. Mulholland's pedal markings will help pianists to maintain clarity in the texture.

Simultaneous duple/triple rhythms

Most of Mulholland's rhythms are dictated by the natural stresses of the English language. While at times the piano will be playing a duple rhythm against a triplet choral part, if singers focus on creating an authentic rise and fall to the language, there will be little confusion about how to execute rhythms correctly. Intone the text regularly in rehearsal to remind singers of the poetry and how the words must "sing."

FREQUENT OCCURRENCE OF INITIAL "W."
Words such as "world," "weight," "wings," and "width" can be tricky to sing well because singers will tend to scoop into the note. Initially, try learning the notes without the text. When they sing "w" words, be sure singers breathe in the position of the vowel that follows, and move as rapidly as possible off the "w" onto that vowel. For instance, on the word "world" in measure 56, singers will breathe as though they plan to sing the "o," and will just lightly touch the "w."

Stylistic Considerations

Mulholland has been quoted as saying: "The text and music, to me, are like parents. They are mother and father—and that is ideal. You certainly play them one off of the other very often. Sometimes you go to your mother for certain things and sometimes you go to your father for certain things. And yet I don't look at them as separate entities, I look at them as a unit." Mulholland's choice of consistently high-quality texts is doubtless part of why he is so frequently commissioned for new choral works. His melodies are singable and often sound effortless, but they are never lacking in complexity.

Most of Mulholland's choral music is accompanied, a feature that allows him to create fullness and depth in the sound (think of the effect of the piano part in his frequently performed folksong setting "O My Love's Like a Red Red Rose").

Mulholland's style could be characterized as Romantic, with long-breathed phrases, a tonal harmonic framework with expressive dissonances, and rubato designations in virtually every composition he has written. Mulholland's secular texts tend to emphasize love and the beauty of nature. He is equally at ease composing sacred music, such as his setting of the Mass entitled *Missa Romantica*.

Form and Structure

Form: A B A'

SECTION	MEASURE	EVENT AND SCORING
A section	mm. 1–4	Piano Introduction
	mm. 5–13	2 phrases (5 + 4)
	mm. 14–25	3 phrases (4 + 4 + 4)
	mm. 26–33	2 phrases (4 + 4)
	mm. 33–36	Piano Interlude (overlaps with end of choral phrase in mm. 33)

SECTION	MEASURE	EVENT AND SCORING
B section	mm. 37–39	1 phrase (3)
	mm. 40–43	transition material with imitative entrances in key of C Major
A' section	mm. 44–51	2 phrases (4 + 4)
	mm. 52–61	2 phrases (4 + 6)
	mm. 62–65	Ending phrase with two bars *a cappella* singing followed by piano closing material

Text and Translation

The text of "Measure Me Sky" appears in the poem of same title by American poet Leonara Speyer (1872–1956). in the *Bookman Anthology of Verse* (1922).

Note: There is a typo in measure 37 of the Colla Voce edition. The text reads "Horizon, reach but," and the original poem reads "Horizon, reach out."

Measure me, sky!
Tell me I reach by a song
Nearer the stars;
I have been little so long!

Weigh me, high wind!
What will your wild scales record?
Profit of pain,
Joy by the weight of a word.

Horizon, reach out,
Catch at my hands, stretch me taut,
Rim of the world; (check semi-colon)
Widen my eyes by a thought.

Sky, be my depth,
Wind, be my width and my height,
World, my heart's span;
Loneliness, wings for my flight!

Additional References and Resources

Burton, Sean. "James Mulholland: For the Love of Music." *Choral Director* August/September (2005).

Durow, Peter. *The Choral Music of James Mulholland An Analytical Study of Style*. PhD diss., Florida State University, 2007.

Thornton, T. *The Influence of Poetry Upon James Mulholland's Compositional Process and Musical Style*. DMA diss., University of Arizona, 2008.

Mulholland, James and Giselle Wyers, telephone interview, August 27, 2008.

Wine, Tom, ed. *Composers on Composing for Choir*. Chicago: GIA Publications Inc. (2007).

Contributed by:

Giselle Wyers

Teacher Resource Guide

Scarborough Fair

Mary Goetze

SSA
Boosey & Hawkes: 48004182
Overall: 2
Vocal: 2
Tonal/Rhythm: 2

Composer

Mary Goetze is an emerita faculty member of the Indiana University School of music. She created the children's chorus at IU in 1980 and conducted the group until 1995. She currently conducts the International Vocal Ensemble, which emphasizes world music, and teaches few courses, but previously, she was the chair of Music in General Studies department. Her work with children's choirs and world music has made her an internationally acclaimed and in-demand clinician, conductor, author, and arranger. Her numerous arrangements, mainly for children's or women's voices, appear in the Mary Goetze Choral Series (Boosey & Hawkes). Besides numerous articles, she has also written books and a multimedia series. She was a major author on McGraw-Hill's *Share the Music* and *Spotlight on Music* series, which are standard texts for K–6 music education. Dr. Goetze is a co-chair and co-founder of the Mountain Lake Colloquium for Teachers of Music Methods, a biannual conference for general music teachers. A graduate of Oberlin Conservatory of Music, Indiana University, and the University of Colorado, she has received several awards and honors for her impact on and teaching in the music world, including the President's Award in Recognition of Distinguished Teaching from Indiana University in 1991.

Composition, Genre, and Historical Perspective

Written in 1987, this is an arrangement of an English folk ballad; its duration is approximately 3 minutes 45 seconds. The voicing is for three-part, a cappella treble (SSA) choir. Goetze arranged this piece while teaching at Indiana University, two years after receiving her doctorate, but eight years after creating the university children's chorus. She was already a well-established arranger at this time, and had ample experience with children's choirs to employ her knowledge of what works best for the education and growth of young voices.

Musical Elements and Technical Considerations

Although the piece looks like it is in the key of E minor (natural), in reality, the folk melody is in the dorian mode (natural minor with a raised 6th). The recurring C-sharps in the music serve as evidence of this modality. For the most part, the mode appears melodically, as part of the main melody of the piece. Harmonically, natural minor seems to be more dominant. Therefore, the modality should not cause too much of a problem for the singers once they learn the scale. Use a dorian scale in a few warmups to help the singers get the feel for the mode. If the singers are adept in solfège, singing *re* to *re* diatonically delineates the dorian scale. (However, I would not recommend singing the piece itself in solfège unless you solfège on E minor and simply use an adjusted syllable for the raised 6th. Use the key signature as your guide in determining tonic.) The piece remains in E minor except for verse 4, which takes a turn to B minor. This transition, and the transition back to E minor at the end of the verse, might cause a small challenge initially, but singers can easily learn it if they understand the harmonic direction of each transition. Rehearsing with a chordal accompaniment, which reflects the modulation, while learning this transition, will quicken the process and tune the singers' ears to the changing harmonic direction.

The texture is homophonic in some verses and polyphonic in others. It is a nice piece to use for teaching children both of these textures and how to handle singing with others in each situation. The contrapuntal areas are almost exclusively two-way, only two rhythmic lines contrasting each other, even when all three voices are singing. The countermelodies are often imitative, which makes learning them easier. The three parts sing unique rhythms only in short transitional areas.

Harmonies in this arrangement are simple and often quite open. Short yet pervasive dissonances throughout the piece create a plaintive sound. Although they are blatant, for the most part the dissonances are approached melodically in stepwise motion. If the singers learn the individual lines well, the dissonances should simply occur as a result of combining those lines. Teaching the music with a horizontal approach, instead of a chord-by-chord vertical approach, may help the singers in this respect (i.e., teach individual lines/melodies, make them firm, then combine).

The dynamics of "Scarborough Fair" are subdued, as is fitting for the nature of the text. However, young voices, in an attempt to maintain this dynamic, may sing with tension and a stinted breath flow. Singers must be encouraged to approach these dynamics with an easy throat and an energized breath. Otherwise, the performance will create fatigue and will lack appropriate resonance and line.

Goetze used moderate and appropriate ranges in this arrangement; singers will easily handle the vocal aspect. As always, when the melody occurs in the lower voices (i.e., verse 4), the higher voices must be careful not to sing too loud so as to not dominate the texture.

The rhythmic content is straightforward in a gentle 3/4 meter. An eighth-note pickup (mm. 12, 69, and 95), which occurs at each appearance of the first verse text, is the only possible rhythmic difficulty since it is unique from the dominating rhythmic vocabulary of the piece.

Stylistic Considerations

A simple, folk-like tone is most appropriate for this piece; romantic resonance and vibrato would detract from the delicate dissonances and exposed lines in this arrangement. It is perfectly suited to children's voices. The singing should be gentle, legato, and relatively quiet (the loudest dynamic is *forte* and it does not last very long). Attention to proper word stress, melodic direction, and musical phrasing will help to give variety and interest to the lilting meter and prevent the overly "sing-song" feel that often bogs down songs that use a moderate three meter.

Form and Structure

The piece is strophic and uses five different verses of text. The first verse is brought back at the end.

Section	Measure	Event and Scoring
Introduction	mm. 1–4	S1, S2 duet; A counterpoint
Verse 1	mm. 5–20	(same as Intro)
Verse 2	mm. 21–36	mostly 3-part homophonic
Verse 3	mm. 37–54	S2 and A counterpoint
Verse 4	mm. 54–72	S1 and A counterpoint
Verse 5	mm. 72–87	S1, S2 duet; A counterpoint
Verse 1 again	mm. 88–103	mostly 3-part homophonic
Codetta	mm. 104–112	homophonic except for echoing, fade-out ending)

Text and Translation

There are a variety of opinions about the meaning of the phrase "parsley, sage, rosemary, and thyme," but there seems to be no conclusive data. The text itself has gone through many variants, and is still used in multiple forms. The variant used by Mary Goetze is found below.

Are you goin' to Scarborough fair?
Parsley, sage, rosemary and thyme.
Remember me to one who lives there.
She was once a true love of mine.

Bid her to make me a cambric shirt,
Parsley, sage, rosemary and thyme,
Sewn without seams or needlework,
If she would be a true love of mine.

Have him to find me an acre of land,
Parsley, sage, rosemary and thyme,
Lying between sea-foam and the sea-sand,
Or he'll not be a true love of mine.

Tell him to plough it with a lamb's horn,
Parsley, sage, rosemary and thyme,
And sew it well with one peppercorn,
Ere he be a true love of mine.

When at last he has finished his work.
Parsley, sage, rosemary and thyme.
He'll come to claim his cambric shirt,
And ever be a true love of mine.

Contributed by:

Joni Jensen

Teacher Resource Guide

The Birds

Benjamin Britten

(1913–1976)

Unison/piano accompaniment
Boosey & Hawkes: 48011406
Overall: 2
Vocal: 2
Tonal/Rhythm: 2

Composer

Benjamin Britten, a compositional prodigy of 20th century England, was born in Lowestoft, Suffolk in 1913. His mother, a gifted pianist and singer, recognized the young boy's musical potential and when Britten was six years old she began his earliest musical training with piano lessons, followed by viola lessons when he was ten. By the time the he turned fourteen, Britten had already written over a hundred opus numbers. Although most of these works remain unpublished, his juvenilia is filled with rich, early creativity.

Britten's Mozartian compositional ability caught the attention of composer Frank Bridge, who became his teacher. In 1928 Britten entered a public school called Gresham's where he became quite distraught and homesick. After completing his school certificate in 1930, he successfully applied for a scholarship to the Royal College of Music (RCM; *The Birds* was one among the several pieces that were included as part of the application) where he continued to study composition.

After winning several awards for his composition and leaving RCM, Britten wrote his first film scores. It was in 1935 that he began his friendship and collaboration with the poet W. H. Auden. In 1939, Britten sailed to Canada and later moved to New York with his partner, tenor Peter Pears.

Britten returned to Suffolk in 1942 and composed some of his most popular choral works, *Hymn to Saint Cecilia* and *Ceremony of Carols*. Among his most notable musical and professional achievements was his work toward reviving English opera, initiated by the success of *Peter Grimes* in 1945. There is much written about his obsession with the idea of loss of innocence, his love for men and boys, and his fiercely held political beliefs, especially pacifism, which is most evident in his most major choral work, the *War Requiem*, composed in 1961.

Britten's compositional style and harmonic language expanded in the 1950s as he explored dodecaphony and various non-Western musical traditions. His diverse output includes opera, choral, and orchestral works, and music for film, radio, and stage. Britten is a key figure in the development of the twentieth-century British musical tradition.

Composition, Genre, and Historical Perspective

Among his earliest published works, *The Birds* (1929) was composed during his time at Gresham's. The harmonic language of the sixteen-year-old Britten is conservatively beautiful. Not surprisingly, Britten dedicated this work to his mother, with whom he corresponded with exceptionally intimate letters during his years as a schoolboy. (See *Letters from a Life*, vol. i.) *The Birds* has long been considered his "first" song, though he wrote many unpublished songs which pre-date it. "It has the advantage of suggesting the emotional directness of childhood albeit expressed in deceptively sophisticated terms" (Johnson 21). The piece sets the text of the prominent Catholic writer Hillaire Billoc, who poeticizes the story of Jesus creating birds out of clay, a non-canonical story found in 2nd- and 3rd-century Gnostic writings and the Qu'ran. As a youth, Britten wrote a great deal of Christian-themed music that reflected his religious interests.

Technical Considerations

This work requires a very simple, almost childlike approach to the text to obtain the color that was intended by the composer. Strongly encourage your singers to use closed vowels throughout. While the text may pose religious issues for some ensembles wishing to perform the text, minor alterations to the text may allow use of the piece. The work is a stunning example of Britten at his most direct, childlike, and inward compositional self. The starkly sensitive and beautiful accompaniment adds a haunting element to the simple character of this child's view of Christmas.

Stylistic Considerations

Although the piece was composed with intentional naïveté, the choir should be careful not to sound immature. The difficulty level is definitely suited to the abilities of a children's choir. The choir should work toward not only unification of pitch throughout this unison music, but also toward unification of English diction, which can contribute to the desired light and buoyant tone. The piece is strophic and, as with any of Britten's work, the various contrasts in character, tempi, and dynamics are well marked from verse to verse. His phrasing is also clearly indicated and should be examined and followed. *The Birds* is a wonderful piece for teaching key relationships to a choir and for demonstrating how to approach various altered pitches (for example, *fi* and *si*) in modulations.

Even at a young age, Britten demonstrated a gift for setting the English language to music. Point out to the choir examples of his trouble-free prosody and careful treatment of the text. For instance, by ending each phrase with suspended dominant harmonies, he reflects both the soaring of the birds and the soaring of the "soul to Paradise" as unresolved chords hang at the cadences.

Form and Structure

The Birds is strophic.

Section	Measure	Event and Scoring
Intro	1–2	Piano introduces simple, child-like accompaniment.
Verse 1	3–10 (2+2, 2+2)	The unison voices sing in E Major (last measures modulate up a major third to A♭ Major).
Verse 2	11–17 (2+2, 2+1)	Voices sing embellished melody in new key and modulate up another major third to C major in the last two bars.
Bridge	18–21 (2+2)	The C major climax of the piece occurs on the Latin text "Tu creasti Domine," with a sudden *esultante* burst of vocal line and 16th note movement in the accompaniment.
Verse 3	22–28 (2+2, 1+2)	Final prayerful, introspective verse in C major occurs with a return to E major in the final two measures.

SECTION	MEASURE	EVENT AND SCORING
Coda	29–30	The closing two measures of staccato piano evokes small hands carefully negotiating the keyboard.

Text and Translation

When Jesus Christ was four years old,
The angels brought Him toys of gold,
Which no man ever had bought or sold.

And yet with these He would not play.
He made Him small fowl out of clay,
And blessed them till they flew away.

Tu creasti, Domine.
Jesus Christ, Thou child so wise,
Bless mine hands and fill mine eyes,
And bring my soul to Paradise.

Text: Hillaire Billoc

Suggested Listening

James Jordan, Conductor:
The Voices of Anam Cara, track 12. Angels in the Architecture (GIA ChoralWorks Series). GIA CD-837.

Additional Resources

Britten, Benjamin. *Letters from a Life: The Selected Letters and Diaries of Benjamin Britten, 1913–1976*. Ed. Donald Mitchell and Philip Reed. Berkeley: University of California, 1991.

Cooke, Mervin, ed. *The Cambridge Companion to Benjamin Britten*. Cambridge, UK: Cambridge University Press, 1999.

Evans, Peter. *The Music of Benjamin Britten*. London: J. M. Dent & Sons, 1979.

Johnson, Graham. *Britten, Voice, & Piano: Lectures on the Vocal Music of Benjamin Britten*. Aldershot, UK: Ashgate, 2003.

Contributed by:

Richard Hutton

Teacher Resource Guide

Weep No More

David Childs

(b. 1969)

SSA/piano
Santa Barbara Music: SBMP 249
Overall: 2
Vocal: 2
Tonal/Rhythm: 2

Composer

David Childs is Associate Professor of Choral Studies at the Blair School of Music, Vanderbilt University, Nashville, Tennessee where he teaches symphonic and chamber choirs, Collegium Vocale, conducting, and choral methods. A native of New Zealand, he completed a Bachelor of music degree from Canterbury University, Christchurch, in musicology, theory, harmony, and composition. In 1993 he attended the Florida State University where he completed a M.M. in conducting. Childs then returned to New Zealand, where he taught high school general and choral music. In 1999 he returned to the United States and earned a D.M.A. in conducting at Louisiana State University. In 2000 he was appointed assistant professor at the Blair School of Music. He is married to Lesley French Childs, who is a talented singer and surgical resident in otolaryngology. Childs' many choral compositions are published by Santa Barbara Music Publishing Company, Alliance Music Publications, Inc., and Walton Music.

Composition, Genre, and Historical Perspective

Weep No More is a setting of the first stanza of a John Keats poem Fairy's Song. The work was composed in 1998 for Havelock North High School's Voix de Femmes, a newly-formed select women's choir in New Zealand. At the time I was selecting repertoire for the New Zealand equivalent of contest or festival, which was actually more of a choral competition. The top twenty choirs in the country were selected to compete for gold, silver, and bronze awards. In their first year of existence, Voix de Femmes won gold, silver, and bronze medals. This work is dedicated to a friend and colleague, Meryn, with whom I taught high school music in New Plymouth, New Zealand before I moved to the other coast. The composition grew out of a haunting sixteenth-note pattern that I one day shaped at the keyboard. From there the work gradually took form, whereby it maintained the wistful sixteenth notes (known in New Zealand as a semi-quavers) in all but eighteen measures of the work.

Despite the title, there is a bittersweet beauty to the work; it instructs one to be hopeful, expectant, and positive, but this is difficult to do in a predominantly minor key! The tonality does change to a more positive A major at the critical line: Dry your eyes—O dry your eyes, but this does not last. The overall mood of Weep is intentionally somber and melancholic—intending to reach to the core of the soul and to stir up emotions. However, we can be morose for only so long! The most important themes that should be drawn from the piece are optimism and anticipation; a sincere belief that life situations change for the better. Many believe that, even in death, "life" situations change for the better. (This was a widely held belief during Keats's lifetime and earlier, when many citizens lived in miserable and atrocious living conditions, and looked forward to the afterlife).

Musical Elements and Technical Considerations

One of the most difficult challenges in a successful performance of this work is to accurately tune the opening section. Partly because the second altos are set so low and also because of the unusual shift from the tonic (F-sharp minor) to a flatted supertonic major chord (G major) in measure 6 (complicated by a 4-3 suspension in the sopranos), attaining stable intonation has proved a great challenge for many—including myself. Measures 9 to 12 tend to flatten quite considerably; it is essential that the singers understand the size of each interval, and that they maintain good breath support throughout this long phrase. Encouraging them to "imagine" the falling notes of the phrase (and also tied or repeated notes) as "rising," may help them hold pitch. Imagery and breath/technical instruction should be supplied by the director as necessary at these critical junctures.

Care should be taken to avoid eliding the "-re" of "more" into the "O" in measures 37 to 44. A small glottal stop or attack is encouraged. The same is true in measures 45 to 52 with the words "eyes/O" and "For/I." Avoid "eye/zo" and "Foh/rye" at all costs. At measure 37 consider leaning into the "Weep" (there is a tenuto marking below each of the notes), and also shape the phrase dynamically. There is a tendency to keep all three iterations of "Weep no more" the same. Consider a slight crescendo into each succeeding "weep" before diminishing in sound on the long five-count note after the third statement. Measure 45 should be buoyant, full-toned, and vibrant—in stark contrast to the preceding music. It may be necessary to change the balance of voices between sopranos and altos in measures 49 to 53, where the parts enter in imitation. Feel free to divide the soprano and alto lines of music sections into equally balanced sections of soprano and alto voices on top, and soprano and alto voices reading the second line of music. This should also be a consideration when the music splits three ways in measure 68. Here there is a directive in the music to "divide into three equal parts."

Stylistic Considerations

An overall feeling of legato should be maintained throughout the work. Despite the use of much textual repetition and subsequent punctuation (i.e., measures 37 to 44), care should be taken in deciding when to breathe, as this will disrupt the flow. The tenuto markings should be interpreted as providing gentle emphasis to the notes, not accents. They should therefore be prepared—in both directions—with softly tapered dynamics. It is suggested that a full, round tone be maintained throughout, even in the instances of soft singing. Avoid a breathy quality at all costs. An effective use of dynamics (that do not appear in the score) is to begin the final choral section at measure 60 softly (say mp or p), and then taper off at measure 64 (half a dynamic softer), and again at measure 68—a tiered dynamic effect. The accompaniment is much more challenging than it appears at first glance. It is imperative that rhythmic integrity be maintained at all times; there should be no rubato or other alterations of tempo until the final page. The right hand should be played with a light touch; the left hand should present the melodic interest when apparent (i.e., the opening four measures, which anticipate the soprano melody).

Form and Structure

This work loosely resembles a rondo form (there are variations of these, such as ABA, ABACA, ABACABA), whereby the A material begins and concludes the work, and appears in the middle of the composition as well. The overall structure can divided as follows:

SECTION	MEASURE	EVENT AND SCORING
Introduction:	mm. 1–4	(comprising two phrases). This anticipates A.
A	mm. 5–12	(primary material); then repeated in mm. 13-20
A'	mm. 21–28	(secondary material based on A)
Transition/Bridge	mm. 29–36	(new material that has harmonic roots in Introduction)
B	mm. 37–44	(derived from A)
C	mm. 45–59	(new material, centered around the key of A major)
B	mm. 60–71	(material from 37–44 but further expanded)
Transition/Bridge	mm. 72–79	(based on mm. 29–36)
Coda	mm. 80–85	(uses material from Introduction and based on A)

Text

Fairyís Song by John Keats, English, 1795–1821

Shed no tear—O shed no tear!
The flower will bloom another year.
Weep no more—O weep no more!
Young buds sleep in the rootís white core.
Dry your eyes—O dry your eyes,
For I was taught in Paradise
To ease my breast of melodies—
    Shed no tear.

Overhead—look overhead
íMong the blossoms white and red—
Look up, look up—I flutter now
On this flush pomegranate bough—
See me—ítis this silvery bill
Ever cures the good manís ill—
Shed no tear—O shed no tear!
The flower will bloom another year.
Adieu—Adieu—I fly, adieu,
I vanish in the heavenís blue—
    Adieu, Adieu!

Recordings

Santa Barbara Music Publishing CD 8—Octavos 4, performed by the Haltom High School, Haltom City, TX, Amy Allibon, conductor.

Contributed by:

David N. Childs

Teacher Resource Guide

Yo Le Canto Todo El Dia

David Brunner

(b. 1953)

SATB/piano
Boosey & Hawkes: 48004679
Overall: 2
Vocal: 2
Tonal/Rhythm: 2

Composer

David L. Brunner is one of today's most active and versatile composers and conductors. He is Professor of Music and Director of Choral Activities at the University of Central Florida in Orlando and is well known for his compelling work with singers of all ages, conducting All-State and regional honor choirs in over thirty states at the elementary, middle, and high school levels.

As an inspired teacher, he is also a popular clinician at choral festivals and educational workshops throughout North America and Europe, including the American Choral Directors Association, Music Educators National Conference, and American Guild of Organists; the Association of British Choral Directors and the Kodály Societies of Canada and Australia; the International Cathedral Music Festival at Salisbury and Canterbury; the International Honor Band and Choir Festival at the Hague and Brussels; and the Choral Music Experience International Institute for Choral Teacher Education in England, Scotland, and Wales.

Brunner is an imaginative composer who has received numerous ASCAP awards and in 2000, joined a prestigious group of American composers when he was named Raymond W. Brock Commissioned Composer by the American

Choral Directors Association. He has over one hundred publications in print and forthcoming, over eighty-five works written on commission, and is represented on over forty recordings. The *New York Times* has noted him as a "prolific choral writer whose name figures prominently on national repertory lists." His music has been performed and recorded worldwide in venues such as Royal Festival and Queen Elizabeth Halls in London, Canterbury Cathedral, Disney Concert Hall in Los Angeles, EPCOT, and Carnegie Hall.

Dr. Brunner received his BME at Illinois Wesleyan University, an MM in Conducting at Northwestern University, and the DMA in Choral Literature and Conducting at the University of Illinois. He has served on the editorial board for *The Choral Journal*, is the author of articles in both *The Choral Journal* and *Music Educators Journal*, and is a contributing author to *The Choral Director's Cookbook: Insights and Inspired Recipes for Beginners and Experts* (A. J. Gumm, *ed.* Galesville, MD: Meredith Music Publications, 2006). His works are published by Boosey & Hawkes, Inc.

Composition, Genre, and Historical Perspective

Yo Le Canto Todo El Dia was commissioned by the Miami Children's Chorus and premiered in Miami on May 19, 1996, conducted by Timothy A. Sharp. A performance by the Children's Honor Choir, conducted by Anton Armstrong at the national American Choral Directors Association (ACDA) convention in San Antonio happened the following year. Two years later, an SATB version followed the original version for two-part treble voices. The work has appealed to a wide variety of singers of all ages and abilities.

Although many of my works tend to be melodically oriented, lyrical, thoughtful, and reflective, there are also works that have a strong rhythmic focus and are angular and bold. *Yo Le Canto Todo El Dia* is certainly one of these!

Musical Elements and Technical Considerations

Many choirs have performed this piece quite successfully, and with great enthusiasm. The ranges are comfortable and melodic contours lie well in the voice. The sectional form and repetition of musical ideas facilitate both learning and memorization. The technical demands center mostly on rhythmic ideas, particularly the clear articulation of both rhythm and language.

Here are some suggestions for rehearsal and performance:

- The singing should be "forward" in the mouth, with a brighter, rather than darker, quality.

- As in all my works, the construction of phrases and rhythmic ideas are closely tied to the natural rhythm and accentuation of the spoken text, so it should "sing as it speaks." The language shapes the rhythm. Feel the syllables of emphasis and shape the phrase to enhance this text inflection. The *la* (mm. 37–39 and elsewhere) section should be light, bright, and forward: on the tip of the tongue. There may be instances where the emphasis seems to be more in the middle of the measure rather than on the downbeat (e.g., mm. 33–36), and shaping the phrase in this way will add interest and forward momentum.

- Elided syllables (e.g., *do el* in m. 27, *y a* in m. 34, and *y e* in m. 36) move quickly to the second syllable.

- The melodies are playful in character and should be sung with buoyancy. Sing with light-hearted energy.

- The flavor of this piece is inspired by Latin music—highly rhythmic and characterized by dotted, syncopated, and triplet rhythms. The singing style should clearly and precisely delineate the rhythms and have a dance-like quality. Enjoy the angular nature of the syncopations!

- The triplets are an important feature of the rhythm and should never be rushed. Allow the triplet grouping some space. The final note in the figure *Yo le can-TOH* has been shortened in the SATB publication from a quarter note to an eighth note—an exclamatory release I like—and should be utilized in the SA version as well.

- Clapping should be precise—crisp, bright, and together!

- There is a sense of forward momentum, moving often toward words of emphasis or importance. Be careful, however, not to rush.

- Although the musical ideas are rather short, they are often linked together to form longer phrases. The B section (mm. 33–42) is a good example. Make this section flow by observing the dotted (no break) lines and carrying through with breath energy.

- The rather virtuosic piano part should be clear and fairly dry, so use pedal sparingly. The piano is an important partner to the voices and should interact in a way that provides a strong rhythmic sense, a steady pulse, and stylistic inflection.

Stylistic Considerations

I first heard the text of this piece sung to a different tune by a solo singer in a group of world percussionists. The intensely rhythmic nature of that ensemble was a strong influence for my writing. Though there was not a conscious effort to imitate a specific tradition or style of Latin music, the character and vitality is apparent. The performance suggestions in the preceding paragraphs will enable singers to identify stylistic traits and connect with them in their bodies and singing voices.

Form and Structure

The piece is built from short melodic ideas—each with a distinctive rhythm—that are combined to form larger contours, often by means of repetition or sequence. These phrases are arranged to form larger sections, which I'll call A and B. Section A is comprised of three short ideas: "a" (the broad two-measure phrase *Ya me voy de Corazon* repeated for the words *ya me voy con un tambor*), "b" (an angular, more rhythmic two-measure idea, again repeated), and "c" (the triplet exclamation *Yo le canto!* that is also repeated). The B section is constructed in a similar fashion: "d" presents the text in a more active rhythm that combines both syncopated features and triplets, essentially a one-measure idea descending sequentially. This is followed by a repeat of "d" on a *la* syllable (let's call it d^1), followed by "e," a longer and rhythmically altered version of the *Yo le canto!* exclamation. The large sections appear several times, usually with an asymmetrical number of measures, due to the varied length of the shorter melodic ideas, and the piece proceeds as follows. The first and second presentations of section A are ten measures long (4 measures + 4 measures + 2 measures). The third appearance of A omits the "a" material, so is only six measures long. B is ten measures long when it first appears (4 + 4 + 2) and eleven measures the second time because the "e" motive is repeated (4 + 4 + 3). The piano introduction is eight measures long, with subsequent interludes of four and eight measures, incorporating material from the introduction. A four-measure coda based on the "c" motive ("*Yo le canto!*") closes the piece. An overview of the form looks like this:

SECTION	MEASURE	EVENT AND SCORING
Introduction	(mm. 1–8)	[8]
A (abc)	(mm. 9–18)	[10] (4+4+2)
Interlude	(mm. 19–22)	[4] piano
A (abc)	(mm. 23–32)	[10] (4+4+2)
B (dd^1e)	(mm. 33–42)	[10] (4+4+2)
A (bc)	(mm. 43–48)	[6] (4+2)
B (dd^1e)	(mm. 49–59)	[11] (4+4+3)

Section	Measure	Event and Scoring
Interlude	(mm. 60–67)	[8] piano
Coda (c)	(mm. 68–71)	[4]

Text and Translation

The Spanish text translates as follows:

So I am moving with my heart,
So I am leaving with a drum,
I sing to you all day long
  With affection and joy,
So I am leaving with a drum
  With affection and emotion.

Although I have often heard performances where *yo* and *ya* are sung with a "j" sound, I prefer the harder "d a" pronunciation, as was suggested by a student singer of mine from Venezuela. He said that would be more prevalent in everyday speech and I like the rhythmic bite it provides.

Contributed by:

David Brunner

Teacher Resource Guide

Back to Ethiopia

arr. Paul Rardin

(b. 1965)

TTBB/a cappella
Santa Barbara Music: SBMP 155
Overall: 2
Vocal: 2
Tonal/Rhythm: 2

Arranger

Paul Rardin is associate director of choirs at the University of Michigan, where he teaches undergraduate conducting and conducts the Men's Glee Club and University Choir. He taught previously at Towson University in Towson, Maryland, where for twelve years he served as director of choirs.

Rardin is a graduate of Williams College and the University of Michigan, where he received the M.M. in composition and the D.M.A. in conducting. He has studied conducting with Theodore Morrison, Jerry Blackstone, and Gustav Meier, and composition with Leslie Bassett, George Wilson, and Robert Suderburg. His settings of spirituals and folk songs are published by Santa Barbara Music Publishing.

Composition, Genre, and Historical Perspective

According to Olive Lewin, "Back to Ethiopia" is a Rastafarian song, "an expression of longing for the country [the singers] regard as home." For many, this country was Ethiopia, whence thousands of slaves were brought to Jamaica first under Spanish rule (beginning 1494) and then British rule (beginning

1655). Lewin asserts that slavery "continued to flourish until the nineteenth century" and that, as of 1973, Afro-Jamaicans constituted more than 90 percent of the Jamaican population.

Lewin expounds on the Rastafarian tradition: "True Rastafarians are deeply religious and lean in varying degrees toward the beliefs of the Coptic or Ethiopian Orthodox Churches. Some revere Haile Selassie[1]* of Ethiopia as a god—others consider him one of Jahweh's chosen prophets, but all Rastafarians consider Ethiopia their homeland." It is little wonder that the piece bears numerous similarities to the African-American spiritual, another genre characterized by texts that describe longing for another place (usually heaven, with the secret meaning of the northern states).

Musical Elements and Technical Considerations

Pitch and Rhythm

Singers should find that pitches and rhythms of this arrangement honor the simplicity of the original tune. Only in two brief passages does the harmony require accidentals outside D Major. Gentle syncopations occur in the verse and refrain and repeat throughout. Releases on eighth rests during the "oh, yes" refrain should always be at or below the prevailing dynamic. Choirs selecting faster tempos may consider putting the final "s" on beat 4 rather than on the "-and" of beat 4. The 4th-beat "father" (m. 57) and subsequent syncopation (m. 59) are perhaps the only areas in which the intermediate choir may need repeated rehearsal.

Tone and Onset

As mentioned, "Back to Ethiopia" shares numerous attributes with the African-American spiritual: the text plaintively longs for a different place; the "verses" in the verse-and-refrain structure are merely repetitions of a single line of text; and the melody suggests very slow harmonic rhythm. We might consider this piece a Jamaican equivalent of the African-American spiritual. Sometimes considered African-America's classical music (where Gospel would be its popular cousin), the spiritual invites us to use our best classical sound: low breath, lifted soft palate, and tall, rich vowels. This is especially important in the *forte* section, measures 52 through 59, when singers may initially sing too heavily in chest register in higher tessituras.

With the refrain "oh, yes," conductors face the challenge of achieving rhythmically precise entrances on a vowel, and should consider practicing

1 Haile Selassie, whose birth name was Ras Tafari Makonnen, was emperor of Ethiopia from 1930–1974. The Rastafarian movement, a "messianic religio-political movement" (*Concise Oxford Dictionary of World Religions*) was founded by Marcus Garvey in the Jamaican slums in the 1920s and claims over one million members worldwide. The current arrangement of "Back to Ethiopia" omits the second verse, which reads "Haile Selassie is our God an' King."

balanced onset during warm-up exercises. Balanced onset refers to the way singers bring the vocal folds together to produce sound; overactive adductor muscles will produce an accented, belted onset, while underactive adductors will produce a breathy, unsupported onset. Choirs can achieve balanced, rhythmically unified onset by initiating vowels with an added, inaudible "h" before the beat. Rehearse "oh" as is, then ask singers to begin with an audible "h" before the beat ("hoh"), then to use the same "h" but inaudibly. The effect should be one of the choir sneaking in rather than stepping in.

Line

Choirs should give primary focus to a beautiful, sustained legato; this may indeed prove to be the greatest challenge to the choir. The metronome marking of quarter note = 72 should be considered flexible, with smaller ensembles selecting a faster tempo and larger ensembles taking a noticeably slower tempo (perhaps in the 50s).

Conductors should consider stamina-building breathing exercises in preparing this piece. These might include daily, timed exhalations after a full intake of air (these exhalations should increase in duration throughout the rehearsal schedule); singing the piece on a pitched lip trill (lips buzzing together); and warm-up scale patterns repeated until singers run out of air. In addition, conductors should encourage *physical movement* during sustained notes that will remind singers to continue their breath support lest the tone lose its core. Such movement might include "fishing" (casting imaginary fishing rod high and long through the duration of the pitch), "tug of war" (pulling on an imaginary rope to mirror conductor), and pulling an imaginary string forward from the forehead.

Intonation

Divisi events occur in a total of 13 measures and should present minimal challenge melodically. The conductor should listen for audibility of the melody and the bass part at all times. The re-harmonization of "oh, yes" in each of the three verses presents a wonderful intonation exercise; each time, the F-sharp of the melody should predominate slightly in the chord, and should be equally high at every iteration in order to ensure good intonation in the changing chord around it. Conductors might want to experiment with which F-sharp sounds "highest" and most in tune: measure 17 (as the third in a D-major chord), measure 35 (fifth in a B-minor chord), and measure 62 (root of an F-sharp major chord).

The *forte* in the climactic section should not come at the expense of good intonation, particularly from the tenors initially and then baritones as they leap to D-natural in measure 56. Remember Robert Shaw's rule of dynamics: "Never louder than lovely."

Stylistic Considerations

There is very little to this piece that does not meet the eye. The choir that sings this piece with excellent breath support, tall vowels, and beautiful tone will largely capture the essence of this simple but haunting tune.

Conductors should ask for a warm and rich tone, one that resonates fully throughout the face, mouth, and throat. The sound will need enough brightness to stay in tune (ask for "mask" resonance by having the choir sing the piece on an "ng" combination) but should otherwise have warmth (ask the choir to "coax" their sound to the back of the mouth by having singers move a free hand by the side of their face, from the front of the mouth to the back of the throat).

Conductors should encourage dynamic motion through the long-held notes (subtle crescendo–diminuendos are especially welcome on the text "oh, yes"), and should ensure that dynamics are kept below *mezzo-piano* until the climactic crescendo beginning in measure 48.

The words "back" and "lan'" should have a very tall, vertical vowel (think more British than American), as should the first syllable in the word "Africa."

Form And Structure

Section	Measure	Event and Scoring (length of phrases)
Introduction	mm. 1–10	first iteration of "oh, yes" refrain (4+6)
Verse 1	mm. 11–27	tenor I melody, refrain, prolonged repeat of refrain (6+4+7)
Verse 2	mm. 28–42	tenor I melody, refrain (re-harmonized), repeat of refrain (6+1+4+4)
Bridge	mm. 43–51	new harmonization of refrain (4+5)
Verse 3	mm. 52–69	baritone melody, refrain, repeat of refrain (8+2+4+4)
Coda	mm. 70–76	final iteration of refrain (7)

Text

Take me back to Ethiopia lan', take me back to Ethiopia lan'.
Take me back to Ethiopia lan', O yes Rastafari, O yes.

Wan go back to Ethiopia lan', wan go back to Ethiopia lan',
Wan go back to Ethiopia lan', O yes Rastafari, O yes.*

Africa is our father's home, Africa is our father's home,
Africa is our father's home, O yes Rastafari, O yes.

*The original text substitutes "wan go back" for "take us back" for strains 2 and 3. Omitted verse reads:
"Haile Selassie is our God an' King, Haile Selassie is our God an' king,
Haile Selassie is our God an' King, O yes Rastafari, O yes."

Additional References and Resources

Religion Facts, "Rastafari," http://www.religionfacts.com/a-z-religion-index/rastafarianism.htm#1

Lewin, Olive. *Forty Folk Songs of Jamaica*. Washington, DC: General Secretariat of American States, 1973.

Bowker, John, ed. *Concise Oxford Dictionary of World Religions*. New York: Oxford University Press, 2000.

Contributed by:

Paul Rardin

Teacher Resource Guide

Byker Hill

arr. Mitchell Sandler

TTBB
Hinshaw Music: 1448
Overall: 2
Vocal: 2
Tonal/Rhythm: 2

Arranger

Bass/baritone Mitchell Sandler studied music at the University of California at Berkeley, and completed a secondary study of Baroque Music Performance Practice at the Royal Conservatory in The Hague, Netherlands. Prior to his study in The Hague, Sandler was a member of the internationally known men's chorus Chanticleer. He has been in Holland since 1989 and has performed as a soloist with leading European conductors of early music, the Netherlands Opera, Ton Koopman's Amsterdam Baroque Choir, the Netherlands Radio Chorus, and is a founding member of the vocal quartet with piano, Song Circle.

Composition, Genre, and Historical Perspective

The text and melody of "Byker Hill" need to be discussed separately in order to completely understand the history of the song. The text is native to Northeast England and the melody is found in the shape-note style of the early United States folk hymn tradition.

The text is representative of the mining song folk ballad of Northumberland, England. In the foreword to *Northumbrian Minstrelsy* A. L. Lloyd wrote: "The heart of Northumbria is the country of the river Tyne.... Moreover, it is the only part of England with a local music-dialect in which certain of its melodies are distinct from the tunes of any other region. Nor is the folk song of this area all of a piece; it is as varied as the landscape itself." "Byker Hill" stays true to that tradition of variance as the stanzas are found in a variety of forms, one such variation, dated 1812, John Bell listed the text as "Walker Pits" in his book, *Rhymes of Northern Bards*. A. L. Lloyd lists the same text in 1952 in the book, *Come All Ye Bold Miners*, albeit with minor changes of contractions and spelling. The third stanza is found in the ballad text of "Elsie Marley," which is the story of its namesake, an innkeeper's wife, who caught fever; to cool down she went out into a field and ended up falling into and drowning in a coal pit full of water. Maxine Baker recorded the song in 1965 and included the fourth stanza referencing Geordie Johnson's, rather than Geordie Tarlton's, pig, and after the pig was hit with a shovel it danced a jig all the way to Byker Hill, rather than to Walker Shore. The folk tradition was and continues to be an oral tradition and so derivation from, and variation of, the original form is common.

The Irish and Northumbrian melodies that are associated with any parts of this text are: "Off She Goes," a jig in a major key, "Elsie Marley," a jig in mixolydian, and "Dorrington Lads," a slip jig in major. Sandler set an adaptation of "The Hebrew Children," which is published in the *White & King Sacred Harp*. The *Denson Revision of the Sacred Harp* (1966) lists the minister Peter Cartwright as having composed the tune sometime between 1820 and 1825 although he had used the tune in camp meetings prior to its notation. The original title was "Where Now Are the Hebrew Children?" a phrase that is repeated three times followed by the answer. During the camp meetings it was common for a congregation or group of vocalists to improvise new texts for continuous singing.

Musical Elements and Technical Considerations

"Byker Hill" is a fun and energetic strophic mining song that has an attractive Dorian melody. Constant quarter notes, in a driving 4/4 rhythm, reflect the difficult work of the miners in the coal pits. The arrangement is homorhythmic and provides excellent opportunities for acquiring skill in large leaps for the bass section. Spending time during voice building that concentrates on defining leaps, such as solfège or numbers, will help prepare the bass section for singing this jumping line successfully. Using solfège to navigate the melody of this Dorian tune will give singers an opportunity to identify with the note relationships in a different way, and will increase singers' modal vocabulary.

Tenor 2 and Baritone sections will get the opportunity to work on linear/horizontal part independence due to the part crossing at measure 3 (Bass and Tenor 2), and in measures 11 through 14, 16, and 18 (Baritone and Tenor 2). Experiment with standing arrangements so that each section is in its own circle and can hear their fellow singers louder than the ensemble until they feel confident and stable. Test for independence by using a standing arrangement that incorporates the sections whose parts cross: an example would be to arrange the Bass and Tenor 2 in one circle and rehearse through measure 3.

This arrangement follows the typical voicing of *The Sacred Harp* in that an inner voice sings the melody throughout, in this case, Tenor 2. Singers with harmonic parts should be sure that they can hear the melody at all times, being sensitive to the low tessitura of the Tenor 2 melody.

Time should be spent defining the foreign words that relate to Northeastern English Mining, as singers are most likely unfamiliar with them. Once the singers have an understanding of what is being communicated, they can use the text to deduce the following: Where would this text be sung? Why are they singing those particular texts? Who would sing the song and why?

Stylistic Considerations

Geographically, Ireland and Northumberland are relatively close and their music traditions have shared forms such as jigs, ballads, and melodies. Their music most likely had similar performance practices as well; when you listen to the Chanticleer recording you will notice how Celtic it sounds. Chanticleer frequently elaborates on the melodic line by including nonharmonic tones such as accented lower neighbors, especially on the opening Dorian tonic (*re*), which reinforces the Dorian mode.

Singers of folk music frequently improvise within the structure of the melody, so experiment with elements of improvisation by changing the texture, adding notes to the melody, or by changing some rhythms to reflect the natural rhythmic inflection of the text.

Form and Structure

This song is strophic with alternations of verse and refrain in a homo-rhythmic texture. The arrangement was written for Chanticleer, however, the notated version and the recording differ a great deal, the differences are detailed below. Even when the notated texture and recording texture match, Chanticleer does employ liberties outside of the vocal score in their voice leading.

Section	Phrase	Voicing	Chanticleer Voicing
Verse 1	(4+4)	TTB	Unison Melody T2
Refrain	(4+4)	TTB	TTB
Verse 2	(4+4)	TTBB	TTBB

SECTION	PHRASE	VOICING	CHANTICLEER VOICING
Refrain	(4+4)	TTB	TTB
Verse 3	(4+4)	TTBB	T2B1
Refrain	(4+4)	TTB	TTB
Verse 4	(4+4)	TTBB	2 part Improvisation
Refrain	(4+4)	TTB	TTB
Verse 5	(4+4)	TTBB	TTBB
Refrain	(4+4)	TTB	TTB

The definitive Chanticleer recording adds the following to the end:

Verse 1	(4+4)	Beginning *pp* with cresendo into the chorus
Refrain	(4+4)	Claps are added on beat 1 of each measure and on beat 4 of the fourth measure of the phrase, which reinforces the cadence.

Text

If I had another penny,
I would have another Jill*,
I would pay the piper play me the
Bonny lass of Byker Hill.

Refrain
Byker Hill and Walker Shore,
Collier* lads forever more,
Byker Hill and Walker Shore,
Collier lads forever more.

When first I came down to the dirt,
I had no trousers, no pit shirt.
Now I've gotten two or three,
Oh, Walker Pit's done well by me.

The pitman* and the keel* man Trin,
They don't drink bumbo* made from gin,
Then to dance they do begin,
To the tune of Elsie Marley.

Geordie Tarlton he had a pig,
He hit it with a shovel and it danced a jig.
All the way to Walker Shore,
To the tune of Elsie Marley.

Gentle Jenny she's behind the barn,
With a pint of ale underneath her arm.
A pint of ale underneath her arm,
And she feeds it to the baby.

*Definitions

Jill (Gill): A measure of capacity, one fourth of a pint. In context, a quantity of ale.

Collier: One in the business of digging, transporting, or dealing in coal.

Pitman: A man who works in the mining pit.

Keel: A barge or lighter, used on the Tyne River for carrying coal from Newcastle.

Bumbo: A pint of beer with a shot of spirits, usually gin.

Additional References and Resources

Bell, John, ed., *Rhymes of Northern Bards*. Newcastle: Frank Graham, 1812. Reprint, 1971.

Brown, Theron, and Hezekiah Butterworth. *The Story of the Hymns and Tunes*. New York: George H. Doran, 1906.

Bruce, J. Collingwood, and John Stokoe, ed., *Northumbrian Minstrelsy: A Collection of the Ballads, Melodies, and Small-Pipe Tunes of Northumbria*. Newcastle-Upon-Tyne: Society of Antiquaries, 1882. Reprint, Hatboro, PA: Folklore Associates, Inc., 1965.

Dawney, Michael, ed., *Doon the Wagon Way: Mining Songs from the North of England*. London: Stainer & Bell, 1973.

Lloyd, A. L., ed., *Come All Ye Bold Miners: Ballads and Songs of the Coalfields*. London: Lawrence & Wishart, 1952.

Stokoe, John, ed., *Songs and Ballads of Northern England*. Darby, PA: Norwood Editions, 1973.

White, B. F. *Original Sacred Harp (Denson Revision)*. Cullman, AL: Sacred Harp Publishing, 1966.

White, B. F. *The Sacred Harp*. Facsimile of 1859 3rd ed. Nashville, TN: Broadman Press, 1968.

Web sites:

The La-Primavera Ensemble: www.la-primavera.nl/engligh/mitchell.htm (accessed August 15, 2008)

The People's Dictionary: www.dictionary.co.uk (accessed August 15, 2008)

The Session: www.thesession.org (accessed August 15, 2008)

Suggested Listening

Byker Hill, *Chanticleer The Anniversary Album 1978-1988*. Chanticleer, CR-8801.

Contributed by:

Christopher S. Owen

Teacher Resource Guide

Flanders Fields

Roger Emerson

TTB/piano
Hal Leonard: 8741443
Overall: 2
Vocal: 2
Tonal/Rhythm: 2

Composer

Known for creating "songs kids love to sing," composer Roger Emerson is one of the most widely performed choral composers and arrangers in America today. He has published hundreds of pieces with over 15-million copies in circulation. His works have been performed at the Kennedy Center, the White House, and Carnegie Hall. A frequent lecturer on popular choral music, Emerson has addressed many major music education organizations, including MENC. Emerson earned a degree in music education from Southern Oregon University and has taught in both the public schools and at the College of the Siskiyous in Northern California, where he concluded his teaching career. Emerson now devotes all of his time to composing, arranging, and consulting. "In Flanders Fields" was created in collaboration with fellow composer and founder of America Sings, John Jacobson.

Composition, Genre, and Historical Perspective

Flanders, a former county on the North Sea, has been the scene of war and strife throughout the centuries. Emerson's "In Flanders Fields" is a lovely and simple setting of a 1915 poem of the same title written by Dr. John McCrae (1872–1918). McCrae was a poet and a surgeon, and he served as a medical officer in the Canadian Army. "In Flanders Fields" is the sole work by which McCrae is remembered; it commemorates the thousands of men who died in a terrible battle in the Ypres salient in the spring of 1915.

Musical Elements and Technical Considerations

This is a great teaching piece"for young or inexperienced ensembles. Though it does not present many technical challenges for the conductor or singers, it affords an opportunity for young students to learn about many musical concepts. For example, with their instructor's guidance, students will learn how to beautifully shape a phrase, work to achieve dynamic contrast, and execute suspension–resolutions with care. The texture varies throughout, with unison, two-part, and three-part textures all represented. Emerson does not call for any one section to sing alone; this is a wonderful thing for young choirs that are small, with singers who might be apprehensive. The higher tessitura of the refrain might pose difficulties for some young tenors and baritones. This presents teachers with another pedagogical opportunity, as they continue to work with their students on how to properly and healthily execute these phrases.

Stylistic Considerations

Emerson's stylistic markings indicate that the piece should be sung pensively with rubato. The first verse may be sung in unison or as a solo, if desired. Verse 2 is marked *mezzo forte* and verse 3 is *forte*, per Emerson's dynamic markings. Within the specified dynamics, it is important that phrases are sung with direction and intention. If each phrase is sung identically, the piece will not be communicative.

Conductors will need to make decisions with regard to the fermatas; Emerson writes fermatas at many of the phrase endings. If one is too indulgent, and holds these for a substantial amount of time, it can severely interrupt the overall flow and momentum of the piece. It is my feeling that the music is best served if most of them are thought of as very slight pauses.

Finally, it is of utmost importance that teachers spend time discussing the text with their students, and of course, the circumstances under which the poem was created. Emerson and Jacobson offer the following words regarding the importance and poignancy of McCrae's poem.

> On Veterans or Remembrance Days in North America we often wear a poppy blossom on our lapel to salute our fallen warriors. This beautiful gesture was encouraged by the vivid words of Dr. McCrae's poem. From the intrepid battlefields of Gettysburg and Bull Run, Europe and the

Pacific, Korea, Vietnam, the Persian Gulf and all of the battles before and after, we do our best to remember the sacrifice of others who protected our dreams and realities. Lest we forget, *In Flanders Fields* will be there to remind us.

Form and Structure

Emerson's strophic setting of the text is guided by the structure of McCrae's three-stanza poem. Sung after verses two and three, then repeated a third time as a close, the refrain uses text from the final lines of stanzas two and three.

SECTION	MEASURE	PHASE STRUCTURE
Introduction	1–4	(2+2)
Verse 1	5–13	(4+4)
Verse 2	14–21	(4+4)
Refrain	22–26	(2+2)
Verse 3	27–34	(4+4)
Refrain	35–38	(2+2)
Refrain	39–44	(2+3)

Text

The Arlington National Cemetery Web site offers the following information regarding the creation of McCrae's "In Flanders Fields."

> A young friend and former student [of McCrae's], Lieut. Alexis Helmer of Ottawa, had been killed by a shell burst on 2 May 1915. Lieutenant Helmer was buried later that day in the little cemetery outside McCrae's dressing station, and McCrae had performed the funeral ceremony in the absence of the chaplain. The next day, sitting on the back of an ambulance parked near the dressing station beside the Canal de l'Yser, just a few hundred yards north of Ypres, McCrae vented his anguish by composing a poem. The major was no stranger to writing, having authored several medical texts besides dabbling in poetry. In the nearby cemetery, McCrae could see the wild poppies that sprang up in the ditches in that part of Europe, and he spent twenty minutes of precious rest time scribbling fifteen lines of verse in a notebook...it [the poem] was very nearly not published. Dissatisfied with it, McCrae tossed the poem away, but a fellow officer retrieved it and sent it to newspapers in England. *The Spectator*, in London, rejected it, but *Punch* published it on 8 December 1915.

In Flanders fields the poppies blow
Between the crosses, row on row,
That mark our place; and in the sky
The larks, still bravely singing, fly
Scarce heard amid the guns below.

We are the Dead. Short days ago
We lived, felt dawn, saw sunset glow,
Loved and were loved, and now we lie
In Flanders fields.

Take up your quarrel with the foe:
To you from failing hands we throw
The torch; be yours to hold it high.
If ye break faith with us who die
We shall not sleep, though poppies grow
In Flanders fields.

—Dr. John McCrae

Additional References and Resources

"Biography." Roger Emerson Music. http://rogeremerson.com/ (accessed August 30, 2008).

"In Flanders Fields." Arlington National Cemetery. http://www.arlingtoncemetery.net/flanders.htm (accessed August 30, 2008).

"John Jacobson: Music Educator, Choreographer, Presidential Point of Light." http://www.johnjacobson.com/index_music.shtml (accessed August 30, 2008).

Contributed by:

Bradley Miller

Teacher Resource Guide

How Can I Keep from Singing

arr. Bradley Ellingboe
(b. 1958)

TBB/piano and oboe
Neil A. Kjos: 5572
Overall: 2
Vocal: 2
Tonal/Rhythm: 2

Composer

Bradley Ellingboe is a native of Lakeville, Minnesota. He graduated from Saint Olaf College with a degree in music theory and composition, and sang in the Saint Olaf Choir under Kenneth Jennings. He holds degrees in vocal performance and in choral conducting from the Eastman School of Music, studying with Jan DeGaetani, Donald Neuen, Sam Adler, and Alfred Mann. Ellingboe has done additional study at the University of Oslo, the Aspen Music Festival, and the Vatican. Since 1985 he has been on the faculty of the University of New Mexico, where he is Professor of Music and Director of Choral Activities.

Ellingboe is well known as a composer and arranger of choral music, with over 100 pieces in print. His music has been recorded by the Harvard Glee Club, the Saint Olaf Choir, Philip Brunelle's VocalEssence, Craig Hella Johnson's Conspirare, the Santa Fe Desert Chorale, and choirs from Luther College and the University of Michigan, among many others. He regularly serves as a guest conductor for festival choruses in the United States and abroad. In 2007, Ellingboe was named *Maestro del Coro* for the Tuscia Opera

Festival in Viterbo, Italy. He made his Carnegie Hall conducting debut in 2008. An expert in the vocal music of Scandinavia, Ellingboe was knighted by King Harald VII of Norway in 1994.

Composition, Genre, and Historical Perspective

In the mid-1990s, a member of my church choir suggested I write an arrangement for men's chorus of this beloved hymn. At that time I did not know the piece, but he very helpfully gave me a copy of it taken from a "fake book" that had only the melody line and suggested chordal accompaniment.

It turned out that this source was inaccurate on two counts. First, it listed the piece as "traditional American." (I have also seen the hymn attributed to both the Quakers and the Shakers.) As I later found out, the hymn was, of course, written in the 1860s by the American Baptist minister Robert Lowry. Second, this version had eliminated many of the most Christian features of Lowry's text. This re-wording was in keeping with the way Pete Seeger popularized the song during the folk revival of the 1960s.

The idea to make a choral arrangement of "How Can I Keep from Singing?" lay dormant for a few years, until I was invited to conduct the Florida ACDA Male Honor Choir in 1997 and I decided to prepare something special for my visit. Since that time I have also arranged the piece for SATB and SSA choruses.

Musical Elements and Technical Considerations

This arrangement is for 3-part men's chorus, divided TBB. However, (and here I am presuming an ensemble that is fairly balanced between tenors and basses) rather than having all the tenors on the top part and then dividing the basses in two, I suggest dividing the men equally among the three lines and even perhaps adding a few more voices to the bass 2 part. When the piece divides into four parts, arrange the men into four equal parts. This means that some of the inner voices will switch between tenor 2 and baritone in order to achieve a good balance.

The piece opens with a solo oboe line. Oboe is one of my favorite instruments. When it is played well, the oboe, as with the cello, comes closest to approximating the human voice. If possible, get an excellent oboist to play. Encourage the player to "sing" through the instrument and allow him or her to use a goodly amount of rubato.

The opening line for the chorus should be sung legatissimo with only a bit of vibrato and in imitation of the oboist's musicality. I deeply love chant and the unison lines should be sung as smoothly and placidly as one of those ancient melodies.

Please note that when played on the piano, the opening choral line is a single pitch, which then divides into three. All things being equal, when played on the piano the three tones will sound louder than the one tone. But in a choir, a unison sung by all the men is now divided into three parts and will sound softer, unless the crescendo in measure 7 is observed. Therefore, the crescendo is not so much an expressive device as a technical one seeking to counteract the weakened sound that often occurs when an ensemble goes from unison into parts.

Although it is not written anywhere, I have a tendency to go slightly faster and use more marcato whenever the refrain "No storm can shake my inmost calm...," first found in measures 13 to 18, is sung. This seems to me to be a natural response to the strong affirmation of the text in that spot. Indeed, even Lowry's tune is more martial in character there than in the opening lyrical phrases. Measure 19 is transitional, moving back into the legato character of the opening and setting up the entrance of the piano. This alternation between legato and marcato should be observed in later stanzas as well.

The piano's right hand echoes the opening theme of the oboe and should follow the oboe's phrasing and rubato to the extent possible. When the text describes the "music ringing" and the "echo," the piano subtly reinforces this idea in measure 25 and again in measure 42.

Stylistic Considerations

The alternation between legato and marcato mentioned above is, by nature, both technical and stylistic. The interplay between the two articulation styles should be embraced. The singers should be encouraged to make the words come alive by singing the meanings and not just the notes.

I proceeded from the assumption that this hymn, when sung in its normal congregational setting, would tend to be marcato throughout. However, as a choral piece that would feel a little relentless, so as an arranger I marked the piece *legato*. To put it another way, I assumed that singers who already knew this hymn would tend to sing it marcato, so I tried to emphasize the lyrical features of the tune. Yet it must be said that to sing this entire piece in a legato manner would be just as uninteresting as to sing it entirely marcato.

Form and Structure

The piece is a hymn arrangement and therefore strophic. The introduction, interludes, and coda are apparent. There are two extensions, one in measures 44 and 45, and one in measures 55 to 57, for the sake of variety.

Text and Translation

Only after the piece was published did I learn that this was not an American folk hymn, but rather entirely the work of Robert Lowry. By then the piece had been published in all three voicings and had sold tens of thousands of copies.

The biggest divergence between the text as I first learned it and Lowry's original, is found in my arrangement between measures 39 and 58. owry's text reads as follows:

What though my joys and comforts die?
The Lord my Savior liveth:
What though the darkness gather 'round!
Songs in the night he giveth:
No storm can shake my inmost calm
While to that refuge clinging;
Since Christ is Lord of heaven and earth,
How can I keep from singing?

In the last ten years, Lowry's hymn has seen a resurgence in popularity, finding its way once again into many new hymnals, missals, and supplements. In that time I have received letters complaining that I watered down Lowry's text to make the piece more palatable for secular choirs. As explained in the opening paragraphs, it was not my intention to subvert the original, but was simply ignorance on my part. The changes came from receiving faulty source material at the outset. I am grateful that both school and church choirs find this piece to be useful and attractive, and I encourage choirs to consider using the original or my text, as the situation warrants.

Contributed by:

Bradley Ellingboe

Teacher Resource Guide

Streets of Laredo

Timothy C. Takach

Unison with TBB solo/piano
Graphite Publishing: GP T-006
Overall: 2
Vocal: 2
Tonal/Rhythm: 2

Composer

Timothy C. Takach has received a number of commissions from various organizations including the St. Olaf Choir, Cantus, the Bowling Green State University Men's Chorus, The Singers: Minnesota Choral Artists, The Young New Yorker's Chorus, the Appleton North High School Varsity Men's Chorus, and the Western Michigan University Chorale. His compositions have been heard on NPR and have been recorded by various groups in North America. The *Washington Post* said of one his works, "the gorgeous part-song harmonies never obscured the text, making the lyrics an equal partner to the music." Takach graduated with honors from St. Olaf College, Northfield, Minnesota in 2000 with a BA in Music Theory/Composition and a BA in Studio Art. He sings with and was a co-founder of the professional male vocal ensemble, Cantus. In his work with Cantus, Tim clinics thousands of students across the country each year. He effectively and passionately conveys small but important fundamental ideas about music making both as an ensemble and as an individual singer; his contagious enthusiasm encourages young singers to commit to their art and to keep singing. As a singer, Takach gives over eighty concerts a year and has had his works performed in concert halls across the United States, Canada, and Europe. Takach lives in Minneapolis, Minnesota.

Composition, Genre, and Historical Perspective

As a composer, I spend most of my time writing original works. When I'm asked to do an arrangement, I always try to bring something new to the piece. This typically includes new countermelodies that can be sung concurrently with the original melody, meter changes to accent word stress and narrative connotation, and an updated look at a familiar tune.

"The Streets of Laredo" is a traditional American folk song, and when I was commissioned by Jayne Windnagel to write an arrangement of it for the Children's Choir of the Church of St. Michael, the beautiful melody was an easy inspiration. The original ballad is called "The Cowboy's Lament," and contains no less than eleven verses. The song has been recorded by Johnny Cash (he sang eight verses), Marty Robbins (five verses), the Smothers Brothers (two...um...altered verses) and many others. The ballad includes the line: "Go gather around you a crowd of young cowboys, And tell them the story of this my sad fate." Although I didn't include this verse, it certainly sets the scene of the story and the voicing in my arrangement mirrors the narrative. Since I originally wrote the unison line for a children's choir, it carries with it the innocence of those young cowboys, and the men's voices assume the role of our tragic hero.

Musical Elements and Technical Considerations

One of the main challenges in rehearsing and performing "The Streets of Laredo" will be to find a good balance between the unison voices and the men's choir. The piece can be done with many different combinations of voicing—unison children's choir with TBB trio, solo with TBB choir, SATB choir with unison SA and TBB divisi—and each combination will provide it's own unique set of challenges. The end goal for any combination of voices is to make sure that the melody comes shining through in every verse, and that the supportive lines never obstruct the story, as they could, for example, in measures 28 to 35.

In measures 40 to 43, I ask the baritones to sing high and to use a light head voice. If needed, feel free to add a few tenors to help that high D stay light and in tune, but have them blend their color toward the baritones' sound. Those versatile tenors would complete the baritone line in measure 43 and then go back to the tenor line at the downbeat of measure 44.

Starting in measure 43, the men get their own *a cappella* section. This verse can be tricky harmonically for some singers. I would suggest rehearsing the men separately on this section, and simultaneously work with the unison voices (especially if they are learning the part by rote) to rehearse the rhythmic changes in measures 73 to 89, which are different from the other three verses. For the men's *a cappella* verse in measures 43 to 62, experiment with rubato and work toward committed, emotionally charged singing. Some rubato happens naturally with the change in time signature at measure 49, but be sure to take your time and enjoy that moment as it cadences in measure 50. Conversely, don't lose any steam in measure 58 and press on to the end of the phrase in measures 61 and 62. The ensuing piano part should take its energy from the men.

In measures 62 to 73, the piano part must stay strong and in tempo. In measure 73, have the pianist bring out the high D so the unison voices can hear their starting pitch. It's an easy one to lose during the preceding measures. The piano provides the melody of the fife in verse 4, measures 93 to 100. Don't be afraid to bring this out of the texture. I wrote the melody high so it won't conflict with the vocal ranges. The piano returns to its original motive in measure 101, so let it resume the role of supporting and balancing the voices.

Stylistic Considerations

In this piece, as well as all folk songs, the narrative is essential. Encourage your singers to really dig into the characters and to sing the words, not just the notes. Musically, find legato in the phrases, and keep the phrases energized through the long melodic lines. It is easy for the singers to punch the quarter notes separately instead of keeping them all part of one musical gesture.

Form and Structure

Section	Measure	Event and Scoring
Introduction	mm. 1–8	piano
Verse 1	mm. 9–24	unison voices
Interlude	mm. 23–26	piano
Verse 2	mm. 28–43	unison voices with TBB support
Interlude	mm. 43–46	TBB *a cappella*
Verse 3	mm. 47–62	TBB *a cappella*
Interlude	mm. 62–73	piano
Verse 4	mm. 74-89	unison voices and TBB
Interlude	mm. 89–92	piano
Verse 5	mm. 93–109	unison voices and TBB
Tag	mm. 108–114	piano

Text and Translation

As I walked out in the streets of Laredo,
As I walked out in Laredo one day,
I spied a poor cowboy wrapped up in white linen,
Wrapped up in white linen as cold as the clay.

"I see by your outfit that you are a cowboy,"
These words he did say as I boldly stepped by.
"Come sit down beside me and hear my sad story;
I was shot in the breast and I know I must die.

"Get six jolly cowboys to carry my coffin;
Get six pretty maidens to bear up my pall.
Put bunches of roses all over my coffin,
Put roses to deaden the clods as they fall.

"Go bring me a cup, a cup of cold water,
To cool my parched lips," the cowboy said;
Before I turned, the spirit had left him
And gone to its Giver, -- the cowboy was dead.

We beat the drum slowly and played the fife lowly,
And bitterly wept as we bore him along;
For we all loved our comrade, so brave, young, and handsome,
We all loved our comrade although he'd done wrong.
~*Anonymous*

Contributed by:

Tim Takach

Level 3

Mixed voices:

Ave Maria Dett, Robert Nathaniel...267
Hodie Whitbourn, James...271
In Remembrance Ames, Jeffery L....275
"In Splendoribus Sanctorum" from *The Strathclyde Motets* MacMillan, James...281
Jesu dulcis memoria de Victoria, Tomás Luis...285
Lebenslust Schubert, Franz...291
Magnificent Horses Ling-Tam, Jing...297
O vos Omnes Casals, Pablo...301
Oremus Sisask, Urmas...305
Pater, Noster Stravinsky, Igor...309
Prayer Before Sleep Robinovitch, Sid...315
Psalm 100 Jauchzet dem Herrn Mendelssohn, Felix...321
Revoici venir du Printemps Le Jeune, Claude...327
Sir Christèmas Mathias, William...333
The Water Is Wide Paulus, Stephen...339
This We Know Jeffers, Ron...345
To the Mothers of Brazil: Salve Regina Jansson, Lars/arr. Eriksson, Gunnar...349
We Shall Walk through the Valley Moore, Undine Smith...355

Treble voices:

Magnificat in A minor Porpora, Nicola...361
Vus vet zayn Hatfield, Stephen...371

Men's voices:

Greater Love Chatman, Stephen...375

Teacher Resource Guide

Ave Maria

Robert Nathaniel Dett

(1882–1943)

SATB with baritone solo
Hinshaw Music: HMC333
Overall: 3
Vocal: 4
Tonal/Rhythm: 3

Composer

Robert Nathaniel Dett (commonly known as R. Nathaniel Dett) was born on October 11, 1882 in Drummondsville, Ontario. He began formal piano instruction at the age of 5, eventually taking lessons ay the Lockport Conservatory and then at the Oberlin Conservatory of Music. He received his Bachelor of Music degree with honors in composition and piano from Oberlin in 1908 and began touring as a concert pianist. After brief stints as a professor at Lane College in Tennessee and at the Lincoln Institute in Jefferson City, Missouri, he became the director of music at the Hampton Institute in Virginia in 1913, a post he held until 1932. During his tenure at that traditionally African American institution he founded the Hampton Institute choir, the Hampton Choral Union, and the Musical Arts Society; he also served as the president of the National Association of Negro Musicians from 1924–1926.

Dett continued his studies throughout his life, attending different summer institutes, including Harvard in 1920 and 1921 and the Fontainebleau School of Music under Nadia Boulanger in 1929. He eventually earned his master's degree from Harvard in 1932, having already been granted an honorary doctorate from Oberlin in 1926. At Harvard, he won two awards; the Francis Boot Award for his choral composition *Don't Be Weary, Traveler*, and the Bowdoin Prize for his essay "The Emancipation of Negro Music."

After leaving the Hampton Institute, he was Visiting Director of Music at Bennett College in Greensboro, North Carolina from 1937 to 1942. He was serving as a choral advisor to the United Service Organization when he died of a heart attack while on tour with a choir in Battle Creek, Michigan on October 2, 1943.

Composition, Genre, and Historical Perspective

R. Nathaniel Dett published approximately a hundred pieces, mainly for piano, solo voice, and choir. His choral compositions include two major works: the extended motet *Chariot Jubilee* and the oratorio *The Ordering of Moses*, both of which use African-American spirituals as their main thematic material. A hallmark of Dett's compositions is his ability to combine a neo-Romantic compositional style with the spiritual, a technique seen most often in his earlier compositions. In addition to numerous piano compositions, he also compiled two collections of spirituals: *Religious Folk-Songs of the Negro as Sung at Hampton Institute* and *The Dett Collection of Negro Spirituals*.

Dett's *Ave Maria* is a short (three-and-a-half minute) through-composed piece for SATB choir and baritone solo, set to the text of the traditional Latin prayer. In the G. Schirmer edition (now held by Hinshaw) an English text is included under the Latin, but that text is certainly not a singing translation of the Latin—it is instead freely written prose that does not even attempt a singing translation of the original Latin. While the piece does not employ melodic material from a spiritual, it most certainly exemplifies Dett's neo-Romantic style. This can be seen in the tempo indications, for example, the opening indication for *Molto moderato e con espressione*, the numerous dynamic markings, and other indications, such as *ritard* and *con espressivo*; the harmonies as well, are full and rich with numerous (albeit brief) chromatic passages.

Technical Considerations

Several issues will present challenges to even the most accomplished choral groups when rehearsing and performing the *Ave Maria*. The overall tessitura for all the vocal parts is relatively low: sopranos have numerous middle Cs and the D directly above, and altos sing mainly at the bottom part of the staff (or below—including several low Gs), and their highest note is B above middle C, which occurs only once in measure 11. The tenor line requires several low Cs and Ds and is elsewhere primarily in the center of the staff; the basses sing notes that do not rise out of the bass clef (nothing higher than A below middle C, which only occurs on two occasions) and they sing several low Es and Fs (and a low D in measure 16 and a low C in measure 31—however, *ossia* notes are provided an octave above in those two instances). This being said, the tenors do have a high G in measures 10 and 11, and the sopranos have one high A in measure 38. The overall low tessitura makes for a fairly dark sound; this, combined with the fact that the piece is written in F major, will make maintaining proper intonation a significant challenge for the choir. To offset the inevitable dark sound of the piece, the director might encourage the choir to sing with a tone and vowel formations that are fairly bright and forward; certainly, the director should discourage a covered sound from the choir.

Rhythmically the piece is not difficult, as it is comprised primarily of half, quarter, and eighth notes, and is for the most part homophonic. However, the melodic lines of each individual voice part will on occasion be challenging. While the melodies move mainly in stepwise motion, larger leaps must be negotiated at times, and there are numerous examples chromatic accidentals that must be sung with extremely accurate intonation. Examples of larger leaps occur most often in the tenor and bass lines, for example, measures 3 and 4 in the tenor line (a fifth upward followed immediately by a tritone downward), a skip of a seventh up to a high G in the tenor line in measure 10, the bass line in measures 11 and 12 (a skip of a sixth downward followed immediately by a seventh upward), a seventh downward in the tenor line in measure 15—and numerous other examples. The conductor should sing through each line individually before beginning the rehearsal process; it will become readily apparent where the lines are relatively disjointed. Examples where chromatic accuracy is important are also plentiful, including measures 6 through 8 in the alto line (C–B natural–B-flat–G–A–B-flat), the bass line in measures 6 and 7 (A-natural–A-flat–G–A-natural–B-flat–C), the alto line in measures 12 and 13 (D–C-sharp–D–C-natural–B-natural–C), and others. Once again, by singing through each part individually, the conductor should be able to identify problematic passages.

The baritone solo appears in the last nine measures of the piece. It is mainly a chant on A below middle C on the text *Ave Maria, gratia plena, ora pro nobis peccatoribus, in hora mortis nostrae,* with the choir holding chords under the soloist. The final six measures are metered *Amen* statements by the choir and soloist.

While the solo is certainly accessible to any male singer, some individual work might need to be done in order to obtain the effect desired by the conductor. It should also be noted that the final series of chords in the choir will need special attention with regard to tuning, as they are set low in the voice and are fairly chromatic in nature. The ending three measures are interesting, as the tenors hold a high F—a fourth above the sopranos on middle C. Rescoring so that only tenors who are capable of floating out that note on a *pianissimo* sing it and having the remaining tenors sing the optional C below middle C given in the bass line, might be a judicious choice to end the piece.

Stylistic Considerations

As stated before, Dett has written the *Ave Maria* in a neo-Romantic style, so a Romantic style of singing should be stressed. Encourage the choir to attend to dynamic indications, be flexible in the rhythmic pulse with rubato, and create long, sustained phrases with a rich and full tone. Of special note is the fact that Dett was known for extreme dynamics when conducting his own choirs, so a wide range of dynamics should be especially emphasized. Although the sopranos should predominate the texture for the most part, there are short passages in the lower voices that should emerge from the texture on occasion, as they are of more melodic and/or rhythmic interest.

Form and Structure

Ave Maria is through composed and revolves mainly around the primary key of F major; even so, there are a fair number of secondary dominant and borrowed chords. Sections can be easily divided into 4-bar phrases, but many times those shorter phrases can and should be combined to create 8- or even 12-bar phrases. Definite cadential points occur in bars 8, 16, 32, and 41, but the conductor should exercise his or her own best judgment as to the combination of phrases elsewhere.

Text

Ave Maria, gratia plena, Dominus tecum;
benedicta tu in mulieribus, et benedictus fructus ventris tui, Jesus.
Sancta Maria, Mater Dei, ora pro nobis peccatoribus,
nunc et in hora mortis nostrae. Amen.

Hail Mary, full of grace, the Lord is with thee;
blessed art thou among women, and blessed is the fruit of thy womb, Jesus.
Holy Mary, Mother of God, pray for us sinners,
now and at the hour of our death. Amen.

Contributed by:

David Scholz

Teacher Resource Guide

Hodie

James Whitbourn

(b. 1963)

SATB with soprano solo/organ
Encore Publications
Overall: 3
Vocal: 4
Tonal/Rhythm: 3

Composer

James Whitbourn is a versatile composer with an international reputation for choral music and music for film, television and concert hall. After studying music at Oxford University, he began his career as a BBC producer. His compositional output has been influenced by that background and is admired for its direct connection with performers and audiences worldwide. His largest composition is the concert-length choral work, *Annelies*, which sets words from The Diary of Anne Frank, and which was premiered by Leonard Slatkin at London's Cadogan Hall in 2005. The chamber version of the work for piano trio and choir was commissioned and premiered by the Westminster Williamson Voices of Westminster Choir College, James Jordan, Conductor.

James Whitbourn's choral works have been performed on every inhabited continent in the world, especially the *Son of God Mass*, which is regularly performed throughout the United States, Europe and other parts of the world. His Film and TV work includes the lush orchestral score for the BBC landmark series Son of God, together with music for 9/11, the Cenotaph and the Queen Mother's funeral. Artists who have performed and broadcast Whitbourn's music include Katherine Jenkins, Daniel Hope, Arianna Zukerman,

BBC Philharmonic and the choirs of King's College Cambridge and Westminster Abbey.

It should be noted that another major work, *Luminosity*, written in 2008, was written for an unusual combination of choir and dancers, and was conceived as a visual counterpoint to the music. The work was commissioned and premiered by the Westminster Williamson Voices, James Jordan, conductor, the Blair Academy Choir, William Hammer Conductor, the violist Daniel Stewart and the Archedream Blacklight Dance Theater.[1]

Composition, Genre, and Historical Perspective

In the liner notes of the recording *James Whitbourn: A finer truth*, the composer states:

> *Hodie*, like the *Mystery of Love*, is the result of a collaboration with my friend Robert Tear. The words were written on 5 June 1999, during a trip to Hong Kong; it was set to music a few days later. The music, after its slow introduction, becomes a lively dance, reflecting the original meaning of the word "carol" (Fr. *Carole* = round dance). The exuberance of *Hodie* affirms the Divine gift of Love which was present on the first Christmas Day.

Technical and Stylistic Considerations

This exciting work presents challenges for both the choir and the organist. The work is very approachable by most levels of choirs, but a great deal of care must be taken when teaching the tenor and alto parts. The alto line has some intervallic and harmonic challenges for the singers. It is suggested that (1) the alto and tenor be rehearsed together and (2) that the work be rehearsed very slowly on a neutral syllable to work out the quickly moving harmonic rhythm as well as the rhythmic character of the piece. It is highly recommended that closed vowels be used throughout to enable better intonation. In the piano sections of the work, *forte* consonants should be emphasized to maintain the rhythmic character of the work.

Form and Structure

The first stanza of the poem is used as the main theme of the piece and recurs regularly like a refrain or as a rondo-like form. After the slow introduction, the dance-like section is grouped in a 4-bar phrase structure combined with an irregular phrasing of the instrumental ritornello. The harmonic language is largely modal with mixtures of mixolydian, dorian, and often with lydian and phrygian inflection.

1 Source: http://www.jameswhitbourn.com/#/about/shortbiography

Section	Measure	Event and Scoring	Key Area
Intro	mm. 1–11		G
Stanza 1	mm. 12–14	3; instrumental ritornello	G
	mm.15–18	4	
	mm. 19–22	4	
Stanza 2	mm. 23–26	4	D
	mm. 27–30	4	
Stanza 3	mm. 31–32	2; instrumental ritornello	G
	mm. 33–36	4	
	mm. 37–40	4	
Stanza 1	mm. 41–44	4	D
	mm. 45–48	4	
Stanza 4	mm. 49–53	4	E–D–A
	mm. 54–57	4	
Stanza 5	mm. 58–61	4	D
	mm. 62–65	4	
Stanza 6	mm. 65–70	6; instrumental ritornello	G
	mm. 71–74	4	
	mm. 75–78	4	
Stanza 7	mm. 79–82	4; = Stanza 1	D
	mm. 83–86	4	
Coda	mm. 86–87	2; instrumental ritornello	G
	mm. 88–89	2	
	mm. 90–91	2	
	mm. 92–100	9(3+1+1+4)	
	mm. 101–103	3	

Text

By Robert Tear (b. 1939)

Hodie Christus natus est.
The holy child is born.
In his LOVE man's hope does rest
On this eternal morn.

Cherubs with trumpets shatter the starts.
Seraphs touch their strings.
Saints, angels, choirs are massed
The Word seeds the heaven in rings.

In a blessed stable a picture is seen.
Parents, Jesus there.
An ass looking on, an ox beaming
At the best hay of the year.

The wise men are no longer wise:
God in his crib has bewildered them.
They place their gifts around the sides.
Kneel and pray. Adore him.

Yet in this joy is sensed a shadow,
An intimation of loss.
A ghostly fear of a dark tomorrow
With thorns and a heavy cross.

But now the heavens spin fast around,
It's jubilation day,
Infinity's ears are whipped by sound,
Would this day so stay.

Hodie Christus natus est.
The holy child is born.
In his LOVE man's hope does rest
On this eternal morn.

Suggested Listening

James Whitbourn: Luminosity. Matthew Berry, conductor, performed by Commodio. Naxos 8.572103 ("Luminosity" plus other motets by Whitbourn).

James Whitbourn: A finer truth. Timothy Brown, conductor, performed by Clare College Choir Cambridge. Et Cetera KTC 1248

Angels in the Architecture. James Jordan, conductor, performed by The Voices of Anam Cara. GIA CD-836

Web site:

http://www.jameswhitbourn.com

Contributed by:

K. Steve Kim

Teacher Resource Guide

In Remembrance

Jeffery Ames

(b. 1969)

SATB/piano and horn
Walton Music: 8501547
Overall: 3
Vocal: 3
Tonal/Rhythm: 3

Composer

Jeffery L. Ames serves as Director of Choral Activities at Belmont University in Nashville, Tennessee. His prior appointments include Assistant Director of Choral Activities at Baylor University and Director of Choral Activities at Edgewater High School and Lincoln High School in Florida.

As a choral clinician, Ames has conducted senior and junior high school mixed and male choirs at the state and regional conventions of the American Choral Directors Association and the Music Educator's National Conference, including the inaugural Florida Male All-State Chorus. He has performed internationally in Italy and Costa Rica. An accomplished accompanist, he has performed with well-known conductors such as André Thomas, Allen Crowell, Jo-Michael Scheibe, Lynne Gackle, Bradley Ellingboe, and most recently with Anton Armstrong and the Texas All-State Mixed Choir.

Ames's reputation as a distinguished and well-respected composer and arranger is growing and his music has been premiered by the Florida Music Educators Association, the Florida American Choral Directors Association, the Southern Division of ACDA, the National ACDA Conference in Los Angeles, and the National ACDA Conference in Miami.

Ames holds the PhD in Choral Conducting/Choral Music Education and a master's degree in Choral Music Education from Florida State University, and a Bachelor of Music degree with at double major in Vocal Performance and Piano Accompanying from James Madison University. He is the first recipient of the ACDA James Mulholland Choral Music Fellowship.

Composition, Genre, and Historical Perspective

> *In Remembrance* may be described as "a piece that goes deep into the heart…a piece that heals, comforts and gives a voice to those feelings we all have when we experience adversity in our lives."
>
> – Mary Ellen Loose

This anthem is in response to the tragic accident that took the lives of Dr. William (Bill) Potts and his two daughters, Becca and Anna, on July 4, 2002. Bill was a choral parent and Becca was one of my students during my tenure as Director of Choral Activities at Lincoln High School in Tallahassee, Florida. This piece is written in their memory and dedicated to the surviving members of the immediate family: Jayne, wife and mother; Elisabeth, eldest daughter and sister; Jason, Elisabeth's husband, and Will, son and brother.

Musical Elements and Technical Considerations

In Remembrance is a moving work filled with lush harmonies, a sonorous climax, and an abundance of text painting. Overall, the anthem requires long, connected phrases. Envision "bowing" long notes within the musical line.

Introduction

The peaceful introductory material found in measures 1 to 6 calls for an effective balance within the tenor and bass sections. The cascading passage on "Domine" must be approached with a light vocal mechanism in order to avoid intonation issues. This passage may be viewed as God coming down to earth for humankind, or God extending His hand to humankind.

Section A

Careful balance is needed for the unison melody found in measures 6 to 9. Just as the cascading passage found in the introductory material is viewed as God coming down to humankind, the P4 and P5 leaps in measures 6 and 8 may be viewed as humankind's attempt to reach up to God. A change in the harmonic structure begins in measure 14. The dissonance found in the alto line in measures 15 to 18 is a "point of interest" within the phrase. This part of the phrase contains the key element that begins the harmonic and emotional shift in the work. The horn solo in measures 19 to 23 is also an integral part in setting the mood.

Section B

The soprano and alto melody in measures 23 to 30 may be viewed as a prayer to God for graciousness as they sing of their heart-felt pain and despair. The treble melody may also be interpreted as a plea to the tenors and basses for graciousness. The tenor and bass entrance in measure 31 may join the communal prayer to God, or perhaps be interpreted as a plea to the sopranos and altos for comfort. The slurred articulation on the word "distress" builds tension, and the horn entrance at measure 39 helps to make an effective crescendo leading into the climax of the piece.

Section C

The voice leading in measure 40 distinguishes measures 41 to 48 as the ultimate despairing moment of the anthem. This section requires a sonorous tone, filled with emotion, from the entire ensemble.

The soprano and alto duet at measure 48 calls for a sense of hopelessness and is most effective if the slurred articulation is strictly followed. The tenor and bass lines in measures 49 to 52 should function as a seamless, solid harmonic foundation. A different mood emerges in measures 53 to 59. Here, the harmonic and rhythmic structure found in the piano accompaniment offers a sense of hope and optimism. A slight ritardando is effective in measure 56. The "light" chord needs to shimmer with energy, without vibrato, to portray a sunrise cresting over a mountain range. A true *mezzo di voce* is essential to the text painting. Lastly, the horn cadenza is written to be performed freely and plaintively.

A reprise of the introductory material functions as a transition to a recapitulation of the main theme. However, the unison treatment on the word "Domine" in measures 73 to 75 may be interpreted as one's acceptance to the tragedy, or may be compared to the sovereignty of God.

Coda

The coda, which begins in measure 76, brings a message of reassurance and is performed in *recitativo* style allowing a deeper impact upon the listener/performer. In measures 78 and 79, the descending line found in the alto and bass parts is the "point of interest" and should lead the crescendo for the ensemble. Within these two measures, the image of the dearly departed returning to the earth is brought to life. The final chords in measures 80 to 83 contain suspensions and end on an F major chord with an added 2nd scale degree wanting to "rest forevermore."

Stylistic Considerations

In Remembrance is to be performed in a romantic style and the conductor should determine how much rubato to use.

Form and Structure

SECTION	MEASURE	EVENT AND SCORING
Introduction	mm. 1–6	freely composed; F major (TTBB)
A Section	mm. 6–14	(SATB)
Transition	mm. 15–22	with dissonance leading to relative minor
B Section	mm. 23–39	D minor (SA & SATB)
C Section	mm. 40–59	D minor and N^6 (SATB & SA)
Transition	mm. 60–61	with horn cadenza
Abbreviated introductory material	mm. 62–65	F major (TTBB)
A^1 Section	mm. 66–75	(SATB)
Coda	mm. 76–83	

Text and Translation

It was my desire that the text of *In Remembrance* serve as a celebration of the Potts's lives in addition to portray the hurt and despair felt by many about their deaths. The process of finding the appropriate text took nearly two years to complete. I was comforted by the initial line *Lux aeterna luceat eis Domine*, but also became inspired by the Psalms of David asking God for His mercy and deliverance. Furthermore, the most profound passage of the piece may be recognized as the words of Christ on the cross, "My God, my God, why hast thou forsaken me?" Yet amid despair and hopelessness, *In Remembrance* carries a message of healing, peace, and hope applicable to many situations and personal circumstances.

Lux aeterna luceat eis Domine. (from the "Communion" of the *Requiem Mass*)
May light eternal shine upon them, O Lord.
Turn to me and be gracious, for my heart is in distress. (Psalm 4:1)
Oh God, my God, why hast thou forsaken me? (Matthew 27:46)

My tears linger at night, but joy comes in the morning light. (Psalm 30:5)
Lord, in Your infinite mercy, grant them rest forevermore. (Based on the "Requiem aeternam" from the *Requiem Mass*.)

Additional References and Resources

Jeffers, Ron. *Translations and Annotations of Choral Repertoire Volume I: Sacred Latin Texts*. Corvallis, Oregon: earthsongs, 1988.

Suggested Listening

Ride On! The Stangeland Family Youth Choral Academy: Oregon Bach Festival.
Anton Armstrong, conductor. (2006).
2005 ACDA High School Honor Choir. Jeffery Redding, conductor. (Via Media)

Contributed by:

Jeffrey Ames

Teacher Resource Guide

"In Splendoribus Sanctorum"

from *The Strathclyde Motets*

James MacMillan

(b. 1959)

SATB/a cappella with trumpet or organ obbligato
Boosey & Hawkes: 48019895
Overall: 3
Vocal: 3
Tonal/Rhythm: 3

Composer

James MacMillan studied music at Edinburgh University and took Doctoral studies in composition at Durham University with John Casken. After working as a lecturer at Manchester University, he returned to Scotland and settled in Glasgow. The successful premiere of *Tryst* at the 1990 St. Magnus Festival led to his appointment as Affiliate Composer of the Scottish Chamber Orchestra. Between 1992 and 2002 he was Artistic Director of the Philharmonia Orchestra's Music of Today series of contemporary music concerts. MacMillan is internationally active as a conductor, working as Composer/Conductor with the BBC Philharmonic between 2000 and 2009, and was appointed Principal Guest Conductor of the Netherlands Radio Chamber Philharmonic in 2010. He was awarded a CBE in January 2004.

In addition to *The Confession of Isobel Gowdie*, which launched MacMillan's international career at the BBC Proms in 1990, his orchestral output includes the percussion concerto *Veni, Veni, Emmanuel*, premiered by Evelyn Glennie in 1992 and which has since received over 400 performances and has been programmed by leading international orchestras and conductors including the New York Philharmonic under Leonard Slatkin, the Philadelphia Orchestra under Andrew Davis, and the Detroit Symphony under Neeme Järvi.

Works by MacMillan also include *Seven Last Words from the Cross* for chorus and string orchestra, screened on BBC TV during Holy Week 1994, *Inés de Castro*, premiered by Scottish Opera and toured to Porto in 2001, a triptych of orchestral works commissioned by the London Symphony Orchestra (LSO): *The World's Ransoming*, a Cello Concerto for Mstislav Rostropovich, and Symphony: "Vigil" premiered under the baton of Rostropovich in 1997, and *Quickening* for The Hilliard Ensemble, chorus and orchestra, co-commissioned by the BBC Proms and the Philadelphia Orchestra.

Recent MacMillan works include Piano Concerto No.2 first performed with choreography by Christopher Wheeldon at New York City Ballet, *A Scotch Bestiary* commissioned to inaugurate the new organ at Disney Hall with soloist Wayne Marshall and the Los Angeles Philharmonic conducted by Esa-Pekka Salonen, and *The Sacrifice* premiered and toured by Welsh National Opera in 2007. His *St. John Passion*, co-commissioned by the LSO, Royal Concertgebouw Orchestra, Boston Symphony Orchestra, and Berlin Radio Choir, had its premiere under the baton of Sir Colin Davis in 2008. Future premieres include a new violin concerto for Vadim Repin co-commissioned by the LSO, Zaterdag Matinee, and the Philadelphia Orchestra, and a piano concerto for the Minnesota Orchestra. James MacMillan is published exclusively by Boosey & Hawkes.

Reprinted by kind permission of Boosey & Hawkes.

Composition, Genre, and Historical Perspective

"In Splendoribus Sanctorum" is a communion motet for Nativity Midnight Mass composed as part of *The Strathclyde Motets*.

> *The Strathclyde Motets* grew out of ongoing discussions between Alan Tavener, Brendan Slevin, the Roman Catholic Chaplain at Strathclyde University, and me. We drew the Strathclyde University Chamber Choir into an ongoing project at the Chaplaincy—now at St. Columba's Church in Maryhill—that they would come a few times a year and sing the liturgy for us, and I would write a series of new Communion motets for them.... Of course the culmination of that great movement in the liturgy is the sacrifice of the Eucharist and the reception of the Eucharist; therefore, in a sense the peak of all that is the moment where communicants and congregation are deep in introspection as individuals, and as a community, reflecting on this mystical and loving union that they have.... There's a greater concern for color, I think, and also a different approach to time—liturgical time—maybe because of having spent a lifetime attending liturgies and being interested in what a choir can bring to sacred worship, especially while people are in quiet meditation after receiving Communion.

> Having heard these motets in context, there's a kind of suspended animation about them. They don't seem to go anywhere, they kind of float as an entity, and there are one or two ideas that sort of ease into being and just exist, and then it stops. For that reason I have noticed a different mood and a different sensation about these motets."
>
> ~James MacMillan

In writing the *Strathclyde Motets* MacMillan set out to write a series of communion motets of moderate difficulty that would be of real and lasting use for average church or concert choirs. Aware that much of his choral music to date could be too challenging for average use, these new motets provide a very welcome opportunity for almost any choir of reasonable attainment and ambition to sing some contemporary music of real value.

"In splendoribus sanctorum" is a motet of pure simplicity written in short sections that are interspersed with trumpet (or organ) obbligato passages. As the piece progresses through a number of repetitions, the trumpet increasingly plays its part more freely, which creates a feeling of development and progression even though the choral parts remain unvaried. It is hugely effective writing and demonstrates the fact that simple means can often deliver the strongest message.

From: http://www.boosey.com/cr/composer/James+MacMillan

Technical Considerations

This striking work is within performance of any SATB at any level of development. The tenor is, in essence, the only moving part in each section, and the other sections of the ensemble form an ostinato-like accompaniment to that line. Because of the improvisatory nature of the work, its performance can be as long as eight minutes, or shorter if desired. A virtuosic trumpet player is required. However, the trumpet part can be played on the organ if a trumpet player of sufficient ability is not available.

Stylistic Considerations

MacMillan's homophonic, simple, and chant-like writing with use of parallel fifths throughout harkens back to organum. Given the meditative ethos and the low tessitura of "In Splendoribus Sanctorum," the choir should work to develop a rich and focused sound quality appropriate to the liturgical atmosphere of the piece. Similarly, the trumpeter or organist must approach the interpolations with sensitivity and reverence. The conductor should not keep strict time, but rather emulate the metrical freedom of chant. Basses with an easily produced low F are needed.

Form and Structure

Section	Measure
1	mm. 1–7
Obbligato Interpolation #1	
2	mm. 8–14
Obbligato Interpolation #2	
3	mm. 15–21
Obbligato Interpolation #3	
4	mm. 22–27
Obbligato Interpolation #4	

Repeat three or four times; during subsequent repetitions, the trumpeter (organist) may vary the obbligato passages by jumping from line to line or from phrase to phrase *ad lib.*

Text and Translation

Roman Breviary, Psalm 109:3

In splendoribus sanctorum,
ex utero ante luciferum genuite.

In the splendor of the holy ones:
I have begotten you from the womb
before the rising of the day-star.
~Jeffers

Suggested Listening

James Jordan, *Angels in the Architecture*, The Voices of Anam Cara, GIA CD-836

Additional Resources

Web Site: http://www.boosey.com/cr/composer/James+MacMillan

Contributed by:

Richard Hutton

Teacher Resource Guide

Jesu dulcis memoria

Tomás Luis de Victoria

(1548–1611)

SATB
E.C. Schirmer: 2995
Overall: 3
Vocal: 3
Tonal/Rhythm: 3

Composer

Tomás Luis de Victoria is most certainly the greatest Spanish composer of the sixteenth century. He was held in such high regard that he was given the greatest compliment a composer could be given: he was called "the Spanish Palestrina." Palestrina was considered by many to be the greatest composer of his time; he was a master of polyphony, adhering to the strict rules of counterpoint, which were so important to the Roman Catholic Church at the time. Despite Palestrina's seeming restrictions, his music possessed an unmatched simple beauty and clarity. Given Victoria's study and work in Rome and his mastery of this style, he is certainly worthy of that title.

Victoria, born in Ávila, Spain, most likely knew that once he completed his youthful studies, that he must travel to Rome to become a master composer and church musician. In 1565 he went to Rome to study at the Jesuit Collegium Germanicum and stayed there until 1569 when he returned to Spain to assume the role of organist and cantor (leader of worship) in Monserrat. After completing his studies, he returned to Rome in 1571 to teach at the Collegium. Soon after, in 1573 he was appointed *maestro di cappella* at the Collegium.

Victoria enjoyed a renowned career as a teacher, composer and church musician, and remained in Italy for sixteen years. In 1587 he returned to Spain to work as Chaplain and Choirmaster at Real Convento de las Clarisas Descalzas in Madrid, where the empress Maria had retired. He remained that position until 1603 in spite of being courted by many of the most prestigious Cathedrals in Spain and Italy. After 1603 and until his death, he remained at the convent as an organist, virtually unknown by the new generation of composers writing in a dramatic new style that would become known as *Baroque*.

When researching his music, be aware of alternate spellings, as some editions refer to him by variants of his Italianized name, Tomas Luis da Vittoria, or Ludovico Tommasso da Vittoria, and others.

Composition, Genre, and Historical Perspective

Victoria is the most significant composer of the late Renaissance in Spain. He mastered the craft of Roman counterpoint, that is, creating compositions in which vocal parts move independently of one another, yet his music was distinct from that of Roman composers as he imbued the counterpoint with a more personal style. It is thought that perhaps Victoria's freedom in composition came from working in Spain, where he was less directly ruled by the limitations imposed by the Roman Catholic Church.

Victoria's compositional voice might be considered similar to Palestrina's—only spicier. His music seems to have a more mystical intensity with greater personal emotional expression than that of his Roman contemporaries. He used dissonance more freely and also used intervals that were frowned upon by strict application of the rules of counterpoint. His free use of counterpoint, dissonance, voice leading, and texture allowed him to create dramatic word painting that is most often found in madrigal composition.

"Jesu dulcis memoria" is an excellent example of Victoria's style. This motet for the Blessed Sacrament is in the traditional style of the Roman Renaissance: it is in Latin, sung *a cappella*, and scored in a simple and clear style with a fine balance between homophony and simple polyphony; also, voices imitate one another clearly, the text is clearly understood as the writing utilizes only very short melismas, and phrases are "dovetailed," that is, they begin and end independently of one another. We hear Victoria's personal stamp in the high degree of chromaticism, long tones in the bass line (which give the bass part not only more melodic function, but also a more mysterious quality), and finally, the sustained pitch in the soprano at the final cadence, which takes away from the soprano's typical melodic function, and helps create a static and other-worldly color.

Musical Elements and Technical Considerations

Many major considerations face conductors prior to beginning rehearsal on any work from the Renaissance. The first is to determine in what key to sing the piece. "Jesu dulcis memoria," as with many works from the Renaissance, is published in numerous different keys. The important issue to remember is that it is not in any key at all, but rather, a mode. The actual pitch on which the piece begins is less important than the relationships between pitches. Many things affect the actual pitch at which the work might have been sung—from the pitch of the local organ, to the standard pitch of a given town, to the clef combination with which a piece was written, to the relative pitch given to the choir by the priest of cantor's intonation. In today's classroom we often find that certain pitch levels seem to fit different groups, so in light of all these variables feel free to experiment. Try beginning this piece on A, if the tessitura is too low for any part, or if the piece tends to go flat, try beginning on B. Choose a pitch level that ultimately reinforces the mystical mood of the piece and highlights the chromaticism.

The next consideration in music of the Renaissance is one of meter and tempo. Once again, as would be the case with much music of this time, in perusing various editions of this piece we see numerous choices by editors as to the relative note values. Good questions to ask are: "How often does the harmony change?" "How often do the text syllables change?" "What is the mood of the text?" "If I were to sing one of these lines by myself, how fast would I need to go to make it through in one breath?" Answers to these questions provide the conductor with practical insight into the needs of the composition, the intended mood for the audience, and the needs of the singers—the exact practical matters Victoria must have considered. In the case of "Jesu dulcis memoria," determine the note value of the tactus (beat) by the first three syllables. If "Je-su dul-" is written in whole notes, then give the whole note the beat, if they are written in half notes, let the half note be the tactus. The manner in which the text is set (and the way the harmony moves) shows that those notes become the tactus. But how fast? This music is sung to support the most mysterious moments of the Roman Catholic Mass, the Lord's Supper. The music needs to create a mysterious effect, not drawing attention to the performer but to the sacrament being shared—too fast and the music seems hurried and loses the sense of mystery, too slow and the singers will run out of breath before the end of the phrase. Find that "window" of appropriate tempo and be flexible.

Once pitch level and tempo have been chosen (and remember, stay flexible), begin to focus on the performance issues. This music looks slow, so it tends to sound slow. When sight singing, count-sing or subdivide into syllables such as [nu-ni] to emphasize the underlying rhythm of the work.

Firmly establish tactus throughout the choir, as the horizontal nature of these lines will encourage sections to lose a sense of ensemble.

Chant the text in real time, as if the singers were native speakers, emphasizing the accent of text, the momentum of the phrase of text, the ebb and flow of the syllables, and the pressure and release of weight. Intone the text on one pitch emphasizing these elements. Have the entire choir sing one part in unison, applying these elements with the rhythms and pitches given. Draw the choir's attention to textual and musical momentum that drives toward the penultimate syllable of the piece.

Help sections learn their individual functions in polyphony. First, help all singers, especially basses, to think horizontally, melodically. Emphasize the direction and forward motion of their lines, especially when notes are long, parts sustained, or tessitura static. Second, help them learn in each phrase, when their text or piece of the melody is to come to the fore and then when to recede. Have them highlight or bracket those few notes or syllables in each phrase that highlight the polyphony, emphasize the dissonance, and text paint.

Stylistic Considerations

Musical and stylistic ideas are again best discovered by asking pragmatic questions: "What is the mood and function of the piece?" "How soft or loud can my singers sing beautifully?" "When does a *crescendo* or *diminuendo* begin to draw attention to itself, rather than enhance the music?" "Does the tempo or phrase need to move here a bit for greater energy and momentum, or does the phrase need to relax?" The answers to these questions can result in a natural approach to phrasing, with as much flexibility and spontaneity possible.

The mystical mood of "Jesu dulcis memoria" might be best be conveyed by a delicate and deliberate tempo, somewhat slow to begin. On the phrase "gaudia" the text becomes more personal, less about God and more about the one conveying the text. Allow the tempo to move a bit and the dynamics to increase naturally. After the cadence, the tessitura falls during the words "above all else"—allow the dynamic to diminish and become inward and intimate. The final phrase should be the most mystical and restrained of all.

Form and Structure

The form of this motet, as in all Renaissance polyphony, is determined by its text. As there are four lines of text, conservative Roman compositional rules of counterpoint would necessitate four phrases of music. These four phrases create two essentially equal parts to the motet, the first half concluding with the cadence on "gaudia."

Phrase one begins in aeolian mode, ending on the dominant. The text is proclaimed in a very clear style. Phrase two sees Victoria employing greater freedom in text painting: for "granting the heart true joy" he abandons any strict imitation and allows the voices to seemingly move freely in long and repeated melismas. Phrase three, "but above all else," employs more traditional imitation combined with greater chromaticism. Phrase four seems to capture the mystery of Roman Catholic communion through the delicate writing and light texture of "your sweet presence."

Text and Translation

Jesu dulcis memoria	Jesus, sweet remembrance,
Dans vera cordis gaudia:	Granting the heart true joy,
Sed super mel et omnia	Above all things
Ejus dulcis praesentia.	Is Your sweet presence.

Editions

Jesu Dulcis Memoria. E.C. Schirmer 2995

Four editions are available at Choral Public Domain Library:
www.cpdl.org/wiki/index.php/Jesu%2C_dulcis_memoria_%28Tomás_Luis_de_Victoria%29

Contributed by:

Geoffrey Boers

Teacher Resource Guide

Lebenslust

Franz Schubert

(1797-1828)

SATB
Hinshaw Music: HMC-425
Overall: 3
Vocal: 3
Tonal/Rhythm: 3

Composer

Franz Schubert (1797–1828) was an Austrian composer who made notable contributions to the symphonic, chamber, piano, and solo song repertoires. Like Beethoven, Schubert found himself on the cusp of the Classical and Romantic periods. Both composers knew well the conventions of the day, and broke free of them whenever possible. This was especially true in terms of harmonic language and formal structure. As a composer, Schubert is known for his gift of melody, expressive approach to harmony, symbolic or representative elements woven into his music, the originality and depth of his accompaniments, and elegant formal and thematic construction.

Born and raised in Vienna, Schubert benefited from the active musical life of the city. At age seven, he began musical studies with Antonio Salieri and it has been reported that he began composing in early adolescence or before. During his formative years, he was enrolled in school, but his musical activities eventually compromised his grades. He eventually left his schooling to move home and become, like his father and brothers, a school teacher. He hoped that this would provide income while he pursued his greatest love:

composition. Although he did not enjoy teaching, his plan worked: during this time Schubert was incredibly prolific.

Schubert placed a heavy emphasis on social interactions, and his music often reflected the social facets of his day-to-day life. Throughout his life, he maintained close-knit circles of friends that often included musicians, poets, librettists, and other artistic types. At gatherings—referred to as "Schubertiads," as Schubert and his music were a primary focus—his friends often doubled as performers and audiences for Schubert's solo voice, piano, and chamber music. Without this group, Schubert's career might not have gotten off the ground in the first place, as they gave him food, lodging, and even underwrote his earliest publications. Despite being penniless and having poor professional luck in the early years, his friendships sustained him. Perhaps for this reason, Schubert was often drawn toward texts that espoused deeper aspects of friendship.

Despite his lack of reliable income, Schubert led a life of excess: almost constant smoking, binge drinking, and promiscuity that most likely led to his probable contraction of syphilis. He eventually died at the early age of thirty-one. Despite this short life, his immense compositional output has contributed significantly to the Western musical canon.

Composition, Genre, and Historical Perspective

Schubert wrote masses, motets, and other music intended for performance by choirs. He also wrote more than 150 part songs, of which "Lebenslust" (originally titled "Die Geselligkeit") is one.

Part songs come in such variety that they largely elude strict definition. They are usually unaccompanied, but not always. They are usually homophonic, but not always. The melody usually stays in the top voice, but not always. The text is usually a previously existing secular poem, but not always. They are usually scored for male voices, but not always. The difficulty level is usually low, but not always. Most typically, the term refers to small-scale secular pieces for two or more voice parts. The term has broadened to encompass madrigals, glees, catches, rounds, quodlibets, even barbershop songs, and certain folk-song arrangements (Blezzard). Part singing peaked in popularity in the nineteenth century, and was especially popular in England and Germany. According to Judith Blezzard: "Later in the 19th century, mixed choirs and competitive choral festivals were established. The partsongs of composers including Schubert, Schumann, Franz, Mendelssohn, Cornelius and Brahms set much German Romantic poetry, and show parallels with their lieder in both style and sentiment."

Most of Schubert's part songs are for male vocal ensembles, but the next largest category is for mixed voices. Some actually carry generic drinking-song titles, but most often Schubert was drawn to the same kind of poetry he set in the solo song. Given its deviation from Schubert's typical part-song style, "Lebenslust" was most likely written to be played and sung as part of a Schubertiad. Indeed, the meter, tempo, scoring, jaunty rhythms, and subject matter of the song make it suitable for the atmosphere of a party with close friends. If this was the case, it is likely that the vocal parts were sung by friends in attendance, and that Schubert played the piano part himself.

1815 is often dubbed Schubert's "Miracle Year" for the immense output that occurred during this time. In contrast, the year 1818 is considered a low-output year for Schubert. "Lebenslust" is one of the pieces Schubert penned in 1818, written in January of that year.

Musical Elements and Technical Considerations

- The difficulty level is such that "Lebenslust" would be an appropriate choice for the start of the school year with an advanced high school choir, or as a challenge piece for the end of the year with younger choirs.
- About half of the thirty-five measures sung by the choir have basically the same rhythm (see m. 6). Teaching this rhythm before anything else might save rehearsal time.
- Schubert begins employing more chromaticism in measure 13, while simultaneously slowing the rhythm more or less by half. What is the reason for this significant change? Clearly, Schubert is looking at the same lines of text we heard in measures 5 through 9, but now from a different perspective. Until this point, Schubert seems to be illustrating the "zest for life" spoken of in the text, but the music starting in measure 13 seems instead to focus on the line: "To be alone is tedious." Whatever the reason, assigning a dramatic impetus to these bars will help the singers have more emotional attachment to them.
- This is party music. There is a dance-like quality, a let-loose quality. It is full of wit and intensity. Taking a proper, refined, and stylistically perfect approach will certainly work, but it might miss Schubert's point in composing the piece. As discussed above, there is a huge roller coaster of emotion packed into just 39 measures! This is evidenced by the widely varying textures for the accompaniment, the disparity of harmonic styles from phrase to phrase, the dynamic extremes, the several ritards/fermatas, and so on. How would Schubert and his friends have sung this piece? Probably by paying great and humorous attention to these extremes—it might have even gotten raucous! So feel free to recreate a bit of this party atmosphere in your performance.

- This is great for any age, starting from 8th grade. I was introduced to the piece in 10th grade chorus and later sang it as part of a faculty quartet in a recital to welcome new music students to our college choral program. It is great for festival choirs, and would also work for small groups at a contest. I have even heard this piece sung well in its original scoring by a junior high chorus. I programmed it when I conducted the Kentucky Junior High All-State Choir (altering a few notes in the tenor part).
- Regardless of the age of the singers, a capable pianist is certainly required. The piano part, which Schubert almost certainly wrote to his own considerable skill, is truly collaborative.

Stylistic Considerations

- It is stylistically appropriate to perform part songs with any number of voices on a part, from quartet to large choirs. This allows flexibility in programming: perform with your full choir in concert, present it for a large group contest, and assign a quartet or octet to sing it for a solo and ensemble contest—all in a single year.
- Generally, rubato is an appropriate expressive device to use in music of the Romantic period. Given the tempo and dance-like quality of "Lebenslust," a very fine performance of this piece can be given without employing rubato at all. However, if rubato is desired, it is best to keep the tempo constant on the upbeat sections, employing rubato only in the melodramatic moments, such as measures 12 through 19 and 27 through 29.
- There are a variety of editions available of Schubert's original SATB voicing. The most readily available are from Tetra/Continuo and Hinshaw; both of these include singable English translations in the music. Heritage offers a 3-part mixed version that might still be in print. Perhaps the highest quality edition available is published by Faber (available through Hal Leonard) under the title, *Four Partsongs*—it includes four of Schubert's most popular secular SATB works: "Lebenslust," "Der Tanz," "An die Sonne," and "Schicksalslenker."

Form and Structure

Note: The following measure numbers include the initial anacrusis as measure 1, although some editions count the first full measure as measure 1.

The overall form is AB.

Section	Measure	Event and Scoring
Piano introduction		mm. 1–5
	mm. 1–3	Drawn from mm. 24–25 or 34–35 and varied
A	mm. 5–19	Lines 1 & 2
	mm. 5–9	Lines 1 & 2
	mm. 9–14	Lines 1 & 2; increased chromaticism and surprise cadence on flattened subtonic lend this section a melodramatic quality
	Mm. 14–15	Piano echo of mm. 13–14
	Mm. 15–19	Re-statement of line 2, variation of mm. 11–14 with increased chromaticism
B	mm. 19–39	Lines 3 & 4
	mm. 19–29	Lines 3 & 4; music is quasi-imitative fugato
	mm. 29–39	Lines 3 & 4; music is variation of mm. 19–29

Text and Translation

Note: Unger's original poem includes three stanzas. As Schubert set only the first stanza, only that stanza has been translated. However, all three are included here for the reader's convenience.

Wer lebenslust fühlet, der bleib nicht allein,	He who feels a zest for life is never alone,
Allein sein ist öde, wer kann sich da freu'n?	To be alone is tedious, who can enjoy that?
Im traulichen Kreise, beim herzlichen Kuss,	To live together in an intimate circle,
Beisammen zu leben, ist Seelengenuss.	With a loving embrace, That is joy to the soul!

Das lehrt uns der Tauber, für Liebe und Lust
erhebt sich dem Täubchen die seidene Brust,
es gurret der Tauber, er lehret im Kuß
beisammen zu leben, sei Herzensgenuß!
Geselligkeit fesselt die ganze Natur,
in Lüften, im Wasser, auf lachender Flur.
Er selber gebot es, der alles erschuf,
beisammenzuleben ist Menschenberuf!
~Johann Karl Unger (1771–1836)

Additional References and Resources

Blezzard, Judith. "Sing, Hear: the German Romantic Partsong." *Musical Times*, cxxxiv (1993).

Contributed by:

Drew Collins

Teacher Resource Guide

Magnificent Horses
arr. Jing Ling-Tam

SATB
Alliance Music: AMP 0324
Overall: 3
Vocal: 3
Tonal/Rhythm: 3

Composer

Jing Ling-Tam is Director of Choral Studies at University of Texas, Arlington, at the time of this writing. Her biography states that she is a native of Taiwan with degrees from the New England Conservatory and the University of North Texas. She has worked in Asia and tours there with Western choirs. Her music series, published by Alliance Music, includes arrangements of folk songs from China, Jamaica, and the Hebrides as well as other, more typically Western music. Her work as a conductor and vocal clinician also spans several continents.

Composition, Genre, and Historical Perspective

Mongolia is an "independent country of Inner Asia and landlocked between the Russian Federation to the North and China to the east, west, and south."[1] The culture has been centered on horses for hundreds of years and the importance of these animals manifests in a rich tradition of folk music and visual arts.

The popularity of "Magnificent Horses"—an arranged folk song—is merited on its immediate appeal. In the current enthusiasm for multicultural experiences, this short piece gives the sense of an excursion to the Far East, yet avoids the difficulty of Eastern languages for Western singers; the choir imitates the thrilling sound of bells on horses. The piece indeed sounds foreign enough to spark our curiosity, yet maintains approachability with predominantly Western harmony.

Musical Elements and Technical Considerations

Much of the Eastern effect of "Magnificent Horses" derives from the hexachordal scale employed: A–F-sharp. However, it reads fairly easily in B minor and may be effectively taught on solfège using the flat seventh scale degree "te."

The piece opens with four-part men's chorus. For some young choirs that might otherwise be excluded from performing the piece, the first tenor line can almost always be sung by altos with a little judicious planning when the men have four-way divisi. The introduction can easily be lengthened by repeating any portion of measures 3 through 7 in order to make a suitable processional—no galloping please!

A few notes on possible pitfalls:

- Note that measure 3 includes opposing dynamic shifts, fading out the initial calls and increasing the sound of imitated bells, as horses approaching from afar.
- Current scores require a page turn from measure 7 to 8, which may require some rehearsal for the men to find their voice part with the addition of women's voices and instruments.
- Placing the grace notes can be difficult; they are outside the usual idiom for Western choirs. It may help to learn the lines without the grace notes, then add them later at a sufficiently slow tempo.
- In current editions, measure 8 contains a likely error in the soprano line: the grace note preceding beat three should almost certainly be on the pitch C—instead of the printed A—to match the instrumental and alto parts. This would also match measure 9.
- Achieving a proper tempo is imperative for communicating the character of the horses. Make a plan to attain the final tempo in advance of the first performance so that acrobatics required of the singers' tongues can become natural and so the tempo can become ingrained in the performers' bodies. In this piece choirs can easily begin to race downhill and out of control. Note that the directive: "Robust, spirited" may feel different in various spaces and for more or less experienced singers.

- Singing 16th notes on "di-li-di-li" must employ fleet tongues. Practicing with "di-di-di-di" may encourage the necessary tip-of-the-tongue action, akin to double-tonguing a brass instrument.
- Note that measure 31 begins with crescendo only—no tempo change—and accelerando is added at measure 33. Acceleration is only possible to the point of allowing the 16th notes to ring—and not run away.
- Shouts of "hei" beginning in measure 33 require a healthy shout, and must infuse the growing climax with precise rhythm.
- The final measure stands in stark contrast to the rest of the piece.
  - First, memorization must be in order so there are no soloists here.
  - The utterance of "sha" is a dramatic and picturesque moment. It can seem to bring the rushing horses to a grinding halt or send them soaring over the landscape.
  - Don't underestimate the final foot stomp. It can be tricky, but is enormously effective if coordinated, surprising, and sonorous.

"Magnificent Horses" is highly effective when memorized, but requires careful attention. It has many repetitive motives, but bars 35 and 36 are the only two successive measures that are exactly the same for all voices. The transition from holding scores to singing from memory may require singers to make their own mnemonic devices. Once fully memorized, a choir without score can enhance the performance with posture and facial expression in the free nature of folk music. Singing without music should also allow concentration on the conductor, who will hold the reins of the tempo.

It is possible to execute the song without instruments, but they add much to the flair of the performance, the energy of the singers, and they save some choral fatigue by assuming some of the rhythmic responsibility and by frequently doubling the melody.

Stylistic Considerations

The *erhu* listed in the score is a fairly modern Chinese stringed instrument from the family of instruments called *huqin*, which "all have a thin, round, fretless neck mounted to a relatively small resonating chamber of varying shapes, with (usually) two strings between which the hair of the bow passes."[2] Should finding an experienced player prove difficult, the score allows a flute to be substituted. The Chinese flute is generally a transverse bamboo instrument. Sleigh bells are also required, preferably mounted on a stick, rather than a strap, for the rhythmic precision required here.

Since the singers are imitating the bells, it may be instructive—and fun—to experiment with varying the vocal colors: nasal, hollow, or tinny, for example. The tone can be changed from one section of the piece to another or differentiated among the sections of the choir.

The grace notes are surely intended to sound before the beat as a general rule. However, a stronger effect may be achieved in the first two measures by landing the grace notes on the beat. These bars can be taken somewhat out of tempo. The grace notes function as a type of accent and need not be overtly precise. Frankly, it's a piece that can sustain a few bumps and bruises as long as the choir takes it seriously.

Form and Structure

Several formal divisions of the piece are possible and compelling, at least of the first few bars. One possibility follows:

Measure	Event and Scoring
mm. 1–15	A single musical gesture—an introduction. mm. 1–7 add continually new elements and lead to the introduction of the bells in m. 8 as a significant event; m. 11 is the peak of energy.
mm. 15–28	5 phrases (2+2+4+4+2)
mm. 15–28	repeat as above
mm. 29–37	5 phrases (2+2+2+2+1) Thinking in two-bar phrases is helpful, but this section is truly additive, not structural, similar to the opening section.

Text and Translation

The text consists entirely of sound syllables intended to imitate the jingling of bells.

Contributed by:

Andrew Crow

1 Pegg, Carole. "Mongolia." *Grove Music Online*. accessed 27 August 2008.

2 Thrasher, Alan R. "China: Musical Instruments." *Grove Music Online*. accessed 27 August 2008.

Teacher Resource Guide

O vos Omnes

Pablo Casals

(1876–1973)

SATB
Tetra: TC–128
Overall: 3
Vocal: 3
Tonal/Rhythm: 4

Composer

Spanish composer Pablo Casals was given his first musical instruction by his father on piano, violin, and organ. At the age of 11, after hearing a recital on the instrument, he turned to the cello as his principle means of artistic expression. In 1888, he enrolled in the Escola Municipal de Música, in Barcelona, Spain, graduating in 1893, and then began an international career as a performer, teacher, conductor, and composer. A fierce opponent of the Franco regime, which took power in Spain in the late 1939, Casals moved to the border town of Prades in France and vowed never again to perform in a country that publicly acknowledged the totalitarian government. Throughout his life he continued to fight against tyranny, injustice, and inequality, using his international fame to champion the rights of oppressed peoples, eventually winning the Nobel Peace Prize for his efforts. Casal's artistry as a performer and composer was inspired by three things he revered: God, nature, and the music of Bach, especially the six suites for solo cello. After discovering a volume of the suites in a Barcelona bookstore in 1890, he practiced the set for a dozen years before playing them in public, and for the rest of his life he played at least one of the suites every day.

Composition, Genre, and Historical Perspective

O vos Omnes is a sacred motet for *a cappella* voices dating from 1932. Composed for the Benedictine monks of Montserrat, it was originally for men's voices; it was rewritten for SATB divisi choir in 1965. The short text is drawn from the Lamentations of Jeremiah, and the words are freely repeated throughout, resulting in an overall duration of roughly three minutes. Casals had a particular disdain for what he called the "experimental" music that was in vogue at the time; as a result his own compositions are strongly rooted in the compositional style of the Romantic Era and are best viewed in that light. Looking specifically at *O vos Omnes*, this Romantic style is readily apparent: rich and expressive harmonies, dramatic changes in dynamics and vocal ranges, a plethora of short crescendos and decrescendos, and an overall arching form created with climactic events occurring in the middle of the piece countered by a quietly reflective opening and conclusion.

Technical Considerations

Primarily, this motet is syllabically homophonic and offers no real rhythmic challenges; indeed, the most difficult rhythm would be a dotted quarter note followed by and eighth note. Phrases are no longer than four measures (with one exception when a six-bar phrase occurs from m. 25, beat 3, to m. 31, beat 3), so frequent breathing opportunities are present throughout, even when the tempo indication of quarter note equals 54 is strictly followed. Although some sections are primarily four-part writing, divisi in all voices occurs frequently, and the ranges are for the most part comfortable for each vocal part. Certain exceptions must be noted; tenors and sopranos have high Gs and the basses a high E-flat in bar 16, first sopranos are required to sing a high B-flat in bar 20, and there is an optional low C for the basses in the concluding chord of the piece.

A wide range of dynamics is employed, and as mentioned before, those shifts are sometimes sudden and dramatic, most notably in bars 16 through 22, where shifts from *forte* to *piano*, back to *forte*, and then *piano* again occur; each dynamic marking encompasses only two measures. These shifts in dynamics should be relatively easy to accomplish, as there is a corresponding change from a high tessitura for the *forte* measure to a relatively low tessitura for the bars marked *piano*.

The lines are on occasion somewhat chromatic, but nearly always in the context of the tonalities employed; accidentals are mostly functional as part of secondary dominant or borrowed chord, although on occasion appear as neighbor notes or passing tones. Once the tonal language is in the ears of the singers, the individual lines are not particularly difficult. Some larger skips must be negotiated, but in general the lines are stepwise in motion. Of greater difficulty is the sudden unexpected shifts in tonality that occur on occasion;

for example, moving from a cadence in G major in bar 15 to a *fortissimo* E-flat major chord to begin the following phrase, and the shift in tonality at bar 33 (again to an E-flat major chord) from the C major chord that concludes the previous phrase.

Stylistic Considerations

Due to the largely syllabic setting of the text, care must be taken that the lines are sustained and connected. This may be particularly challenging in bars 22 to 31, where there is a preponderance of quarter notes; the choir must be encouraged to make sure that each note leads to the next without any decay. The same might be said regarding bars 31 to 42, where the lower three voices must sustain half notes, dotted half notes, and whole notes at dynamics no louder than *mezzo-piano*, yet must maintain the energy of the phrases throughout.

The importance of the dynamic indications cannot be overestimated and those indications, given in great detail, should be followed closely. Even though ritards and a tempo indications are never given in the score, when considering the Romantic nature of Casals's writing, a fair amount of rubato can be employed, especially a slowing of the tempo when concluding phrases. However, due to the numerous short phrases throughout, care must be taken in shaping and defining the overall form of the piece, lest the work become merely a series of short phrases.

Musical Elements and Form and Structure

O *vos omnes* is basically through composed and is essentially homophonic and syllabic. Some phrases are repeated, but they are invariably modified and/or extended. This being said, the piece can be divided into several sections by viewing both the melodic material and the text set in each section. Section one, the text O *vos omnes qui transitis per viam* encompasses bars 1 through 15. Bars 1 and 2 serve as a short introduction, bars 7 through 11 are an modification and extension of bars 3 through 6, and bars 12 through 15 introduce new melodic material (on the same text) and serve as a transition to section two. This next section, the climatic moment of the piece, sets the text *attendite, et videte* and lasts a relatively short six bars, measures 16 through 21. Bars 16 to 17 and 20 to 21 are set high in the tessitura and at a *forte* dynamic; these measures are interrupted by bars 18 to 19, set for divisi men's voices at a contrasting low tessitura and *piano* dynamic. The next section is the most extended, encompassing bars 22 through 36, and sets the text *si est dolor sicut dolor meus*. Bar 22 through the first two beats of bar 25 introduce new melodic material that is extended (beginning a fourth higher than the initial statement) from bar 25 (beats three and four) through beats one and two of bar 31. Beats three and four of bar 31 through bar 36 provide a reflective ending to the section that is made more dramatic by the insertion of two beats of silence to begin bar 33.The final section in bars 37 through 42 essentially recalls bars 1 through 6 in both melodic and harmonic material as well as the text O *vos omnes qui transitis per viam*, but differs from the opening bars in that the final six bars begin on a C major chord before the piece is concluded in the primary key of C minor. Over the course of the piece Casals takes us away from C minor through sections in G major, E-flat major, and F major (of particular beauty is the series of fifths in mm. 25 through 31, moving from F to B-flat to E-flat to A-flat to D-flat to G-flat to C and finally back to F).

Text

O vos omnes qui transitis per viam,
attendite et videte si est dolor sicut dolor meus.

O all you who pass along this way,
behold and see if there is any sorrow like unto my sorrow.

Contributed by:

David Scholz

Teacher Resource Guide

Oremus

Urmas Sisask

(b. 1960)

SATB choir/a cappella
Boosey & Hawkes: 48016261
Overall: 3
Vocal: 4
Tonal/Rhythm: 3

Composer

Original notes by Kristel Pappel from the performance edition:

> Urmas Sisask (b. 1960) possesses a vision unique among Estonian composers; his music contains magical primeval power rather than polished mannerisms, a sincere sense of beauty rather than distanced aestheticism. Sisask is unique because he does not strive to be different. He is bravely and honestly himself. Sisask makes use of everything that is available and from which he can learn: Gregorian chant, early polyphony, Renaissance dance rhythms, early Baroque monody, Palestrina, 16th-century madrigals, the music of Tormis and Pärt, and so on. The most important periods in Sisask's education were the Tallinn Special Music School, from which he graduated from René Eespere's composition class in 1980, and the Tallinn Conservatory, where he continued his studies with Eespere and from which he graduated in 1985.
>
> Sisask has gained international recognition primarily as a choral composer, although the *Starry Sky Cycle* for piano was among the first

pieces by him to attract attention. Apart from choral works, Urmas Sisask has written chamber, instrumental, and orchestral music. He has developed his own, expressive language with an idiom closer to the old church modes than to functional harmony.

Composition, Genre, and Historical Perspective

Original notes by Kristel Pappel from Forward to Gloria Patri:

> Sisask went through an "enrichment period" in 1987–1988. He participated in courses on early music and familiarized himself with Gregorian chants and early Baroque music. At the same time, he studied the solar system and worked out theoretical sound values for the rotations of Mercury, Venus, Earth, Mars, Jupiter, Saturn, Uranus, Neptune and Pluto, obtaining what he calls the "planetal scale." This reduces to a row of five tones: C-sharp, D, F-sharp, G-sharp, and A. To his surprise, Sisask discovered that this scale matched that of a basic mode of Japanese Music called *kumayoshi*. Sisask considers it both symbolic and ironic that at the same time he was given a Catholic Prayer book with Latin texts.
>
> Sisask wrote *Gloria Patri* in 1988 from which "Oremus" is No. 23 of 24 hymns for mixed choir. All the songs are based on the *kumayoshi* mode. The order of the songs can be freely varied, for it is a collection, not a cycle. The most important aspect of *Gloria Patri*... for Sisask himself, apart from the use of *kumayoshi*, is no doubt the counterpoint.
>
> [All] of [the] motets in the *Gloria Patri* are like exercises in counterpoint, vocal inventions of a sort: *Alleluia* is a fugue, *Deo gratias* is a passacaglia, *Agnus Dei* is a canon, and so on. *Benedicamus* is derived from the juxtaposed choirs of the Venetian school, while *Confitemini* is related to Renaissance dances. These works provide a wealth of performance material for choirs at many levels, and is especially suited to both large ensembles and more intimate sounds of a chamber choir. The free recitation of *Pater noster* harks back to Gregorian chant, as does the melismatic *Ave Maria*, which is dedicated to Estonian choir conductor Ene Üleoja.

Technical Considerations

There is no text for "Oremus" in the performance edition by the composer. It uses only *ad libitum* voweling by the choir to create a sustained sound palate that seems connected to the cosmos, and also reflective of deeply inward, personal prayer. For American choirs, it may be difficult to maintain good intonation without some structure around the voweling, especially because the composer asks for an "mm" throughout, which is difficult to maintain pitch. Conductors may choose to assign vowels to the choir to stabilize pitch in their ensembles. For the recording that accompanies this text, two performance adjustments were made in the score. First, various vowel sounds were added to lend interpretative color to our performance. Second, choral parts were doubled with hand chimes. In our work and explorations with this piece, we found that the addition of these chimes adds an acoustic shimmer to the piece that enhances its truly mystical and spiritual qualities.

There is another interesting compositional feature in this work. If one examines each section, while there is no melodic rhythm in any one part, there is an overall ostinato-like rhythm present. It is helpful to the ensemble to know the overall rhythm pattern for each section. Also, the use of solfège is encouraged in order to anchor intonation of this piece. Conductors are encouraged to use a non-legato/non-expressive beat to achieve a crystalline clarity to the attacks on each change of pitch.

Interpretatively, this work is stunning because of its inward and spiritual qualities. The sounds produced from the choir should begin in a very personal place in order to provide a warm tone. Intense listening at all times is required by the choir, especially during the sustaining of very long tones, to maintain intonation. It is also very helpful when learning the work to count-sing to clarify and stabilize pitch attack.

Stylistic Considerations

Because of the 5-note mode Sisask employs in "Oremus," the same sonorities recur throughout the piece in different inversions. Again, while the composer asks for only an "mm" sound throughout, employ voweling as is performed on the companion recording to this text. Each section of the choir should always be aware of the progression of pitches in the other voice parts, as opportunities to tune to octaves, perfect fifths, and major thirds abound. The choir must maintain rhythmic integrity despite the ethereal nature of the piece. As the unaltered pitches of the *kumayoshi* mode cycle through, it is both the gradual and sudden contrasts in dynamics that are key to the effectiveness of this piece. The conductor should strive to achieve a large arch of dynamic shape to the *fortissimo* section of the work.

Form and Structure

Section	Measure	Event and Scoring
1	mm. 1–23	Entrances in order of Bass, Tenor, Alto, Soprano on "M..."; voices move one by one to a new note in the series via a composite rhythm of half, half, half, half

Section	Measure	Event and Scoring
2	mm. 24–59	Alto and Soprano duet on *ad libitum* vowels, then tenor and bass entrances; composite rhythm: half, quarter, quarter, half, half
3	mm. 60–79	Entrances in order of Bass, Alto, Tenor, Soprano; composite rhythm: quarter, quarter, quarter, quarter, half, half
4	mm. 80–111	Bass and Tenor duet, then Alto and Soprano entrances; composite rhythm: half, quarter, quarter, half, half
5	mm. 112–127	All voices with the composite rhythm: quarter, quarter, quarter, quarter, half, half
6	mm. 128–143	Full texture as rate of harmonic change increases to a new sonority every beat
7	mm. 144–147	Entrances on "M…" in order of Bass, Alto, Tenor, Soprano with a return to composite rhythm of section 3
8	mm. 148–155	Full texture with a return to composite rhythm of section 2
9	mm. 152–175	Full texture slows to original pace of section one ending in order of Soprano, Alto, Tenor, Bass

Text and Translation

M…
U-O-A-E-I-Ü-Ö…

Suggested Listening

James Jordan, *Angels in the Architecture*, The Voices of Anam Cara, GIA CD-836

Contributed by:

Richard Hutton

Teacher Resource Guide

Pater Noster

Igor Stravinsky

(1882–1971)

SATB/a cappella
Boosey & Hawkes: 48009527
Overall: 3
Vocal: 2
Tonal/Rhythm: 3

Composer

Leonard Bernstein once declared Igor Stravinsky to be "the greatest and most significant composer of the 20th century." Indeed, careful study of Stravinsky's works reveals his influence on and mastery of many of the century's musical tendencies, including neo-nationalism, neo-classicism, and serialism.

Stravinsky was born in the seaside town of Oranienbaum near St. Petersburg, Russia in June 1882 into what might be considered a family of nobility. His mother, Anna Kholodovskaya, was the daughter of a high-ranking official in Kiev. His father, Fyodor Stravinsky, was descended from a long line of Polish senators and landowners. Fyodor, one of Russia's leading operatic bass-baritones, regularly brought into the home many of Russia's premiere conductors, operatic singers, and composers, including Borodin and Mussorgsky. The young Stravinsky enjoyed sight-reading at the piano through his father's diverse collection of scores and demonstrated great interest in the music of the Russian masters, Mozart, Beethoven, and most particularly, Wagner. Stravinsky had wanted to pursue a career in music, but his father persuaded him to enter law school at the University of St. Petersburg instead. He reluctantly agreed, provided that he would be allowed to study harmony and counterpoint alongside his legal studies.

While at university, Stravinsky befriended the son of Nicolai Rimsky-Korsakov, who put him in touch with the famed composer. Soon he would begin weekly lessons with Rimsky-Korsakov and eventually abandon the study of law. Rimsky-Korsakov offered the twenty-year-old composer discipline and ample opportunity to hear his works performed. Stravinsky's first major assignment was a four-movement piano sonata. Soon he was writing larger symphonic and choral works. In 1909, less than a year after Rimsky-Korsakov died, Stravinsky's orchestral music caught the attention of Sergei Diaghilev (founder of the famed Russian Ballet). Diaghilev commissioned the young composer to contribute music for the company's season the following year in Paris. The 1910 premiere of *The Firebird* ballet established Stravinsky as a brilliant and innovative composer, and other ballets containing Russian folk elements (rhythms, melodies, and folk legends) followed, earning Stravinsky worldwide acclaim. The 1913 ballet *The Rite of Spring*, with its angular rhythms, jarring dissonances, and primitive scenario (a pagan sacrifice), incited the audience first to yelling, then to fist fighting in the aisles, and finally to a full riot in the theater. This ballet completed its seven performances (without any more rioting) and endures today as a masterpiece.

In 1920 Stravinsky took up permanent residence in Paris. During this era between the world wars, his influences were composers such as Poulenc and Debussy and artists like Picasso and Matisse. His music during this time, now defined as "neo-classical," saw a more economical use of instrumentation, clearer harmonies that seemed to look back to Mozart and Bach, and simpler combinations of rhythm and melody, as represented in Stravinsky's choral masterpiece *Symphony of Psalms*.

After World War II, Stravinsky moved to the United States and settled in Hollywood and later in New York City. In his final years he experimented with serialism, producing *Requiem Canticles* and *Cantata*. True to form, Stravinsky departed from "traditional" serial techniques as developed by Schoenberg and devised his own methods for use of the tone row. He died in April 1971 in New York City and was buried in Venice. Stravinsky's legacy as a composer seems to lie in his ability to adapt to novel ideas and experiences, absorb new idioms, and then innovate in directions not seen by other composers.

Composition, Genre, and Historical Perspective

Stravinsky's first sacred choral piece, *Pater Noster* (Lord's Prayer) was composed in 1926 after two profound religious experiences. The first such occurrence took place in Venice when Stravinsky had a contract to perform his piano sonata. He was deeply concerned that a deep abscess on his right index finger would adversely affect his performance, and he apologized to the audience for what he thought would be a sub-standard performance. Stravinsky then looked down, lifted the bandage, and saw that his finger had been healed.

Stravinsky's second religious encounter occurred in Padua, Italy during the 700th anniversary celebration of St. Anthony. He writes in his *Dialogues* that upon entering the basilica, just as a saint's body was exhibited, he made a personal (and undisclosed) request to God: "I saw the coffin, I knelt, and I prayed. I asked that a sign of recognition be given when and if my prayer was answered." His prayer had been granted, and Stravinsky did "not hesitate to call that moment of recognition the most real in my life."

After these profound religious experiences, Stravinsky returned to the faith tradition of his youth by becoming a communicant in the Russian Orthodox Church in Nice, France. Soon after, Stravinsky would publish the *Pater Noster* (Otche nash), *Ave Maria* (Bogoroditse Devo), and *Credo* (Simvol veri) in Church Slavonic, the liturgical language of the Russian Orthodox Church. These works, for 4-part unaccompanied mixed chorus, were eventually adapted by the composer and published in Latin in 1949.

The soprano line of *Pater Noster* is modeled on an Orthodox chant (although the melody is original) and uses only four pitches. (It has been surmised—but never suggested by the composer himself—that Stravinsky used this 4-tone cell to denote the points of the cross.) The homophonic piece is musically restrained and devoid of dynamic or harmonic contrast. Stravinsky once said, "I have always considered that in general it is more satisfactory to proceed by similarity than by contrasts. Music gains strength in the measure that it does not succumb to the seductions of variety. What it loses in questionable riches it gains in true solidity." The staid nature of the piece is exactly the point, according to the composer: "The more art is controlled, limited, worked over, the more it is free... The more constraints one imposes, the more one frees oneself of the pains that shackle the spirit."

Musical Elements and Technical Considerations

Musically, *Pater Noster* is simple and straightforward and will be quite accessible to choirs of modest size. This piece is written in harmonic minor, and could serve as an excellent introduction to the minor mode. Begin instruction by reading through the piece on solfège. Use the metronome early and often in the process to ensure a motoric, forward-moving musical line. Once the choir is able to sing the entire piece on solfège absolutely in tune, move to a neutral syllable. A good syllable choice for the work will be a dark, rounded /u/ ("oo") vowel with an initial consonant /d/. (In any case, choose a neutral syllable that will develop a "French" vowel color, since Stravinsky wrote this piece while he was a French citizen.) Require the choir to sing the entire piece on the neutral syllable with as little change in the integrity of the vowel as possible when moving from note to note. This will ensure a true legato. If the choir drops pitch, vocalize with lip trills and re-sing on the neutral vowel. If at any time the choir becomes harmonically unstable or sings incorrect pitches, return to solfège. Next, the choir will be ready to move to the Latin. Color all vowels toward the French Latin, with dark, rich vocal colors, as Italianate Latin might be a bit too bright for this piece. If intonation problems persist, eliminate the consonants, and insist that the chorus move fluidly from one vowel to the next. Then add back in the consonants, but do not allow these to disrupt the legato phrasing. Avoid "over-pronouncing" the text or disturbing the musical line with undue emphasis of specific syllables or pitches.

Some notes on diction for this piece: Dentalize, but do not aspirate, the /t/ sounds. Ensure that all /s/ sounds do not become /z/ sounds. When an /r/ is between two vowels, "flip" the /r/; when the /r/ sits next to a consonant, "roll" the /r/. When a /t/ sits between two vowels, it is pronounced /ts/. When a "c" begins a word and is followed by a vowel, it is pronounced "ch" as in "church." The "qu" sound is pronounced like /kw/ as in "quick."

Generally speaking, avoid overt shaping of the line. Instead, opt for a restrained approach to the piece with minimal dynamic contrasts. Do not labor at cadential points or add time to any phrases. Keep the line always moving forward in strict time. At points where voices cross, expect the choir to achieve absolute unison, as if one part drops out.

Stylistic Considerations

Stylistically, the piece calls for a simple, modest approach. Remember that Stravinsky designed this piece with self-imposed limits on melodic range, dynamic contrast, and harmonic language. Your performance should be understated and a bit emotionally detached. Listen to recordings of the piece that achieve this neo-classical detachment, and share these recordings with the choir. Strive for a French coloration of the Latin and a forward-moving, motoric musical line. The underlying eighth note does not change amid the constantly shifting meters. The quarter note = 72, and the piece when performed is a bit over a minute long.

Form and Structure

Pater Noster is through composed, but with recurring melodic motives or "cells" in each vocal part. The time signatures and bar lines align with the text, but do not necessarily call for particular emphasis on downbeats. Important cadential points fall either on the dominant or tonic chord. The piece is homophonic, with one or two pitches aligned with each syllable.

Text and Translation

Pater noster qui es in coelis,
sanctificetur nomen tuum:
adveniat regnum tuum: fiat voluntas tua,
sicut in coelo et in terra:
panem nostrum cotidianum da nobis hodie:
et dimitte nobis debita nostra,
sicut et nos dimittimus debitoribus nostris:
et ne nos inducas in tentationem:
sed libera nos a malo. Amen.

Our Father in heaven, hallowed be your name,
your kingdom come, your will be done,
on earth as in heaven.
Give us today our daily bread.
Forgive us our sins as we forgive those who sin against us.
Save us from the time of trial and deliver us from evil.
For the kingdom, the power, and the glory are yours
now and forever. Amen.

Additional References and Resources

Craft, Robert, and Igor Stravinsky. *Dialogues*. Garden City, NY: Doubleday, 1963.
Stravinsky, Igor. *Autobiography*. London: Calder and Boyars, 1975.
Stravinsky, Igor, and George Seferis. *Poetics of Music in the Form of Six Lessons*. Cambridge, MA: Harvard University Press, 1942.
Summer, Robert J. *Choral Masterworks from Bach to Britten*. Scarecrow Press, 2007.
Walsh, Stephen. "Stravinsky, Igor." *Grove Music Online*, 2009.
Walsh, Stephen. *The Music of Stravinsky*. Routledge, 1988.

Contributed by:

James Bowyer

Teacher Resource Guide

Prayer Before Sleep

Sid Robinovitch

(b. 1942)

SATB divisi
Alfred Publishing: VEI 1091
Overall: 3
Vocal: 3
Tonal/Rhythm: 2

Composer (provided by the Canadian Music Centre)

A native of Manitoba, Sid Robinovitch received his Doctorate in Communications from the University of Illinois and taught social sciences at York University in Toronto. Since 1977 he has been devoted to musical composition, having studied at Indiana University and at the Royal Conservatory of Toronto with Samuel Dolin. He presently lives in Winnipeg, Canada, where he works as a composer and teacher.

Having written for a wide variety of musical media, Robinovitch has received commissions from performers such as the Elmer Iseler Singers, the Canadian Piano Trio, and the Winnipeg Symphony Orchestra. His works have been frequently broadcast on CBC radio, including original pieces based on folk tales from around the world and arrangements of Judeo-Spanish folk songs. In 1990 his *Sons of Jacob* for violin and piano was nominated for a Juno award as best classical composition, and in 1991 his *Adieu Babylon* was the commissioned work at the Eckhardt-Gramatté National Music Competition.

While many of Robinovitch's works are rooted in traditional or folk material, they often have a distinctly contemporary flavor as well. *Dreaming Lolita*, for example, is a dramatic retelling in poetic form of the famous Nabokov novel *Lolita*, and in *Psalms of Experience* the choral textures are infused with elements of Balinese music and rhythmic chanting.

In addition to his concert works, Robinovitch has written music for film, radio, and TV, where he is probably best known for his theme for CBC-TV's satirical comedy series, "The Newsroom."

Klezmer Suite, a recording devoted entirely to his music performed by the Winnipeg Symphony under the direction of Bramwell Tovey, was nominated for a 2002 Juno award and received a Prairie Music Award for outstanding classical recording.

Compositional/Genre/Historical Context

"Prayer Before Sleep" is the final movement in a collection of six settings of texts from the Hebrew Talmud. The larger work is entitled *Talmud Suite* and was commissioned by the Elmer Iseler Singers of Toronto through a grant from the Ontario Arts Council. The entire *Talmud Suite* includes the following movements:

I. Thanksgiving Upon Awakening
II. Funeral Oration
III. Song of Protest
IV. On the Death of a Child
V. The Advent of the Messiah
VI. Prayer Before Sleep

Musical Elements

Melody

The melody of "Prayer Before Sleep" occurs first in the bass voice before being traded among the higher voice parts. The graceful melodic contor—either derived from or imitating chant—follows a predictable pattern: a large leap from an anacrusis to the first down beat of a phrase followed by lyrical step-wise motion until the cadence at the end of the verse. The pitch vocabulary of the melody falls within the confines of G major, save for a passing F-natural, referencing the mixolydian mode.

Harmony

The harmonic vocabulary of this piece falls almost entirely within the context of G major. The only chromatic alterations occur in the primary melody—a lowered seventh (F-natural) borrowed from the mixolydian mode. There is conservative use of extended tertian harmonies, built mostly to accommodate passing or neighboring non-chord tones. Robinovitch is thoughtful with his use of dissonance and voice leading, although there are several instances where tendency tones resolve in an unexpected way. In stanza three, the tenor countermelody rises up to the leading tone (F-sharp) before descending again to scale-degree three. Similarly, the treatment of seventh chords within the last three measures of the piece is unconventional; here, the second sopranos move from the seventh of A minor (G), to the seventh of D major (C), before descending a tri-tone to the seventh of G major (F-sharp), and then resolving to the tonic (G).

Rhythm

Robinovitch draws on a simple, chant-inspired rhythmic palette within "Prayer Before Sleep." He almost exclusively uses quarter notes and eighth notes, with an occasional sixteenth note or two thrown in to accommodate necessary text underlay. Robinovitch alters the meter in measures 64 and 65 to facilitate additional text.

Texture

"Prayer Before Sleep" is unaccompanied and, at its thickest, divides into eight parts. The texture of this work varies by verse; the opening stanza is in unison; the second verse poses a secondary melody against the primary material now in the tenor voice; the third verse offers the melody in the soprano and alto lines and a countermelody in the tenor over a near drone in the bass; verse 4 presents the melody in the soprano line with a harmonization in the lower voices.

Form and Structure

Robinovitch sets the text strophically with each of the four verses set slightly differently. The melody occurs first in the bass voice and is then passed to each of the higher voices. The phrasing of the first verse (three short 4-bar phrases followed by a 5-bar phrase) may inform those following.

Verse 1: Unison Basses
Verse 1: Tenor and Bass Duet
Verse 3: Soprano, Alto, and Tenor Trio over a Bass drone
Verse 4: Four Voice Harmonization of Soprano Melody with some additional divisi

Other: Dynamics, Articulation, Tempo, Range

Dynamics: *piano* to *forte* (relating to texture and narrative arc)
Articulation: legato
Tempo: andante, quarter note = ca. 58, liberal slowing at the end
Range: Soprano: D–F'
Alto: B–D
Tenor: D–F-sharp
Bass: G'–C

Technical Considerations

Although "Prayer Before Sleep" is straightforward, there are several technical issues that might arise in your rehearsals. Here are four challenges you might encounter and some rehearsal remedies to help you along the way:

1. *Hebrew Diction*

   If you have no experience singing in Hebrew, fear not—there is likely someone within your community who would love to visit your rehearsal to coach your choir on Hebrew pronunciation. The guide provided by the composer is quite helpful and may suffice. In general, be quite careful with the initial "ch" sound, the apostrophe (a bright schwa sound), and diphthongs, as they are quite different from German.

2. *Intonation*

   When I have performed this piece, the choir often had more success maintaining pitch when they sing it in G-sharp instead of G.

3. *Controlling the Ritard and New Tempo in the final ten bars of the piece*

   Try subdividing from beat two of measure 64, and conduct at the eighth note pulse from there on. From measure 68, be careful not to beat too much—less is more here. Make sure you make eye contact with the voice sections that have moving notes, as a choir can easily lose count when they are camped out on long notes (altos in 68, tenors on beat two of 69, altos on beat two of 71, and second sopranos and tenors on measure 72.)

4. *Voice Leading and Divisi*

   If your choir is smaller in size, you might consider re-voicing this work. The initial verse could be sung by all of your men, for instance. From measure 52 to 69 and measure 71 to 72, consider using a three-way division in the women so that each voice part is equally balanced. Likewise for the men from measure 65 to 71.

Performance Practice

As this is a recently composed work, performance practice can only be speculative. The score is a good source for most information. Dynamic, articulation, and tempo modifications are indicated clearly. Decisions about phrasing and breathing can be derived from the text and the music, but be practical—if you have a small choir and staggered breathing is not an option, use your best judgment and insert some additional corporate breaths as you see fit.

Text and Translation

This Hebrew text is drawn from the Jewish *Talmud*, a compilation of laws, commentaries, legends, and philosophy originating in Palestine and Babylonia during third and eighth centuries. According to the composer, this particular excerpt is from a group of prayers found in the Babylonian Talmud that are recited at home before retiring at night.

Baruch atah Adonai *Eloheinu melech ha-olam* *Hamapil chavlei sheina* *Al einai* *Ut'numah al afapai*	Exalted art Thou, O my Lord Who art God and King of the World, Who weighs down my eyes With gentle bonds of sleep, And refreshes my tired spirit with slumber.
Vihi ratson milfanecha *Adonai Elohai Velohei Avotai* *Shetashkiveini l'shalom* *V'ta-amideini l'shalom*	May ever it be Thy will, Lord my God, and God of all my fathers, To lay me down in untroubled peace And raise me up in peace once
V'al y'vahaluni rayonai *Vachalomot ra-im* *V'harhorim ra-im* *U-t'hi mitati shleima l'fanecha*	Do not let dark imaginings disturb me With thoughts of sin and despair. O heal my fear and my suffering – May my bed be enclosed in Thy care.
V'ha-er einai *Pen ishan hamavet* *Ki atah hame-ir* *L'ishon bat-ayin* *Baruch atah Adonai* *Hame-ir la-olam kulo* *Bichvodo*	Give light unto my eyes Lest the sleep of death o'ertake me. For 'tis Thou who breathes life Into our slumb'ring soul. Exalted art Thou, O Lord, Who illuminates all the world With His Glory.

A Hebrew pronunciation guide is supplied in the score by the composer.

Recordings

Robinovitch, Sid. "Prayer Before Sleep" from *The Talmud Suite*, performed by the Elmer Iseler Singers (Elmer Iseler, conductor). On *Gloria: Sacred Choral Works*. CBC Records: MVCD 1058, 1993.

Robinovitch, Sid. "Prayer Before Sleep" from *The Talmud Suite*, performed by the University of Miami Chorale (Jo-Michael Scheibe, conductor). On *Voices and Light*. Albany Records: TROY 215, 1996.

Contributed by:

Emilie Amrein

Teacher Resource Guide

Psalm 100 (Jauchzet dem Herrn)

Felix Mendelssohn

(1809–1847)

SATB

GIA Publications, Inc.: G-5929

Overall: 3

Vocal: 4

Tonal/Rhythm: 3

Composer

Felix Mendelssohn was born in Hamburg to a wealthy Jewish banking family in 1809. Felix and his siblings Fanny, Rebecka, and Paul were baptized as Protestants in 1816, by interesting coincidence on March 21, the birthday of Johann Sebastian Bach. Felix was given the names Jacob Ludwig, and the surname Bartholdy was added after his parents' conversion in 1822, resulting in the name Felix Jacob Ludwig Mendelssohn-Bartholdy.

Mendelssohn and his older sister Fanny both became accomplished pianists and composers at an early age, and both developed successful musical careers; Fanny as a concert pianist and composer and Felix as an internationally recognized conductor, organist, and composer. His compositional oeuvre includes chamber works, symphonies, art songs, choral works, and of course his two completed oratorios, *St. Paul* and *Elijah*.

Mainly recognized during his life as a conductor, Mendelssohn is credited with stimulating a renewed interest in the music of J. S. Bach, which began with young Felix directing a performance of the *St. Matthew Passion* in 1829. Mendelssohn served as a guest conductor throughout Europe during his relatively short career, and as he was frequently asked to be a guest conductor at the annual Birmingham Festival, he was one of the first conductor-composers to make numerous trips to England. He became director of the Leipzig Gewandhaus Orchestra in 1835 and brought that ensemble to the forefront of European orchestras during his 12-year tenure.

Due to his studies at the Berlin Singakademie with Carl Friedrich Zelter, Mendelssohn developed a strong appreciation for the great composers who preceded him, notably Handel, Mozart, Beethoven, and of course Bach. As a result, his music is a fascinating fusion between Romantic, Baroque, and Classical compositional techniques. He died in late 1847 from a series of strokes brought on by continually declining health and the shock of his sister Fanny's sudden death in May of that year.

Composition, Genre, and Historical Perspective

Many of Mendelssohn's earlier, shorter works can be placed into his oeuvre not only as worthy compositions in their own right, but also as pseudo-preparatory studies. The compositional style he explored in these early pieces led to his more ambitious undertakings, notably the oratorios *St. Paul* and *Elijah*. This is the case with a series of psalm settings composed between 1837 and 1844. The settings of Psalms 42, 95, 98, and 114 are for chorus, orchestra, and soloists in multiple movements and can be thought of in the same style as his eight chorale cantatas. Among the *a cappella* Psalm settings, there are two in English (Psalms 5 and 31), the well-known opus 78 (including Psalms 2, 43, and 22, all in German), and a setting of psalm 100, *Jauchzet dem Herrn* (1844). Many of the *a cappella* settings are for 8-part divisi choir or double choir, but *Jauchzet dem Herrn* is primarily set for SATB choir, with the middle section set for SATB divisi soloists (although these solo lines can be sung by the entire chorus, as discussed later). This is Mendelssohn's second setting of Psalm 100; the earlier setting is for straight SATB choir.

Technical Considerations and Musical Elements

Like most of Mendelssohn's smaller choral works, this piece is well crafted in terms of tonal motion, melodic lines, and formal structure. In fact, at initial glance it appears to be straightforward, almost easy. Careful study of the score will, however, reveal certain aspects that should be considered before programming. At the top of that list would be the extended 8-part divisi in the middle section, which also happens to be in the somewhat problematic key of F major. While Mendelssohn has marked this middle section to be sung by soloists, it is certainly possible, perhaps even preferred, to use the entire choir or perhaps only a smaller portion of the choir for this section.

Ranges for all voice parts are within the capabilities of a good high school choir, but it should be noticed that all voice parts do need to negotiate an octave and a half in range. As in much of Mendelssohn's choral writing, the tenor line often lies fairly high in the voice, with the tenor I singing several high Gs and a high A in the concluding phrase. A strong bass section that is capable of sustaining a low G and F will be needed, but the soprano and alto lines are more accessible, with primarily a high F needed for the sopranos and low C and B-flat for the altos.

Melodic lines for each voice are for the most part tuneful and easily sung; they are in fact largely stepwise in motion. Although the piece is largely through composed, melodic fragments return periodically throughout and serve as subtle unifying elements. The occasional accidentals found in each part should feel natural to the singers after relatively little rehearsal, especially after the choir understands where the piece is headed tonally. This being said, the basses will need to sing octaves and intervals of a 4th or 5th accurately, and there are certain slightly more unexpected leaps on rare occasion in each voice part. There are numerous suspensions throughout, but all are well prepared and easily sung.

Mendelssohn is not nearly as tonally adventurous as later Romantic composers such as Bruckner or Brahms, so the tonal motion of phrases is relatively straightforward. When there are chords outside of the main key, they last only a beat or two and are almost invariably a secondary dominant of some sort, resolving naturally to the appropriate chord. Since the main keys of C and F major are so closely related, the transitions between the main sections will be easily negotiated as well.

Rhythmic aspects are extremely simple. The most difficult rhythm involves a dotted-quarter note followed by an eighth note, and this occurs only five or six times in the entire piece. An equal balance of homophonic and polyphonic writing is found throughout, and any rhythmically independent lines last for no more than a few measures. Dynamics are not extreme, extending only from *forte* to *piano*, but there are numerous *crescendo–decrescendo* markings that occur over a single measure that need to be observed. All in all, the most problematic aspect of the piece might be the fact that it is in German (and this will slow down the learning process only if the choir is not used to the language).

Stylistic Considerations

As in much Romantic music, the conductor should feel free to experiment with rubato, but this should follow the natural rise and fall of the vocal lines. There should certainly be a slowing of the tempo when approaching cadential points, but the amount of *ritard* should vary in relation to the finality of the cadence. Cadences marked with a *fermata*, for instance, should be approached with more *ritard*, whereas a more gentle relaxation in tempo should occur leading to cadential points in the context of a larger section. In any instance, it is vital that a return to the original tempo happen following any cadential point.

Mendelssohn marks *Andante con moto* for the opening section (mm. 1 to 31) of this psalm setting. As he writes in common time, the feel of a decently quick four should be felt, verging on the feel of a broader two. This must be contrasted with the return to C major in measure 64, where *Andante* is marked and a distinct feel of four should be felt. Marked *Poco Lento*, the middle section in F major (mm. 32 to 63) should be more expansive in tempo than either the opening or concluding sections.

A full yet healthy tone should be used for the *forte* sections of the piece and a subdued yet sustained tone for the *piano* sections, always with the recognition that dynamics are not as extreme as those found in late Romantic music. Since the word underlay is largely syllabic throughout, the choir may have a tendency to sing with a slight decay on each note, resulting in a pulsing effect. The singers must instead concentrate on singing through each phrase, sustaining and energizing each note.

Obviously the teaching of this piece should begin by eliminating the German, using instead a neutral syllable. However, with relatively few accidentals, this could be an excellent piece on which to employ solfège as part of the learning process, at least on the four-part sections. When adding in the text, good diction must be consistently encouraged, with special emphasis placed upon robust German consonants.

Form and Structure

The work is *a cappella*, through composed, in three sections (F major, C major, and F major respectively), and uses the first five verses of Psalm 100.

Section	Measures	Event and Scoring
I (verses 1–3)	mm. 1–31	SATB, *andante con moto*, homophonic with occasional points of imitation
II (verse 4)	mm. 32–63	SSAATTBB, *poco lento*, primarily homophonic, opening with antiphonal writing between women's and men's sections
III (verse 5)	mm. 64–84	SATB, *andante*, almost entirely homophonic

Text and Translation

Psalm 100: 1–5. English is from the King James version of The Holy Bible.

Jauchzet dem Herrn alle Welt!
Dienet dem Herrn mit Freuden, kommt vor sein Angesicht mit Frohlocken.
Erkennet, dass der Herr Gott ist. Er hat uns gemacht
und nicht wir selbst zu seinem Volk und zu Schaafen seiner Weide.
Gehet zu seinen Thoren ein, mit Danken, zu seinen Vorhöfen, mit Loben
danket ihm, und lobet seinen Namen.
Denn der Herr ist freundlich und seine Gnade wahret ewig,
und seine Wahrheit währet für und für.

Make a joyful noise unto the Lord, all ye lands,
Serve the Lord with gladness, come before his presence with singing.
Know ye that the Lord, he is God; it is he that hath made us,
and not we ourselves, we are
his people, and the sheep of his pasture.
Enter into his gates with thanksgiving,
and into his courts with praise;
be thankful unto him, and bless his name.
For the Lord, he is good; his mercy is everlasting,
and his truth endureth to all generations.

Contributed by:

David Scholz

Teacher Resource Guide

Revoici venir du Printemps

Claude Le Jeune

(1528/30–c.1600)

SATB
Belwin Mills: DMC 1203
Overall: 3
Vocal: 3
Tonal/Rhythm: 3

Composer

Claude Le Jeune was born in either 1528 or 1530 in (or around) the town of Valenciennes in the north of France, near the modern border with Belgium. His first published works appear in print in the early 1550s within *chanson* collections. Le Jeune's next published work, *Dix Pseaumes de David,* appears in 1564 and is dedicated to two Huguenot members of Charles IX's court. As a Protestant, he relied on the protection of Huguenot nobles such as William of Orange and Henri of Navarre during the sporadic wars of religion that plagued France in the late sixteenth century. Le Jeune probably lived in Paris during most of the 1560s and published his works through a local publisher there.

In 1570 he joined with poet Jean-Antoine Baïf and composer Thibault de Courville to compose, perform, and promote *musique mesureé à l'antique*, a new style of music that sought to combine contemporary French verse with classical ideals of declamation and text accent. As part of their collaborations, Le Jeune (and others) set a large number of Baïf's texts to music, including "Revoici venir du Printemps." In addition to *musique mesureé*, Le Jeune also composed many settings of psalm tunes and texts from the Genevan Psalter intended for liturgical use in Huguenot churches.

Le Jeune was employed as *maistre des enfants de musique* in the court of François, Duke of Anjou, from 1582 until the Duke's death in 1584. Even though Le Jeune had composed much music by this time, he had published very little. This was due in part to the fact that Baïf's *Académie de Poésie et de Musique*, to which Le Jeune belonged, was focused on developing their new art form within the relative secrecy of their own fellowship. Baïf's grand plan did not include exposing their work to the general public until after their style and ideals were well established and well recognized among the intellectual class. This point never arrived, and although he planned to publish many of his works in the late 1590s, much of it was only published after his death in the first decade of the 1600s. Once published, his large body of works influenced many later French composers, including Olivier Messiaen (1908–1992), whose *Cinq rechants* (1948) is an homage to Le Jeune's work.

Composition, Genre, and Historical Perspective

As mentioned above, this work is an example of a unique style known as *musique mesureé à l'antique*. The striking feature of *musique mesureé* is the fact that the rhythms are all predetermined by the long and short stresses of text, with a long stress receiving double the duration of a short stress. The result is an overwhelmingly irregular meter.

Unlike the contemporaneous *chanson*, *musique mesureé* tended more toward homophony. While "Revoici venir du Printemps" on the whole is evocative of springtime, it is not very madrigalian in its localized word painting.

Musical Elements and Technical Considerations

The varying rhythmic accents will undoubtedly be the most difficult aspect in the learning of this piece. For the conductor, identifying the groupings of two and three that arise from the text is essential. The next step is communicating those groupings to the choir, both through well-prepared scores (an angle bracket above groupings of three and a square bracket above groupings of two are employed in this edition) and through slow and careful speech and response of the text in rhythm. Adding a physical gesture on the first syllable of each beat grouping will be helpful in achieving a dance-like final product.

Another difficulty lie in dealing with the issue of language. The French of "Revoici venir du Printemps" dates from the late sixteenth century, and the fact that Baïf was a champion of his own idiosyncratic spelling methods further complicates matters. Within the many editions of this piece, both historical and modern, I count no fewer than five spellings of the word "revoici" ("revecy," "revesy," "revoicy," "revoici," and "revesi,"), sometimes used interchangeably within one edition! In addition, some early printed versions of the piece include a modified, rhyming version of the text that was carried out after the death of both Le Jeune and the poet Baïf. For simplicity, this edition uses a modern French realization of Baïf's original text.

When approaching a sixteenth-century French text, the performer is invited to explore the possibility of performing the text with historically accurate pronunciation, for which I refer the performer to the excellent book *Singing Early Music*. (See the reference list below for more information on this title.) One should note that the issue of historically accurate pronunciation is perhaps a little more problematic than usual in this case due to the fact that Baïf's original spellings seem to imply pronunciations that are possibly not even in keeping with his own contemporary French dialect.

The sections of the piece alternate between the *Rechant à 5* and *Chant* for 2, 3, 4, and 5 parts. The *rechants* are to be sung by the entire choir, while the *chants* may be sung as written, by semi-choirs from within those sections, or by soloists. Where practical, I believe that performing the *chants* with a semi-chorus or soloists helps to provide textural variety and makes the buildup to the final *rechant* more compelling.

In keeping with early editions, no tempo is indicated in this edition. The piece calls for a tempo that allows the piece to take on the airy, joyous atmosphere that the text describes, while not being so fast that the text is lost in the commotion. For most spaces and choirs, I would suggest something in the range of half note = 104–138. Also, in keeping with early editions, barlines only appear at the ends of the lines of text.

Stylistic Considerations

A successful performance of this piece calls for a sense of dance as conveyed through the sprightly changing rhythms and clarity of text through well-expressed diction. In order to effectively render the swiftly changing harmonies and to best portray the springtime atmosphere, it is advisable to stick to a lighter tone with minimal vibrato.

Form and Structure

As noted above, "Revoici venir du Printemps" alternates between *rechants*, which act as a sort of refrain, and *chants*, which are like verses. The first *chant* is a duet. Over the course of the piece, the *chants* add one more voice each time, building to the final *Chant à 5*. The *rechants* are all direct repetitions of one another, but the *chants* have the sense of a developing variation.

Rechant à 5 [x 2]
    Chant à 2
Rechant à 5
    Chant à 3
Rechant à 5
    Chant à 4
Rechant à 5
    Chant à 5
Rechant à 5

Text and Translation

Revoici venir du printemps,
L'amoureuse et belle saison.

Le courant des eaux recherchant
Le canal d'été s'éclaircît:
Et la mer calme de ces flots
Amollit le triste couroux:
Le canard s'égaie se plongeant,
Et se lave coint dedans l'eau;
Et la grue qui fourche son vol
Retraverse l'air et s'en va.

Revoici…

Le soleil éclaire luisant
D'une plus sereine clarté;
Du nuage l'ombre s'enfuit,
Qui se joue et court et noircit
Et forêts et champs et couteux.
Le labeur humain reverdit,
Et la pré découvre ses fleurs.

Revoici…

De Vénus le fils Cupidon
L'univers semant de ses traits,
De sa flamme va réchauffer,
Animaux, qui volent en l'air,
Animaux, qui rampent aux champs,
Animaux, qui nagent aux eaux.
Ce qui mêmement ne sent pas,
Amoureux se fond de plaisir.

Revoici…

Rions aussi nous: et cherchons
Les ébats et jeux du printemps:
Toute chose rit de plaiser:
Célébrons la gaie saison.

Revoici…

[1]Here comes the spring again,
the beautiful season of love.

The flow of the water seeking its
summer channel becomes clear,
and the calm sea with its waves
mollifies its grim danger;
the duck enjoys diving
and bathes himself in the water;
and the crane, which forks its wing,
criss-crosses the sky and goes away.

Here comes…

The sun shines
with brightness more serene;
it chases shadows from the clouds
which play and run and darken
the forests and fields and hills.
The fields the men work become green,
and the meadow reveals its flowers.

Here comes…

Venus' son, Cupid
sowing the world with arrows,
will inflame with his fire
creatures that fly in the air,
creatures that crawl in the fields,
creatures that swim in the water.
Even the being with not sensation
will feel love and drown in pleasure.

Here comes…

Let us laugh too,
and let us seek the revels and games
of spring:
everything laughs with pleasure:
let us celebrate the merry season.

Here comes…

1 This uncredited translation is found underlain in the *Oxford Partsongs and Madrigals* edition. The copyright notice for the entire volume reads: © Oxford University Press, 2001.

Additional References and Resources

Le Jeune, Claude. *Airs*. 1608. A modern edition edited by D. P. Walker with introduction by François Lesure and D. P. Walker. Rome: American Institute of Musicology, 1951.

———. *Printemps*. 1603. A modern edition edited by M. Henry Expert. New York: Broude Brothers, n.d., ca. 1950. [This edition includes a facsimile of Baïf's text in its original spelling.]

———. *Recent Researches in the Music of the Renaissance*. Edited by James Haar. Vol. 98, *Les cent cinquante pseaumes de David, mis en musique a quatre [a cinq] parties*, edited by Anne Harrington Heider. Madison, WI: A-R Editions, 1995.

———. "Revoici venir du printemps," in *Oxford Choral Classics*. Edited by John Rutter. *Madrigals and Partsongs*, edited by Clifford Bartlett. Oxford: Oxford University Press, 2001. [See pp. 194–201, 373.]

McGee, Timothy J., A. G. Rigg, and David N. Klausner, eds. *Singing Early Music: the pronunciation of European languages in the Late Middle Ages and Renaissance*. Bloomington: Indiana University Press, 1996.

Contributed by:

Gregory Brown

Teacher Resource Guide

Sir Christèmas

William Mathias
(1934–1992)

SATB/organ
Oxford University Press: 3430088
Overall: 3
Vocal: 3
Tonal/Rhythm: 4

Composer

William Mathias (1934–1992) was a Welsh composer. He began his music studies at a young age and began composing at the age of 3. Formal music training took place at the University College of Wales, Aberystwyth and the Royal Academy of Music. In addition to being a prolific composer throughout his life, Mathias also taught at the University College of North Wales, and founded the North Wales International Music Festival in St. Asaph in 1972, which he directed until his death in 1992. Mathias wrote in various genres including an opera *The Servants* (1982), three piano concertos, significant organ music, an organ concerto, and so on. Many of his works, such as his clarinet and harp concertos, have entered the repertoire of many orchestras. His most famous works are his choral works, especially the sacred works. Perhaps most notable is *Let the People Praise Thee, O God*, which was written in 1981 for the royal wedding of the Prince and Princess of Wales.

Composition, Genre, and Historical Perspective

"Sir Christèmas" comes from the larger work *Ave Rex*, Op. 45, a carol sequence for choir and orchestra. This work was commissioned by the Cardiff Polyphonic Choir and was first performed in 1969. *Ave Rex* is a work in four movements with texts inspired by anonymous medieval lyrics:

I. "Ave Rex" (Hail, King of angels)
II. "Alleluya, a new work is come on hand"
III. "There is no rose of such virtue"
IV. "Sir Christèmas"

Mathias himself created a reduction of the orchestral version for organ. It is not appropriate for the accompaniment to be played on piano. "Sir Christèmas" works well in performance on its own and provides a well-needed up tempo seasonal sacred option to a holiday program.

Musical Elements and Technical Considerations

Many carols with Medieval texts have multiple languages, typically English and Latin, within one setting. This is known as a *macaronic* text. "Sir Christèmas" is a macaronic carol, but is unique in that the two languages are English and French. Because of the mixed languages, the Medieval nature of the English, and the rhythmic complexity of the piece, it makes most sense to introduce this piece through the text. Speak through the French, go over unfamiliar English words such as "brayed" (pronounced "braid" to rhyme with "maid"), and odd turns of phrase such as "and be right merry." In this style it is important to insist upon British pronunciation of the English text and to eliminate as many "Americanisms" as possible. For instance, the word "nowell" should have a open "o" sound for the first vowel without the presence of a diphthong, and the second syllable should begin with a fast "w" glide, followed by an open "eh" sound, and concluding with a forward, flipped "l" sound.

Once the choir has internalized the correct pronunciation of both the English and French it is helpful to speak the text in rhythm. Make sure to use a higher pitched speaking voice with the appropriate articulation and accents. Mathias is very clear about the placement of accents, and speaking the text allows the choir time to focus on this level of detail without worrying about singing correct pitches. Be sure to point out the one moment of dynamic variation: the *crescendo* in measure 30 to *fortissimo* through conclusion.

Mathias's writing is frequently based on short melodic motives, which he often develops through modal treatments. In learning the pitches. it might be effective to work the "Nowell" sections paying attention to the subtle changes that Mathias adds:

1. Mm. 2–3: S and T in unison
2. Mm. 12–13: S and T in unison, A: countermelody.
3. Mm. 19–20: same as 12-13.
4. Mm. 24–25: S&T in union, A and B in unison at the perfect fifth.
5. Mm. 31–32: same as 31–32, a dynamic level louder.

Understanding the construction will help the singers to know where they are heading in each coming section.

It is worth taking time to break down the pitches of measures 8 to 11. The modal feeling of this section may be elusive to some singers. It is advisable to create a 3-part women's divisi for this section. Measures 26 through 31 require special attention as well, especially with the tricky transition out of measure 25. For these complicated note sections, remove the articulation and text, sing legato on a neutral syllable so the pitches tune, and lock into their open sonorities.

Stylistic Considerations

The most important factor in preparing Mathias in a stylistically appropriate way is articulation. Although the score has no markings to this effect, it is clear that the composer intends a variety of articulation within the phrases. Measures 2 and 3 (and respective repetitions) should be rather clipped and marcato, yet performed with a clear sense of the larger phrase. The conductor must make a decision as to how to treat the final "l" of the word "Nowell." Clearly the sound should be a forward "l" and, depending on the acoustics of the performance space, might be best served by a shadow schwa following the "l."

The sectional solo phrases of measures 4, 6–7, 14–17, and 20–23 lend themselves to a more lyrical articulation. Diction should be clear, and each note should spring directly to the vowel, yet with more of an arching phrase structure and line than the "Nowell" ritornello.

The sections with the homophonic, thick harmony as in measures 8 to 11 and 26 to 30, are perhaps the most difficult. The harmonies change at a fast pace, so the pitches must be immediately clear. Each part must be able to sing its respective line with complete clarity, springing to the center of each pitch. Having said this, these sections can very quickly become very note heavy, especially with the constant long-short-long-short note values. Care must be taken to make sure that the larger phrase structure is always clearly defined. The phrasing of measure 8 should go to the first syllable of "Christèmas," probably with an eighth rest breath at the end of the measure. The measure 9 phrase should move forward to the downbeat of measure 10 on the word "near." Make sure the notes marked staccato in measure 10 are not so short that the sonority is not clear. Perhaps a clearer indication for most singers would be staccato with a tenuto mark. Measures 26 and 27 should be treated as one phrase with singers phrasing across the eighth rest in measure 26. The staccato indication on beat four in measure 27 most likely indicates that the choir should re-sing the vowel, which provides a jovial sense to the phrase. Measures 28 through 30 into measure 31 should be sung without a collective breath and with the phrase moving forward to the climax of measures 31 through 34. The tie to the eighth note on beat two of measure 34 is standard British notation for the placement of the final consonant. The presence of the accent mark indicates a strong shadow schwa following the final "l."

Shouted final endings can frequently be problematic. One must consider where to place the shout in the voice, how to articulate the two syllables, and most importantly, how to express the appropriate joyful emotion without sounding apathetic on one end or over the top on the other. The shout must be fully supported in nature, with the sound coming from the chest not from the throat. The shout should be pitched in the upper register of the speaking voice, and both syllables of the word "Nowell" should receive equal weight.

Form and Structure

"Sir Christ̹èmas" is a miniature form with sections often 2- or 3-bars long. There are three distinct sections within the piece that create a modified rondo form. The composite form is: ABABCABABACA.

A: Nowell ritornello: increases in complexity with each repetition.
B: Sectional solo lines: relates the story of the carol.
C: Full choir statements: strongest, most joyful moments.

Section	Measure	Event and Scoring
Introduction	m. 1	
A	m. 2	soprano and tenor, unison
B	m. 4	alto solo line
A	m. 5	soprano and tenor, unison
B	mm. 6–7	bass solo line
C	mm. 8–11	full choir
A	mm. 12–13	soprano and tenor, unison; alto, countermelody.
B	mm. 14–17	bass solo line
A	mm. 18–19	soprano and tenor, unison; alto, countermelody.
B	mm. 20–23	soprano solo line
A	mm. 24–25	soprano and tenor, unison; alto and bass, unison at the 5th.

SECTION	MEASURE	EVENT AND SCORING
C	mm. 26–30	full choir
A	mm. 31–33	soprano and tenor, unison; alto and bass, unison at the 5th.

Text and Translation

Anonymous, ca. 1500:

Nowell, nowell.
Who is there that singeth so,
Nowell, nowell?
I am here, Sir Christèmas.
Welcome, my lord Sir Christèmas!
Wlecome to all, both more and less, come near.
Dieu vous garde, beaux sieurs, [God keep you, kind sirs]
Tidings I you bring:
A maid hath borne a child full young,
Which causeth you to sing:
Nowell, nowell.
Christ is now born of a pure maid;
In an oxstall he is laid,
Wherefore sing we at a brayde:
Nowell, nowell.
Buvez bien par toute la compagnie. [Good health to everyone]
Make good cheer and be right merry,
And sing with us now joyfully:
Nowell, nowell!

Additional References and Resources

Craggs, Stewart R. *William Mathias: A Bio-Bibliography*. Westport, CT: Greenwood Press, 1995.

McCray, James. "The choral music of William Mathias." *The Diapason*. Vol. 84, no. 9, September, 1993: pp. 14–15.

Slawson, John. "The choral music of William Mathias." DMA thesis, University of Cincinnati. 1985.

Contributed by:

W. Bryce Hayes

Teacher Resource Guide

The Water Is Wide

Steven Paulus

(b. 1949)

SAB/harp or piano
European American Music: 49012822
Overall: 3
Vocal: 3
Tonal/Rhythm: 4

Composer

Stephen Paulus is regarded as one of the leading American composers of the last quarter century. He has been commissioned by leading orchestras such as the New York Philharmonic, Atlanta Symphony, and Dallas Symphony. He has been commissioned to write works for some of the world's leading soloists such as Evelyn Lear, Thomas Hampson, Doc Severinson, Håkan Hågegard and others. He is a leading opera composer, holding residencies at leading festivals such as Aspen, Santa Fe, and Tanglewood, and composed for opera companies around the United States.

Typically, a composer of this stature composes little in the way of choral music, save for large works for chorus and orchestra. A Minnesota resident, Paulus has had a strong relationship to the vibrant choral community there, and his music was championed at a very young age by Dale Warland and his Singers. As a result he has written a great deal of quality works for choirs of all ability levels. Paulus has written large scale choral works such as *The Meditations of Li Po*, as well as small works for young voices and church choirs, such as "Sing Hallelu," and "The Water Is Wide."

His style is distinctly American in harmony, melody, texture, and rhythm. His harmony is in descendant of Copland's American sound, yet with the deeply moving harmonies of the late twentieth century. His melodies are often lyrical, easily sung, and flattering to the voice. Rhythm and textures combine to create music of great energy and momentum.

Composition, Genre, and Historical Perspective

"The Water Is Wide" is an arrangement of one of America's most beloved and familiar folksongs. As with most folksongs, or music of the people, exact origins are hard to discover. It is known that the tune we recognize as "The Water Is Wide" was originally set to the text of "O Waly, Waly"—a text of Scottish or English origin. The song has been sung since the 1600s and continues its popularity today. As conductor and choir together study the history and journey of this timeless song, much can be learned about how music changes with the times yet remains the same, and how different cultures adopt and adapt music from other places, peoples, and times.

The texts of both "O Waly, Waly" and "The Water Is Wide" tracks the course of failed love, from the warmth of new love, through initial disillusionment, then loss. "O waly, waly" means, roughly, "Oh, woe is me." As with many folksongs, there are many variations of text and subtle variations of tune, but the major text points and sentiment remain.

For a good introduction to the Scottish version, play Benjamin Britten's setting of "O Waly, Waly" from his *Folksongs from the British Isles*. American versions to share with your choir are recordings by Samuel Barber, James Taylor, Joan Baez, and many others, such as on the *Lilith Fair* tour of the 1990s when it was sung by Jewel, Sarah McLachlan, and the Indigo Girls.

Musical Elements and Technical Considerations

"The Water is Wide" sets a great example that leading composers can write art music for young voices. This arrangement of a familiar tune is impressively simple with just enough twists to be interesting and satisfying to beginning groups as well as to the Dale Warland Singers, who premiered this work.

The vocal texture throughout this strophic setting is unison, save for the third verse. Verse 1 is soprano and alto in unison, verse two is men in unison, verse three is a suggested baritone solo with soprano and alto adding delicate harmony, and the fourth verse is unison chorus.

This piece is a great beginning of the year piece for the SAB choir, or a simple concert addition for other choirs. Paulus is a brilliant composer, and his voice is heard in the exquisite accompaniment, which is scored for harp, but is also effective on piano. His music is distinctly American in its harmony, employing tasteful dissonance, beautiful extended harmonies, and open texture to create a melancholy atmosphere. Whereas the unison voices strictly adhere to the melody, Paulus's substitutions of harmony, shifting chord types that occur at the same point in the melody, teach young singers to sing dissonance and other chord tones all the while they are singing the same melody.

The only challenging section of the work is verse 3. Paulus sets the soprano and alto to sing a simple counterpoint to the melody in the baritone voice (for younger groups feel free to use soli, a small group of soloists). The soprano and alto accompaniment is also scored in a disjunct, open style, reflecting the American sound described above. Leaps of 7ths and 4ths are common, and at times the women sing nonharmonic tones and color tones in extended chords. When possible, Paulus assists the singers by approaching the dissonant notes by step, or by doubling pitchesin the piano.

Vocally, Paulus is careful to assist untrained voices by providing numerous breaks in the melody for breaths. He asks the singers to sustain the first two phrases of each verse, for example "The water is wide, I cannot get o'er" and "And neither have I wings to fly." For the remainder of each verse, Paulus inserts rests after each short phrase of text. Young choirs of course will instinctively want to breathe in these places, and in many arrangements this breaks the flow of the phrase. Here, Paulus builds in the breaks and asks the singer and conductor to shape each short statement, ending each phrase in a way that creates continuity through the rests.

Form and Structure

Strophic, with two measure intro and six-measure outro.

Verse 1: SA unison
Verse 2: Men unison
Verse 3: Baritone solo with SA
Verse 4: Choir unison

Text and Translation

As the text is English or Scottish in origin, it is good to remember that American English is a foreign translation of the original text. For that reason, included here is a version of Scottish origin, perhaps more closely tied to the original, followed by the variation of the text used in this arrangement.

Waly, Waly, gin Love be bonny

O Waly, waly, (a lament—"woe is me") up the bank,
And waly, waly, doun the brae (hill),
And waly, waly, yon burn-side (riverside),
Where I and my Love wont to gae (go)!

I lean'd my back unto an aik (oak),
I thocht it was a trustie tree;
But first it bow'd and syne (soon) it brak (broke)—
Sae my true love did lichtlic (lightly) me.
O waly, waly, gin love be bonnie (beautiful),
A little time while it is new!
But when 'tis auld (old) it waxeth cauld (cold),
And fades awa' like morning dew.
O wherefore should I busk my heid (adorn my head),
Or wherefore should I kame (comb) my hair?
For my true Love has me forsook,
And says he'll never loe me mair (more).
Now Arthur's Seat
Sall (shall) be my bed (burial place),
The sheets sall ne'er be 'filed by me;
Saint Anton's well sall be my drink;
Since my true Love has forsaken me.
Marti'mas wind, when wilt thou blaw (blow),
And shake the green leaves aff the tree?
O gentle Death, when wilt thou come?
For of my life I am wearìe.
'Tis not the frost, that freezes fell,
Nor blawing snaw's (snow) inclemencie,
'Tis not sic cauld (such cold) that makes me cry;
But my Love's heart grown cauld to me.
When we cam in by Glasgow toun,
We were a comely sicht (sight)to see;
My Love was clad in the black velvèt,
And I mysel in cramasie (crimson).
But had I wist (known), before I kist (a coffin = died),
That love had been sae ill to win,
I had lock'd my heart in a case o' gowd (gold),
And pinn'd it wi' a siller (silver) pin.
And O! if my young babe were born,
And set upon the nurse's knee;
And I mysel were dead and gane,
And the green grass growing over me!

The Water is Wide

The water is wide, I cannot get o'er,
And neither have I wings to fly.
Give me a boat that can carry two,
And both shall row, my love and I.

I leaned my back 'gainst some young oak,
Thinking it was a trusty tree.
But first it bent and then it broke,
Just as my love proved false to me.

Oh, love is handsome, love is fine,
Bright as a jewel when first it's new,
But love grows old and waxeth cold,
And fades away like morning dew.

The water is wide I cannot get o'er,
And neither have I wings to fly.
Give me a boat that can carry two,
And both shall row, my love and I.

Recordings

"The Water is Wide." Stephen Paulus, *Lux Arumque*, Dale Warland Singers, Dale Warland. Gothic Records

Web Site

www.StephenPaulus.com

Contributed by:

Geoffrey Boers

Teacher Resource Guide

This We Know

Ron Jeffers

SATB
Earthsongs: S-002
Overall: 3
Vocal: 2
Tonal/Rhythm: 4

Composer

Ron Jeffers is best known as founder and owner of *earthsongs* publishing company. Based in Corvallis, Oregon, earthsongs has distinguished itself as the premiere American publisher of global choral music. Jeffers is also the author of a four-book series titled *Translations and Annotations of Choral Repertoire*. Volume I is Sacred Latin Texts, Volume II is German Texts, Volume III is French and Italian Texts, and Volume IV is Hebrew Texts. These resources are a staple of every conductor's library. Jeffers is Professor of Music Emeritus at Oregon State University.

Composition, Genre, and Historical Perspective

The *earthsongs* edition of "This We Know," with English, German, French, and Spanish translations, was prepared for the First World Symposium on Choral Music held in Vienna, Austria in August, 1987. The "Performance Notes" on the back cover read:

> *It is dedicated to the International Federation for Choral Music (I.F.C.M.) and to the abiding wisdom and spirit of Chief Seattle. Dona nobis pacem.*

Chief Seattle or Sealth (Lushottseed c. 1786–June 7, 1866) (also spelled Seathle, Seathl, or See-ahth), was a leader of the Suquamish and Duwamish Native American tribes and tribes in what is now the state of Washington. A prominent figure among his people, he pursued a path of accommodation to white settlers. The city of Seattle, Washington was named after him. There is significant dispute over whether Chief Seattle actually spoke the words attributed to him. Nonetheless, whatever the origin, the text serves as an excellent teaching tool for environmental awareness, and as a poignant reminder of the interconnectedness and sanctity of life.

Musical Elements

"This We Know" is a short (41 measures) homophonic piece. The simple rhythms gently follow the speech pattern of the text. The occasional metric shifts are used for text emphasis. There is no tempo marking, but the harmonic rhythm lends itself to quarter note = 60. Except for the presence of three eighth notes, the entirely homophonic work uses principally quarter-note and half-note motion. While the piece is written and begins in the key of A minor (and ends in A major), the use of chromaticism throughout gives the work a sense of momentary key shifts.

This is a simple work accessible to any choir able to sing in four-part harmony. However, due to its somewhat austere hymn-like structure, directors and singers will need to focus on accurate intonation, subtle use of dynamic markings, and clear enunciation of text. Word stress is mostly accommodated through the use of rhythmic declamation.

The voice leading is simple, but the harmonies will require repetition and familiarity for clear vertical clarity. Additionally, tidy, crisp and unified consonants are necessary for intelligibility and sustained vowels.

The opening harmonic scheme (mm. 1 through 5) is echoed in measures 9 through 13. Finding these rhythmic and harmonic similarities will assist in the learning process. "This We Know" is an excellent teaching tool for voice leading and chord inversions. It is also a wonderful piece for exercising choral intonation, as the harmonies move so slowly as to allow singers to engage in active listening.

One concern for younger choirs are the slightly compressed tenor and bass parts, especially in measures 7, 10, 11 to 12, 18 to 19, 25 to 26, and 28 to 29. The very low tenor parts written a third above the bass will require careful attention to balance. Conductors may want to consider moving some baritones to the tenor part and some tenors to the alto at moments.

Much of the piece stays within a small range with limited tessitura. For this reason, the vocal demands are restricted and the tonal range is narrow. As a result, vocal color must come from dynamic shading and vowel shading.

Stylistic Considerations

While the overall style of "This We Know" is monochromatic, the interest and color in the performance must come from the subtle use of dynamics and careful attention to vowels. The conductor and singers would be well advised to view long notes as opportunities for dynamic expression, either expanding or fading.

Form and Structure

The work divides itself according to the partitions of the text. The text phrase, "This we know" functions as a refrain and is an affirming exhortation that is used four times in the work with a fermata on the final word each time.

Section	Measure	Event
Part 1	mm. 1–10	Text: *The earth does not belong to us; we belong to the earth.*
Part 2	mm. 11–27	Text: *All things are connected like the blood that unites one family. Whate'er befalls the earth, befalls the children of the earth.*
Part 3	mm. 28–41	Text: *We did not weave the web of life, we are merely a strand in it. Whatever we do to the web, we do to ourselves.*

Text

This we know. The earth does not belong to us; we belong to the earth.
This we know. All things are connected like the blood that unites one family.
All things are connected.
Whate'er befalls the earth, befalls the children of the earth.
This we know.
We did not weave the web of life, we are merely a strand in it.
Whatever we do to the web, we do to ourselves. This we know.

Additional References and Resources

The Performance Notes on the back cover of this publication include the following words:

> *The simplicity and strength of Chief Seattle's text has been translated into various languages so that many different choirs might be able to express these profound sentiments in their native language. Simultaneous multi-lingual performances are possible—encouraged—as a symbolic manifestation and celebration of the web that connects all things. Complete performances in*

any language are also welcomed. And some choirs have found that speaking the text in a canonic multilingual format followed by singing it in the native language gives both the sense of the multi-cultural connection and a clear understandable expression of the text in the native language.

And finally, as Black Elk says in his book The Sacred Pipe, it is hoped that this piece "will help in bringing peace upon the earth, not only among humankind, but within each person and between the whole of creation."

Contributed by:

Jerry Ulrich

Teacher Resource Guide

To the Mothers of Brazil: Salve Regina

Lars Jansson

(b. 1951)

arr. Gunnar Eriksson

(b. 1936)

SATB

Walton Music: 8501635

Overall: 3

Vocal: 3

Tonal/Rhythm: 3

Composer

Lars Jansson, born in 1951 in Örebro, Sweden, studied classical piano as a child. At the age of thirteen, inspired by recordings of Miles Davis and John Coltrane, Jansson developed an interest in the organ and in jazz piano. By 1970 Jansson had moved to Göteborg to study dentistry. Eighteen months later he left the dental school to pursue formal musical training at the Göteborg College of Music. During these two years Jansson collaborated with a number of renowned jazz musicians, and in 1973 he left the conservatory to perform professionally. He has earned international acclaim touring and recording with the Arild Andersen Quartet, the Lars Jansson Trio, and the Jan Garbarek Group, among others. In 1998 he began teaching at the Royal Academy in Århus, Denmark, and in 2001 he received the Grammy award in Denmark for best international album. He has composed music for jazz ensemble, big band, choir, strings, saxophone quartet, and woodwind quartet.

Arranger

Swedish conductor and composer Gunnar Eriksson (b. 1936) studied with renowned choral conductor Eric Ericson at the Royal Music Academy in Stockholm. Currently Eriksson serves as professor of choral conducting at the State College of Music and the State Opera College at the University of Göteborg. He is founder and director of the Rilke Ensemble, a twelve-voice mixed ensemble committed to expanding the choral form both vocally and spatially. Eriksson has conducted and toured with the Göteborg Chamber Choir for more than 25 years and has recorded more then twenty albums with the ensemble. A specialist in the art of choral improvisation, he is in demand worldwide as a clinician and workshop leader.

Composition, Genre, and Historical Perspective

"To the Mothers of Brazil" was originally recorded in 1991 on the album *A Window Towards Being* by the Lars Jansson Trio, with jazz piano, percussion, and string bass. Gunnar Eriksson adapted the piece for chorus by adding the Latin text "Salve Regina" and then premiered the work in 1995 with Eric Westberg's Vocal Ensemble in Rio de Janeiro. The arrangement can be performed *a cappella* as written or, at the conductor's discretion, with added instrumental improvisation.

Musical Elements and Technical Consideration

Without question, rhythmic precision is essential to the success of "To the Mothers in Brazil: Salve Regina." Introduce singers to this piece first with counting exercises, setting the metronome to eighth note = 108. The aim of these exercises is to develop ensemble unity on syncopated rhythmic patterns in 6/8 time. Scaffold the exercises so that the chorus is at first able to simply stay in sync *on the beat*, and then move to exercises that maintain rhythmic precision *on the off-beat*.

Using the metronome, speak the rhythm for a 6/8 bar by repeating "one two three four five six…" until the ensemble is absolutely together and does not accent any beat. Next, work on subdivision by adding "and" in between each counted number; repeat the pattern until the ensemble is rhythmically precise and does not accent any beat: "one and two and three and four and five and six and…" Finally, using measures one and two from the piece as your model, speak the rhythm only on the given pitches (the dashes indicate a sixteenth note length of space between the notes): "one -- two -- three -- four and -- and -- and one -- two -- three -- four and -- and -- --." Speak the rhythm for other ostinati found throughout the piece.

After these initial rhythmic exercises, the choir is ready to read through the piece using solfège. It is preferable to use a *la*-based minor, but any sight-singing system—provided the system is used consistently—can work. Establish the tonic chord by outlining the minor triad *la–do–mi*. Then sing the natural minor scale ascending (*la-ti-do-re-mi-fa-so-la'*) and then descending. Note that sopranos and altos need the raised seventh scale degree, so the harmonic minor scale may be sung next: *la-ti-do-re-mi-fa-si-la'*. Read through the piece on solfège and if desired, invite students to write the solfège syllables above the notes in their voice part. Use of the Curwen hand signs throughout the process is highly encouraged.

After the piece has been fully learned on solfège, move to a neutral vowel. The rounded [u] vowel with an initial [d] consonant is very helpful for keeping spaciousness and warmth in the tone. Keep the lips very forward (as though sipping through a straw) and the vowels closed (teeth close together). Sing the piece on [du] until a true legato can be achieved without accenting any notes. Avoiding accents may seem counterintuitive since this piece employs a Latin dance rhythm. The syncopation, however, is "built in" to the music. Accenting notes will destroy the legato and cause intonation problems.

When the choir is able to sing every note on the neutral vowel absolutely in tune, add the Latin text. (If the choir struggles with pitches at any time, return to solfège.) Precise diction is the other key to success with this piece, and it begins with uniform vowel shapes. Work to maintain uniform lip positioning (forward and rounded) when moving from vowel to vowel. The more consistent (or similar) one vowel is to the next, the more legato the musical line will be. Four of the Latin vowels are already closed: [i], [e], [o], and [u]. These will be easier to keep uniform than the open—but not too forward or "bright"—vowel "ah." Use the "ah" sound as found in "wah" as opposed to "yah."

The consonants pose other issues to consider. Avoid aspirating the [t]. Make sure that the [s] is as in "Sam" and not the [z] sound as in "zebra." Flip the initial "r" and any "r" between two vowels. Roll the "r" when it sits next to a consonant on either side.

As noted earlier, avoid accents of individual notes in the piece. This is particularly true of the last note of a melodic line and of syncopated pitches.

This piece is well suited for choruses of varying sizes. Smaller mixed ensembles with sixteen to eighteen members (to cover all divisi) will enjoy the gentle, intimate nature of the piece. Larger performing forces will capitalize on the tremendous power of the piece as it unfolds section by section.

Stylistic Considerations

Because "To the Mothers in Brazil" was originally composed for jazz trio (without text), commence score study by listening to several recordings of the piece by various jazz ensembles. An obvious recording to begin with is the Lars Jansson Trio's 1991 rendition with piano, percussion, and string bass. Then listen to other incarnations, such as on saxophonist Hans Ulrik's 1994 album *Strange World*. These recordings reveal the rhythmic and melodic subtleties on which the choral arrangement is based. This step is enormously important because these recordings will establish a clear path to your teaching process. Share these recordings with the choir to model clarity and simplicity of the musical lines.

With these jazz recordings "in the ears" of your singers, achieving the gentle, forward-moving melodic lines will be well within reach. A precise, yet legato and nonpercussive, approach to the piece will ensure a spirited, buoyant sound. The conductor is encouraged to experiment with a multiplicity of sound combinations by voice type for variety throughout. One section might use only women, with male voices joining at the repeat. Instrumentalists, such as flute or saxophone, in addition to percussionists, may be invited to improvise at given points as well. This is a piece in which choral and instrumental improvisation may be instituted inventively and effectively.

Work up to a tempo of dotted quarter note = 54.

Form and Structure

The form of this piece is a series of four- and eight-bar phrases, each to be repeated at the discretion of the conductor. Within each section, there is room for experimentation to achieve variety in musical color and mood. Instruments and voice combinations can be added or omitted. According to the arranger, the use of canon, poetry readings, and tone clusters can be added for texture. Included in the arrangement is a page of suggested rhythms for percussion improvisation. Also, the arranger has denoted a number performance suggestions by section for the chorus. These are *suggestions* only. The beauty of this piece is that every performance will be unique to the ensemble.

Text and Translation

Salve, Regina, mater misericordiae	Hail holy Queen, Mother of Mercy
Ad te clamamus exules filii Havae.	To thee do we cry, poor banished children of Eve.
Regina coeli laetare, alleluia.	Queen of Heaven, rejoice, Alleluia.
O Clemens, O pia, O dulcis virgo Maria.	O clement, O loving, O sweet Virgin Mary.
Et Jesum, benedictum fructum ventruis tui.	And Jesus the blessed fruit of thy womb.

Salve Regina is one of four Marian antiphons that, in the Catholic tradition, are non-Psalm chants sung in veneration for the Virgin Mary during the time of the liturgical calendar most appropriate to the text. The four antiphons are: *Alma redemptis mater* (Advent to February 1), *Ave regina caelorum* (February 2 to Wednesday of Holy Week), *Regina caeli* (Easter Sunday to Friday after Pentecost), and *Salve regina* (Trinity Sunday to the Saturday before Advent).

Contributed by:

James Bowyer

Teacher Resource Guide

We Shall Walk through the Valley

Undine Smith Moore
(1904–1989)

SATB
GIA Publications, Inc.: G-6434
Overall: 3
Vocal: 3
Tonal/Rhythm: 3

Composer

Undine Smith Moore, pianist, organist, choral conductor and composer, was born in rural southern Virginia in 1904. She grew up and began her academic teaching career in the midst of a segregated society (the Brown v. Board of Education Supreme Court ruling to end segregation did not occur until 1954). Despite these obvious impediments, Undine Smith Moore's parents helped her to have a culturally rich upbringing:

> [T]he determination of my parents to create for us a haven so fortified with love and support that assault from the larger, dominant group could not pierce our armor; we lived life with gusto in the midst of oppression, even flourishing in situations often designed to humiliate us.

Smith Moore attended Fisk University for her undergraduate degree in music, and Columbia University for her MA and Professional Diploma in Music. While in New York, she also took courses at the Manhattan School of Music and workshops at the Eastman School of Music. Her primary teaching position was at Virginia State University, where she taught courses in composition for 45 years, and mentored many students who went on to have distinguished careers in music. While at Virginia State University, she co-founded the project, "The Black Man in American Music," a four-year initiative to promote performances and the study of music by African Americans.

Smith Moore viewed herself as a practical composer who often wrote music because there were not enough scores in the choral library. Her background in public school teaching and passion for academia led her to consider herself "a teacher who composes" more than "a composer who teaches." Despite the humility of such statements, she celebrated impressive achievements in composition.

Smith Moore reached her zenith as a composer in 1981 when her oratorio, *Scenes from the Life of a Martyr* (a cantata for narrator, chorus, soloists, and orchestra outlining the life and death of Martin Luther King, Jr.) was premiered in Carnegie Hall and received a Pulitzer Prize nomination. Her achievements as a composer of choral, orchestral, and dramatic works, as well as solo instrumental music, earned her an honorary doctorate from Indiana University in 1976. Smith Moore died in 1989 at the age of 84, leaving over fifty choral works of varying length and difficulty. Her daughter, Mary Moore Easter, is still living and teaches dance at Carleton College in Northfield, Minnesota.

Composition, Genre, and Historical Perspective

"We Shall Walk Through the Valley" was composed in 1974 as the final movement of a 7-movement set entitled *Choral Prayers in Folk Style*. Each of the four movements averages one to three minutes in length, and the work was intended for liturgical use. Despite the accessibility of all seven works as a whole, "We Shall Walk through the Valley" is probably the best-known movement, perhaps because the universal theme of its text makes it easier to program. Smith Moore chose to shorten the original text significantly, emphasizing the universal, more general elements of the text.

Choral Prayers in Folk Style

1) Lord Have Mercy
2) Glory to God in the Highest
3) I Believe This Is Jesus
4) O Holy Lord
5) Come Along in Jesus' Name
6) O That Bleeding Lamb
7) We Shall Walk through the Valley in Peace (original title)

Musical Elements and Technical Considerations

The most difficult element of the piece is probably in the first bar, where the sopranos are asked to float up to a high G after a skip of a sixth. Coach your sopranos to "breathe for the high note," so they are ready with an elevated soft palate and comfortable breath support. Although the vowel "ah" often works well for sopranos, rehearsing the passage on a more closed vowel such as "oo" or "ee" might also help them find the right focus and placement. In rehearsal, if sopranos tend to scoop to the high G, try having them start the phrase on the G, then drop lightly down to the B-flat. By alternating starting pitches of G and B-flat, sopranos will learn how to move from middle register to high register with ease. The same rehearsal technique would be useful for the tenor entrance in measure 3.

Balance between sections might also be a challenge, since the melody of "We Shall Walk through the Valley" is occasionally held by altos. Notice bar 9, where the altos sing the melody in a low part of their range in duet with the tenors, who are high enough to project easily. Consider adjusting the balance by asking a couple of lower tenors to join the baritones, who have to divide in bars 11 through 13. The extra tenors will help the bass divisi to project, while taking some of the volume away from the tenors. A similar adjustment with the women's voices could help: have a few second sopranos join the alto melody, then skip to their own line at the next entrance.

The text contains many commas that should not automatically denote a breath. Identify breath points soon in the rehearsal process and insist that singers keep a seamless quality by not "sneaking" breaths at the commas. An example is in bars 29 to the end, where all voices should attempt to sing the 5-bar phrase in one breath.

The dynamics in general do not exceed *mezzo forte*, but there may be points when singers are tempted to get louder as the texture thickens (see the soprano entrance in measure 13). Remind your chorus to lay their entrances into the overall fabric of the sound to avoid uncalled for "spikes" in dynamics.

A certain amount of *rubato* will help the text to resonate with the audience. An example is in measure 13, where the word "peace" should be carefully placed, not metrically cut off, because a hasty treatment of the "c" sound will detract from the sensation of serenity.

"We Shall Walk through the Valley" is an excellent choice for teaching students to "walk a piece" in Dalcroze rhythms. Have your singers move to the rhythms of their own parts, singing while stepping forward on each new note. As they move through the room, singers will begin to notice which line is moving quickly, and which line is holding back. Identifying the "texture of movement" helps singers to hear all of the parts, not just their own, and bring out important melodic lines.

Stylistic Considerations

Carl Harris, in his article "Three Schools of Black Choral Composers and Arrangers 1900–1970," considers Undine Smith Moore a "Black Innovator," a member of "third generation" African-American composers who inherited ideas and traditions from the past, but tended to be innovative in how they used original material. Although this may be true of Smith Moore's major works, "We Shall Walk through the Valley" is decidedly conservative in style. In an interview, Smith Moore described her intent to keep spiritual settings simple:

> In making these arrangements, my aim was not to make something "better" than what they had sung. I thought the spirituals so beautiful that I wanted to have them experienced in a variety of ways—by concert choirs, soloists, and instrumental groups. To attempt this has given me such musical pleasure and has strengthened the memories of the people who loved me and gave direction to my life.

The simplicity of Smith's Moore's harmonies and rhythms allows the source melody to be clearly heard in the style of hymn singing. Smith Moore notated many of the spiritual melodies herself from childhood recollections of hearing her mother sing quietly while preparing dinner.

Form and Structure

Strophic form, predominantly homophonic.

Section	Measure	Event and Scoring
Introduction	mm. 1–8	(4 + 4)
Verse 1	mm. 9–24	(4 + 4 + 4 + 4)
Coda	mm. 24–32	(2 + 2+ 2+ 2) single section bars, followed by 5-bar homophonic closer
Verse 2	mm. 9–24	(new text)
Coda	mm. 24–32	(identical to the Coda to Verse 1)

Text and Translation

As is the case in many African-American spirituals, the text appears in many different versions, with few or many stanzas depending on the context. Undine Smith Moore's text appears below:

We shall walk through the valley in peace
We shall walk through the valley in peace
If Jesus himself shall be our leader
We shall walk through the valley in peace

There will be no trials there
There will be no trials there
If Jesus himself shall be our leader
We shall walk through the valley in peace

An alternate version of the text, quoted from the Web site www.negrospirituals.com, is noted below:

We shall walk through the valley and the shadow of death
We shall walk through the valley in peace
If Jesus Himself shall be our leader
We shall walk through the valley in peace

We shall meet our brother there
We shall meet our brother there
If Jesus Himself shall be our leader
We shall walk through the valley in peace

There will be no weeping there
There will be no weeping there
If Jesus Himself shall be our leader
We shall walk through the valley in peace

Additional References and Resources

Books:

Briscoe, James R., ed. *Contemporary Anthology of Music by Women.* Bloomington and Indianapolis: Indiana University Press, 1997.

Articles:

Brunelle, Philip. "The Centenary Year of Undine Smith Moore: Dean of Black Women Composers." *Choral Journal* Vol. 44 (2004): 39–41.

De Lerma, Dominique-Rene, Doreene McKenzie, and Leroy Vlaun, eds. "A Concordance of Scores and Recordings of Music by Black Composers." *Black Music Research Journal* Vol. 4, (1984): 60–140.

Harris, Carl. "Three Schools of Black Choral Composers and Arrangers 1900–1970." *Choral Journal* Vol. 14, No. 8 (1974): 11–18.

Harris, Carl Jr. and Undine Smith Moore. "Conversation with Undine Smith Moore, Composer and Master Teacher." *The Black Perspective in Music* Vol. 13, No. 1 (1985): 79–90.

———"The Unique World of Undine Smith Moore, Teacher—Composer—Arranger." *Choral Journal* Vol. 16, No. 5 (1976): 6–7.

Book Chapters:

"Undine Smith Moore." In *The Black Composer Speaks*, edited by David N. Baker, Lida M. Belt, and Herman C. Hudson, pp. 173–202. Metuchen, NJ: Scarecrow Press, 1978.

Discography:

The Undine Smith Moore Songbook. This CD, released by Richsound Records 4112N10 of 1975, features the Virginia State College Concert Choir singing Smith Moore's compositions, under the direction of Carl Harris, Jr., a conductor who worked closely with Smith Moore and published a number of articles and interviews about her work.

Dissertations:

Jones, J. R. D. "The Choral Works of Undine Smith Moore: A Study of Her Life and Work." PhD diss. Jun 1981, vol. 41, New York University, 1980.

Contributed by:

Giselle Wyers

Teacher Resource Guide

Magnificat in A minor

Nicola Porpora
(1686–1768)

SSAA
Hal Leonard: 7766
Overall: 3
Vocal: 4
Tonal/Rhythm: 3

Composer

Born in Naples, Italy, Nicola Porpora (1686–1768) was the son of a bookseller. At the age of ten, he entered a conservatory to study music performance and composition. His quick success led to teaching responsibilities only three years later. After his schooling, the majority of Porpora's accomplishments came from his compositions, mainly opera, and teaching.

Porpora completed his first opera in 1708 and continued to receive commissions throughout his life. His most productive period of operatic composition was from 1718 to 1741, after which time the steep decline of public enthusiasm for the genre slowed production. He composed forty-four operas in total. His most successful works include *Eumene* (1721), *Siface* (1725), *Ezio* (1728), *Semiramide riconosciuta* (1729), and *Arianna in Naxo* (1733). His operatic style is characterized by da capo arias filled with technically difficult and ornamental vocal lines; it is possible that he was partially responsible for the trend in the Baroque period for composers to write ornamental melodies. Porpora traveled throughout Europe composing and producing operas—even spending several years in England as a rival to Handel. Although he was obviously popular in his time, Porpora's operas are rarely performed today.

Porpora received many appointments to teaching positions, often in response to his operatic success. Most of these appointments were as *maestro di cappella* to dignitaries and courts. He also found much success with positions teaching at the famous Venetian Ospedali orphanages (four located in Venice), primarily for girls. It was for these Ospedali that Porpora wrote many of his sacred works. The pieces are scored for various combinations of voices and instruments, but a fair number of them call for only women's voices.

While maintaining these positions and working on commissions, Porpora became well known for teaching voice privately. Some of his most famous students included Farinelli and Caffarelli (two renowned castrati); he even taught voice and composition to a very young Franz Joseph Haydn. Porpora focused on building strong technique through repetition of exercises to obtain ultimate control over all aspects of the voice. He was influential enough as a pedagogue that his students passed his techniques down to their students for many years.

Composition, Genre, and Historical Perspective

In the introductory notes of this edition of the *Magnificat in A minor*, the editor states that Porpora wrote it for the Ospedali degli Incurabili in Venice between the years of 1726–1738. However, more recent research (Whittemore) confirms that Porpora wrote the work later, in 1745, for the Ospedale di Santa Maria dei Derelitti, one of the other orphanages in Venice. The work is approximately ten minutes long and is scored for women's voices in four parts, with soloists from the upper three voice parts, string orchestra, and organ. Porpora composed the work just after his era of success as an opera composer.

Many sources indicate that the musicians at the Ospedali were highly skilled and they always amazed visitors with their performances. Not only did Porpora write music for them but he also taught many of the singers privately. Porpora most likely wrote this Magnificat, which is generally labeled a "motet," for a Vespers service in the chapel at the Ospedali. As was typical for the time, it is likely that around forty musicians (10 to 12 instrumentalists, 30 singers) participated in the performances. Motets of this kind were common in the late Baroque period, often written especially for major feast-day services.

Musical Elements and Technical Considerations

The Baroque harmonic progressions in the *Magnificat* are easy to understand and sing. The harmonic rhythm in the fast sections is generally one chord per measure. For the slower parts, the changes can occur as many as four times per measure. There are long sections in general key areas, which are mostly in the tonic, dominant, and their relative keys, with a few references to secondary dominants. Devices such as suspensions and suspension chains, circle of fifth movement, sequences, chromatic passing tones, minor mode variations (usually melodic, sometimes harmonic), and pedal tones punctuate this simple harmonic skeleton. A favorite harmonic device of Porpora in this work was the use of long sections of continuous circling progressions. Cadences within these progressions are often hidden because the music passes through them so quickly. What frequently seems like the end of a phrase is actually the beginning of another string of long sequential progressions. This happens continually, creating cadential extensions one after another (the longest of these by far occurs in the Sicut Erat section). This can be exhausting for a singer and difficult to follow as a listener. Help the performers shape these long sections of progressions as a whole, and work on shaping the phrases within them. With this bigger picture, singers will not get lost in all the notes and consequently you will more likely keep the audience engaged through a more organized and meaningful presentation of the seemingly unresolved extended sequences.

Melodies in this work rise out of these harmonic progressions. They are not very disjunct in structure but are often highly ornamented, melismatic, and sometimes chromatic. This is certainly a consequence of Porpora's expertise in opera and the voice. This aspect makes the piece more appropriate for advanced choirs. The singers must be able to produce melismas and ornaments accurately and hopefully musically. Teach these florid sections on nonsense syllables, with an initial consonant (such as "du" or "no"), then gradually remove consonants until the singers can perform the notes clearly without the oral articulation. If the melismas become overly slurred, do not use "h," staccato, or glottal inflections to clarify the notes. Articulate slightly slower tempi with abdominal muscles and breath (martellato singing); articulate faster tempi with vibrato (subtle vibration in tempo concurrent with the changing pitches). It is best to explain and teach these techniques in simple terms to avoid exaggeration. For instance, you can tell your singers to give the notes "jiggle."

Porpora also used repeating melodic motives, passing them from one voice to another. Make sure to bring out the musical conversation/interaction of between these motives. He also employed dueting throughout the piece, which further contributes to the conversational character. By far the most disjunct melodies occur in the second alto part, which often moves in a reflection of root motion. Performing this line with precision is especially important, as the other voice parts will rely on its harmonic foundation for intonation accuracy.

The texture of the *Magnificat* is both homophonic (Et exultavit) and polyphonic (Et misericordia). However, Porpora filled even the homophonic movements with polyphonic punctuation by way of alternating duets, early or late entrances of just one part, counter rhythms, and ornaments. To the listener's ear, the busy texture of this work can become cluttered and difficult to understand. Early in the learning process, decide which vocal lines are important, and help the singers understand the appropriate role of their part at those particular times. For instance, in the Sicut erat, measures 68–80, the two soprano voices duet over a pedal tone sung by both alto parts. The duet is obviously more musically significant, but the altos singing together on one note can be a formidable dynamic force unless held in check. Each part should know how it best fits into the musical whole. The first sopranos are not always the best part to emphasize, since Porpora spread melodic interest across all parts and in the accompaniment.

Within this perpetually active texture, there is also a fair amount of voice crossing. Spending time with each section to strengthen parts, and helping the singers become aware of when voice crossings occur, will prevent these areas from causing confusion. Also, seek to rehearse the more polyphonic parts in sectionals until the singers know their specific phrase shapes and breaths and can maintain their shapes while singing with the other parts. Then, when combined, help the singers know which parts need to be brought to the musical fore and how to make musical conversations with their individual lines through interactions with other parts.

The rhythms in this work are relatively straightforward. Issues that might cause problems lie in differentiating between straight and dotted rhythms, syncopated entrances, some more highly ornamented solo portions, and subtle variations in rhythms between the parts in homophonic passages. Simply making singers aware of these variants will help them prepare and prevent problems. Speaking the text in rhythm and singing lines on a neutral syllable will also help to clean up the rhythmic difficulties. Metrically, the *Magnificat* is not complicated, except that the compound meter sections create difficulties for both the conductor and performers. The editorial markings indicate that these sections should be conducted with one beat to the measure. This makes sense musically, but gives very few options to the conductor in the realm of controlling shape. Consider re-barring your score in these sections to create macro meters. It is not necessary to give these changes to performers, but it gives the conductor more options for shaping lines instead of using perpetual downbeats. These new patterns, if placed conscientiously, will inherently shape the phrases. The singers will also need assistance in these compound meter sections to maintain a lilting feeling in the performance. Emphasising the first beat of the three subdivisions is important, but even more effective is the de-emphasis of the other two beats. Using this attention to metric feel will also prevent the nonmusical pounding that often occurs with quick tempo compound meters.

The vocal ranges in the *Magnificat* are not extreme. However, the first sopranos spend the majority of the piece at the top of the treble staff. This range, lying directly in the secondo passaggio of most sopranos, is an unfortunate tessitura. The sopranos' voices will tire quickly if conductors do not guide them in making appropriate registration decisions. This situation could lead to not only fatigue, but also to serious intonation problems. Encourage the first sopranos to sing with more of the head register in their vocal mixture, maintain a relaxed singing mechanism (I find that teaching them to sing with an "extra buffer of air" helps them do this), and/or match their tone to that of a flute rather than to an oboe. As the first sopranos often stay on the dominant pitch (E in A minor), to build their tonal foundation they need to tune their ears to harmonic roots often found in the second alto line and the bass parts of the accompaniment. Second sopranos and first altos sing mostly in the middle of the staff, and the second altos spend much of their time on the bottom of the staff. As you can imagine, these four voice parts, remaining mainly on the staff together, create tightly closed chord positions. The part spacing feels quite narrow, and the proximity of these voices is the primary cause for most of the voice crossing in the work.

For the majority of the *Magnificat*, phrases are very long, too long to execute in one breath for most singers. It is best to study each part individually, deciding where and when to breathe or to stagger breathing. When making these decisions, take into account not only the text, but also the melodic syntax. It is common practice when approaching Baroque music of this sort to choose places to breathe not only to resupply air, but also to shape the music appropriately. Conductors often use string idioms to guide their decisions, lifting vocally when a string player would lift the bow, even if this place occurs in the middle of a word. For instance, when notes are tied over a barline to an eighth note, followed by continued eighth-note movement, consider removing the tied eighth note and breathing in its place. You do not need to use this technique at all times. Use it with discretion, but realize that it is appropriate for music such as this (see Sicut Erat measure 36 in the first alto voice for a perfect place to employ this tool). Remember that these breaths may often occur in the middle of a musical phrase and are best approached in a way that will not disrupt the line but will propel it in the appropriate direction.

This piece is in Latin; conductors must give particular attention to ensuring the appropriate pronunciation of the language. It is obvious that Italianate Latin is the most suitable for this work. A big challenge when singing in Latin is in achieving a pure vowel (this is especially difficult with "i," pronounced [i]). Use warm-ups and constant reminders to help your singers get the feel of this language. Also, be aware of the tendency of singers to use diphthongs in their pronunciation. Simple vocalises, recordings, and repetition can aid in reducing this inclination. The *Magnificat* is also full of long phrases occurring on one syllable, via held notes or melismas. Give special care to maintaining the proper vowel throughout long phrases, as singers will have a tendency to relax the purity as they hold out the sound. Remind singers to continually renew the vowel as they approach these long lines. Rehearse by even re-saying the vowels (without a glottal attack) on every new pitch or beat if necessary until the singers' attention remains on vowel purity.

There are six main sections in this work (see Fig.1), several of which may be extracted and performed separately. However, the piece works best with all sections together to create a more unified whole. For instance, sections 1 and 2 would be difficult to perform individually because section 1 ends on a half cadence, which steps directly into a resolution in section 2. These two sections could be performed apart from the others and work quite well together. Section 4 also stands alone well. All other sections do not even have a proper introduction, but are best prefaced by their respective previous sections. Extracting sections to perform separately requires thought and understanding of the work in order to be successful.

This edition of the *Magnificat* is a vocal/keyboard score. The keyboard part is for use in lieu of an orchestra, and organ is preferred over a piano for such a performance. The reduction however is often very pianistic in style. Most of the faster sections need to be performed on manuals only, unless the conductor or organist makes significant adjustments to the score. The instrumental parts are available via rental from the publisher.

Many of these issues are inherent in the music of the Baroque time period and are valuable in the education of singers. Teach principles that they can carry into future performances of music of this style and era. For comments on tone, articulation, dynamics, tempi, soloists, and ornamentation, please refer to the **Stylistic Considerations** section of this guide.

Stylistic Considerations

Scholars agree that the singing style of the Baroque era had a lighter quality than the more Romantic style ideals of today. In addition, Porpora wrote this piece with younger voices in mind. A healthy way to achieve this sound is to teach the singers to use more head voice than is typical in their registration. They should carry it down lower in larger amounts and relinquish any full chest sounds. Telling the singers to sound like boy sopranos seems to be effective as long as they can do so without a breathy quality. Singers should keep vibrato to a minimum also. Not only did singers of the Baroque use it more ornamentally than now, but the use of obvious vibrato in such a busy and melismatic work will only muddy the performance. Remember that these sacred works were often performed in churches where there was a great deal of reverberation; this is yet another reason to keep the sound pure and simple. Singers can learn to do this healthily without detriment to their solo voices. Using the singing tone mentioned above is the first step. Help the singers moderate the vibrato down low in their breathing mechanism and leave the throat free and relaxed. This is simply a device to prevent the singers from using the throat to stop the vibrato, which is a major cause of vocal health issues in this situation. Avoid extreme variations in dynamics while using this technique.

Conductors should take the time in their study of the music to determine the articulation he/she prefers. Performers often execute Baroque music in an overly legato or overly marcato style. Approach musical lines with a subtle finesse instead of large swooping gestures. Articulate the voices similarly to your instrumental articulation. Shape phrases and motives similar to string performance practice, which would often be a bit off the string. The dynamic markings and specific tempo markings in the score are editorial. Use these at your discretion, but if they are close to Romantic expressiveness, they are not appropriate for this music. Porpora chose his tempo markings to indicate a feel rather than to dictate an actual speed. Determine at which tempo each section feels most appropriate within the context of the tempo descriptor. Never go so fast that you cannot perform the smallest note values accurately or so slow that the music loses interest and impetus.

There are a few vocal solos indicated in this music. These can be sung by soloists or small groups as necessitated by the group's skill set. Ornamentation is a large part of the Baroque style; include the indicated trills if possible. When using ornaments, such as trills in a group, it is helpful to simply notate the desired realization for the singers. In general, approach trills from the upper neighbor and end them with a turn when it suits the cadence. Soloists may add other ornaments, such as other trills and appoggiaturas, but Porpora himself wrote out most ornaments for the choral singing. In all aspects, when performing period music, do what makes the music "work" for the piece and for the ensemble.

Form and Structure

Although this piece appears as one larger work in the score, Porpora separated it into six distinct sections. I have addressed them separately below. For ease in the use of this guide, and since there are no measure numbers marked in the score, I restarted measure numbering with each section. The movements alternate slow and fast tempos, the slower always in simple meter, and the faster in compound.

There are two charts presented below. The first (Fig. 1) will give general information about each section of the work, the second shows the specific form of each section (Fig. 2). As indicated below, Porpora organized the piece well, but most certainly wrote in a through-composed fashion. Harmonic trends, significant cadences, motivic materials, and text usage all contribute to the formal organization represented in Fig. 2.

Fig. 1, *Magnificat in A Minor* by Porpora: section information.

	LENGTH	TIME	TIME SIG.	TEMPO	KEY(S)	
1	Magnificat anima mea	9 mm.	0:45	C	Adagio	A minor, ends on the dominant
2	Et exultavit	100 mm.	1:50	3/8	Allegro	A minor, C major, transitional, A minor
3	Et misericordia	19 mm.	1:40	C	Adagio	F major, ends on the dominant
4	Fecit potentiam	118 mm.	2:05	3/4	Allegro	C major, A minor, C major, A minor, through D major to G major
5	Gloria Patri	12 mm.	1:00	C		E minor, A minor
6	Sicut Erat	117 mm.	2:00	3/8	Allegro	A minor, E minor, A minor (Picardy third)

Fig. 2, *Magnificat in A Minor* by Porpora: form analysis.

1. Magnificat anima mea
   mm. 1–9, 1 phrase (3.5+5.5)
2. Et exultavit
   mm. 1–18, 3 phrases (7+5+6)
   mm. 19–36, 2 phrases (9.5+8.5)
   mm. 37–73, 3 phrases (9[3+3+3]+18.5[3+8+4+3.5]+9.5[2+7.5])
   mm. 74–100, 4 phrases (5+4+9.5+8.5)
3. Et misericordia
   mm. 1–19, 2 phrases (13[5+8]+6)
4. Fecit potentiam
   mm. 1–21, 2 phrases (8[5+3] +13[6+7])
   mm. 22–40, 2 phrases (8[3+5]+11[6+5])
   mm. 41–58, 2 phrases (7+11)
   mm. 59–87, 3 phrases (8+13+8)
   mm. 88–118, 2 phrases (12[6+6]+19[7+7+5])

5. Gloria Patri
   mm. 1–12, 2 phrases (4+8[3+5])
6. Sicut erat
   mm. 1–55, 2 phrases (13+41[9+13+6+14])
   mm. 56–117, 4 phrases (12+12+36[10+10+10+6]+2)

Text and Translation

The text of this work appears in the Gospel of St. Luke in the New Testament of the Bible (Luke 1:46-55) and is one of the canticles of the Bible. In the Gospel, it appears as Mary, the mother of Jesus, responds to the exclamation of her cousin, Elizabeth, who praises Mary for her role as the mother of the Messiah. However, it is most often used at the end of the Vespers, or evening service.

1. Magnificat anima mea Dominum:

2. Et exsultavit spiritus meus in Deo,
salutari meo.
Quia respexit humilitatem ancillae suae:
ecce enim ex hoc beatam me dicent
omnes generationes.
Quia fecit mihi magna qui potens est:
et sanctum nomen eius.

3. Et misericordia eius a progenie in
progenies timentibus eum.

4. Fecit potentiam in bracchio suo:
dispersit superbos mente cordis sui.
Deposuit potentes de sede,
et exaltavit humiles.
Esurientes implevit bonis:
et divites dimisit inanes.
Suscepit Israel, puerum suum,
recordatus misericordiae suae.
Sicut locuts est ad patres nostros,
Abraham et semini eius in saecula.

5. Gloria Patri, et Filio,
et Spiritui Sancto.

6. Sicut erat in principio, et nunc,
et semper, et in saecula saeculorum.
Amen.

1. My soul doth magnify the Lord:

2. And my spirit hath rejoiced in God
my Saviour.
For he hath regarded: the lowliness of his
handmaiden.
For behold, from henceforth: all
generations shall call me blessed.
For he that is mighty hath magnified me:
and holy is his Name.

3. And his mercy is on them that fear
him : throughout all generations.

4. He hath shewed strength with his
arm: he hath scattered the proud in the
imagination of their hearts.
He hath put down the mighty from their
seat: and hath exalted the humble and
meek.
He hath filled the hungry with good
things: and the rich he hath sent empty
away.
He remembering his mercy
hath holpen his servant Israel:
as he promised to our forefathers,
Abraham and his seed forever.

5. Glory be to the Father, and to the Son
and to the Holy Ghost:

6. As it was in the beginning, is now,
and ever shall be, world without end.
Amen.

Bibliography and Suggested Resources

Baldauf-Berdes, Jane J. *Women Musicians of Venice: Musical Foundations 1525–1885*. Rev. ed. Oxford Monographs on Music. New York: Oxford University Press, 1996.

White, Chris D. "Nicola Porpora's Magnificat in A Minor: A Baroque Masterpiece for Women's Voices." *Choral Journal* (February 1997): 13–19.

Whittemore, Joan. E-mail message to author. August 21, 2010.

Whittemore, Joan. *Music of the Venetian Ospedali: A Thematic Catalogue*. New York: Pendragon Press, 1995.

Whittemore, Joan. "Research Report: Venetian Ospedali, Setting the Record Straight." ACDA Choral Journal Online (April 2009). http://www.acdaonline.com. Retrieved August 20, 2010.

Whittemore, Joan. "The Revision Repertoire of the *Ospedali Veneziani*." *Choral Journal* (March 1994): 9–13.

Contributed by:

Joni Jensen

Teacher Resource Guide

Vus vet zayn

Stephen Hatfield
(b. 1956)

SSA
Colla Voce: 21-20112
Overall: 3
Vocal: 3
Tonal/Rhythm: 3

Composer

Stephen Hatfield lives in the rain forest on Vancouver Island and teaches English at the University of Victoria. His first music lessons were from an old vaudeville performer who had squatter's rights to a shack behind his parents' house. Although choir teachers told him that his voice was pretty terrible, Stephen bounced back to become a noted choral conductor and composer, especially noted for his arrangements of multicultural music. He enjoys composing for the theatre and training terrified actors to sing onstage.

A notable consistency among Hatfield's arrangements is his expressive markings, which often evoke more than just technical performance instructions, but also describe the spirit of the music or the intended visceral experience of singing it. This reveals his clever, sometimes quirky, always insightful perspective on their music and its performance.

Composition, Genre, and Historical Perspective

The historical notes given on the inside cover of the published edition are useful and thorough. They do not mention the klezmer tradition, which is mostly secular, though often devotional, and is performed with dancing at celebrations like weddings. Not just a folk style, klezmer is a pop style like jazz, blues, and Portuguese *fado*.

Because the deepest roots of the tradition are in Central Asia, there are echoes of the non-Western modes (particularly, in this case, the lack of fixed, rigid scale allows for what sounds to Western ears like raised and lowered versions of the same scale degree) and characteristic inflections of liturgical chant (such as the scooping and fast-moving embellishments).

Musical Elements and Technical Considerations

Like most of Stephen Hatfield's arrangements, "Vus vet zayn" is written with very singable parts. There are some unique pitch issues because of the suggestions of alternate modes—like augmented seconds and flatted sixths. Getting the flexible mode in your singers' ears will be important. Using solfège warmups with lots of *so–le–ti–do–ra* combinations, and alternating between *mi* and *me* before you rehearse, will help to acclimate their ears to the modality of the song.

Singing on solfège could be useful to get the singers to remember where, for example, A is flat and where it is natural, but do not let the altered notes get your choir thinking of a particular mode, or even that the piece changes modes. Instead, impress upo them that the song is in one mode that provides several possibilities, sort of like one of those *Choose Your Own Adventure* books. It's a single mode that contains *mi* and *me*, just never at the same time.

The rubato at the beginning and the increasing tempo in the middle of the song are the only rhythmic challenges. The degree of challenge will depend on the size of the ensemble and their level of experience. Begin with flexibility from the very beginning, particularly if you are sure of your chosen tempi. Certainly, the singers need to have the pitches in their ears before you ask them to superimpose rhythmic changes on what they are learning, but after the very earliest introduction of notes they should begin experiencing the rubato. Just as if you were teaching any other rhythmic problem, the sooner you start, the more thoroughly incorporated into their learning it will be.

Like the rhythmic idiosyncrasies, the vocal effects, like sliding and scooping, should be incorporated as early into rehearsals as possible. Basic pitches come first, but what Western eyes might consider ornamentation actually indicates pitches that can't be notated on a staff in a traditional way. These notes are part of the tunes, not just additions piled on top of what is really the "correct" melody.

Though mostly in three parts, there are divisi sections in the lowest part, creating moments of four-part harmony. Divide your choir into three unequal parts with the majority of voices on the lowest part and the fewest on the highest part; this should create a balanced sound.

Stylistic Considerations

"Vus vey zayn" contains some common stylistic elements of klezmer music, including the rubato at the beginning, then increasing tempo at the end, scat-like, onomatopoeic sounds that imitate instruments, and scooping slides up into notes—which so many teachers must work to get their singers *not* to do—are called for (m. 17 of part two). These are stylistic elements that this arrangement shares with jazz and pop music, so the singers can apply their experience in these Western styles (which they undoubtedly hear incessantly, even in the mall and in elevators) to inform their performance.

Good singing is always important, but lovely vocal technique need not be the main focus of performing "Vus vet zayn." Because this is music that is traditionally shared among loved ones, the performance must not be characterized by polished refinement, but rather by a casual, uninhibited friendliness. Intensity, passion, abandon, and freedom are the goal. "Vus vet zayn" has the potential to be the most fun your singers have in the whole concert.

Stephen Hatfield's final expressive marking, "increasingly ecstatic," is the essence of the stylistic considerations. A choir that stands and sings this obediently following their conductor's tempo changes but never getting carried away by the joy, is missing the point. There must be some spontaneity to the performance, preferably a lot of actual euphoria. If it helps your singers connect with the spirit of the music, clapping or using hand percussion like tambourines could add even more energy. Better still, have them come up with a story about why they're singing it: for the wedding or birthday party of one member of the choir, perhaps. Maybe every rehearsal you sing for a different singer's wedding. Whatever makes it personal for every singer, will make the performance more expressive and authentic.

Form and Structure

Section	Measure	Event and Scoring
Verse	mm. 1–9	a slow introduction with drone; "moody and mystical"
Verse (repeated)	mm. 10–17	with homophonic harmony lines; "a little faster… with more spring"
Refrain	mm. 18–25	
Refrain with embellishments	mm. 26–33	"a little faster and springier"
Verse	mm. 34–41	melody in part two
Refrain	mm. 42–49	melody in part two
Refrain (repeated)	mm. 50–57	greater independence between parts

SECTION	MEASURE	EVENT AND SCORING
[Coda]	mm. 34–57	"repeated as desired" and "gradually increase tempo through the end, increasingly ecstatic"

Text and Translation

The text is traditional Yiddish.

> Fin papir veln mir/ Boyen, boyen oy a brik./ Katshn zikh, katsn zikh/ In undzer land tsurik./ Vus vet zayn, vus vet zayn,/ Az Mesheikh vet kimen tsi geyn?/ Gebrotene toybm vet men lkoybm/ Ovfn gasn breg.

The translation, as provided in the editorial notes of the piece, is as follows:

> "From paper we will build a bridge and we'll roll along back to our land. What will be when the Messiah comes? We'll gather roasted doves from the side of the road."

Note: Yiddish is a very forgiving language when it comes to diction. The editorial notes describe it as "protean," which indicates that it is not only flexible, but adapts to different circumstances, changing character as needed. Unlike French, Italian, and even English, there is no set of rules for pronunciation of Yiddish. One community will pronounce it differently from another with no animosity between them about who is right or wrong: both acknowledge that either is legitimate. So, what might be an irritatingly vague transliteration is actually a usefully flexible guide. Instead of worrying about accuracy of open and closed vowels or voices and unvoiced consonants, feel free to use the pronunciation that is most useful for your group—whatever vowel they sing the best, whatever they can learn the fastest, or whatever the Yiddish speaker in your choir or the staff of your school recommends.

One important characteristic sound is the schwa between two consonants where there is no vowel, as in "*kloybm*" and "*gasn*." Also, words that look like English words, such as "*land*," have the possibility of distracting English-speaking singers and making them forget that this is a foreign language and not to be pronounced as they expect.

Contributed by:

Amelia Nagoski Peterson

Teacher Resource Guide

Greater Love

Stephen Chatman

(b. 1950)

SATB
E.C. Schirmer: 7–0552
Overall: 3
Vocal: 3
Tonal/Rhythm: 3

Composer

Stephen Chatman (b. 1950 in Faribault, Minnesota) is considered one of Canada's preeminent composers. Chatman studied with Joseph Wood and Walter Aschaffenburg at the Oberlin Conservatory and with Ross Lee Finney, Leslie Bassett, William Bolcom, and Eugene Kurtz at the University of Michigan in Ann Arbor, completing a D.M.A. degree in 1977. He also received a Fulbright grant for study with Karlheinz Stockhausen at the Hochschule für Musik in Cologne.

Since 1976, he has been Professor and Head, Composition Division at the University of British Columbia, in Vancouver. Chatman is recognized internationally as a composer of choral, orchestral, and piano music. His approximately sixty choral works—widely performed and published by Highgate Press, Boosey & Hawkes, Oxford University Press, earthsongs, Waterloo, E.B. Marks, Hal Leonard, and Alfred—have sold more than 350,000 printed copies.

Chatman's music is generally accessible for choirs of varying abilities and maturity, and is consistently harmonically and melodically engaging. Stylistically, many of Chatman's pre-1982 works are complex, virtuosic, and atonal. By the late 1970s, Chatman's music suggests a more complete musical expression, encompassing a broad range of musical traditions, eclecticism, and post-modern aesthetics: collage techniques, simplified musical language, tonality, modality, minimalism, traditional forms, popular music influences, counterpoint of styles, veiled references, and theatrical elements.

Chatman has remarked: "It's easy to enjoy all types of music—I don't want to be pigeon-holed. A composer must be true to himself." In 1982, Chatman began composing choral music influenced by various traditional musical styles. "You Have Ravished My Heart" for SATB (1982), a transitional work and the first of many "accessible" or "popular" choral works, signals Chatman's gradual departure from modernism and a path toward post-modernism, spirituality, and a wider audience. These post-1982 secular and sacred choral works, in addition to many educational piano pieces, embrace a predominantly pan-diatonic tonal language, lyricism, melody, folk song, and more traditional musical gestures, forms, and compositional techniques.

Composition, Genre, and Historical Perspective

Greater Love derives its inspiration from an evocative and powerful Wilfred Owen poem. The transparent vocal writing allows the words to speak clearly and eloquently to both singer and listener. The work is essentially strophic and structured in four clearly delineated verses. The only accompaniment to the work is a solo oboe (or soprano saxophone), producing an austere, melancholic effect. The work is tonal (C Dorian) with many open fifth chords.

Musical Elements

Greater Love is a deceptively difficult piece to study and perform. While the voice leading is sensible and accessible throughout, the difficulty in performing the work is in the intense, sustained, and exposed vocal lines. There are many helpful pedagogical elements within this relatively short work. The range of dynamics and vocal flexibility required for performance make it an ideal teaching piece.

Additionally, the dark and stark nature of the poetry gives the work a somber and grave quality and requires vocal and emotional maturity. *Divisi* alto and bass throughout much of the work necessitates careful attention to balance among singers. The range and tessitura of all parts is both reasonable and comfortable, with the possible exception of the alto on the third verse.

The opening baritone solo requires a singer of reasonable control and expressivity. Much of the tessitura of the solo lies from middle C to the E-flat above.

The concluding verse calls for significant attention to subtlety and control.

Stylistic Considerations

The composer has indicated exactly what expressive details are required for an effective performance of this work. Careful attention to these markings by both conductor and singers will produce the most successful results.

For example, musical instructions include specific directives for staggered breathing, tempo nuances, broadening of tempo, detailed breathing, and tenuto marks. Meticulous information provided by the composer ensures minimal ambiguity on the part of the conductor and performers.

Form and Structure

Measure	Event and Scoring
mm. 1–14	Two bar instrumental introduction; 12-bar baritone solo with open fifth sonority, chorus sustained "nn" background; dynamics remain soft
mm. 15–30	Soprano and tenor melody (imitative paired voices) with *divisi* alto/bass "ah" background; dynamics increase to *mf*
mm. 31–44	Soprano and bass melody (imitative paired voices) followed by tenor and background; dynamics increase to *ff* at the conclusion of this section, which ends on an open fifth
mm. 45–57	Unison verse, sung *sotto voce*; *pp*

Text and Poet

Red lips are not so red
As the stained stones kissed by the English dead.
Kindness of wooed and woo'r
Seems shame to their love pure.
O Love, your eyes lose lure
When I behold eyes blinded in my stead!
Your slender attitude
Trembles not exquisite like limbs knife-skewed,
Rolling and rolling there
Where God seems not to care;
Till the fierce Love they bear
Cramps them in death's extreme decrepitude.
Your voice sings not so soft,
As wind murm'ring through rafter'd loft,
Your dear voice is not dear,
Gentle, and evening clear,
As theirs whom none now hear,
Now earth stopped mouths that coughed.
Heart, you were never hot,

Nor full like hearts made great with shot;
And though your hand be pale,
Paler are all which trail
Your cross through flame and hail:
Weep, you may weep, for you may touch them not.

Wilfred Edward Salter Owen MC (1893–1918) was an English poet and soldier, regarded by many as one of the leading poets of the First World War. His shocking, realistic war poetry on the horrors of trench and gas warfare was heavily influenced by his friend Siegfried Sassoon; his verses sat in stark contrast to both the public perception of war at the time and to the confidently patriotic verse written earlier by war poets such as Rupert Brooke. Some of his best-known works—most of which were published posthumously—include *Dulce Et Decorum Est*, *Insensibility*, *Anthem for Doomed Youth*, *Futility*, and *Strange Meeting.*

The preface he wrote intended for a book of poems to be published in 1919, contains numerous well-known phrases, especially "War, and the pity of War," and "the Poetry is in the pity."

Benjamin Britten incorporated nine of Owen's poems into his *War Requiem*, opus 66, along with words from the Latin Mass for the Dead (*Missa pro Defunctis*). The *Requiem* was commissioned for the reconsecration of Coventry Cathedral, and was first performed there on May 30, 1962.

Owen is perhaps just as well-known for being killed in action at the Battle of the Sambre just a week before the war ended, which caused news of his death to reach home as the town's church bells declared peace.

Contributed by:

Jerry Ulrich

Level 4

Mixed voices:

A Boy and a Girl Whitacre, Eric .. 381
Also hat Gott die Welt geliebt Schütz, Heinrich .. 385
Balulalow Custer, Gerald .. 393
Best of Rooms, The Thompson, Randall .. 399
Calme des Nuits Saint-Saëns, Camille .. 403
Chindia Pascanu, Alexander .. 409
El Hambo Mäntyjärvi, Jaakko .. 413
In Paradisum Fissinger, Edwin Russell .. 419
Lay a Garland Pearsall, Robert Lucas (de) .. 423
Lo, How a Rose E'er Blooming Sandström, Jan .. 429
My Flight for Heaven Henson, Blake R. .. 433
Stars I Shall Find Dickau, David .. 439
"Sure on This Shining Night" from *Nocturnes* Lauridsen, Morten .. 443
Valiant for Truth Vaughan Williams, Ralph .. 449

Treble voices:

Ain't No Grave Can Hold My Body Down arr. Caldwell, Paul/Ivory, Sean .. 455
Hotari Koi arr. Ogura, Ro .. 463
I Thank You God Walker, Gwyneth .. 469
LAWA Sadler, Katheryn .. 477
Les étoiles Sirett, Mark .. 483
O bone jesu Brahms, Johannes .. 489
Psalm 121 Raminsh, Imant .. 493
There Is Sweet Music Here Gawthrop, Daniel E. .. 499

Men's voices:

Come Sing to Me of Heaven arr. McDermid, J. Aaron .. 503
Credo Martini, Giovanni Battista .. 507
Crucifixus Lotti, Antonio/arr. Davison, Archibald T. .. 515
Four Cummings Choruses, Opus 98 Persichetti, Vincent .. 519
Love Never Ending Zinter, Aaron .. 527
Ramkali Sperry, Ethan .. 533
Rustics and Fishermen Britten, Benjamin .. 539

Teacher Resource Guide

A Boy and a Girl

Eric Whitacre

SATB divisi
Hal Leonard: HL08744627
Overall: 4
Vocal: 4
Tonal/Rhythm: 5

Composer

As one of the leading composers of contemporary choral music, Eric Whitacre has received composition awards from the Barlow International Composition Competition, the American Choral Directors Association, and the American Composers Forum. In 2001 he became the youngest recipient ever to be awarded the Raymond C. Brock commission by the American Choral Directors Association. His formal training, which did not begin until he was an undergraduate student, culminated under the tutelage of Pulitzer Prize and Oscar-winning composer John Corigliano at The Julliard School. Whitacre's published works have received thousands of performances and have become the subject of many doctoral dissertations and other scholarly works.

Composition, Genre, and Historical Perspective

"A Boy and a Girl" may be best classified as a twentieth-century secular motet. The work is a setting of a poem by Nobel Laureate Octavio Paz and was commissioned in 2002 for the California All-State Chorus. Whitacre provides the following comments regarding the work. "A Boy and a Girl is such a tender, delicate, exquisite poem; I simply tried to quiet myself as much as possible and find the music hidden within the words."

Musical Elements and Technical Considerations

Whitacre's setting of Paz's poem is exquisite. The imagery in the poetry is brought to life through local text painting and the overall mood of the work. The piece is similar to many of Whitacre's other unaccompanied compositions in terms of its harmonic and melodic language; however, the vocal lines are less virtuosic than many of his other works, undoubtedly because it was commissioned for an ensemble of high school singers. That being said, it is not an easy sing. At times, the sopranos and tenors must be able to sing in their upper registers with great control, and the low basses must be able to sound below the staff with resonance.

One of the most challenging aspects of this piece is making the cluster chords come to life. Much care must be taken to ensure that each chord is balanced and tuned perfectly. In order to achieve this, the conductor must understand how the sonorities are constructed and how they function within the phrase. More specifically, it is imperative to be aware at all times of which pitches are doubled, and in which voice parts. Whitacre often changes the texture from chord to chord within a phrase. For example, in measures 16 and 17, he writes five-, six-, and seven-part sonorities. A clear plan should be devised as to how this will be handled, as it can present significant problems in terms of balance. It is helpful if the singers know the function of their particular pitches as well. This helps them open their ears to the sound around them, and adjust if necessary. Additionally, conductors must make decisions regarding vowel shape and color, and vibrato.

The voice leading in this piece, particularly in the alto and soprano parts, may present challenges; Whitacre often writes in parallel seconds. Singers who are not accustomed to these harmonies may find this difficult. Some conductors have found that teaching a piece such as this using solfège can be very helpful for the singers. This method not only provides assistance in learning the pitches, but also helps students understand the function of each pitch within the various sonorities.

Stylistic Considerations

In order to capture the true essence of this piece, an ensemble must be attentive to the small details. Whitacre provides very clear dynamic markings throughout; these, more than anything, are related to text stress. An ensemble should work to observe all of these markings, thus allowing the piece to embody the natural sense of ebb and flow inherent in the poetry. The composer indicates that the piece should be sung with *rubato* and very tenderly. He gives specific instructions at various moments, such as *slowly* in measures 11 and 12; but for the most part, each conductor must determine how he or she prefers to shape each phrase in terms of *rubato*. Let the text be the guide when making these decisions; it is often helpful to speak the text aloud to internalize the natural rhythm of the verse.

Whitacre uses silence to great effect throughout the work, and the music lives and breathes because of the polarity between motion and stillness. Conductors must be very careful to ensure that rests are observed for their full duration. In a performance situation, adrenaline can easily cause one to rush through these stunning moments. That being said, phrases should be thought of in large groupings, not in one- or two-measure fragments. An understanding of how the short phrases work together to create large phrases is critical. For example, in the first six measures of the piece, there are clearly four short phrase fragments, but the four together constitute the first complete poetic thought. Even with the composer's employment of rests, a listener should be able to understand the syntax of the poem.

The final eight measures, although sung on a hum, must be approached as if there were text. The shaping of these final phrases is essential to ending the piece with artistry. Whitacre has marked very specifically the dynamic scheme he envisions. Lastly, the final chord should be held for the full eight beats *in the slow tempo*.

Form and Structure

"A Boy and a Girl" is homophonic throughout and constructed in modified-strophic form. The strophes are dictated by the three-stanza structure of Paz's text. Whitacre extends the work beyond the final strophe with an eight-measure coda.

Section	Measure	Event and Scoring
Stanza 1	mm. 1–13	no divisi
Stanza 2	mm. 14–27	divisi in all parts at varying moments
Stanza 3	mm. 28–44	enharmonic common-tone modulation from B9 to CmM9; divisi; one ensemble melismatic passage in mm. 35–37
Coda	45–52	no divisi; sung on "mm"

Text

Stretched out on the grass
a boy and a girl.
Savoring their oranges, giving their kisses
like waves exchanging foam.

Stretched out on the beach
a boy and a girl.
Savoring their limes, giving their kisses
like clouds exchanging foam.

Stretched out underground
a boy and a girl.
Saying nothing, never kissing,
giving silence for silence.

—Octavio Paz, translated by Muriel Rukeyser

Additional References and Resources

Layton, Stephen, conductor. *Eric Whitacre: Cloudburst and other choral works.* Polyphony. Hyperion CDA67543. 2006.

Web Site:

Eric Whitacre. http://www.ericwhitacre.com (accessed August 30, 2008).

Contributed by:

Bradley Miller

Teacher Resource Guide

Also hat Gott die Welt geliebt

Heinrich Schütz

(1585–1672)

SATTB
GIA Publications, Inc.: G-6524
Overall: 4
Vocal: 3
Tonal/Rhythm: 4

Composer

Heinrich Schütz was born in 1585 in the small town of Köstritz, part of the principality of Reuss in Saxony. As a young boy, Schütz excelled in the subjects of counterpoint and plainchant, and his singing voice was impressive enough to earn him the opportunity to serve as a choirboy in Kassel and receive an education at the renowned Collegium Mauritianum, the court school. Further studies in composition with the aged Giovanni Gabrieli in Italy solidified Schütz's commitment to a career in music, despite his parents' initial desire for him to be a lawyer instead.

Schütz's first major collection of compositions, written after two years of study with Gabrieli, was also his only major contribution of secular music to the field. *Il primo libro de madrigali* of 1611 features madrigals for SAB, SATB, and double mixed chorus without accompaniment, revealing Gabrieli's belief (as Schütz's teacher) that young composers should first write music in the "stile antico" before attempting modern, accompanied works.

Although Schütz's confidence as a composer was slow to solidify, a fortunate opportunity came his way after his Italian studies, to serve in Dresden in 1615 as the Kapellmeister for elector Johann Georg. Any possibility of this being only an interim position was short-lived—his work as organist, composer, and music director was so prized that Schütz was promoted to Hofkapellmeister in 1621, where he put in over thirty years of service to the Saxon court before his retirement. Schütz's primary duties were to educate the choirboys, audition and conduct his chorus and instrumental ensembles, and compose music for royal occasions and court ceremonies.

Despite the promise of prosperity usually associated with such royal appointments, Schütz's life and compositional output was gravely affected by the onset of the 30-Years War, a bitter religious—and eventually political—battle that engulfed most of Europe from 1618–1648. The direct impact of the war on Schütz's output is clear when one compares his first collection of sacred music, *Psalmen Davids* of 1619, written before the war broke out, with his *Kleine geistliche Concerte* of 1636. *Psalmen Davids* is a collection of psalm settings for multiple choruses of singers and instruments, written in the grand Italian Baroque style, while *Kleine geistliche Concerte* is a lean, economical collection of vocal concertos for one to five voices without instruments (except continuo). Not only was Schütz limited in terms of the number of musicians who could perform his work, but often his collections of music could not be published at all due to lack of financial support from the court. Although the 30-Years War came to a close in 1648, even as late as 1651 Schütz's court musicians were feeling the financial pinch, as the court attempted to repay the war's debts. Schütz describes in a 1651 letter the conditions of one of his singers:

> ...[he] lives like a sow in a pigsty, has no bedding, lies on straw, has pawned his coat and his jacket. His wife came to me yesterday and begged me for God's sake to render fatherly aid and help them get away...I find it neither praiseworthy nor Christian that in a land so highly esteemed less than twenty musicians can or will not be supported...

That Schütz continued to compose with such fervor despite adverse conditions is testament to the force of his creative voice. Schütz is credited with writing over 500 works during his lifetime, the vast majority of which are choral or vocal in nature. Notable collections not previously mentioned include his *Geistliche Chormusik*, *Cantiones Sacrae*, *Symphoniae Sacrae* (submitted in three collections in 1629, 1647, and 1650), and his *Musicalische Exequien*. Schütz is hailed by music historians as the greatest German composer of the seventeenth century, credited with bringing German music to a new level of sophistication and depth, and fusing Italian elements with German style in a cohesive manner.

Composition, Genre, and Historical Perspective

"Also hat Gott die Welt geliebt" is a setting of the biblical text, "For God so loved the world" for SATTB chorus and basso continuo. It appears in the collection *Geistliche Chormusik*, Opus 11 Nr. 12 (SWV 380), and was published in the final year of the 30-Years War (1648). The collection contains over 25 compositions for mixed chorus in five parts of various voicings. That these masterworks are accessible to today's high school and college singers is due in part to Schütz's response to limited forces in his own chorus, which dropped from 27 voices when he started in Dresden to only 10 voices at the height of the war.

The official name of this piece's genre is "aria," a confusing term used in the Baroque period for various forms of music, including instrumental and sacred choral settings, as well as opera.

Musical Elements and Technical Considerations

Below is a list of musical and technical issues that arise in this piece, and suggestions for how to address them.

FIVE-PART MIXED CHORUS WITH A DIVIDED TENOR LINE

Consider dividing your chorus unconventionally. Take a few sopranos down to altos, a few lower altos to Tenor I (have them omit the lowest notes), and a few baritones to Tenor II. Even if you are unable to provide a full basso continuo, consider doubling the bass line with a talented student cellist or bass player, or use the piano accompaniment indicated in the GIA Publications edition to round out the richness of the harmonies. If you decide to sing the work *a cappella*, feel free to take it up a half or whole step for ease of range (the concept of exact pitch is a modern one).

THE PIECE STARTS OUT "FEELING LIKE" IT'S IN A MINOR, BUT ENDS IN E MAJOR

Although Schütz wrote during an era that was as much "modal" as "tonal," modern ears are accustomed to singing toward a tonic, which in this piece is felt as E major. Help your students to understand the "direction" of the harmony, and to feel the anticipation of building toward the E-major cadences in measures 12, 24, 47, 70, and 75, as well as resting on "plagal" A-major cadences in measures 36 and 59. Giving a linear feeling to how the phrases are sung (rather than attempting to tune every chord vertically as it comes) will help students move the phrase towards logical points of rest.

FREQUENT METER CHANGES

What appears in a modern edition as meter changes would have been seen as proportional divisions of a central "tactus," the rhythmic "heartbeat" of music during the Renaissance and Baroque eras. Schütz once wrote that the tactus "represents the soul and life of all music." Conductors often feel a responsibility to find the right tempo and correct proportions, but perhaps what is more reasonable is to aim to be "HIP" (have a "historically informed performance"—term borrowed from Christopher Hogwood). Here are some basic principles:

1. Encourage your singers to feel a long rhythm as the main pulse (in this piece, the half note, which would have been a "semi-breve" in Schütz's time, is the main pulse, but in other settings even the whole note may be the "tactus," depending on the original notation).
2. Set your tempo around the principle that the "tactus" will be around 60 or slightly faster. This suggestion is rooted in the early music writers' assertion that the tactus should equal the heartbeat of a "healthy person at rest." In this edition, a tempo of half note = 60–72 is suggested.
3. When changing "meters," maintain some kind of proportional relationship between the rhythms. A glance at the original document (or one of the urtext editions of the piece) is the only way to determine with certainty, which proportion to take. In the GIA edition, it is suggested that when moving from 2/2 to 3/2, the whole note should equal the dotted-whole note.
4. Keep in mind that while proportionality is often desirable, the ultimate test of what works should be determined by the text, the affect of the piece, and the needs of your performers. Alexander Blachly, a renowned scholar of tempo issues in the 15th century, has written, "the speed of the beat may be decided by the performer according to the perceived needs of each piece...Tempo is thus removed from the domain of non-musical, mathematical criteria and restored to the domain of performance, where it keeps company with such notions as phrasing, tone color, mood, expression, declamation, gesture, and volume."

CLOSE IMITATIVE ENTRANCES ARE OFTEN ONLY A QUARTER-NOTE BEAT APART

If your singers are feeling the larger pulse, aligning their shorter rhythms into that larger pulse will be easier. Emphasizing the importance of proper declamation by observing the stress marks indicated in the GIA score, will help singers to move their lines with a dance-like, almost spoken quality.

Teach the 3/2 sections first, where the entrances fall mostly on downbeats. Encourage singers to feel the 3/2 section in a "slow 1," to give this section a lilting, light quality.

LONG SOLO PASSAGES FOR TENOR VOICES

The solo indications are editorial, based on the historical practice of alternating soloists with chorus. If you prefer, omit the solo designation and have the entire section cover these parts.

Advantages to Programming This Piece

- The German text is relatively short, allowing you to teach the diction in less rehearsal time.
- The universality of the text's theme allows you to program it during any time of year.
- The five-part setting, although challenging, features voice ranges that are fairly close together and easier to manage.
- There are only three major sections that alternate. Rather than teaching the piece straight through, teach bars 37 through 46 at the same time as bars 60 through 75, and teach bars 24 through 36 at the same time as bars 47 through 59. Then you only have bars 1 through 24 left to teach.
- Singing a piece by Heinrich Schütz allows students to learn elements of Baroque vocal style. Students will enjoy hearing about Schütz's perseverance through life's challenges, while discovering clever examples of text painting. Note the descending melody (bars 9 through 12), representing God's gift "down" to earth, the repetition of the word "alle" (bars 24 through 26 and elsewhere) to represent "all" people, as well as his repetition of the text "sondern das ewige Leben" (bars 37 through 47 and elsewhere) to represent unending life, with a steady ascent of pitches into musical "heaven."

Stylistic Considerations

Eva Linfield notes in her essay on Heinrich Schütz in the NGD that, "Over-respectful, 'pious' performances of his sacred works have been largely replaced by more vibrant interpretations, and these in turn have deepened appreciation of the sensitive and complex manipulation and enrichment of the text that is one of the chief hallmarks of Schütz's best music." Let Linfield's words be an inspiration to us all to not over-think our path to a "HIP" performance. Much of Schütz's choral music was influenced by dance forms, and the music must move and dance with vitality and a sense of spontaneity and freedom.

Form and Structure

The following measure numbers correspond to GIA Publications' edition of *Also hat Gott die Welt geliebt*, 2007.

AABBCBBC

In the case of overlapping phrase sections, the measures are stated twice.

Section and Scoring	Measure	Event
A solo	mm. 1–12	(2 + 3 + 3 + 4)
A choral	mm. 13–24	(2 + 3 + 3+ 4)
B solo	mm. 24–30	(3+ 2 + 2)
B choral	mm. 30–36	(3 + 1 + 3)
C choral	mm. 37–47	(3 + 2 + 2 + 3)
B choral	mm. 47–53	(3 + 2 + 2)
B choral	mm. 53–59	(3 + 1 + 3)
C choral	mm. 60–75	(3 + 2 + 2 + 3 + 5)

Text and Translation

Bible: John 3:16

Translation: For God so loved the world that he gave his only-begotten son, so that all who believe in Him would not be forsaken, but would have everlasting life.[1]

Additional References and Resources

Plank, Steven Eric. *Choral Performance: A Guide to Historical Practice*. Lanham, Md.: Scarecrow Press, 2004.

A brief and clearly written introduction to performance practice in early music from a choral perspective.

Price, Curtis, ed. Music, Society and The Early Baroque Era. Englewood Cliffs, NJ: Prentice Hall, 1993.

An accessible, entertaining account of the early Baroque focusing on aspects of society and culture as much as music.

Smallman, Basil. Schütz. Oxford: Oxford University Press, 2000.

A well-written, concise biography.

Winold, Allen and Ray Robinson. The Choral Experience: Literature, Materials, and Methods. New York: Harper's College Press, 1976.

A helpful general guide to performance practice in choral music in all style periods, with an especially useful historical notation chart.

1 Translation compiled by Ron Jeffers, *Translations and Annotations of Choral Repertoire, Volume 11: German Texts*, edited by Gordon Paine, copyright 2000 earthsongs publications

Collected Editions

Heinrich Schütz: *Sämtliche Werke*, ed. P. Spitta and others (Leipzig, 1885–1927/R)

Heinrich Schütz: *Neue Ausgabe sämtlicher Werke*, ed. W. Bittinger, W. Breig, W. Ehmann and others (Kassel, 1955–)

Heinrich Schütz: *Sämtliche Werke*, ed. G. Graulich and others (Stuttgart, 1971–)

Catalogue

Schütz-Werke-Verzeichnis (SWV): kleine Ausgabe, ed. W. Bittinger (Kassel, 1960); suppl. in W. Breig (1979); complete, ed. Breig (in preparation)

Contributed by:

Giselle Wyers

Teacher Resource Guide

Balulalow

Gerald Custer

SATB/a cappella
GIA Publications, Inc.: G-7190
Overall: 4
Vocal: 4
Tonal/Rhythm: 4

Composer

Gerald Custer grew up in Metuchen, New Jersey alongside the children of poet John Ciardi, and with pianist Robert Taub and a young man named Dave Cotkin, better known to the rest of the world as illusionist David Copperfield. Like his high school director Dr. Dennis Shrock, he attended Westminster Choir College, where he hoped to become a professional singer. Since it was quickly evident that as a singer he made a better conductor, he took a degree in choral music education instead, followed by a master's in orchestral conducting from The George Washington University, and is now pursuing a doctorate in choral conducting at Michigan State University. Custer has been in Michigan since 1979, and most of his career has been spent conducting: as interim conductor of the Saginaw Choral Society; as conductor of The Arbor Consort, the Jefferson Street Chorale, and the Orchard Ridge Choral Society; guest conductor of the Dodworth Saxhorn Band, and most recently as Director of Music at First Presbyterian Church in Farmington Hills, a suburb of Detroit.

Composing began as an avocational pursuit. Even so, he had the good fortune to have works commissioned and premiered by the Williamson Voices, the Schola Cantorum, the Summer Vocal Institute, and the Westminster

Choir of Westminster Choir College of Rider University; his works have been sung by the choirs of Hofstra, Wayne State, and Case Western Universities and the Interlochen Arts Academy chorus; and works have been performed by organist Marilyn Mason. His setting of "Innisfree" is the title track for the debut recording of The Voices of Anam Cara; the group's second CD, *Inscape*, is devoted entirely to selections of his choral music. You can find more of Custer's work in the *Evoking Sound*, *Music from Westminster*, and *Calvin Institute for Sacred Worship* series published by GIA Publications and in the catalogues of Morningstar Music and Augsburg Press. In his spare time, he writes. He has published articles in the ACDA *Choral Journal*, regularly writes the "Choral Master Class" column in each issue of the GIA *Quarterly*, and has contributed a number of chapters to the multivolume text *The Choral Rehearsal* by Dr. James Jordan.

Composition, Genre, and Historical Perspective

Ever since my college days, it's been my habit to mark Christmas by composing a carol. Two of these—"Winter's Cold" and "Richard Crashaw's Carol"—have made their way into print; "Balulalow" (2006) is the latest to join their company. Setting this particular text gave me pause, because it remains strongly identified with Britten's elegant setting in his *Ceremony of Carols*. But just days before writing this carol, I had finished a commission for the Williamson Voices on another text associated with great composers across the ages: *O Magnum Mysterium*. "Fools rush in where the wise fear to tread," so in I rushed; when the carol was finished I sent it (as I do with almost everything I write) to my colleague and friend James Jordan, who proposed we give it to Dr. Joe Miller to celebrate his first Christmas as Director of Choral Activities at Westminster, an idea with which I immediately and enthusiastically agreed.

"Balulalow" is a homo-rhythmic carol for unaccompanied SATB voices. Like much of my choral output since 1990, it exhibits the characteristic traits of what theorists call *pandiatonicism*: music grounded in traditional tonal practice, with recognizable cadences and attention to careful voice leading, but using an enriched harmonic vocabulary that includes chords of the seventh and the ninth, bitonality, and occasional quartal structures. At the same time, it reflects my abiding interest in the linear modal writing of Tallis, Byrd, Gibbons, and other Renaissance masters, and hopefully it shows the stylistic impact of twentieth-century composers such as Vaughan Williams, Hindemith, and Lauridsen, and my own teacher Sir Malcolm Williamson, all of whom continue to influence my work.

Musical Elements and Technical Considerations

"Balulalow" has two distinct challenges: harmony and text. Because this piece is essentially an accompanied melody, sing the soprano line first (in octaves) at *mp* on "voo" or "noo." This carol is classical rather than romantic in its aesthetic—the climax of each section comes in the middle of the phrase (except the third, which is a long crescendo)—so have singers "somatize" the music by leaning forward into these peaks or by pointing forward with an index finger as they sing through the melody. Do the same when singing the piece in parts as well.

Next, rehearse the outer (S/B) parts until the harmonic envelope and overall direction are well established. Then tackle the rest, rehearsing multiple voices (given the harmony here, S/A and T/B pairs are best) to lock the notes in place. The only intervallic challenges are in the tenor voice: the approach to the CM9 chord in bar 12 and the C-sharp in the last bar. The remainder is harmonically straightforward, except measure 4, beat 4 and measure 13, beat 1, but the voice leading works reasonably well in both cases (I hope). Finally, sing the entire work, "listening louder than you sing" to ensure the melody is always clear and that sustained notes pull back slightly to let moving parts be heard without extra effort.

Since the text of "Balulalow" is in Scottish dialect, it should be sung with tall, spacious and closed vowels; for example, the opening sound is far closer to "oo" in "soon" than the diphthong "oh" in "home." The recording accompanying this text offers a definitive guide to performing the text. A few points deserve some particular attention:

- Carefully shape polysyllabic words (credill, sangis, evermoir) by singing the unaccented syllable a bit more softly and with a slightly darker vowel.
- Consider using a shadow vowel ("schwa") to clarify declamation in measure 7 ("in/my"), measure 10 ("rock/thee"), and measures 12 and 13 ("and/never").
- Similarly, in the second verse, consider using a shadow vowel in measures 9 and 10 ("of/my") and measures 12 and 13 ("and/sing").

Additional information about performing this work can be found in subsequent sections of this chapter.

Stylistic Considerations

Straightforward declamation is the key to performing this carol well—not just vocally but rhythmically as well. Choirs should minimize vibrato when singing this work to enable the music to tell its story directly and simply. Let the natural rise and fall of the melodic line fuel dynamic motion, singing the second verse one dynamic level quieter than the first, and do not ritard the last phrase of the work either time. Since "Balulalow" belongs to the "cradle song" genre of carol, it should be performed as all lullabies are: tenderly, as a love song sung by a mother to her child. The performance on the CD with this text is authoritative and I collaborated in its making.

Form and Structure

"Balulalow" is a homo-rhythmic, strophic work centered on D, whose form is driven by the structure of the text it sets. Its verses are musically identical, organized as shown below:

Section	Phrase/Measure	Event and Scoring		
Period 1	Phrase 1: mm. 1–4	DM:	$\begin{smallmatrix}4\\3\#\end{smallmatrix}$	I → V^6
	Phrase 2: mm. 5–8			I → V
Period 2	Phrase 3: mm. 9–12	dm:	$\begin{smallmatrix}4\\3\#\end{smallmatrix}$	i → VII^9
	Phrase 4: mm. 13–17			VI → V

The final phrase violates expectations generated by the preceding three 4-bar phrases by melding measures 13 and 14 and a cadential extension in measures 15 through 17 to heighten the emotional intensity given to the penultimate word in verse one and the last word in verse two. And yes: it *is* a fragment of Vaughan Williams's *Mass in G Minor* you hear in the alto voice at measure 16.

Text and Translation

The text of "Balulalow" is a translation (likely made in the 16th century by the Wedderburn family of Aberdeen) of Luther's Christmas hymn for children, "Von Himmel Hoch." Only the final stanza is used for this carol. The full text as translated reads:

I come from hevin heich to tell the best nowells that e'er befell.
To you thir thythings trew I bring and I will of them say and sing.
This day to you is born ane child of Marie meik and Virgin mild.
That blissit bairn bening and kind sall you rejoyce baith hart and mind.

Lat us rejoyis and be blyth and with the Hyrdis go full swyth
And see what God of his grace hes done throu Christ to bring us to his throne.
My saull and life stand up and see what lyis in ane cribbe of tree.
What Babe is that, sa gude and fair? It is Christ, God's Son and Air.

O my deir hart, yung Jesus sweit, prepair thy creddill in my spreit!
And I sall rock thee in my hart and never mair fra thee depart.
Bot I sall praise thee evermoir with sangis sweit unto thy gloir.
The kneis of my hart sall I bow and sing that rycht Balulalow.

Choirs preferring to sidestep the challenges of the original may prefer the following modernized adaptation:

O my dear heart, young Jesu sweet, prepare thy cradle in my sp'rit![1]
And I shall rock thee in my heart, and nevermore from thee depart.
But I shall praise thee evermore, with songs so sweet unto thy glor'.[2]
The knees of my heart shall I bow and sing that true[3] Balulalow.[4]

Contributed by:

Gerald Custer

1 Pronounce "spreet" to rhyme with "sweet."

2 Pronounce "glor" to rhyme with "evermore."

3 "Rycht" is literally right, apt, fitting.

4 Pronounce "lau" to rhyme with "bow."

Teacher Resource Guide

Best of Rooms

Randall Thompson

(1899–1984)

SATB/a cappella
E.C. Schirmer: 2672
Overall: 4
Vocal: 4
Tonal/Rhythm: 4

Composer

Ira Randall Thompson was born in New York City, April 21, 1899, and died in Boston, July 9, 1984. Although his family was musical, young Thompson was not encouraged to take up music as a profession. His early musical pursuits began at an old reed organ on the family summer farm in Vienna, Maine. As a student at the Lawrenceville School in New Jersey, where his father was an English teacher, Thompson was raised in an academic environment and was engaged as a school organist. His first attempts at composition began around 1915 with a piano sonata and a Christmas part song. In 1916 he entered Harvard University where he auditioned for the chorus but was turned down by its conductor, Archibald T. Davison. Davison eventually became his mentor. Thompson later mused, "My life has been an attempt to strike back."

By the time Thompson received his MA in 1922, he had also studied with Swiss-born American composer Ernest Bloch. In that year, he won the Damrosch Fellowship to study at the American Academy in Rome. There he began what turned out to be a lifelong friendship with the Italian people, their music, and their language. He also started writing the first of his significant musical compositions: the five *Odes of Horace*, set for chorus and completed in 1924. On his return to the United States, Thompson lived in Greenwich Village, taking on various musical jobs, including composing songs and music for musical revues. A year later, he married Margaret Quayle Whitney of Philadelphia, who was a lifelong supporter of her husband's musical ambitions.

In 1927, Thompson was appointed Assistant Professor of Music, Organist, and Choir Director at Wellesley College, and was awarded Guggenheim fellowships. From then on, his academic and directorial career included becoming a lecturer at Harvard; a guest conductor of the Dessoff and Madrigal choirs and the Julliard chorus in New York; and a professor of music successively at Berkeley, the University of Virginia, Princeton, and Harvard. In one interval he was Director of the Curtis Institute of Music in Philadelphia, where his student assistants included Samuel Barber and Leonard Bernstein. With the latter, he continued to maintain a close personal and professional friendship and was often a source of guidance for the younger composer and conductor. However, Thompson disliked the administrative work that robbed him of time for composing.

Between 1932 and 1935, Thompson was the chief architect of a survey that ultimately revolutionized the teaching and performance of music on American's campuses. The results of this published study (*College Music*, 1935) provided the impetus toward professional competence and higher standards in academic choral performance.

Composition, Genre, and Historical Perspective

Randall Thompson was sometimes criticized for his "backward looking" neo-romantic style of composition. However, his writing demonstrates a strong affinity for text and clearly reveals a congruous marriage of music and poetry. Thompson was a tonal, melodic composer who relied on poetic inspiration for musical drama.

Although Thompson wrote three symphonies and two string quartets, the bulk of his composition is vocal and choral. His oeuvre includes one opera, *Solomon and Balkis*. His choral works are mostly settings of Biblical texts but also include American poets and writers. His music is distinctly American in its harmonic and melodic language.

The note at the end of the 2003 edition of "The Best of Rooms" includes *Gstaad 15-24.I.'63*, indicating the work was composed in Gstaad, Switzerland from January 15–24, 1963. It was published by later that year by E.C. Schirmer.

Musical Elements

"The Best of Rooms" is unaccompanied, and the piano reduction of the vocal parts will be invaluable in rehearsal preparation. The relatively short work (50 measures) remains in A-flat major throughout, yet the presence of G-flat early on gives it a decidedly modal character. Additionally, measures 20 through 27 contain progressive elements of chromaticism that require particular attention to intonation.

A particular challenge of Thompson's choral writing is his use of protracted melismas that gradually increase in range and dynamics. It is important for the vowel sounds to remain consistent throughout the melismas. These are often accompanied by a gentle chromaticism that demands careful tuning and accurate treatment of intervals. The voice leading is sensible, but often includes skips and leaps that are quite demanding for younger singers. Examples include the soprano octave leaps in measures 26 and 27, alto octave leaps in measure 26, and the challenging alto voice leading in measure 25. These sections might require piano doubling in the learning process.

Another feature of Thompson's music (used extensively in both "The Last Words of David" and "Alleluia") is the use of a half note tied to an eighth note followed by three eighth notes. It is important to begin these half notes softly and *crescendo* through the tied eighth note. They are often paired, as in measures 29 and 30 (alto/bass) and measure 33 (soprano/tenor). As each successive pairing unfolds, paying attention to dynamics will allow the melodic and harmonic lines to sound in a transparent manner.

Thompson uses very specific and detailed dynamic markings in all his music. Measures 33 to 44 include a dynamic range from *ff* to *pp*, as well as the following markings: *poco piu mosso*, *poco rall.*, *sfz*, *trattenuto*, multiple *diminuendi*, *sfz*, two *fermati*, *meno mosso*, and various dynamic gradations. The conductor and singers must pay careful attention to each and every detailed nuance that contributes to the romanticized effect of Thompson's choral writing.

While the score indicates that this work is to be performed unaccompanied, a less-experienced chorus might also perform the work with a soft organ or piano accompaniment providing support for the voices.

Form and Structure

Measure	Event and Scoring
mm. 1–15	Opening two verses of the poem, principally homophonic in nature, with short imitation and voice pairing. This portion of the work can be very easily grasped by choirs of even modest ability. The dynamics range from *pp* to *mp*.
mm. 16–38	After the initial text "Give Him the choice" the following 21 bars are an increasingly dramatic setting of the words "Grant Him the nobler part of all the House."

mm. 39–50 The concluding section to the text "the best of all's the heart" is a more reflective and introspective conclusion, remaining largely in A-flat with gradually slowing rhythmic values.

Text and Translation

"The Best of Rooms" is a setting of the Robert Herrick poem, *Christ's Part* (1647). Herrick was a seventeenth-century English poet who lived during the Civil War. His reputation rests on the spiritual works *Hesperides* and the much shorter *Noble Numbers*, published together in 1648. This particular poem is an allegory of offering Christ the best of rooms in the human body, the heart. Although Herrick wrote very sensual and suggestive secular poetry, this poem is distinctly sacred in nature. Public school teachers must be aware that it uses the word Christ and subsequent capitalized pronouns referring to "He" and "Him."

Christ, He requires still, wheresoe'er He comes,
To feed, or lodge, to have the best of rooms;
Give Him the choice; grant Him the nobler part
Of all the house: the best of all's the heart.

Contributed by:

Jerry Ulrich

Teacher Resource Guide

Calme des Nuits

Camille Saint-Saëns

(1835–1921)

SATB
GIA Publications, Inc.: G-7605
Overall: 4
Vocal: 4
Tonal/Rhythm: 3

Composer

Camille Saint-Saëns, composer, organist, pianist, and music historian, was regarded by his peers as one of the most influential—and controversial—French composers of the nineteenth century. His leadership as founding director of the *Societé Nationale de Musique*, an organization devoted to supporting the creation and premieres of new French compositions, helped place Paris in the center of musical innovation, allowing French composers to forge a national identity.

Saint-Saëns was born in 1835 in Paris. His father, a civil servant of humble means, died of consumption when Saint-Saëns was only three months old, leaving Saint-Saëns to be raised by his mother and great aunt. In his first year, Saint-Saëns showed signs of an inherited weakness toward consumption, and his mother, following medical advice, sent her son to the country where the air was cleaner and he could be cared for by a full-time nurse. Despite a difficult start to life, Saint-Saëns' prodigious talents rivaled even that of the young Mozart. Saint-Saëns could read, write, and compose by the age of three (his first piano piece was written in March of 1839). Saint-Saëns' mother worked to create balance in her son's life: while allowing him opportunities to shine as a child prodigy by performing in frequent public venues, she attempted to protect him from being overworked or mistreated.

Saint-Saëns' formal education was at the Paris Conservatoire beginning in 1848, where he studied composition and organ, as well as singing. He showed an impressive appetite for knowledge outside the subject area of music, leading him eventually to publish articles about topics as diverse as philosophy, astronomy, biology, and mathematics. Fauré once said that Saint-Saëns "sought to understand everything that he might love everything." After graduating from the Paris Conservatoire, Saint-Saëns served for twenty years as organist at the Madeleine, and for a brief four-year period, on the composition faculty at the Ecole Niedermeyer, where he became Gabriel Fauré's teacher.

Although Saint-Saëns was well traveled, he enjoyed being centered primarily in Paris, where he fostered collegial relationships with other French composers such as Berlioz, Liszt, Gounod, and especially Fauré. His relationship to Fauré approached that of a father/son relationship, perhaps due to the tragic loss of both of his own sons, six weeks apart, in the same year (1878). His marriage to Marie-Laure Truffot, already tenuous at best, dissolved within three years of the tragedy. The death of his mother in 1888 was another severe blow, but his creative work and frequent concert tours managed to give him purpose. His first visit to America was in 1906, where he was hailed as one of the finest living composers, and in 1913 he received the coveted Grande Croix of the Légion d'Honneur.

Saint-Saëns was one of the first nineteenth-century composers to, like Mendelssohn, "rediscover" early music composers such as Lully and Charpentier. Saint-Saëns' impressive scholarly ability led to his work as editor of collected editions of J. S. Bach, Rameau, Gluck, Mozart, and Beethoven. The influence of eighteenth-century style and form on his music is evident in his charming and accessible *Oratorio de Noël* of 1863, for chorus, soloists, string quartet, harp, and organ. Other well known choral works include his *Mass* Op. 4 (1857), *Requiem* (1878), and numerous short, simple church motets for chorus and organ. Although Saint-Saëns composed twelve complete operas, the only one still regularly performed is *Samson et Dalila* (Op. 47) from 1873. It is ironic to note that one of Saint-Saëns' most beloved instrumental works, *Le Carnaval des animaux* (1886), was a source of embarrassment to him, and he feared its subject matter would tarnish his reputation as a "serious composer." Saint-Saëns' output also features well-crafted art songs and a large body of piano and organ music, not surprising due to his career as a performer on both instruments. His final public performance on piano was in 1921 at the late age of 75, and he died only a few months later. He was buried in the Madeleine and given a state funeral.

Composition, Genre, and Historical Perspective

The part song "Calme des Nuits" was written in 1882, and in the following year it was paired with another part song entitled "Les fleurs et des arbres" (of 1883) into a set entitled *Deux choeurs*, Op. 68, with "Calme des Nuits" appearing first in the set. Because the two part songs were written a year apart, it is certainly feasible to perform only one or the other, depending on the needs of the chorus.

To place Saint-Saëns in historical perspective, consider this useful quote: "The life of Saint-Saëns began in the Paris of Chopin and Berlioz and ended away from the Paris of Stravinsky and Les Six." Such a wide span of musical styles is hard to fathom within a single composer's lifetime, however long. But in the case Saint-Saëns, his style remained relatively close to that of his predecessors, specifically Schubert and Mozart.

"Calme des Nuits" was written when Saint-Saëns was 52, already well established in his compositional style. The simplicity of the writing may be linked to his dedication of the work to Charles Gounod, a fellow composer who placed melody at the top of the compositional hierarchy, and favored the transparent textures of the Renaissance composer Palestrina.

Musical Elements and Technical Considerations

Like all choral works written in French, a certain amount of time will need to be devoted to realizing the pronunciation accurately; however, the relatively short text and homophonic texture makes rehearsal of the diction a fairly straightforward process. Practice intoning the text in "Julia Child" style before actually singing the notes in French. (Heightened spoken pitches are easier than "droning" text to translate to singing when pitches are added back in.) A brief introduction to the French vowels will really help students grasp the color of the language. Invite your school's French instructor (or a native speaker) to visit the class, perhaps once near the beginning of the language teaching and once again after the choir has prepared the piece for performance.

The most challenging issue in "Calme des Nuits" probably lies in achieving excellent intonation and blend for the following reasons:

- Texture is often exposed with wide spaces between voice ranges;
- Sung phrases are long, averaging 6 bars in a slow tempo;
- Dynamics of the A and A' sections are pianissimo, making breath support and blend extremely important;
- Large melodic skips such as the soprano's octave skip in bar 16 must be achieved within a pianissimo dynamic.

Although Saint-Saëns specified that piano could be used "ad libitum," it is difficult to imagine how to properly improvise a piano part that fits seamlessly with this delicate texture; in most cases its presence probably isn't necessary. What is more important is to build the singers' understanding of the harmonic structure so they can properly tune all their chords. When a singer knows that his or her pitch is the third of a triad, he or she will sing it higher than if it is the root. Taking time to identify how chords are built will save scores of rehearsal time later, and will give students the tools to tune chords in each new performance (which might take place in venues with varying acoustics).

Another way to build excellent intonation is to rehearse parts in various combinations (sopranos with tenors, sopranos with basses, tenors with altos and basses, etc.) so that singers can hear the chords in different contexts. Since you might postpone rehearsing the music with text, experiment with singing on closed vowels (oo, ee, or the French ü) to help the chorus "hone in" on proper intonation; this will prepare singers for how "closed" French vowels need to feel.

Encourage long, relaxed breaths so that singers can really pause to prepare their support mechanism. Ask singers to stand frequently, with elevated ribs, relaxed shoulders and a sense of freedom in their bodies. Coordinate "relay" or "stagger" breathing, choreographing where individual singers will breathe, so that the long phrases stay alive without singers having to struggle.

Stylistic Considerations

The interpretation of "Calme des Nuits" must be driven by the poem, which will dictate the phrase shape and rhythmic flow of the lines. An added layer of meaning exists in the text: a glimpse at the solitary, inner life of a poet. Ask your singers to intone the poem's lines in every rehearsal, and help them to slowly memorize not only the words, but also the meaning, so that as they sing they will understand what they are singing about. This technique will bring an authenticity to the performance, despite the "foreign" language. French music has been said to be "unmetered," but there is a cadence and flow to the language that is distinct and worth pursuing.

Because Saint-Saëns remained conservative in his choral writing style, it is best to avoid excessive outward expression. Maintain simplicity in the interpretation, allowing the text to guide any contrasts. Apart from the short burst of "extroversion" heard in bars 28 through 32, the piece is remarkably serene.

Saint-Saëns favored shifting chords based on tertial relationships. Notice the shifts in harmony in the chorus in bar 29 (from the B minor triad on the downbeat, to the G major triad in first inversion on the second note). Only one part changes notes—the altos—but every singer needs to feel that shift and respond musically. This kind of chord progression is a hallmark of composers of the Romantic era.

Form and Structure

The overall form is A B A'.

Section	Measure	Event and Scoring
A	mm. 1–6	one phrase
	mm. 7–13	one phrase
	mm. 14–18	one phrase
	mm. 19–27	one phrase, one bar of rest
B	mm. 28–32	one phrase
	mm. 33–36	one phrase that segues directly into A' section
A'	mm. 33–38	return to A' occurs in middle of the phrase
	mm. 39–40	one phrase
	mm. 41–48	one phrase
	mm. 49–58	one phrase

Text and Translation

Scholarly texts claim that the authorship of the poem "Calme des Nuits" is anonymous. However, the large number of poems written and published by Saint-Saëns has led some to wonder if Saint-Saëns himself wrote the text. The full text and a translation are provided below:

Calme des nuits, fraîcheur des soirs,
Vaste scintillement des mondes,
Grand silence des antres noirs
Vous charmez les âmes profondes.
L'éclat du soleil, la gaité,
Le bruit plaisent aux plus futiles;
Le poète seul est hanté
Par l'amour des choses tranquilles.

Calmness of night, coolness of
evening,
Vast sparkling of worlds,
Great silence of dark caverns,
You charm the deeper souls.
The flash of sunlight, merriment,
And noise please those more
frivolous;
Only the poet is haunted
By the love of quiet things.

Additional References and Resources

Studd, Stephen. *Saint-Saens: A Critical Biography*. London: Cygnus Arts, 1999.

Flynn, Timothy. *Camille Saint-Saëns: A Guide to Research*. New York: Routledge, 2003.

Saint-Saëns, Camille and Gabriel Fauré, Jean Michel Nectoux and J. Barrie Jones. *The Correspondence of Camille Saint-Saëns and Gabriel Fauré: Sixty Years of Friendship*. England: Ashgate, 2004.

Catalogues

Catalogue général et thématique des oeuvres de Saint-Saëns. Durand & Cie (Paris, 1897, rev. 1908).

Rather, S.T., ed. A *Thematic Catalogue of the Complete Works of Camille Saint-Saëns, i: The Instrumental Works*. (Oxford, forthcoming).

Contributed by:

Giselle Wyers

Teacher Resource Guide

Chindia

Alexandru Pascanu
(1920–1989)

SATB
Santa Barbara Music: SBMP44
Overall: 4
Vocal: 4
Tonal/Rhythm: 4

Composer

Composer Alexander Pascanu was born in 1920 in Bucharest, Romania, and died there in 1989. A member of the faculty of the Music Conservatory in Bucharest, he was known as a champion of Romanian folksong, and he published several books and journal articles on the subject. He also published several articles on the art of choral arranging, on music theory, and on composition. In addition to his choral works, he composed for orchestra and chamber ensembles as well.

Santa Barbara Music Press, in its introductory remarks on the inside cover of the octavo, thanks the President of Uniunea Compozitorilor Si of Bucharest for permission to publish *Chindia*. The press quotes the President: "Pascanu was a wonderful man, both in professional as in human respect. We should be glad to see this masterpiece becoming accessible to American choirs."

Composition, Genre, and Historical Perspective

Chindia, Pascanu's most popular choral piece, is meant to capture in sound a vigorous Romanian folk dance of the same name. This piece is based on the instrumental accompaniment to this dance, and is to be performed in a robust, festive manner befitting its origin. Singers are encouraged to imitate the instruments that would have originally accompanied the dance. Folk music traditions in Romania are quite diverse and vary from region to region. Popular Romanian folk instruments include violin, panpipe, cozba (a cousin of the lute), and cimbalom (hammer dulcimer).

The word *chindia* also refers to a specific time of day—dusk—as well as to the horizon, where the sun sets. This word embodies the mysterious passage of day into night, a time when the *Chindia* dance is most often performed.

Musical Elements and Technical Considerations

Vocal articulations and dynamics are clearly marked throughout the piece, and following the composer's suggestions promises a performance full of festive drama. The list below notes musical and technical issues that arise in this piece, as well as suggestions for rehearsal and performance.

Rapid Execution of Rhythms

The melody, which first appears in the soprano line at measure 5, remains prominent throughout the piece. The lower voices function primarily as accompaniment to the melody, providing the rhythmic impetus for the propulsion of the work. The challenge comes in rapidly executing the syllables while maintaining rhythmic accuracy. To best accomplish this, consider the syllables as an imitation of an instrument rather than as vehicles for beautiful vowel sounds. The integrity of the vowel is not as important as the crisp, precise delivery of the consonant. Thus, rather than trying for an [a] vowel in the 16th-note passages, use more of a schwa, or [ ]. The [a] vowel is more appropriate for note durations of a quarter note or greater.

Simultaneous Duple/Triple Rhythms

In measures 69 through 72, the alto, tenor, and bass continue to accompany the soprano melody. While the soprano line features eighth-note rhythms, the alto, tenor, and bass simultaneously share triplet rhythms against sopranos' rhythms. The sopranos must resist the urge to "swing" the second eighth note in each grouping, while the supporting voices must accurately execute the triplets without rushing.

Melismatic Melodic Passages

In measure 64, the percussive opening of the piece gives way to a lyrical variation of the melody originally featured in the opening soprano line. Here, however, there are no consonants to help propel the melody. Great care must be taken to articulate repeated pitches, perhaps with a soft onset each time. The melody in this section centers on the pitch D, and the melismatic flourishes above and below this pitch are primarily ornamental. Encourage singers to keep these "flourishes" light in production and remain focused on the resonance of the head register, and to resist allowing chest register to invade the tone in these passages.

Dynamic Extremes

Part of the excitement of *Chindia* is in its dynamic range. The composer asks for *crescendi* from *piano* to *fortissimo* in the space of only a few short measures (as in mm. 55 through 58), and even a *pianissimo* to *forte* and to *subito piano* (mm. 29 through 30). Finding the the true *piano* and true *forte* for the choir becomes important here; the *piano* dynamic must be soft without being airy, and the *forte* must be powerful without becoming a shout.

Balance

The soprano has the melody for much of the piece, and only on a few occasions does it move into another voice. The bass section enjoys a brief presentation of melodic material in measures 43 through 50, but aside from that deviation the sopranos dominate throughout. Altos, tenors, and basses must be aware of their supporting role and work to avoid overpowering the melodic line. This is especially difficult when the choir moves homophonically (as in mm. 17 and 18).

Stylistic Considerations

Because of the folk nature of the piece, and because the text is essentially nonsense syllables, every effort should be made to create the feel of a folk dance band. The outer sections, which are vigorous and lively, require a primarily staccato feel with great precision in the rhythm. The tempo, once established, remains constant until the *rallentando* into the B section at measure 61. The B section, essentially a more lyrical presentation of the melody from the A section, is more legato in nature. The return of the A section in measure 80 demands the choir revert to the original staccato execution, this time at an even brisker tempo.

According to Santa Barbara's program notes in the octavo, the composer preferred the piece to be done *a cappella*, even though he provided a piano accompaniment.

Form and Structure

Chindia appears to be in ABA^1 form; the B section is deceptive, however, in that it is basically a slower, more legato presentation of the melody rather than an evolution and development of the melody. The transitions in measures 61 through 63 and measures 77 through 79 provide musical "bookends" to the slower section, making it feel like a separate musical event, even though the melodic material is essentially unchanged. The return of the A section material in measure 80 brings back the original material at an even faster tempo. Measure 108, which correlates to measure 29 in the A section, begins a coda of sorts that extends to the end of the piece. The final measure is a dramatic shout, "muf!" from the chorus.

Text and Translation

The syllables in place of text are meant to imitate the instruments that would ordinarily accompany the dances. Rapid execution of the syllables and free, light vocal production are key to capturing the folk essence of the work. As mentioned above, the importance of the driving consonants supercedes the importance of the vowel. All "r"s should be flipped, and singers should resist the use of an American "r" production.

Contributed by:

Karen Kennedy

Teacher Resource Guide

El Hambo

Jaakko Mäntyjärvi
(b. 1939)

SATB
Walton Music: 8501354
Overall: 4
Vocal: 4
Tonal/Rhythm: 4

Composer

Jaakko Mäntyjärvi was born in Turku, Finland in 1963. He studied music theory and conducting at the Sibelius Academy, Finland's music university. Mäntyjärvi was employed for several years as a translator and computer system manager at The English Centre Helsinki, a private translation company.

Mäntyjärvi has a vast background singing in ensembles such as Savonlinna Opera Festival Choir, the Sibelius Academy Vocal Ensemble, and the Tapiola Chamber Choir for which he was the assistant conductor from 1998 to 2004 and composer-in-residence from 2000 to 2005. He was conductor of the Savolaisen Osakunnan Laulajat student choir from 1988 to 1993.

Most of Jaakko Mäntyjärvi's compositions are for choir. A brief listing of his choral works include: *Four Shakespeare Songs* (1984), "Ave Maria" (1991), "Pseudo-Yoik" (1994), "Kouta" (1996), "El Hambo" (1997), *More Shakespeare Songs* (1997), *Deux ballades de François Villon* (2001), *Agnus Dei in combinationibus* (2006), and "Alleluia delle pietre dure" (2006). His work *Canticum Calamitatis Maritimae* received third prize in the European composition competition for cathedral choirs in 1997. Mäntyjärvi's major commissions include those for the Cork International Choral Festival, for the 700th Anniversary of the Consecration of Turku Cathedral, and for Chanticleer and the King Singers.

His works are published by Bu Sulasol in Finland and Walton Music in the United States.

Composition, Genre, and Historical Perspective

In the octavo notes from 1998, Jaako Mäntyjärvi states:

> "El Hambo" is the second installment in a rather loosely defined series that I have decided to call *Justly Forgotten Peoples*. (The first installment was, of course, "Pseudo-Yoik.") The *hambo* is a Swedish folk dance in 3/4 time. This augmented hambo in 5/4 time is something of a tribute to those folk musicians whose enthusiasm much exceeds their sense of rhythm, and the increasingly desperate punctuations should be interrupted as an attempt to keep the performance in some sort of metrical shape. The somewhat arrogant title is intended to suggest (rather like *La Valse*) an apotheosis of the genre, The Mother of All Hambos if you like, or perhaps even The Hambo to End All Hambos. It also embraces the pan-European ideal; for those who find themselves distressed by the fact that the piece does not in fact contain anything remotely identifiable as Spanish, it may be of interest to note that *elhambo* means "electric hambo" in Swedish and could also be an alternative transliteration of the Welsh *y llam bodd* ("the jump of joy"). Further cognates are welcome.
>
> Sources of inspiration for this piece include, surprisingly, genuine Norwegian choral folk song arrangements and of course the Swedish Chef from *The Muppet Show*. The text is, or is supposed to be, completely meaningless, as those who are familiar with "Pseudo-Yoik" will already have suspected. The first three chords of the piece are violin tunings actually used in Norwegian folk music.
>
> "El Hambo" and "Pseudo-Yoik" should not be performed one after another because they are embarrassingly similar.

"El Hambo" was commissioned by Rita Varonen for the Cantinovum choir of Jyväskylä, Finland, and premiered in June 1997 at the Tampere Choir Festival.

Musical Elements and Technical Considerations

This is a very difficult work that can be incredibly effective and entertaining performed by an advanced ensemble. Conductors who consider programming this work should be aware of the inherent challenges that it presents. In determining whether the piece will work with a given ensemble, the conductor must clearly weigh the amount of time that the work will take in rehearsal against the performance return to consider if it will be worth the time of learning. Several considerations are listed below.

Some extreme vocal ranges will provide challenges and singers might have to shift to an alternate part from time to time in order to access a singable part and create appropriate ensemble balance. Depending on the ranges and facility of the singers, this might require extra preparation on behalf of the conductor and careful score markings by singers. The ensemble will need to have particularly strong low basses in order to create the full effect of this work. The ranges are as follows:

Sopranos	high: A5	low: F3
Altos	high: D5	low: F3
Tenors	high: G4	low: A2
Basses	high: D4	low: D2

The work contains both unison singing (often displaced at the octave—parallel octaves) and frequent divisi into eight parts. The basses sometimes divide into three parts. The work also includes various claps and stamps for effect.

Perfect fifths are present almost consistently throughout the composition and when they are not, they are frequently inverted to perfect fourths. These fluctuating parallel intervals give the work a rustic feel. Parallel thirds also regularly occur in the work. The consistent use of parallel intervals demands that the choir have impeccable intonation.

Changing meter and the changing back and forth between triplets and dotted-quarter and eighth-note patterns will present significant challenges to the ensemble. Most of the work alternates back and forth every few measures between 5/4 and 3/4 time. There is also one measure of 6/4 to extend a sound effect.

Most American choirs will find the text, at least initially, confusing or difficult to pronounce. As noted under the Text and Translation section ahead, the made-up words should be pronounced as in Finnish. The conductor should slowly isolate and practice vowel and consonant sounds so that a firm base is laid for understanding the production of sounds needed. When the rules of pronunciation are understood, the conductor should slowly speak the text with exaggerated diction and have the choir repeat it back. The next step would be to speak the text slowly in rhythm. This kind of practice should be repeated over many rehearsals so that the text will flow fluently from the singers' lips. As the singers develop their knowledge, skills, and fluidity, the speed of the recitations should be increased. It is most probable, based on the involvedness of the text, that the best way for the choir to learn the notes will be by singing on neutral syllable.

One of the main difficulties of the work is the fast tempo. The composer has marked it at quarter note = 152. The conductor should rehearse under tempo until the ensemble is ready to succeed at a faster pace. The addition of claps and stamps to the tricky text, rhythmic assertion, quick tempo, and constant in and out of divisi make this work a worthy contest for a daring ensemble.

Stylistic Considerations

The humor of this work is found in the parody of the text. The work sounds as if it could be a setting of a rustic folk song, which values sounds that traditional Western music does not (e.g., parallel fourths, fifths, and octaves, and open fifths). There is a lack of harmonic invention in favor of repetition of the previously mentioned elements. In this sense the work is similar to folk-song arrangements by Aaron Copland, Benjamin Britten, and Béla Bartók.

Form and Structure

The large structure of this work is ABA[1].

SECTION	MEASURE	EVENT AND SCORING
Introduction	mm. 1–3	
A	m. 4	based on G tonic alternating with the dominant with C-sharps and F-naturals (mixolydian feel)
	m. 17	based on D with many C-sharps
	m. 25	F-sharp enters
B	m. 31	open fifth drone throughout, subdominant mixed mode area (C major and C minor) instead of the expected dominant
	m. 38	end of subdominant
A[1]	m. 64	a tempo

Text and Translation

In the octavo notes from 1996, Jaako Mäntyjärvi states: "the text, such as it is, of "El Hambo" should be pronounced as Finnish, flavoured with amusing imitations of the vowel colours of any Scandinavian language except Danish."

A comprehensive and indelible guide for the pronunciation of vowels and consonants is included in the octavo.

düdelidamm
oi aadi oodi düüdi üüdi dam
oi aadi oodi düüdi aadi düüdi düdelidamm
hei jäkkä däkkä düüdi aadi hei jäkkä düüdi dambo
hei jäkkä däkkä düüdi aadi oodi aadi üüdi ambo
dam dördi jördi bork bork

düdeli dingi dingi düii düii
o' hei jäkkä däkkä düüdi aadi hei jäkkä düüdi dambo
hei jäkkä däkkä düüdi aadi oodi aadi üüdi ambo
dam dördi jördi bork bork
aaba deebe deebe düüap

lei aani aani lüüdi aanaa
lei aani ooni aanaa
lüüdi aadi oodi aanaa
oi aadi oodi düüdi üüdi dam
oi aadi oodi sveeba deeba deeba duuba duubi duubi dam

dap duu ap düdelidamm bap duu ap
dap du ap düdeli dingi dingi duu ap
oi aadi oodi düüdi üüdi dam
oi aadi oodi aaba eeba deeeba dam dam hambo

Additional References and Resources

Octavo:

Mäntyjäri, Jaako. *El Hambo*. Chapel Hill: Walton Music Corporation. 1997. (WW1264).

Recording:

Jaako Mäntyjäri: Choral Works. Tapiola Chamber Choir. Hannu Norjanen, conductor. (Finlandia Records 0927-41563-2).

Contributed by:

Joseph Ohrt, DMA

Teacher Resource Guide

In Paradisum

Edwin Fissinger
(1920–1990)

SATB
Plymouth Music: 55-51105
Overall: 4
Vocal: 4
Tonal/Rhythm: 4

Composer

Edwin R. Fissinger, born June 15, 1920, received both his bachelor's and master's degrees from the American Conservatory of Music in Chicago, where he specialized in composition and studied under Leo Sowerby. Fissinger later became director of the choir and held that position from 1947 to 1954. In 1965, he earned a doctorate from the University of Illinois, where he was a graduate assistant in music theory from 1954 to 1957. From 1957 until 1967, he was chairman of the music department and director of the choir and madrigal singers at the University of Illinois at Chicago Circle. Fissinger joined the faculty of North Dakota State University (NDSU) in 1967, was chairman of the music department and served as the director of the University Concert Choir and Madrigal Singers, both of which received recognition and numerous awards under his direction.

Edwin Fissinger was a charter member of the American Choral Director's Association and had an active career as a conductor and composer for forty-five years. In addition to orchestral, piano, and vocal compositions, he wrote 183 choral works. Fissinger was nationally recognized as a composer and editor of choral music, and published numerous works. From 1958 to 1962

Fissinger was consulting editor for Summy-Birchard Publishing Co. He was a distinguished choral director, and in 1973, 1977, and 1983 the NDSU Concert Choir, under his direction, was selected to perform at the opening session of the National Convention of the American Choral Directors Association. At the 1977 convention, his choir participated in an American choral music documentary produced by Zweites Deutsches Fernsehen (Second German Television Network). He retired in 1985 but continued composing until his death in Fargo, North Dakota on October 16, 1990.

Fissinger has been included in editions of Who's Who in the Middle West, the International Who's Who of Musicians, Men of Achievement, Personalities of America, and Who's Who in American Classical Music. The following companies publish his choral music: Associated, Colla Voce, Hal Leonard, Kjos, Meadowlark, Pavane, and Walton.

Composition, Genre, and Historical Perspective

In Paradisum (Latin: *Into Paradise*). The title comes from the first words of the Latin text. The original chant is sometimes sung during the funeral liturgy of the Roman Catholic Church, usually while the casket is taken from the Church for burial. The reference to Lazarus calls to mind the story in the Gospel of Jesus raising his friend from the dead after being moved to tears by the grief of Mary and Martha, the sisters of Lazarus.

This setting of *In Paradisum* was written in 1988 for Dr. Ed Thompson and the University of Utah Concert Choir. Since its first performance, *In Paradisum* has been performed in many prestigious concerts, including several National ACDA Conventions as well as many all-state performances.

Musical Elements and Technical Considerations

In Paradisum, a motet, features asymmetrical musical phrases designed to follow the text very closely. Fissinger tended to wrap the notes and rhythm around the text in a very syllabic style, which results in a mixed-meter setting with asymmetrical phrases.

I find that the most challenging part of this piece is in keeping the singers "on the breath" so that the asymmetrical phrases, and therefore the text lines, can stay intact. Otherwise, the choir typically tends to fall off the breath at spots like measures 2 and 3, 7 and 8, 14 and 15, 44 and 45, 50 and 51, and 57 and 58. Warmups that emphasize legato singing would be most helpful in preparing the choir for singing these beautiful phrases. I would suggest not rushing ends of phrases but rather separating phrases with a tenuto; don't be concerned with staying in a strict tempo. In this way, the chant style that I believe Fissinger intended will be more easily realized. Examples of this happen especially in measures 11 and 26.

The harmonic language of this piece is very refreshing and almost surprising to the choir as they begin to rehearse it. Chordal structures and phrases that the choir would anticipate in a typical motet are quite different in this setting, and the choir might need a few hearings to settle in on these differences.

An interesting feature that sets this motet apart from other settings is an "unsynchronized" section about two-thirds of the way into the composition (mm. 35 through 41, three phrases) in which the conductor is instructed in the music to divide each section of the choir into three groups to sing the phrases either in long, medium, or short tempos at random starts. The "phrasers" are instructed to *crescendo* and *diminuendo* randomly, especially as they hear the dissonances created by the "unsynchronization." The result is an ethereal sound especially if sung in a hall with rather live acoustics. As each section finishes its phrases, the conductor brings the choir into the final third of the piece, which repeats the text from "Chorus Angelorum." I have also experimented with other treatments of this section that have worked well but are dependent on the standing placement of the choir at the time of performance. I would suggest experimenting with this section to see how the choir can best achieve the desired effect.

Stylistic Considerations

The style of this motet is very legato and chant-like. As in Gregorian chant, the music always moves along freely. It is safe to assume that textual accents are always on the penultimate syllable, unless indicated by an acute accent (e.g., há-be-as, sus-cí-pi-ant); other syllables are sung lightly.

The considerations for the choir will be to place the word stress appropriately to give the overall phrase an authentic chant-like feel. The approximate timing for this piece is four and a half minutes.

Form and Structure

Measure	Event and Scoring
mm. 1–5	(5 bars) 2+3: In paradisum deducant te angeli
mm. 6–11	(6 bars) 2+4: in tuo adventu suscipiant te martyres
mm. 12–18	(6 bars) 3+3: et perducant te in civitatem sanctam Jerusalem
mm. 18–22	(5 bars) 3+2: Chorus angelorum te suscipiat
mm. 23–30	(8 bars) 4+4: et cum Lazaro quondam paupere aeternam habeas requiem
mm. 31–34	(4 bars) solo: In paradisum
mm. 35–41	(7 bars) unsynchronized section: In paradisum deducant te angeli: habeas requiem
mm. 42–46	(5 bars) 3+2: Chorus angelorum te suscipiat

Measure	Event and Scoring
mm. 47–53	(7 bars) 5+2: et cum Lazaro quondam paupere aeternam, aeternam
mm. 54–59	(6 bars) 4+2: aeternam habeas, habeas
mm. 60-62	(3 bars): habeas requiem

Text and Translation

Latin text:
In paradisum deducant te angeli,
in tuo adventu
suscipiant te martyres,
et perducant te
in civitatem sanctam Jerusalem.
Chorus angelorum te suscipiat,
et cum Lazaro quondam paupere
aeternam habeas requiem.

English translation:
May the angels lead you into
paradise,
may the martyrs receive you
in your coming,
and may they guide you
into the holy city, Jerusalem.
May the chorus of angels receive you
and with Lazarus once poor
may you have eternal rest.

Additional References and Resources

Edwin Fissinger Papers, 1948–1990 (Mss 226). Biography. Institute for Regional Studies, North Dakota State University Home Page, http://www.lib.ndsu.nodak.edu/ndirs/collections/manuscripts/lit&music/Fissinger/biography.html, October 24, 2000.

Edwin Fissinger. Pavane Publishing, copyright 2008. http://www.pavanepublishing.com/Site/33/.

Spirtual and Religious Texts. National Public Radio: All Things Considered. *The End of Life: Exploring Death in America*. Copyright 2008. http://www.npr.org/programs/death/glossary.html#paradisum.

Contributed by:

Michele Holt

Teacher Resource Guide

Lay a Garland

Robert Pearsall

(1795–1856)

SSAATTBB
Oxford University Press
Overall: 4
Vocal: 3
Tonal/Rhythm: 4

Composer

Robert Lucas [de] Pearsall (1795–1856) began his training as a lawyer near Bristol, England. He began his first composition studies began following a move to Germany in 1825. Pearsall's composition training was in strict counterpoint under Joseph Panny. The early works were mostly choral Latin motets in the "pure" style. Pearsall returned to England in 1836 and became involved in the founding of the Bristol Madrigal Society in 1837. Through this affiliation Pearsall began writing madrigals in the style of Morley. His first madrigals were simple imitations of the Renaissance style, and his later works expanded the madrigal style by incorporating his counterpoint training and sense of Classical line. Fuller Maitland believed his larger madrigals to be, "... real masterpieces in a form that has seldom been successfully employed in modern times." The end of Pearsall's career brought a return to sacred composition, with music written for both Anglican and Catholic traditions. Pearsall considered his almost unknown *Requiem* to be his finest work.

Composition, Genre, and Historical Perspective

"Lay a Garland" was written on June 4th, 1840, scored for SSAATTBB. Written during Pearsall's madrigal period, most likely for the Bristol Madrigal Society, this piece departs from earlier madrigal settings by Pearsall that were simple adaptations of Morley's style. In "Lay a Garland," Pearsall explores combining his earlier German training in counterpoint with his interest in the madrigal form. This madrigal is a study in Classical line and a marvel of advanced counterpoint technique.

Musical Elements and Technical Consideration

The categorization of "Lay a Garland" as a madrigal is deceiving to those unfamiliar with the piece. This work is far more complicated, both to prepare and to sing, than a simple "fa-la –a" Morley madrigal. Concurrent with that is the issue of appropriate performing forces. While one would imagine a madrigal being sung by a small ensemble of 12 to 20 singers, this is not necessarily the best solution for this piece. A small ensemble of professional singers with years of vocal training and endless breath support might be able to sustain an effective performance of this piece, but for most upper level high school and college choirs the piece works better with 40-plus singers. The length of the phrases, sostenuto, and independent nature of the individual lines are best served, for most choirs, by at least 4 or 5 singers on each part (in the SSAATTBB configuration).

As in any polyphonic writing, singers in each part must be able to understand clearly the contour and phrasing of their line. Therefore, an effective technique for early rehearsals might be to work in sectionals, perhaps using section leaders on each part.

Younger singers will no doubt have difficulty keeping continuity of line and phrasing through the very long sustained notes. For instance, the Alto I part in bar 3 is difficult to keep moving through the whole note tied to a half note on the word "on." Imagery and kinesthetic tools can be helpful in getting through these long passages: have the singers draw the line with their hands or move through the room as the phrase extends. The analogy of a duck floating seamlessly along the surface of a lake while its legs are busily kicking under the water helps singers to visualize the role of breath support in long phrases. This piece is also an effective tool for teaching the skill of free breathing through long phrases: listening to the singers on either side of you, staggering your breathing, and never waiting until the end of your air supply to take a breath. These are all good skills to reinforce through this piece.

Stylistic Considerations

Once the singers have command of the notes, contour, and phrasing of their individual lines it is appropriate to begin to fit the parts together. The major challenge in fitting the parts together is harmonic understanding of the larger structures, especially through the modulatory sections. It seems appropriate to talk about using an accompanist during rehearsal of this piece. Most editions of this piece do not contain a reduction, and even the finest accompanists have difficulty reducing 8-part polyphonic scores at sight. Having said this, it is very effective to have a keyboard player provide a harmonic underpinning to the chordal structures. If your accompanist is unable to do this at sight, it might be helpful to provide him or her with a basic harmonic analysis.

The most difficult section harmonically begins at measure 27. The combination of E-flats and F-sharps can be difficult to look at, and difficult to hear. This is compounded by the addition of the D-flat into the harmonic language, first in measure 32. The harmonic unrest settles at the return of the dominant in measure 40. If the singers can effectively hear the harmonic motion of the passage, even with the aid of harmonic structures from the keyboard, they will have better chance at staying in tune when the keyboard is removed.

Once the individual lines are learned and the harmonic structures are understood, it is important to illustrate how the nonharmonic tones are used and what the implications are for the phrasing. This is a wonderful way to open students' ears to parts other than their own, and to mold more sensitive, musical singers. It is helpful to point out all the suspensions and explain the technique of slight crescendo into a suspension. An effective place to illustrate this technique is in measure 27 as the voices enter and stack suspensions to text paint the "false love" of the coming phrase.

British diction is obviously appropriate for this piece. No American "r" sounds at all; all "r"s should be replaced with a schwa. Diphthongs should be treated very carefully, placed as late as possible on words such as "lay." Make sure to use an open round vowel on words such as "thou" and pure [u] sound on the word "yew."

Finally, take care to understand the text of the piece and its overall gentle and peaceful character, which must pervade in an effective performance. Perhaps the most delightful (and treacherous!) moment of the piece is the passage into and out of the deceptive cadence in measure 53. Be careful to gently place the chord on the word "earth," being both mindful of the diction issues (no American "r") and aware of the motion of the phrase. The slightest rallentando is appropriate as the phrase unfolds into the restful final cadence.

An effective tempo for performance of this piece is half note = 56.

Form and Structure

The form of this piece lies mostly in its harmonic structure and creates a simple ternary form:

Section	Measure	Event and Scoring
A	mm. 1–10	Establishment of tonic.
	mm. 10–27	Moving toward development through relative minor.
B	mm. 28–40	Development, harmonically unstable; ends on dominant of E-flat major.
A[1]	mm. 40–58	Return of E-flat major key structure; final phrase arch into cadence.

Text and Translation

Text by Francis Beaumont (1584–1616) and/or John Fletcher (1579–1625), (dramatists who frequently collaborated) "Aspatia's song" from *The Maid's Tragedy* published 1610. This lyric is a song sung by Aspatia in Act II, Scene I of the play *The Maid's Tragedy*. Aspatia is distraught because her betrothed is forced into marriage to the kind's mistress. Pearsall's version of the lyric changed the voice from the first to the third person, removed one line and changed a few words. This lyric has also been set by other composers such as Parry, Warlock and Andriessen, but the Pearsall is clearly the most well-known setting.

Lay a garland on her hearse,
Of dismal yew,
Maidens, willow branches (wear),[1]
Say she died true.

Her love was false, but she was firm
[From my hour of birth;]
Upon her buried body lie
Lightly, (thou)[2] gentle earth.

1 Changed from the original "bear."

2 Added by Pearsall.

Additional References and Resources

Hunt, Edgar. *Robert Lucas Pearsall: The "Compleat gentleman" and His Music (1795–1856) Based on the Researches of the Late Dr. Hubert Hunt.* Chesham Bois, 1977.

Wilson, T. Rex. *The Musical Writings and Music of Robert Luca Pearsall.* PhD Musicology: North Texas State University. 1975.

Contributed by:

W. Bryce Hayes

Teacher Resource Guide

Lo, How a Rose E'er Blooming

(Es ist ein Ros entsprungen)

Jan Sandström

(b. 1954)

Solo quartet and mixed eight-voice choir (SATB/SSAATTBB)
Sveriges Körförbunds Förlag (Stockholm),
Walton Music: 8500322
Overall: 4
Tonal/Rhythm: 4
Vocal: 3

Composer

Jan Sandström was born in Vilhelmina in Lapland on January 25, 1954, and grew up in Stockholm. He began his university education by studying counterpoint in Stockholm (with Valdemar Söderholm) and then went north, to the top of the Gulf of Bothnia, studying at University School of Music in Piteå from 1974 to 1976. He completed his training back at the Royal Academy of Music in Stockholm, studying music theory (1978–82) and composition with Gunnar Bucht, Brian Ferneyhough and Pär Lindgren (1980–84). In 1982 he was asked to join the developing of new music of the young and expanding University School of Music in Piteå. So he returned there, teaching composition and music theory (1985–89), and after a year out, in Paris (1984-85); he was appointed professor of composition at the university 1989. Sandström is among the most frequently performed Swedish composers on the international scene today.

Composition, Genre, and Historical Perspective

The Walter performance edition of *Es ist ein Ros entsprungen* states that the music is written by Michael Praetorius and Jan Sandström. This can mistakenly be interpreted to mean that Praetorius wrote the chorale tune. The tune and text is a traditional German chorale. German composers such as Praetorius (1571–1621), Heinrich Schütz (1585–1672), and Hugo Distler (1908–1942) are among the many composers who have harmonized the melody. Hugo Distler's version is perhaps the least known treatment of the tune, but in many ways correlates with Sandström's choral texture. For programming considerations, both versions would make an attractive "sonic" set for any program.

In this composition by Sandström, the composer takes the harmonization by Praetorius and treats the tune and harmonic structure to both expansion and fragmentation that creates an impressionist-like palate of transparent choral colors that creates a stunning sonic effect. The chorale tune, almost mystically, appears and then disappears into the texture. When it reappears, it always reappears as a fragment embedded in a rich harmonic template. The composer uses rests and pauses between treatments of the verse in a masterful way. The dramatic use of those silences should be explored by conductors performing this work.

Technical Considerations

There are several matters to consider when performing this piece. First, depending on the performance acoustic, it is effective to have the quartet separated from the larger chorus. The larger the space of separation and the more reverberant the room, the more the sonic effect of the work is heightened for the audience. The work can also be performed in the round, with the solo quartet at the front of the performance space. Tuning is an issue in this work. Tuning problems can be avoided if solfège is employed while learning the work, and if closed vowel sounds that are tall and narrow are used throughout. Particular care needs to be taken in the tuning within the first and second tenor parts prior to the final entrance of the chorale tune. Whether English or German is chosen for the choral tune text and whatever performance choice is made, the overall vowel concept should remain closed for intonation reasons. Conducting throughout should remain non-espressivo with a light ictus to ensure that each pitch is attacked cleanly and rhythmically throughout. It is suggested that either one soprano or three sopranos sing the final G ostinato on the final cadence.

Stylistic Considerations

"Es ist ein Ros entsprungen" ("Lo! How a Rose E'er Blooming") is written for double choir. The first choir sings the first verse of the Michael Praetorius chorale. The blooming of the rose is represented by the second choir, in divisi, singing *con bocca chiusa (c.b.ch.)*, that is, with closed lips.

Because the texture and the function of the two choirs are completely different, it would be best for each choir to learn the parts separately. Then combining the beauty of the chorale text with the sound of the impressionist SSAATTB will create a magical effect.

Form and Structure

In this piece, Sandström only uses the first verse of the traditional text. The chorale tune is sung by the first choir (harmonization by Praetorius) and then dissapperas into the texture of the second choir. The second choir depicts and mirrors the harmonic colors the Praetorious setting of the text with sonorous harmony and augmentation of the harmonic rhythm of the work. The illusion of the suspension of time is one of the masterful compositional achievements of this work.

Choir I (chorale):	Musical phrase	Song form
Es ist ein Ros entsprungen	*a*	Part I
aus einer Wurzel zart,	*b*	
als uns die Alten sungen:	*a*	
von Jesse kam die Art	*b*	
und hat ein Blümlein bracht	*c*	Part II
mitten im kalten Winter	*a'*	Part III
wohl zu der halben Nacht.	*b*	

Text and Translation

(1st translation)

Es ist ein Ros entsprungen	Lo! How a rose e'er blooming,
aus einer Wurzel zart,	From tender stem hath sprung,
als uns die Alten sungen:	Of Jesse's lineage coming
von Jesse kam die Art	As seers of old have sung;
und hat ein Blümlein bracht	It came a blossom bright,
mitten im kalten Winter	Amid the cold of winter
wohl zu der halben Nacht.	When half-spent was the night.

English translation by Theodore Baker

(2nd translation)

Es ist ein Ros entsprungen	A rose has come forth
aus einer Wurzel zart,	from a tender root,
als uns die Alten sungen:	as the prophets of old sang to us.
von Jesse kam die Art	From Isaiah came the lineage,
und hat ein Blümlein bracht	and it has brought us a flower
mitten im kalten Winter	in the cold midwinter,
wohl zu der halben Nacht.	right at the midnight hour.

Suggested Listening

Angels in the Architecture: The Voices of Anam Cara. Performed by The Westminster Williamson Voices, James Jordan, conductor. GIA CD-836

Additional Resources

Jeffers, Ron and Gordon Paine. *Translations and Annotations of Choral Repertoire, Vol. II: German texts*. Corvallis, OR: earthsongs, 2000.

Shrock, Dennis, *Choral Repertoire*. New York: Oxford University Press, 2009.

Slonimsky, Nicholas, and Laura Kuhn, ed. *Baker's Biographical Dictionary of Musicians*, Vol. V, Centennial ed. New York: Schirmer Books, 2001, pp. 3138–3139.

Contributed by:

K. Steve Kim

Teacher Resource Guide

My Flight for Heaven

Blake R. Henson
(b. 1983)

SATB divisi
GIA Publications, Inc.: G-7189
Tonal: 4
Vocal: 3
Overall: 4

Composer

Born in Dallas, Texas, Blake Henson currently resides in Columbus, Ohio, where he taught music theory and aural skills while completing his Doctor of Musical Arts in music composition at The Ohio State University. He holds a bachelor's degree in music theory and composition as well as a master's degree in composition from Westminster Choir College in Princeton, New Jersey. He has studied composition with Thomas Wells, Donald Harris, Joel Phillips, Jay Kawarsky, Ron Hemmel, Michael Cox, and John Parker, and has collaborated with such noted composers as Mark Adamo, Stephen Paulus, Tarik O'Regan, and Gerald Custer.

Sought after for his choral, vocal, and orchestral work, Henson has received numerous commissions from professional ensembles, colleges and high schools, churches, and community choruses and orchestras, including Chanticleer, Westminster Kantorei, Westminster Williamson Voices, Anam Cara, Masterwork Chorus and Orchestra, and the New Jersey Chamber Singers. His music has been performed in some of the finest venues in the United States, including Carnegie Hall, The National Cathedral, and Spivey Hall, as well as in concert halls in Canada, Mexico, England, South Africa,

Taiwan, and Japan. His choral works have been performed at ACDA National Conventions as well as by numerous All-State choirs.

An active author and pedagogue, Henson is completing a book on composition pedagogy and is writing on a text for aural training submersion with James Jordan and David Conte. In 2011, he will begin a recording project of his choral works with the Philadelphia chamber ensemble Anam Cara, to be released under the GIA ChoralWorks label.

As a performer, Henson has appeared with the Westminster Choir, Westminster Kantorei, Fuma Sacra, New York Philharmonic (Davis, Dutoit, Maazel, Gilbert, Hickocks), Cleveland Orchestra (Boulez), New Jersey Symphony (Labadie, Järvi), Dresden Philharmonic (Fruhbeck de Burgos), and Dallas Symphony Orchestra (Litton), and has collaborated with such noted conductors as Joseph Flummerfelt, James Jordan, Andrew Megill, and Emmanuell Villaume.

Henson is a member of the American Choral Directors Association (ACDA), Society for Music Theory (SMT), Society of Composers, Inc. (SCI), and American Society for Composers, Authors, and Publishers (ASCAP); he is also a volunteer for the American Cancer Society.

In May 2010, Henson received a distinguished alumni award from Westminster Choir College. In autumn 2010, he joined the faculty of St. Norbert College as Assistant Professor of Music Theory, History, and Composition.

Blake Henson is published by GIA Publications, Inc. A complete listing of his choral works can be found at www.giamusic.com as part of the *Evoking Sound Choral Series* and the *Music from Westminster Series*.
Accessed: http://www.blakerhenson.com/about.htm

Composition and Historical Perspective

The process of composing a musical work is much more than the forging of a vehicle for artistic communication; it's the act of turning a very intimate, inward journey into an outward expression—a chance to touch someone's life and, in so doing, change the world. As such, the composition process can be exceptionally thrilling and rewarding. This piece, on the other hand, is the result of an incredible struggle. I had initially intended to use a different text, and had completed several sketches for how the work would evolve. But as luck would have it, the copyright section in the back of the poetry anthology from which I was working wasn't exactly complete. Despite several phone calls and letters to publishers and poets' estates, I began to realize that I would have to start over with a new text. I set the project aside indefinitely. Several months later, I was having dinner with an old friend and I began to recount my story of textual misfortune. Almost instinctively, he quipped, "Why don't you use that Robert Herrick poem? The one that begins, 'Charm me asleep.'" I was absolutely stunned. I had been looking for a chance to set *To Music, Becalm His Fever* for nearly ten years but had always passed on the opportunity, feeling that my own limited life experience stood in the way of the text. This time, however, I felt rather at home with the depth of the words and their meaning. I cut our dinner short to get home to my piano and begin writing.

The resulting work, *My Flight for Heaven*, takes Herrick's text about seeking comfort in the welcome embrace of death and shifts the point of view to one invoking music while striving toward a new life without pain, suffering, war, and famine. The Westminster Choir (for whom the work was composed) and I share a very strong, unique passion for music and its profound ability to change the world; this text seemed perfectly in keeping with our common goal. When the choir premiered the piece in the Spring of 2007, I was overwhelmed by the number of audience members who spoke to me afterwards, touched by the work, seeing the text as a metaphor for their own hardships and finding comfort in the music itself. The experience was exceedingly humbling, and I soon realized that, while I set out to touch the lives of others, I was the one who had been touched. I tried to change the world, but the world, it seemed, changed me.

—Blake R. Henson

Technical Considerations

The compositional style of the composer lends itself well to any choir who should decide to perform this work. It is suggested to conductors to use the musical pauses throughout the piece to give dramatic shape to the work. Care should be taken to achieve proper text stresses and declamation. Conductors should strive for a different color in the sound of the choir on the final return of the work's introductory measures to highlight interpretative elements in the text.

Stylistic Considerations

A unique feature of this piece is that every single cadential gesture is with a subdominant chord. There are many added chord tones, such as added 9th (2nd) or added 11th (4th), that create beautiful sonorities of the harmony. It is important for the singers to identify the function of the notes in relationship to the chord. Finding the right balance for each chordal sonority will bring about the beauty of this piece. At the same time, the linear movement, the phrasing should follow the structure of the sentences of the poem so the momentum of the piece flows right and appropriate for the text.

Form and Structure

Section	Measure	Phrase Structure
Intro	1–5	5
Part I (A)	6–10	5(2+3)
	11–14	4
	15–18	4
Part II (B)	19–22	4
	23–27	4
Part III (C)	28–31	4
	32–35	4
Part IV (A')	36–42	7(3+2+2)
	43–48	6
	49–50	2
	51–53	3
Ending	54–60	7(3+2+2)

Text

from *To Music, Becalm His Fever*
by Robert Herrick (1591–1674)

Charm me asleep, and melt me so
With thy delicious numbers;
That, being ravish'd, hence I go
Away in easy slumbers.
Ease my sick head, and make my bed,
Thou Pow'r that canst sever me
From me this ill;
And quickly still,
Though thou not kill
My fever.

Fall on me like a silent dew,
Or like those maiden showers,
Which, by the peep of day, do strew
A baptism o'er the flowers.
Melt, melt my pains
With thy soft strains;
That having ease me giv'n,
With full delight,
I leave this light,
And take my flight,
For Heaven.

Suggested Listening

Angels in the Architecture. The Voices of Anam Cara. James Jordan, conductor. (GIA GIA CD-836).

Additional References and Resources

Web site: http://www.blakerhenson.com

Contributed by:

K. Steve Kim

Teacher Resource Guide

Stars I Shall Find

David Dickau

SSATBB
Walton Music: HL 08501496
Overall: 4
Vocal: 4
Tonal/Rhythm: 4

Composer

Dr. David Dickau is a choral conductor and composer residing in Mankato, Minnesota where he is Director of Choral Activities at Minnesota State University, Mankato. As a part of his duties, Dickau conducts the Concert Choir and Chamber Singers and teaches conducting and composition. His university has awarded him the status of Distinguished Faculty Scholar. Dickau holds advanced degrees in Choral Music from Northwestern University in Evanston, Illinois and the University of Southern California, Los Angeles. He has taught choral music on both the high school and college levels and has conducted community and church choirs. He served for thirteen years as music director of Magnum Chorum, a Twin Cities-based chamber choir.

Dickau has received commissions to compose for choral festivals, colleges and universities, foundations, churches, and schools. Some significant commissions have included *Dresden Canticles*, composed in honor of the rebuilding of the Frauenkirche in Dresden, Germany; "View from the Air," commissioned by the Charles and Anne Morrow Lindbergh Foundation in honor of the seventieth anniversary of Charles Lindbergh's historic trans-Atlantic flight; and the choral suite "Of Life and Love," commissioned by the Arkansas Chamber Singers in celebration of their twenty-fifth anniversary.

Composition, Genre, and Historical Perspective

A wonderful benefit of teaching in a university or college is the occasional opportunity to take a sabbatical. Such an opportunity was awarded me in 2002. I gathered several commissions and departed for St. Simons Island, Georgia to compose. I find it difficult to compose during the school year because of my duties as Director of Choral Activities at the university. I truly appreciated this extended time to focus on composition.

The Illinois Music Educators, District VII, chose me to compose a piece to be performed the following year. I chose Sarah Teasdales' remarkable poem, "There Will Be Rest." An important image in this text is stars. As I walked the Georgia beach at night, the stars seemed to be close enough to touch. This was the context in which I composed "Stars I Shall Find."

The image of stars as "beacons of hope" influenced this setting of the text. I had previously been deeply moved by Frank Ticheli's setting of this poem. While his composition focused more on rest, I decided to focus on conveying the potential that the stars represent. In my setting, the music involves striving and arriving at whatever the stars symbolize. The beauty of great poetry is that it can represent different things to different people. Because of the significant piano accompaniment, I chose to dedicate this piece to my life-long friend, one of my piano teachers, Jane Robinson.

Musical Elements and Technical Considerations

This piece requires careful listening and flexible tonal production throughout. Pay careful attention to the meaning of words and reflect that meaning in your tone quality. For instance, the word "rest' and the words "sure stars shining" connote different images. See if you can depict this through your tone quality. Also, take care to articulate the natural word stress of each phrase. Words such as ROOF-tops, se-RENE, for-GET-ting, and so on. must be carefully articulated. This is especially true when connecting STILL-ness to HO-ly in measures 32 and 33 and meaures 54 and 55. This attention to detail really makes the text come alive for the audience. It also makes each musical phrase much more elegant.

This text is filled with pitched consonants. Take care to execute these ahead of the beat, otherwise the rhythm will not be as crisp as it needs to be. This is especially true with the opening line of the text, "There will be rest."

There are many "color" notes in the choral parts. This is an essential element of contemporary harmonic language. These notes are added to contribute harmonic interest and add musical meaning to the text. Students should be aware when they are singing such notes and listen carefully so that they perform them with sensitivity to the sonority of the chord and the context of the phrase.

The basses often sing the third of the chord in order to keep a phrase moving ahead toward the cadence. This can cause tuning issues. Make the basses aware of these passages and work with them to listen carefully. (Some examples are mm. 15 and 16, m. 25, and m. 38, among many others.) The basses also must sing flexibly and sensitively in passages where they are performing exposed passages high in their range (e.g., mm. 21, m. 40, and m. 48).

In measures 31 to 34 and 53 to 56, it can be challenging to let the text speak naturally without_breaking between "stillness" and "holy." Pay careful attention to word stress. This is an important expressive moment in the piece that is much more effective without a break. In the final statement of this text in measures 87 and 88, I recommend a breath on beat 4 of measure 87 since it is the final statement in the piece.

As the voices rise to the top of their range in measures 36 through 46, take care to keep the tone free and flowing and work to make sure it does not become shrill. In measure 58, the emotion of the text changes to a more active quality. Try to reflect this in the choir's tone. The climax of this section occurs in the dramatic cadence in measures 76 and 77. Again, work to keep the vocal production free and flowing as you approach the top of the singers' ranges.

The final statement beginning in measure 88 has a different feel from the rest of the piece. My interpretation of the text is that you are now at that place you have been striving to reach. The tone quality should be weightless and sound almost ethereal and floating.

Stylistic Considerations

"Stars I Shall Find" is written in a Romantic style. Each phrase has its own importance and individuality—although one should avoid extremes. The most important consideration is the text. Articulating the word stress and meaning of each phrase of the text will make the piece come to life. Use a wide variety of tonal color to express this evocative poem. Rich dynamic contrasts and varieties of tonal color related to the meaning of the text will contribute greatly to a successful performance.

The accompaniment must also flow with each phrase. Measures 1 through 4 comprise a different entity than measures 5 through 8 and so on. These separate statements are articulated by the accompanist. The accompanist should take great freedom in releasing the energy of the climactic cadence in measure 76 and in the subsequent passage in measures 78 and 79 in order to prepare the final section for the chorus beginning in measure 82. Be sure the pianist plays "deep into the keys" in measures 76 through 79. A brief pause between measures 79 and 80 would be appropriate.

Form and Structure

This piece is through composed, although there are many unifying elements throughout. The sections can be divided as follows:

SECTION	MEASURE	EVENT AND SCORING
Introduction	mm. 1–12	(4+4+4)
A	mm. 13–35	First statement of opening verse of text (4+4+4+10+1)
A¹	mm. 36–56	Second statement of opening verse of text (4+4+3+10+1)
B	mm. 56–77	Contrasting section based on second verse of text (4+4+4+8)
	mm. 76–79	Piano transition to final statement (4)
A²	mm. 80–91	Final statement of theme based on opening material (2+4+6)

Text and Translation

American poet Sara Teasdale (1874–1933) was known for the simple beauty and lyricism of her poems. She published several collections in her lifetime. "There Will Be Rest" was her last published work. Throughout her life, Teasdale suffered from depression and wrote about stars as beacons of hope. She eventually took her own life at the age of 48. In my setting of this poem, I emphasized the theme of hope.

There Will Be Rest
There will be rest, and sure stars shining
Over the roof-tops crowned with snow
A reign of rest, serene forgetting,
The music of stillness, holy and low.

I will make this world of my devising
Out of a dream in my lonely mind,
I shall find the crystal of peace above me
Stars I shall find.

Recording

"Stars I Shall Find," performed by the Minnesota State University, Mankato Concert Choir, conducted by the composer. Available at Waltonmusic.com.

Contributed by:

David Dickau

Teacher Resource Guide

Sure on This Shining Night from *Nocturnes*

Morten Lauridsen

(b. 1943)

SATB/piano
Peermusic: 621281220
Overall: 4
Vocal: 4
Tonal/Rhythm: 4

Composer

Morten Johannes Lauridsen was born on February 27, 1943 in Colfax, Washington. He grew up in Portland, Oregon and attended Whitman College in Washington and the University of Southern California (USC). Lauridsen is currently Distinguished Professor of Composition at the USC Thornton School of Music where he has been on the faculty since 1972. He was head of the Composition Department at USC from 1990 to 2002. Lauridsen served as Composer-in-Residence with the Los Angeles Master Chorale from 1994 to 2001.

Lauridsen's choral cycles include: *Mid-Winter Songs* (1980), *Madrigali: Six "Fire Songs" on Renaissance Italian Poems* (1987), *Les Chansons des Roses* (1993), *Lux aeterna* (1997), *and Nocturnes* (2005). His *a cappella* motets include: "O magnum mysterium" (1994), "Ave Maria" (1997), "O nata lux"—the middle movement of *Lux aeterna*—(1997), "Ubi caritas et amor" (1998), and "Ave dulcissima Maria" (2004). "O magnum mysterium," "O nata lux," and "Dirait-on" from *Les Chansons des Roses* are the all-time best-selling choral octavos distributed by Theodore Presser, which has been in business since 1783. Lauridsen has also composed anthems, solo songs, and two cycles for solo voice.

Morten Lauridsen was named an "American Choral Master" by the National Endowment of the Arts in 2006 and was presented the prestigious National Medal of the Arts by George W. Bush in 2007. The vocal music of Lauridsen holds a permanent place in the standard repertoire of the twentieth and twenty-first century.

Composition, Genre and Historical Perspective

"Sure on This Shining Night" is the third movement in the cycle entitled *Nocturnes*. The first song, "Sa Nuit d'Été," is on French text by Rainer Maria Rilke and the second, "Soneto de la Noche," is on Spanish text of Pablo Neruda. The first and third songs have piano accompaniment and the second is *a cappella*. The *Nocturnes* can be performed independently or as part of the cycle in the order listed.

Lauridsen composed *Nocturnes* for the American Choral Directors Association as part of the Raymond W. Brock Memorial Commission program. The commission guidelines state that the compositions should be "substantial and accessible" and "be of a kind and quality that will live and last for a long period of time." "Sure on This Shining Night" fulfills these directives completely and in addition, has immediate appeal to both singers and audiences. The other two movements in the cycle are more difficult.

"Sure on This Shining Night" carries the thumbprint of one of the great composers of our time. Musicians today, or those far in the future, who come across this masterpiece, will immediately recognize it as the work of Morten Lauridsen. His signature use of inverted chords, dissonance, long flowing melodies, deep expression, and the creation of ethereal atmospheres are all present here.

The premiere performance of *Nocturnes* was given by the Donald Brinegar Singers at the ACDA National Convention in Los Angeles in February, 2005, with the composer at the piano.

Musical Elements and Technical Considerations

The work begins with a simple and flowing piano accompaniment, which plants deep roots for the tonality and sentiment of the work. The piano is an active partner in the music and not simply an underlying feature.

It is imperative in this work, as in much of Lauridsen's output, that the singers sustain a legato line "on the breath," with great expression in relationship to text. Sometimes beautifully disjunctive in nature, the vocal lines must be approached linearly and with consistent placement of the voice so that all notes remain aligned and the phrases remain sustained and musical. Great attention must be given to vowel unification. All of the voice parts contain what at first might seem to be difficult passages due to unexpected intervals, but as the piece becomes familiar to the ears of the singers, these serendipitous passages will be recognized as beautifully and creatively crafted lines that are immensely singable.

It is wise for the conductor to do, at minimum, a simple harmonic analysis to notice where dissonances lie. Seconds, sevenths, and ninths are examples of usual dissonances of consequence. The voice parts that sound these specific intervals should be emphasized to ensure their effectiveness. Musicians should then identify the purpose of the discord. Building toward a climax, creating tension, preparing for the release of tension, emotional drawing in, and text painting are examples of why such dissonances are present. The level of overt expression of the dissonance should be considered in order to create the most profound experience.

The work is firmly grounded in D-flat major in the accompaniment but the first three measures of the primary theme in the voices are pentatonic. It will be easy to begin here on solfège or neutral syllable.

Stylistic Considerations

This work of Morten Lauridsen sounds inherently American. The use of open harmonies between the lower voices conjures thoughts of Aaron Copland, and the deft text setting reminds us of Randall Thompson. The hallmark of Lauridsen's music, time and time again, is its inherent singability.

Contemporary music, as mentioned above, necessitates an aural understanding of, and careful attention to, dissonance. It is imperative that the choir members learn to hear important dissonances and to understand relationships between their specific voice parts and other notes sung by others within a given chord. Frequently, the effectiveness and beauty is diminished in performances of contemporary music due to unbalanced, misunderstood, or unexpressed dissonances.

Form and Structure

The overall structure of the work is $AA^{1}BCA^{2}$Coda.

Section	Measure	Event and Scoring
Piano introduction	mm. 1–5	Establishes a strong D-flat major tonality.
A	mm. 6–15	First statement of the primary theme by tenors and basses in unison; poetry stanza 1.

Section	Measure	Event and Scoring
A^1	mm. 16–24	Second statement of primary theme starting with sopranos and altos; tenors introducc the secondary theme, which is heard together with the primary theme; voice crossing exists between the tenors and altos; poetry stanza 1.
	mm. (24)25–26	Piano.
B	mm. 27-37	New material appears in the tenor and bass parts as they sing in unison; the primary motive of the secondary theme is used but varied; this theme is new yet sounds familiar to the ear, this must be at least partially attributed to its continual grounding in D-flat as with most of the material in the work; this section continues with the women entering with the new theme and there is interplay between the male and female voices before settling into homophonic movement for all; poetry stanza 2.
C	mm. 38–47	This section builds to the climax of the work on the subdominant and then relaxes in measure 47 to a dominant chord on top of a subdominant in the bass creating a beautiful suspended feeling; poetry stanza 3.
A^2	mm. 48–56	The D-flat pedal is firmly established again and the basses sing the primary theme as the sopranos enter with the beginning of the secondary one, the other voices enter with imitative counterpoint and fill out the harmonic structure; poetry stanza 1.

Section	Measure	Event and Scoring
Coda	mm. 57–64	The D-flat pedal once again grounds the work, a subdominant on top of the tonic chord in measure 60 establishes another beautiful suspended moment that prolongs the anticipated ending, continuing on in measure 61 a dominant on top of a tonic chord suspends time once more before the resolution to D-flat major; first line of poetry stanza 1.

Text

The text was written by Pulitzer-prize winning author James Agee (1909–1955). It is included in his only volume of poetry, *Permit Me Voyage*, from 1934. Many people are familiar with the popular setting of this text by American composer Samuel Barber.

Sure on this shining night
Of star-made shadows round,
Kindness must watch for me
This side the ground.

The late year lies down the north.
All is healed, all is health.
High summer holds the earth.
Hearts all whole.

Sure on this shining night
I weep for wonder
Wandering far alone
Of shadows on the stars.

Additional References and Resources

Wine, Tom, editor. *Composers on Composers for Chorus*. Chicago: GIA Publications, Inc. 2007.

Recordings

Dialogues Volume 1: Morten Lauridsen, Paul Salamunovich, and James Jordan. Chicago: GIA Publications, Inc. 2008. (CD-773)

Morten Lauridsen: Nocturnes. Polyphony, Britten Sinfonia. Stephen Layton, conductor. (Hyperion CDA67580).

Web Sites

www.acdaonline.org
www.mortenlauridsen.com

Contributed by:

Joseph Ohrt, DMA

Teacher Resource Guide

Valiant for Truth

Ralph Vaughan Williams
(1872–1958)

SATB
Oxford University Press: 3535297
Overall: 4
Vocal: 4
Tonal/Rhythm: 5

Composer

Ralph Vaughan Williams was the leading English composer of his generation, and a central figure in the resurgence of British music in the twentieth century. He is notable throughout his long career, for composing works accessible to a wide range of musicians including many works appropriate for amateurs.

As a young man, Vaughan Williams developed slowly as a composer. For many years he was conscious of a lack of technique that he attempted to address through several years of study both at home and abroad. By his late thirties, he had arrived at his personal voice, and fully embraced his national identity; he became most strongly influenced both by English folk song and by the great English composers of previous centuries. Vaughan Williams once remarked, "the greatest artist belongs to his country as much as the humblest singer in a remote village"[1] and that the folk-song revival "gave a point to our imagination; far from fettering us, it freed us from foreign influences which weighed on us."[2]

1 Machlis, 6th ed, p. 451
2 Machlis, 6th ed, p. 451

Composition, Genre, and Historical Perspective

Valiant-for-truth is generally listed as a motet for mixed voices with organ or piano. While it is certainly a motet (a choral composition of moderate length, generally sacred), it should really be considered an *a capella* work. The opening five measures are marked as optional, and Vaughan Williams is clear that the keyboard is not to play from measure 6 onward.

As a mature work of Vaughan Williams, the work shows his love of the English choral sound and the influence of Parry and Stanford, both who were once his teachers. This is a truly sober work, notwithstanding the sense of triumph with which it ends, dealing specifically with the end of life.

Musical Elements and Technical Considerations

Most of the text in this piece is first presented in a single section of the choir and marked *quasi recitativo*; these lines are interspersed with choral responses. Although the *recitativo* line is generally marked *piano* or *mezzo piano*, it is best to treat these dynamic markings as you would for a solo line, making sure the part is clearly heard. Where applicable, ensure such lines are more prominent than those choral sections marked *piano* or *pianissimo*. Ask singers to differentiate clearly in their own minds (and in their scores) whether their section is leading at any given moment, or is simply part of the choral texture. In measure 20 and throughout the passage that follows, the upper voices must sustain their chords very softly indeed in order for the basses' line to be distinctly heard.

Be careful in treatment of diphthongs such as "I," and "going," especially when these are set to longer pitches, where each singer will have his or her own concept of where the diphthong will occur, and whether the change in vowel ought to happen quickly or slowly. After making singers aware of what the diphthong is, it is often useful in rehearsal to have them associate a hand gesture with each vowel, and to have them demonstrate with a gesture where the diphthong occurs.

Certain other words call for special attention in order that beautiful vowels can be maintained in spite of the presence of certain problematic consonants. Work to unify the timing and treatment of the final "r" sound in such words as "father's," "sword," and "rewarder" (a particularly dangerous customer in this regard!), as well as those that end in an "l," such as "skill." My preference is to replace the letter "r" with an [a]-colored schwah sound, and to use a very short "l" sound, with the tip of the tongue.

Add an accent to the alto E on the first beat of measure 56 to match the earlier appoggiaturas in the bass and tenor.

Many modern conductors generally choose to acknowledge commas in choral music by asking their choirs to breathe or inflect where commas occur. While this is normally an aid to intelligibility, habits of punctuation were somewhat different in the seventeenth century, when Bunyan wrote this text. The modern conductor should *not* feel obligated to acknowledge every comma in this piece even with an inflection, let alone a breath. Examples of commas you may choose to ignore in order to establish longer musical phrases include:

My sword, I give to him…
and my courage and skill, to him that can get it.
My marks and scars I carry with me, to be a witness for me…
When the day that he must go hence, was come…
into which, as he went, he said…

In measures 66 to 70, take the *marcato* instruction to indicate a very clear and somewhat sharp attack on each note. In a resonant acoustic, each eighth note can be slightly detached. The 32nd notes will only work if each one is accented, and if the preceding note is made quite short to create acoustic space in advance.

Stylistic Considerations

Written in 1940 and published the following year, this mature work of Vaughan Williams is accessible to most choirs. The composer would have initially expected the work to be performed by cathedral choirs of men and boys, but that is no reason to avoid performing it with any mixed choir with whom you may be working.

However, the original performing forces do give us a clue as to how to interpret the performance instruction *quasi recitativo*. There is no indication that Vaughan Williams expected these lines to be sung by soloists, but rather that he meant to involve the entire section. The implication of these facts is that we as conductors are not being directed toward the dramatic tempo fluctuations and highly personal expression seen in, for example, some performances of opera recitative. Rather, what is likely expected here is a somewhat measured delivery with such added inflections as would be natural to the language. Of course, the question of how much inflection or tempo variation to employ in the *recitativo* lines will be influenced by many other factors in each conductor's particular situation, including the acoustic: in a large and resonant cathedral, too fast a tempo will simply render the text unintelligible, whereas the drier acoustic found in many dedicated concert spaces will permit a greater range of tempo. Those who prefer a single tempo will take comfort from the fact that many recordings of English choirs singing this piece exhibit a steady tempo from beginning to end.

As with all English cathedral music, the primary aesthetic values in approaching this music must include clarity and excellent intonation. There is nothing virtuosic or particularly showy here, although there is certainly a sense of faith, and of tremendous depth. If at all possible, arrange to perform the work in a resonant acoustic. Use vibrato sparingly, if at all, in the upper voices, and work toward an exceedingly well focused sound in the lower voices.

Form and Structure

SECTION	MEASURE	EVENT; SCORING; KEY
Intro.	mm. 1–5	5; opt. organ; Key: D (modal)
	mm. 6–18	13(3+5+5); text alternates altos/chorus
	mm. 19–30	12(6+6); basses lead while chorus mediates on "I am going…"; Key: D major
	mm. 31–40	10(3+2+5); chorus homophonic, declamatory; Key: G, B-flat, B minor
	mm. 41–46	6; imitative section; Key: D major
	mm. 47–56	10(6+4); Altos lead, stacked choral entrances; Key: E minor
	mm. 57–63	7(1+6); choral entrances repeat and expand
	mm. 64–78	15(2+5+3+5); crescendo and repetition of "trumpet" motives; Key: B-flat, G

Text and Translation

The text is drawn word-for-word from John Bunyan's great Christian allegory *The Pilgrim's Progress from This World to That Which Is to Come*, better known simply as *Pilgrim's Progress*. While those readers familiar with the book will understand the context immediately, many singers will benefit from some explanation. Bunyan's allegory was very direct; he personified certain human characteristics in figures such as Mr. Worldly Wiseman and Mr. Legality, and created memorable depictions of such places as Vanity Fair and the Valley of the Shadow of Death. Subtlety was in no way Bunyan's goal; rather, the book was written to instruct the reader on certain principles and perils of the spiritual life.

Mr. Valiant-for-truth is not the protagonist of the story (that role is filled by Christian, the "everyman" character who fails many times along the journey and whose need of grace and mercy are made clear), but is rather a paragon on the courageous pilgrim, one who presses on despite every difficulty, and who bravely fights against the powers of evil when necessary. This excerpt is a description of the end of his life and his eternal reward.

Pilgrim's Progress is a work of prose, not of poetry. The excerpt set by Vaughan Williams reads as follows:

After this it was noised abroad that Mr. Valiant-for-truth was taken with a summons…; and had this for a token that the summons was true, "That his pitcher was broken at the fountain." When he understood it, he called for his friends, and told them of it. Then, said he, "I am going to my Father's, and though with great difficulty I am got hither, yet now I do not repent me of all the trouble I have been at to arrive where I am. My sword, I give to him that shall succeed me in my pilgrimage, and my courage and skill, to him that can get it. My marks and scars I carry with me, to be a witness for me, that I have fought his battles, who now will be my rewarder." When the day that he must go hence, was come, many accompanied him to the riverside, into which, as he went, he said, "Death, where is thy sting?" And as he went down deeper, he said, "Grave, where is thy victory?" So he passed over, and all the trumpets sounded for him on the other side.

Contributed by:

John Trotter

Teacher Resource Guide

Ain't No Grave Can Hold My Body Down

Traditional Spiritual

arr. Paul Caldwell and Sean Ivory

SSA(A) and Piano (also available in SATB and piano
Earthsongs: S-243
Overall: 4
Vocal: 4
Tonal/Rhythm: 4

Arrangers

Paul Caldwell and Sean Ivory have collaborated on several choral arrangements and compositions that have been performed and recorded by choirs around the world. Some of their recent works were written for performances at the Sydney Opera House, Carnegie Hall, and Minneapolis Orchestra Hall. Paul Caldwell is Artistic Director of the Youth Choral Theater of Chicago, a member of the Board of Directors for Chorus America, a former composer-in-residence for the Choral Music Experience training course for conductors at Elon University, and former Music Director of the American Boychoir's summer festival held in Princeton, New Jersey. Sean Ivory received his Master's Degree in Choral Conducting from Michigan State University. He is a graduate of Calvin College and conducts that college's Campus Choir. He is also affiliated with Forest Hills Central High School and the North American Choral Company. Caldwell and Ivory's pieces are primarily available through earthsongs and GIA. Their newest works are self-published.

Composition, Genre, and Historical Perspective

This stirring concert arrangement was inspired by a traditional spiritual refrain. Caldwell and Ivory used the refrain as the basis of the arrangement and added verses with original texts and melodies. This acknowledges that songs from the oral tradition evolve over time. A visit to youtube.com will present the listener/viewer with several versions of the song ranging from a solo gospel rendition, including one by Jessie Mae Renfro with guitar accompaniment, which undoubtedly reflects more of the song's spiritual roots. At the time of writing, over sixty recordings containing the same refrain ("Ain't no grave can hold my body down") were available on Apple's iTunes. The recordings range from bluegrass and country, to gospel and field recordings from the south, to Library of Congress recordings of Bozie Sturdivant, and finally the Fisk Jubilee Singers. It is important for the choral director to acknowledge the traditional roots of the piece while helping students understand the originality and effectiveness of the arrangement as it transforms the song for concert use.

Caldwell and Ivory arranged "Ain't No Grave Can Hold My Body Down" for a collegiate women's chorale. Due to the weight of the text, the vocal ranges, and the divisi writing, it is best suited for advanced high school treble choirs, collegiate, and community women's ensembles. Unlike Caldwell and Ivory's rousing arrangement of "Go Where I Send Thee," this piece calls for a more mature sound, a connection to the text that comes with age and experience, and an ability to convey the "weightiness" of the piece. In short, the range of expression and depth of interpretation makes this arrangement more appropriate for older singers. Caldwell and Ivory's "Ain't No Grave" also requires a pianist with a strong sense of gospel style, a powerful left hand, and a commanding presence.

Stylistic Considerations

This spiritual has a feeling of weight, conviction, and resolve that Caldwell and Ivory refer to as "determination and assurance." It is also a soaring declaration of tenacity, willpower, and fortitude. The song calls for a strength and grit in performance that will be lost if the tempo is too fast. Moses Hogan used to remark in conference sessions that non-black conductors have a tendency to choose a tempo that is too quick when performing spirituals. This can cause the choral sound to lighten and brighten in tone color, which is less appropriate for a text that calls for a dark, mature, and almost ominous tone. The weight of the text will be lost if the tempo feels rushed. The powerful accompaniment and vocal performance will also seem frantic rather than strong and grounded.

The arrangers have specifically used "sistuh" (sister), "wanna" (want to), "get cho" (get your), "mornin'" (morning), "numbuh" (number), and other dialectic spellings of words in the score to give an authentic sound to the text. Giving the choir license to cut off the final "r" on such words as "sistuh" and "numbuh" encourages a freer lower jaw and tall vowel shapes. It also encourages proper syllabic stress on the accented syllable.

Caution should be used in the sections that call for hand clapping and foot stomping. Neither action should be understated, but the percussive sounds can overpower the singing. Clapping and stomping must be done with conviction but not at a high volume (in spiritual style, finger snapping should not be substituted for hand clapping). Choirs have a tendency to rush the tempo when the claps and stomps are added. The conductor should take care to maintain a clear, steady, and almost heavy beat pattern to keep the choir from racing (i.e., if the conductor tries to join the clapping, the "train" may speed out of the station). Again, the ensemble should be reminded of the weight of the text and try to resist the temptation to rush.

Musical Elements and Technical Considerations

From the first entrance, singers need to think of the rests as active "holes"—spaces in the line that add drama, emphasis, and rhythmic vitality. When the measure begins with a rest (mm. 5, 7, 9), singers can rehearse with a stomp on the rest that prepares and/or propels the entrance on the "and" of beat 1. It is equally important to observe rests in other parts of the measures; singers need to avoid carrying sound through the rests. Those spaces are incredibly important to the dramatic delivery of the text, which almost seems halted or fragmented at times. Those spaces also provide opportunities for crisp final consonants and chances to take necessary breaths that will keep the tone rich and full (e.g., m. 8: "grounD," m. 18: "sounD," mm. 107 and 109: "graVe," and m. 116: "tricK"). At measure 10, the altos need to have a commanding sound and accurate entrance on beat 1 to fill the rest in the first and second soprano parts. In m. 13, the second sopranos need to take care to make a clean, clear entrance on the "and" of beat 1 in contrast to the first soprano and alto entrances on beat 1. Measure 17 demands careful attention, with each voice part entering within a half beat of the others. Observing the rests to create spaces is of paramount importance in measures 130 to 140, where the two separate choirs are in dialogue, literally tossing the sound back and forth almost every beat or half-beat.

As noted above, the arrangers have dropped the final consonant of several words in the text. When incorporating the spiritual style into the performance of the piece, the conductor might be tempted to use a stopped "t" on the word "ain't" rather than a released "t," or drop the "t" altogether like the "r" in "sistuh." However, the released "t" should be used here as a rhythmic event to help create vitality and momentum, and add to the sense of determination in the text.

Choirs might be tempted to over sing this piece using *forte* dynamics from start to finish. Individual phrases and entire sections need to be shaped to create dynamic contrast. For example, measure 27 could *crescendo* as the notes ascend to the downbeat of measure 28 (on the accented syllable of "eternally") then *decrescendo* quickly—almost as a *sforzando*—and then grow again steadily through the long note on beats 3 and 4. This will direct the energy to the downbeat of the new section at measure 29. A *crescendo* in measure 36 followed by a *subito piano* at the entrance in measure 37 can provide welcome and dramatic contrast. The same is true for a *subito piano* entrance at measure 69. When the first sopranos take the lead as soloists in measure 93, pay careful attention to the long notes as they shape each of the four phrases individually and as a progression leading to the entrance of the second sopranos in measure 100.

Beware of potentially difficult notes. The first soprano part at measure 16, beat 3, begins chromatically but does not continue in that fashion. Be sure to sing a B-flat on beat 4 (in the key signature) rather than a B-natural, which singers expect as a continuation of the motion by descending semitones. Take care with the second soprano part at measure 30; the chords change on every beat (i v i vii°) and require careful tuning. Watch the alto part in measure 102 with B-naturals on "grave could," in contrast to the B-flats on "hold my" in measure 104. Listen for accurate tuning of the chromatic passage in the second soprano part in measure 100 and in the alto part in measure 105. The first soprano line at measure 105 is not a repeat of measure 99; watch the descending minor second in measure 99 on beat 3 compared with the descending minor third in measure 105. The unison descending passage in measure 148 is a challenge. Then in measure 149, be sure to sing the D-sharp and B-natural high enough in relation to the D-natural and B-flat in the previous measure. It is possible for the pitch to sag with the descending bell chord and the rapid chromatic pattern in the piano accompaniment.

Throughout the piece the syncopated patterns (e.g., mm. 29, 31) will have more life if the notes that fall off the beat are detached slightly—denoted here with italicized syllables: "Sist*uh* *you better* get cho ticket if *you wanna ride*." Detached notes will also make the section at measure 69 have a stronger feeling of syncopation (and almost rhythmic tension), but separating the notes can also cause the choir to rush the tempo. Put enough space between the detached notes to maintain a strong sense of the beat and the tempo.

Observing the correct word stress and syllabic stress in the text will help shape each phrase and give the necessary weight to downbeats and important words. This is especially true in measures 53 to 65. Use strong accents on the downbeat and accented syllable in each short phrase: "*I* will...fly to *JE*sus... in the *MORN*in'...when I *DIE*" and "*I* know...he will *TAKE* me...home to *LIVE* with...him on *HIGH*."

Approach this piece as a 3-part SSA arrangement. When divisi occurs, it can be done within the existing section(s) without shuffling voices to new parts. The exception would be measures 130 to 141. At this point, the arrangers call for a switch from SSA division to two choirs, each with two parts. Shifting to four equal sections can facilitate this directive: Choir I comprised of first soprano and first alto and Choir II comprised of second soprano and second alto. This gives each choir enough singers for the high notes and enough singers to provide a dark, rich sound for the lower notes. The choir returns to the original 3-part division at measure 142.

The choir should work hard to create a sense of dialogue between voice parts (mm. 45–52) when the melody line is literally tossed back and forth from section to section, and when one section seems to answer another. Placing the singers in a traditional choral arrangement will enhance that dialogue. If the choir is arranged in a mixed formation, singers should be encouraged to be physical with the piece—perhaps using the slightest lean or shift of weight when singing the fragment of the melody or response to the melody—to help the audience track the text moving through the sections. Regardless of the choral formation, each singer should be involved physically to stay connected to the rhythm and momentum of the piece. A static performance of this piece will be less evocative and may not strike the audience in a visceral and emotional way.

Finally, this piece requires great vocal stamina and intensity in performance. It is difficult to maintain that intensity from start to finish. Conductors might want to consider making a cut at the repeated section at measures 77 through 92. If the optional 8 bars at measure 121 intended for a sign-language version of the refrain are not used, conductors might also consider a cut from measure 121 through 129 leading directly from the climactic point in measure 120 to the double choir "dialogue" beginning at measure 130.

Form and Structure

Section	Measure	Event and Scoring
Introduction	1–4	Piano
Refrain	5–20	Full choir in three parts (with some divisi)
Verse	21–36	Full choir in three parts
Refrain	37–44	Full choir in three parts (repeat of 5–12)
Ref. Variation	45–52	Melody moving through parts with rest of choir in response

SECTION	MEASURE	EVENT AND SCORING
Verse 2	53–76	Full choir in three parts with sop 1 divisi (modulation at 61)
Refrain	77–92	Full choir in three parts with some divisi in sop 1 and sop 2
Ref. Variation	93–112	Soprano section with responses from sop 2 and alto
Verse 3	113–120	Full choir in three parts with divisi in sop 1 and sop 2
Interlude	121	Optional 8-bar interlude—American Sign Language in silence
Ref. Variation	122–129	Full choir in three parts
Verse 4	130–145	Double choir—two parts in each choir
Coda	146–150	Ending—full choir with divisi in soprano 1 and soprano 2
Alt. Coda	147b–150	Ending—full choir with divisi all parts

Text

Ain't no grave can hold my body down.
They ain't no grave can keep a sistuh underground.
Oh, I will listen for the trumpet sound.
Ain't no grave can hold my body down.

You know they rolled a stone on Jesus.
And then they tried to bury me.
But the
So we could live eternally.

Sistuh you better get cho ticket if you wanna ride.
In the mornin' when Jesus call my numbuh, I'll be on the other side.

Ain't no grave is gonna hold me.
Ain't no man is gonna bury me.
Ain't no serpent gonna trick me.
Ain't now grave can hold my body down.

I will fly to Jesus in the mornin' when I die.
I know he will take me home to live with him on high.
I will fly with Jesus in the mornin'.
Don't look here. I'll be way up in the sky.

Soon one day he's gonna call me up to heaven for a chariot ride.

Ain't no grave dug deep enough to hold me.
Ain't no devil been slick enough to trick me.
Ain't no grave digguh man enough to bury me.
You cain't hold me down!

Ain't no grave evuh been dug so low.
No grave digguh evuh been born so strong.
Ain't no man that can, ain't no devil can,
Ain't no grave can hold me.
Ain't no grave dug low enough down.

Suggested Recordings

Calvin College Women's Chorale, Pearl Shangkuan, conductor. Calvin College Web site:
http://www.calvin.edu/academic/music/ensemble/wmnschor/.

One World, Many Voices. Calvin College Women's Chorale, Pearl Shangkuan, conductor. earthsongs CD-07; earthsongs DVD S-249: Sign language. http://www.earthsongschoralmusic.com. E-mail: info@ earthsongschoralmusic.com. Phone: 541-758-5760.

Maryland All-State Concert, 2008. All State Senior Women's Chorus, Mary Jane Pagenstecher, conductor. Maryland Music Educators Association. http://www.mmea-maryland.org. E-mail: exdirector@mmea-maryland.org. Phone: 800-94-MUSIC.

Additional Audio Resources

Negro Religious Songs and Services (1999). Bozie Sturdivant. The Library of Congress Archive of Folk Culture. Rounder.

Negro Religious Field Recordings from Louisiana, Mississippi, Tennessee Vol. 1 1934–1942. Silent Grove Baptist Church Congregation with Bozie Sturdivant. Document Records DOCD-5312.

The Unaccompanied Voice: An A-Cappella Compilation (2000). Richard Buckner. Secretly Canadian Records.

The Swingin' Gospel Queen (2006). Sister Rosetta Tharpe. epm.

Contributed by:

Mary Jane Pagenstecher

Teacher Resource Guide

Hotari Koi

Japanese Children's Song

arr. Roh Ogura

(1916–1990)

SSA/a cappella
CORO: WOM–109
Overall: 4
Vocal: 3
Tonal/Rhythm: 4

Composer

Roh Ogura (1916–1990) was a prolific composer and writer as well as an admired teacher. As a student, Ogura was influenced by French modernist composers and then by Beethoven and Brahms. Later in life, Ogura returned to the music of his native Japan for inspiration and found success in arranging traditional folk songs and nursery rhymes for chorus. He composed many works for orchestra, as well as several miniatures for piano. Hotaru Koi is the fifth movement from his 1958 work, *Nine Pieces on Children's Songs of Tohoku Region* for *a cappella* women's chorus. The entire work is comprised of the following movements:

I. Karasu
II. Komori-uta
III. Yuki Kon Kon
IV. Tedeboko
V. Hotaru Koi
VI. Saruko Ga San-Man

VII. Yubin Haitatsu
VIII. Owaiyare
IX. Begoko Sambiki

Composition, Genre, and Historical Perspective

Classically trained composers have long engaged in the practice of borrowing or inventing melodies from folk cultures and inserting them into their own work. From Dvorak and Grieg to Vaughan Williams and Copland, folk-inspired art music can reflect a diversity of cultural experience and can offer an accessible alternative to the mainstream.

In choral music, folk *singing* has played an equally significant role in the inclusion of folk melodies in art music. This is to say that the manner in which folk music was produced—largely in gender segregated cultural forums—has helped to promote a vast repertoire of music written for men's and women's choirs. Dvorak's *Moravian Duets* and Vaughan Williams's *Folk Songs for the Four Seasons* come to mind as excellent examples of folk-inspired art songs for women's choir. Japanese composer Roh Ogura's 1958 work for women's voices, *Nine Pieces on Children's Songs of Tohoku Region*, from which Hotaru Koi is drawn, builds on this tradition.

Technical Considerations and Musical Elements

This is a fairly straightforward piece and will not present too many issues for you. However one potential problem deserves mentioning.

Staccato = Arhythmia

The rhythm and meter of this piece is simple and predictable. Yet, if the quarter notes passed among the voices in the ritornello (on the text *Ho, ho, ho...)* are too short, many issues can arise, from rushing of tempo to poor vowel matching and intonation.

A staccato articulation is a fundamentally a-rhythmic one—less experienced musicians will likely rush or produce vocal tension in these instances. This simple opening, which recurs throughout the piece, can be highly treacherous if the quarter notes are too short. Try singing the composite rhythm in a legato fashion.

Melody

The melody in this short work is shared by all three voices in the canonic ritornello, and derived from a pentatonic inflected A minor scale. The use of repetition and frequent intervals of major seconds and minor thirds contribute to the childlike character of the melody. In the more homophonic episodes between citations of the ritornello, melodic material is found in the duet between the two soprano voices and features a constant eighth-note pulse. Meanwhile, the alto line—derived from the soprano melodic material—is displaced by two quarter notes from the duet. Overall, the melodic features of this work are eclipsed by the textural phenomenon of the three voices in tight canon at the unison found in the ritornello.

Harmony

The harmonic language of this piece is derived from A natural minor with a recurring pentatonic inflection. There is a brief chromaticism in the bridge section—measures 22 to 23—where the harmony travels from E minor to D minor by means of borrowed chromatic chords such as A major and B major.

Rhythm

The rhythmic palette of this piece is appropriately simple and childlike, with a prevalence of quarter notes and eighth notes.

Texture

The dominant texture of Ogura's arrangement is canon; the ritornello material (occurring on the repeated text *Ho, ho, hotaru koi*) is built on a simple melody in a unison canon at the quarter note. Even the homophonic episodes found between the ritornellos display features of canon. As two voices duet homophonically, the third voice enters out of phase with the first two.

Other: Dynamics/Articulation/Tempo/Range

Dynamics: *pianissimo* to *più forte*
Articulation: only *fortepianos* are indicated
Tempo: *Allegro ma non tanto*, quarter note = 152
Ranges:

S1: E4–E5
SII: E4–B4
A: B3–B4

Stylistic Considerations

Whenever one performs a piece of music that has heavy folk inflection, it begs the question of authenticity in our performance practices. Can any choir successfully reproduce the musical culture of a country other than their own? The larger philosophical question is one that we cannot delve into here, but it is an important one. If we are to program cross-culturally, I think it is our responsibility to pursue authenticity with due diligence. This means doing some research about the culture from which we are borrowing.

With Hotaru Koi, that might involve listening to Japanese choirs or Japanese folk musicians in order to approximate a "Japanese" sound. Similarly, you might consider that these songs are children's songs; you may want to make your choir sound more youthful. That said, you might argue that since the arranger indicates that these are children's songs for women's voices and that he was an admirer of the traditions of Western Art music, you would rather ask your choir to sing with a more mature, "Western" (bel canto) sound. Both arguments are valid and can be manifested in a variety of musical and vocal ways.

Form and Structure

The form of this short piece is dictated by textural and harmonic shifts. A schematic of these shifts follows:

Measure	Event and Scoring
mm. 1–10	Canon
mm. 11–14	Soprano Duet with Alto Imitation
mm. 15–17	Canon
mm. 18–21	Soprano Duet with Alto Imitation
mm. 22–25	Chromatic Homophony
mm. 26–36	Canon
mm. 37–38	Duet-like Canon
mm. 39–46	Canon

In this way, the form most closely resembles ABABCABA, a modified rondeau or ritornello form. This is an appropriate formal design for a children's song in that it prominently features repetition.

Text and Translation

Japanese:
Ho, ho, hotaru koi
Atchi no mizu wa nigai zo
Kotchi no mizuwa amai zo

Ho, ho, hotaru koi
Ho, ho, yama michi koi
Hotaru no otosan kanemochi da
Do ri de oshiri ga pikapika da

Ho, ho, hotaru koi
Ho, ho, yama michi da
Hiruma wa kusaba no tsuyu no kage
Yoru wa ponpon taka chichin

Tenjuku agari shitareba
Tsunbakura ni sarawarebe

Ho, ho, hotaru koi
Atchi no mizu wa nigai zo
Kotchi no mizu wa amai zo

Ho, ho, hotaru koi yama michi da
Ando no hikari o chotto mite koi

Ho, ho, hotaru koi
Ho, ho yama michi koi
Ho, ho, ho…

English translation by David Larson:
Ho, ho, ho, firefly
Come, there's some water that's bitter to taste
Come, here's some water that's sweet to your taste

Ho, ho, ho, firefly
Ho, ho, up this mountain path
Firefly's daddy struck it rich, so he's got lots of dough
No wonder that his rear end sparkles in the dark

Ho, ho, ho, firefly
Ho, ho, up this mountain path
In the daytime hiding 'mongst the dewy blades of grass
But when it's night, his lantern burns bright

E'en though we've flown all the way from India, zoom!
And those sparrow swarm to swallow us

Ho, ho, ho firefly
Come, there's some water that's bitter to taste
Come, here's some water that's sweet to your taste

Ho, ho, ho firefly up this mountain path
Look! See a thousand lanterns sparkling in the dark

Ho, ho, ho firefly
Ho, ho, up this mountain path
Ho, ho, ho...

Recordings

Ogura, Ro. "Hotaru Koi" performed by Libana on *Fire Within*. Lady Slipper Records: B0000000A2, 1993.

Ogura, Ro. "Hotaru Koi" performed by Le Choeur de femmes Sibylla, Céline Castaño, conductor, on *Inspirations Contemporaines: Oeuvres Pour Choeur de Femmes a Cappella Du Xxème siècle*. DBA Productions: B00168PUQY, 2002.

Ogura, Ro. "Hotaru Koi" performed by Tokyo Philharmonic Chorus, Kenji Otani, conductor, on *Japan's Concert: 20-21—History of the 21st Century Composers, Vol. 14*. VA Classics: ECJC-014, 2001.

Contributed by:

Emilie Amrein

Teacher Resource Guide

I Thank You God

Gwyneth Walker
(b. 1947)

SSA
E. C. Schirmer: 5331
Overall: 4
Vocal: 4
Tonal/Rhythm: 4

Composer

Gwyneth Walker was born in 1947 in New York City. When she was one, her parents moved to New Canaan, Connecticut and she lived there throughout her childhood. Walker attended High school at Abbot Academy, the sister school to Phillips Andover, rather than New Canaan Public School because her parents believed that Abbot featured an excellent sports and music program. While there, she sang in every available choral group and even arranged several pieces for her choral groups to perform. Walker completed her undergraduate studies at Brown University and her masters and doctoral studies at Hartt School of Music. She was very advanced in music theory by the time she entered Brown and that allowed her to skip most entry-level courses and study independently with Paul Nelson. One of her orchestral compositions actually received a reading by the Rhode Island Philharmonic Orchestra. At Hartt, Walker studied composition with Arnold Franchetti. She also sang in a women's choral group for which she did a great deal of arranging. Walker took a teaching position at Oberlin where she taught music theory and composition to advanced students. She stayed at Oberlin for four years and then began to notice that she did not have enough time to compose. She left Oberlin in 1980 and moved to the Brainstorm Dairy Farm in Braintree, Vermont to pursue a full-time career as a composer surrounded by 400 Holstein cows.

Walker was active in the United Church of Christ before becoming a Quaker, taking after her maternal relatives of Dutch heritage seven generations back. The influence of the Quaker heritage on Walker's music is profound and can be seen in her attempt to make her music understandable and clear to anyone who hears it. Walker lives her life and approaches her career with an egalitarian way. Her belief in this philosophy is especially apparent in the way in which she accepts commissions from groups of all types, sizes, and musical status, from professional orchestras to elementary school choirs.

Gwyneth Walker loves the theatrical, but prefers to make her choral music theatrical in other ways besides setting a libretto or extended theatrical work to music. She prefers to use texts by twentieth-century American poets like Lucille Clifton, May Swenson, e.e. cummings, and Virginia Adair. She has also arranged many American folk songs, which she enjoys because the melodies are familiar to people. She has no desire to write her own lyrics.

Poetry that is readily comprehensible attracts her. Because she is a Quaker, she prefers poetry that expresses beauty over works that express violence or praises one person above another. In setting a poem, her process begins by attempting to fully understand the meaning of poem. She does not literally express the words but rather the underlying meaning of the poem. The last thing she believes a composer should worry about is which note goes with which word. Her music tends to create imagery and feelings based on the poetry. Walker said in an interview during the 1999 American Choral Directors Association Convention in Chicago, where *I Thank You God* was premiered, "Everything about me comes out in my music."[1]

Composition, Genre, and Historical Perspective

I Thank You God was a Raymond W. Brock Memorial Commission, which is the highest honor bestowed upon a choral composer by the American Choral Directors Association. Gwyneth Walker was given this commission in 1998, and the work was performed on the closing evening of the 1999 National Convention in Chicago, Illinois, by the ACDA National Women's Honor Choir, conducted by Diane Loomis. The piece is published by E. C. Schirmer. It was originally voiced for SSA, with piano accompaniment, but Walker added a mixed-voice arrangement to the E. C. Schirmer catalog several years later. The work is about four minutes in length.

Musical Elements and Technical Considerations

This composition can be thought of as loosely constructed, with four verses or sections and a repeated section or refrain that changes slightly by key and bar length each time it is repeated. Although the verses are written metrically in mixed meter to allow a natural flow of the text, many accelerando, ritard, and fermata markings give the verses a rubato feel while actually remaining in time. After setting up the poem using ascending arpeggios in the piano (seemingly connecting earth to heaven), Walker continues to thank God:

for the leaping greenly spirits of trees
and a blue true dream of sky; and for everything which is natural
which is infinite which is yes

Be sure to observe the staccato markings on "leaping" and "greenly" as this style marking, along with the alto punctuation of beats 3 and 6, gives the listener the feeling of skipping. If executed well, this is a wonderful effect.

Refrain—i thank You God

The refrain is varied in both tonality and length each time it is sung. It is made up of running eighth notes. Of this passage Walker says: "Do not sing the eighth notes as if you are plodding along! They are meant to be emphasized, as in speech, and accented according to their meaning. Do not sing them all alike!"[2]

Walker's words should be taken very seriously on the refrain. The choir should be feeling like the words are simply pouring out and not thinking about placing the words on exactly the right beat. I tell my choir that they should feel almost rushed and breathless. Each time the choir sings "amazing," they should be sure to stress (almost elongate) the second syllable.

(i who have died am alive again today
and this is the sun's birthday; this is the birth
day of life and love and wings: and of the gay
great happening illimitably earth)

The accelerando that takes place in measures 29 and 30 is extremely important, as these measures are the set-up bars for the stretching effect that happens in measure 31, "gay great happening." Have the choir take a bit of time after breath mark after "happening" to help set that measure apart from the ritardando that follows.

Refrain—i thank You God

The refrain this time is shortened to include only the theme of the refrain.

how should tasting touching hearing seeing
breathing any—lifted from the no
of all nothing—human merely being
doubt unimaginable You?
(now the ears of my ears awake and
now the eyes of my eyes are opened.

Walker uses some wonderful word painting on the word "doubt." To emphasize this, be sure to have the choir place the "t" right on the rest. The exception is in measure 54 where the choir holds through on the word "doubt." I would suggest having the choir breathe after "You?" in that measure to set the next phrase apart. Measures 60 to 63 (one of my favorite moments of the piece) should be sung with an open, moving sound. I find this to be one of the emotional highlights in this composition and makes the following refrain simply pour out of the choir.

Refrain—i thank You God

The work continues with a piano solo—choir ornaments with an ascending arpeggio over the top; the Refrain i thank You God (fragment); a Reprise of "i who have died am alive again today"; an extended Refrain; and then the coda. My singers found this piece, especially the coda, to be an extremely personal and emotional expression. Observe the accelerando and crescendo markings to make this happen. Walker includes markings like "fervently" and "in celebration," which I think the performers will find to be ultimately correct.

Stylistic Considerations

Walker says of this work that *I Thank You God* is about "vastness and grandeur." *I Thank You God* portrays some of this through its journey from C minor eventually ending in C major. The coda invites the choir to be open to and full and appreciative of the "creator" for the gifts of the earth. It is a remarkable journey through many recitative-like passages in a reflective minor mode to an awakening in C major that happens in the coda (measures 88 to 100). The piece has traveled from low C in the piano (the opening note) to high C in the soprano (the highest note of the final chord).

Form and Structure

I Thank You God begins with a page-long bar of piano introduction. Walker begins by having the piano open with three sets of ascending arpeggios that seem to be climbing to heaven. The arpeggios are played almost rubato, marked with accelerando and ritard. An almost dreamy stage is set as the singers enter over a repeated four note pattern.

Measure	Event and Scoring
mm. 2–5	(4bars) 2+2 "i thank You God for most this amazing day"
mm. 6–9	(4 bars) 2+2 "for the leaping greenly spirits of trees and a blue true dream of sky" Here Walker uses word painting on the word "leaping" (6/8 bar with descending leaps for one bar).
mm. 10–13	(4 bars) "and for everything which is natural which is infinite which is yes" Walker uses an ascending passage with mixed meter (6/8, 5/8, 4/4) leading to "God" of the next phrase.
mm. 14–17	(4 bars that overlap the upcoming 4-bar piano interlude by the middle bar) This is the first of four times the phrase "i thank You God" will be repeated. The setting of this phrase resembles a moving personal prayer.
mm. 17–20	Piano interlude
mm. 21–22	(2 bars) As in the beginning of the piece, Walker uses a 2-bar piano introduction to set up a dreamy atmosphere using a repeated descending 5-note pattern what introduces the next verse.
mm. 23–26	(4 bars) "i who have died am alive again today" This verse features altos with a soprano accompaniment figure.
mm. 27–32	(6 bars) 2+2+2 "and this is the sun's birthday this is the birth day of life and love and wings /and of the gay great happening illimitably earth" This phrase is marked accelerando, moving quickly toward the climax of the phrase where the emphasis is placed on the last two bars with fermatas over the words "gay" and "great."
mm. 33–36	(4 bars) "i who have died am alive again today" This phrase marks the end of this verse. Walker considers this line important enough to repeat again later in the work.
mm. 35–40	A 6-bar piano interlude. Bars 35 and 36 overlap the end of the previous vocal phrase. Sopranos sing a fragment of the refrain.
mm. 41–42	As before, Walker uses the descending 5-note repeated pattern in the piano to introduce the next verse.
mm. 43–46	(4 bars) (marked *quasi recitative*) "how should any human being doubt You?" Walker uses word painting every time the word "doubt" is sung by following the word with a rest before singing the next word "You," suggesting faltering or doubt.
mm. 47–50	(4 bars) "how should tasting touching any human merely being doubt You?" Walker uses word painting on the words "doubt You" once again.
mm. 51–56	(6 bars) 4+2 The text from the last phrase is expanded to end with "doubt unimaginable You." The word "unimaginable" is stretched over a bracketed sextuplet over the bar for emphasis.

Measure	Event and Scoring
mm. 57–59	(3 bars) "lifted from the no of all nothing, doubt You?" The end of this phrase features a very dramatic moment as the choir is instructed to crescendo from *piano* to *forte* as the tempo moves forward and marked in the score as *Grandly*. Walker uses this phrase as a lead into the expansive next phrase.
mm. 60–63	(4 bars) 2+2 "now the ears of my ears awake. now the eyes of my eyes are opened" Walker sets up this phrase as the climax of the work by its fullness and homophonic grandeur. It is the last line of the verse and is marked *forte* as well as accelerando. It is unlike any of the preceding treatments of the text in that it is sung with a full sound in homophonic fashion, unlike the quasi-recitative sections that precede it. This statement leads directly into another refrain.
mm. 64–65	(2 bars) Refrain: "i thank You God"
mm. 66–69	(4 bars) Piano interlude ornamented by the choir on the words "awake" and "opened."
mm. 70–71	2 bars) Refrain: "i thank You God"—this time is changed to a call and response between a solo soprano and solo alto.
mm. 72–81	(10 bars) 2+2+6 "I who have died am alive again today." This text is repeated here (from m. 33 to m. 36), placing a greater importance on this line for Walker. Besides the refrain text, it is the only repeated text in her setting. There is some speculation that Walker was greatly affected by the death of her mother, an event that took place just before she composed this piece. The repetition of this line seems to suggest a rebirth for Walker after that solemn event. In an interview, Walker says of this line: "One could take that in the Christian manner, but also in a personal manner. We all have times when we feel our spirit has died through the death of a loved one, through depression, or through an experience of spiritual or emotional death. Then for some reason or other, we feel alive again today. That poem really speaks to me."[3]
mm. 82–88	(7 bars) 4 + 3 Extended refrain: "i thank You God." The last bar of this refrain overlaps the first bar of the coda.
mm. 88–100	Entwines the words "i thank You God" and "this day." Finally arrives in C major as the sopranos are invited to sing a high C on the final chord.

Text and Translation

The text is adapted from "i thank You God for most this amazing" from *Complete Poems: 1904–1962* by e.e. cummings, edited by George J. Firmage. Adaptations for Walker's setting were made with permission of the Trustees for the e.e.cummings Trust.

i thank You God for most this amazing day:
for the leaping greenly spirits of trees
and a blue true dream of sky; and for everything
which is natural which is infinite which is yes
(i who have died am alive again today,
and this is the sun's birthday; this is the birth
day of life and of love and wings: and of the gay
great happening illimitably earth)
how should tasting touching hearing seeing
breathing any—lifted from the no
of all nothing—human merely being
doubt unimaginable You?
(now the ears of my ears awake and
now the eyes of my eyes are opened)

Additional References and Suggested Resources

There are no books published on Gwyneth Walker's music, although there is a one-page entry in *The Norton/Grove Dictionary of Women Composers*. The largest source of information about the composer's music is found in the articles, reviews, essays, program notes, and correspondence published on her Web site: www.gywnethwalker.com. Information on her Web site falls into three categories: biographical data about the composer, general statements from the composer, critics, conductors, or fellow composers about Walker's work, and reviews of her music.

Walker, Gwyneth. "*I Thank You God*: Notes by the Composer." Web site of Gwyneth

Walker—Composer http://www.gwynethwalker.com/forevera.html Accessed May 13, 2003.

Walker, Gwyneth. Assisting in rehearsal: *I Thank You God*. National Women's Honor Choir Rehearsal. American Choral Directors' Association National Convention. Chicago, IL. April 13, 1999.

Burrichter, Vicki Lynne. *The Choral Music of Gwyneth Walker: An Overview*, Doctor of Arts diss. University of Northern Colorado, December 2003.

Burrichter, Vicki. Interview with Gwyneth Walker. Tape recording. Chicago, IL, April 14, 1999.

Walker, Gwyneth to Vicki Burrichter. "Family history." Personal e-mail, May 13, 2003.

Contributed by:

Michele Holt

1 Gwyneth Walker, assisting in rehearsal, "I Thank You God," National Women's Honor Choir Rehearsal, American Choral Directors' Association National Convention, Chicago, IL, 13 April 1999.

2 Gwyneth Walker, assisting in rehearsal, "I Thank You God," National Women's Honor Choir Rehearsal, American Choral Directors' Association National Convention, Chicago, IL, 13 April 1999.

3 Brooks, Gene. "An Interview with Gwyneth Walker." *Choral Journal*. February 1999. *Website of Gwyneth Walker—Composer* http://www.gwynethwalker.com/walkinf5.html>. 13 May 2003.

Teacher Resource Guide

LAWA

Katheryn Sadler

SSAA
Boosey & Hawkes: 48018827
Overall: 4
Vocal: 4
Tonal/Rhythm: 4

Composer

Although most of her life and career occurred in Australia, Kathryn Sadler was born and raised in England. She studied voice and music education at Trinity College of Music in London. After immigrating to Australia, she continued her studies in opera and music theatre at The Victorian College of the Arts, which is part of the University of Melbourne. She also studied advanced conducting at the University of Toronto with Doreen Rao. Her singing career includes performances at most of the major opera companies in Australia as well as many public and private venues in the Melbourne area.

Sadler has ample and varied experience as a conductor as well, leading ensembles at the University of Melbourne and the Defence Force School of Music. She has also worked with the Melbourne Chorale, the Royal Melbourne Philharmonic Choir, and Gloriana. Sadler created the Mac. Robertson Chamber Voices in 1992, which continued to perform until 1999. With this ensemble she produced a recording, *In dulci jubilo*, which reached international acclaim. She currently teaches private voice and conducts ensembles at Melbourne Girls' Grammar School and is musical director for Vox Synergy, an ensemble that is part of Melbourne Youth Music.

Her involvement in many ensembles has been the catalyst for most of Sadler's compositions and arrangements. Boosey & Hawkes publish many of these pieces in its Choral Music Experience series. Sadler continues to be active as a clinician, coach, and conductor.

Composition, Genre, and Historical Perspective

LAWA, published in 2005, was conceived as a recessional and is dedicated "With love and gratitude to the Mac.Robertson Chamber Voices & Chamber Ensemble, Mac.Robertson Girls' High School, Melbourne, Australia." It is likely this was written while Sadler conducted the ensemble from 1992–1999. The title is an acronym for the four angel voices presented in the work: Love, Art, Wisdom, and Adventure.

Musical Elements and Technical Considerations

This work is a combination of five different musical elements: Chorale, Angel(s) of Love, Angel(s) of Art, Angel(s) of Wisdom, and Angel(s) of Adventure (for more on how this all works together, please refer to the section on Form and Structure). When broken down into its various elements, this piece seems relatively simple. However, the combination of these elements creates a complex texture. The conductor should take care to teach the individual elements well before combining them. This should ensure more certainty in the singers as they approach the time for performance.

The individual parts of this work involve some rhythmic complexity. There are syncopations, super triplets, and some sixteenth-note ornamental figures. Alone, the rhythms are readily manageable; however, they often occur simultaneously in different parts. Take special care to learn each rhythm accurately, and spend time isolating difficult combinations, like sixteenth notes against super triplets, before approaching the work on its larger scale.

The chorale rhythms are homophonic but syncopated in almost every measure, and although they are repetitive and not overly difficult, the tight chords and syncopated rhythms must be performed on "ng." This will not only make rhythmic accuracy and unity difficult but may also make the chords more difficult to tune, as the singers might have a hard time hearing each other. This will become even more challenging if performed dispersed in hall in any way.

The sense of tonality in this work is unsure; however, it is diatonic and usually feels somewhat like C major or A minor. The real harmonic foundation occurs through the chords in the Chorale part, which are almost all seventh chords. Any other harmony comes by means of combining the Angel melodies. Although the Angel parts are based on the harmonies of the Chorale, they each employ many extra melodic elements, such as passing tones, appoggiaturas, and suspensions, which wander in and out of the harmonic context.

All the Angel voice parts are melodic. Each enters successively, and as it does, each part, respectively, gets more and more complicated. Because of the lack of tonal center and the pervading seventh chords, the melodies are not always intuitively obvious. There are large leaps, some into dissonances, and unexpected turns in the melodic shapes. The melody for Adventure, indicative of its name, is the most difficult melodically, rhythmically, and in its range. Within two measures, it spans one whole step shy of two octaves. Adventure singers must be versatile at the top and bottom of their vocal range.

Although the combination of these melodies produces a complicated musical texture, the singers should have little issue putting the piece together once they learn each individual melody. The sheer amount of repetition of each line in the piece will give the singers ample opportunity to practice their lines. However, each melody should be studied individually until the singers achieve a good sectional unity in phrasing, tone, and all other polishing elements, otherwise they will most likely not succeed when the parts are combined.

The text should not cause too much difficulty in this work. There is an abundance of the [e] vowel in words like "Angel" and "may" that the singers repeat throughout the piece. Make sure the singers maintain roundness in their lips and are careful about timing the diphthong to avoid the bright, brazen sounds that often accompany that vowel. The conductor will also need to make a decision as to how to perform the "r" in the word "spirit." Whether you choose to use an American "r" or a flipped "r" depends on your personal preference; either way, the singers need to know which to do.

The piece will be the most successful if memorized by the singers. This should not be too difficult in lieu of the amount of repetition. The singers should also be admonished to watch the conductor carefully. Watching the conductor is especially crucial in this work if you use it as a recessional or in any theatrical, dispersed way. Guide singers to use their eyes to achieve alignment, instead of their ears. If they do not do this, the result would be cacophony.

Stylistic Considerations

There are program notes included with this work, which are as follows:

> *LAWA* was designed to be a recessional item, but it can be equally used as a processional or as a concert item. It was found to be most effective when the "Angels" were randomly placed in the ensemble, rather than grouped together and the Chorale dispersed among them. There's plenty of scope for theatrical effect in *LAWA* and choir directors are encouraged to be daring in this respect!

Please feel free to create an ending to suit your purpose and use dynamics as appropriate. That method of "fade out" can be at the director's discretion.

If the ensemble is not big enough to sustain the Chorale, it can be adapted for guitar, piano, or string quartet. Chord symbols are provided for your convenience. It has been effectively performed with four celli providing the Chorale. Male singers should be given the Chorale to accompany the Angels. For the original performance the orchestra sharing the concert program became Chorale, so that the entire company could exit together.

In consideration of these musical and theatrical elements of the piece, it would probably be most successful if performed with a more simple and pure vocal tone. The tight chords of the Chorale and the syncopated and sometimes difficult rhythms will be more difficult to perform accurately if the singers use a more complicated, romantic tone (especially if the work is performed using theatrical elements that would disperse the singers during the performance). Using a sound typical to the British style of singing would create the right aural atmosphere for the work. If the singers are moving during the performing, one should give special consideration as to how this would be best accomplished in the venue and rehearsed beforehand. As far as the performing and/or theatrical style, you can present the piece as simply or as intricately as you desire.

Form and Structure

There are five separate musical-textual units included in the structure of this piece. Each unit is eight measures long and is repeated multiple times, without variation (except for the text of the chorale). They are as follows:

Chorale: Employs four-part chords in mostly closed position, the majority of which include sevenths. There are one to two chords per measure occurring on a gently syncopated rhythm. The text for the most part is "ng," but opens to "LAWA, Amen" in the middle of the work.

Four Angels:

Love—A single melody sung by a soloist and group to the text of verse 1. The 8 measures of Love is always aligned exactly with the 8 measures of the Chorale. The voices singing this part will eventually join the chorale and function as second altos.

Art—A single melody sung by a soloist and group to the text of verse 2. The 8 measures of Art always begin one measure after the beginning of the Chorale. The voices singing this part will eventually join the chorale and function as first altos.

Wisdom—A single melody sung by a soloist and group to the text of verse 3. The 8 measures of Wisdom always begin two measures after the beginning of the Chorale. The voices singing this part will eventually join the chorale and function as second sopranos.
Adventure—A single melody sung by a soloist and group to the text of verse 4. The 8 measures of Adventure alway begins one measure after the beginning of the Chorale. The voices singing this part will eventually join the chorale and function as first sopranos.

Measure	Event and Scoring
1. mm. 1–8	Love solo
2. mm. 9–16	Chorale
3. mm. 17–24	Chorale and Love group
4. mm. 25–32	Add Art group (m. 26)
5. mm. 33–40	Add Wisdom group (m. 35)
6. mm. 41–48	Add Adventure group (m. 44) Note: There are repeat brackets in mm. 44–51 that would simply repeat all five parts in their respective progression. The music instructs the choir to use as needed.
7. mm. 49–56	Continuation of number 6.
8. mm. 57–64	Half of the singers in each Angel group join the Chorale successively at the end of their previous repetition (Love: m. 57, Art: m. 58, Wisdom: m. 56, Adventure: m. 58). The remaining singers of each Angel group remain on their respective parts.
9. mm. 65–72	The remaining singers of each Angel group join the Chorale successively at the end of their previous repetition (Love: m. 65, Art: m. 66, Wisdom: m. 67, Adventure: m. 68). The Angel soloists remain on their respective parts.
10. mm. 73–80	Angel soloists join the Chorale successively at the end of their previous repetition (Love: m. 73, Art: m. 74, Wisdom: m. 75, Adventure: m. 76). All singers finish the Chorale together.
11. mm. 81–88	Optional: repeat the Chorale if necessary.

Text and Translation

Kathryn Sadler wrote the text for this piece as well as the music. It repeats multiple times throughout the piece, each verse often occurring simultaneously with the others. The only verse presented alone, and thus the only verse that will be readily understood by the listeners, is the first.

I am the Angel of Love,
May your heart be warmed by my spirit.
I am the Angel of Love,
May your heart be whole.

I am the Angel of Art,
May your soul be deepened by my spirit.
I am the Angel of Art,
May your soul be whole.

I am the Angel of Wisdom,
May your mind be attuned to my spirit.
I am the Angel of Wisdom,
May your mind be whole.

I am the Angel of Adventure,
May your life be enhanced by my spirit.
I am the Angel of Adventure,
May your life be whole.

Contributed by:

Joni Jensen

Teacher Resource Guide

Les étoiles

Mark Sirett

(b. 1932)

SSA
Alliance: AMP0687
Overall: 4
Vocal: 4
Tonal/Rhythm: 4

Composer

Dr. Mark Sirett (b. 1952) is a native of Kingston, Ontario, and a graduate in choral conducting and pedagogy from the University of Iowa. He has taught at the University of Western Ontario, the University of Alberta, and Queen's University where he directs Queen's Choral Ensemble. He is the founding Artistic Director of the Cantabile Choirs of Kingston, a seven-choir educational program involving over 250 singers.

Dr. Sirett has won two international awards in choral conducting: the Jury Prize for Imaginative Programming and Artistry at the Cork International Choral Festival, 2002 in Ireland, and the Outstanding Conductor Award from the Young Prague 2004 Music Festival. Choirs under his direction have won numerous provincial, national, and international honors, including First Prize in the CBC Choral Competition in the Church Choir Category, and a Gold Award at the Young Prague Music Festival, 2004.

Dr. Sirett is also an award-winning choral composer whose works have been performed and commissioned by some of Canada's leading choirs including the National Youth Choir of Canada, the Toronto Mendelssohn Choir,

Toronto Children's Chorus, Amabile Youth Singers, Ottawa Regional Youth Choir, Richard Eaton Singers, and the Elora Festival Singers.

Dr. Sirett is frequently in demand as a guest conductor, choral clinician, and adjudicator. He has been guest conductor of the Ontario Youth Choir, the Peterkin Chorale (Youth Choir), and the Alberta Honours Children's Choir. *(Bio courtesy ECS Publishing)*

Compositional, Genre, and Historical Context

Conductor William Brown and the Oriana Women's Choir commissioned six Canadian composers to write works for their Poetry and Music Project in 2004. For this project, composers Stephen Chatman, Eleanor Daley, Ruth Watson Henderson, Donald Patriquin, Imant Raminsh, and Mark Sirett selected poetry by Toronto students. Mark Sirett writes: "It was a great pleasure for me to join in this unique commissioning project of the Oriana Singers. I am sure that each of the composers involved in the project were astounded by remarkable richness of the poetry provided by so many young, talented writers in the Toronto region. William Brown and the extraordinary singers in the choir must be commended for their vision in launching such a project, and for the exceptional evening of premieres we all enjoyed in May [2004]."

Technical Considerations and Musical Elements

Melody

Sirett's treatment of melody within "Les étoiles" is less assertive than his use of harmony and rhythm. The melody is found exclusively within the soprano 1 voice and is characterized by chromatic pitches and a pervasive alternation between duple and triple subdivisions of the primary pulse. Sirett repeats the melody in full for the second strophe of the poem, before concluding with a sweet and simple coda where the harmonic rhythm slows considerably and the accompaniment drops out for two whole bars.

Harmony

The harmonic palette for this piece is highly romantic—chromaticisms, borrowed chords, third relations, enharmonic pivot chords, and nonfunctional harmonies abound, resulting in a relatively unstable harmonic landscape reminiscent of the French romantics Debussy and Ravel. The augmented triad makes several appearances as well, lending a mystical air to the work. The final cadence seems almost anachronistic in its simplistic F major with a suspended second.

Rhythm

Congruent with his romantic treatment of harmony, Sirett seems intent on destabilizing the pulse subdivision within this piece. Although squarely in four, Sirett is constantly alternating between duplet and triplet subdivisions of the pulse, often putting the two in direct opposition between the voices or within the piano accompaniment. Other than this, Sirett's treatment of rhythm is fairly straightforward. (There are several instances where one might highlight a syncopated rhythm; however, this would be ill-advised as the general character and articulation markings would indicate that every effort should taken to downplay the feeling of syncopation within this piece.)

Texture

"Les étoiles" is written for women's chorus and piano. Although it calls for three-part chorus (soprano 1, soprano 2, and alto), the piece occasionally employs divisi in four parts. The texture of the piece is homophonic with the melody most often occurring in the soprano 1 line.

Form and Structure

"Les étoiles" is divided into two strophes of twelve bars and ends with a brief coda. Within the parallel strophes, the phrasing is similar but not identical; each strophe begins with a two-bar piano introduction and two two-bar phrases moving from F major to D minor and E-flat major to a C major minor ninth. Within the middle phrase that follows, there is some variation, however the function remains the same in both strophes—to travel from B-flat major to D major. Finally, there is a two-bar extension of harmonic ambiguity with two prominent augmented chords (sharing two pitches in common: F and A). After the second strophe, there is a five-bar coda where the final augmented chord is resolved to D-flat major (where the root is enharmonically equivalent to the root preceding it) before cadencing simply in F major.

Other: Dynamics/Articulation/Tempo/Range

Dynamics: pianissimo to forte with neo-romantic messa di voce
Articulation: Legato with occasional tenuto indicated
Tempo: Moderato with rubato and a generous ritardando at the end.
Range: Soprano I: C-f'
Soprano II: A-d'
Alto: F-bb

Technical Considerations and Musical Elements

There are three obvious technical issues that might challenge your choir:

Rhythm

The constant duplet versus triplet subdivision of pulse is easy enough to teach but less experienced singers might be overwhelmed when the two are put into opposition. You might consider practicing this rhythmic mode mixture outside the context of rehearsing of this piece—perhaps in a warmup with antiphonal clapping. Once the students get the hang of the rhythm in the abstract, reintroduce the skill within the context of the piece for easier learning.

Harmony

The romantic harmonies that Sirett works with in this piece may also seem daunting to a young singer. Again, consider working out these harmonies separate from the piece itself, and work on the individual vocal lines discretely before re-contextualizing the whole.

French Diction

For non-native speakers, singing in the French language can be very intimidating. There are many sounds in French that are unique to that language, and developing the ability to create these sounds can take time. Although there is an adequate pronunciation guide provided in the score, a native French speaker may be a more effective guide in teaching this text. If there are no native speakers in your community, consider consulting one of the many available published guides to French diction for singers. My favorite is *Diction for Singers: A Concise Reference for English, Italian, Latin, German, French, and Spanish Pronunciation* by Joan Wall. Once you have a sense of the language, introduce the sounds to your choir in small increments. Slow repetition of each phrase will help immensely.

Stylistic Considerations

As this is a recently composed work, performance practice can only be speculated. The score and the premiere recording are good sources for most information—as is the composer himself. That said, dynamics, articulation, and tempo modifications are indicated clearly in the score; an interpretation based on this information should not be hard to derive. In general, be liberal with your tempo and dynamic gestures in order to emphasize the romantic characteristics of the work.

Text and Translation

As one of six commissioned composers for Oriana's Poetry and Music Project, Mark Sirett chose a poem by Ryan O'Reilly on the subject of stars. On the Oriana Women's Choir Web site, Sirett writes: "Ryan O'Reilly's poem Les étoiles is an atmospheric text full of beautiful imagery; this inspired a musical setting that is appropriately neo-romantic and at times, impressionistic in feeling." For more information about this project and links to recordings, please visit http://www.orianachoir.com.

French

Les étoiles brillent pendant la nuit,
Toutes petites et jolies.
Des milliers de petits soleils au Coeur
 de l'immensité,
L'immensité noire.

Elles clignotent toute la nuit
Et puis elles s'enfuient.
Quand le jour vient, il n'y a plus rien.
Tout est éphémère.

English

The stars shine through the night,
All small and pretty.
Some thousands of tiny suns in the heart
 of infinity,
Black infinity.

They blink all night
And then they flee.
When the day arrives, they are no more.
All is fleeting.

Recordings

Sirett, Mark. "Les Etoiles," on *Child with the Starry Crayon*, performed by Oriana Women's Choir, William Brown, Conductor. Self-published, 2004. Available for purchase at http://www.orianachoir.com.

Contributed by:

Emilie Amrein

Teacher Resource Guide

O bone jesu

Johannes Brahms

(1833-1897)

SSAA
Peters: P66141
Overall: 4
Vocal: 4
Tonal/Rhythm: 4

Composer

Johannes Brahms (1833–1897) was born in Hamburg, Germany and died in Vienna, Austria. A leading figure in German Romanticism, Brahms was known for having an outwardly more conservative voice than other great Romantic period figures, such as Wagner and Strauss. He began his career as a concert pianist and early in his career he was mentored by Robert and Clara Schumann. Brahms was an avid student and scholar of Renaissance music, which is clearly seen in his writing style, especially in his choral music. Throughout his career Brahms served as a choral director for various ensembles, and many of his shorter choral works were written specifically for these ensembles. While the majority of his choral music was written in the first half of his career, Brahms's popularity was launched with the performance of his *Ein deutsches Requiem*, his largest choral work, in 1868.

Composition, Genre, and Historical Perspective

"O bone jesu" is number one in a set of three sacred pieces for women's chorus entitled aptly, *Drei Geistliche Chore*, Op. 37. The set also includes a setting of "Adoramus te" and "Regina coeli" for choruses two and three, respectively.

Drei Geistliche Chore is an early work (1859) and was inspired by motets of the late Renaissance.

This Latin motet is intended for liturgical performance on Good Friday. The text is a combination of references to Christ, combined with a variety of passages from the psalms (12, 30 and 38).

Musical Elements and Technical Considerations

For a short eighteen-measure piece lasting only ninety seconds "O bone jesu" is surprisingly dense in terms of musical material. Brahms is a master of the miniature, and he fits a large number of sophisticated musical devices into a brief period of time. Do not be tempted to consider this an easy read because of its length and apparent homophonic structure; this piece presents some formidable challenges.

The first and most difficult consideration is the independence of the vocal lines. Here Brahms is truly writing under a Renaissance model. There is significant cross voicing within the parts, even entire phrases where parts are flipped from their typical voicing. For instance in measures 11 to 14, the Soprano II and Alto I parts are inverted from their normal order. Because this cross voicing occurs in every part, it would be ideal if each section of the choir sounded alike rather than different. Clearly there are moments when the range extends to the extremes, especially for Soprano I and Alto II; at these moments the color of each section should be clear, even though the majority of the writing contains interweaving mid-range lines that should be rather homogenous in sound.

Another complex layer to "O bone jesu" is the variation of voice pairings and fluidity in the ways the voices are paired. Rather than pairing voices for entire phrases, Brahms endlessly moves through a kaleidoscope of vocal combinations that require the utmost awareness and sensitivity on the part of the singer. In this instance, it would make sense to rehearse every voice part in duet with each of the other three voice parts, and point out all sections of pairings. While time consuming, this exercise provides the singers with a rich understanding of the music surrounding them. In addition, it might work best for this piece to eventually be performed in a formation of mixed quartets so that ultimate listening can occur.

The final obvious technical consideration is tuning. Brahms's writing is harmonically quite adventurous, for such a brief piece, and the modulations must be handled very carefully. The first difficult tuning moment is in measures 4 to 5. The Soprano I ascent of a tritone and then a major third up to F-sharp is rather tricky to keep in tune, especially as it crosses the break of the voice. The Soprano II and Alto II voice pairing in measure 5, with the sharp shift from B-natural back to B-flat, is also worthy of close attention. The C-major chord on the downbeat of measure 6 must sparkle with all the hope of the resurrection, and Soprano II clearly shoulders the difficulty in making this happen with the approach to the third of the chord ascending through the passaggio in the middle of a diminuendo to pianissimo. The second tuning spot to look out for is measures 9 and 10, especially as the modulation occurs in Alto I and Alto II parts. Watch out for the tritone in Alto I and the descending octave in Alto II. Finally, the harmonic resolution back to F major in the last three measures of the piece is difficult: the E-natural in Soprano I shifts function from the fifth of an A-minor triad to the third of a C-dominant seventh chord, so the center of pitch must also change.

An effective rehearsal technique for improving tuning in a piece such as this is to remove text entirely and sing on one, easily unified vowel, where all focus can be on the center of pitch. Closed vowels such as "ee" and "u" are better for tuning work rather than open vowels, which offer too much variation in shape and sound for a clearly focused pitch. Work with parts in pairs and then in groups of three to assure consistency of tuning before trying all four voices together.

Stylistic Considerations

When choosing the appropriate sound for a piece one should always consider the era the piece comes from. While "O bone jesu" is a mid-nineteenth century piece, which may suggest a more full, round, dramatic sound, it is also clearly based on a Renaissance model, which would suggest a thinner, perhaps more reedy sound. How, then, does the choral conductor go about choosing an appropriate sound for this work? The answer is clear within the score that there should be a balance between the aforementioned extremes. Because of the interweaving nature of the four independent lines, each part must sound somewhat similar in timbre and color. This is especially true of adjacent voices. Effectively matching the colors of the sections will allow the true beauty of the cross voicing to shine through. The sound does require an element of Romantic heft, especially within the dynamic contrasts. It is through these nineteenth-century touches that the piece distinguishes itself from a Renaissance motet.

"O bone jesu" is a piece that can be helped significantly by a performance space with appropriate acoustics. Brahms more than likely intended this piece to be performed liturgically, most likely in a church with a strong reverberation. One cannot always control the space and acoustics, but if at all possible, this piece, much like a Bruckner motet, would work much better in a large, reverberant church rather than a small auditorium.

Form and Structure

MEASURE	EVENT AND SCORING
mm. 1–3:	2 phrases (2+1)
mm. 4–6:	2 phrases (1+2)
mm. 7–11:	2 phrases (2+3)
mm. 12–18:	1 phrase (7)

Text and Translation

O bone Jesu,
miserere nobis,
quia tu creasti nos,
tu redemisti nos
sanguine tuo praetiosissimo.

O blessed Jesus,
have mercy upon us,
because You have created us,
You have redeemed us
With your most precious blood.

Additional References and Resources

Botstein, Leon. *The Complete Brahms: A guide to the Musical Works of Johannes Brahms*. New York: W.W. Norton, 1999.

Evans, Edwin. *Historical, Descriptive & Analytical Accounts of the Entire Works of Johannes Brahms, Volume I: Vocal Works*. New York: B. Franklin, 1970.

Hancock, Virginia. "Brahms's Performances of Early Choral Music." *19th-Century Music*, Vol. 8, No. 2 (Autumn, 1984), pp. 125–141.

Swafford, Jan. *Johannes Brahms: a Biography*. New York: Alfred A. Knopf, 1997.

Contributed by:

W. Bryce Hayes

Teacher Resource Guide

Psalm 121

Imant Raminsh

SA
Overall: 4
Vocal: 4
Tonal/Rhythm: 4

Composer

Latvian born Imant Raminsh moved with his family to Canada in 1948. His earliest musical training was at the Royal Conservatory of Toronto, followed by a Bachelor of Music degree at the University of Toronto. He enjoyed further study at the Akademie Mozarteum in Salzburg. Since that time he has become a national treasure in Canada for his compositions, and is well known as a conductor, teacher, and performer.

He currently resides in British Columbia and has founded numerous groups in the region, among them, the Prince George Symphony, NOVA Children's Choir, and AURA Chamber Choir.

Raminsh's compositions have been performed by professional choirs and orchestras around the world, among them the Stockholm Chamber Choir, the Tokyo Philharmonic Chamber Choir, and Ave Sol (the Latvian Chamber Choir). In 2002, his nine-movement, eight-language *Symphony of Psalms* was premiered in Carnegie Hall with a massive choir of 170 voices plus orchestra.

Composition, Genre, and Historical Perspective

"Psalm 121" is indicative of the renaissance of children's choral literature composed in Canada during the last quarter of the twentieth century. Canadian children's choral music, Raminsh's music in particular, endeavors to create true art music for young voices. These works challenge young singers to grow by providing vocal lines, shapes, and melodies that encourage good singing. The music is at once challenging and rewarding.

Historically, Psalm settings highlight the unique nature of the original Hebrew poetry. There is no rhyme scheme as in European poetry, rather, the "rhyme" comes from the duality of most verses. Verses either come in two parts, as in "the Lord shall not smite thee by day, nor the moon by night," or in pairs, such as "I lift up mine eyes to the hills, from whence cometh my help. My help cometh from the Lord..." Verses come in opposites, "the Lord preserve thy going out and thy coming in," or in restating an idea, "the Lord is thy keeper, the Lord is the shade upon thy right hand." Handel's Messiah is perhaps the most famous setting of Hebrew poetry that reflects this continual and shifting duality. "Psalm 121" is a gem in this regard.

Musical Elements and Technical Considerations

"Psalm 121" is an excellent piece to challenge a choir that typically sings in two parts, and would be ideal for a contest or end-of-year project. It is also a good beginning-of-the-year teaching piece for the three-part treble choir, with many teachable moments with regard to tone, range extension, and expression.

The opening motive, "I will lift up mine eyes," is a static line introduced by the soprano and echoed by the alto. Take care to ensure that the singers focus on the flexibility and musicality of textual declamation. After the opening motive in the first section, measures 10 to 19 immediately demonstrate Raminsh at his lyric best. The lines are full of moving, fluid eighth-note melodies, with well-voiced leaps upward of the fourth. The melody continues to unfold with rhythmic energy always propelling the singer across the barline. Think "and 1 and 2 and 3 and 4," rather than "1 and 2 and 3 and 4 and."

In section 2, the tessitura sits below the treble clef. Now Raminsh the teacher is apparent while he attempts to keep the lines lyric, moving, and flexible, even as he encourages a darker tone needed for text painting. Take care to retain a light upper register and buoyant moving breath through these phrases.

The second half of section 2, measures 45 to 60, is the most challenging of the entire work. Introduce these phrases using a neutral syllable that encourages buoyant, light, and forward moving articulation, such as [de], [pe], or [te], changing often to keep voices relaxed. Keep air moving on ascending intervals, encourage the singers to use the high tones as points of departure rather than as the high pitch to "shoot for." Once the vocal lightness and movement of tone and breath are evident, intone the text on a unison pitch, much like the opening of the piece. Challenge the singers to sing legato even at times when the text moves on every eighth note. Also lead them to keep the vowel moving on the long pitches and reinforce singing lightly at the onset of the syllables that will be paired with the highest tones.

The final section is a terrific tool for teaching beauty of tone in the lower register: the text, key, and vocal writing combine to allow the voices to naturally resonate without pushing the chest register. Younger voices love how they sound. Learn this section first and then apply this relaxed, lifted lower color to section 2 where the tendency might be to push.

Stylistic Considerations

This work is a wonderful teaching tool for conveying the idea of musical energy flowing from weak to strong, rather than strong to weak, which is so often the habit of younger singers. Peruse the work and notice how many phrases begin and end on offbeats. Encourage singers to use body movement, such as stepping forward as they sing the off-beat entrance and to feel the momentum toward the next step or beat.

In the same manner, many young artists will approach a high note with great energy and effort. The concept of weak to strong can encourage singers to approach high notes with ease and relaxation. In measure 56 *ff*, both parts are asked to repeatedly approach high notes from below. Of course the natural inclination is to push, press, or exert some kind of extra effort to "reach" the higher pitch. This creates a phrase in which the high tone is the arrival point. which is only the case in measure 60, on the word "soul." In every other case (and this is true in most music) the high pitch propels the phrase forward and should be thought of as a departure point for creating momentum rather than receiving momentum. Have the singers sing 8–5–3–1 on many different syllables, help them feel open and light on the descending interval, draw their attention to how the tone and exercise begins on the top. Next, sing 5–8–5–3–1, opening to the feeling of the top note before they sing the top, then reinforce the feeling of the tone being light and starting again on the top. Next, use the text of this section in the exercise. Apply these concepts to this section.

Finally, the idea of weak to strong will help singers develop a more healthy lower register. Often singers feel they have more strength in the lower voice, where they can "belt" a bit, and are weaker in the middle voice. As mentioned before, the closing section always makes choirs sound rich and colorful. It is in the lower register, but it approaches from the repeated chant on f "I will lift up mine eyes..." the descent of the fourth from the weaker register into the lower register provides the correct lift and balance of lightness with richness.

Build warm up exercises that descend by fourth from the light middle register down into the lowest tones. Then approach measure 29 *ff* with this same technique.

Form and Structure

Raminsh plays with the text of Psalm 121 to create unity in his composition. The opening phrase "I will lift up mine eyes" is repeated numerous times to punctuate the beginning and end of sections of the work.

The work opens in B-flat major in 4/4 to a static piano accompaniment that introduces the lush harmony built on seconds and fourths. The reoccurring motive "I will lift up mine eyes," a static chant or intonation on a single pitch F, is then introduced. Section 1, measures 1 to 10, concludes with a reiteration of this opening motive in measures 20–24. Section 1 includes 2 measures (mm. 16–17) in which Raminsh divides the choir into three parts, other than this it is a strictly SA texture.

The middle section begins in measure 25 as it modulates to F-sharp minor and is set in 6/8 time. The mood is much darker and the tessitura lower, creating a more ominous effect. In measure 45 the work modulates to D major, and as the relative tessitura begins to rise, the text becomes more hopeful and the mood brightens. In measure 55, the tempo broadens and the key modulates upward again to F major as the choir sings "the Lord shall preserve thee from all evil." The work comes to a dramatic climax in measures 60 and 61, with sopranos above the staff singing "He shall preserve thy soul."

Measures 65 to 68 see a return to tempo 1 in 4/4 and the reappearance of the opening motive. Raminsh modulates back to B-flat major as the choir sings again in a low tessitura the benediction "The Lord shall preserve thy going out and thy coming in." Rather than the ominous color in section 2, the choir now sings with depth and warmth as they sing of promise.

Text

I will lift up mine eyes to the hills from whence cometh my help.
My help cometh from the Lord which made heaven and earth.
He will not suffer thy foot to be moved: He that keepeth thee will not slumber.
Behold, He that keepeth Israel shall neither slumber nor sleep.
The Lord is thy keeper, the Lord is thy shade upon thy right hand.
The sun shall not smite the by day, nor the moon by night.

The Lord shall preserve you from all evil, He shall preserve thy soul.
The Lord shall preserve thy going out and thy coming in,
From this time forth, e'en for evermore.

Recording

Raminsh, Imant. "Psalm 121," *Echo in My Soul.* Northwest Girls Choir, Rebecca Rottsalk.

Contributed by:

Geoffrey Boers

Teacher Resource Guide

There Is Sweet Music Here

Daniel E. Gawthrop

(b. 1949)

SSAA
Belwin: SCHCH 77111
Overall: 4
Vocal: 3
Tonal/Rhythm: 4

Composer

Composer Daniel E. Gawthrop was born in 1949 in Fort Wayne, Indiana. He has been the recipient of over one hundred commissions to write original music. His works have been published by Dunstan House, Warner Brothers (now Alfred Publishing Co.), Theodore Presser, Sacred Music Press, and others.

Gawthrop served for three years as Composer-in-Residence with the Fairfax Symphony Orchestra, Fairfax, Virginia, and has been the recipient of four grants from the Barlow Endowment for Musical Composition. He has been commissioned by dozens of institutions including the American Choral Directors Association through their prestigious Raymond Brock Memorial series, and has had works première in the Concert Hall of the John F. Kennedy Center for the Performing Arts, the Salt Lake City Mormon Tabernacle, and Washington National Cathedral. His choral pieces have been performed and recorded by such eminent ensembles as the United States Air Force Singing Sergeants, the Gregg Smith Singers, the Turtle Creek Chorale, the Paul Hill Chorale, the American Boychoir, the Mormon Tabernacle Choir, the

Cathedral Choral Society (of Washington National Cathedral), and literally hundreds of other groups in the United States and abroad.

In addition to his work as a composer, Gawthrop has been active as a broadcaster, clinician and adjudicator, organist, conductor, teacher, and writer, including a period as music critic for the *Washington Post*. Gawthrop is a Life Member of the American Choral Directors Association, a member of the American Guild of Organists, and a member of Phi Mu Alpha Sinfonia, the music fraternity. Gawthrop currently serves on the Board of Advisors of the Barlow Endowment for Music Composition at Brigham Young University.

Composition, Genre, and Historical Perspective

"There Is Sweet Music Here" is a secular motet for unaccompanied four-part treble voices (SSAA). Although a relatively early work (ca. 1985), this piece already demonstrated the characteristic harmonic language that has come to identify my writing style. Frequent and unprepared shifts of the tonal center and close part writing render performing the piece a bit trickier than a first glance at the printed page might suggest. Like all of my music, this piece is clearly tonal and uses mostly familiar harmonies, although they frequently turn in radically unexpected directions. Singers and conductors who are familiar with the better known "Sing Me to Heaven" will find this piece similar in style and difficulty.

Although conceived for a treble choir, word has reached me that the occasional TTBB group performs this piece essentially unaltered, but pitched down an octave. I confess to being somewhat startled (though in no way offended) by the idea. The very fine male ensemble Cantus has recorded the work with this voicing (see Additional References and Resources) to excellent effect.

Musical Elements and Technical Considerations

An effective and moving performance of this piece will depend upon the choir's ability to sustain the intensity of extended lines at quiet dynamic levels while maintaining sensitive balance and exquisite intonation. Singers will need to be frequently reminded that singing quietly requires the constant application of great energy. On an effort scale of one to ten, soft singing rates at a full ten, whereas *bustagutto* needs only about an eight.

The dynamic level of the piece never exceeds *mezzo piano*. Variety, therefore, is achieved through focused attention to microdynamics. Ranges are quite modest for all parts except the heroic second altos—a solid low F is required of them. Wheaties™ should be served prior to all rehearsals. First sopranos get only one note above the staff, a mere G, but are required to sit for an entire whole note on top-line F, completely alone, and at a dynamic marking of *pianissimo*. Urge restraint and delicacy upon them at this point, for it may not occur to them otherwise.

Take care not to permit the singers to widen minor seconds. Remind them that the resolution (which always follows—that's just the sort of composer I am) will be all the sweeter if the discord has an edge to it. Under no circumstances should singers be permitted to slide into notes. If necessary, have them mark their scores "*non scoopando*" as a reminder.

In measures 20 and 21, the word "tir'd" ("tired") is spread across two pitches for the first sopranos and they will want to change the vowel at the point where the pitch changes. That's fine, but be sure that all the other singers do the same thing at the same time, even though their pitches do not change.

The suggested tempo (half note equals ca. 54) may be interpreted with some latitude, particularly in response to the acoustics of the performance space. A dry room may demand something a bit quicker. A reverberant space, by contrast, may invite you to linger at certain points. By all means feel free to do so, but do remain aware of the possibility that you might be allowing things to grind gradually slower and slower until focus and intensity are lost. You'll know when this has happened by the glazed looks in your singers' eyes and the barely muffled snores from the audience.

Stylistic Considerations

The warm harmonies may tempt some of your singers toward a pop style of vocalization, with its characteristic mannerisms, inflections, ornaments, and excesses. However, this piece was actually conceived with the sound of an English boy choir in mind. Strive, therefore, for purity of tone, carefully matched vowels and an effortless manner that conceals all the hard work, discipline, dire threats, and histrionics required to bring it about.

Form and Structure

At a total length of only forty measures, form obviously plays a very minor role in the effectiveness of this piece. Nevertheless, you might say that it follows an arch structure, with the apex at the fermata of measure 25. Don't let this distract you—the piece is through composed and depends far more on sensitivity to the text than to any formal considerations. This is a restful little gazebo for the soul, not the Taj Mahal.

Text and Translation

The poem "Song of the Lotos-Eaters" is by Alfred, Lord Tennyson (1809–1892) and is currently in the public domain. Only the first eleven lines are used in this setting.

There is sweet music here that softer falls
Than petals from blown roses on the grass,
Or night-dews on still waters between walls
Of shadowy granite, in a gleaming pass;
Music that gentlier on the spirit lies,
Than tired eyelids upon tired eyes;
Music that brings sweet sleep down from the blissful skies.
Here are cool mosses deep,
And thro' the moss the ivies creep,
And in the stream the long-leaved flowers weep,
And from the craggy ledge the poppy hangs in sleep.

Additional References and Suggested Resources

While You Are Alive (2008). Cantus. CD or MP3 download available on their Web site: http://www.cantusonline.org.

Other than the above recording, I did not consult anyone. All blame for inaccuracies of fact and the general lack of respect for musicological niceties remains my own.

Contributed by:

Daniel Gawthrop

Teacher Resource Guide

Come Sing to Me of Heaven

arr. J. Aaron McDermid

TTBB
Mark Foster: MF1502
Overall: 4
Vocal: 4
Tonal/Rhythm: 3

Arranger

J. Aaron McDermid is Director of Choral Activities at Jamestown College in Jamestown, North Dakota. His appointment at the university includes conducting the Concert and Chapel Choirs, and teaching applied voice and conducting. McDermid has held the posts of Conductor and Artistic Director of the Tucson Masterworks Chorale, Assistant Conductor of the University of Michigan Men's Glee Club, and Director of Choral Activities at Northfield High School in Minnesota.

The American Choral Director's Association of Minnesota named him Outstanding Young Choral Conductor in 1999. His compositions have been performed at ACDA Division and National Conventions, in addition to All-State Choirs, and international honor choirs in Germany and Australia. He is the Artistic Director and member of the professional *a cappella* male vocal ensemble *Chanson* and is an active clinician, guest conductor, and tenor soloist. McDermid has earned degrees in Music Education and Choral Conducting from Concordia College in Moorhead, Minnesota and the University of Michigan, and is finishing a doctorate in Choral Conducting at the University of Arizona.

Composition, Genre, and Historical Perspective

The folk hymn tune, "Sing to Me of Heaven" was presented to McDermid in July of 1995 by a friend whose mother was dying of cancer; his friend wanted that text sung at his mother's funeral. McDermid composed a TTBB setting and it was sung to the ailing woman in August, three weeks prior to her passing.

The arrangement is a setting of the hymn tune "Sing to Me of Heaven," found in *The Sacred Harp*: in the *Denson Revision of the Sacred Harp* (1966). John Massengale is credited as having composed the tune between the years 1860 and 1869. Mrs. Mary Staney Bunce Schindler, formerly, Mrs. Dana, wrote the hymn in 1840 on the occasion of the death of a pious friend.

Musical Elements and Technical Considerations

"Come Sing to Me of Heaven" is a lyric and beautiful arrangement of a folk hymn that calls music to act as the bridge between mortal and immortal life. Verses 1 and 2 (mm. 1–32) maintain a steady 3/4 meter that seems to suggest the earthly dwelling place. It is during the transition (mm. 33–43) that the meter is constantly in flux, passing through 4/4 (2 measures), 3/4 (1 measure), 2/4 (1 measure), 4/4 (4 measures), 3/4 (2 measures), 4/4 (1 measure), before arriving at the Maestoso 3/4. McDermid repeats the text ("come sing to me of heaven") over seven times during this transition with a variety of underlying rhythms, it is these ever changing meters and changing rhythmic accents of the text that suggest the turbulent yet beautiful crossing over of the soul into heaven. The Maestoso marking at measure 43 is the arrival into heaven, the first verse text is repeated but is altered by adding one beat to measures 45 and 53. The 4/4 bars draw out the beginning of the phrase, and when combined with the full texture fortissimo of all parts singing on text, it is the musical greeting in heaven. The verse plays out with contentment and calm release, ultimately ending on a very peaceful flat-VII to ⇨I (Picardy) cadence.

Though the arrangement is beautiful there are a host of difficulties a choir will need to overcome to portray the beauty within. The opening unison passes through the chest and head registers in measures 5 to 6, using a lighter approach with a softer volume while passing from the C-sharp to E will facilitate a smooth transition between the registers.

When the texture passes from 2 parts back to unison in measure 14 the choir will need to be sensitive to the force of sound they produce; since there are more singers singing the unison it is easy to overpower the piano dynamic marking, care should be taken to listen for and control the dynamic level.

Verse 2 begins with a Tenor 2 soloist and the choir accompanying on the [oo] vowel in measures 17 to 32. It is imperative that the Tenor 1, Baritone, and Bass maintain a legato connection through the phrase until the breath markings. Common mistakes are rearticulating the [oo] with a percussive glottal stop or aspiration; interrupting the flow of the musical phrase will distract the listener away from the melody. Another common mistake is to not phrase the musical movement of the accompaniment figures. I suggest musicians marking their scores where the climax point of the phrase is with an asterisk, or other meaningful marking, and then filling in the appropriate crescendos and decrescendos to support the buildup and then repose of the phrase.

Difficulty in tuning may happen at measure 45 as a result of the ambiguous harmony in the transition in measures 37 through 42, a pedal tone on E destabilizes the harmonic structure, which has been hovering around D major. Although the cadence at measure 43 arrives in D major, it is weakened by the baritones as they move up a whole step, which changes the tonality to a first inversion B minor chord, this ambiguity in tonality creates difficulty in locating the A major chord at measure 45. The isolation of measure 42, beat 4, through measure 45, beat 2, may be necessary to tune this transition.

Tuning issues are prevalent from measure 57 to the end due to the use of seventh chords and dissonances. This is especially true at measure 59, beat 3: after a 4-beat rest the Baritone on B and Tenor 1 on A enter on the interval of a minor 7th over an incomplete second inversion Bmm^7. There is a similar entrance at measure 61, the Bass B against the Tenor 2 A, and Tenor 1 C-sharp minor 7th and major 9th, respectively. In this situation it may be useful to approach the tuning as a root position F-sharp minor chord with a non-harmonic B in the bass, ascending stepwise to the harmonic tone C-sharp.

The pronunciation of the contraction "heav'n" used throughout the piece will present difficulty to some less experienced singers. There are three treatments of the contraction, off the beat release, on the beat release, and the elision of the consonants to the following word sound. In all instances, it is beneficial to put the syllabic stress on the penultimate syllable. This is particularly helpful for creating a legato transition at measure 39, beat 3, as the absence of breath marks requires the "-v'n" to elide to the following word "come" creating the consonant cluster "-v'nk."

Form and Structure

SECTION	MEASURE	PHRASE	EVENT AND SCORING
Verse 1	mm. 1–8	(4+4)	Unison
	mm. 9–16	(4+4)	2 parts, unison, 4 parts at
cadence			
Verse 2	mm. 17–24	(4+4)	Tenor 2 solo, choral "oo" accomp
	mm. 25–32	(4+4)	Tenor 2 solo, choral "oo" accomp
Transition	mm. 33–43	(5+5+2)	Meter fluctuations, passes through a variety of meter signatures

Section	Measure	Phrase	Event and Scoring
Verse 1	mm. 44–51	(4+4)	Melody in Tenor 2 other sections sing mostly homo-rhythmically
	mm. 52–56	(4)	Melody in Tenor 2 other sections sing mostly homo-rhythmically
	mm. 57–65	(4+2+2)	Phrase extension, Ending

Text:
Come sing to me of heav'n,
When I am called to die.
Sing songs of holy ecstasy
To waft my soul on high.

When the last moment comes
Let one sweet song begin.
Let music cheer me last on earth;
To greet me first in heav'n.

Additional References and Resources

Horn, Dorothy. *Sing to Me of Heaven*. Gainesville, FL: University of Florida Press, 1970.

White, B. F. *Original Sacred Harp (Denson Revision)*. Cullman, AL: Sacred Harp Publishing, 1966.

White, B. F. *The Sacred Harp*. Facsimile of 3rd ed. Nashville, TN: Broadman Press, 1968.

Web sites:

The Tucson Masterworks Chorale Notes: www.tucsonchorale.org/newslettermarch.pdf (accessed June 20, 2008)

Jamestown College Concert Choir: www.jc.edu/users/mleidhol/choir/director.htm (accessed August 20, 2008)

Contributed by:

Christopher S. Owen

Teacher Resource Guide

Credo

Giovanni Battista Martini
(1686–1786)

TTB
Hinshaw Music: HMC2059
Overall: 4
Vocal: 4
Tonal/Rhythm: 3

Composer

Giovanni Battista Martini (1706–1784) was one of 18th-century Italy's most celebrated composers and pedagogues. An ordained priest, he spent almost his entire career in his native Bologna, where in 1725 he was appointed maestro di cappella of the Franciscan church at the age of nineteen.

Throughout his long life, Martini was avidly devoted to all aspects of his art. He amassed a personal music library that is estimated at 17,000 volumes, collected 300 portraits of the most prominent musicians of his day and of the past, and undertook a comprehensive history of music, titled *Storia della musica*, managing to get only as far as the medieval period by the fourth incomplete volume. Martini was well connected in the music world and corresponded enthusiastically with the leading musical figures of his time. He was also one of the few Italian composers at the time fortunate enough to become acquainted with the music of J. S. Bach.

We don't hear much of Martini's music today, with the possible exception of a setting of "Domine, ad adjuvandum me festina," a perennial favorite. He is probably best remembered today for the many composers he mentored. At least sixty-nine composers could claim Martini as their teacher, including

Jommelli, J. C. Bach, and most famously, Wolfgang Amadeus Mozart, who once wrote of his teacher, "I never cease to grieve that I am far away from that one person in the world whom I love, revere and esteem most of all."

Martini's sacred choral music is appealing, well crafted, and certainly worth a second look by any conductor hoping to find music that is musically gratifying and that can be performed well by a volunteer ensemble without a huge investment of precious rehearsal time.

Composition, Genre, and Historical Perspective

It will not surprise you to learn that Martini, having spent over five decades as a chapel master for the Roman Catholic Church, composed a large number of mass settings—approximately thirty-two. He also composed several settings of individual sections of the Ordinary of the Mass including two Kyries, three Glorias, and twelve Credo settings.

The Ordinary of the Mass refers to those portions of the Mass liturgy that do not change with the liturgical calendar: Kyrie, Gloria, Credo, Sanctus/ Benedictus, and Agnus Dei. The Credo is the longest text of the Ordinary, a statement of the central tenets of the Christian faith based on the Creed approved by the Council of Nicea in the year CE 325.

We do not know when this Credo setting, unpublished during Martini's lifetime, was composed, although certain stylistic features point toward a date on the early side of his overall output. Martin Banner's new edition is based on a hand-copied score and set of instrumental parts found in Bologna's Civico Museo Bibliografico Musicale.

Musical Elements and Technical Considerations

This particular Credo setting draws more from the contrapuntal style of Baroque church music than the more transparent homophonic style that became popular as Martini grew older. Nevertheless, a "modern" expressive sensibility is detectable in the variety of the melodic language and in the range of textures. These are the two primary elements—melodic variety and textural variety—that will allow the piece to come across as vital and engaging to an audience.

Because of its general wordiness, the Credo often presents a particular challenge for composers and performers. Martini chooses a common solution by dividing the text into four individual movements ("Patrem omnipotentem," "Et incarnatus," "Crucifixus," and "Et resurrexit"), allowing for built-in variety of tempo and key.

The first movement, composed over a perpetually moving bass line, is imitative in texture, moving freely between solo, duet, and trio writing.

Particularly expressive are the closing measures, which describe the descent of the Son from heaven in the use of a chain of descending suspensions in the upper two voices. For liturgical reasons, the chant setting of the first line ("Credo in unum Deum") would have been intoned by the celebrant before the beginning of the polyphonic setting on the words "Patrem omnipotentem." You will probably want to assign this short, *a cappella* chant line to a soloist from within your group.

The second movement, a concise eight measures, provides a stark, homophonic contrast to the first. The text here describes the transformation of God into man, and the music is a somber Adagio in minor mode. The third movement consists of the two lines of the Credo that describe the crucifixion and burial of Christ. It may seem surprising to a 21st-century listener to find that Martini has chosen to set this portion of the text as a gentle and tuneful duet in F major, but such a setting would not have seemed unusual to Martini's audience. The final movement returns to the key, tempo, and overall texture of the opening movement, and after a brief Adagio excursion to the parallel minor during the description of the coming day of judgment, offers up the expected fugue on the text "and the life of the world to come."

Martini indicates *Tempo Giusto* for the first and last movements. Literally, "just time," this term was sometimes used to indicate a return to strict tempo after a freer passage but in this context refers to the abstract concept of an ideal tempo—not too fast, not too slow.

Vocal ranges are within the expected limits, but might extend a bit beyond the comfort zone of some adolescent men: Tenor 1: (D)G to G1; Tenor 2: (C)E to F1; Baritone: G to C(E-flat). The tonal language should not present great challenges, however, even for less experienced singers. Chromaticism is minimal and modulations are limited for the most part to the expected dominant, subdominant, and relative minor and major key areas.

Stylistic Considerations

There are plenty of choices to be made here.

First of all, how large a choir? Martini would have probably expected solo voices or only a few singers to a part, but as with most questions of historical authenticity, the choice of performing forces is not purely objective. Martini might have been delighted to hear a piece like this performed by a much larger choir, particularly a group that is able to sing in tune and with a good sense of style.

What constitutes good style in a piece of 18th-century Italian sacred choral music? That's a big question with many answers, but a few guidelines go a long way:

1) Never allow an inattentive sameness to creep into the performance. Pay close attention to the construction of each individual line. What does the shape of the melody suggest about how it should be sung? Can the notes in a long phrase be grouped into smaller units, and if so, how can you help the audience to hear those smaller groupings? When you analyze each individual melodic line, do you see opportunities for variety in articulation? Finally, how does each vocal line interact with the others? Martini writes some wonderfully dissonant suspensions and you will want to make sure that these come across to the listener.

2) No dynamic indications appeared in the original manuscript and the editor's suggested dynamic markings are appropriately minimal. But considerable dynamic variation, always using the text and the musical material as your guide, is absolutely necessary for an effective performance.

3) A careful, elegant, and varied declamation of the text, with proper accentuation and attention to meaning, is paramount. Italian pronunciation of the Latin text is appropriate, which is good news. The pure, unchanging vowels are conducive to good vocal production and ensemble unity.

4) Vocal tone should be clear, pure, and vibrant. While it is not necessary (perhaps even inadvisable) to sing without vibrato, it should be recognized that Martini was composing well before the norms of modern vocal production, as we understand them, were established. Vibrato was considered an embellishment, not a constant. It is also worth noting that the job of keeping contrapuntal textures clear is made much more difficult when vibrato is excessive.

5) Ornamentation is certainly an option, but it is likely that Martini did not expect much of it in this work. Simple cadential trills at the end of major sections (for example, Tenor 1, measure 39, beat 4 in the first movement) would be the sort of thing you might want to consider adding, and your decision should also depend on the size of the ensemble. The more singers you have, the less effective an ornament is likely to sound.

If you want to do some further reading on 18th-century performance practice as you prepare to conduct this piece, you are in luck. Several of the most important (and easy to find) treatises of the day were written by musicians that Martini knew well, including Agricola, Rameau, and Quantz. A couple of good starting points are recommended below.

One further note on voices: the editor of this edition has suggested the use of solo voices in the third movement. While this is not indicated in the original manuscript, it seems like a good suggestion, because it creates both variety and contrast between this movement and the other three. Could one consider using solo voices, or reduced forces, in other sections for similar reasons? Absolutely. The Adagio section of the final movement comes to mind as one possibility.

Finally, you have several options to consider in terms of accompanying forces. The vocal score provides a keyboard reduction of the orchestral material, and either piano or organ would be perfectly fine in a modern performance. Martini composed the piece for an ensemble of strings, horns, and continuo, and if you have access to instrumentalists, they would provide a great enhancement to your performance (well-prepared instrumental parts, including a realized continuo part, are available from the publisher). A large ensemble of players would not be necessary—even one to a part would be appropriate, depending on the size of your choir. Intermediate to advanced high-school players should be able to deliver a good performance. If you don't have a lot of experience conducting instrumentalists, do yourself a favor and go over the score with an experienced string player.

Form and Structure

I. Patrem omnipotentem (TTB)

Tempo Giusto

m. 1--------------9----------------------------25----------------------38------------|

4 + 4   4 + 4 + 4 + 4   3 + 3 + 3 + 4   2 + 2

Key: C (G) C (G) (a) C (G) C (G) C (a) C

2. Et incarnatus est (TTB)

Adagio

m. 1-----------------|

4 + 4

Key: a (d) a

3. Crucifixus (TT)

Largo andante

m. 1-----------**7**-----------**15**------------------**26**-----------

4 + 2 4 + 4 2 + 3 + 6 4 + 2

Key: F (C) F (C) (B⊠) F

m. 32-----------**39**------------------**50**--------------------------|

3 + 4 2 + 3 + 6 2 + 6 + 4 + 5

Key: F (B) F (B) F

4. Et resurrexit (TTB)

Tempo Giusto

m. 1------------------------------

6 + 6 + 7

Key: C (G) C (a) F C

Adagio

m. 20------------------------------

2 + 3 + 2 + 3

c (G) c (G) c

Primo Tempo

m. 30------------------------------**50**----------------------

5 + 4 + 6 + 5 3 + 5 + 6

C (G) C (a) C (e) (G) (a) C (G) C

(fugue)

64-----------**72**------------------------------**85**--------------------------|

3 + 5 2 + 3 + 4 + 4 2 + 4 + 4 + 2 + 1

C (G)C(G)C (G) (a) (e) C (G) C

exposition *middle entries* *recapitulation* *cadential material*

Text and Translations

[I believe in one God], the Father Almighty,
Maker of heaven and earth,
and of all things visible and invisible.

And in one Lord, Jesus Christ the
only-begotten Son of God.
Born of the Father before all ages.

God of God, Light of Light,
True God of True God.
Begotten, not made,
of one substance with the Father,
By whom all things were made.

Who for us men
and for our salvation came
down from heaven.
And became incarnate by the
Holy Spirit of the Virgin Mary:
and was made man.

He was also crucified for us,
suffered under Pontius Pilate,
and was buried.
And on the third day He rose again
according to the Scriptures.
He ascended into heaven and
sits at the right hand of the Father.
He will come again in glory
to judge the living and the dead and;
his kingdom will have no end.

And in the Holy Spirit,
the Lord and Giver of life,
Who proceeds from the Father and the Son.
Who together with the Father
and the Son is adored and glorified,
and who spoke through the prophets.

And in one holy, Catholic and
Apostolic Church.
I confess one baptism
for the forgiveness of sins.
And I await the resurrection of the dead
And the life of the world to come. Amen.

Bibliography

Agricola, Johann Friedrich. *Introduction to the Art of Singing*. Julianne Baird, trans. New York: Cambridge University Press. 1995.

Jeffers, Ron. *Translations and Annotations of Choral Repertoire, Vol. 1: Sacred Latin Texts*. Corvallis, OR: Earthsongs. 1988.

Neumann, Frederick. *Performance Practices of the Seventeenth and Eighteenth Centuries*. New York: Schirmer Books. 1993.

Quantz, Johann Joachim. *On Playing the Flute*. Edward R. Reilly, trans. New York: Schirmer Books. 1985.

Contributed by:

Jeffrey Douma

Teacher Resource Guide

Crucifixus

Antonio Lotti

(1667–1740)

arr. Archibald T. Davison

TTBB
E. C. Schirmer: 42
Overall: 4
Vocal: 4
Tonal/Rhythm: 4

Composer

Antonio Lotti was born in 1667, most likely in Hannover where his father served as *Kapellmeister*. By 1683 he was living in Venice, studying with Legrenzi, then singing at St. Mark's Cathedral. He rose through the ranks as an organist and became *maestro di cappella* in 1736. In addition to his work at St. Mark's, Lotti composed many sacred and secular vocal pieces for the Ospedale degli Incurabili, an orphanage for girls that was renowned for the singing style of its choir, attributed to Lotti's work there.

Lotti spent the years 1717 to 1719 in Dresden, composing three operas and many sacrd choral works with instruments, including the *Credo in F*. While in Dresden, Handel admired Lotti's work and scholars have noted the influence. Lotti returned to Venice in 1719.

Lotti also composed secular cantatas, oratorios, and some instrumental pieces aside from his significant offerings to the church: masses, mass movements, and other pieces of the liturgy proper. He was among the first to enroll at the formation of a musicians guild, the *Sovvegno di musicisti di Santa Cecilia*. He died in Venice in 1740.

Composition, Genre, and Historical Perspective

"Crucifixus" is a portion of the Credo from the Mass ordinary, which is often set to music apart from the larger liturgy. Ben Byram-Wigfield has asserted that Lotti composed an eight-voice setting of the Credo, from which this piece is drawn, while in Dresden.[1] Composing music for an isolated movement of the Mass was not unusual—like Antonio Vivaldi's *Gloria*, to name a famous and contemporary example. However, this *a cappella* piece differs stylistically from the Vivaldi example: Lotti employed an older, Renaissance style of polyphony with only hints of the more advanced Baroque chromaticism.

In the 1920s, Archibald T. Davison made an arrangement for men's voices in four parts, in accordance with the fashion of that era for the glee club. Of course he sacrificed some continuity of line and extent of range, but the overall effect of Lotti's original is surprisingly well preserved through careful attention to voice doubling and clever adjustment of the text prosody. This arrangement remains a staple of the Men's Chorus repertoire.

Musical Elements and Technical Considerations

"Crucifixus" opens in C minor and closes in C major; the key signature of one flat refers to F major key of the *Credo* from which this segment is excerpted. The translation of Lotti's opening gesture from eight sequential entrances, each to a higher pitch, into four gestures—bass, baritone, tenor 2, tenor 1—then starting over with the lowest voice for a second series of entrances, posed few difficulties for the shift to men's voices. Faithful performance will require careful adjustments to elicit the effect of all eight entrances—in particular, the fifth through seventh statements in the lower voices should not be covered.

Lotti's pattern places dissonance on the strong beats and then resolves the lower voice downward on a weak beat. In conjunction with the syncopation of the head motive, Lotti paints the "cross" of the text, a device for which he was well known and which joins the tradition of many composers in the setting of this pivotal text in the Christian creed.

After each voice has completed the opening statement, Lotti writes in a more homophonic, chordal style, grouping two or three voices together. Davison's compromises become more evident as he fits the harmony and imitative entrances into four voices. He maintains Lotti's idea of imitation and homophony, though the polychoral effect is diminished. In this section also, attention to dissonance is the key to successful rehearsal and interpretation. Young singers often balk at this. Have the singers circle the notes that are dissonant with another part, and rehearse those passages in order to produce a "leaning in" to the conflict, rather than the natural avoidance, which leads to singing out of tune.

1 http://www.ancientgroove.co.uk/lotti/index.html, accessed 1 August 2008

The section that begins with the text "sub Pontio Pilato" at measure 18 places the onus of dissonance on a single voice, the one singing "Passus" on half notes. Davison marks this part *espressivo*. While the term can mean many things in various contexts, here he is certainly guarding against the tendency to sing long notes statically. In order to secure and highlight the expressive nature of the phrase, singers must vocally lean into the last part of the longer note, often by a small crescendo across a barline. The conductor will not be able to direct from the podium every nuance required in this contrapuntal texture; informed singers make the effect possible.

The second phrase of this section, beginning with measure 27, marks a change in the texture and requires a shift in the singers' approach to harmony. While the two inner voices continue the chain of suspensions, the outer voices begin a more Baroque or even Classical pattern of harmonic progression. Basses, especially, must ground the sequence with precise fifths and fourths instead of the conjunct motion of the preceding pages. The arrival at an F minor chord in measure 30 is significant, but it does not feel decisive. Indeed, the fully diminished chord that follows propels the movement forward again. Most conductors include a sizeable lift, adding time at the textual comma before "et sepultus." This marks not only the changing harmony, but also a change to homophony, which closes the piece.

Another lift in measure 32 would not out of order; rather, it might provide a sense of culmination following the intensity of the preceding section. In his arrangement for four voices, Davison omitted, in measure 33, an F sharp that Lotti had included in order to make a dominant progression toward G major. Without the establishment of G major—the dominant of our home key—the final progression to C becomes muddled. Lotti's advanced chromatic harmonies again paint the crossing idea of the crucifixion and the final bars are particularly perilous in the reduced texture without the voice doublings Lotti provided to secure it.

Baritones must carefully navigate the F-natural/F-sharp dilemma from measures 32 to 35. Measure 38 requires them to ascend a diminished fourth, leaping into a tritone against the second tenors. Second tenors will surely need regular repetition of the augmented chord they arpeggiate in measures 38 and 39. A pedal point to anchor the passage is surely wise. Here it appears in the voice of the first tenors, rather than in the basses as we might expect. Indeed, first tenors must be depended on to guide the choir through some treacherous harmonic shifts.

Note, finally, that the piano reduction is missing some accidentals in measure 23.

Stylistic Considerations

Despite the late Baroque provenance and early Classic harmony of the "Crucifixus," Lotti's unaccompanied piece can be effectively approached in the style of a Renaissance motet. The imitative entrances yield an equality of voices characteristic of the earlier period. This counterpoint derives from a "horizontal" compositional technique, focusing on the individual line through most of the piece, rather than the "vertical" sonority, which comes about almost incidentally.

As in Renaissance music, singing with minimal vibrato will allow the composed dissonances to have their full effect. The printed dynamic markings in Davison's arrangement are likely editorial, but they highlight well the harmonic tension, Lotti's main compositional device.

Singing in the key of C is notoriously difficult for *a cappella* singers to tune. If your choir can spare a half step at either end of the range—taking first tenors up to A-flat or basses down to E—the modern keys of B or C-sharp may prove to steady the choir on pitch. The vagaries of absolute pitch in the Baroque period support such an amendment.

Form and Structure

Measure	Event and Scoring
mm. 1–11	a single musical gesture
mm. 12–17	2 phrases (3+3)
mm. 18–30	2 phrases (10+3)
mm. 31–41	3 phrases (2+5+4)

Text and Translation

Latin:
Crucifixus etiam pro nobis sub Pontio Pilato,
passus, et sepultus est.

English:
Crucified also for us under Pontius Pilate,
he suffered, and was buried.

Additional References and Resources

http://www.ancientgroove.co.uk/lotti/index.html

Contributed by:

Andrew Crow

Teacher Resource Guide

Four Cummings Choruses, Opus 98

Vincent Persichetti

(1915–1987)

TB (or SA)/piano
Theodore Presser: 5290697
Overall: 4
Vocal: 3
Tonal/Rhythm: 4

Composer

Vincent Persichetti may be the finest American composer you have never heard of. Born in Philadelphia June 6, 1915, he died in the same city August 14, 1987. He was enrolled at Combs Conservatory in Philadelphia from the age of 5 until earning a bachelor's degree in 1935. Later, he lamented in earnest that his parents let him get such a late start! Persichetti taught at Combs while earning masters and doctoral degrees at the Philadelphia Conservatory, studying piano and composition. He also studied conducting at the Curtis Institute. He served on the faculty of the Julliard School from 1947 and eventually chaired the composition department. He worked in publishing for Elkan-Vogel, and received many awards, honors, and fellowships for his role as composer and as teacher.

When his compositional style reached a distinctive maturity, Persichetti exhibited fluent handling of the many facets of the twentieth century's musical vocabulary. Often his works seem playful, exhibiting the joy of making music.

Persichetti wrote with equal dexterity and interest for children, amateurs, and virtuosi. His piano compositions cover a wide range of possibilities for the instrument. He is little known in the world of choral musicians and vocal soloists, where, again, his oeuvre include appropriate examples for all skill-levels. His music for winds is more frequently performed, owing probably to the smaller core of repertoire for winds and the propensity of those players for modern music. The *Symphony No. 6* for wind ensemble has a cherished place in the canon, and Persichetti's versatility in that medium is reflected in *Celebrations* for chorus and wind ensemble on text by Walt Whitman.

Composition, Genre, and Historical Perspective

Persichetti's *Four Cummings Choruses*, Opus 98, could be called a secular cycle, unified by poet, textual theme, and harmonic contiguity. He composed the set in 1964, approximately in the middle of his career. Considered a mature composer by 1950, Persichetti did not noticeably change his compositional style as time elapsed; rather, he masterfully adapted his compositional language to the medium or text at hand. He turned to American poet e.e. cummings on several occasions throughout his career, and the style of each setting is similar. There are two other opuses called *Cummings Choruses*, plus a set of five cummings poems called *Glad and Very* and a late set called *Flower Songs*. Other choral works stand in stylistic contrast, notably his *a cappella Mass* from 1960.

Walter Simmons stated it succinctly—

> Persichetti's prodigious musical output exemplifies a principle that was also fundamental to his teaching and theoretical writing: the integration into a fluent working vocabulary of the wealth of materials placed at a composer's disposal by the expansion of musical language over the course of the 20th century. Drawing on a wide range of expressive possibilities, from simple diatonicism to complex atonal polyphony, Persichetti produced an array of works whose varied moods, styles and levels of difficulty bewildered those who sought an easily identifiable musical personality or a conventional chronological pattern of development.[1]

In later compositions, Persichetti often quoted or borrowed from his own works across genres, which had a unifying effect on his diverse body of work.

Musical Elements and Technical Considerations

At the bright tempi specified by the composer, Opus 98 is a set of miniatures lasting less than seven minutes altogether. Persichetti designated performance by two choral voices, which can be Soprano/Alto, Tenor/Bass, Men/Women, or any other combination. The poet's masculine voice, or perhaps the

1 Simmons, Walter G. "Persichetti, Vincent." *Grove Music Online*. Accessed 27 August 2008.

frequent necessity for reduced voicing may lead more often to a male chorus performance, but any options will work well. For a terrific section-building exercise and even a bit of healthy competition, divide the set, assigning one piece to each vocal section or two pieces to the women and two to the men.

Perhaps the first requirement for successful performance of Persichetti's Opus 98 is a first-rate pianist (who is not the conductor), to be introduced into the rehearsal process well in advance of the performance. The composer was himself a keyboard virtuoso and these accompaniments present a formidable challenge, fleet fingers atop a list including incisive rhythmic accuracy and sudden, wide dynamic contrast.

By comparison, the vocal parts are very approachable: moderate range, text in English, highly memorable, not to mention fun. The division into two-part harmony with many passages in unison or exact imitation makes for safety in numbers and provides superb pedagogical opportunities. The best approach will include many rounds of efficient repetition. Be prepared for perplexed expressions initially; they will soon yield to pleasant accounts of renditions from the morning shower and "I sang it in my head the whole weekend."

In fact, these pieces present challenges where young singers need most to be challenged: rhythm, independence from accompaniment, and modal or nonfunctional yet diatonic melodies. Persichetti's musical arrivals are intuitive, but his method of quasi-modal progression bends the tonal ear in healthy and useful ways. Singers should note in the score—with a pencil—where they sing in unison or octaves with the other part and also points of imitation. Teach the pieces in short fragments rather than long passages and do not move on until pitches and especially rhythms are precise; sometimes this will mean teaching only three or four notes at a time, then adding a note to the beginning of that motive, then another, and so on.

Some specific suggestions:
"dominic has a doll"

- Begin under tempo, but not so slowly that the edginess is gone.
- Give specific placement, length and character to ending consonants, placing the hard [k] of "dominic" cleanly and forcefully on beat two of bar 5 and every time thereafter. This rhythmic motive unifies the setting.
- Give the same attention and force to the [d] ending of "wired" in bar 7.
- Have the singers perform a physical gesture, like snapping or tapping, on the beats when they sing syncopation, such as on the downbeat of bars 10 and 12.
- Insist on the dynamic contrasts printed, from bar 21 to 22, for example.

- Bar 26, see notes above for singing "dominic" and incorporating syncopation.
- The piano interlude makes an important harmonic connection between the principal pitches of the whole set (G–C, A–D), but the choral re-entry at bar 53 will require some rhythmic acumen from the singers so as not to enter early.
- The sequence of pitches in bars 56 to 60 is an excellent example of the need to isolate individual intervals, removed from rhythm but tied to their text. Start with bar 56, then add the pickup, then advance one more pitch, then one more, and so on.
- The ending chords are rare incidents of four-part harmony. To engender good intonation, rehearse at a comfortable dynamic and move to a comfortable octave first, then add one element at a time until performing as written.
- Notice instances where the piano will help the singers (like at the very end) and where it will confuse them (bars 41 to 46).
- Notice also where the piano range may be more conducive to only the men's or only the women's voices.

"nouns to nouns"

- This is probably the most difficult of the four pieces to put together, but the easiest to pull apart, so start by pulling it apart. Sectional work is best, if possible.
- It is easy to lose the beat in this piece; have each singer make a physical connection to the beat throughout. Note that the final prescription is for one beat to the bar, but begin slow enough to beat each quarter note.
- Note imitation at a fifth in bar 40.
- The eighth rest in bar 44 can be terrifically maddening, but worth pursuing.
- Notice parallels between the first and second verse with modifications:
    - A whole step up from bar 50 to 51—surprise!
    - Bar 56 parallels bar 20 but the lower voice is a fourth higher and a beat sooner.
    - The piano interludes are also linked but modified and their lengths are inconsistent—beware.

"maggie and milly and molly and may"

- This is probably the easiest of the four, although the unequal bars can surely be a trap for the unwary conductor.
- The lower voice works best with a sing-song air of innocence.
- The ultimate tempo must be decided by the clear enunciation of the final line of text—the poem's moral.

- Beware the three final notes; an accidental solo here spoils the effect.

"uncles"

- This poem must be allowed its raucous idiosyncrasies and humorous punch lines from the opening statement.
- Address the elision between the words "my" and "uncle." A slight glottal stroke will clarify the text. An exaggerated glide may add a humorous, inebriated effect. Careless inattention sounds amateurish.
- Prepare the rhythms ruthlessly before your first rehearsal.
- Starting the chorus in bar 50 can be tricky—rehearse with pianist.
- Note the crescendo molto from bar 98 to 102, all the more since it lies low in the voice.

The tempi prescribed by the composer work very well. Once the chorus gets some mastery of the pieces they might be inclined to push beyond the markings. This is highly dangerous! It's best to arrive at performance tempo in advance of the concert and work to ingrain the tempo along with all the other delicate pitches, rhythms, and interpretive details. These catchy pieces sing well from memory.

cummings employed a few references that are now outdated. In "uncles," some singers might need an explanation for "kewpie," and others may balk at whimsical words in "nouns to nouns" like "untheknowndulous." Several of the most poignant poetic lines leave room for multiple interpretations. Encourage your singers to explore the poems in their original form and prepare a interpretations for discussion. For example, to open a discussion, ask: What do we make of the rest on the downbeat of bar 42 in "dominic has a doll"? Is "nouns to nouns" merely wordplay—more evident in the cummings engraving—or a political or religious statement?

Stylistic Considerations

Because of Persichetti's careful attention to the cummings texts, the pieces must be sung with an attitude of speech. Lyrical moments are few, but should be exaggerated for effect. Likewise, ending consonants are carefully placed and serve to display the punctuation Cummings intended, but did not specifically include.

The composer marked meticulous dynamic instructions; effective performance relies on strict adherence. Young singers may find it difficult initially to break out of their conventional mode of lyric choral singing, but encourage them to let out their inner eccentricities for the sake of the poetry. Brief instances of controlled shouting (the very last line of "uncles" reads fortissimo on "castrated pup") must be established in contrast to barely audible, pianissimo, pitched stage whispers. Persichetti's stylistic instructions are in Italian; be sure of each one's meaning. Find a way to highlight the compositional device of canonic imitation, as it occurs frequently.

Form and Structure

"dominic has a doll" divides into two nearly equal sections, measures 1 through 47 and measures 48 through 91. The first section moves from an emphasis on the open fifth on D and A to the fifth on C and G. Significantly, these four pitches are the focal pitches for all four pieces in the opus. The second half returns to D and finishes there with a piano tag. Clearly, Persichetti is not bound by a classical model for phrasing; his musical ideas are governed by the uneven rhythms of the text he illuminated.

Measure	Event and Scoring
mm. 1–14	2 segments (4+10)
mm. 15–47	3 segments (7+22+4)
mm. 48–66	2 segments (5+14)
mm. 67–91	3 segments (3+21+1)

"nouns to nouns" also divides in two nearly equal sections, ruled by an exact repetition of the short text, plus a coda. However, while there are parallel points between the two halves, Persichetti's variations do not break into specifically equal segments.

Measure	Event and Scoring
mm. 1–45	5 segments (4+9+13+12+7)
mm. 46–81	5 segments (3+6+9+8+10)
mm. 82–92	Coda: 2 segments (4+7)

"maggie and millie and molly and may" divides into sections that correspond to the four girls named in the title.

Section	Measure
All 4 girls	mm. 1–9
maggie	mm. 10–14
millie	mm. 15–22
molly	mm. 23–28
may	mm. 29–39
Moral	mm. 40–46

"uncles" also divides according to the characters described. As in all the examples, the piano introductions and interludes often comprise a significant phrase and musical event.

MEASURE	EVENT AND SCORING
mm. 1–15	3 phrases (5+5+5)
mm. 16–27	2 phrases (4+8)
mm. 28–41	3 phrases (2+6+6)
mm. 42–67	3 phrases (9+11+6)
mm. 68–101	4 phrases (9+13+6+6)
mm. 102–107	Coda

Text and Translation

e.e. cummings (1894–1962) was one of America's preeminent poets in the twentieth century. Born to a Harvard professor, cummings may be remembered by high school students as "the guy who didn't use capital letters," but of course, the merit of his work surpasses such idiosyncrasies with eloquence and profound insights, human and divine. Like Persichetti, cummings used conventional poetic devices (e.g., sonnet form, rhyme) when it suited his desired expression, but created his own distinct voice by the use of consistent personal gestures. Many of these gestures, like arranging his words on the page in pictorial ways, do not translate into a musical setting. Many composers have attempted choral settings of cummings's poetry, but none have met the challenge as successfully as Persichetti, whose gift for irony, timing, contrast, counterpoint, and humor seems well suited for work with this poet. Here Persichetti captured the quirky nature of these childlike poems, full of wordplay and nonsensical ideas mixed with startling observations.

Persichetti selected the poems for Opus 98 from various collections; the grouping is the composer's, not the poet's. Looking at the physical layout of the words on the page can be instructive for interpreting their meaning, and provide insight into Persichetti's decisions about phrase structure. (See Additional References and Resources for information on a source for these poems.)

The first and third poems that Persichetti chose come from 95 *Poems*, 1958. "dominic has a doll" tells of a curious friendship and begins:

dominic has

    a doll wired
    to the radiator of his
    ZOOM DOOM

    icecoalwood truck

"maggie and millie and molly and may" ends with the following moral:

For whatever we lose(like a you or a me)
it's always ourselves we find in the sea

"nouns to nouns" comes from *50 Poems*, 1940, and must be seen to be understood. cummings challenged the integrity of even individual words:

w an d
ering

in sin

g
ular untheknowndulous s

pring

"uncles" is properly titled "my uncle" in a large volume from 1926, called *is 5*. cummings playfully described four eccentrics. Of the first, he wrote:

my uncle
Daniel fought in the civil
war band and can play the triangle
like the devil)

The scores state that copyrights are held by Harcourt, Brace and World, Inc.

Additional References and Resources

Persichetti, Vincent, and Rudy Shackelford. "Conversation with Vincent Persichetti." *Perspectives of New Music.* 20:1/2 (Autumn, 1981–Summer, 1982): pp. 104–133.

Vincent Persichetti Society
http://persichetti.org

Theodor Presser Company
http://www.presser.com/Composers/info.cfm?Name=VINCENTPERSICHETTI

cummings, e.e. *Complete Poems 1904–1962*. George J. Firmage, ed. Liveright Publishing, New York, 1991.

Contributed by:

Andrew Crow

Teacher Resource Guide

Love Never Ending

Aaron Zinter

TTBB
Abingdon Press: 712405720
Overall: 4
Vocal: 4
Tonal/Rhythm: 4

Composer

Aaron Zinter is a composer from Fairmont, Minnesota. He did his undergraduate work at Concordia College in Moorhead, Minnesota where he earned a BA in Music Education. He received a MM in Choral Conducting from Illinois State University in 2001. Zinter is currently the director of choirs at Oak Grove Lutheran High School in Fargo, North Dakota. His compositions and arrangements are published by Abingdon Press. As a singer, Zinter is one of the founding members of the professional male vocal ensemble Chanson.

Composition, Genre, and Historical Perspective

"Love Never Ending" can best be described by the term contemporary anthem. While this term gets used in a myriad of ways by today's choral musicians, it's generally believed to incorporate the following key components: sacred English text and the intention to perform it in a liturgical or ceremonial context. This very well known verse of scripture is used in the context of worship, and is one of the favorite verses selected at weddings. It is certainly plausible to see this anthem used in the liturgical or ceremonial context.

This piece draws on three significant influences in Zinter's career: church music, vast choral experience, and his work with the professional male ensemble Chanson, for which the piece was composed. Much of his other published vocal music can be described as written for worship in contemporary style. This anthem however, is best suited for a skilled male ensemble. "Love Never Ending" is a beautiful choral anthem that is as gripping as it is brief. The great irony is that a piece written about unending love can be so fully stated in twenty-five short bars in just under two minutes. Its beauty and sincerity are appealing to singers of all ages.

Musical Elements and Technical Considerations

There are four significant technical challenges to the successful performance of this piece: (1) extended vocal range, (2) number of voice parts, (3) aleatory section, and (4) contemporary harmonic language. Below, I address each of these challenges in detail and provide suggestions for successful navigation.

Extreme Range

The piece is pitched in D-flat major and Zinter uses the full spectrum available to a male ensemble, from high B-flat in the first tenor to low D-flat in the second bass. The demands on the first tenor are of significant concern. For this piece to work successfully, the ensemble must have two or three tenors who can "float" in head voice or falsetto a high A-flat and hold it for an extended period. This is an excellent opportunity to get your young men singing regularly in their head voice and to work through the passaggio. While this musical challenge will test their courage and create a smile or two in rehearsal, working with singers to help them manage this skill is very important. Here are a few suggestions to help them develop these skills.

1. As a part of your daily warm-up process have your men sing on an [u] at or above high B-flat and lightly sing through the passaggio. Be sure to include your baritones and basses in this exercise. Many young voices will have a noticeable "break" going through the passaggio; this is normal and will improve with practice. Have the singers add weight and strength to the voice as it descends. Keep working with your young men toward a mature head voice sound. As the singers voices become more equipped to manage this exercise, experiment with different vowels.

2. It is possible that you will find that there are a few baritones or even basses who can manage the notes more comfortably than the tenors. Don't be afraid to switch them up when they can help.

3. It only needs to be performed by 3–5 singers. Do not feel obligated to use singers in performance whose voices are not prepared.

Let's address the bass 2 requirements. A low D-flat is employed only once and it is the last note of the piece. The composer commented on this particular note in an e-mail exchange:

> The D[-flat] at the end is so gratifying because the rest of the song dances around almost every other pitch in the bass line until our ears so desperately want to hear the low root... I try to outline the harmonic series vertically when I write music so the upper parts usually don't need to sing very loud. The last chord is evidence of this. When you have a strong bass section, it makes the higher parts easier to hear and sing because of where their overtones lie.

Clearly the last note is very important. However, if you discount the final note, the lowest pitch in this piece is an F. I would suggest that the low D-flat (while wonderful) is not absolutely necessary to a successful performance of this piece. If you have a good bass section that can sing to F easily but do not have a low D-flat, revoice the last chord so that all of basses sing the upper D-flat. I would not let this pitch prevent you from programming this wonderful piece.

Number of Voice Parts

Depending on the abilities of your men, this piece is likely to require a significant group of moderately skilled singers. The piece splits into eight parts at times but also at moments has only four-part writing. This is an ideal piece to use with the men of your top mixed ensemble. The good news is that the piece is short and the extreme divisions are not used throughout. The piece provides a challenge for your skilled men and, because of its appeal to young singers and its brevity, will provide your concert a beautiful and artfully crafted men's choir anthem.

Aleatory Section

In bars 10 and 11, Zinter includes a brief aleatory section. *Aleatory*, meaning music that includes an element of chance, in this context means each performance of this section will sound slightly different. The primary variances in this instance are: the voices that come out of the texture, the speed of the repetition, and the overall length of the multiple repeats. This short introduction to aleatory music will require individual voices to sing with confidence. This issue is not a particularly difficult one to solve.
I would approach these two bars in three steps.

1. First, make sure that everyone knows the passage extremely well. Have them sing it in unison multiple times until even the most insecure singers have complete mastery of the pitches.

2. Divide the vocal section in half and start singers at different intervals. Repeat until every member of the section feels comfortable. As they feel confident divide each of the sections in half again and repeat this process until both you and your singers feel in command of this short section.

3. Beat one of bars 11 and 12 ends with a cluster chord. G-flat, A-flat, and B-flat are required. If artfully balanced this will be one of the truly stunning moments of the piece. It will depend on the number of singers available, but I would make sure that the A-flat chord is cleanly in tune and balanced first. Then after the ensemble can hear the A-flat diad, I would add the G-flat and the B-flat. The "color notes" make this chord really shimmer. This may take time to balance so make sure that the G-flat and B-flat are clear and present but are not over sung.

CONTEMPORARY HARMONIC LANGUAGE

The chosen harmonic language requires singers to hold their parts in close harmonic proximity to the next part. I have never had difficulty getting singers to master this technique *as long as I use solfège as my primary tool for teaching.* If I do not use solfège, this challenge can be a problem that will linger through the performance significantly hindering it. I cannot urge you strongly enough to teach this piece with the help of solfège.

Stylistic Considerations

This piece will require your singers to use an elegant and artful legato throughout. Once the students can sing the work on solfège, I would move to the vowel [u] then to [o] before putting it on the English text. Once the singers get the sound in their ears the key to success will be to not allow the text to interrupt the delicate nature of the music while still communicating the text clearly.

Form and Structure

As you can see from the diagram below the piece has two main sections and is short and uncomplicated in nature.

SECTION	MEASURE	EVENT AND SCORING
A	mm. 1–12	two phrases (4+8); bars 9 and 10 repeated aleatory section
B	mm. 13–20	two phrase (3+4)
A	mm. 21–25	two phrases (2+3)

Text and Translation

Zinter selects a very direct and brief text from a more extended passage. In context, this passage is written by Paul the Apostle to a feuding church in Corinth. Paul uses chapter 13 to explain love and the role that it plays within a faithful people.

I Corinthians 13: 4, 7, 8

> Love is patient,
> Love is kind.
> Love never ends.
> Love, it bears all, believes all, hopes all, endures all.
> Love never ending;
> Love divine.

Contributed by:

Brandon Johnson

Teacher Resource Guide

Ramkali

Ethan Sperry

TTBB
Earthsongs: S–251
Overall: 4
Vocal: 4
Tonal/Rhythm: 4

Composer

Born in New York City, Ethan Sperry began studying conducting at the age of eight, cello at the age of twelve, and singing at the age of eighteen. He earned a bachelor's degree in philosophy from Harvard College and received his master's and doctoral degrees in choral conducting from the University of Southern California. Currently, Sperry is Associate Professor of Music at Miami University in Ohio, where he conducts the Men's Glee Club, Collegiate Chorale, and the Global Rhythms Ensemble, and teaches classes in vocal and choral music and the Music of Russia. He is also the editor of the *Global Rhythms* choral series for earthsongs music and serves as the Vice President of the Intercollegiate Men's Choruses. An enthusiastic cook, Sperry has won awards for his baking and his recipes have been printed in *Bon Appetit* magazine and the Cincinnati Enquirer.

Composition, Genre, and Historical Perspective

earthsongs has already published an excellent introduction to this piece and about Indian ragas in general on the back page of the sheet music for *Ramkali*. To save space, I will not repeat that information here.

When I arrived at Miami University (Ohio) in 2000, the last thing I expected was that I would develop a deep love for Indian music . . . that's not an expected consequence of moving to Ohio. However, Miami is a special University and is home to a great number of unique programs, one of which, Global Rhythms, changed my life.

Global Rhythms was created in 1998 by Srinivas Krishnan, a skilled Indian percussionist and vocalist who is also a Miami alumnus (although his degree is in Paper Science). His goal was to teach people to play Indian music, but his priority was purely the music: he encouraged students to learn the unfamiliar Eastern music using the Western instruments they were already comfortable playing. I will never forget the first time I witnessed two flutes, a cello, a trombone, and a drum kit accompanying Srini on his *tabla* playing Classical Indian ragas. The students had learned everything by ear, and some had even traveled to India to learn more after this first exposure. It was clear they were hooked—and so was I. I approached Srini after the concert and we have been collaborating ever since. He selects the repertoire for the ensemble (which now often numbers over a hundred students, including a full SATB choir) while I do most of the arrangements (and coach students and alumni through the process of producing the rest) and conduct the rehearsals and performances.

Now a number of colleges and universities in America have programs and ensembles in Indian music, but none, as far as I know, have students approach the music using their Western instruments. Most ethnomusicology programs teach students the music of a culture using the traditional instruments of that culture. Because many students have already put years of study into their primary instruments, Global Rhythms' tactic of employing that expertise to learn the music of a new culture makes the new music much more accessible. It also allows us to the play music from a variety of cultures: I find it to be a very elegant form of Fusion Ensemble.

Ramkali follows in the Global Rhythms tradition: it was my first attempt to produce an arrangement of a Classical Indian Raga for a traditional Western chorus, using voices not only to sing the melodic lines, but to replace the percussion and the drone of the *shruti box* as well. It follows the trajectory of a Classical raga: first there is an introduction where the notes of the raga are introduced without rhythm; second a "percussion" section where the rhythmic cycle is introduced with no pitch; and finally a *fasts* section combining the scale and the rhythm. While Classical Indian ragas traditionally incorporate a great deal of improvisation in performance, I wanted to write a purely choral piece without using soloists. My compromise was to write vocal lines similar to what an Indian artist might sing when improvising on this raga.

Stylistic Considerations, Musical Elements, and Technical Considerations

To make this piece sound as Indian as possible, it must have a natural flow as if it is being improvised. It should not sound like a robotic reproduction of complex patterns of rhythms and pitches. One way to emphasize the improvisational feel is to highlight the moving of the melody from voice part to voice part. When a new voice section takes over the melody, the singers should sing as if they are reacting to or answering the previous part. This alternation can be either playful or competitive, but it needs to sound like a conversation, one that is growing in intensity and complexity as it progresses.

This is a difficult piece to learn and to teach for many reasons: its length, its language, the unfamiliar scale of its construction, and the unfamiliar vocal techniques it employs, to name a few. So far, I am encouraged by the number of high school and collegiate choir directors who tell me it is worth the challenge. I have found that it is best to rehearse the main sections of the piece separately; connecting them late in the rehearsal process is not difficult. Below is a list, section by section, of ideas many directors have found useful.

I. The "*Allap*" or Slow Introduction (mm.1-20):
- *earthsongs* has excellent audio instructions available on how to teach overtone singing. It's probably not possible to explain well in writing—forgive me for not attempting this here.
- In the parts labeled "*aeiou*," each individual singer should be changing vowels at random. This should effectively obscure the collective vowel sound so the choir sounds more like the drone of an Indian *shruti box* rather than a choir of voices.
- The essence of this section is to hear the melodic line create dissonances with the drone (G and D) and then resolve them to consonances. *Lean* into the dissonant notes (especially F-sharp, A-flat, and C-sharp) and back away to the Gs and Ds.
- If singers with a melody part use a brighter (but not nasal) "*Ah*" vowel, that will solve many balance problems.
- Make sure the drone parts are constantly refreshing the pitch—it's easy for singers to go flat on sustained notes.
- Take your time at each fermata to re-establish the drone before moving the melody from section to section. This can help prevent flattening, and make staggered breathing easier.
- I wrote this section with the intention of giving each voice part a chance to sing the melody, which can make the piece more interesting for the individual singers; but feel free to save rehearsal time by giving each melodic line to a soloist. You can even have the

choir create the drone and have a soloist improvise (if you know a good Indian vocalist) for the entire section and then begin at measure 21 as written.

II. The Percussion Sections (mm. 21–31 and 82–92):

- Perform these sections aggressively. Make the left and right sides of the choir compete for dominance instead of doing call and response. I used to use the "tastes great, less filling" line (from an old commercial) as an analogy for students, but many of the younger ones don't know what I'm talking about anymore.
- The syllables used are traditional Indian percussion syllables called *sollokattu.* They are like a rhythmic solfège—all Indian drummers learn them—and they not only convey the rhythm, but indicate high and low pitches on the drum through choice of vowels: a = low and strong, i = high and weak, e = middle. I also used capital letters for stressed syllables and lower case for weaker ones. Use those cues, don't let the lines be flat. The pitch of the voices should change as the vowels change.
- The basic Western 4/4 measure is divided into eighth notes as STRONG-weak- STRONG-weak- STRONG-weak- STRONG-weak or SwSwSwSw (i.e., all the off beats are weak). The basic Indian 4/4 rhythm is divided eighth notes as follows: SwwSSwwS. It's an alternation or undulation between stressing 1 and 3 with their pickups and letting 2 and 4 be weak. This is what the syllables "Da-din-din-Da-Da-din-din-Da" represent.
- All weak beats create a crescendo into the next strong beat. In the more complex rhythms, crescendo long strings of unaccented notes into the next accented note.
- Make the singers produce the sounds in the very front of their mouths to make the faster parts clearer. Singers who are not fast with their tongues and teeth can choose to speak only the accented syllables and leave the other ones out.
- Do not try to conduct measures 89 through 91 in 4—it'll take you all day and it's not worth it. Just show the accented notes. I use three 2 patterns in each measure.

III. The "*Tintal*" or Verse (mm. 32–81):

- The rhythm parts must dominate this section. If you cannot hear the percussion behind the melody clearly the piece will slow down and lose energy.

- Have the rhythmic parts vastly exaggerate their consonants, especially the basses or any vocal sections singing low in their range. It will help keep alive the rhythmic engine that drives this section, and many ensembles have found it to be the only way to get the rhythmic parts heard at all.
- Stepping or swaying in rhythm during rehearsal helps many choirs keep the beat and find the rhythmic energy in this piece.
- Try to make the parts that sing syllables sound like tabla, the Indian drums with metal plates in them. They have a distinctive *ping* to them that is best represented by using "*ng*" instead of a vowel. The sound "*Dng*" is a hard d going straight to an ng, it is *not* "ding" or "dung."
- After SwwSSwwS, the next most common Indian 4/4 pattern is SwwSwwSw or Ta-ki-ta Ta-ki-ta Ta-ka. This section is based on alternations between these two rhythms and sometimes even combining the two. The rhythms are not difficult, but by simply calling singers' attention to where the changes are and asking them to emphasize the difference brings this piece to life and makes it more fun for them to sing.
- Optional: To make the piece more rhythmic, the main melody can be sung rhythmically as a SwwSwwSw (hoon tho **vaa**-ri **vaa**-ri **ja**-woon **thu**-muh-re **gu**-sai-yan.

Final Note: Many choirs find this piece easier to sing up a half step or even a whole step. This takes pressure off the basses and if the tenors are young it allows them to use their falsetto more, which is vocally less fatiguing.

Form and Structure

SECTION	MEASURE	EVENT AND SCORING
Introduction or "*allap*"	mm. 1–20	5 phrases (6+3+4+3+4)
First percussion break	mm. 21–31	3 phrases (4+3+3)
Verse or "*Tintal*" Part 1	mm. 32–45	3 phrases (5+5+4)
Tintal Part 2	mm. 46–63	4 phrases [(4+5)+(4+5)]
Tintal Part 3	mm. 64–81	3 phrases (4+8+6)
Second percussion break	mm. 82–92	3 phrases (4+3+4)
Tintal (repeated)	mm. 32–81	

Text and Translation

Hoon tho vari vari jawoon thumuhre gusaiyan	I am entirely devoted to you my lord.
Huhmuhri bath kachu maan pyare	At least heed my plea, my love.
Thumuhre mailnuh ki ahsuh pyare	I hope to be united with you, my love.
Chayan na parat mare pyare	Peace of mind is not mine, my love.

The text used in this piece is centuries old and is attached to a melody often sung in a performance of the raga *Ramkali*. It is an old love poem, but one with two distinct interpretations. The traditional interpretation is more literal and has the narrator expressing his true and undying love and devotion. It is unknown whether his love is requited, so the plea becomes more and more animated and even desperate as he awaits a response from his lover. Another interpretation is one in which the narrator has fallen under the sway of a mythical creature called "*naga*," a siren-like creature with a four-armed female torso and the body of a snake (the word "*gusaiyan*" can refer to a *naga* as well a lord or lover). The lover spins in a circle in a hypnotic trance, getting faster and faster as he cedes more and more of his self-control to the *naga*. Under either interpretation, the growing desperation of the narrator is expressed in the music through the constant repetition of the first few words (Hoon tho vari = I am entirely devoted).

Contributed by:

Ethan Sperry

Teacher Resource Guide

Rustics and Fishermen

Benjamin Britten

(1913–1976)

TTBB/a cappella
Boosey & Hawkes: 4033478
Overall: 4
Vocal: 4
Tonal/Rhythm: 3

Composer

Benjamin Britten was born on November 22—Feast Day of Saint Cecilia, patron saint of musicians—in Lowestoft, Suffolk, in 1913. Britten was a precocious musician who at the age of six began taking piano lessons and composing original pieces. At age ten he added viola lessons and by age fourteen he had already composed over one hundred pieces. One of his early choral works, *A Hymn to the Virgin* (now an established part of the repertory), was composed at age seventeen while in the sick bay at his boarding school. From his auspicious early efforts he progressed to the Royal College of Music in London. His works were met with critical success and garnered him many awards during his young career. His works cover a variety of media, including chamber, choral, and orchestral music, ballet, opera, radio, and film. Many of his works display one or more of the following characteristics in varying degrees: a strong sense of British identity through language and subject matter, explorations of Eastern culture and music, a keen interest in social justice and pacifism, and a distinctive melodic and harmonic language that holds textural clarity and an economy of means as compositional ideals.

Composition, Genre, and Historical Perspective

"Rustics and Fisherman" was originally part of Britten's 1953 opera *Gloriana*—an opera that was, by most contemporary accounts, a failure. This initial reception, deemed somewhat harsh by many later critics, is better understood in light of the atmosphere and circumstances of its creation. Britten's general working practice for the creation of a new opera required two major components: ample time for composition and reflection and a close working relationship with the librettist—both of which were in troublingly short supply during his work on *Gloriana*. Britten, starting without even a libretto, had just a little over a year to finish the work in time for Queen Elizabeth II's coronation festivities. Compounding the time constraint was the fact that his librettist, the South African writer William Plomer, was not able to work as closely with Britten as he had in previous, more successful, pairings.

Contributing to negative reception was the fact that the subject matter for the opera was deemed distasteful by many, including, apocryphally, the young Regent herself. Britten's insistence on a solemn and dramatic work for the coronation met with a confused public that seemed to have something more cheerful in mind.

Critics also found fault with the seeming disjunction between scenes that were essentially dramatic or narrative, and scenes that were more pageantry or spectacle. Britten had intended to use these moments of pageantry to highlight "certain facets of English musical life, such as the remarkable ballet and choral singing" against the backdrop of the story of Queen Elizabeth I and Robert Devereux, 2nd Earl of Essex. "Rustics and Fisherman" is only one of six choruses that were excerpted from Act II, scene 1, to form the *Choral Dances from Gloriana*. "Rustics and Fisherman," along with the preceding chorus, "Country Girls," served as songs of offering to the Queen along with the gifts they describe.

Musical Elements and Technical Considerations

This short piece includes potential problems in terms of both range and rhythmic precision. The tenor 1 part calls for fourteen high Gs and two high As. The other parts also have moderately high tessitura, but are not nearly so daunting. Though brief in duration (merely one minute), the piece calls for hearty and energetic singing throughout, which when coupled with the higher ranges, particularly in the tenor 1, can make for a more tiring sing than one might guess at first glance. In order to meet this challenge, encourage energetic, yet open and relaxed singing from all chorus members, even in high range. Along with that, it will also help to ensure that the breathing is open and does not lead to a compounding of tension. The tempo of the piece requires quick rhythmic breaths that almost certainly cannot be full ones. Rather, I would suggest that it is more important that each breath (all occurring on downbeat eighth rests) be impulsive and carry some of the weight of the absent downbeat. On the other hand, be wary of the danger that breathing too heavily or too fully on any downbeat will cause the following entrance to be late and cause the tempo to drag.

Within the piece the only events that occur on downbeats are at the ends of phrases. The effect is one of rhythmic displacement—a sort of aural illusion. With no audible downbeat the ear tends to wonder about its relationship to the pulse, to the stress of the words, and possibly to the tempo as well. In passages such as measure 3 through 5 the effect is clearly apparent and only resolves itself on the downbeat of measure 6. The tendency for performers will be to stretch the last eighth note of measure 5 (and likewise in mm. 11 and 23) in order to place the cadence for "grow" on the perceived downbeat of measure 6, that is, the second eighth-note. It is of primary importance that the choir understands the rhythms and stresses of the text before trying to add other musical elements. Chanting the text, perhaps with the addition of some sort of clap or foot stomp on the downbeats, will help to make rhythmic games within this piece shine, while also allowing the other musical elements to fall into place with far less underlying anxiety.

Stylistic Considerations

Within the opera itself, Britten was careful to evoke a Renaissance sound world while avoiding a simple pastiche of Elizabethan musical styles. As such, it is hard to point to a direct potential model, such as the madrigal, from which we can draw interpretational insights. However, we can note the pastoral elements that suggest folk music or market cries. This observation leads us to a rhythmic and lusty interpretation. Britten's choice of tempo and tessitura, with his declamatory presentation of the simple and direct text captures a certain rough-hewn heartiness, also supports a heavy and spirited interpretation. When performed as part of the complete set of *Choral Dances*, the contrast with the preceding piece, "Country Girls," is made clear not only by the scoring (SA vs. TTBB) and subject matter (flowers vs. more mundane merchandise), but also in the tone color (light and airy vs. full and hearty).

Form and Structure

"Rustics and Fisherman" follows a relatively simple and repetitive structure. All of the choppy phrases begin with one-measure motivic statements that are developed using basic methods such as repetition and/or sequence, building toward a concluding sub-phrase that is longer and more sostenuto.

SECTION	MEASURE
mm. 1–6	1 phrase (1+1+4)
mm. 7–12	exact repetition of mm. 1–6
mm. 13–16	1 phrase (1+1+1+2)
mm. 17–24	1 phrase (1+1+1+4) This phrase is a variation on mm. 1–6.

Text

Text by William Plomer.

From fen and meadow
In rushy baskets
They bring ensamples of all they grow.

In earthen dishes
Their deep-sea fishes;
Yearly fleeces,
Woven blankets;
New cream and junkets,
And rustic trinkets
On wicker flaskets,
Their country largess,
The best they know.

Additional References and Resources

Britten, Benjamin. *Gloriana: an opera in three acts*, op. 53. Libretto by William Plomer. Revised vocal score. London: Boosey & Hawkes, 1968.

Cooke, Mervin, ed. *The Cambridge Companion to Benjamin Britten*. Cambridge: Cambridge University Press, 1999.

Tracey, Edmund. "Benjamin Britten talks to Edmund Tracey." *Sadler's Wells Magazine*, Autumn 1966, 5–7. (Quoted in Cooke, p. 117.)

Contributed by:

Gregory Brown

Level 5

Mixed voices:

Come to Me My Love Dello Joio, Norman . . 545
I Find My Feet Larsen, Libby . . 551
The Hour Has Come Glick, Srul Irving . . 555

Treble voices

Jerusalem Luminosa Betinis, Abbie . . 561

Teacher Resource Guide

Come to Me My Love

Norman Dello Joio
(1913–2008)

SATB/piano
Hal Leonard: 7541
Overall: 5
Vocal: 5
Tonal/Rhythm: 5

Composer

Norman Dello Joio was born January 24, 1913 to Italian immigrant parents in New York City. By the age of four he had begun piano lessons under the tutelage of his father, who was himself an organist, pianist, and vocal coach. In Dello Joio's early teens he began organ studies with his godfather, Pietro Yon, and at the tender age of 14 began his professional musical career as the choir director and organist at the Star of the Sea Church on City Island in New York.

In 1939, Dello Joio received a scholarship to the Julliard School and began compositional studies with Bernard Wagenaar, and by 1941 he had turned all his attention to composition and began to study with Paul Hindemith. It was Hindemith who told the young composer "Your music is lyrical by nature, don't ever forget that." Dello Joio later stated that he eventually understood that statement to mean "Don't sacrifice necessarily to a system, go to yourself, what you hear… Don't say I have to do this because the system tells me to." By the late 1940s Dello Joio had come to the forefront of American composers; in the next decade he gained international recognition. During his life he taught at Sarah Lawrence College and the Mannes College of

Music, and served as dean of the School of Fine and Applied Arts at Boston University. In 1957 he was awarded the Pulitzer Prize for his *Meditations on Ecclesiastes* for string orchestra. Although he was a prolific composer in many genres (wind ensemble, orchestra, television and movie scores, solo voice, piano, and chamber music), he is perhaps best known for his choral works. Many conductors are familiar with his *A Jubilant Song* for mixed or women's chorus and piano. Dello Joio died at his home in East Hampton, New York on July 24, 2008.

Composition, Genre, and Historical Perspective

Dello Joio's oeuvre mainly consists of lyrical and essentially tonal works. It was Hindemith who convinced him to follow this path rather than adhere to the atonal systems of composition in vogue at the time. Dello Joio was influenced by the church music in which he was immersed as a young musician; he was also infludenced by the more popular jazz tunes of the era and 19th-century Italian opera. In 1973, he set *Come to Me, My Love*, to a text based on Christina Rossetti's poem "Echo" and scored it for mixed chorus and piano.

Technical Considerations and Musical Elements

Although essentially tonal in nature, the specific tonal center of *Come to Me, My Love* is somewhat ambiguous. Dello Joio seems to be more interested in the color of chords (high tertian chords abound throughout), than in writing with functional harmonies. This is most readily apparent in the fact that he chooses not to indicate any key signature, but instead writes all notes with accidentals. This makes the music appear much more complicated than it actually is, and more difficult to read (especially for the accompanist). The nonfunctional harmonic movement does not always come easily to the ear, therefore it will require significant rehearsal time to master individual vocal lines. This is especially true in the lower three voice parts, whose lines often serve to fill in harmonies. The piano accompaniment will offer little help to the singers, as it is often almost entirely unrelated to the vocal lines and sometimes is harmonically more a hindrance than a help to the vocalists. Certainly the accompaniment should be thought of as a duet with the voices, not as a supporting instrument.

Melodically the piece is through composed, with short individual phrases bearing little resemblance to each other at first glance. Upon closer examination, however, Dello Joio seems to have chosen two specific intervals on which to base the primary melodic line in the soprano, namely the descending major 2nd and the ascending (usually) perfect 4th (sometimes filled in with passing notes). Look at the primary notes in the soprano line—often the starting and ending notes—for abundant occurrences. There are numerous chromatic passages and awkward larger intervals, especially in the lower three voices; singers will need to perform intervals with extreme accuracy.

All of the above is present opening section of the piece (mm. 1 through 33). Following this section is a three-measure piano interlude, which leads into a section where Dello Joio almost cleanses the ear. C major and D minor chords (both with higher tertian notes added up to the 13th) take up alternating measures, with the chords placed in successive octaves in a steady pulse of quarter notes (mm. 37 through 45). For this section, the vocal lines suddenly without any chromatic movement at all but instead are lyrical and melodious. This soon gives way to a return to the more chromatic motion for the concluding section. The piece finishes on an unadorned E major chord—a tonality not heard until the final note.

Almost all of *Come to Me, My Love* is either homophonic or antiphonal between the men's and women's voices. Determining a logical procedure for teaching the music is therefore fairly straightforward. Begin by teaching the appropriate pairings of voices and individual phrases, then gradually begin to combine them. Obviously, there will be certain points where one of the voice parts will need to be worked by itself, but as individual lines seem almost like a difficult intervallic sight-reading exercise, it is actually easier to teach at least two parts together so they can provide some harmonic basis for each other. Normally, it is helpful to begin the learning process by singing on a neutral syllable, but in this case the natural rhythm of the words is so closely aligned with the notated rhythms, it is more helpful to have the singers learn on the actual text. It should be noted that the poetry of *Come to Me, My Love* is particularly beautiful and should be read and discussed as a work of art in itself. The rhythmic aspects are not terribly difficult, and the piece is set almost entirely in common time, with one 5/4 bar for the singers and a 6/4 bar in the piano interlude (m. 36).

Stylistic Considerations

Dello Joio has given a plethora of musical indications throughout the piece, ranging from general (*andante espressivo* to begin the work, *con colore* at m. 23, and numerous indications of *espressivo*), to very specific ritards and dynamic indications. These specific indications should be followed closely. Where breath marks are not specifically indicated or there is no rest in the vocal lines, the singers should breathe according to the punctuation of the poetry (e.g., in m. 25 and 27 the men's voices should breathe at the comma after the word "years"). A pure, muted tone should be used for sections marked *piano*, which will contrast nicely with the *forte* sections, often marked with indications such as *con colore*, *espressivo*, and even *con intensita* at m. 37.

The natural stress of the text matches well with the rise and fall of the vocal lines, so the singers should be encouraged to bring out text declamation within the context of the phrases.

Form and Structure

Section	Measure	Event and Scoring
Introduction	1–11	piano
I-a	12–16	SATB, piano and *a cappella*, ST and AB paired
I-b	17–22	SATB, primarily *a cappella* with brief piano phrases inserted between vocal phrases
I-c	23–33	SATB, piano, antiphonal between men and women, piano interlude begins in m. 33
Interlude	33–36	piano
II	37–47	SATB, piano, antiphonal between men and women, ends homophonic in all voices
Transition to Coda	48–49	SATB *a cappella*
Coda	50–56	SATB, *a cappella* with brief piano phrases inserted between vocal phrases

Text

Based on the poem "Echo" by Christina Rossetti

Come to me in the night,
Come to me in the silence of the dark'ning night.
Come to me in the speaking silence of a dream;
With soft rounded cheeks and eyes as bright as sunlight on a stream;

O! come back in tears, my love of finished years,
In dreams too sweet, too bitter sweet,
Of Paradise where souls of love abide and meet,
Come back my love, come back to me.

Yet come to me in dreams that I may live my life again;
A mem'ry of those thirsty longing eyes, those eyes so bright,
Come back to me my love that I may give,
Pulse for pulse, breath for breath;

Speak low, lean low,
O! come in silent dreams, my love;
And whisper low, as long ago.

Contributed by:

David Scholz

Teacher Resource Guide

I Find My Feet Have Further Goals

Libby Larsen

(b. 1950)

SSATB
Oxford University Press: 3861526
Overall: 5
Vocal: 4
Tonal/Rhythm: 5

Composer

One of the most performed living composers in the United States, Libby Larsen has produced works in virtually every concert music genre. She was exposed to high quality choral music in her youth, which may help account for the fact that her impressive catalogue of over 400 compositions includes more works for chorus than any other configuration. One significant aspect of Libby Larsen's professional life is that she is a full-time composer, choosing not to hold a regular teaching position at any college, university, or conservatory.

Larsen is a vigorous and passionate speaker and writer. She is interested in the state of music education in schools, and the condition of new music in America generally. She is an articulate thinker on the relationship between the public and concert music, and on the role of the trained musician in society. In 1973, Larsen established the Minnesota Composers Forum, which has since evolved into the American Composers Forum, with a mandate to link communities with composers and performers in the making, playing, and enjoyment of new music. In 2000, at age 50, Larsen received a Lifetime Achievement Award from the American Academy of Arts and Letters.

Composition, Genre, and Historical Perspective

Premiered in 1996 and published by Oxford University Press in 1998, this work was commissioned for the installation of the Senior Minister of Plymouth Congregational Church in Minneapolis, Minnesota. It would be particularly appropriate for such an occasion or for any celebration that looks to the future, such as graduation. It would also be well qualified for a program of American music or American poets.

Musical Elements and Technical Considerations

To approach this piece, singers will need to be comfortable singing *a cappella* and managing parts that are both rhythmically and melodically independent. Although several unusual modulations occur, the voice leading is intelligently written with a view to easing the choir through these passages.

In the opening five measures, take time to unify the color of the "ah" vowel between sections and registers, as well as to clarify the shape of each motive. Clearly, the *tenuti* indicate that the dotted quarter notes are to be given more weight than the eighth notes, but it is for the conductor to decide whether the basses, for example, should lift after the first two notes, or after the first four. The alto part in measure 3 deserves special attention, particularly in the descending part of the line; there is an unusual modulation here that repeats two more times (measures 22 and 43) in the course of the piece.

There is something elusive about the quality of this introduction: Is it to be contemplative, or easy-going, or quietly fervent, perhaps? In any event, there is a kind of call and answer between the bass and alto, so the approach should be unified between the sections, including articulation, length of notes, and dynamic level.

Speaking of dynamics, achieving suitable balance requires considerable vigilance from the conductor and singers; the active text moves from line to line, causing individual parts to change roles from melody to accompaniment quite frequently and in ways that are not always apparent without viewing all the parts together. For example, the tenor entrance at measure 6 should immediately be in the forefront of the texture. The altos in measure 9 should breathe early after the long note *piano*, then take over the melody at the text "that felt so ample"; altos are marked *forte* here, the strongest dynamic we have yet seen, and are in their low register, which will make singing that dynamic a challenge. An early, long, and clearly voiced "th" placed directly on the pitch will help. After a *tutti forte* in measure 11, all voices return to *mezzo piano* before the sopranos in measure 13 recommence the poem, followed by the tenors, basses, and altos. Again, in terms of balance it is very important to distinguish between the accompanying "ah" figures and the melodies set to poetic text.

The second stanza it set beginning at measure 33; Larsen paints the text "something awkward in the fit" with awkwardly fitting harmonic juxtaposition. In order for this technique to be audible, it is crucially important that the tenors and basses maintain their G-flat major chord at a full *mezzo forte* throughout the first half of this measure, where it will clash with the C major of the sopranos and altos.

Take note of the following errata (as well as the corresponding pitches in the keyboard reduction), relative to the Oxford University Press edition of 1998:

m. 2—Last alto note should be A-flat.
m. 3—Last alto note should be A-natural.
m. 18—First syllable in all parts should be "day's" (not "day").
m. 19—Third lower tenor note should be A-flat. In the same measure of the piano reduction, the second note in the right hand should be F.
m. 22—Last alto note should be A-natural.
m. 30—The last bass note should be slurred (on "ah") to the next measure, not slurred from the previous note.
m. 43—Last alto note should be A-natural.

The reason behind the surprising tenor voice leading in measures 50 and 51 has been clarified by the composer herself. The tenor note is deliberately left "as a C to create a semi-quartal harmony (F/G–C–F–B). The F is doubled, so that the C suggests the 5th of F, or the F suggests an added 4th to a C major 7 chord. This creates two potential paths for the continuation of the final chord of the piece. If the tenor sings a D instead of a C, the final chord is a G7, which suggests a specific resolution to C, too directed a goal for the poem."[1]

Stylistic Considerations

Although this text looks to the future and to the possibilities it might afford, this is not a poem of simple optimism or confidence, no anthem to ambition. Its perspective on the human condition is contemplative and somewhat removed, and its view of aspiration rather ambivalent. While acknowledging that there are choices to be made in the future and something to gained thereby, the speaker also maintains a somewhat bemused posture: if each day brings greater expectations than the previous, then one's own goals, which seem all-consuming in the moment, might well prove insufficient all too soon. Larsen's setting certainly amplifies this ambivalence, reflecting the elusiveness of true "arrival" in musical terms.

1 Source: e-mail from Libby Larsen. [AU: To whom was Larsen's e-mail sent, and what was the date of said e-mail?]

This text, then, describes the process of growth, especially the growth of goals and the widening of horizons that result from life experience; what seems a sufficient goal one day is soon "outgrown." A vocal approach consistent with this posture would include a warm tone without any edge or trace of aggressiveness, and diction that is clear while at the same time steering clear of affectation.

Form and Structure

Section	Measure	Event and Scoring	Key
Introduction and Verse 1	mm. 1–12	5 + 7	D-flat (E) C
Verse 1 (altered)	mm. 13–19	7	B-flat
Verse 1 (hesitates, does not complete)	mm. 20–32	4 + 9 (4+2+1+2)	D-flat (E) B
Verse 2	mm. 33–40	8	C
Verse 1 (partial, A-flat C as Coda)	mm. 41–51	4 + 4 + 3	D-flat E

Text and Translation

Larsen has chosen to set the final two-thirds of the Emily Dickenson poem "I could not prove the years had feet—" shown below:

I find my feet have further Goals—
I smile upon the Aims
That felt so ample—Yesterday—
Today's—have vaster claims—

I do not doubt the self I was
Was competent to me—
But something awkward in the fit—
Proves that—outgrown—I see—

Web Site

http://libbylarsen.com

Contributed by:

John Trotter

Teacher Resource Guide

The Hour Has Come

Srul Irving Glick

(1934–2002)

SATB/piano
Gordon V. Thompson Music: VE11105
Overall: 5
Vocal: 5
Tonal/Rhythm: 4

Composer

Srul Irving Glick grew up in Toronto, Ontario where his father was a cantor. He studied composition in Toronto and then in Paris, France. As one of Canada's most prolific composers, he wrote in most major forms. His vocal and choral music are particularly well recognized as both tuneful and emotionally accessible while displaying considerable craft and formal mastery.

Glick was for many years composer-in-residence and choir director at Toronto's Beth Tikvah Synagogue. Both he and Beth Tikvah were recognized with awards for outstanding contributions to Jewish music, to Canadian culture, and for service to humanity at large. In 2000, Glick received the extraordinary Yuvel Award, presented by the Cantor's Assembly of America, for his "life long commitment to the composition of music that captures the heart and touches the soul."

Composition, Genre, and Historical Perspective

"The Hour Has Come" is the finale of a six-movement choral symphony written by Glick to poems by Canadian poet Carole H. Leckner. Musically,

Glick's style, direct and emotional in its appeal, meshes well with Leckner's poems, which are filled with an exuberant appreciation of what it is to be alive. Characteristic attitude of both artists is one of hope, so the piece fittingly ends with an encouragement toward peace and oneness within mankind. As such, it is appropriate for wide use.

Musical Elements and Technical Considerations

This piece is appropriate for a choir of considerable size—and the larger the better. Conceived as a work with orchestra, the gestures are large and the lines long.

The soprano part features both large leaps between registers and a considerable amount of singing at the top of the staff. To meet the first challenge, encourage singers to "live on the top notes" and maintain posture, breath support, and spacious vowels throughout. When singing in the very high register, encourage vowel modification toward "ah" and reduce expectations of distinctness on those consonants (voiced and unvoiced) that cause difficulty in this register. The sopranos' job in such places is to sing beautifully and in tune: let the other sections provide the clear consonants to bring the text to the audience. Consider the very high soprano D in the final three measures of the score as optional: the ending is equally impressive without it. Sopranos who are uncomfortable sustaining a high A in tune for long periods should sing the first alto part beginning at the anacrusis to the third last measure.

A full, resonant, rich, warm sound is appropriate in the *forte* sections. Encourage the singers to make the text, which addresses overarching life issues, as personal as possible. Crescendo power on sustained chords is necessary to realize the many climaxes in the work, for instance: at rehearsal 43, two measures before rehearsal 45, and at the end of the movement. For the most desirable effect at such key places, strive to maintain tuning, tall vowel color, and an open throat with even breath support throughout the crescendo or sustained chord. Many singers respond well to being asked to "expand" or "grow" through the crescendo (rather than "push" or "hold," for instance)

Certain words call for special attention and will provide you as a conductor with an ideal opportunity to acquaint your singers with the differences between spoken and sung English. Work to unify the timing and treatment of the "r" sound in such featured words as "hour," "earth," "short," "fire," "yearning," "heart," and "where." I prefer to replace the letter "r" with [a]-colored schwah sound, but whatever your choice, for the sake of your singers avoid the retroflex "r" (with the tip of the tongue curled towards the back of the throat) that we regularly use in spoken English on words such as "grow." Be similarly careful of the [l] sound in "soul." Habits from spoken English will cause the vowel to become distinctly unbeautiful, as this word is sustained and the final consonant anticipated. A very short Italian (forward) "l" will more than suffice for intelligibility and will allow your singers to maintain the vocal approach we would all like to engender.

Take time to unify vowel color on such words as "love" (my own preference is for a very tall, spacious sound) and "man." After all, the poem encourages unity within the human race; let us strive for the same in our choirs! Agreement on how to treat the diphthong on "fire" is also important. One option is to make the change in vowel sound as late as possible and to de-emphasize it.

If using the Gordon V. Thompson Music edition of 1987, take a moment to correct the spelling in the alto text in the fourth measure of rehearsal 51.

Certain figurations in inner voices will be difficult to balance, for instance the moving alto line two measures after rehearsal 43, or 5 measures after rehearsal 51, where relatively high sustained pitches in the soprano and tenor will likely overcome even the best-willed section. The bass entrance three measures after rehearsal 52 suffers from a similar problem of registration: you might ask some basses to double the first four notes of this entrance an octave higher (which will sound as an overtone, and significantly reinforce the sound). In any event, depending on the age and experience of your singers, it may not be wise to ask them to "project to the back of the hall" in these registers.

Early score study on the part of the conductor will be rewarded when it comes to the treatment of tempi in this work. Of course, rubato must always be organic, and may never be exactly the same from one performance to the next. However, the conductor's task prior to the first rehearsal is to view the piece as a whole, and to arrive at a vision of the piece so that not all climaxes will seem equal, and so that momentum can be maintained to the finish. Some instructions seem unclear with regard to tempo, but are clarified later. The instruction "broadly, legato cantabile" at 45 and *sostenuto* (after 46) are ambiguous with regard to tempo, but the subsequent *a tempo* marking soon after suggests that one or both of these instructions imply a slower tempo, as well as providing information concerning mood.

The approaches to many of this movement's climaxes are accompanied by directions such as *poco ritardando* (before 44) *ritardando* (before 42, and at 54), and *allargando* (four measures from the end). The movement is most effective overall if these directives are not treated as equivalent terms; make the latter more marked than the former.

It is a good idea to consider whether you would like some or all sections of the choir to breathe together in the middle of certain phrases for the sake of textual intelligibility and consistent breath support through what follows. Some places to consider breathing include: upper three voices after "seen" four measures after rehearsal 43 (and one measures before 52), all parts after "intense" two measures later before the subito *pianissimo*, and all parts after "man" in the third measure after 51.

Stylistic Considerations

Choral music lovers appreciate Glick's strong sense of the power of words and his ability to reflect the natural rhythms of speech and syllabic emphases of texts in his vocal lines. The presentation of the bass fugue subject at rehearsal 49 is a case in point: careful disposition of rhythm, rising and falling lines, tenuto, and hairpin dynamic markings work in favor not only of intelligibility but also meaning, and clarify the emotional contour of the line. Here the conductor has the pleasure of working hand in hand with the composer. Do not be afraid to model (sing!) these phrases for your singers as you hear them, and soon the lines will seem to sing themselves. Ensure that as each voice enters in turn, the subject is shaped to match the bass example. The goal is for an aural picture of the gathering of the human family to emerge as the entrances accumulate.

The instruction *espressivo con rubato* is very helpful in accessing the mood and style of this music, which is not primarily objective or intellectual, but rather Romantic. Meant to be immediately accessible, certain of the rhythms and harmonic techniques are also indebted to popular music. All in all, this movement asks to be entered into in an emotional sense. The text is at times a proclamation or exhortation and at others an invitation, which is something much more intimate and personal. There is considerable flexibility within the style, both in terms of vocal color and rubato.

Form and Structure

Section	Measure	Event and Scoring	Key
Instrumental intro.	mm. 1–17	6+7+4	D major
First Stanza	mm. 18–42	6+3+5+4+7	
Second Stanza	mm. 43–55	2+9(4+5)	D minor (to major)
Instrumental intro. (melody begins in m. 53)	mm. 56–70	3+3+4+3+2	D major
Fugue (B–A–T–S)	mm. 71–84	3+4+3+4	B minor to D major
"Where art thou..." Buildup to ending	mm. 85–104	6+8+6	

Text and Translation

The Hour Has Come by Carole H. Leckner

The hour has come
for mankind to embrace,
for the sun blazes
upon the conscience of the earth
and time is growing short
and what is visible must be seen
and the fire is intense
in the consciousness of the planet
and healing is the yearning of her heart.

Our cells are life's tissue,
our bones and marrow her rivers and narrows.
Our heart pumps the cry of her heart
and our soul breathes
the spirit of her song.
Where art thou, O family of man,
sisters and brothers?
The hour has come to love.

Additional References and Resources

http://www.srulirvingglick.com

Recording

Anthology of Canadian Music: Srul Irving Glick. Radio Canada International. ACM 34, CD 1-4.

Contributed by:

John Trotter

Teacher Resource Guide

Jerusalem Luminosa

Abbie Betinis

SA
Neil A. Kjos: 6323
Overall: 5
Vocal: 4
Tonal/Rhythm: 5

Composer

Performed increasingly in the United States and abroad, Abbie Betinis's music has been commissioned by more than forty organizations, including the American Suzuki Foundation, Cantus, Cornell University Chorus, Dale Warland Singers, and the Young New Yorkers' Chorus. Betinis was born in Stevens Point, Wisconsin and studied composition at Saint Olaf College and the University of Minnesota. She also attended the European American Musical Alliance summer sessions in Paris, France, where she studied harmony and counterpoint in the tradition of Nadia Boulanger.

Also a singer, Betinis has performed with the Dale Warland Singers, VocalEssence, and the Saint Paul Chamber Orchestra Chorale.

Betinis's catalog includes two song cycles, music for concert band, and an annual Christmas Carol inspired by her great uncle, Alfred Burt. Her choral music is published by Augsburg Fortress, Fred Bock Music, Graphite Publishing, Kjos, Santa Barbara Music Publishing, and in G. Schirmer's *Dale Warland Choral Series*. She also runs her own self-publishing company, which is accessible on her Web site (see Bibliography and Suggested Resources).

A resident of Saint Paul, Minnesota, she has been a Composer-in-Residence with The Rose Ensemble, The Schubert Club, and The Singers—Minnesota Choral Artists.

Composition, Genre, and Historical Perspective

(These notes were contributed by the composer.) *Jerusalem Luminosa* is an exploration of what it means to make peace. The fifteenth century text, excerpted from a much longer poem, is attributed to Thomas à Kempis (1380–1471) and celebrates the eternal spiritual vitality of the city of Jerusalem, Israel.

> But for me, the text wasn't the end of the story. Knowing that Jerusalem, a significant city for three of the world's major religions, has been the site of much political friction and controversy, I thought it would be interesting—and appropriate—to try to set this text in a way that actively engages in the conscious act of peacemaking. Both the music and the text setting show examples of cooperation, compromise, and, ultimately, resolution. (If only it were so easy in politics!)
>
> *Jerusalem Luminosa* was originally written for two solo voices and premiered in July 2001 at L'Eglise Saint Severin in Paris, France. It was my first commissioned piece.

Musical Elements and Technical Considerations

Jerusalem Luminosa initially poses some rhythmic difficulties, however, in my experience, singers of all ages have risen to the challenge and seem to enjoy the sense of accomplishment and cooperation presented in the challenge.

The music begins in a tranquil state with a unison "Alleluia" chant (taken from a counterpoint worksheet I was supposed to be working on). This short melody is in modern chant notation: no stems, no barlines. It sits squarely in E-flat major.

Almost immediately the voices "play tag": one part constantly trying to catch up with the other, lending and borrowing beats in order to align at cadences and partner at melodic peaks. The fast parts of the piece are mostly in 5/4. A short excursion into 7/8 requires the altos to learn a repeating 2-bar ostinato while the sopranos sing a playful melody over the top. These fast sections are in C minor.

Like much of my vocal work, the syllables of the text are malleable. In this piece, some words compromise by getting squished together, for example, *Luminosa Jerusalem* becomes *Luminosalem*. Other words share their common syllables: *Alleluia, Alleluia* elides into *Alleluia'lleluia*. The piece concludes with an energetic elision: *Luminos'Alleluia!* I like to think that making the text more "cooperative" this way has helped the music achieve the *verae pacis visio* (vision of true peace) that Kempis was imagining.

Needless to say, *Jerusalem Luminosa* should be performed with much care toward rhythmic alignment. Teaching the piece slowly and speaking the text in rhythm will certainly be helpful. Teaching the melodies by ear, phrase by phrase, can also be quite effective. The motives are repetitious and not difficult to learn on their own, but hearing the interplay between them is challenging and can often be made more difficult by staring at the printed page.

Glissandi

Downward glissandi, spanning a major or minor third, are occasionally written from the final quarter note in a measure into the downbeat of the next. For advanced groups, I recommend beginning the quarter-note glissandi as close to the onset of sound as possible. I like the playfulness of this effect. For less advanced groups, it is more important to tune the quarter notes than to worry about the glissandi between them. I have heard the piece done quite effectively without glissandi. They are not there to be worrisome—only to add a sense of play.

Ending

The piece ends with a glissando in both parts up to a high pitch with an "x" notehead. The text is the final *Alleluia!* marked *ff*. I find this ending most effective when the final pitch of the glissando is unspecified and the singers crescendo through the glissando to achieve an effect that is much like a cathartic, high-energy shout on the final syllable.

If performed as a duet, or with men's voices transposed, the ending may sound best by specifying the pitches each part should sing. Consider top part G and bottom part B-flat, or top part D and bottom part G (as written).

Stylistic Considerations

When I sit down to write vocal music, I try to write pieces that I would like to sing. I enjoy energetic singing. I also enjoy playing with rhythmic accuracy as opposed to creating the sensation of being "out of time."

Not surprisingly, I prefer two very different styles of singing on this piece. For the two slow-tempo *Alleluias*, I like the round, chant-style sound with an easy, open throat and minimal-to-no vibrato. For these sections, I imagine deep, dark churches with thick, incensed air and a nice, ringing acoustic resonance. Monks are sitting in a corner somewhere, but you can't really tell exactly where. In fact, it's a bit mysterious.

On the other hand, for the rest of the piece, which is labeled "Ritmico," I prefer a light production. By "light" I don't mean soft (certainly follow the dynamics where indicated), I mean only that singing it feels more like balancing on the balls of your feet than stomping into the ground. The accents are alive. The goal is joyous declamation, even in the soft passages.

Form and Structure

Measure	Section (Length of Phrases in Section)
mm. 1	Slow: Alleluia chant; Eb major (2)
mm. 2–12	Fast: Chorus; C minor (3+2)
mm. 13–17	Fast: Transition (5, overlapping)
mm. 18–22	Slow: Alleluia chant with sopranos transposed up P5; G minor (2)
mm. 23–33	Fast: Chorus, C minor (3+2)
mm. 34–47	Fast: Alto ostinato, Soprano playful "improvised-sounding" melody (7)
mm. 48–51	Fast: Short vamp with repeat signs around it (4)
mm. 52–54	Rit: Chain of suspensions, ritard to ½ step dissonance, fermata, caesura (1)
mm. 55–65	Fast: Chorus (3+2)
mm. 66–69	Fast: Tag, with glissando to an unspecified pitch (2)

Text and Translation

Text: Thomas à Kempis (attrib.) *Trans.: anon.*

Alleluia. Jerusalem luminosa, Verae pacis visio.	*Alleluia.* *Jerusalem, city of light,* *Vision of true peace.*
Alleluia. Totum sanctum, totum mundum, In te quidquid cernitur.	*Alleluia.* *All holy, all elegant,* *Is that which shows itself in thee.*

Bibliography and Suggested Resources

Abbie Betinis Web site: http://www.abbiebetinis.com

Contributed by:

Abbie Betinis

Masterwork

Gloria, RV 589 Antonio Vivaldi . . 567

Masterwork

Gloria, RV 589 (1716)

Antonio Vivaldi

(1678–1741)

SATB with SSA solos and orchestra

Analysis and commentary by Bruce Chamberlain

Biographical sketch and brief history by Emilie Amrein

Antonio Vivaldi's Gloria, RV 589 (1716)

Biographical Sketch and Brief History of Composition

Emilie Amrein

The city of Venice, prosperous and vibrant during the late Middle Ages and Renaissance, declined in stature as a center for trade and commerce throughout the sixteenth and seventeenth centuries. The arts had long played an important role in the identity of the city, however, and as the trade of goods and services declined during this period, the arts—and music in particular—evolved into international commodities in their own right. Renowned Vivaldi scholar Michael Talbot writes that as the seventeenth century progressed, "Culture rather than trade or manufacture was [Venice's] most characteristic field of activity." It was into this environment that Antonio Vivaldi, the preeminent Italian composer of the high baroque period lived.

Vivaldi was born in Venice on March 4, 1678—the first of nine children—to Giovanni Battista and Camilla Calicchio. Giovanni Battista was initially trained as a barber, but played the violin as well. Recent scholarship suggests that Vivaldi's father was a composer in his own right, and may have taught Antonio how to play the violin. As a child, Antonio suffered from a chronic upper-respiratory disorder which today would likely be diagnosed as bronchial asthma. This ailment remained with Vivaldi throughout his life and played a significant role in his evolution.

After his initial musical training, Vivaldi trained for the priesthood. He received tonsure in 1693 and was ordained in 1703. Because of his distinctive red hair, Vivaldi was thereafter nicknamed *il Prete Rosso* (the Red Priest). Though he remained spiritually active and composed often for the church, Vivaldi ceased saying mass in 1706—perhaps because of his struggle with the chronic respiratory illness mentioned above.

Vivaldi continued his musical studies through this period. The first record of a public performance including Vivaldi dates from 1696, where it is noted that he served as a "supernumerary violinist" during the Christmas services as St. Mark's Cathedral. Soon thereafter he took his first professional musical appointment as the *maestro di violino* (violin teacher) at the *Pio Ospedale della Pietà* orphanage in 1703. Interestingly, just one year after this appointment he began to teach other stringed instruments and to acquire instruments for the orchestra as well. Venice's four *ospedali* (literally, *hospitals*)—and the *Pietà* in particular—played a significant role in the Venetian musical scene during the Baroque. Second only to service at St. Mark's cathedral, Venetian musicians and composers were frequently engaged as teachers and performers by the *ospedali*. Michael Talbot describes the *ospedali* as "charitable institutions for orphaned, abandoned, illegitimate or indigent children."

Founded in 1364, the *Ospedale della Pietà* served nearly a thousand children in Vivaldi's time. Young orphaned boys were taught a trade and then released, while young women "were divided into two categories: the *figlie di comun*, or commoners, who received a general education, and the *figlie di coro*, whose education was specifically musical." In this way, the *Pietà* functioned as musical conservatory of sorts and provided Venice's trained musicians and composers with eager students and newly trained ensembles of young women with which to work.

Employment at the *ospedali* was subject to yearly review, and in many instances a contract was terminated for financial reasons or because a suitable instructor could be found "in house." As the young women of the *Pietà* developed and mastered musical skills, they were frequently engaged as teachers for younger students. For this reason, although Vivaldi maintained a lifelong relationship with the *Pietà*, his tenure was discontinuous. Six years after Vivaldi was first contracted by the *Pietà*, he was dismissed in 1709—though he was reinstated in 1711. This off-and-on relationship continued for the rest of his life.

During the early decades of the eighteenth century—and often while on leave from the *Pietà*—Vivaldi pursued musical composition. His first four collections of instrumental works (trio sonatas, violin sonatas, and concertos), his first two oratorios, and his initial forays into opera all date from this period. The most significant composition from this time is his opus three, *L'estro armonico*, which was published in 1711 by the Dutch publisher Etienne Roger. This collection, dedicated to the Grand Prince Ferdinando of Tuscany, is comprised of twelve concertos for one, two, and four solo violins.

According to Michael Talbot, releasing compositions with an international publishing house "reflected not only the superiority of the engraving process of the printing from type still normally used in Italy…but also the enormous growth in demand for the latest Italian music in northern Europe." Evidence of the cultural trade between Italy and northern Europe during this period is plentiful. In addition to the legendary influence of Vivaldi and his works on J. S. Bach (soon after the international publication of *L'estro armonico*, Bach transcribed five of the concertos from the work for keyboard), Germanic composers such as Stölzel, Heinichen, and Pisendel traveled to Venice to meet and study with Vivaldi between 1713 and 1716.

After his reinstatement at the *Pietà* in 1711, Vivaldi continued teaching and performing in Venice. In 1713, Vivaldi's senior colleague at the *Pietà*, Francesco Gasparini (the *maestro di coro*), took a medical leave from the *ospedale* and was never to return. Although Vivaldi was not formally appointed to fill this position, Gasparini's vacancy allowed him a critical opportunity to compose sacred vocal music for the choirs at the *Pietà*. The focus of this study—Vivaldi's *Gloria*, RV 589—dates from this period. Shortly after Gasparini's leave, Vivaldi was honored with a bonus for his compositions. During that year, in addition to a hefty collection of instrumental music, Vivaldi composed an entire mass, a setting of the vespers service, a new oratorio, and over thirty motets for the *Pietà*.

After years of service to the *Pietà* and a vast body of repertoire written for the young women there, the governors of the *Pietà* honored Vivaldi with an appointment to the position of *Maestro di Concerti* in 1716. Remarkably, although it might seem this appointment would have cemented Vivaldi to the *Pietà* for the rest of his life, it proved to be an honorary title for many years. Following this promotion at the *Pietà*, Vivaldi focused his compositional energies on opera, an endeavor that required extensive travel.

Vivaldi took a series of engagements away from Venice in a variety of positions.

1718–20	Served the court of Mantua as the *Maestro di Cappella da Camera*
1720–24	Traveled to Rome to mount several productions of his operas
1726–28	Returned to the Venetian *Teatro San Angelo* for additional operatic productions
1729–33	Traveled broadly, most often in association with productions of his operas, perhaps as far from home as Vienna and Prague. Additional operatic productions likely then took him to Verona, Ancona, Reggio nell'Emilia, and Ferrara.

The *Pietà* was astonishingly supportive of Vivaldi as he traveled around Europe and the Italian peninsula. The governors of the *ospedale* stipulated no residency requirement, but during 1723–29 they asked him to supply the orchestra with two concerti per month to be delivered by post. Ironically, by the 1730s the popularity of Vivaldi's music was in great decline, and those who had once praised the composer became his most bitter critics. In 1735, the *Pietà* reinstated Vivaldi as *Maestro di cappella,* then once again terminated his contract in just three years (1738). From this point on, Vivaldi held no further post with the *Pietà*, although he continued to occasionally compose and direct special performances there through 1740.

In 1740 Vivaldi was persuaded to travel to Vienna for yet another production of one or more of his operas. Unfortunately, the death of the Holy Roman Emperor, Charles VI, interfered with Vivaldi's production—all of Vienna's theaters closed from October, 1740 through Carnival season the following spring in order to commemorate the Emperor's death. At this point, Vivaldi was either too poor or too ill to return home to Venice, where he died in 1741. His last opera, *L'oracolo in Messenia,* was produced posthumously at Vienna's Kartnertortheater in 1742.

Like many composers of the era, a revival of Vivaldi's work and a true understanding of his artistic legacy was delayed for years following his death. Michael Talbot writes, "Vivaldi fell into virtual oblivion, except among a few music historians and lexicographers—to be rescued, like so many of his contemporaries, via Bach scholarship." In the early twentieth century, Vivaldi's reputation was rehabilitated by musicologists Arnold Schering, Alberto Gentili, and Marc Pincherle. Efforts to index Vivaldi's compositional output culminated in the catalogue of his complete works by Danish musicologist Peter Ryom in 1973.

Vivaldi's epic compositional output spans a wide variety of genres. A complete listing of his works and further discussion of his salient style features can be found, among other places, in Michael Talbot's biographical article on the composer in the *New Grove Dictionary of Music and Musicians*. The composer's contribution to the concerto genre in particular should be noted.

In addition to composing over 500 concertos for a variety of individual and groups of instruments, Vivaldi helped to standardize what is now known as *ritornello* form as well as the three-movement concerto form. Additionally, Vivaldi wrote some ninety sonatas for solo instruments and small ensembles.

The composer was equally prodigious in vocal genres. His output includes twenty-one operas, four oratorios, a complete mass in addition to several standalone mass movements, over thirty psalm and canticle settings, more than twenty-five solo motets that often functioned as introductions to larger liturgical settings, and fifty secular solo vocal cantatas and serenatas.

The majority of Vivaldi's sacred vocal music was composed for the choir at the *Pietà* when no *Maestro di Coro* was present; two such periods of vacancy at the *Pietà* occur between the years 1713 and 1719, and 1737 and 1739. Vivaldi's *Gloria*, RV 589 dates from the middle of the first period—1716. Although RV 589 is the focus of our current inquiry, there are in fact two extant settings by Vivaldi of the liturgical *Gloria* text that date from this period (RV 588 and 589). It remains unclear which of these settings was written first. RV 588 is scored for SSATB soloists, SATB choir, and orchestra (including two oboes, trumpet, strings and continuo) while RV 589 is scored for SSA soloists, SATB choir, and orchestra (including oboe, trumpet, strings, and continuo.) There is some documentation of another *Gloria* setting by Vivaldi that has yet to be recovered—although Michael Talbot has speculated that this third *Gloria* may very closely resemble the previous two and may in fact be an arrangement of either RV 588 or 589.

Much like the baroque composers George Frederic Handel and J. S. Bach, Vivaldi was no stranger to the practice of "borrowing" thematic material or full movements from one's own previously composed works or the works of others. In the case of his *Gloria*, RV 589, Talbot suggests that several movements were likely borrowed, although only the final movement has been clearly established as borrowed from a *Gloria* setting by Vivaldi's contemporary, Giovanni Maria Ruggieri (fl. ca. 1690–1720). Other borrowed movements may include the musical material shared in the work's opening movement and the penultimate movement, "Quoniam tu solus Sanctus" as well as the second half of movement four, "Propter magnam Gloriam."

The nature of the first performance of this work has remained somewhat of a mystery to music scholars. Michael Talbot offers several hypotheses of note. He writes, "the occasion on which RV 589 was inaugurated is… elusive. It could well have been written for the celebration of Christmas in 1716 or, earlier in the same year, for the patronal festival of the *Pietà* on 2 July… [Or it may have been] composed for a service of thanksgiving for Venetian military and naval victories over the Ottomans at the end of 1716."

Regardless of the exact circumstances surrounding the work's first performance, certain performance practices are clear. Within the context of the mass, a complementary setting of the *Kyrie* text would have accompanied the *Gloria.* Often these two movements would be sung without a break, unless interrupted by a motet for solo voice. Michael Talbot elaborates on several possible pairings of *Kyrie* settings and solo motets for the *Gloria,* RV 589 in the critical notes that accompany the Critical Edition of the score published by Ricordi in 2002.

In terms of the makeup of Vivaldi's ensembles at the *Pietà*, there remain several theories about how an ensemble of women might have executed Vivaldi's tenor and bass lines which often dip below the range of most female singers. Perhaps not surprisingly, the most credible theory has been proposed by Michael Talbot. If one was interested in performing this work with only women's voices, he suggests that both the tenor and bass lines be sung at pitch with the occasional use of octave displacements to counteract any range issues.

Analysis and Commentary
Bruce Chamberlain

Each movement of Vivaldi's *Gloria* (RV 589) uses one line of text from the Greater Doxology, which gradually assumed its place as the second portion of the Mass Ordinary. A word of explanation is needed to cover the text distribution of "Gratias agimus tibi, propter magnum gloriam tuam." In many editions this text appears as Movements IV and V, and it is true that there is a complete change of style from the setting of the "Gratias..." to the "propter..." However, this analysis recommends that these movements should be performed *attacca*, thus thinking of them as one, making the overall shape of *Gloria* eleven movements, matching one movement per line of text. Since most editions of Vivaldi's *Gloria* do in fact give these movements different numbers, this analysis refers to the movements as Movements IV and V. The *attacca* concept is explained fully in the body of the analysis.

Movement I

Movement I is divided into a seventeen-measure introduction, all in D major, followed by five distinct subsections each employing the entirety of the text "Gloria in excelsis Deo," the first statement of the so-called *Hymnus Angelicus*. The five subsections are labeled in figure 1 as:

Section	Measures
A	17, b. 3 to 28, b. 2
B	28, b. 3 to 37
C	38–48
D	48–59
A'	59–72

Figure 1

Allegro $\frac{4}{4}$

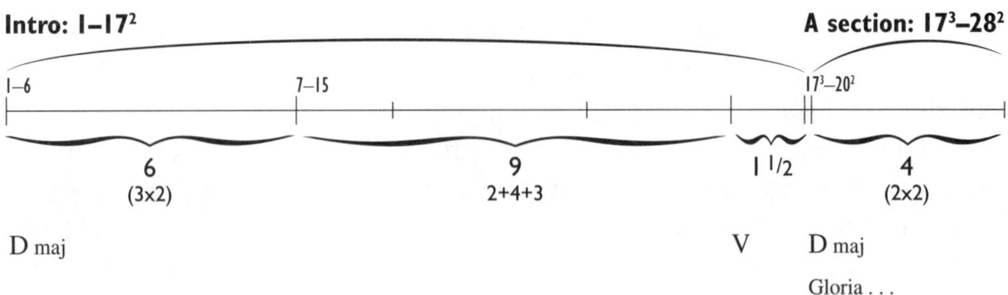

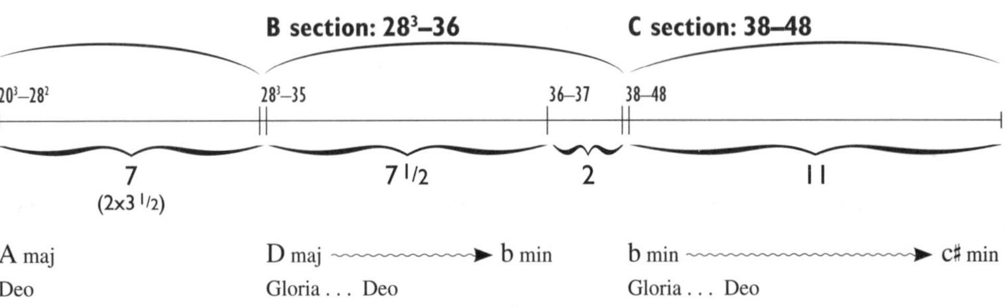

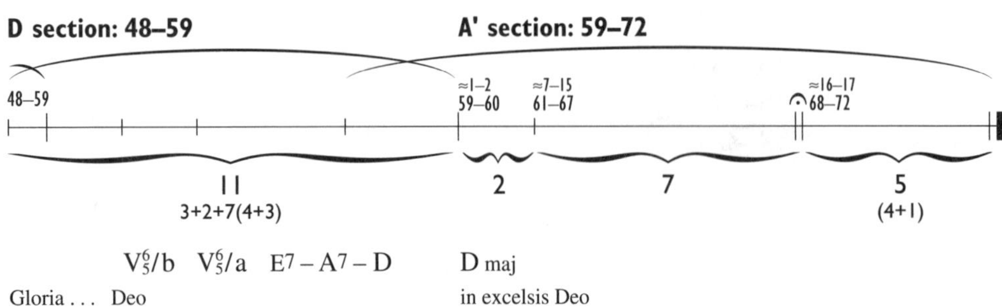

The introduction introduces the musical topic of discourse, seen in mm. 1–4, with the jaunty octave-unison Ds followed by a short scalar motion in m. 2, which is elaborated upon in m. 4. This is truly the full substance of the entire movement and clearly demonstrates Vivaldi's genius in manipulating the smallest amount of material to give the greatest musical effect. The introduction can be organized into three smaller units:

MEASURES	DESCRIPTION
1–6	Two measures repeated three times (3 x 2)
7–15	Grouped in two measures plus a four-measure harmonic sequential descent from C-sharp to G in the bass, culminating in three measures of the dominant-seventh chord in D major
16–17, b. 2	Solidify the perfect authentic cadence in D major, complete with a 4–3 suspension, which ushers in the first statement by the chorus.

Be certain to listen carefully for the subtle change in the final sixteenth-note (m. 8, b, 2), when compared to m. 4. This is easy for less-experienced players to trip over and a quick reminder can avoid lost rehearsal time.

Sections A, B, C, and D are all of similar length (11, 9, 11, and 11 measures respectively) and move from tonic to dominant to submediant and finally to the mediant, C-sharp minor. It is important to keep clear in your mind and ear that the end of one section overlaps the beginning of the next section (e.g., m. 48), as the orchestra will hear m. 48 as the beginning of the new section D, while the chorus will interpret m. 48 as the close of section C. Any momentary indecision or confusion here could be unsettling for all performers.

From an articulation standpoint with regard to the text, baroque performance practices seem to indicate separating each phrase of text one from the other, especially when isolated words repeat. For example, in mm. 17–18, separate between iterations of the word *gloria,* while in mm. 21–24, connect to the text *in excelsis Deo*. Focus on this in mm. 28–35, where the half note on the word *gloria* should be shortened to a quarter note followed by a quarter rest in mm. 29, 30 and 31, but connected to *in excelsis Deo* in m. 32. This general rule may be applied fairly routinely as an axiom throughout the entire movement and work.

One very important conducting decision must be made in m. 67, which is how to handle the fermata. Since m. 67 is analogous to m. 15 (where there is no fermata), consider allowing for three-beats of rest in m. 67 without any further lengthening of time. This will maintain the drive to the end that Vivaldi certainly intended.

Movement II

In stark contrast to Movement I's joy-filled, jaunty opening choral exclamation of *Glory to God in the highest* in D major, Movement II's chorus is in B minor. Its long-breathed double-counterpoint lines will prove a challenge for any ensemble. The conductor must provide shape, continuity, and meaning for this ninety-two-measure chorus. Note that Vivaldi does not provide a single dynamic marking; thus the conductor must help players and singers to understand where the formal aspects of the movement demand tension and subsequent release.

The opening eight-measure instrumental introduction sets the mood and basic affect for the entire movement. Smooth, separate bows for violin, bowed "as it comes" work well. Viola add some interest to the articulation by employing a *portato* bowing, taking two eighth notes per bow. The continuo line also works well with a *portato* bowing for cello, but consider exploring a quarter-note pizzicato approach for the doubling contrabass to provide a solid pulse on each beat.

The main body of the chorus divides nicely into four large sections:

Section	Measures	Subdivision
A	9–40	8 + 16 + 8
B	40–55	5 + 6 + 5
C	55–69	5 + 10
D	69–92	8 + 12 + 4

Figure 2

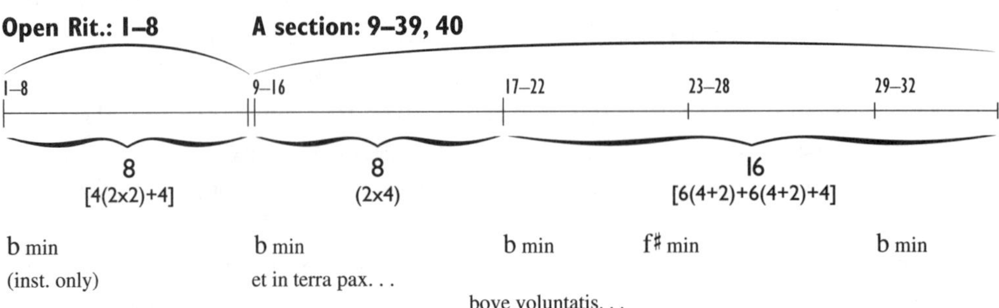

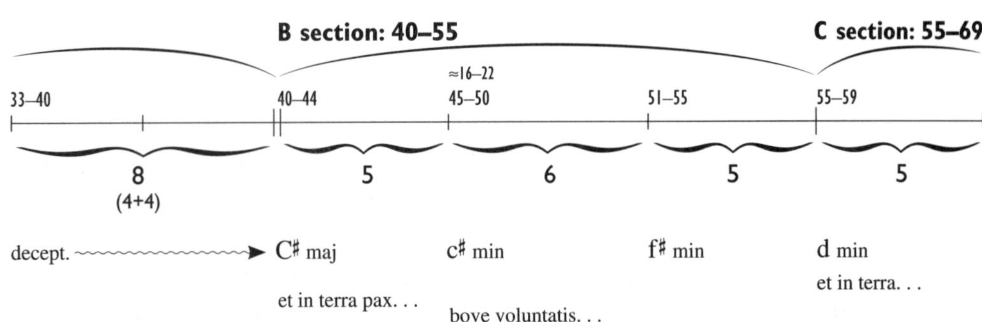

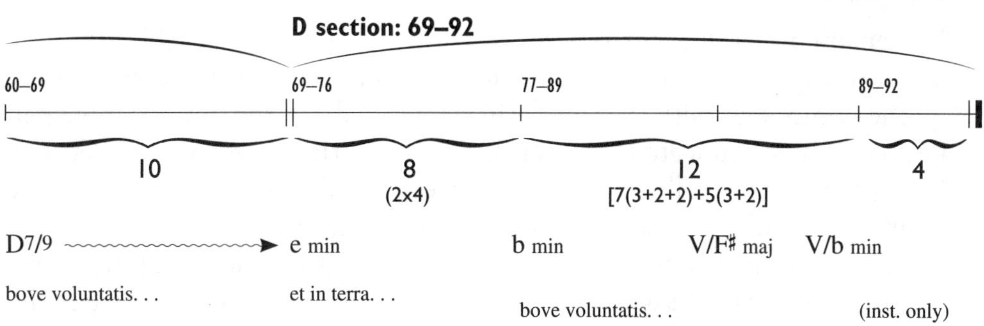

Shape is the main concern for this movement; both short-term within the four- or five-bar phrases and long-term covering the thirty-two or so measures of each large section. An initial example of the short-term shape is the paired counterpoint between bass and tenor in mm. 9–13, which uses only the first phrase of text and demands a slow dynamic intensification to the downbeat of m. 12. This is followed by a release of tension that ushers in an exact repetition in alto and soprano.

Overlapping these two short-term shape opportunities is a long-term dynamic tension beginning with the rising figures in tenor in m. 16 on the second phrase of text. Note that now the tension and drive is unrelenting and upward:

Voice Part	Measures	Motion
Tenor	16–17	C-sharp–D–D-sharp–E–E-sharp–F-sharp
Alto	18–21	F-sharp–G–G-sharp–A–A-sharp–B
Soprano	22–23	C-sharp–D–D-sharp–E–E-sharp–F-sharp
Bass	24	F-sharp–G–G-sharp–A–A-sharp–B

This is followed by a three-measure concluding cadence which establishes F-sharp minor in m. 33. Thus the long-term dynamic tension begins in m. 16 and ascends by half step all the way to m. 29 and finally releases in m. 33. This example of short-term/long-term dynamic/tonal tension/release is central to the success of this movement. Vivaldi often signals the conclusion of a long-term phrase goal with the use of a *hemiola*, as seen at the cadence found in mm. 31–33.

Short-term/long-term shapes can be easily determined through the remainder of the movement by careful examination of the distribution of text: *Et in terra…* is short-term, and *bonae voluntatis…* is long-term. Be sure to maintain steadiness and be helpful in the cadential hemiola spots (mm. 7–8, 31–32, 38–39, 53–54, 67–68, 82–83, and 87–88). Bracketing these hemiola patterns in players' parts will also insure that they understand the subtle shift of harmonic/metric aspect of Vivaldi's musical syntax.

Movement III

Movement III, a duet for two sopranos, has a typical ritornello aria format, featuring opening (mm. 1–17) and closing (mm. 109–125) identical ritornellos in the tonic key, with clearly derived material for the singers interspersed between three truncated ritornellos in contrasting keys. Various entrances for soprano can be a little tricky for less-experienced singers, and thus careful attention to clear cues will help ensure their confidence.

The opening seventeen-measure ritornello features almost all the thematic material for this exciting duet on four of the textual acclimations: *praise*, *bless*, *worship*, and *glorify*. As seen in figure 2, the seventeen measures begin with a two-measure motive followed by a four-measure descending scale, making the first six-measure phrase. The next four measures form a four-measure unit that is really a sequence of the two-measure motive in measures 7–8. The final seven measures can be organized as a four-measure descending step-progression followed by a three-measure unit that signals the first entry of the sopranos.

The three medial ritornellos, mm. 37–42 in D major, mm. 62–66 in E minor, and mm. 75–80 in C major, are all clearly built upon the opening six measures of the initial ritornello. Be sure to observe that the E minor ritornello, however, is only five measures in duration and that the second measure of the pattern has been removed. Further, the E minor ritornello is overlapped by the singers in m. 66; this C section (mm. 67–74) is the only time that soprano does not give forth with the entirety of the text.

Take special care to recognize the *stimmtausch* (voice exchange) that occurs between soprano 1 and 2. This clearly demonstrates that these two voices are equal in Vivaldi's mind's ear and that the two singers must be similar in vocal color, yet independent musicians.

Orchestrally, consider using concertists (one player to a part) during sections A through D, reserving tutti strings for the ritornellos. This will eliminate potential balance issues for the singers and greatly add to the interest in change of texture throughout the movement. If concertists are employed, consider taking the contrabass out during these passages, supporting the singers with a single cello on the bass line instead.

A nice, brisk tempo of a quarter note =112 will truly allow this duet to dance and capture the spirit of the text.

FIGURE 3

Allegro $\frac{2}{4}$

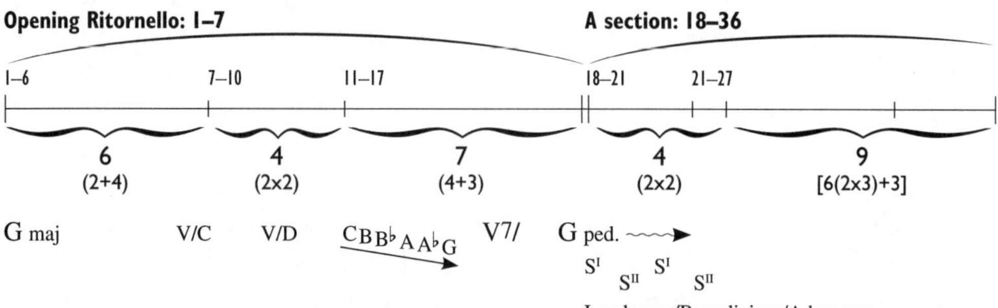

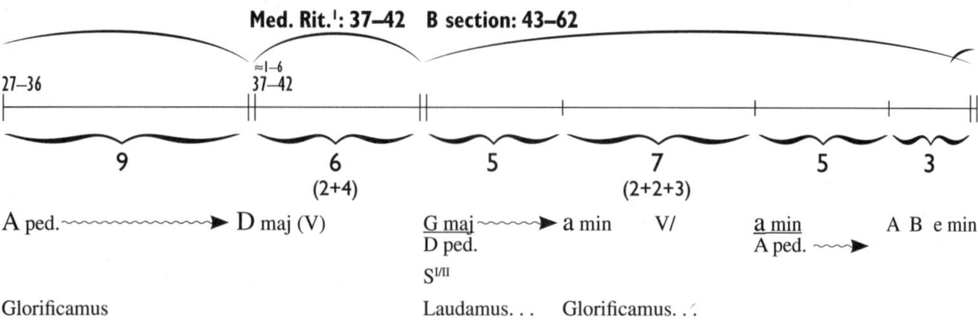

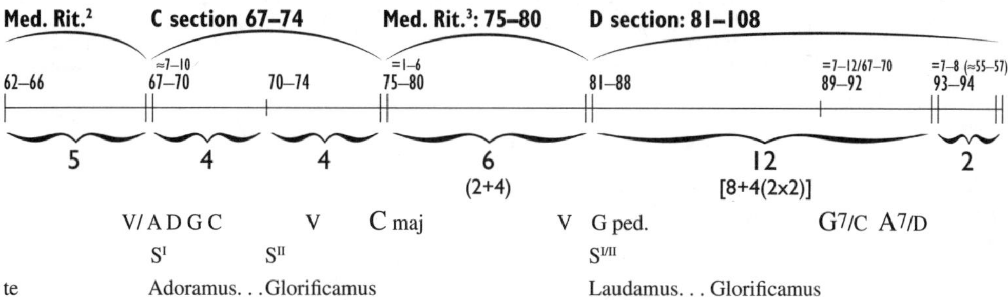

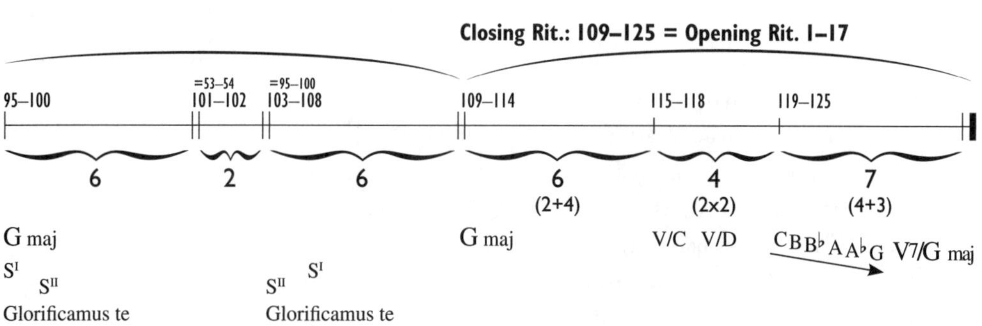

Movements IV and V

As previously noted, these movements are discussed together, as they contain a single line of text—*Gratias agimus tibi, propter magnam gloriam tuam*—and bring the second large section of the *Gloria* text, the so-called acclimations, to a conclusion. These two short movements should be performed *attacca* (attached without pause between them). They represent two stylistic hallmarks of Vivaldi's choral writing. The opening six-measure section is made up of two statements of the first half of the text in two three-measure homophonic choral progressions. The first three measures employ a third relation: E minor–C6–A7; the second three bars confirm B7 as the dominant of E minor, rocking between B major in third inversion, F-sharp major in first inversion, and B major in root position. Be sure to note the scalar motion in the soprano line as it moves stepwise from B to E. The complication is the half step from C-natural to C-sharp and the giant whole step C-sharp to D-sharp.

FIGURE 4

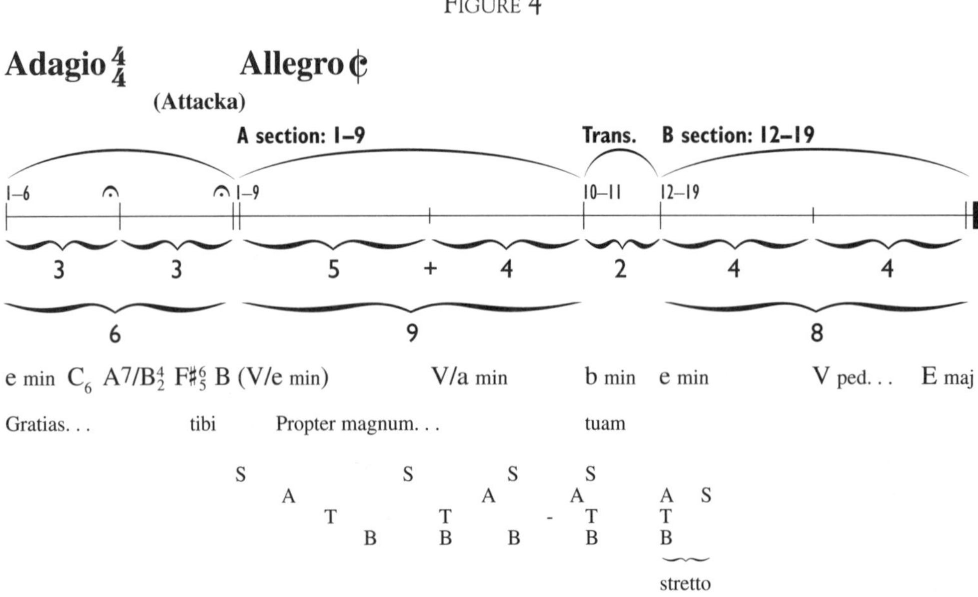

Movement V

Movement V follows Movement IV without pause, and features Vivaldi's other stylistic characteristic of counterpoint. The subject is a two-measure motive that centers on four repeated quarter notes followed by an eighth-note flourish that turns on itself and returns to the opening pitch of the motive. This contrapuntal section falls neatly into two large sections: mm. 1–9 connected by a two-measure transition (mm. 10–11) to mm. 12–19. Section A (mm. 1–9) provides a typical fugal treatment with five statements of the subject alternating between dominant and tonic in *stretto* (overlap) in every measure and rotating through the choral texture from top to bottom, then back to the top again for the fifth statement of the subject. Be sure that sopranos recognize that the last eighth note of m. 5 is an F-natural, not the F-sharp they sing in m. 1.

Following a two-measure transition in mm. 10–12 with a two-beat anacrusis in alto, the eight-measure section B tightens the *stretto* even further (m. 12). Through single statements of the modified subject, the music embarks on a falling melodic-step motion over an enlivened harmonic progression that alternates between root-position major chords and their secondary diminished-seventh chords. This development of sorts lasts for four measures (mm. 12–15), coming to the final four-measure phrase over a dominant pedal point on B, which brings the entire twenty-five-measure package full-circle to a cadence on E major.

Further cementing the two movements together into one is the tempo relationship of Adagio to Allegro that can be made seamless and smooth by making the quarter-note tempo of the Adagio the same as the half-note tempo of the Allegro.

Movement VI

Movement VI, using the Domine Deus text, is a charming, trio sonata-like movement for soprano and oboe, built on a lovely "Siciliano-esque" basso continuo line. This movement works best conducted in four at a tempo of dotted-quarter note = 48–52, rather than in twelve. There are ample opportunities for tasteful embellishments in soprano and oboe with a number of obligatory cadential trills. Be sure to talk with the two soloists prior to rehearsal to make sure that their ornamentation matches, since their melodic material is so interwoven.

There are also several opportunities to employ an echo affect on repeated motivic material:

Measure		Measure
6, b. 1–2	to	26, b. 4
27, b. 1	to	29, b. 3
30, b. 2	to	35, b. 2–3
41, b. 3	to	42, b. 3

These options are at the conductor's discretion and must be decided upon prior to the first rehearsal and clearly indicated in the parts. The choice of continuo group instruments is also up to the conductor; if the budget allows, this is a wonderful opportunity to enhance the continuo line by adding the bassoon color and asking contrabass to play *pizzicato* (plucked) while the cello plays *arco* (bowed). The affect can be truly delightful.

The overall form of this aria is built upon the baroque tradition of instrumental ritornellos alternating with sections for the voice. Vivaldi's internal ritornellos are quite sort and vary considerably in length (e.g., mm. 15–16, 22–24, and 31, b. 3 to m. 32), and really function as connective tissue between phrases and repetitions of the text sung by soprano. The text, which is the first of the three invocations *(Domine Deus…, Domine Fili…,* and *Domine Deus Agnus Dei)*, is stated completely in sections A and C; but in section D (m. 32, b. 2 to m. 36), only the final *Pater omipotens* is used. It may be convenient to think of section D as a kind of codetta to section C.

FIGURE 5

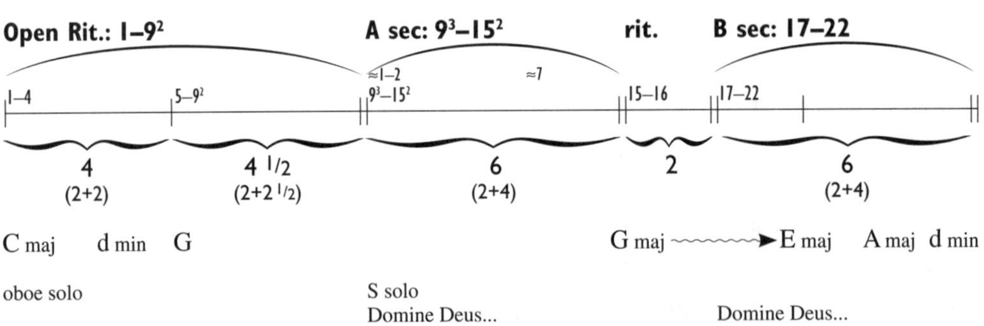

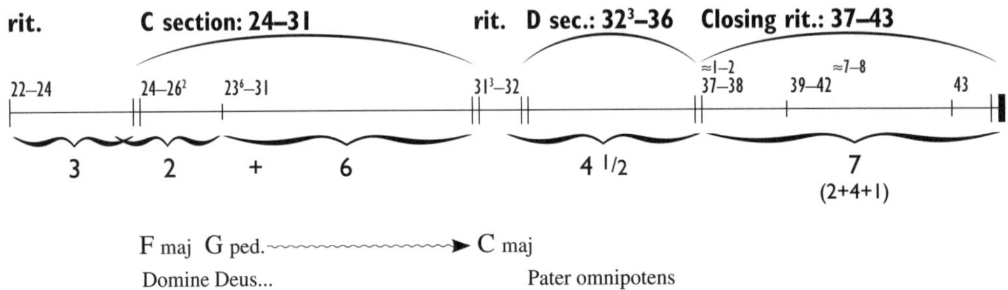

When analyzing this kind of ritornello aria, it is best to examine the opening ritornello very carefully, as it will almost always present all the melodic/ motivic material of the entire movement, as is the case here in mm. 1–9. This material is cleverly modified as the closing ritornello in mm. 37–43. Measures 37–38 are exactly like mm. 1–2, but the passage in mm. 39–40, b. 2 is, in fact, the stepwise progression of m. 6 now extended, while m. 40, b. 3 to m. 41, b. 2 is a repeat of m. 7, and m. 41, b. 3 is similar to m. 8 and leads to a concluding cadence in m. 43.

Pay special attention to places where the ritornello overlaps the soprano solo material and vice versa. These will always be spots where musicians can become confused, thinking that the other line should conclude before they begin. When the conductor knows the score well and is confident with a confirming glance for a cue, everyone is at ease and the dialogue emerges as Vivaldi intended.

Movement VII

Domine Fili Unigenite is one of Vivaldi's most famous choruses. Built upon a jaunty nine-measure example of double counterpoint, this dotted figure may be double dotted for even more rhythmic excitement to underscore the meaning of the text, *the only begotten Son*. If you decide to double dot, be certain to adjust the first beat of mm. 16, 25, 54, and 60 this way:

FIGURE 6

A brisk allegro tempo of quarter note = 132 is recommended.

The movement itself falls into two large sections: mm. 9–53 and mm. 53–90. These are surrounded by identical eight-measure opening and closing ritornellos. The harmonic and contrapuntal interest is found in mm. 26–37, 41–53, and 70–78, where the harmonic rhythm speeds up and the counterpoint involves independence of all four voices. These three sections will require the most rehearsal. Do not hesitate to isolate these spots and then put them back into context.

FIGURE 7

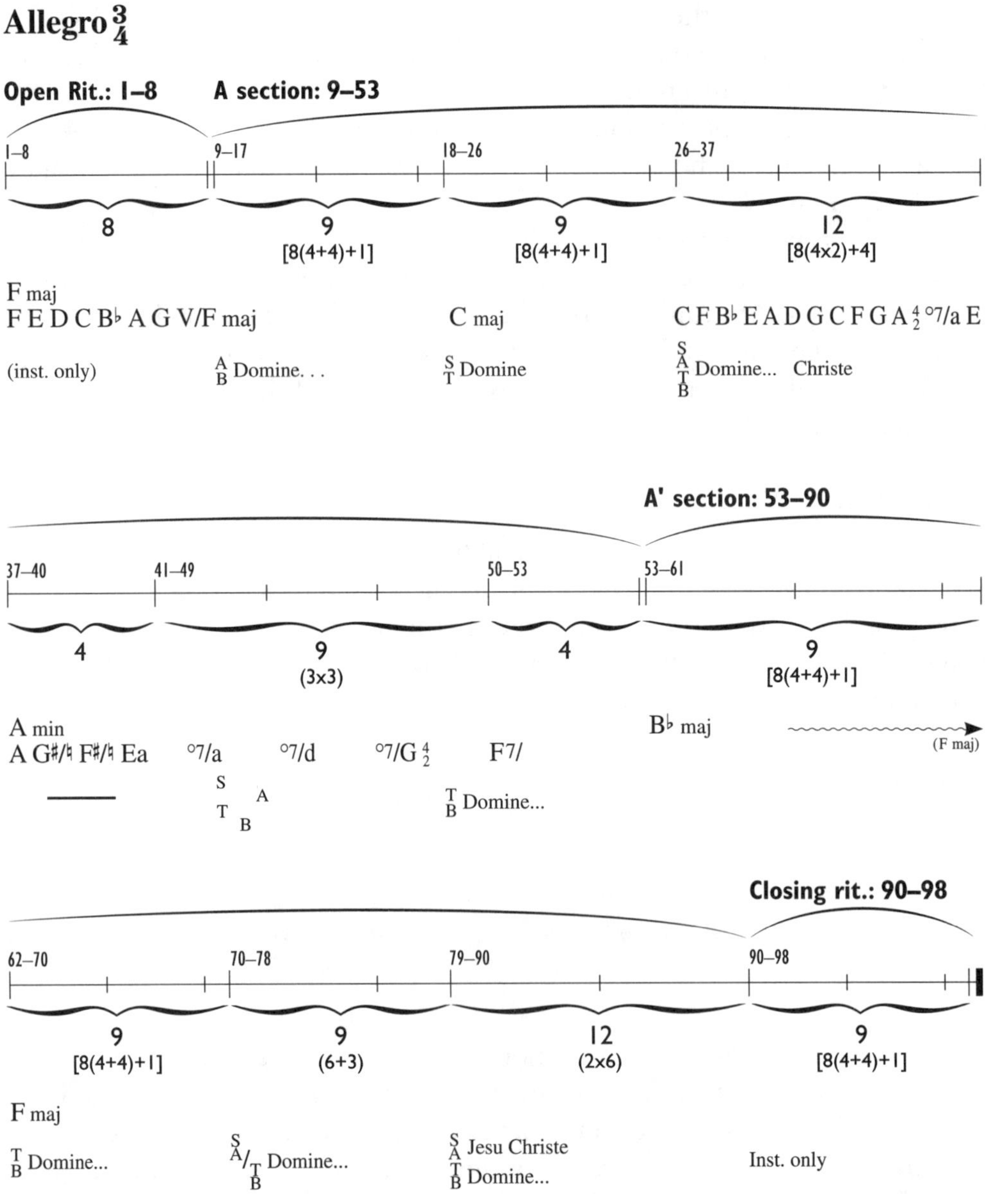

Allegro $\frac{3}{4}$

Open Rit.: 1–8 **A section: 9–53**

1–8 | 9–17 | 18–26 | 26–37

8 | 9 [8(4+4)+1] | 9 [8(4+4)+1] | 12 [8(4x2)+4]

F maj
F E D C B♭ A G V/F maj | C maj | C F B♭ E A D G C F G A $^4_2$ °7/a E

(inst. only) | A/B Domine. . . | S/T Domine | S/A/T/B Domine... Christe

A' section: 53–90

37–40 | 41–49 | 50–53 | 53–61

4 | 9 (3x3) | 4 | 9 [8(4+4)+1]

A min
A G♯/♮ F♯/♮ Ea °7/a °7/d °7/G $^4_2$ F7/ | B♭ maj → (F maj)

—— | S T A B | T/B Domine...

Closing rit.: 90–98

62–70 | 70–78 | 79–90 | 90–98

9 [8(4+4)+1] | 9 (6+3) | 12 (2x6) | 9 [8(4+4)+1]

F maj
T/B Domine... | S/A / T/B Domine... | S/A Jesu Christe, T/B Domine... | Inst. only

It is important to be very clear at the points of cadential hemiola (mm. 35–36 and 51–52) without shifting to a half-note conducting pattern. Also, be very careful that singers do not round out dotted rhythms to sound and feel more like quarter-eighth triplets. Take care as well to keep text stress consistent and accurate with the text itself; do not fall into the trap of accenting final syllables because they fall on downbeats at the ends of long phrases (mm. 17, 26, 37, 43, 53, etc.)

Movement VIII

The last of the three invocations, *(Domine Deus, Agnus Dei Filius Patris)* is set as Movement VIII in a stunning aria for alto solo with choral responses derived from the first of the three petitions, *Qui tollis peccata mundi, Miserere nobis*. Vivaldi distributes the text in a fascinating fashion to co-mingle the invocation to the Lamb of God with the concept of the Redeemer who takes away the sins of the world.

The form of this aria with chorus is typical of the Baroque, employing an opening five-measure ritornello which returns exactly at the close of the movement. Between these two ritornellos are three distinct sections:

Section	Measures
A	6 to 14, b. 2
B	14, b. 3 to 24
C	25–36

In section A the alto soloist presents the entire text of the invocation using a combination of material derived from the opening bass line and her own independent motive. The section concludes with the chorus responding with the opening line of the petition that moves from the A minor cadence (dominant of the key of D minor) to G minor, beginning a rich harmonic progression in section B moving through this sequence: C minor–B-flat–E-flat–A-flat–B-flat–G–C minor–D–G minor–C–F. This allows for the return to D minor in m. 25 and the beginning of section C. During this harmonically rich section B it is important to shape the prosody of the text in concert with the natural syntax of the harmonic language as this motion passes through a series of secondary dominants to their logical resolutions.

In section C, the text distribution is reversed, with the alto soloist using the petition text and the choir responding with invocation text.

FIGURE 8

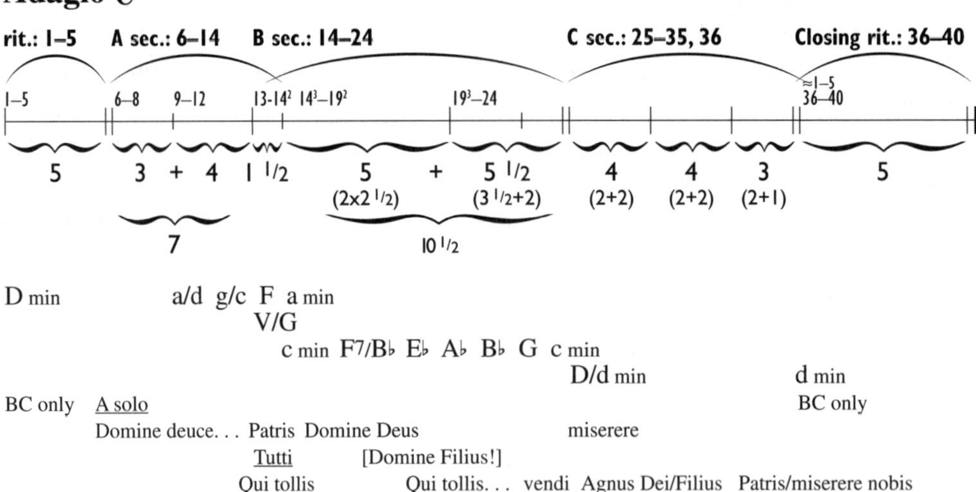

There are a number of possibilities for the treatment of the basso continuo line in this movement that include articulation, bowing versus pizzicato, and removing the contrabass voice at times. These decisions are all up to the conductor, but must be clearly indicated in the parts to avoid confusion and lost rehearsal time. Consider slurring beats 1 and 3 in m. 2 and all subsequent occurrences of this ascending third. It is also possible to double the bass line with contrabass playing *pizzicato* to underscore the walking bass line affect of the movement. Also think about omitting the contrabass when the soloist sings and having it play arco when doubling the choir and playing with the full string section.

Movement IX

Similar in style and function to the *Gratias agimus tibi* movement, Movement IX, *Qui tollis peccata mundi*, features a homophonic, harmonically poignant chord progression moving from A minor to a final cadence on E major. This verse of text, the second of the three petitions, divides into two distinct sections: *Qui tollis peccata mundi* and *suscipe deprecationem nostram*. Vivaldi capitalizes upon this text division by changing the meter and tempo.

FIGURE 9

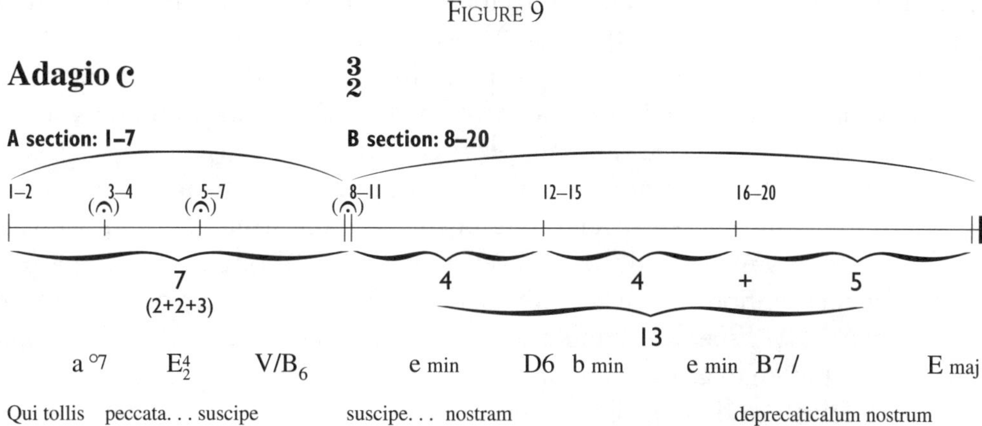

Section A (mm. 1–7) divides into three subsections, each concluding with a fermata. The release of the fermatas in mm. 2 and 4 must function as the downbeat in mm. 3 and 5, while the release of the fermata in m. 7 should set up the new meter and tempo of section B in m. 8. The Adagio works well at a tempo of quarter note = 60.

Section B is also in three subsections: mm. 8–11, 12–15, and 16–20. The new meter of 3/2 implies a quicker tempo: half note = 72. A lift between the repetitions of the word *suscipe* in mm. 8–9 helps make the prosody of the text make sense. The release in m. 15 works best by changing the dotted-whole note to a whole note with half rest. Be sure to clearly delineate the two cadential hemiolas in mm. 13–14 and 18–19. Even though Vivaldi does not indicate any dynamic change in this movement, a quasi-change to *piano* in m. 16 with crescendo to m. 20 adds interest to the repetition of text and harmonic progression of A minor to E major.

Movement X

Movement X is an alto aria and an excellent example of when to use phrasal conducting (e.g., the music is in three but conducted in one, using patterns that illuminate the phrase structure). The phrases in this aria vary considerably and imply numerous hemiolas that make for an exciting and gratifying musical experience. Again, careful examination of the opening ritornello (mm. 1–27) will provide much needed insight into the concepts and shapes of things to come. A tempo of dotted-quarter note = 66 works well to underscore the meaning of the text (the third of the three petitions), and allows the natural *schwung* (swing) of the meter to be a prominent feature of the basic affect of this movement.

The opening ritornello falls into four large phrases. The first phrase, mm. 1–7, is grouped 3 + 4 and thus can be conducted using a clear three pattern followed by a four pattern. The second phrase, mm. 8–13, is in essence a six-measure phrase that is a sequence of two measures; thus choosing a two pattern and using it three times makes this section work nicely.

The third phrase, mm. 14–21, is eight measures that fit nicely into a two pattern four times. Take special note of the hemiola in mm. 20–21. Staying calm, clear, and in two will help players more than shifting to a three pattern with the quarter note as the beat. By marking the hemiola with brackets in the parts, players will see, hear, and understand the momentary shift of harmonic emphasis that enables the hemiola to function.

The fourth and final phrase, mm. 22–26, is five measures that may be grouped 3 + 2. Measure 27, then, is really a downbeat for the next phrase, which ushers in the alto soloist and delineates section A. Note in figure 10 that most often the phrase structure is guided by the orchestra and not the voice. This is very typical of Baroque style in general and Vivaldi's music specifically.

The overall structure of the movement then is:

Section	Measures
R	1–27
A	27–58
R1	58–64
B	64–92
R2	80–84
R3	92–97
C	97–131
R	131–150 (repeat of mm. 8–27)

The three large sections, A, B, and C, are all delineated by the text, beginning with *Qui sedes*... Be sure to note that within section B there is a momentary R2 followed by a continuation of the *miserere* text.

Careful attention to a dynamic shift between the instrumental ritornello music and passages the orchestra plays with the soloist is one of the stylistic features of this kind of ritornello aria. Consider taking out the contrabass in sections A, B, and C when the alto sings, reserving this deepening octave voice for the continuo line only for the ritornellos.

FIGURE 10

Allegro $\frac{3}{8}$

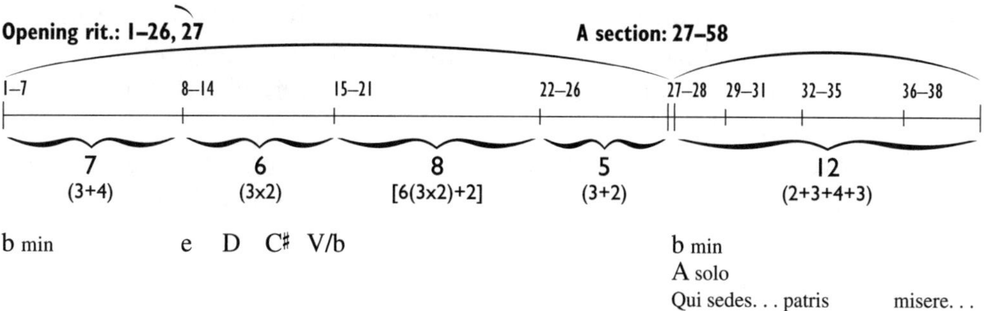

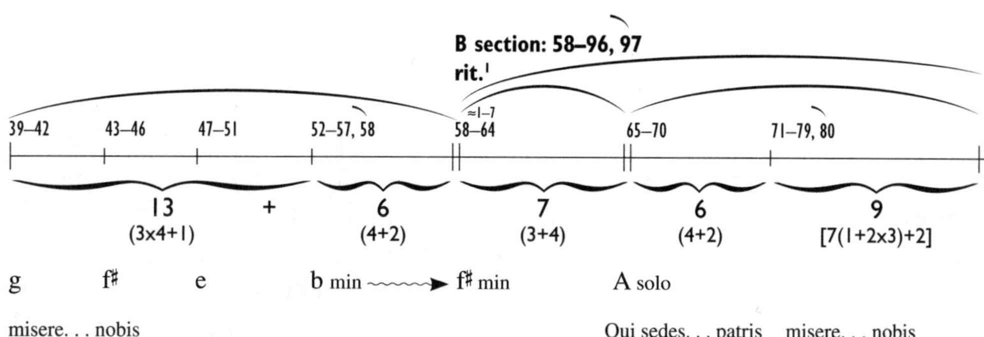

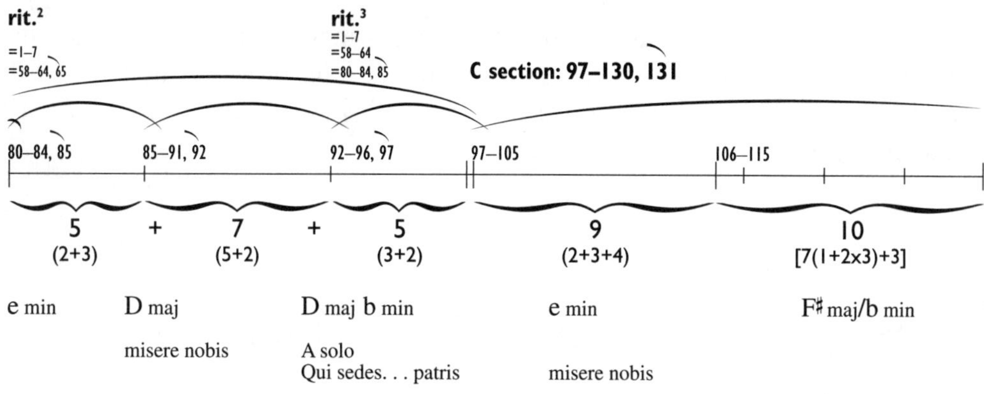

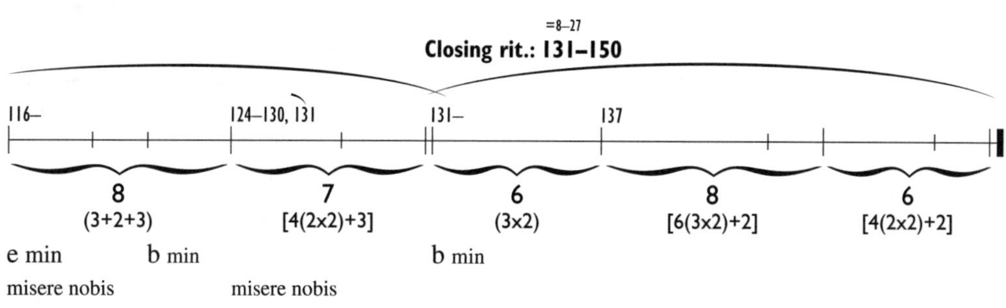

Movement XI

Movement XI employs the first three lines of the final four doxological statements of the *Gloria* text. It also returns to the music of the opening movement, but with some interesting changes that can trip up even a very sophisticated chorus and orchestra; thus some careful attention to this movement is in order.

The two large sections of the movement divide mm. 1–10, b. 2 and m. 10, b. 3 to m. 23. Each large section further divides into smaller subsections:

Section	Measures		
A	[1 to 6, b. 2]	+	[6, b. 3 to 10, b. 2]
B	[10, b. 3 to 16]	+	[17–23]

Section A uses only one line of text *(Quoniam to solus sanctus)*, where section B uses two lines of text *(Tu solus Dominus. Tu solus altissimus, Jesu Christe)*.

When compared to Movement I, this movement uses all the same basic motives and techniques, only in a carefully and cleverly truncated way. For instance, the opening introduction in Movement I is sixteen-and-a-half measures long, where in Movement XI, this instrumental introduction is only five-and-a-half measures. Upon closer inspection you can see that Vivaldi omits mm. 3 and 6–15 of the original introduction in Movement XI. Measures 6, b. 2 to m. 16 of Movement XI is identical to mm. 17, b. 2 to m. 27 of Movement I, with only minor rhythmic adjustments for the text. Measures 17–19 of Movement XI are the same as mm. 57–59 of Movement I. Finally, mm. 22–23 of Movement XI are like mm. 70–72 of Movement I, with the exception of removing beats 2 and 3 of m. 71.

Figure 11

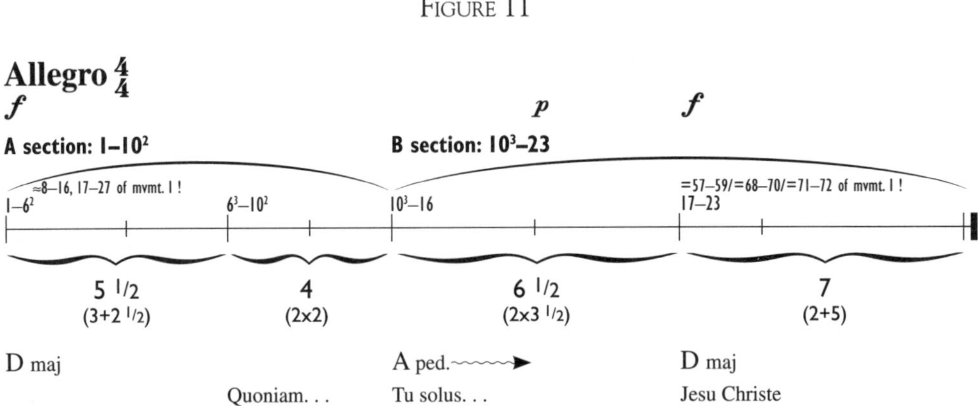

The dramatic restatement yet reworking of music from one movement to another has been used by composers for generations. Vivaldi manages to draw the parallel between the textual concepts of the two movements while highlighting and intensifying the drive to the final movement by truncating his musical ideas from a length of seventy-two to twenty-three measures.

Movement XII

The final movement not only brings to conclusion this doxological statement regarding the third member of the Trinity (the Holy Spirit), but also conforms to a centuries-old musical tradition of employing a large, complicated, contrapuntal movement to round off the entirety of the *Gloria* text. Here Vivaldi uses a fugal structure built upon two contrasting subjects, one predominantly in half and whole notes, the second much more rhythmically articulated with dotted-quarter and eighth-notes. The contrast between the fugue subjects can remain clear and understandable if they also are articulated differently. The first subject should be slightly less articulated, with separation between notes less obvious than the second subject, which lends itself to a highly articulated approach.

Instrumentalists must understand this and match the articulation contrast established by the chorus. A close examination of the entries of subjects and key areas will help the conductor and performers to allow this movement to unfold and conclude nicely. Remember, fugue is not a standardized form, but is really a compositional process. Following an opening exposition which allows the subjects to appear in all voices in a key alternation of tonic to dominant, all fugues are different in shape and scope and boil down to a series of expository sections (fugue subjects stated) and episodes (no fugue subject present).

The opening exposition, mm. 1–16, has three entries of the paired fugue subjects: Bass/soprano in the tonic, alto/tenor in the dominant, and finally soprano/bass back in the tonic. It is important to note that the first two entries are only supported by the basso continuo, allowing the conductor to change the size of the choral forces to only concertists if desired. If you choose this stylistic option, then tutti sopranos should sing in m. 11, tutti tenors joining at m. 11, b. 2, tutti Altos at m. 11, b. 4, and tutti Basses in m. 12 with strings and oboe. This process creates real excitement and brings the opening exposition to a rousing conclusion in m. 16. In episodic passages like mm. 16–23, it is important to help players know when and if their part has material derived from fugue subjects or is simply contrapuntal. The episodes can be some of the most interesting passages in a fugue, where a composer exercises some developmental abilities.

Figure 12 shows that this movement is in fact five expositions separated by four episodes. It is easy to let the energy wane in episode 3 (mm. 45–54) with the movement to F-sharp minor, as well as to allow exposition 4 (mm. 54–60) to become labored and uninteresting. Extra effort must be exerted here to keep the momentum moving forward. Vivaldi has built in a composed crescendo in episode 4, mm. 67–72, with a series of secondary dominants in quick succession leading to the final rousing exposition in mm. 72–78. This brings this exciting and exquisite work to a wonderfully rewarding conclusion.

FIGURE 12

Allegro $\frac{4}{2}$

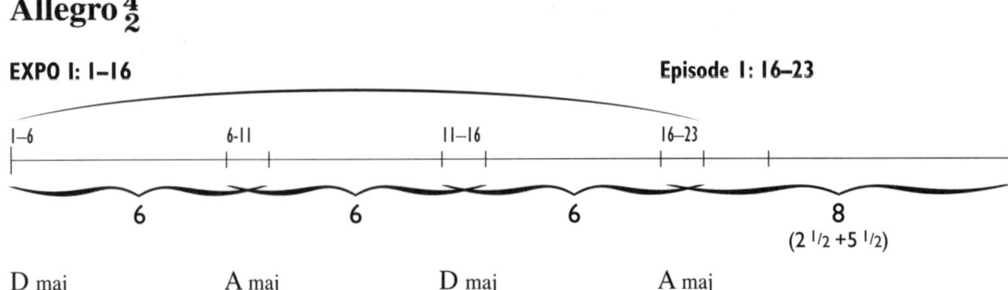

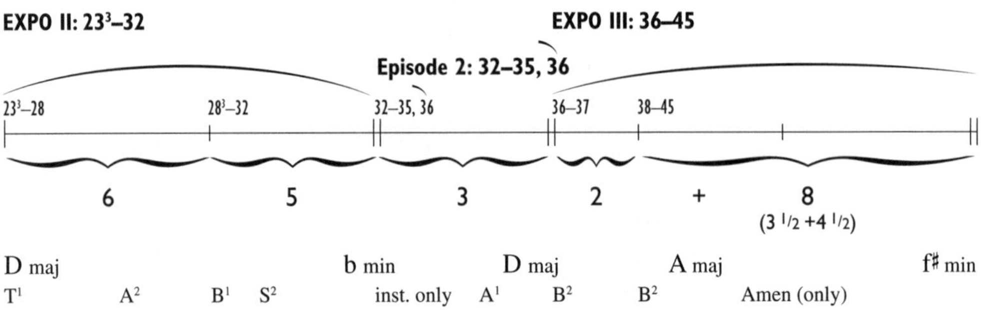

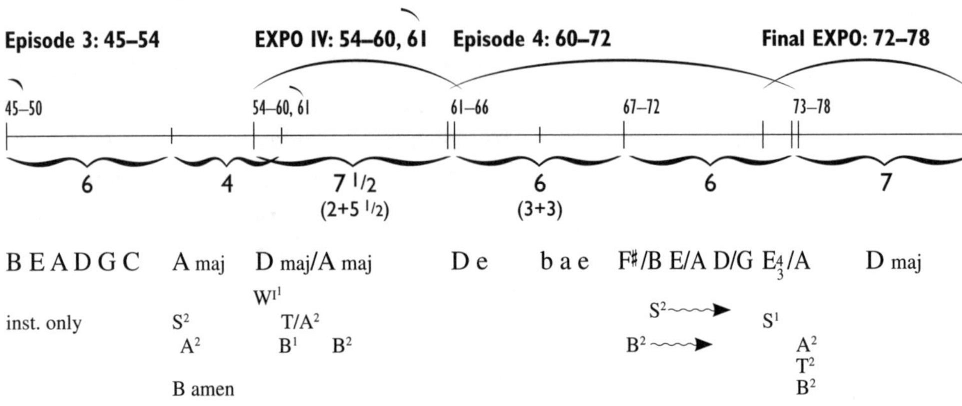

Index by Title for Teaching Music through Performance in Choir Volumes 1, 2, 3

Title	Composer	Vol.	Level	Page
A Boy and a Girl	Whitacre, Eric	3	4	381
A Choral Flourish	Vaughan Williams, Ralph	2	4	495
A Gaelic Blessing	Rutter, John	1	3	208
A New Year Carol				
from Friday Afternoons, Op. 7	Britten, Benjamin	2	1	173
A Procession Winding around Me	Van, Jeffrey	1	5	465
A Spotless Rose	Morton, Graeme	2	4	499
Absalon, fili mi	Desprez, Josquin	1	4	442
Ahrirang	arr. De Cormier, Robert	3	2	127
Ain't No Grave Can Hold My Body Down	arr. Caldwell, Paul/Ivory, Sean	3	4	455
Al naharot Bavel	Rossi, S./ed. Jacobson	2	4	623
Alleluia	Larsen, Libby	1	3	181
Also hat Gott die Welt geliebt	Schütz, Heinrich	3	4	385
Amor de Mi Alma	Stroope, Z. Randall	2	4	505
An die Frauen (To Women), Hob. XXVb:4	Haydn, F./arr. Vancil	2	3	465
An Elizabethan Spring	Chatman, Stephen	2	4	511
April Is in My Mistress' Face	Morely, Thomas	2	2	207
Ave Maria (Angelus Domini)	Biebl, Franz	1	4	446
Ave Maria	Busto, Javier	2	3	315
Ave Maria	Dett, Nathaniel	3	3	267
Ave Maria	Holst, Gustav	1	5	476
Ave Maria	Stravinsky, Igor	2	3	319
Ave Maria, Op. 12	Brahms, Johannes	1	4	426
Ave, maris stella	Loomer, Diane	2	2	293
Ave verum corpus	Byrd, William	1	4	353
Ave verum corpus	Poulenc, Francis	1	5	479
Ave verum corpus, K. 618	Mozart, W. A.	1	3	184
Ave verum corpus, Op. 2, No. 1	Elgar, Edward	1	2	111
Back to Ethiopia	arr. Rardin, Paul	3	2	241

TITLE	COMPOSER	VOL.	LEVEL	PAGE
Balulalow	Custer, Gerald	3	4	393
Be Thou My Vision	Parker, Alice	1	1	89
Beati mortui, Op. 115, No. 1	Mendelssohn/arr. Weber	2	3	469
Benedicamus, Domino	Penderecki, Krzysztof	1	5	487
Best of Rooms, The	Thompson, Randall	3	4	399
Bile Them Cabbage Down	arr. Wilberg, Mack	3	2	131
Bist du bei mir	Bach, J. S.	1	1	93
Black Is the Color of My True Love's Hair	arr. Churchill, Stuart	2	2	211
Bogoróditse Djévo (Mother of God and Virgin)	Pärt, Arvo	1	3	189
Brothers, Sing On! (A Choral Salutation)	Grieg, E./arr. McKinney	2	3	475
Buffalo Gals	arr. Chilcott, Bob	2	3	323
Bullerengue	Rincón, José Antonio	2	2	215
Byker Hill	arr. Sandler, Mitchell	3	2	247
Calme des Nuits	Saint-Saëns, Camille	3	4	403
Cantemus!	Bárdos, Lajos	2	4	517
Cantique de Jean Racine, Op. 11	Fauré, Gabriel Urbain	1	3	193
Chindia	Pascanu, Alexandru	3	4	409
Choral Hymns from the Rig Veda, Set 3	Holst, Gustav	2	5	665
Christ lag in Todesbanden, No. 7 from Opella nova I	Schein, Johann Hermann	2	2	219
Circus Band	Ives, Charles	1	3	199
City Called Heaven	Poelinitz, Josephine	3	2	121
Come Sing to Me of Heaven	arr. McDermid, J. Aaron	3	4	503
Come to Me My Love	Dello Joio, Norman	3	5	545
Confirma hoc, Deus	Handl, Jacob	1	3	325
Credo	Martini, Giovanni Battista	3	4	507
Crucifixus	Lotti, Antonio/ arr. Davison, Archibald	3	4	515
Dadme albricias, hijos d'Eva	Anonymous	1	2	115
Daemon irrepit callidus	Orbán, György	2	4	521
Dance on My Heart	Koepke, Alan	3	2	195
De profundis	Pärt, Arvo	1	4	450
Der Herr segne euch	Bach, J. S.	1	2	157
Die mit Tränen säen, SWV 378 from Geistliche Chormusik, 1648	Schütz, Heinrich	2	4	525
Die Nachtigall, Op. 59, No. 4	Mendelssohn, Felix	1	2	119
Dieu! qu'il la fait bon regarder from Trois Chansons de Charles d'Orleans	Debussy, Claude	2	5	651

TITLE	COMPOSER	VOL.	LEVEL	PAGE
Dirait-on	Lauridsen, Morten	1	3	204
Domaredansen	arr. Collins, Drew	3	2	137
Domine, ad adjuvandum me festina	Martini, Giovanni Battista	2	3	329
Down among the Dead Men	Vaughan Williams, R.	1	3	329
Down by the Riverside	arr. Ames, Roger	2	2	223
Dúlamán	McGlynn, Michael	2	5	673
El Grillo	Desprez, Josquin	1	2	123
El Hambo	Mäntyjärvi, Jaakko	3	4	413
Erev Shel Shoshanim	Hadar, Josef	1	2	127
Ev'ry Time I Feel the Spirit	arr. Dawson, William	3	2	145
Famine Song	VIDA/arr. Culloton, M.	2	2	229
Fillimiooriay	arr. Beery, Lon	3	1	105
Fire	Goetze, Mary	1	2	140
Five Hebrew Love Songs	Whitacre, Eric	2	3	335
Flanders Fields	Emerson, Roger	3	2	253
Four Cummings Choruses, Opus 98	Persichetti, Vincent	3	4	519
Four Pastorales	Effinger, Cecil	2	4	531
Four Slovak Folk Songs	Bartók, Béla	2	4	539
Gate, Gate	arr. Tate, Brian	3	2	199
Geistliches Lied, Op. 30	Brahms, Johannes	2	4	543
Give Us	Winges, Mark	1	5	483
Gloria ad modum tubae	Dufay, Guillaume	1	1	97
Gloria tibi	Bernstein, Leonard	1	2	143
Gloria	Haydn, (Franz) Joseph	1	3	211
God's Bottles	Thompson, Randall	1	3	297
God Is Our Refuge	Mozart, W. A.	3	1	77
God Is Seen	arr. Parker, Alice	3	2	151
Greater Love	Chatman, Stephen	3	3	375
Hallelujah, Amen	Handel, George Frideric	1	3	215
Haneirot Halalu	Hoffman, Stanley M.	1	3	218
Hard Times Come Again No More	Foster, Stephen/arr. Moore	2	1	189
Hark, I Hear the Harps Eternal	arr. Parker, Alice	2	3	343
He, Watching Over Israel	Mendelssohn, Felix	1	3	222
Heart We Will Forget Him	Mulholland, James	2	3	443
Heaven-Haven (A Nun Takes the Veil)	Barber, Samuel	1	4	430
Hello, Girls	arr. Pfautsch, Lloyd	2	1	179
He's Gone Away	Nelson, Ron	1	3	301
Hodie	Whitbourn, James	3	3	271
Hotari Koi	arr. Ogura, Roh	3	4	463
How Can I Keep from Singing	arr. Ellingboe, Bradley	3	2	257

TITLE	COMPOSER	VOL.	LEVEL	PAGE
Hvalite imi Ghospodne (Praise the Name of the Lord)	Tchaikovsky/Chesnokov	1	4	455
I Am His Child	Hogan, Moses	2	2	269
I Find My Feet Have Further Goals	Larsen, Libby	3	5	551
I Have Had Singing	Sametz, Steven	2	4	549
I Love My Love	Holst, Gustav	1	4	358
I Once Loved a Lad	arr. Neaum, Michael	2	2	273
I Thank You God	Walker, Gwyneth	3	4	469
Ich wollt', meine Lieb'	Mendelssohn, Felix	2	2	277
If Music Be the Food of Love	Dickau, David	2	3	349
Ihr Heiligen, lobsinget dem Herren, SWV 288	Schütz, Heinrich	1	3	304
Il est bel et bon	Passereau, Pierre	1	4	361
I'm A-Rollin'	arr. Rardin, Paul	2	3	481
I'm Going Home on a Cloud	arr. Deibler, Seán	2	1	141
In Paradisum	Fissinger, Edwin	3	4	419
In Remembrance	Ames, Jeffery	3	3	275
"In Splendoribus Sanctorum" from *The Strathclyde Motets*	MacMillan, James	3	3	281
Innisfree	Custer, Gerald	2	3	353
Innoria (Huron Dance Song)	Patriquin, Donald	1	3	225
Ipharadisi	arr. Ulrich, Jerry	3	2	155
It Takes a Village	Szymko, Joan	3	2	159
I've Been 'Buked, Children!	arr. Dilworth, Rollo A.	2	2	233
J'entends le moulin	arr. Patriquin, Donald	2	2	281
Japanese Garden	Culloton, Matthew	3	2	205
Jasmine Flower	Ling-Tam, Jing	1	2	131
Jauchzet dem Herrn alle Welt, SWV 36	Schütz, Heinrich	1	4	364
Jerusalem Luminosa	Betinis, Abbie	3	5	561
Jesu dulcis memoria	Victoria, Tomás Luis de	3	3	285
John the Revelator	arr. Caldwell and Ivory	2	4	553
Johnny Has Gone for a Soldier	Parker, A./Shaw, R.	1	3	228
Jordan's Angels	Dilworth, Rollo	3	2	209
Jubilate Deo	Wilberg, Mac	1	4	369
Jubliate Deo in C	Britten, Benjamin	1	3	231
Ka Hia Manu	Hatfield, Stephen	2	3	359
Komm, heil'ger Geist	Schumann, Georg	1	4	372
Kyrie	Beethoven, Ludwig van	1	4	376

Title	Composer	Vol.	Level	Page
La Muerte del Angel	Piazzolla, A./arr. Zadoff	2	4	559
Las Amarillas	Hatfield, Stephen	2	4	605
LAWA	Sadler, Katheryn	3	4	477
Lay a Garland	Pearsall, Robert	3	4	423
Lebenslust	Schubert, Franz	3	3	291
Les étoiles	Sirett, Mark	3	4	483
Let Down the Bars, O Death, Op. 8, No. 2	Barber, Samuel	2	4	565
Let Their Celestial Concerts All Unite	Handel, George Frideric	1	3	237
Let Us Now Praise Famous Men, Op. 35	Finzi, Gerald	1	2	160
Lirum bililirum	Mantovano, Rossino	2	2	237
Little Innocent Lamb	arr. Bartholomew, M.	2	2	299
Lo, How a Rose E'er Blooming	Sandström, Sven-David	3	4	429
Love and Pizen (Springfield Mountain), Op. 60, No. 3	Mechem, Kirke	2	3	365
Love Never Ending	Zinter, Aaron	3	4	527
Love Walked In	Gershwin, G./arr. Zegree	2	3	371
Magnificat in A minor	Porpora, Nicola	3	3	361
Magnificent Horses	arr. Ling-Tam, Jing	3	3	297
Manly Men	Knecht, Kurt	2	4	629
Measure Me Sky	Mulholland, James	3	2	215
Medieval Gloria	Singh, Vijay	3	1	111
Messe basse	Fauré, Gabriel	2	3	449
Mon coeur se recommande à vous	Weckerlin, Jean-Baptiste	2	2	241
Morning Moon	Silvey, Philip E.	2	2	285
Muié Rendêra	Pinto Fonseca, Carlos	1	3	242
Musicks Empire	Pfautsch, Lloyd	1	3	246
My Bonnie	Parker, A./Shaw, R.	1	2	164
My Flight for Heaven	Henson, Blake	3	4	433
My Spirit Sang All Day	Finzi, Gerald	1	4	380
Ngana	Leek, Stephen	1	4	384
Nigra sum	Casals, Pablo	1	3	308
Nine Hundred Miles	Silvey, Philip	3	1	99
Nis'ka Banja	arr. Page, Nick	2	3	455
Noel!	Sametz, Steven	1	3	334
Not While I'm Around	Sondheim, S./arr. Page	2	2	305
Notre Père	Duruflé, Maurice	1	3	250
O aula nobilis	Mathias, William	2	4	611
O bone jesu	Brahms, Johannes	3	4	489

Title	Composer	Vol.	Level	Page
O Jesu Christ, mein Lebens Licht, BWV 118	Bach, Johann Sebastian	2	3	377
O magnum mysterium	Lauridsen, Morten	2	4	571
O magnum mysterium	Victoria, Tomás Luis de	2	3	383
O Music	Mason, Lowell/arr. Rao	2	1	145
O Occhi, manza mia	de Lassus, Orlande	3	2	163
O schöne Nacht, Op. 92, No. 1	Brahms, Johannes	1	4	387
O Sing Joyfully	Batten, Adrian	2	3	387
O vos Omnes	Casals, Pablo	3	3	301
Old Abram Brown	Britten, Benjamin	1	1	102
Old Time Religion	arr. Hogan, Moses	3	2	167
Oremus	Sisask, Urmas	3	3	305
Os justi	Bruckner, Anton	1	5	461
Ose Shalom (The One Who Makes Peace)	Leavitt, John	2	1	149
Our Father (Otche Nash)	Kastal'sky, Alexandr	1	3	312
Past Life Melodies	Hopkins, Sarah	2	3	393
Pater Noster	Stravinsky, Igor	3	3	309
Poor Man Lazrus	Hairston, Jester	1	2	167
Praise His Holy Name!	Hampton, Keith	2	2	245
Prayer Before Sleep	Robinovitch, Sid	3	3	315
Psallite	Praetorius, Michael	1	2	134
Psalm 96	Sweelinck, Jan P.	1	4	395
Psalm 100 (Jauchzet dem Herrn)	Mendelssohn, Felix	3	3	321
Psalm 117	Hoffman, Stanley	2	4	633
Psalm 121	Raminsh, Imant	3	4	493
Ramkali	arr. Sperry, Ethan	3	4	533
(Rejoice O Virgin) Bogoroditse Devo	Rachmaninoff, Sergei	1	4	398
Requiem	Fauré, Gabriel Urbain	1		493
Requiem	Gilkyson, Eliza/ arr. Craig Hella Johnson	3	2	173
Revoici venir du Printemps	Le Jeune, Claude	3	3	327
Rise Up, My Love, My Fair One	Raminsh, Imant	1	4	434
Rustics and Fishermen	Britten, Benjamin	3	4	539
Salmo 150	Aguiar, Ernani	1	3	254
Salut au chevalier printemps, Op. 151, No. 2	Saint-Saëns, Camille	2	4	617
Sam Was a Man	Persichetti, Vincent	2	2	309
Savory, Sage, Rosemary and Thyme	Patriquin, Donald	1	2	147
Scarborough Fair	Goetze, Mary	3	2	221

TITLE	COMPOSER	VOL.	LEVEL	PAGE
Sea Shanties	arr. Jeffers, Ron	2	1	195
Sehnsucht	Schubert, Franz	2	4	637
Set Me as a Seal	Clausen, René	1	3	258
Sfogava con le stele	Monteverdi, Claudio	2	4	577
Shall I Compare Thee	Paulus, Stephen	2	4	643
She Moved through the Fair	Takach, Timothy	1	2	170
Shenandoah	Erb, James	1	3	261
Si iniquitates observaveris	Wesley, Samuel	1	2	172
Sicut cervus	Palestrina, Giovanni	1	3	264
Sicut locutus est	Bach, J. S.	1	4	402
Silent Devotion and Response	Bloch, Ernest	1	2	137
Simple Gifts (Shaker Song)	Copland, Aaron	1	1	105
Sing Me to Heaven	Gawthrop, Daniel	2	3	399
Sing We and Chant It	Morley, Thomas	3	1	81
Sing Ye Praises to Our King, Op. 20, No. 4	Copland, Aaron	2	4	583
Sir Christèmas	Mathias, William	3	3	333
Sometimes I Feel Like a Motherless Child	Gilbert, Nina	1	2	175
Song for the Mira	MacGillivray/arr. Calvert	2	1	183
Song of Peace	Persichetti, Vincent	1	3	337
Soon Ah Will Be Done	Dawson, William L.	1	3	340
Sorida	arr. Powell, Rosephanye	3	1	87
Sounding Joy	Walker, Gwyneth	2	2	249
Stabat Mater	Pergolesi, Giovanni	1	3	316
Stars I Shall Find	Dickau, David	3	4	439
Steal Away	arr. Dennard, Brazeal W.	2	1	201
Streets of Laredo	Takach, Timothy	3	2	261
Suite Nordestina	arr. Miranda, Ronaldo	2	3	403
Sure on This Shining Night	Barber, Samuel	1	3	268
Sure on This Shining Night	Lauridsen, Morten	3	4	443
Te Quiero	Favero, Alberto	1	4	406
The Battle of Jericho	arr. Hogan, Moses	2	3	409
The Birds	Britten, Benjamin	3	2	225
The Blue Bird	Stanford, Charles Villiers	2	4	589
The Choir Inivisible	Harris, Ron	2	5	657
The Divine Image	Shank, Joshua	2	2	253
The Hour Has Come	Glick, Srul Irving	3	5	555
The Last Words of David	Thompson, Randall	1	3	234

Title	Composer	Vol.	Level	Page
The May Night (Die Mainacht)	Brahms, Johannes/ arr. Frackenpohl, Arthur	3	1	93
"The Pasture" from *Where the Earth Meets the Sky*	Stroope, Z. Randall	3	2	179
The Path to the Moon	Thiman, Eric	2	1	155
The Promise of Living	Copland, Aaron	1	4	391
The Silver Swan	Gibbons, Orlando	2	3	415
The Snow	Elgar, Edward	1	2	151
The Turtle Dove	arr. Spevacek, Linda Steen	2	1	159
The Water Is Wide	Paulus, Steven	3	3	339
There Is Sweet Music Here	Gawthrop, Daniel	3	4	499
There Is Sweet Music Here	Lightfoot, Mary Lynn	2	2	289
There Will Be Rest	Ticheli, Frank	1	4	411
This Little Light of Mine	arr. Berg, Ken	2	1	165
This We Know	Jeffers, Ron	3	3	345
Three Choral Pieces	Berger, Jean	1	2	154
Three Madrigals	Diemer, Emma Lou	2	2	257
Three Whitman Settings	Clausen, René	2	4	593
Time and Concord	Britten, Benjamin	1	3	272
To Be Sung of a Summer Night on the Water	Delius, Frederick	1	4	415
To the Mothers of Brazil: Salve Regina	arr. Eriksson, Gunnar	3	3	349
Três Cantos Nativos	arr. Leite, Marcos	2	3	421
Two Hymns to the Mother of God	Tavener, John	1	4	418
Ubi caritas	Duruflé, Maurice	2	3	427
Va pensiero (Chorus of the Hebrew Slaves)	Verdi, Giuseppe	1	4	422
Valiant for Truth	Vaughan Williams, Ralph	3	4	449
Vamuvamba	Mganga, Boniface	1	3	276
Varjele, Jumala, soasta (God, Protect Us from War)	Tormis, Veljo	2	5	677
Venite exultemus Domino	Sweelinck, Jan P.	2	3	433
Verbum caro factum est	Hassler, Hans Leo	2	3	439
Verleih uns Frieden	Mendelssohn, Felix	2	1	169
Vier Gesänge für Frauenchor, Op. 17	Brahms, Johannes	1	4	437
Viva Tutti	anonymous 18th century	3	1	115
Vorspruch from Mörike-Chorliederbuch, Op. 19	Distler, Hugo	2	4	599
Vus vet zayn	Hatfield, Stephen	3	3	371
Wade in the Water	Hogan, Moses	1	3	280

TITLE	COMPOSER	VOL.	LEVEL	PAGE
Wanting Memories	Barnwell, Ysaye M.	3	2	185
Water Night	Whitacre, Eric	1	5	470
We Shall Walk through the Valley	Moore, Undine Smith	3	3	355
Weep No More	Childs, David	3	2	229
What Shall We Do with the Drunken Sailor	arr. Parker and Shaw	2	3	487
What'll I Do?	Berlin, I./arr. Shaw, K.	2	3	459
When David Heard	Weelkes, Thomas	1	3	283
Where the Music Comes From	Hoiby, Lee	3	2	191
Widerspruch, D. 865	Schubert, Franz	1	3	345
Wie lieblich sind deine Wohnungen	Brahms, Johannes	1	5	473
Wir eilen mit schwachen, doch emsigen Schritten	Bach, J. S.	1	3	322
With Drooping Wings	Purcell, Henry	1	3	287
Yet Gentle Will the Griffen Be, No. 3 from What Grandpa Told the Children	Nuñez, Francisco J.	2	2	263
Yo Le Canto Todo El Dia	Brunner, David	3	2	235
Zigeunerleben, Op. 29, No. 3	Schumann, Robert	1	3	291

Index by Publisher for Teaching Music through Performance in Choir Volumes 1, 2, 3

TITLE	COMPOSER	VOL.	LEVEL	PAGE
A Boy and a Girl	Hal Leonard	3	4	381
A Choral Flourish	Oxford University Press	2	4	495
A Gaelic Blessing	Hinshaw Music	1	3	208
A New Year Carol from Friday Afternoons, Op. 7	Boosey & Hawkes	2	1	173
A Procession Winding around Me	Walton Music Corp.	1	5	465
A Spotless Rose	Augsburg Fortress	2	4	499
Absalon, fili mi	Broude Brothers	1	4	442
Ahrirang	Hal Leonard	3	2	127
Ain't No Grave Can Hold My Body Down	earthsongs	3	4	455
Al naharot Bavel	Broude Brothers	2	4	623
Alleluia	E. C. Schirmer Music Co.	1	3	181
Also hat Gott die Welt geliebt	GIA Publications, Inc.	3	4	385
Amor de Mi Alma	Walton Music Corp.	2	4	505
An die Frauen (To Women), Hob. XXVb:4	Southern Music Co.	2	3	465
An Elizabethan Spring	Waterloo Music	2	4	511
April Is in My Mistress' Face	E. C. Schirmer Music Co.	2	2	207
Ave Maria (Angelus Domini)	Hinshaw Music	1	4	446
Ave Maria	Walton Music Corp.	2	3	315
Ave Maria	Hinshaw Music	3	3	267
Ave Maria	Collegium Music Pub.	1	5	476
Ave Maria	Boosey & Hawkes	2	3	319
Ave Maria, Op. 12	C. F. Peters Corp.	1	4	426
Ave, maris stella	Cyprus Choral Music	2	2	293
Ave verum corpus	Editions Salabert	1	5	479
Ave verum corpus	Oxford University Press	1	4	353
Ave verum corpus, K. 618	Hinshaw Music	1	3	184
Ave verum corpus, Op. 2, No. 1	Novello Publications	1	2	111
Back to Ethiopia	Santa Barbara Music	3	2	241

TITLE	COMPOSER	VOL.	LEVEL	PAGE
Balulalow	GIA Publications, Inc.	3	4	393
Be Thou My Vision	Hinshaw Music	1	1	89
Beati mortui, Op. 115, No. 1	Alliance	2	3	469
Benedicamus, Domino	Schott Musik International	1	5	487
Best of Rooms, The	E. C. Schirmer Music Co.	3	4	399
Bile Them Cabbage Down	Hinshaw Music	3	2	131
Bist du bei mir	Gordon Thompson	1	1	93
Black Is the Color of My True Love's Hair	Shawnee Press	2	2	211
Bogoróditse Djévo (Mother of God and Virgin)	Universal Edition	1	3	189
Brothers, Sing On! (A Choral Salutation)	J. Fischer & Bro./Alfred	2	3	475
Buffalo Gals	Oxford University Press	2	3	323
Bullerengue	Third Planet Music	2	2	215
Byker Hill	Hinshaw Music	3	2	247
Calme des Nuits	GIA Publications, Inc.	3	4	403
Cantemus!	Editio Musica Budapest	2	4	517
Cantique de Jean Racine, Op. 11	Hinshaw Music	1	3	193
Chindia	Santa Barbara Music	3	4	409
Choral Hymns from the Rig Veda, Set 3	E. C. Schirmer Music Co.	2	5	665
Christ lag in Todesbanden, No. 7 from Opella nova I	Alexander Broude	2	2	219
Circus Band	Peer-Southern	1	3	199
City Called Heaven	Colla Voce	3	2	121
Come Sing to Me of Heaven	Mark Foster	3	4	503
Come to Me My Love	Hal Leonard	3	5	545
Confirma hoc, Deus	Alliance	1	3	325
Credo	Hinshaw Music	3	4	507
Crucifixus	E. C. Schirmer Music Co.	3	4	515
Dadme albricias, hijos d'Eva	Associated Music Pub.	1	2	115
Daemon irrepit callidus	Hinshaw Music	2	4	521
Dance on My Heart	Santa Barbara Music	3	2	195
De profundis	Universal (Out of Print)	1	4	450
Der Herr segne euch	Edition Peters	1	2	157
Die mit Tränen säen, SWV 378 from Geistliche Chormusik, 1648	GIA Publications	2	4	525
Die Nachtigall, Op. 59, No. 4	Golden Music	1	2	119
Dieu! qu'il la fait bon regarder from Trois Chansons de Charles d'Orleans	Durand/Theodore Presser	2	5	651
Dirait-on	Peer-Southern	1	3	204
Domaredansen	earthsongs	3	2	137

Title	Composer	Vol.	Level	Page
Domine, ad adjuvandum me festina	Concordia Publishing	2	3	329
Down among the Dead Men	E. C. Schirmer Music Co.	1	3	329
Down by the Riverside	Hinshaw Music	2	2	223
Dúlamán	Hinshaw Music	2	5	673
El Grillo	Alfred Publishing Co.	1	2	123
El Hambo	Walton Music	3	4	413
Erev Shel Shoshanim	World Music Press	1	2	127
Ev'ry Time I Feel the Spirit	Neil A. Kjos	3	2	145
Famine Song	Santa Barbara Music Pub.	2	2	229
Fillimiooriay	Alfred	3	1	105
Fire	Boosey & Hawkes	1	2	140
Five Hebrew Love Songs	Walton Music Corp.	2	3	335
Flanders Fields	Hal Leonard	3	2	253
Four Cummings Choruses, Opus 98	Theodore Presser	3	4	519
Four Pastorales	G. Schirmer	2	4	531
Four Slovak Folk Songs	Boosey & Hawkes	2	4	539
Gate, Gate	earthsongs	3	2	199
Geistliches Lied, Op. 30	GIA Publications	2	4	543
Give Us	Alliance	1	5	483
Gloria ad modum tubae	GIA Publications	1	1	97
Gloria tibi	Boosey & Hawkes	1	2	143
Gloria	Alfred Publishing Co.	1	3	211
God's Bottles	E. C. Schirmer Music Co.	1	3	297
God Is Our Refuge	National	3	1	77
God Is Seen	Hal Leonard	3	2	151
Greater Love	E. C. Schirmer Music Co.	3	3	375
Hallelujah, Amen	Alfred Publishing Co.	1	3	215
Haneirot Halalu	E. C. Schirmer Music Co.	1	3	218
Hard Times Come Again No More	Warner Bros./Alfred	2	1	189
Hark, I Hear the Harps Eternal	Warner Bros./Alfred	2	3	343
He, Watching Over Israel	E. C. Schirmer Music Co.	1	3	222
Heart We Will Forget Him	National Music Publishers	2	3	443
Heaven-Haven (A Nun Takes the Veil)	G. Schirmer, Inc.	1	4	430
Hello, Girls	Lawton-Gould/Alfred	2	1	179
He's Gone Away	Theodore Presser Co.	1	3	301
Hodie	Encore	3	3	271
Hotari Koi	CORO	3	4	463
How Can I Keep from Singing	Neil A. Kjos	3	2	257

TITLE	COMPOSER	VOL.	LEVEL	PAGE
Hvalite imi Ghospodne				
(Praise the Name of the Lord)	Musica Russica	1	4	455
I Am His Child	Alliance	2	2	269
I Find My Feet Have Further Goals	Oxford University Press	3	5	551
I Have Had Singing	Steven Sametz Pub.	2	4	549
I Love My Love	G. Schirmer, Inc.	1	4	358
I Once Loved a Lad	Theodore Presser Co.	2	2	273
I Thank You God	E. C. Schirmer Music Co.	3	4	469
Ich wollt', meine Lieb'	National Music Publishers	2	2	277
If Music Be the Food of Love	Plymouth Music Co.	2	3	349
Ihr Heiligen, lobsinget dem Herren, SWV 288	C. F. Khant	1	3	304
Il est bel et bon	Bourne Company	1	4	361
I'm A-Rollin'	Santa Barbara Music Pub.	2	3	481
I'm Going Home on a Cloud	Ascolta	2	1	141
In Paradisum	Plymouth Music	3	4	419
In Remembrance	Walton Music	3	3	275
"In Splendoribus Sanctorum"				
from *The Strathclyde Motets*	Boosey & Hawkes	3	3	281
Innisfree	GIA Publications	2	3	353
Innoria (Huron Dance Song)	earthsongs	1	3	225
Ipharadisi	Neil A. Kjos	3	2	155
It Takes a Village	Santa Barbara Music Pub.	3	2	159
I've Been 'Buked, Children!	Santa Barbara Music Pub.	2	2	233
J'entends le moulin	earthsongs	2	2	281
Japanese Garden	Neil A. Kjos	3	2	205
Jasmine Flower	Alliance	1	2	131
Jauchzet dem Herrn alle Welt, SWV 36	Barenreiter	1	4	364
Jerusalem Luminosa	Neil A. Kjos	3	5	561
Jesu dulcis memoria	GIA Publications	3	3	285
John the Revelator	earthsongs	2	4	553
Johnny Has Gone for a Soldier	Alfred Publishing Co.	1	3	228
Jordan's Angels	Hal Leonard	3	2	209
Jubilate Deo	Hinshaw Music	1	4	369
Jubliate Deo in C	Oxford University Press	1	3	231
Ka Hia Manu	Boosey & Hawkes	2	3	359
Komm, heil'ger Geist	earthsongs	1	4	372
Kyrie	Broude Brothers	1	4	376
La Muerte del Angel	Editorial Lagos	2	4	559
Las Amarillas	Boosey & Hawkes	2	4	605

TITLE	COMPOSER	VOL.	LEVEL	PAGE
LAWA	Boosey & Hawkes	3	4	477
Lay a Garland	Oxford University Press	3	4	423
Lebenslust	Hinshaw Music	3	3	291
Les étoiles	Alliance	3	4	483
Let Down the Bars, O Death, Op. 8, No. 2	G. Schirmer	2	4	565
Let Their Celestial Concerts All Unite	Alfred/E. C. Schirmer	1	3	237
Let Us Now Praise Famous Men, Op. 35	Boosey & Hawkes	1	2	160
Lirum bililirum	Faber Music Ltd.	2	2	237
Little Innocent Lamb	G. Schirmer	2	2	299
Love and Pizen (Springfield Mountain), Op. 60, No. 3	G. Schirmer	2	3	365
Love Never Ending	Abington	3	4	527
Love Walked In	Hal Leonard	2	3	371
Magnificat in A minor	Hal Leonard	3	3	361
Magnificent Horses	Alliance	3	3	297
Manly Men	Walton Music Corp.	2	4	629
Measure Me Sky	Colla Voce	3	2	215
Medieval Gloria	Alfred	3	1	111
Messe basse	Broude Brothers	2	3	449
Mon coeur se recommande à vous	E. C. Schirmer Music Co.	2	2	241
Morning Moon	Santa Barbara Music Pub.	2	2	285
Muié Rendêra	earthsongs	1	3	242
Musicks Empire	Alfred Publishing Co.	1	3	246
My Bonnie	Out of Print (copy from Warner-Chappell)	1	2	164
My Flight for Heaven	GIA Publications	3	4	433
My Spirit Sang All Day	Boosey & Hawkes	1	4	380
Ngana	Musical Resources	1	4	384
Nigra sum	Tetra	1	3	308
Nine Hundred Miles	Santa Barbara Music Pub.	3	1	99
Nis'ka Banja	Boosey & Hawkes	2	3	455
Noel!	Alliance	1	3	334
Not While I'm Around	Hinshaw Music	2	2	305
Notre Père	Editions Durand	1	3	250
O aula nobilis	Oxford University Press	2	4	611
O bone Jesu	C. F. Peters Corp.	3	4	489
O Jesu Christ, mein Lebens Licht, BWV 118	Carus-Verlag	2	3	377
O magnum mysterium	Lauridsen, Morten	2	4	571
O magnum mysterium	Peer Music	2	3	383

Title	Composer	Vol.	Level	Page
O Music	Boosey & Hawkes	2	1	145
O Occhi, manza mia	G. Schirmer	3	2	163
O schöne Nacht, Op. 92, No. 1	G. Schirmer	1	4	387
O Sing Joyfully	Oxford University Press	2	3	387
O vos Omnes	Tetra	3	3	301
Old Abram Brown	Boosey & Hawkes	1	1	102
Old Time Religion	Hal Leonard	3	2	167
Oremus	Boosey & Hawkes	3	3	305
Os justi	C. F. Peters Corp.	1	5	461
Ose Shalom (The One Who Makes Peace)	Hal Leonard	2	1	149
Our Father (Otche Nash)	Musica Russica	1	3	312
Past Life Melodies	Morton Music	2	3	393
Pater Noster	Boosey & Hawkes	3	3	309
Poor Man Lazrus	Bourne Company	1	2	167
Praise His Holy Name!	earthsongs	2	2	245
Prayer Before Sleep	Alfred	3	3	315
Psallite	Bourne Company	1	2	134
Psalm 96	Theodore Presser Co.	1	4	395
Psalm 100 (Jauchzet dem Herrn)	GIA Publications	3	3	321
Psalm 117	Ione Press/ECS Pub.	2	4	633
Psalm 121		3	4	493
Ramkali	earthsongs	3	4	533
(Rejoice O Virgin) Bogoroditse Devo	Musica Russica	1	4	398
Requiem	Hinshaw Music	1		493
Requiem	Schirmer	3	2	173
Revoici venir du Printemps	Belwin Mills	3	3	327
Rise Up, My Love, My Fair One	Boosey & Hawkes	1	4	434
Rustics and Fishermen	Boosey & Hawkes	3	4	539
Salmo 150	earthsongs	1	3	254
Salut au chevalier printemps, Op. 151, No. 2	Roger Dean Pub.	2	4	617
Sam Was a Man	G. Schirmer	2	2	309
Savory, Sage, Rosemary and Thyme	earthsongs	1	2	147
Scarborough Fair	Boosey & Hawkes	3	2	221
Sea Shanties	earthsongs	2	1	195
Sehnsucht	Santa Barbara Music Pub.	2	4	637
Set Me as a Seal	Shawnee Press	1	3	258
Sfogava con le stele	National Music Publishers	2	4	577
Shall I Compare Thee	Paulus Publications	2	4	643
She Moved through the Fair	Neil A. Kjos	1	2	170

Title	Composer	Vol.	Level	Page
Shenandoah	Alfred Publishing Co.	1	3	261
Si iniquitates observaveris	Oxford University Press	1	2	172
Sicut cervus	GIA Publications, Inc.	1	3	264
Sicut locutus est	Hal Leonard Corporation	1	4	402
Silent Devotion and Response	Broude Brothers	1	2	137
Simple Gifts (Shaker Song)	Boosey & Hawkes	1	1	105
Sing Me to Heaven	Dunstan House	2	3	399
Sing We and Chant It	Schirmer	3	1	81
Sing Ye Praises to Our King, Op. 20, No. 4	Boosey & Hawkes	2	4	583
Sir Christèmas	Oxford University Press	3	3	333
Sometimes I Feel Like a Motherless Child	Shawnee Press	1	2	175
Song for the Mira	Cabot Tr./G.V. Thompson	2	1	183
Song of Peace	Theodore Presser Co.	1	3	337
Soon Ah Will Be Done	Neil A. Kjos	1	3	340
Sorida	Hal Leonard	3	1	87
Sounding Joy	E. C. Schirmer Music Co.	2	2	249
Stabat Mater	Edwin F. Kalmus	1	3	316
Stars I Shall Find	Walton Music	3	4	439
Steal Away	Shawnee Press	2	1	201
Streets of Laredo	Graphite Publishing	3	2	261
Suite Nordestina	earthsongs	2	3	403
Sure on This Shining Night	G. Schirmer, Inc.	1	3	268
Sure on This Shining Night	Peermusic	3	4	443
Te Quiero	earthsongs	1	4	406
The Battle of Jericho	Hal Leonard	2	3	409
The Birds	Boosey & Hawkes	3	2	225
The Blue Bird	Stainer & Bell	2	4	589
The Choir Inivisible	Woodland Mus./Carl Fisc.	2	5	657
The Divine Image	Santa Barbara Music Pub.	2	2	253
The Hour Has Come	Gordon V. Thompson	3	5	555
The Last Words of David	E. C. Schirmer Music Co.	1	3	234
The May Night (Die Mainacht)	Hal Leonard	3	1	93
"The Pasture" from *Where the Earth Meets the Sky*	Colla Voce	3	2	179
The Path to the Moon	Boosey & Hawkes	2	1	155
The Promise of Living	Boosey & Hawkes	1	4	391
The Silver Swan	E. C. Schirmer Music Co.	2	3	415
The Snow	Novello Publications	1	2	151

Title	Composer	Vol.	Level	Page
The Turtle Dove	Hal Leonard	2	1	159
The Water Is Wide	European American Music	3	3	339
There Is Sweet Music Here	Belwin	3	4	499
There Is Sweet Music Here	Heritage Music Press	2	2	289
There Will Be Rest	Hinshaw Music	1	4	411
This Little Light of Mine	Colla voce	2	1	165
This We Know	earthsongs	3	3	345
Three Choral Pieces	Neil A. Kjos	1	2	154
Three Madrigals	Boosey & Hawkes	2	2	257
Three Whitman Settings	Shawnee Press	2	4	593
Time and Concord	Boosey & Hawkes	1	3	272
To Be Sung of a Summer Night on the Water	Boosey & Hawkes (rental)	1	4	415
To the Mothers of Brazil: Salve Regina	Walton Music	3	3	349
Três Cantos Nativos	earthsongs	2	3	421
Two Hymns to the Mother of God	Chester Music Ltd.	1	4	418
Ubi caritas	Durand/Theodore Presser	2	3	427
Va pensiero (Chorus of the Hebrew Slaves)	Alfred Publishing Co.	1	4	422
Valiant for Truth	Oxford University Press	3	4	449
Vamuvamba	earthsongs	1	3	276
Varjele, Jumala, soasta (God, Protect Us from War)	Boosey & Hawkes	2	5	677
Venite exultemus Domino	GIA Publications	2	3	433
Verbum caro factum est	GIA Publications	2	3	439
Verleih uns Frieden	Oxford University Press	2	1	169
Vier Gesänge für Frauenchor, Op. 17	Peters Music Publishers	1	4	437
Viva Tutti	Alfred	3	1	115
Vorspruch from Mörike-Chorliederbuch, Op. 19	Bärenreiter Verlag	2	4	599
Vus vet zayn	Colla Voce	3	3	371
Wade in the Water	Hal Leonard	1	3	280
Wanting Memories	Musical Source	3	2	185
Water Night	Walton Music Corp.	1	5	470
We Shall Walk through the Valley	GIA Publications	3	3	355
Weep No More	Santa Barbara Music Pub.	3	2	229
What Shall We Do with the Drunken Sailor	Warner Bros./Alfred	2	3	487
What'll I Do?	Hal Leonard	2	3	459
When David Heard	Associated Music Pub.	1	3	283
Where the Music Comes From	G. Schirmer	3	2	191

Title	Composer	Vol.	Level	Page
Widerspruch, D. 865	Alfred Publishing Co.	1	3	345
Wie lieblich sind deine Wohnungen	G. Schirmer	1	5	473
Wir eilen mit schwachen, doch emsigen Schritten	E. C. Schirmer Music Co.	1	3	322
With Drooping Wings	Bourne Company	1	3	287
Yet Gentle Will the Griffen Be, No. 3 from What Grandpa Told the Children	Boosey & Hawkes	2	2	263
Yo Le Canto Todo El Dia	Boosey & Hawkes	3	2	235
Zigeunerleben, Op. 29, No. 3	Alfred Publishing Co.	1	3	291

Index by Composer and Arranger for Teaching Music through Performance in Choir Volume 3

Composer	Title	Level	Page
Ames, Jeffery	*In Remembrance*	3	275
anonymous 18th century	*Viva Tutti*	1	115
Barnwell, Ysaye M.	*Wanting Memories*	2	185
Beery, Lon	*Fillimiooriay*	1	105
Betinis, Abbie	*Jerusalem Luminosa*	5	561
Brahms, Johannes	*O bone jesu*	4	489
Brahms, Johannes/ arr. Frackenpohl, Arthur	*The May Night (Die Mainacht)*	1	93
Britten, Benjamin	*Rustics and Fishermen*	4	539
Britten, Benjamin	*The Birds*	2	225
Brunner, David	*Yo Le Canto Todo El Dia*	2	235
Caldwell, Paul/Ivory, Sean	*Ain't No Grave Can Hold My Body Down*	4	455
Casals, Pablo	*O vos Omnes*	3	301
Chatman, Stephen	*Greater Love*	3	375
Childs, David	*Weep No More*	2	229
Collins, Drew	*Domaredansen*	2	137
Culloton, Matthew	*Japanese Garden*	2	205
Custer, Gerald	*Balulalow*	4	393
Dawson, William	*Ev'ry Time I Feel the Spirit*	2	145
De Cormier, Robert	*Ahrirang*	2	127
Dello Joio, Norman	*Come to Me My Love*	5	545
Dett, Nathaniel	*Ave Maria*	3	267
Dickau, David	*Stars I Shall Find*	4	439
Dilworth, Rollo	*Jordan's Angels*	2	209
Ellingboe, Bradley	*How Can I Keep from Singing*	2	257
Emerson, Roger	*Flanders Fields*	2	253
Eriksson, Gunnar	*To the Mothers of Brazil: Salve Regina*	3	349
Fissinger, Edwin	*In Paradisum*	4	419

Composer	Title	Level	Page
Gawthrop, Daniel	*There Is Sweet Music Here*	4	499
Gilkyson, Eliza/arr. Craig Hella Johnson	*Requiem*	2	173
Glick, Srul Irving	*The Hour Has Come*	5	555
Goetze, Mary	*Scarborough Fair*	2	221
Hatfield, Stephen	*Vus vet zayn*	3	371
Henson, Blake	*My Flight for Heaven*	4	433
Hogan, Moses	*Old Time Religion*	2	167
Hoiby, Lee	*Where the Music Comes From*	2	191
Jeffers, Ron	*This We Know*	3	345
Koepke, Alan	*Dance on My Heart*	2	195
Larsen, Libby	*I Find My Feet*	5	551
de Lassus Orlande de	*O Occhi, manza mia*	2	163
Lauridsen, Morten	*Sure on This Shining Night*	4	443
Le Jeune, Claude	*Revoici venir du Printemps*	3	327
Ling-Tam, Jing	*Magnificent Horses*	3	297
Lotti, Antonio/arr. Davison, Archibald	*Crucifixus*	4	515
MacMillan, James	"In Splendoribus Sanctorum" from *The Strathclyde Motets*	3	281
Mäntyjärvi, Jaakko	*El Hambo*	4	413
Martini, Giovanni Battista	*Credo*	4	507
Mathias, William	*Sir Christèmas*	3	333
McDermid, J. Aaron	*Come Sing to Me of Heaven*	4	503
Mendelssohn, Felix	*Psalm 100 (Jauchzet dem Herrn)*	3	321
Moore, Undine Smith	*We Shall Walk through the Valley*	3	355
Morley, Thomas	*Sing We and Chant It*	1	81
Mozart, W. A.	*God Is Our Refuge*	1	77
Mulholland, James	*Measure Me Sky*	2	215
Ogura, Roh	*Hotari Koi*	4	463
Parker, Alice	*God Is Seen*	2	151
Pascanu, Alexandru	*Chindia*	4	409
Paulus, Steven	*The Water Is Wide*	3	339
Pearsall, Robert	*Lay a Garland*	4	423
Persichetti, Vincent	*Four Cummings Choruses, Opus 98*	4	519
Poelinitz, Josephine	*City Called Heaven*	2	121
Porpora, Nicola	*Magnificat in A minor*	3	361
Powell, Rosephanye	*Sorida*	1	87
Raminsh, Imant	*Psalm 121*	4	493
Rardin, Paul	*Back to Ethiopia*	2	241
Robinovitch, Sid	*Prayer Before Sleep*	3	315

Composer	Title	Level	Page
Sadler, Katheryn	*LAWA*	4	477
Saint-Saëns, Camille	*Calme des Nuits*	4	403
Sandler, Mitchell	*Byker Hill*	2	247
Sandström, Jan	*Lo, How a Rose E'er Blooming*	4	429
Schubert, Franz	*Lebenslust*	3	291
Schütz, Heinrich	*Also hat Gott die Welt geliebt*	4	385
Silvey, Philip	*Nine Hundred Miles*	1	99
Singh, Vijay	*Medieval Gloria*	1	111
Sirett, Mark	*Les étoiles*	4	483
Sisask, Urmas	*Oremus*	3	305
Sperry, Ethan	*Ramkali*	4	533
Stravinsky, Igor	*Pater Noster*	3	309
Stroope, Z. Randall	"The Pasture" from *Where the Earth Meets the Sky*	2	179
Szymko, Joan	*It Takes a Village*	2	159
Takach, Timothy	*Streets of Laredo*	2	261
Tate, Brian	*Gate, Gate*	2	199
Thompson, Randall	*Best of Rooms, The*	4	399
Ulrich, Jerry	*Ipharadisi*	2	155
Vaughan Williams, Ralph	*Valiant for Truth*	4	449
Victoria, Tomás Luis de	*Jesu dulcis memoria*	3	285
Walker, Gwyneth	*I Thank You God*	4	469
Whitacre, Eric	*A Boy and a Girl*	4	381
Whitbourn, James	*Hodie*	3	271
Wilberg, Mack	*Bile Them Cabbage Down*	2	131
Zinter, Aaron	*Love Never Ending*	4	527

Index by Title for Teaching Music through Performance in Choir Volume 3

Title	Composer	Level	Page
A Boy and a Girl	Whitacre, Eric	4	381
Ahrirang	arr. De Cormier, Robert	2	127
Ain't No Grave Can Hold My Body Down	arr. Caldwell, Paul/Ivory, Sean	4	455
Also hat Gott die Welt geliebt	Schütz, Heinrich	4	385
Ave Maria	Dett, Nathaniel	3	267
Back to Ethiopia	arr. Rardin, Paul	2	241
Balulalow	Custer, Gerald	4	393
Best of Rooms, The	Thompson, Randall	4	399
Bile Them Cabbage Down	arr. Wilberg, Mack	2	131
Byker Hill	arr. Sandler, Mitchell	2	247
Calme des Nuits	Saint-Saëns, Camille	4	403
Chindia	Pascanu, Alexandru	4	409
City Called Heaven	Poelinitz, Josephine	2	121
Come Sing to Me of Heaven	arr. McDermid, J. Aaron	4	503
Come to Me My Love	Dello Joio, Norman	5	545
Credo	Martini, Giovanni Battista	4	507
Crucifixus	Lotti, Antonio/arr. Davison, Archibald	4	515
Dance on My Heart	Koepke, Alan	2	195
Domaredansen	arr. Collins, Drew	2	137
El Hambo	Mäntyjärvi, Jaakko	4	413
Ev'ry Time I Feel the Spirit	arr. Dawson, William	2	145
Fillimiooriay	arr. Beery, Lon	1	105
Flanders Fields	Emerson, Roger	2	253
Four Cummings Choruses, Opus 98	Persichetti, Vincent	4	519
Gate, Gate	arr. Tate, Brian	2	199
God Is Our Refuge	Mozart, W. A.	1	77
God Is Seen	arr. Parker, Alice	2	151
Greater Love	Chatman, Stephen	3	375
Hodie	Whitbourn, James	3	271

TITLE	COMPOSER	LEVEL	PAGE
Hotari Koi	arr. Ogura, Roh	4	463
How Can I Keep from Singing	arr. Ellingboe, Bradley	2	257
I Find My Feet Have Further Goals	Larsen, Libby	5	551
I Thank You God	Walker, Gwyneth	4	469
In Paradisum	Fissinger, Edwin	4	419
In Remembrance	Ames, Jeffery	3	275
"In Splendoribus Sanctorum" from *The Strathclyde Motets*	MacMillan, James	3	281
Ipharadisi	arr. Ulrich, Jerry	2	155
It Takes a Village	Szymko, Joan	2	159
Japanese Garden	Culloton, Matthew	2	205
Jerusalem Luminosa	Betinis, Abbie	5	561
Jesu dulcis memoria	Victoria, Tomás Luis de	3	285
Jordan's Angels	Dilworth, Rollo	2	209
LAWA	Sadler, Katheryn	4	477
Lay a Garland	Pearsall, Robert	4	423
Lebenslust	Schubert, Franz	3	291
Les étoiles	Sirett, Mark	4	483
Lo, How a Rose E'er Blooming	Sandström, Jan	4	429
Love Never Ending	Zinter, Aaron	4	527
Magnificat in A minor	Porpora, Nicola	3	361
Magnificent Horses	arr. Ling-Tam, Jing	3	297
Measure Me Sky	Mulholland, James	2	215
Medieval Gloria	Singh, Vijay	1	111
My Flight for Heaven	Henson, Blake	4	433
Nine Hundred Miles	Silvey, Philip	1	99
O bone jesu	Brahms, Johannes	4	489
O Occhi, manza mia	Lassus, Orlande de	2	163
O vos Omnes	Casals, Pablo	3	301
Old Time Religion	arr. Hogan, Moses	2	167
Oremus	Sisask, Urmas	3	305
Pater Noster	Stravinsky, Igor	3	309
Prayer Before Sleep	Robinovitch, Sid	3	315
Psalm 100 (Jauchzet dem Herrn)	Mendelssohn, Felix	3	321
Psalm 121	Raminsh, Imant	4	493
Ramkali	arr. Sperry, Ethan	4	533
Requiem	Gilkyson, Eliza/arr. Craig Hella Johnson	2	173
Revoici venir du Printemps	Le Jeune, Claude	3	327
Rustics and Fishermen	Britten, Benjamin	4	539

Title	Composer	Level	Page
Scarborough Fair	Goetze, Mary	2	221
Sing We and Chant It	Morley, Thomas	1	81
Sir Christèmas	Mathias, William	3	333
Sorida	arr. Powell, Rosephanye	1	87
Stars I Shall Find	Dickau, David	4	439
Streets of Laredo	Takach, Timothy	2	261
Sure on This Shining Night	Lauridsen, Morten	4	443
The Birds	Britten, Benjamin	2	225
The Hour Has Come	Glick, Srul Irving	5	555
The May Night (Die Mainacht)	Brahms, Johannes/arr. Frackenpohl, Arthur	1	93
"The Pasture" from *Where the Earth Meets the Sky*	Stroope, Z. Randall	2	179
The Water Is Wide	Paulus, Steven	3	339
There Is Sweet Music Here	Gawthrop, Daniel	4	499
This We Know	Jeffers, Ron	3	345
To the Mothers of Brazil: Salve Regina	arr. Eriksson, Gunnar	3	349
Valiant for Truth	Vaughan Williams, Ralph	4	449
Viva Tutti	anonymous 18th century	1	115
Vus vet zayn	Hatfield, Stephen	3	371
Wanting Memories	Barnwell, Ysaye M.	2	185
We Shall Walk through the Valley	Moore, Undine Smith	3	355
Weep No More	Childs, David	2	229
Where the Music Comes From	Hoiby, Lee	2	191
Yo Le Canto Todo El Dia	Brunner, David	2	235

About the Editors

Australian born conductor Heather J. Buchanan is Associate Professor of Music and Director of Choral Activities at Montclair State University, where she conducts the 170-voice Chorale, 55-voice University Singers, and 24-voice Vocal Accord. She holds degrees from The Queensland Conservatorium of Music of Griffith University, Australia (Bachelor of Music in music education), Westminster Choir College of Rider University (Master of Music with distinction in choral conducting and music education), and a PhD candidate from the University of New England in Australia. A certified Andover Educator, Ms. Buchanan specializes in the teaching of Body Mapping and somatic pedagogy for musicians. In addition to the *Teaching Music through Performance in Choir* choral series, she published the DVD/VHS *Evoking Sound: Body Mapping and Basic Conducting Technique* (GIA) with James Jordan of Westminster Choir College and co-edited three choral octavos with Matthew Mehaffey in the *Evoking Sound Choral Series* (GIA).

Choirs under Ms. Buchanan's direction have received critical acclaim for their "heartfelt conviction," "vibrant sound," and for singing with the "crispness and dexterity of a professional choir." Her choirs have been recognized for their performances in a variety of prestigious venues, including Carnegie Hall, Alice Tully Hall, the Ferenc Liszt Zeneakadémia (Budapest), St. Nicholas Church (Prague), Rachmaninoff Hall (Moscow), and the Russian Museum (St. Petersburg) as invited U.S. representatives for the Imperial Garden Festival. The MSU Chorale regularly appears with the New Jersey Symphony Orchestra, and has performed Howard Shore's *The Lord of the Rings Symphony*, Beethoven's *Ninth Symphony*, Orff's *Carmina Burana*, and Verdi's epic *Messa da Requiem*. The University Singers continues their collaborations with renowned composer-artist Meredith Monk, with *Songs of Ascension* performed in the Guggenheim Museum (March 2009) and recorded in November 2009 on ECM Records under legendary producer Manfred Eicher. Ms. Buchanan is in demand as a guest conductor and clinician in the United States, Europe, and Australia. She resides in Princeton Junction, New Jersey, with her husband and daughter.

Matthew Mehaffey is Associate Professor of Music at the University of Minnesota, where he conducts the University Singers and the Men's Chorus, and teaches graduate and undergraduate courses in Conducting and Literature. A native of Pittsburgh, Pennsylvania, Dr. Mehaffey holds degrees from Bucknell University (B.M.), Westminster Choir College (M.M.), and the

University of Arizona (D.M.A). Recent professional conducting engagements include work with Washington National Opera, St. Paul Chamber Orchestra, Minnesota Orchestra, Carnegie Hall, VocalEssence, Minnesota Chorale, Air America Radio, and Turner Network Television. He is in frequent demand as a lecturer and guest conductor, and has published extensively with GIA Publications. Additionally, he is Artistic Director of the Oratorio Society of Minnesota and serves as Director of Music at St. Clement's Episcopal Church in St. Paul. An avid sports fan, he enjoys golf, baseball, and curling in his spare time. He lives with his wife Libby and their two daughters, Veda and Colette.